A TRUE AND FAITHFUL RELATION

OF WHAT PASSED FOR MANY YEARS
BETWEEN DR. JOHN DEE
AND SOME SPIRITS

BY

DR. JOHN DEE

Golem • Media
BERKELEY, CA
www.golemmedia.com

Golem Media

BERKELEY, CA

Golem Media
1700 Shattuck Ave #81
Berkeley, CA 94709
www.golemmedia.com

Golem Media edition, 2008.
Printed in the United States of America
ISBN 1-933993-56-1

A True & Faithful
RELATION
OF
What paſſed for many Yeers Between
Dᴿ. JOHN DEE
(A Mathematician of Great Fame in Q. Eʟɪᴢ.
and King Jᴀᴍᴇs·their Rᴇɪgnes) and
SOME SPIRITS:
Tᴇɴᴅɪɴɢ (had it Succeeded)
To a General Alteration of moſt S T A T E S *and*
K I N G D O M E S *in the World.*

His *Private Conferences* with Rᴏᴅᴏʟᴘʜᴇ Emperor of *Germany*, Sᴛᴇᴘʜᴇɴ
K. of *Poland*, and divers other Pʀɪɴᴄᴇs about it.
The Particulars of his Cauſe, as it was agitated in the *Emperors* Court;
By the Pᴏᴘᴇs Intervention: His Baniſhment, and Reſtoration in part.

Aₛ Aʟₛᴏ
The LETTERS of Sundry Great Men
and Pʀɪɴᴄᴇs (ſome whereof were preſent at ſome of theſe
Conferences and Apparitions of Sᴘɪʀɪᴛs:) to the ſaid D. Dᴇᴇ.

Oᴜᴛ Oꜰ
The Original Copy, written with Dʳ. Dᴇᴇs own
Hand: Kept in the LIBRARY of
Sir T H O. C O T T O N, Kᵗ. Baronet.
WITH A
PREFACE
Confirming the *Reality* (as to the Point of Sᴘɪʀɪᴛs) of
This RELATION: and ſhewing the ſeveral good Uₛᴇs that
a Sober Chriſtian may make of All.
B Y
Mᴇʀɪᴄ. Cᴀsᴀᴜʙᴏɴ, D.D.
L O N D O N.

MAHOMET *receives his Law by Inspiration.*

APPOLONI. TYANEUS *in Domitians tym.*

Edw: Kelly *Prophet or Seer to D.r Dee.*

Roger Bacon *an English man*

PARACELSUS *Receits from the Inspiration of Spirits.*

D.r Dee *avoucheth his Stone is brought by Angelicall*

PREFACE.

WHAT is here presented unto thee (Christian Reader) being *a True and Faithful Relation, &c.* (as the Title beareth, and will be further cleared by this Preface) though by the carriage of it, in some respects, and by the Nature of it too, it might be deemed and termed, *A Work of Darknesse*: Yet it is no other then what with great tendernesse and circumspection, was tendered to men of highest Dignity in *Europe*, Kings and Princes, and by all (*England* excepted) listned unto for a while with good respect. By some gladly embraced and entertained for a long time ; the Fame whereof being carryed unto *Rome*, it made the Pope to bestir himself, not knowing what the event of it might be, and how much it might concern him. And indeed, filled all men, Learned and Unlearned in most places with great wonder and astonishment : all which things will be shewed and made good (to the utmost of what we have said) in the Contents of this book, by unquestionable *Records* and evidences. And therefore I make no question but there will be men enough found in the world whose curiosity will lead them to Read *what I think is not to be parallell'd in that Kind by any book that hath been set out in any Age to read*: I say, though it be to no other end then to satisfie their curiosity. But whatsoever other men, according to their several inclinations, may propose to themselves in the reading of it , yet I may and must here professe in the first place, in Truth and Sincerity, that the end that I propose to my self (so far as I have contributed to the Publishing of the Work) is not to satisfie curiosity, but to do good, and promote Religion. When we were first acquainted with the Book, and were offered the reading of it, having but lately been conversant in a Subject of much Affinity ; to wit, of *Mistaken Inspiration* and *Possession*, through ignorance of Natural causes (which labour of ours, as it was our aime at the first in publishing of it, to do good, so we have had good reason since to believe, that we did not altogether misse of what we aimed at) we could not but gladly accept of it. And as we gladly accepted , so we read unto the end with equal eagernesse and Alacrity : Which when we had done, truly it was our Opinion , That the Publishing of it could not but be very Seasonable and Useful, as against *Atheists* at all times, so in these Times especially, when the Spirit of Error and Illusion, not in profest *Anabaptists* only, even of the worst kind that former Ages have known and abhorred, doth so much prevail, but in many also , who though they disclaim and detest openly (and heartily too, I hope, most of them) the fruits and effects that such causes have produced in others, yet ground themselves neverthelesse upon the same principles of *Supposed Inspiration* and imaginary *Revelations* ; and upon that account deem themselves, if not the Only, yet much better Christians then others. And I was much Confirmed in this Judgment when I was told (as indeed I was, at the first, by them that knew very well) that the Most Reverend, Pious and Learned *Archbishop of Armagh,* lately

deceas-

deceafed, upon reading of the faid book, before his death, had declared himfelf to the fame purpofe, and *wifhed it Printed.* But becaufe it is very poffible,
that every Reader will not at the firft be fo well able of himfelf to make that
good ufe by good and Rational Inferences and Obfervations of this fad Story
as is aimed at, my chiefeft aim in this Preface is to help fuch. And becaufe it is
not leffe probable that this Licentious Age will afford very many, who with the
Saduces of old (that is, Jewifh Epicures) believe no *Spirit,* or Angel, or Refur-
rection; who therefore being prepoffeffed with prejudice when they hear of fo
many Spirits as are here mentioned, and fo many ftrange Apparitions, in feveral
Kinds, will not only fling back themfelves, but will be ready to laugh at any
other that give any credit to fuch things. Although I will not take upon me to
convert any by Reafon that are engaged into fuch an opinion by a wicked life,
that is, Unjuft practifes, Luxurious lewd courfes, open profaneneffe, under the
name of Wit and Galantry, and the like, becaufe, I think, it is very juft with
God to leave fuch to the error and blindneffe of their Judgments; fo that without a Miracle there can be little hopes of fuch. Yet I fhall hope that fuch as are
Rational men, fober in their Lives and Converfations, fuch as I have known
my felf; yea, men of excellent parts in other things, men that are both willing
to hear and able to confider: that fuch, I fay, may receive fome fatisfaction by
what I fhall fay and propofe to their Ingenuous confideration in this matter. Were
we to argue the cafe by Scripture, the bufineffe would foon be at an end; there
being no one Controverted point among men, that I know of, that can receive
a more Ample, Full, Clear and fpeedy determination, then this bufinefs of *Spirits,* and *Witches,* and *Apparitions* may, if the Word of God might be Judge. But
I will fuppofe that I have to do with fuch, who though they do not altogether
deny the Word of God, yet will not eafily, however, admit of any thing that
they think contrary to Reafon, or at leaft not to be maintained by Reafon. I
fhall therefore forbear all Scripture Proofs and Teftimonies in this particular,
and defire the Chriftian Reader (who otherwife might juftly take offence) to
take notice upon what ground it is that I forbear.

But though I will not ufe any Scripture for proof, yet by way of Application
I hope I may be allowed to ufe fome Scripture words, which may direct us
perchance to a good Method in the examination of this bufineffe. The Apoftle
faith in a place, φάσκοντες ἶναι σοφοὶ, ἐμωράνθησαν: (*profeffing themfelves to be wife, they became
fools*) I fhall not enquire of whom, and upon what occafion it was fpoken: I
draw no argument from it; only becaufe there is a fhew of great Wifdom in
this Opinion; and yet, as I conceive, as much of Error and falfhood (that is,
Folly, as the word is often ufed) as in any other falfe opinion that is leffe popular.
I will frame my difcourfe to this iffue, firft, to enquire what it is that makes
it fo popular and plaufible, among them efpecially that pretend to more then
ordinary Wifdom; and then fecondly, lay it open (as I am able) to the view in its
right colours, that the *Folly* or falfhood of it may be difcernable even to ordinary judgments.

Firft then, (as for them that *deny Spirits,* &c.) we fay, The world is full of impofture; to know this, to obferve it in all Trades, in all Profeffions, in all ranks
and degrees of men, is to know the world, and that is to be wife. Though we
call them *Juglers,* yet they deferve to be thought the plaineft dealing men of the
world that fhew their tricks openly in the ftreets for money; for they profeffe
what they are. They are the trueft Juglers that do their feats (and they for mo-

ny too, moſt of them) under the Veil and Reputation of Holineſſe, Sanctity, (or, Saintſhip) Religion, Virtue, Juſtice, Friendſhip ; fine words to catch men that are of eaſie Belief, and thinks that every thing that gliſters muſt needs be gold. Hence it is, that men that have had the Reputation of Wiſe men in the world, have commended this unto us as greateſt Wiſdom, Not Easily To Believe : Νῆφε, ὶ μέμνησο ἀπιστεῖν : ἄρτρα ταῦτα τῶν φρενῶν *Epicharmus* got more credit for this one ſaying (and hath done more good too, perchance) then many that have been the Authors of vaſt Volumes. Now if thoſe things that are expoſed to ſenſe, the proper Objects of our Eyes and Eares, be lyable to ſo much Impoſture and Deceit, that the wiſeſt can ſcarce know what to believe : How much more caution do we need in thoſe things that are ſo much above Senſe, and in ſome reſpects contrary to Senſe (and that is *Spirits*) that we be not deceived ? If we conſider the Nature of man, his Bodily frame, the Affections of his ſoul, the Faculties of his mind, we ſhall have no occaſion at all to wonder if moſt men are apt to believe and to be cheated. But as no cauſe to wonder, ſo as little cauſe to imitate : *Felix qui rerum potuit cognoſcere cauſas* ! τεραλολογία, *a deſire of, or to ſtrange things that may cauſe amazement*, is the proper affection of the vulgar, that is, of moſt men, which they bring into the world with them, (it is the obſervation of the wiſeſt of men that have written concerning the affairs and actions of men) and cannot be rid of but by wiſdom, which is the happineſſe of few : *Errandi, non neceſſitas tantum, ſed amor*. *Seneca* ſomewhere ſpeaking of the Nature of Man ; There was a time when the world was much governed by *Oracles* ; private men went unto them as unto God, Kings and Princes ſent unto them to be adviſed about greateſt matters : and ſo much faith was aſcribed unto them, generally, that the very word became a Proverb appliable unto thoſe things, whereof no queſtion can be made. Yet thoſe very ancient Heathens, that tell us of theſe Oracles, tell us of their vanity ; and though they ſay not, That all were falſe and counterfeit, yet whileſt they acknowledg it of ſome, they give us juſt occaſion to ſuſpect that it might have been found as true of the reſt alſo, had like care been taken to examine the truth of them alſo.

Again, there was a time (and that time not many hundred years yet paſt) when *Miracles* were the only diſcourſe and delight of men : Ghoſts and Spirits were in every houſe ; and ſo prone were men to receive what was delivered unto them in that kind, that Miracle-makers were much put to it, not to make their ſtories probable, (for that was not ſtood upon) but to make them wonderful enough ; inſomuch that ſome have been forced ^{See the Life of Albertus M.} to complain publickly of the credulity of the people, who yet themſelves tell us much more, I dare ſay, then was ever true. As of Miracles, ſo of *Exorciſmes* : How many Divels and Spirits have been driven out of men and women, ſuppoſed to be *poſſeſſed*, by ſolemn Exorciſmes, to the great wonder of the beholders, which afterwards upon further ſearch and examination, have been convicted to have been nothing but the artifices and ſubtil contrivances of men ? Sentences and Judgments have paſſed upon ſuch cheats when they have been diſcovered in moſt places of Europe, which have been publiſhed. But they have done ſtrange things though (ſome that were thought poſſeſſed) and things impoſſible, to ordinary ſenſe, to be done by Nature. It is very true, ſome have : But they that know what ſtrange things may be done to the amaze-

ment

ment of all not acquainted with such mysteries, by long *Use and Custome*, they will not easily wonder (so as to make a supernatural thing of it) though they see things, which, to their sight and of most, cannot but seem very wonderful, and almost impossible. As for the bodily temper of man and of his *Brain*, it hath been sufficiently by some late books of that subject (*Enthusiasme*) both by reasons from Nature, and by sundry examples proved, that a very little distemper of the brain, scarce discernable unto any, but those that are well versed in the study of Natural causes, is enough to represent Spirits, Angels and Divels, Sights and Stories of Heaven and Hell to the Fancy : by which sober kind of Madnesse and deliration, so little understood vulgarly, many have been, and are daily deceived ; and from these things, through the ignorance of men, strange things sometimes have ensued, and the peace of Common-weales hath suffered not a little.

Aristotle, in his Meteors, tells of one that alwayes saw (so he thought, at least) another man's shape before his eyes, and how they happened unto him naturally, he gives a reason. *Hyppocrates*, Περὶ παρθενίων, (a very short Discourse, but full of excellent matter) sheweth how some, both men and women, through Natural causes, come to fancy to themselves that they see δαίμονας, Divels and Spirits, and to be tormented in their Souls, even to the making away of themselves by their own hands. The Author of the book, *De Morbo Sacro*, (very ancient too, but not right *Hyppocrates*, as many are of opinion) hath excellent matter too, to the same purpose ; but I have not the book at this time by me. *Hyppocrates*, (where before) sheweth how many in that case were gulled by the Priests of those times, making them believe, That this happened to them through the anger of some god. " They that are verst in the *Opticks* know, That there is a " way, through the help of *glasses* that shall not be seen, to make moving sha- " dows that shall appear like Ghosts, to the great terror of the ignorant behold- " er : and it is said, That pretended Astrologers and Fortune-tellers cheat many " by those sights. It is the opinion of some Jewish Rabbins, That what Ghosts or Souls are raised by *Necromancy*, they alwayes appear *inverso corpore*, that is, their head dowards and feet upwards. Though nothing is to be wondered at in Rabbins, who (commonly) are, as full of ridiculous conceits as ever came into the head of any Bedlam : Yet my opinion is, " That the first ground of " this wild conceit was, some appearance by the *Species* of an object, gathered " through a little *glasse* into a dark room. For so indeed the objects must ap- " pear *inverso corpore* if it be done in a high room, and the objects from whence " the *Spiecies* are gathered be lower then the glasse through which they passe. And the reason of it is very Demonstrable to the sight of any reasonable man. Certainly, by this secret (which yet is no great secret, being commonly seen and practis- ed among them that are any thing curious) strange things may be done by a Cunning man, to their great amazement that know not the cause. There would be no end if I should attempt to gather from several Authors what hath been invented by men, and what may be done by Art to cheat men in matters of this nature. Let any man, that is yet a stranger to it, but read the life of *Alexander the false Prophet*, or Prognosticator, written by *Lucian*, and he shall see notable examples of successeful Cheats and Impostures, scarce credible indeed, but that the thing was yet then fresh and famous, and that all circumstances of

Histo-

Hiſtory confirm the truth of the relation. And let him that reads it judge, what dull and dry fellows the Mountebank-Aſtrologers, Prognoſticators and Fortune-tellers of theſe dayes are, to this Noble., Renowned *Alexander*. Only let him know that reads, that *Lucian* was a profeſt Atheiſt, and therefore no wonder if he find *Epicurus* ſpoken of with great reſpect, whom all Atheiſts, and Atheiſtically inclined are ſo much obliged to honour. This excepted, I think, the Story is very worthy to be known, and much more worthy to be read by all men (conſidering the good uſe that may be made of it) then many books that are daily tranſlated out of other languages.

But laſtly, If there were any ſuch thing, really as Divels and Spirits that uſe to appear unto men; to whom ſhould they (probably) ſooner appear, then to ſuch as daily call upon them, and devote their Souls and Bodies unto them by dreadful Oaths and Imprecations? And again, then to ſuch, who through damnable curioſity have many times uſed the means (the beſt they could find in books, by Magical Circles, Characters and Invocations) and yet never, neither the one nor the other ſaw any thing?

I have ſaid as much as I mean to ſay (though ſomewhat perchance might be added) to ſhew the plauſibleneſſe of the opinion, in oppoſition to vulgar apprehenſions and capacities, whereby (as I conceive, for I have not wittingly omitted any thing that I thought material) it chiefly intitles it ſelf to wiſdom, and more then ordinary prudence, which all men generally are ambitious of. Yet I would not have it thought that all men that hold this concluſion, That there be no Spirits, *&c.* go ſo rationally to work, or can give this account or any other more rational and plauſible for what they hold. God knows there be many in the world, men of no learning, and mean capacities, who can ſpeak as peremptorily as the beſt, not becauſe they have conſidered of it, and underſtand the grounds of either opinion, but becauſe they know, or have heard it is the opinion of ſome Learned, and they hope they ſhall be thought learned too if they hold with them. Beſides an ordinary (for ſome have been learned) *Epicurean,* who makes it his Motto (to himſelf and in his heart) Ἐν τῷ μηδὲν ἰδέναι, ἥδιστος βίος: and ſeeks his eaſe in this world (ἀπαραξίαν their own word, which imports *Tranquility* both of mind and body; a good word but ill applyed) as his *ſummum bonum,* or chiefeſt happineſſe: It is a great eaſe to him when any ſtrange things doth happen by Witches, Wizards and the like; and other ſome to ſatisfie their faith, others their reaſon and curioſity, are put to it to enquire of men by conference, and to ſearch into books ancient and late, Sacred and Profane, and all little enough. A great eaſe, I ſay, for him, then, and upon all ſuch occaſions, to poſſeſſe his Soul in ſecure ignorance, and to ſave his credit (yea, and to gain credit with ſome) by barely ſaying, *Fabula eſt, I do not believe it.* We ſhall hear ſome of them by and by acknowledg, in effect, as much as I have ſaid: I impoſe nothing upon them. I will not take upon me to judge of a book that I never read; I cannot ſay that I ever ſaw it. But becauſe I have heard ſome men magnifie an Engliſh book written of this ſubject to prove that there be no Witches, I will impart unto the Reader that hath not obſerved it, the judgment of one of the Learnedſt men that ever *England* ſaw (I wiſh he had been more gently dealt with when time was) of that book, whereby it may appear (if his judgment be right, as I am very inclinable to believe

lieve, becauſe of his great Learning, and wonted circumſpection in his cenſures) what great undertakers many men are upon very little ground, and how prone others to extol what doth favour their cauſe, though to the prejudice of their better judgments, if they would judge impartially. Dr. *Rainolds* in thoſe elaborate *Prælectiones de libris Apocryphis*, where he doth cenſure ſome opinions of *Bodinus* as prejudicial to the Chriſtian Faith. *Reginaldus Scotus, noſtras,* (ſaith he) *qui contrariam Bodino inſanit inſaniam, ait Papiſtas confiteri, non poſſe Demonas ne audire quidem nomen Jehovæ. Acceperat ille à Bodino, & attribuit Papiſtis in genere, tanquam omnes Papiſta in eo conſpirarent. Pergit ipſe, & quoniam animadverterat quaſdam fæminas maleficas, aliquando iſtius modi narrationes ementiri, putavit omnia eſſe ficta; ex imperitia Dialectica, & aliarum bonarum artium: Ut qui nullo judicio, nullâ methodo, nullâ optimarum artium ſcientiâ, eodem modo aggreſſus ſit hanc rem, quomodo Poeta loquitur,*

——— *Tenet inſatiabile quoſdam Scribendi cacoëthes: & eodem prorſus modo ratiocinatur,* &c. We have been the more willing to produce this paſſage out of the writings of that Learned man, becauſe we alſo in our anſwers may have occaſion to ſay ſomewhat to the ſame purpoſe; not of that Author or his book, which he judgeth, any thing, but of the ground upon which he builded, which we ſhall find to be the ſame upon which others alſo, that deny Spirits have gone upon. But we will go Methodically to work, and take every thing in order, as we have propoſed in the objections.

Firſt, We ſaid, The world was full of Impoſture. It is granted, of Impoſtors and Impoſtures. But what then ſhall the concluſion be, That therefore there is no truth in the world, or at leaſt not to be attained unto by mortal man? Truly, many books of old have been written to that effect. *Sextus Empiricus* is yet extant, a very learned book it cannot be denied, and of excellent uſe for the underſtanding of ancient Authors, Phyloſophers eſpecially. I could name ſome Chriſtians alſo, by profeſſion, men of great learning that have gone very far that way. But this will not be granted by ſome I am ſure that are or have been thought great oppugners of the common opinion about Witches and Spirits; ſome Phyſicians I mean, and Naturaliſts by their profeſſion. But may not we argue as plauſibly againſt that which they profeſſe, as they have done or can do againſt Spirits and Apparitions? We would be loath to make ſo long a digreſſion; we have had occaſion elſewhere to ſay ſomewhat to this purpoſe: and they that will be ſo curious may ſee what hath been written by *Cornel. Agrippa* (who is very large upon this ſubject) about it, not to name any others. It is not yet a full twelve-moneth, that a friend of mine, a Gentleman of quality, brought his Lady to *London* (ſome 60 miles and upwards from his ordinary dwelling) to have the advice of Phyſicians about his wife (a very Virtuous and Religious Lady) troubled with a weak ſtomack and ill digeſtion; which cauſed grievous ſymptoms. I think he had the advice of no leſſe then a dozen firſt and laſt: I am ſure he named unto me five or ſix of the chiefeſt in Credit and practice that the Town affordeth. Not one of them did agree in their opinions, either concerning the Cauſe, or the means to be uſed for a Cure. So that the Gentleman went away more unſatisfied then he came. What he did I know not: I know what ſome men would have inferred upon this. Yet I, for my part, for the benefit that I have received by it, and the effects that I have ſeen of

it,

it, both upon my felf, and others in my life-time, upon feveral occafions (where *learned Artifts*, not *Empiricks* have been employed) though all the world fhould be of another opinion, I think my felf bound to honour, as the profeffion, fo all Learned, Ingenious Profeffors of it : and I make no queftion but the worft of *Agrippa's* objections, by any man of competent judgment and experience, may eafily be anfwered. I fay therefore that as in other things of the world, fo in matters of *Spirits and Apparitions*, though lyable to much error and impofture, yet it doth not follow but there may be reality of truth and certainty difcernable unto them that will take the pains to fearch things unto the bottom, where truth commonly is to be found, and are naturally endowed with competent judgments to difcern between fpecious arguments and folidity of truth.

But this proveth nothing. No : but the removing of this common objection may difpofe the Reader, I hope, to confider of what we have to fay with leffe prejudice. And that fhall be our next task, what we have to fay for *Spirits*, &c. before we come to particular Objections. Wherein nevertheleffe I will be no longer then I muft at this time, becaufe I fhall have a more proper place in two feveral Tractates, the one whereof hath been a long time in loofe notes and papers, not yet digefted, to wit, my Second Part of *Enthufiafme*: the other, in my head yet wholly, but in better readineffe to be brought to light, becaufe of later conception; to wit, *A Difcourfe of Credulity and Incredulity, in things Natural, Civil and Divine, or Theologgical.* We fhall meet there with many cafes not fo neceffary here to be fpoken of, which will help very much to clear this bufinefs.

¶ But here I fay, firft of all, It is a Maxim of *Ariftotle's* the great Oracle of Nature, which many have taken notice of, and applyed to their feveral purpofes : O' πᾶσι δοκῆ, τοῦτο εἶναι φαμὲν, *That which is generally believed, is moft likely to be true.* Who alfo in another place of the fame book doth approve the faying of *Hefiod*, φήμη δ' οὔτιγε πάμπαν ἀπόλλυται, ἥντιρα λαοὶ Πολλοὶ φημίζωσι. Now if any opinion whereof queftion is made can juftly pretend to a general affent and confent of all people, places, ages of the world, I think, nay, I know, and it will be proved that this of Witches, Spirits, and Apparitions may. I do not know fcarce any ancient book extant of Philofopher or Hiftorian (the Writings of profeffed Epicureans excepted, of *Ariftotle* we fhall give an account by and by) but doth afford fome pregnant relation, teftimony or paffage to the confirmation of this truth. I dare fay, fhould a man collect the relations and teftimonies out of feveral Authors and books (that are come to our knowledge) within the compaffe of two thoufand years, of Authors well accounted of, generally, and vvhofe teftimonies (Hiftorians efpecially) vve receive in other things; a man might make a book of the biggeft fize and form that ordinary books (vvhich vve call *Folioes*) are. It is true, many Authors may vvrite one thing vvhich may prove falfe, as the famous hiftory of the *Phenix*, perchance, or fome fuch; but upon examination it vvill appear that thofe many take all from one or tvvo at the moft, vvho firft delivered it. They add nothing in confirmation of their ovvn knovvledg or experience. But here it is quite othervvife, thofe many Authors that I fpeak of (Hiftorians efpecially of feveral ages) they tell

us

us different things that hapned in their own times, in divers places of the world: and of many of them we may say they were such as knew little of former books, or stories of other Nations but their own. Within these 200 years the world, we know, by the benefit of Navigation hath been more open and known then before; yea, a great part of the world discovered that was not known before. I have read many books, the best I could meet with, in several Languages, of divers Voyages into all parts of the world: I have conversed with many Travellers, whom I judged sober and discreet. I never read any book of that argument, nor yet met with man, that I have had the opportunity to confer with, but was able of his own knowledg to say somewhat whereby my belief of these things might be confirmed.

Now for the *Epicureans* (of all Philosophers the most inconsiderable in matters of knowledg, as former ages have described them) no man need to wonder if they denyed those things which by *the solemn engagement of their Sect* they were bound and resolved, notwithstanding any sight or sense, experience or evidence to the contrary, not to believe, at least not to acknowledg. This doth clearly appear by one that may be believed (though I have met with it in more) in such things. *Lucian* (himself a profest *Epicurean* Atheist) who doth commend *Democritus*, *Epicurus* and *Metrodorus* (the most famous of that Sect) for their ἀσαμαντιστὸν γνώμην, as he calls it, their *fixed*, *irrevokeable*, *unconquerable resolution*, when they saw any strange thing that by others was admired as miraculous, if they could find the cause or give a probable guesse, well and good, if not, yet not to depart from their first resolution, and still to believe and to maintain that it was false and impossible: It is a notable passage, and which excellent use may be made of. I will therefore set down his own words for their sake that understand the Language: —— ὅςι πάτι τὸ μηχάνημα (speaking of some of *Alexander the false Prophet* his devices)

Lu ian in Alex. Ald. ed. p. 179.

ἐδύτο Δημοκρίτε τινος, ἢ ἐ αὐτὸ Ἐπικούρου, ὁ Μητροδώρου, ἀσαμαντιστὸν πρὸς ταῦτα ἐ τὰ τοιαῦτα γνώμην ἔχοντος, ὡς ἀπιστῆσαι, ἐ ὑπὸ ἣν εἰκάσαι ἐ εἰ μὴ εὑρεῖν τὸν τρὸπον ἐδύνατο, ἐκεῖνο γοῦν προπεπεισμένου, ὅτι λέληθεν αὐτὸν ὁ τρὸπος τῆς μαγγανείας: τὸ δ' οὖν πᾶν ψεῦδος ἐςι, ἐ γενέσαι ἀδύνατον. Who doubts that this is the resolution of many also in these dayes, not of them only who are Epicureans, whose manner of living (as we have said before) doth engage them to this opinion, but of others also, who think it not for their credit (the vanity of which belief nevertheless might easily appear, there being nothing so mean and ordinary in the world wherein the Wisdom of the wisest, in the consideration of the causes, by the confession of best Naturalists, may not be posed) to believe any thing that they cannot give a probable reason of. Not to be wondred then if we see many, notwithstanding daily experience to the contrary, to stick so close to those tenets which they have wedded themselves unto with so firm a resolution from the beginning, never to leave them, be they right or wrong.

As for *Aristotle*, I confesse his authority is very great with me; not because I am superstitiously addicted to any of his opinions, which I shall ever be ready to forsake when better shall be shewed unto me; but because

(be-

(befides the judgment of all accounted wife and learned in former ages) I am convicted in my judgment, that fo much folid reafon in all Arts and Sciences never iffued from mortal man (known unto us by his writings) without fupernatural illumination. Well: *Ariftotle* doth not acknowledg Spirits, he mentions them not in any place. Let it be granted : And why fhould it be a wonder to any man that knows the drif. and purpofe of *Ariftotle's* Phylofophy ? He lived when *Plato* lived ; he had been his fellow Scholer under *Socrates*, and for fome time his Scholer ; but afterwards he became his *æmulus*, and pleafed himfelf very much to oppofe his Doctrine, infomuch as he is cenfured by fome Ancients for his ingratitude. The truth is, *Plato's* writings are full of Prodigies, Apparitions of Souls, pains of Hell and Purgatory, Revelations of the gods, and the like. Wherein he is fo bold that he is fain to excufe himfelf fometimes, and .doth not defire that any man fhould believe him, according to the letter of his relations, but in groffe only, that fomewhat was true to that effect. Indeed he hath many divine paffages, yea, whole Treatifes, that can never be fufficiently admired in their kind ; but too full of tales, for a Phylofopher, it cannot be denyed. *Ariftotle* therefore refolved upon a quite contrary way : He would meddle with nothing but what had fome apparent ground in Nature. Not that he precifely denyed all other things, but becaufe he did not think that it was the part of a Phylofopher to meddle with thofe things that no probable reafon could be given of. This doth clearly appear by a Divine paffage of his, *De part. anim. l.* 1. *t.* 5. where he divides Subftances in ἀγεννήτους ἢ ἀφθάρτους, *Eternal and Incorruptible*, that is, in effect, *Spiritual* (for even Spirits that were created might be termed ἀγέννητα, that is, properly, *That have not their beginning by Generation* ; but we will eafily grant, that the creation of Angels, good or bad, was not known to *Ariftotle* : (we may underftand *Gods* and *Intelligences*) and thofe, that μέλλχυσι γενέσεως ἢ φθορᾶς, that is, *are mortals.* He goes on, *As for Divine Subftances, which we honour, we can fay but little of them, though we defire it ; becaufe fo little of them is expofed to fenfe* [and Reafon.] *. Mortal things that we are familiarly acquainted and daily converfe with, we may know if we take pains. But much more fhould we rejoice in the knowledg (yea though we know but a very little part) of things Divine for their excellency, then in the knowledg of thefe worldly things though never fo perfect and general But the comfort that we have of them (which doth make fome amends) is the certainty, and that they come within the compaffe of Sciences.* What could be faid more Divinely by a man that had nothing by revelation ? Truly, there appeareth unto me (if I may fpeak without offence and mifconftruction) more Divinity in thofe words, then in fome books that pretend to nothing elfe. Add to this another place of his in his *Metaphyficks*, where he faith, That though things fupernatural be of themfelves clear and certain, yet to us they are not fo , who fee them only with Owles eyes. Can we fay then that *Ariftotle* denyed thofe things that he forbore to write of, becaufe they were (their natures and their qualities) above the knowledg of man ? Neither is it abfolutely true that *Ariftotle* never wrote of Spirits and Apparitions. *Cicero* in his firft book *De Divinatione*, hath a long ftory out of him of a fhape or Spirit that appeared in a dream to one *Eudemus* (his familiar friend and

ac-

acquaintance) and foretold him ſtrange things that came to paſſe. *Clemens Alexandrinus* hath a ſtrange ſtory out of him, of a Magical Ring, one or two, which *Excestus*, King of the Phocenſes did uſe, and foreſaw things future by them. It is to be found and ſeen among the fragments of *Ariſtotles* works. And that he did not deny Witches, may appear by that mention he makes of them in more then one place. How much he aſcribed to common report and experience, though no reaſon could be given, doth appear by his Preface to his Treatiſe *De Divinatione per inſomnia*: where he propoſeth the caſe, how hard it is for a rational man to believe any thing upon report which he can ſee no reaſon for ; nay , which ſeemeth contrary to reaſon : as, for a man to foretel by dream what ſhall happen in another Kingdome far off without any apparent cauſe. But on the other ſide, ſaith he, not leſs hard to deny that which all men, or moſt men , do believe, to wit, that there be ſuch predictions. For to ſay (his own words) that ſuch dreams come from God , beſides what elſe might be objected (which might eaſily be underſtood by them that underſtand his Doctrine) it is moſt unreaſonable to believe that God would ſend them to men either vitious in their lives, or idiots and fools, of all men the moſt vile and contemptible , who have been obſerved to have ſuch dreams oftner then better and wiſer men. So leaving the buſineſſe undetermined, he doth proceed to the conſideration of thoſe Prophetick dreams, for which ſome probable reaſon may be given. Yet in the ſecond Chapter he ſaith directly, That though dreams be not

*The Latine Inter- βιοπεμπτα, yet they may be perchance * δαιμονια, for ſuch
preter tranſlates it he acknowledges Nature to be, not θεια, but δαιμονια on-
Dæmonia; & I know ly. I will not enquire further into the meaning of theſe
not how it can be words; it is not to be done in few words. It plainly ap-
better expreſſed, pears that nothing troubled him ſo much (for he repeats
though lyable to the objection twice or thrice) as that God ſhould be thought
ambiguity.

to favour either wicked men or fools. I wiſh no worſe Doctrine had e-ver been Printed or Preached concerning God. But ſtill let it be remembred that he knew of no Divine Word or Revelation. Yet *Jul. Scaliger* in his Commentaries upon *Hypocrates De Inſomniis*, doth wonder that *Ariſtotle* ſhould ſtick ſo much at this, and ſeems himſelf to give a reaſon grounded in Nature. Indeed he ſaith ſomewhat as to the caſe of fools and idiots, but nothing (that I remember) that reacheth to wicked men alſo. Let theſe things be conſidered, and let the Reader judge of how different temper *Ariſtotle* was from that of ancient or later *Epicures.* This mention of *Ariſtotle* and *Plato* puts me in mind of *Socrates* their Maſter, *his Familiar Spirit*; no Shape but a Voice only, by which his life and actions were much directed. The thing is atteſted by ſo many, ſo grave Authors whereof ſome lived at the very time, others not long after, or in times not very remote, that I know not how it can be queſtioned by any man. Neither indeed is it, that I remember, by any Heathens or Chriſtians of ancient times, and there have been books written of it, divers, in Greek and Latine, whereof ſome are yet extant. But whether it were a good Spirit or an evil, ſome men have doubted, and it is free for any man to think what he pleaſeth of it. For my part I ever had a Reverend opinion of *Socrates*,

and

and do believe (if there be no impiety in it, as I hope not) that he was, as among Heathens in some respect, a fore-runner of Christ, to dispose them the better when the time should come to imbrace (and it did it effectually) the Gospel. Many other Phylosophers, that have been of greatest fame, were certainly great Magicians, as *Orpheus, Pythagoras, Empedocles*, and the like, as by those things that have been written of them by several ancient authors may be collected. But above all I give the pre-eminence to *Apollonius Thianeus*, a man of later times, and of whom we may speak with more confidence and certainty; This was the man whom ancient Heathens very tenacious of their former worship and superstitions, did pitch upon to oppose unto Christ. His Life hath been written by divers, four of them were joyned together and opposed to the four Gospels : and *Hierocles*, a famous Phylosopher of those times, made a Collation of his Miracles with those of Christs, who was answered by *Eusebius*, yet extant. Sure it is, they prevailed so much, that he was for a long time worshipped by many, and in sundry places as a very God; yea, by some Roman Emperors, as we find in History. *Philostratus* hath written his Life in very Elegant stile (as *Photius* judged) in 8 books, which are extant. And though they contain many fabulous things, as any man may expect by the undertaking, yet have they so much truth and variety of ancient learning, that I think they deserve to be better known then commonly they are ; but cannot be understood, I am sure, as they should be, by any translation either Latine or French that ever I saw : For the *Paris* Edition, though it boast of great things (as the manner is) yet how little was performed may easily appear unto any that will take the pains to compare it with the former edition of *Aldus* : Which I speak not to find fault, but because I wish that some able man would undertake the work ; there is not any book, by the Translations yet extant, that more needeth it. What use *Scaliger* made of him, may appear by his frequent quotations in his Notes upon *Eusebius*, in the History of those times. As for *Appollonius* his Miracles or wonderful Acts (which is our businesse here) though many things have been added, some, probably, done by Imposture, yet I do not see how it can be doubted but he did many strange things by the help of *Spirits*, which things may be judged by due observation of circumstances ; as for example, That being convented before *Domitian* the Emperor in the presence of many, he presently vanished and was seen a great way off (at *Puteoli* I think) about the same time. That at the very time when *Domitian* was killed at *Rome*, he spake of it publickly and of the manner of it at *Ephesus* : and so of many others, which seem to me (as unto most) almost unquestionable. The greatest wonder to me is, that such was his port and outward appearance of Sanctity and Simplicity, that even Christians have thought reverently of him, and believed that he did his wonders by the power of God, or by secret Philosophy and knowledg of Nature not revealed unto other men. So *Justine Martyr*, one of the ancient Fathers of the Church judged of him, as is well known. Most later Phylosophers that lived about *Julians* time, and before that, as also the Emperors themselves, many of them, were great Magicians and *Necromancers*, as may easily eafily appear, partly by their own writings, and partly by the Hiftory of thofe times.

I do very much wonder whether any man, being a Scholer, and not ftrongly prepoffeffed, that doth not believe *Spirits,* &c. can fay that he e-ver read the books of Tryals and Confeffions of Witches and Wizards, fuch I mean, as have been written by learned and judicious men. Such as, for example, I account *Nichol. Remigius,* his *Demonolatria : ex judiciis capitalibus* 900 *plus minus hominum,* &c. grounded efpecially upon the Confeffions and Condemnations of no leffe then 900 men and women in *Lorraine* within the compaffe of few years. That he was a learned man, I think no body will deny that hath read him; and that he was no very credulous and fuper-ftitious man (though a Papift) that alfo is moft certain: and I have won-dred at his liberty many times. I know not how it is now in thofe pla-ces; but by what I have read and heard of the doings of Witches and Sor-"cerers in *Geneva* and *Savoy* in former times (I could fay fomewhat of my "felf, how my life was preferved there very ftrangely, but my witneffes are "not, and I will not bring their credit in queftion for fuch a bufineffe.) I am of opinion, That he that fhould have maintained there that there was no fuch thing as Witches, or Spirits, &c. would have been thought by moft either mad and brain-fick (fo frequent and vifible were the effects to fober eyes) or a Witch himfelf. For indeed it is ordinary enough, that thofe that are fo really, are very willing (which deceiveth many) to be thought Impoftors, and there is good reafon for it: I fhould fooner fuf-pect him an Impoftor that doth profeffe himfelf (except it be by way of confeffion, as many have done) and is ambitious to be counted a Witch or Sorcerer. I remember I faw a book fome years ago, intituled, *De l'incon-ftance des mauvais Anges & Demons,* printed at *Paris* 1612. in *quarto,* and ano-ther of the fame Author, and fize, intituled, *L'incredulite & mefcreauce du for-tilege,* Paris 1642. Strange ftories are told there of a Province of *France,* a-bout that time (or little before) marvelloufly infefted with Witches and Sorcerers, infomuch that people did not know one another (in fome one place) in the ftreets, by reafon of evil Spirits appearing publickly in the fhape of men; and that the proceedings of juftice (which doth not hap-pen often) were fometimes difturbed by them. I think the Author him-felf was one that was fent to the place by the King with fome authority, and to make report. But as I do not altogether truft my memory, having had but a fight of the books (it was at the *Bell* in St. *Pauls* Church-yard:) So I befeech the Reader not to reft upon this account that I give him upon my beft remembrance, but to perufe the books himfelf. I am confident he may receive good fatisfaction, being things that were not done in a corner, but very publickly and well attefted as I remember. However the reader muft give me leave (though it be not to this purpofe, left my fi-lence be drawn to the prejudice of the truth) to tell him, that I met with one great falfhood there concerning my own fa-ther, (of *Bl. M.*) which I have abundantly refuted, and all others of that nature, when I was yet very young. But that (as I conceive) which in all thefe ftories would moft puzzle a rational man, is the fignes which are fet

Tom 11. p 6c8.
Nec. Caf. Pictus.

down

down by many how witches may be known, as *Teats*, *swimming upon the water*, *dry eyes*, and the like : which things indeed have some ground of truth, being limited to particular times and places, but are not of general application. Mr. *Vossius* had therefore reason to find fault with *Springerus* and *Bodinus* for making that a certain token of a Witch that she cannot weep. Who also in the same place doth well except against the tryal of γυναικολύσεως, as he calls it (commonly, *purgatio per aquam frigidam*) condemned by many. But he had done well to have limited his exception, and to have shewed how, and when, and how far such observations may be used. For certainly they are not altogether to be neglected. But the reasons of such observations or marks that are given by some, are so ridiculous, that they would make a sober man (that hath not patience enough to ponder all things diligently) to suspect all the rest. So one tels us, That when the Cock croweth the solemn meetings of Witches (which opinion perchance may prove ancient enough, as we shall shew elsewhere) are dissolved : and he thinks a reason may be because of the crowing of the Cock in the Gospel, when St. *Peter* denyed Christ. Another tells us, That Witches being well beaten *trunco vitis* (with a Vine stick or club) *Maleficia illata solvere sævillina coguntur*, have no more force to do hurt, or, that the party bewitched recovereth. And the reason (he thinks, and yet he no ordinary man neither) *ex mysterio vini & vineæ dilectæ Deo, ex cujus mysterio quotidie Sacramentum Sacrosancti Sanguinis Domini conficitur*, &c. But I shall have a more proper place for the full examination of these things in one of the two Treatises before mentioned. It cannot be denyed but this whole businesse of Witches, what through ignorance, what through malice, is very lyable to many mistakes and divers impostures. And it were to be wished that in all such Trials some prudent Divines, and learned experienced Physicians might be joyned. But hence to conclude with *Wierius* (who neverthelesse doth acknowledg Spirits, and the Illusions and Apparitions of Divels, and their mischievous opperations as much as any, and tells as strange things of them) and some others, that therefore there are no Witches and Sorcerers, is as if a man should deny the power of herbs because a thousand things have been written of them of old, and are yet daily falsely and superstitiously. And indeed it so fell out once in *Rome*, as by *Plinie* is recorded at large, Where when some ascribed such power unto Herbs, as though Sun and Moon had been subject unto them, the dead might be raised, armies vanquished, and what not ! which was not very well relished by many : at last came *Asclepiades*, who perswaded men that were very well disposed to be perswaded, that all Physical use of Herbs and Simples was a meer cheat, and that men were better want them, there being other means easier and lesse troublesome to restore health and overcome diseases, which he professed to teach : and prevailed so far for a while, that they were laid aside, and a new course of Physick introduced. Which for a while, as I said, (so prone are men commonly to entertain new divices) gave good content generally. It is well observed by *Aristotle* (and I think a great part of humane wisdome

Voss. de Idolol. 111. 180,181.

So in my Copy, it may be it should be, *vitis & vin.*

de-

dependeth on it) that in all things of the world that are commendable, as there is somewhat which is true and real, so somewhat also which is counterfeit and false. There is beauty Natural, saith he, and there is Artificial beauty by painting and trimming. A true, sound, healthy complexion, and that which makes a good shew, but is not sound. True, real gold and silver, but divers things also that may be taken for gold and silver at a distance, or by them that judge at the outward appearance. So, true, sound Ratiocination, and that which seems so to the unlearned, or to corrupt judgments, though it be very false. They that consider well of this, may the sooner come to the knowledg of truth in all things.

Well: we go on.

There was in *Aix* (*Aquæ Sextiæ* anciently, now *Aquensis Civitas*) in *Provence* (a County of *France* so called) in the year of the Lord 1611. a Romish Priest tryed, convicted, and by Sentence of the Court or Parliament condemned to be burned alive for abominable practises, and horrid things by him upon divers (some persons of quality) committed with and by the Divel. He had long desired it and sought it; at last the divel appeared to him in the habit of a Gentleman. The story is in divers books, *French* and *Latine*, and translated (at that time I believe) in divers languages. I would goe forty miles with all my heart to meet with that man that could tell me any thing whereby I might but probably be induced to believe, or at least to suspect, that there might be some mistake in the particulars of his Sentence. For my reason, I must confesse, was never more posed in any thing that ever I read of that nature. *Gassendus* indeed in *Pereskius* his life, hath somewhat (as I remember) of *Pereskius* his Opinion, as if he thought some of those things he confessed might be ascribed unto imagination; but I see no reason given: neither are the things of that nature, that can admit any such suspicion. Besides, *Tristan, of the Lives of the Emperors and their Coynes,* will tell you somewhat which may make a doubt, whether *Gassendus* ought to be believed in all things that he reporteth concerning that famous man. I am not very much satisfied of what Religion (though truly a very learned man) *Gassendus* was. And by the way (which is somewhat to the case of Witches in general) if I be not mistaken (for I have it not at this time) there is a relation in that very book of somewhat that hapned to *Pereskius* by Witches when he was a child. That wicked Sorcerer which was burned at *Aix*, foretold before his death that some misfortune would be done at the time and place of his execution, which hapned accordingly, and very strangely too. Somewhat again, I must confesse, I have seen printed (*Mimica Diaboli*, &c.) to take away the scandal of some part of his confession, or the Devils saying of Masse, &c. some part of which things might perchance with some colour be ascribed to imagination: but that is not it that troubles me. But enough of him.

What man is he, that pretends to learning, that hath not heard, and doth not honour the memory of *Joachimus Camerarius*, that great light of *Germany*? so wise (and for his wisdom, and other excellent parts, sought unto by many Princes) so moderate a man (an excellent temper for the

attain-

attaining of Truth) and so versed in all kind of learning, that we shall scarce among all the learned of these later Times find another so generally accomplished. The strangest relations that ever I read, or at least as strange as any I have read of Witches, and Sorcerers, and Spirits, I have read in him : such as either upon his own knowledge he doth relate, or such as he believed true upon the testimonie of others known unto him. The last work that he ever went about for the publick was, *De generibus Divinationum*, but he did not live (the more the pity) to make an end of it. But so much as he had done was set out by one of his learned sons, *Lipsiæ*, *an. Dom.* 1576. There *p* 33. he hath these words, *De Spirituum verò, quæ sunt Græcis δαιμόνια admirabili non solum efficacitate, sed manifesta Specie, quæ φάσματα perhibentur, præsentiâ; incredibiles extant passim veterum narrationes, & nostris temporibus superantia fidem comperta sunt, extra etiam γοητείας de quibus posteà dicetur.* So *p.* 89. & *p* 151. again and more fully. But his strangest relations are in his *Proæmium* to *Plutarchs* two Treatises, *De Defectu Oraculorum*, and *De Figura* EI *Consecratâ Delphis*, set out by him with Notes. Here I could come in with a whole cloud of witnesses, name hundreds of men of all Nations and professions that have lived within this last hundred years, and not any among them but such as have had, and have yet generally the reputation of Honest, Sober, Learned and Judicious, who all have been of this opinion that we maintain. But because we have to do with them especially who by their Profession pretend to the Knowledge of Nature above other men, I will confine my self for further testimony to them that have been of that Profession. I have been somewhat curious for one of my Calling, that had no other end but to attain to some Knowledge of Nature, without which a man may quickly be lead into manifold delusions and Impostures. I have read some, looked into many : I do not remember I have met with any professed Physician or Naturalist (some one or two excepted, which have been or shall be named) who made any question of these things. Sure I am, I have met with divers strange relations in sundry of them, of things that themselves were present at, and saw with their own eyes, where they could have no end, that any man can probably suspect, but to acknowledge the truth, though with some disparagement to themselves (according to the judgment of many) in the free confession of their own ignorance and disability to give reasons, and to penetrate into causes. Well : what then shall we say to such as *Jul. Cæsar, Scaliger, Fernelius, Sennertus*, the wonders and Oracles of their times ? As Physicians so Phylosophers, men of that profound wisdom and experience (much improved in some of them by long life) as their writings shew them to have been to this day. What shall we make of them ? or what do they make of themselves, that will censure such men as either cheaters or ignorant idiots ? *Henericus Saxonia*, a Learned Professor and Practiser of Physick in *Padua*, in that Book he hath written of that horrible Polonian Disease, which he calls *Plicam*, which turneth mens hairs (in sight) to Snakes and Serpents; in that book he doth ascribe so much to the power of Witches and Sorcerers in causing Diseases, not private only but even publick, as Pestilences and the like, as himself confesseth he could never have believed, until he

was

was convicted by manifest experience; and indeed is wonderful, and may well be thought incredible unto most, yet is maintained and asserted by *Sennertus De Febribus*; and in his sixth book (as I remember) *De Morbis à fascino, incantatione, & veneficiis inductis*. I will forbear the names of many men of fame and credit, Physicians too, because most of them are named (and commonly enough known) by *Sennertus* upon this occasion. There is one, whom I think inferiour to none, though perchance not so commonly known or read, and that is, *Georgius Raqusaius* a Venetian, who by his first education and profession was an Astrologer, cast many Nativities, and took upon him to Prognosticate; but afterwards conscious to himself of the vanity of the Art (that is, when the Divel doth not intermeddle, as alwayes must be understood: for some Astrologers have been Magicians withall, and have done strange things) gave it over, and hath written against it very Learnedly and Solidly. Read him, if you please, in his Chapters *De Magis, De Oraculis*; yea, through his whole Book *De Divinatione*, and you may be satisfied what he thought of these things : he also was a Physician. But I must not omit the Learned Author that set out *Musæum Veronense*, a great Naturalist and a Physician too; he handles it at the end of that work somewhat roundly and to the quick, I must confesse, but very Rational y and Solidly, in my judgment, against those pretended Peripateticians, that would be thought to defend the opinion of *Aristotle* herein. I could say somewhat of ancienter Physicians too, and give some account of those many Spels and Charmes that are in *Trallienus*, in all his books; an ancient Physician, in high esteeme with some eminent Physicians of these late times, as they themselves have told me; though not for his Charms, but for his other learning and excellent experience, which they had found good use of But this I reserve for another place & work. And this mention of that eminent Physician who commended *Trallienus* unto me, puts me in mind of what he imparted himself, not long before his death; of his own knowledge and experience; and particularly of the account he gave me of the examination of a Conjurer in *Salisbury*, at which, he said, none were present but King *James*, (of most Blessed Memory) the Duke of *Buckingham*, and himself: It is likely some others may have heard the same, and I had rather any body should tell it then I, who was then a patient under him, and durst not, were I put to it, trust to my memory for every circumstance

Hitherto I have gone by Authorities rather then Arguments, partly because I thought that the shortest and the clearest way for every bodies capacity, and partly, because such Arguments (if any besides these we have here) as have been used against this opinion, may be found fully answered in those I have cited. The truth is, it is a Subject of that nature as doth not admit of many Arguments, such especially as may pretend to subtilty of Reason, Sight, Sense, and Experience (upon which most Humane Knowledge is grounded) generally approved and certain, is our best Argument. But before I give over, I will use one Argument which perchance may prove of some force and validity, and that is, A consideration of the strange shifts and evasions and notorious absurdities that these men are put

to,

to, who not being able to deny the *ὅτι*, or *matter of Fact*, would seem to say somewhat rather then to acknowledg Spirits, and Divels, and Witchcraft. *Pomponatius*, who hath not heard of? I once had the book, I know not now what is become of it. But I remember well, I never was more weary of reading then when I read him; nothing that ever I read or heard of *Legends* and old womans tales did seem to me more groundlesse and incredible. But because those men bear themselves very much upon the power of imagination (which indeed is very great, and doth produce strange effects) I shall commend to the sober Reader that hath not yet met with him, *Tho. Eienus* his Learned Tractat, *De Viribus Imaginationis*, a very Rational and Philosophical discourse. Of their miserable shifts and evasions in general, the Author or Observator rather of *Musæum Veronense*, before quoted, will give you a good account. I have at this present in my hands the writings of a Physician, *Augerius Ferrerius* by name. What he was for a Physician I know not; all (I doubt) of that profession will not allow very well of his Preface to his *Castigationes Practicæ Medicinæ*, whatever they think of the *Castigationes* themselves. But in general, his Stile, and various reading, and knowledge of good Authors, speak him a Learned man sufficiently. *Thuanus* in his History gives him a most ample *Elogium*, and makes him to have been *Jul. C. Scaliger* his intimate acquaintance and much respected by him. But I doubt whether *Thuanus* had ever seen this book of his: it doth not appear by that *Elogium* that he had. Well, this Learned man in his Chapter *De Homerica* (so he calls it) *Medicatione*, where he treats of cures done by Charms and Spels, by Words and Characters, which others impute commonly to Witchcraft: first, for the *ὅτι*, he doth not deny it: (*Nam iis quæ sensibus exposita sunt contravenire, sani hominis non est.*) He thinks them little better then mad men that will deny that which is approved by so visible experience. Yet it seems he was one of them that did not believe, or would not believe (though he doth not say so positively) Spirits and Witches, and Supernatural Operations. What then? he plainly maintaineth and argueth it (though he quote no Gospel for it) that such is the nature of the Soul of man (if he know how to use it) that by a strong faith and confidence it may work any miracle without a miracle: *Verum confidentia illa, ac firma persuasio* (that you may have some of his words if you have not the book) *comparatur indoctis animis per opinionem quam de Caracteribus & sacris verbis conceperunt. Doctis & rerum intelligentiam habentibus, nihil opus est externi, sed cognitâ vi animi, per eam miracula edere possunt. &c.* And again alittle after, *Doctus verô. & sibi constans solo verbo sanabit.* I do not hence conclude that this *Ferrerius*, though he speak as though he were, and names no body else, that he was the first or only that hath been of this opinion. *Avicenne* the Arab was the first, as I take it, that set it on foot: some others have followed him in it. But since these men acknowledg the strange effects that others deny, let the sober Reader judge whether of the two more likely to grant *Spirits* and Divels, or to make the Soul of man (of every man, naturally) either a God or a Divel. But let men take heed how they attempt to do Miracles by their strong faith and confidence, for that is the ready way to bring the Divel unto them, and that is it which hath made many Witches and Sorcerers. As for that Faith whereby men did work Miracles in the Primitive times, spoken of in the Gospel, commonly called, *The Faith of Miracles*, that is quite another thing, which I shall not need to speak of in this place. Of a strong confidence in God, even in them that are not otherwise very godly, whether it may not, according to Gods first order and appointment, produce sometimes some strange effects; we have had a consideration elsewhere, where we treat of *Precatorie Enthusiasm*. But this also is quite another thing, as may appear by what we have written of it.

But to conclude this part; upon due consideration of the premises, and what else I have in readiness upon the same Subject (if God give me life and health) I cannot satisfie my self how any Learned man, sober and rational, can entertain such an opinion (simply and seriously) That there be no *Divels* nor *Spirits*, &c. But upon this account which I give my self (leaving all men to their own judgments herein) that if there be any such truly and really, it must needs be because being at first prepossessed upon some plausible ground, and being afterwards taken up with other thoughts and employments, they are more willing to stick to their former opinion without further trouble, then to take the pains to seek further. Ο῾ῦτως ἀταλαίπωρος τοῖς πολλοῖς ἡ ζήτησις τῆς ἀληθείας, καὶ ἐπὶ τὰ ἕτοιμα μᾶλλον τρέπονται, as *Thucydides* doth very well observe. And when we say, *A Learned man*, there is much ambiguity in that word. For a man may be (not to speak of the ignorance of the common people, in those climates especially, who think all Learning concluded in Preaching; and now in these times too; them best Preachers that in very deed have least Learning, but preach by *Instinct* and *Inspiration*, as they call it) but a man, I say, may be a *Learned Man*, a very Learned man in some one kind or profession, even to Excellency and Admiration, who neverthelesse is and may be found ignorant enough in other kinds: but a general Learned man is a thing of a vast extent, and not often seen: It is a businesse of an infinite labour, besides that it requireth Natural parts answerable; without which (judgment specially) the more pains sometimes the more ignorance. I aim not by this at any particular man or men (*Deum testor*) I would much rather submit to the censure of others my self, then take upon me to censure any; but the observation is of very good use, I know it, and may give much satisfaction in many cases, and have given an instance of it in *Tertullian*, and some others elsewhere.

I have done for this time; I come now to the Objections, wherein I shall not need to be very long, because they run much upon one thing, Imposture, which hath already been spoken of and answered. But yet somewhat more particularly shal be answered.

First, Of *Miracles*. It cannot be denyed but the world is full of horrible Impostures in that particular: Yet I believe, that some supernatural things, as cures, &c. do happen in every age, for which no reason can be given, which also for the strangenesse may be called Miracles. But if we limit (with most) the word to those things that proceed immediately from God or divine power: I shall not be

very

very ready to yield that many such Miracles are seen in these Dayes. But I will not further argue the Case in this place. Well, let us take *Miracles* in the ordinary Sense : I verily believe that many such things do happen in many places; but that through negligence partly, and partly through incredulity, they are not regarded oftentimes, or soon forgotten. And wiser men, sometimes, though they know or believe such things, yet are not they very forward to tell them, lest they bring themselves into contempt with those supposed wise men, who will sooner laugh at any thing they do not understand, then take the pains to rectifie their ignorance or inform their judgments. I hope I shall do no wrong to the Memory of that Venerable, Incomparable Prelate, B I S H O P A N D R E W E S, for Sound Learning and True Piety whilest he lived, one of the greatest Lights of this Land; if I set down two Stories, which we may call *Miracles*, both which he did believe to be true, but for one of them, it seemes, he did undertake upon his own knowledge : The one, concerning a noted, or at least by many suspected Witch or Sorceress, which the Divel, in a strange shape, did wait *upon* (or *for* rather) at her death. The other, concerning a man, who after his death was restored to life to make Confession of a horrible Murder committed upon his own Wife, for which he had never been suspected; both these, as he related them to my F. (in familiar conversation) and my F. did enter them for a remembrance into some of his *Adversaria.* In the substance I believe there could be no mistake, but if there be any mistake in any Circumstances, as of Names, or otherwise, that must be imputed to my F. who was a stranger, not to the tongue only, but to all businesses (more then what might be known by printed books, and such publick wayes) of *England.*

The First, thus :

L. Vetula Londinensis, cui morienti Diabolus affuit.

Mira Historia quam narrabat ut sibi compertissimam Dom. Episcopus. Fuit quædam L. mulier ditissima, et curiosis artibus addictissima : vicina ædibus Fulconis, *qui fuit pater Domini* Fulconis, *totâ Angliâ celeberrimi; atque adeo lectissimæ matronæ, matri ejusdem* Fulconis, *familiarissima. Hæc per omnem vitam sortilegiis dedita, & eo nomine infamium muliercularum amica et patrona : (Cui morienti cum adstarent quà viri, quà fæminæ gravissimi; animadversum est sub horam mortis, adstitisse ad pedes lecti hominem vultu terribilem, vulpinis pellibus amictum, quem ipsa contentis oculis intuebatur; ille, ipsam. Quæsitum est à janitore, quare illum admisisset ille negarè se vel vidisse. Tandem secedunt ad fenestram duo vel tres, consilium capturi quid illo facerent. Erat quidam Senator ingentis nominis . . . . . qui bis Prætor Londinensis fuit : item Pater* Fulconis, *et alii. Placet illis ipsum compellare et rogare quis esset. Hoc animo repetunt priora loca sua ad lectum. Interim* L. *vocem magnam edit, quasi animam ageret; omnes illam curare, spectare, sublevare; mox redit ad se illi ignotum illum requirunt oculis. Nusquam apparet. Ante horæ spatium moritur ægra.*

The other thus,

Kalend. August. Narrabat hodie mihi rem miram, Reverendiss. Præsul, Domin. Episcop. Eliensis : quam ille acceptam auribus suis à teste oculato & auctore, credebat esse verissimam. Est vicus in Urbe Londino,

qui

qui dicitur, Vicus Longobardorum. In eo vico Parœcia est, & œdes parœcialis, in qua fuit Presbyter, homo summœ fidei, et notœ Pietatis, ... An. 1563. *quo anno, si unquam aliàs, pestis grassata est per hanc Urbem Londinum. Narravit igitur hic Parrochus et passim aliis, et ipsi quoque Dom. Episcopo sibi hoc accidisse. Erat illi amicus in suâ Parœciâ insignis; vir, ut omnes existimabant, probus et pius. Hic peste correptus advocavit Presbyterum illum suum amicum, qui et œgrotanti affuit, et vidit morientem nec desernet nisi mortuum; ita Demum repetiit domum suam. Post horas satis multas à morte hujus, cùm ipse pro mortuo esset relictus in cubiculo; uxor illius idem cubiculum est ingressa, ut ex arcâ promeret Lodicem, sine linteamen ad ipsum* ἀπολιθων, *ut est moris. Ingressa audit hanc vocem, operi intenta. Quis hic est? terreri illa, et velle egredi, sed auditur iterum vox illa: Quis hic est? Ac tandem comperto esse mariti vocem, accedit ad illum: Quid, ait, marite; tu igitur mortuus non es? et nos te pro mortuo compositum deserveramus. Ego verò, respondit ille, vere mortuus fui: sed ita Deo visum, ut anima mea rediret ad corpus. Sed tu uxor, ait, Si quid habes cibi parati, da mihi esurio enim. Dixit illa veruecinam habere se, pullum gallinaceum, et nescio quid aliud: sed omnia incocta, quœ brevi esset paratura. Ego, ait ille, Moram non fero; panem habes, ait, et caseum? quum annuisset, atque petiisset afferri, comedit spectante uxore: deinde advocato Presbytero, et jussis exire è cubiculo omnibus qui aderant; narrat illi hoc: Ego, ait, verè mortuus fui; sed jussa est anima redire ad suum corpus, ut scelus apperiram ore meo, manibus meis admissum, de quo nulla unquam cuiquam nota est suspicio. Priorem namque uxorem meam ipse occidi manibus meis, tantâ vafritie, ut omnes res lateret: deinde modum perpetratı sceleris exposuit; nec ita multò post expiravit, ac verè tum mortuus est.*

There is no necessity that any body should make of either of these relations an Article of his Faith; yet I thought them very probable, because believed by such a man, and therefore have given them a place here. So much of *Miracles.*

Of *Exorcismes* we must say as of *Miracles.* One notable example of a counterfeit Possession, and of great stirs likely to have insued upon it in *France,* we have out of *Thuanus,* in our late *Treatise of Enthusiasme.* The *History of the Boy of Bilson* is extant, who by the Wisdom and Sagacity of the R^t R^d F. in God *Thomas,* Lord Bishop of *Lichfield* and *Coventry,* was discovered to be an Impostor on purpose set up and suborned to promote the Romish cause, *An. Dom.* 1620 Such examples and stories most Countries have afforded good store, which are extant in divers Languages. Neither must it be concealed (by them that seek truth without partiality) that some, once called *Disciplinarians,* now more known by another name, have attempted to deal in those things, hoping thereby to gain great advantage to their cause. It was a famous Story in Q. *Elizabeth's* Reign, though now perchance out of the knowledg of many, and beyond the remembrance of any living, how one Mr. *D.* a very zealous man of that Sect, did take upon him by long prayers to cast out Divels, so maintained and asserted with great vehemency by him and some others that favoured that cause, though upon legal examination they proved otherwise, which occasioned many books on both sides in those dayes, but two, *melioris notœ,* as we say, written by Dr. *H.* concerning *Exorcismes;* the one against Papists, the other against *P.* I have them both somewhere yet, I hope, but can not come at

them

them at this time, which is the cause that I cannot particularize that businesse with circumstances of times, and names or persons as I would. But there were many other books written (some very big, which I have seen) about it, as I said before; so that the whole businesse, with very little inquisition, if any have a mind, may quickly be found out. One Bookseller in Little *Britain* did help me to the sight of six or seven at once; yet one of the books then written, and as I was told, upon this occasion much commended unto me by some very Learned, to wit, Dr. *Jordan, of the Suffocation of the Matrix,* I long sought before I could meet with it. And such was the ignorance of some Booksellers, that I could not perswade them there was any such book extant: but now at last I have got it. All the use I shall make of it at this time is, that whereas the whole drift of the book tends unto this, to shew the error of many in ascribing natural diseases to supernatural causes; which might be thought by some to favour their opinion that believe not *Witches,* &c. The Author doth very prudently and piously make this profession in the Preface, *I do not deny but that God doth in these dayes work extraordinarily for the deliverance of his children, and for other ends best known to himself; and that among other there may be both possessions by the Divel, and obsessions, and Witch-craft,* &c. *and dispossession also through the Prayers and Supplications of his servants, which is the only means left unto us for our relief in that case, but such examples being very rare now adayes,* &c. Yet for all this I do not conclude that Mr. D. was guilty of any Imposture: he might do it through ignorance being cozened by others. I have heard he was an honest man, and dyed piously, and disclaimed to the very last that he did any thing in that businesse otherwise then *Bonâ Fide* I would judge charitably, even of those men that are not guilty of much charity towards others, whose judgments and consciences will not suffer them (though men of approved worth and piety otherwise) to say as they say, and to do as they do in all things. Be it granted therefore, that this businesse of *Exorcismes* is lyable to much Imposture: however, no man that hath read the relations of men and women possest, in several places, with due observation of circumstances; some of which relations, besides other persons of credit, have been attested; yea, some penned and published by learned Physicians and Naturalists, who have been employed about the Cure, observed their carriage, heard some of them speak strange Languages: silly women possest, discourse of highest points of Phylosophy, or the Mathematicks and the like. No man, I say, that is not a stranger to these things (besides what some Travellers, no way interessed in the cause, can aver upon their own knowledge) will make any question either of the real possession of divers, according to relations that have been made, or of the Divels speaking in them and by them when they have been Exorcised; and sometimes upon bare conference. And though some Protestants are of opinion, That it is not lawful or warrantable for any man to take upon him to Exorcise upon such occasions, that is, (as I conceive) by way of absolute power and authority, and by superstitious wayes and means, as is ordinarily done: Yet where a man hath a Calling, as if he be lawfully Called to the Ministry, and set over such a Parish where any happen to be possessed (as indeed
deed

deed my felf have a Parifh, that is, right to a Parifh as good as the Laws of the Land can give me, which hath been grievoufly haunted, though not altogether in the fame kind, this many years, to the undoing of many there; but I muft not come near it, nor have the benefit of the Law to recover my right, though never told why) and he find himfelf zealoufly moved, yet without prefumption, I would not defpair, but his prayers, with other performances of devotion, and the affiftance of fome others of the fame calling, might prove available before God: but ftill prefuppofed, as moft expedient and neceffary, that the opinion and refolution of fome Learned and confcionable Phyfician, one or more, be had in the cafe; and their prefence alfo in all actions, if it may be had, obtained. Some, it may be, will thank me, and I hope it will offend none, if I impart unto them what I have found in my F. his *Ephemeris* (or, *Daily account of his life*) tending to this purpofe.

Anno Dom. 1603. Kal. Junii. *Quem memfem, et reliquos omnes velis ô Deus,* &c. *Hunc q. lætum egimus, cum matre, uxore, affine, et viro nobili, Dom. de Counf. et nobili item matrona, D de St. Pons: qui omnes in re pietatis* ὁμοφρονοῦντες, *Ecclefiam hujus loci afsiduè celebravimus. Inter alios Sermones quos habui cum D. de St. Pons, de miniftro provinciæ Vivaretii fumus locuti, cui nomen* Mercero: *Regit ille in eo tractu plures parvas Ecclefias; habitat a. in loco, qui dicitur,* Chafteau-double. *Acceperam de eo ex vulgi rumoribus, quod vim Dæmonas ejiciendi haberet; quæfivi,* ἀκριβέστερον *de D. de St. Pons quid rei effet. Illa feriò affirmavit, plures Dæmoniacos (decem aut circiter) in Ecclefiam anductos, eo concionante primùm, dein orante, palam, et Confefsione omnium fuiffe fanatos. Quofdam Demonas ita eum certis fignis erupiffe, ut res apud omnes fieret teftatifsima. Porrò autem omnes qui fanati funt, Religionem Catholicam Romanam ante femper profeffos. Mercerum verò impatientiffimè ferre, fi qnis inter loquendum, ut fit, diceret, Mercerum Diabolos ejicere, non enim fe, verùm Ecclefiam Dei effe nominandam, cujus precibus ardentiffimis Dei aures patuerint. Dom et illi et univerfo gregi fuorum benedicat.* Amen.

In Englifh (for their fakes that underftand no Latine, and that it be not required alwayes, for it would be very tedious) this is the effect, At fuch a time, in fuch a place, he had the opportunity to meet with a grave (whether Lady or Gentlewoman) Matron, one he had a very good opinion of; her name *M. de St. Pons,* and having often heard by common report of a certain Proteftant Minifter that was faid to caft out Divels, he did accurately inform himfelf by her (fhe living, it feems, very near, if not in the fame parifh) of all particulars concerning that bufineffe; who did averre it to be moft true, and that ten, or thereabouts, Demomoniacks, or poffeffed men (all making profeffion of the Roman Catholick Religion) had been brought to the Church (at feveral times, as I take it) and that publickly, and by the generall confefsion of all then prefent, and by fome notable fignes (fometimes) at the going out of the Devils; they were, upon his Praying after Sermon, all delivered. But that he took it very hainoufly if any faid, that he had caft out Devils; For, not I, faid he, but the earneft Prayers of the Church, have prevailed with Almighty God to work this wonderful thing.

As for *Oracles*: It is true, Heathens themfelves acknowledg, that fome
were

were the jugglings of men. Sometimes Princes; sometimes private men: (as now of Religion, of Preaching, and Praying, and Fasting; of Masses and Processions: most Princes and States in all places) made good use of them to their owne ends; and made them speak what themselves had prompted. But a man might as probably argue; because some have been so freely acknowledged to have been by compact and subornation, it is the more likely, that those of which never any suspicion was, should be true. We read of many in *Herodotus*: of one, which was contrived by fraud; but there we read also, that when it came to be known (though care had been taken that it might not:) the chief Contriver, a great man, was banished, or prevented worse, by a voluntary Exile; and the *Sacred Virgin* or *Prophetesse*, deposed. But not to insist upon particulars, which would be long, it is most certain, and it will cleerly appear unto them that are well read in ancient Authors and Histories, That all Heathens, generally the wisest and learnedest of them, those especially, that lived when Oracles were most frequent, did really believe them to be, which they pretended unto: and that they were so indeed, for the most part (taking it for granted that their Gods were *Divels* or *Evil Spirits*) by many circumstances of Stories, and by other good proofs, may be made as evident: neither was it ever doubted or denyed (alwayes granted and presupposed, that, as in all worldly things, much imposture did intervene and intermingle) by ancient Christians acknowledged, I am sure, by most, if not all. But I have spoken of them elsewhere already, and therefore will be the shorter here.

Our *last Objection* was: If there be *Devils* and *Spirits*, Why do they not appear unto them, who do what they can, as by continual curses, so by profane curiosity to invite them? First, We say, ἀπ᾿ἐξωδίνξια τὰ κείμαξια αὐτῶ, ὡ̓ ἀπ᾿ἐξιχριασοι αἱ ἰδίι αὐτῶ. When we have good ground for the ὅτι, to stick at the διότι, because we do not understand the reason, is as much as to say, that we think we should be as wise as God. *Aristotle* did not meddle with things that he could give no reason of; yet he did not deny them (as we have shewed) and it is one thing to require a reason of things meerly natural; and another of those that happen by a meer secret Providence. But this will give them no great satisfaction who perchance believe a God (some) as much as they believe a Devil. *Secondly*, Therefore we say, There may be some natural reason too, upon *Aristotles* grounds. *Aristotle* (as hath been shewed elsewhere) compares the effects of *Melancholy*, from whence he deriveth all kind of *Enthusiasm*, to the known effects of *Wine*. What is the reason, that some men with little wine will quickly be drunk, and become other Creatures, being deprived for the time of the use of reason? Others though they drink never so much, will sooner burst then reel, or speak idly. as some in their excess grow merry, others sad: some calm and better natured; others furious: some talkative, others stupid. The Devil knowes what tempers are best for his turn; and by some in whom he was deceived, he hath got no credit, and wished he had never meddled with them. Some men come into the world with *Cabalistical Brains*; their heads are full of mysteries; they see nothing, they read nothing, but their brain is on work to pick somewhat out of it that is not ordinary; and out of the very *A B C* that children are taught, rather then fail, they will fetch all the Secrets of Gods Wisdom, tell

you

you how the world was created, how governed, and what will be the end of all things. Reason and Sense that other men go by, they think the acorns that the old world fed upon; fools and children may be content with them but they see into things by another *Light.* They commonly give good respect unto the *Scriptures* (till they come to profest *Anabaptists*) because they believe them the Word of God and not of men; but they reserve unto themselves the Interpretation, and so under the title of *Divine Scripture,* worship what their own phansie prompts, or the devil puts into their heads. But of all *Scriptures* the *Revelation* and the obscure Prophesies are their delight; for there they rove securely; and there is not any thing so prodigious or chimerical, but they can fetch it out of some Prophesie, as they will interpret it. These men, if they be upright in their lives and dealings, and fear God truly, it is to be hoped that God will preserve them from further evil; but they are of a dangerous temper; Charitable men will pity them, and sober men will avoid them. On the other side, some there are whose brains are of a stiff and restive mould; it will not easily receive new impressions. They will hardly believe any thing but what they see; and yet rather not believe their eyes, then to believe any thing that is not according to the course of nature, and what they have been used unto. The devil may tempt such by sensual baits, and catch them; but he will not easily attempt to delude them by magical Shews and Apparitions. And what sober man, that believeth as a God, so a divel, doth doubt, but they that make it their daily practice to damn themselves, by such horrid oaths and curses, are as really poslest, yea far more in the posselsion of the devil, then many that foam at the mouth, and speak strange languages?

But 3*dly* Some have tried and used the means, but could never see any thing but what if others that never desired it really, but in some wanton curiosity, unadvisedly, that they might be the better able to confute the simplicity of some others as they thought, rather then that their faith wanted any such confirmation, have tryed some things, or have been present at some experiments and have seen (with no small astonishment) more then they expected or desired? Some persons of credit and quality, I am sure, have made it their confession unto me, that it hath so hapned unto them; who have been so affected with it, that they would not for a world be so surprized again.

But 4*ly* and lastly, The Confessions of some *Magicians* are extant in print, who tell very particularly what means they used, what books they read, &c. and they saw and found (if we believe them; and what should tempt them to lye, no melancholy men, I know not) till they were weary, and Gods grace wrought upon their hearts to bring them to repentance. There be such confessions extant, but the Reader shal pardon me, if I give him no further account. It would much better becom them therefore, that have made such essays without succesle, to repent, and to be thankful unto God, then to make that an argument, that theres no divel, and perchance no God. There is a terrible saying (if well understood) in the Scripture; Ὁ ῥυπῶν ῥυπάτω, *He that is filthy let him be filthy still* Let them take heed (I advise them as a friend) if they persist in their hardness of heart and infidelity, lest God in just judgment, though they seek still, and provoke as much as they can, will not suffer that they shall see any thing, lest they should fear and be converted.

I come

I Come now to Dr. D E E, and to *This Book* of his, which hath been the occasion of all the Discourse hitherto. As for his Person or Parentage, Education and the like, I have but little to say more then what he saith himself in his first Letter to the Emperor (RODOLPHE) of *Germany*, that being yet very young he was sought unto (*ambiverunt me*) by two Emperors, CHARLS the 5th and FERDINANDO his Brother and Successor in the Empire. Mr. *Cambden* indeed in the year 1572 makes honourable mention of him, and calls him, *Nobilis Mathematicus*. He dedicated his *Monas Hieroglyphica* to MAXIMILIAN Successor to FERDINANDO; first printed at *Antwerp, An. Dom.*1564. and afterwards at *Francford*, 1591. and what other places I know not. In the year 1595. he did write (and was printed 1599 I am sure, but whether before that or no, I cannot certainly tell) *A discourse Apologetical*, &c. directed to the then *Archbishop of Canterbury*, wherein he hath a Catalogue of books written by himself, printed and unprinted, to the number of 48. in all, and doth also mention the books of his Library about 4000 volums in all, whereof 700 ancient Manuscripts, Latin, Greek, and Hebrew. There also doth he produce a Testimony of the University of *Cambridg*, dated 1548. But this whole Discourse of his being but short, for the better satisfaction of the Reader, I thought good to have it here reprinted the next after this Preface. His *Mathematical Preface* before *Euclid*, is that I think which of all his writings published hath been most taken notice of in *England*, and added much to the worth and commendation of that Edition of *Euclid*. He was a married man and had divers children, as will appear by this Relation; a great Traveller, and lived to a great age. But as I said before, I do not pretend to give an account of his life in general, unto others, which my self am yet a stranger to. What concerneth this *Relation* I am to give an account, and I hope there shall be nothing wanting to that. Four things I propose to my self to that end,

First, Somewhat to confirm the truth and sincerity of this whole *Relation*.

Secondly, To answer some Objections that may be made against some parts of it.

Thirdly, To give some light to some places, and to satisfie the Reader concerning the perfection and imperfection of the book, as also, concerning the Original Copy.

Fourthly, and lastly, To shew the many good uses that may be made of all by a sober Christian.

I. It seems that Dr. *Dee* began to have the reputation of a *Conjurer* betimes. He doth very grievously complain of it in that *Preface* to *Euclid* but now spoken of, about the end of it, and yet there doth also term himself, *An old forworn Mathematician*. For my part whether he could ever truly be so called, I yet make some question: But I am very confident, that himself did not know or think himself so, but a zealous worshipper of God, and a very free and sincere Christian. How this is to be reconciled with the truth of this *Relation*, shall be afterwards considered of. For the truth and sincerity of the *Relation*, I hope

no

no body will fo grofly miftake us as though we intended thereby to juftifie what is here printed againft any fufpition of forgery; as if any man taking the advantage of Dr. *Dees* name and fame of a *Conjurer*, could be fufpected to have devifed and invented thefe things in his own brain to abufe the world. I fhould be forry my name fhould appear in any kind to any book lyable to fuch a fufpition; and the very name and credit of that fo much and fo defervedly prized *Library* from whence this is pretended to be taken, is fufficient (with civil underftanding men) to prevent the groffeneffe of fuch a miftake. Befides the Original Copy it felf, all written with Dr. *Dees* own hand, there kept and preferved. But by *Truth and Sincerity*, intending not only Dr. *Dee's* fidelity in relating what himfelf believed, but alfo the *reality* of thofe things that he fpeaks of, according to his relation : his only (but great and dreadful) error being, that he miftook falfe lying Spirits for Angels of Light, the Divel of Hell (as we commonly term him) for the God of Heaven. For the *Truth* then, and *Sincerity* or *Reality* of the *Relation* in this fenfe, I fhall firft appeal to the Book it felf. I know it is the fafhion of many (I will not fay that (I never did it my felf) that are buyers of books, they will turn five or fix leaves, if they happen upon fomewhat that pleafeth their fancy, the book is a good book, and when they have bought it, it concerneth them to think fo, becaufe they have paid for it : but on the other fide, if they light upon fomewhat that doth not pleafe (which may happen in the beft) they are as ready to condemn and caft away. It is very poffible that fome fuch buyer lighting upon this, and in it, upon fome places here and there, where fome odd uncouth things may offer themfelves; things ridiculous, incredible to ordinary fenfe and conftruction, he may be ready to judge of the whole accordingly. But for all this, I will in the firft place appeal to the book it felf; but with this refpect to the Reader, that he will have patience to read in order one fourth part of the book at leaft before he judge; and if by that time he be not convicted, he fhall have my good will to give it over. Not but that all the reft, even to the end, doth help very well to confirm the truth and reality of the whole Story : but becaufe I think there is fo much in any fourth part, if diligently read, and with due confideration, that I defpair of his affent, that is not convicted by

Sir *Thomas Cotton* Knight Baronet.

it. For my part, when the book was firft communicated unto me by that Right worthy Gentleman who is very ftudious to purchafe and procure fuch Records and Monuments as may advantage the truth of God (all truth is of God) and the honour of this Land, following therein the example of his noble Progenitor, by his very name, Sir *Robert Cotton*, known to all the Learned as far as Europe extendeth. I read it curforily becaufe I was quickly convinced in my felf that it could be no counterfeit immaginarie bufineffe, and was very defirous to fee the end, fo far as the book did go. Afterwards, when I underftood that the faid worthy Gentleman (efpecially, as I fuppofe, relying upon my *Lord of Armagh's judgment and teftimonie*, which we have before fpoken of) was willing it fhould be publifhed, and that he had com-

mitted

mitted the whole bufinefs unto me; I read it over very exactly, and took notes of the moft remaikable paffages (as they appeared unto me) truly I was fo much confirmed in this firft opinion by my fecond reading, that I fhall not be afraid to profefs that I never gave more credit to any Humane Hiftory of former times. All things feemed unto me fo fimply, and yet fo accurately, and with fo much confirmation of all manner of circumftances written and delivered, that I cannot yet fatisfie my felf, but all judicious Readers will be of my opinion. But neverthelefs, to help them that truft not much to their own judgments, let us fee what can be faid.

Firft, I would have them, that would be further fatisfied, to read Dr. *Dee* in that forecited Preface, where he doth plead his own caufe, to acquit himfelf of that grievous crime and imputation of a *Conjurer*. But that was written, I muft confefs, long before his Communication with Spirits: yet it is fomewhat to know what opinion he had then of them that deal with Divels and evil Spirits. But after he was made acquainted, and in great dealings with them, and had in readinefs divers of thefe his books, or others of the fame Argument, containing their feveral conferences and communications, to fhew, and the manner of their appearing exactly fet down; obferve, I pray, with what confidence he did addrefs himfelf to the greateft and wifeft in Europe. To Queen *Elizabeth* often, and to her Council, as by many places of this Relation doth appear; but more particularly by his Letter to Sir *Francis Walfingham*, Secretary, &c. That he did the like to King *James* and his Councel, may eafily be gathered by the Records (in this *Relation*) of 1607. but much defective. But then to the Emperor.*Rodolphe*, to *Stephen* King of *Poland*, and divers other Princes and their Deputies; the wifeft and learnedft, their feveral Courts did afford for the time: the particulars of all which addreffes and tranfactions are very exactly fet down in the book. Nay, fuch was his confidence, that had it not been for the *Nuncius Apoftolicus* his appearing againft him at the Emperors Court by order from the Pope, he was, as by fome places may be collected, refolved for *Rome* alfo, not doubting but he fhould approve himfelf and his doings to the Pope himfelf and his Cardinals. In all thefe his addreffes and applications being ftill very ready to impart all things unto them that would entertain them with that refpect he thought they deferved; yea, readily, which is very obfervable, even to receive them into this Myftical Society, whom he thought worthy, and in fome capacity to promote the defign; as de facto he did divers in feveral places: *Albertus A-lafco*, Prince Palatine of *Polonia*, *Puccius* a learned man, and Prince *Rofemberg* in *Germany*, who were long of the Society, befides fome admitted to fome Actions for a while, as *Stephen* King of *Poland*, and fome others. We will eafily grant (as elfewhere hath been treated and handled at large) that a diftempered brain may fee, yea, and hear ftrange things, and entertain them with all poffible confidence, as real things, and yet all but fancy, without any real found or Apparition. But thefe fights and Apparitions that Dr. *Dee* gives here an account, are quite of another nature; yea, though poffibly the Divel might reprefent divers of thefe things to the fancy inwardly

which

which appeared outwardly : Yet of another nature, I say, and not without the intervention and operation of Spirits, as will easily appear to any man by the particulars. Besides the long Speeches, Discourses, Interlocutions upon all occasions and occurrences in the presence of more then one alwayes; and externally audible to different persons, for the most part or very frequently. That these things could not be the operation of a distempered Fancy, will be a sufficient evidence to any rational man.

Again, let his usual preparations and Prayers against an Apparition or Action (as he called them) his extraordinary prayers upon some extraordinary occasions, as upon *Edward Kelley* his temporary repentance, and another for him when he was about to forsake him (in Latine a long one) *Stephen* King of *Poland* being then present. And again, when his Son *Arthur* was to be initiated to these Mystical Operations and Apparitions, in the place of *Edward Kelley*, and the like. And again, his Humility, Piety, Patience, (O what pity that such a man should fall into such a delusion! but we shall consider of the causes in its right place afterwards) upon all occasions, temptations, distresses, most eminent throughout the whole Book. Let these things be well considered, and above the rest, his large and punctual relation of that sad abominable story of their *Promiscuous, carnal Copulation*, under the pretence of obedience to God.——— Let these things, I say, be well considered, and I think no man will make any question but the poor man did deal with all possible simplicity and sincerity, to the utmost of his understanding at that time. And truly, this one thing (as we said before) excepted, his mistaking of evil Spirits for good, it doth not appear by any thing but that he had his understanding, and the perfect use of his Reason to the very last, as well as he had had any time of his life.

Again, let it be considered, that he carryed with him where ever he went A STONE, which he called his *Angelicall Stone*, as *brought unto him by an Angel, but by a Spirit sure enough*, which he shewed unto many; to the Emperor among others, or the Emperors Deputy, Dr. *Curts*, as I remember : But more of this *Stone* afterwards. We may therefore conclude surely enough, That Dr. *Dee* in all this Relation did deal with all simplicity and sincerity. I shall only add, That whereas I used the word *Reality* before, concerning those things that appeared, according to this Relation : I would not be mistaken, as though I intended that whatsoever the Divel did seem to do or represent; it was *Really* and *Substantially* as it seemed and appeared, that would be a great and gross mistake. The very word *Apparition* doth rather import the contrary. All I understand by *Reality*, is, that what things appeared, they did so appear by the power and operation of Spirits, actually present and working, and were not the effects of a depraved fancy and imagination by meer natural causes. By which, strange things, I confess, may be presented and apprehended too, sometimes by the parties with all confidence, as we said before, though all be but fancy and imagination. But all circumstances well considered, make this Case here to be of another nature; and it may be it was the policy of these Spirits to joyn *two* of purpose in this business, to make the truth and reality of it the more un-

que-

queſtionable ; hoping (if God had given way) they ſhould have paſſed, in time for good Spirits abroad generally, and then we ſhould have ſeen what they would have made of it. From leſſe beginnings , I am ſure, greateſt confuſions have proceeded and prevailed in the world, as we ſhall ſhew elſewhere. And ſince that in all this buſineſs, as we ſaid but now , Dr. *Dee* did not deal alone , but had a conſtant Partner or Aſſiſtant, whom ſometimes himſelf calleth his *Seer*, or S*kryer*, one by name *Edward Kelly* : it will be requiſite before we proceed further, that we give ſome account of him alſo. According to Dr. *Dee's* own relation here, *An. Dom.* 1587. *April* 7. *Trebonæ* : in the particulars of his Son *Arthur's Conſecration* (after his manner, which he calls, *His offering and preſenting of him to the ſervice of God :*) *Uriel* (one of his chiefeſt Spirits) was the author of their *Conjunction* : but when and how it hapned (being but *obiter* mentioned there) we do not find any where ; and more then what I find here I have nothing to ſay : For certain it is by this whole ſtory , from the beginning to the end of it, that *Kelley* was a great Conjurer , one that daily converſed by ſuch art as is uſed by ordinary Magicians, with evil Spirits , and knew them to be ſo. Yet I would ſuppoſe that he was one of the beſt ſort of Magicians , that dealt with Spirits by a kind of *Command* (as is well known ſome do) and not by any *Compact* or agreement : this may probably be gathered from ſundry places. But that he was a Conjurer, appeareth firſt by that, where he proffered to raiſe ſome evil Spirit before the Poliſh Prince Palatine , *Albert Lasky* (of whom more by and by) for a proof of his Art. But Dr. *Dee* would not ſuffer him to do it in his houſe. Wicked ſpirits are caſt out of him to the number of 15. *p.* 32. But I make no great matter of that in point of proof , becauſe all there upon his bare report only. But ſee *p.* 63. &c. where it is laid to his charge, and he anſwereth for himſelf and his Spirits. See alſo where at laſt he yielded to bury not to burn his Magical books. But read his own confeſſion (where you ſhall find him ſpeak like one that knew very well what did belong to the Art) and the record made by Dr. *Dee* concerning a ſhrewd conteſt that hapned between Dr. *Dee* and him , (it was about ſome Magical things) wherein *Edward Kelly* carried himſelf ſo fiercely, that Dr. *Dee* being afraid of his life , was forced to call for help. Peruſe well this place and I preſume you will require no further light as to this particular concerning *Kelly*.

As for the ſeveral *Epiſtles* (in Latin moſt) that will be found here, as alſo Narratives of ſeveral meetings and conferences, they carry ſo much light with them, being ſet out with ſo many remarkable circumſtances of time, place, perſons, &c. that no man of judgment that hath any knowledge of the world, will or can make any ſcruple of the ſincerity and fidelity of either reports or Deeds and monuments (ſuch I account the Letters to be) herein contained. A man might with little labour (that had all kind of books at command) have found ſomewhat concerning moſt (outlandiſh) perſons in them mentioned. I could not intend it , and I think it would have been a needleſs labour. If any make any queſtion let them make ſearch , I dare warrant it unto them they ſhall find all things to agree punctually. But becauſe *Albert Lasky* (next to *Edward Kelley*) is the man moſt
in-

interreſſed in this ſtory; I will give you ſome account of him out of Mr. *Cambden* his *Annals*.

Anno Dom: 1583. *E Polonia, Ruſſiæ vicinâ hac æſtate venit in Angliam ut Reginam inviſeret,* Albertus Alaſco, *Palatinus Siradienſis vir eruditus, corporis lineamentis barbâ promiſiſſimâ, veſtitu decoro, & pervenuſto; qui perbenignè ab ipſa nobilibuſque magnoque honore & lautitiis, et ab Accademia Oxonienſi eruditis oblectationibus, atque variis ſpectaculis exceptus, poſt 4. menſes ære alieno oppreſſus, clam receſsit.*

But of all Letters here exhibited, I am moſt taken, I muſt confeſs, with the Biſhops Letter that was *Nuncius Apoſtolicus*: he ſeemes to me to ſpeak to the caſe very pertinently (take *Puccius* his account along in his long letter to Dr. *Dee,* of his conference with the ſaid Biſhop concerning the ſame buſineſs) and to have carryed himſelf towards Dr. *Dee* very moderately and friendly.

I I. Now to Objections:

The firſt ſhall be this: Although 'tis very probable that Dr. *Dee* himſelf dealt ſimply and ſincerely; yet ſince he himſelf ſaw nothing (for ſo himſelf acknowledgeth in ſome places) but by *Kelley's* eyes, and heard nothing but with his ears. Is it not poſſible that *Kelley* being a cunning man, and well practiſed in theſe things might impoſe upon the credulity of Dr. *Dee* (a good innocent man) and the rather, becauſe by this office under the Doctor he got 50 *l.* by the year, as appeareth. Truly this is plauſible as it is propoſed; and like enough that it might go a great way with them that are ſoon taken, and therefore ſeldom ſee any thing in the truth or true nature of it, but in the outward appearance of it only. But read and obſerve it diligently and you will find it far otherwiſe: It is true indeed, that ordinarily, Dr. *Dee* ſaw not himſelf; his buſineſs was to write what was ſeen (but in his preſence though) and heard by *Kelley.* Yet that himſelf heard often immediately appeareth by many places; I ſhall not need any quotations for that himſelf feeleth as well as *Kelley.* In the relation of the *Holy Stone,* how *taken away* by one that came in at a window in the ſhape of a man, and *how reſtored;* both *ſaw* certainly. In the ſtory of the *Holy Books, how burned* and how reſtored again (part of them at leaſt) which Dr *Dee* made a great Miracle of, as appeareth by ſome of thoſe places; there alſo both ſaw certainly. And *Albert Lasky, the Polonian Palatine ſaw as well as Kelley.* Beſides, it doth clearly appear throughout all the book that *Kelley* (though ſometimes with much adoe perſwaded for a while to think better of them) had generally no other opinion of theſe Apparitions but that they were meer illuſions of the Divel and evil Spirits, ſuch as himſelf could command by his art when he liſted, and was æquainted with, inſomuch that we find him for this very cauſe forſaking, or deſirous to forſake Dr. *Dee,* who was much troubled about it; and is forced in a place to *Pawn his Soul* unto him (to uſe his own words) that it was not ſo, and that they were good Spirits ſent from God in great favour unto them. But for all this *Kelley* would not be ſatisfied, but would have his Declaration or Proteſtation of his ſuſpicion to the contrary entred into the book; which you ſhall find, and it will be worth your reading. I could further

al-

alledge, that if a man confiders the things delivered here upon feveral occafions, being of a different nature, fome Moral, fome Phyfical, fome Me-
taphyfical, and Theological of higheft points (though fometimes wild e-
nough, and not warrantable; yet for the moft part very remote from vulgar
capacities) he will not eafily believe that *Kelley*, who fcarce underftood Latine) not to fpeak of fome things delivered in *Greek* in fome places) and be-
took himfelf to the ftudy of Logick long after he had entred himfelf into
this courfe, could utter fuch things : no, nor any man living perchance,
that had not made it his ftudy all his life-time. But that which muft needs
end this quarrel (if any man will be pertinacious) and put all things out of
doubt, is, that not *Kelley* only ferved in this place of *Seer* or *Skryer*, but o-
thers alfo, as his fon *Arthur*, and in his latter dayes, when *Kelley* was either
gone or fick, one *Bartholomew*, as will be found in all the *Actions* and Apparitions of the year 1607. which (as I fufpect) was the laft year of the Doctors life, or beyond which I think he did not live long.

Secondly, It may be objected, or ftuck at leaft, How Dr. *Dee*, fo good, fo
innocent, yea, fo pious a man, and fo fincere a Chriftian as by thefe papers (his delufion and the effects of it ftill excepted) he doth feem to have
been, God would permit fuch a one to be fo deluded and abufed, fo rackt
in his foul, fo hurried in his body for fo long a time, notwithftanding his
frequent, earneft, zealous prayers and addreffes unto God, by evil Spirits
(even to his dying day, for ought we know) as he is here by his own relation fet out unto us.? Truly, if a man fhall confider the whole carriage
of this bufineffe, from the beginning to the end, according to this true and
faithful (for I think I may fo fpeak with confidence) account of it here
prefented unto us, this poor man, how from time to time fhamefully,
grofly delayed, deluded, quarrelled without caufe, ftill toled on with fome
fhews and appearances, and yet ftill fruftrated and put off: his many
pangs and agonies about it, his fad condition after fo many years toil, travel, drudgery and earneft expectation, at the very laft (as appeareth by the
Actions and apparitions of the year 1607.) I cannot tell whether I fhould make
him an object of more horror or compaffion; but of both certainly in a
great meafure to any man that hath any fenfe of Humanity, and in the examples of others of humane frailty : and again, any regard of parts and
worth, fuch as were in this man in a high degree. True it is, that he had
joyes withal and comforts, imaginary, delufory, it is true; yet fuch as he enjoyed and kept up his heart, and made him outwardly chearful often times,
I make no queftion ; fuch as the Saints (as they call themfelves) and *Schifmaticks* of thefe and former times have ever been very prone to boaft of, per-
fwading themfelves that they are the *effects* of Gods bleffed *Spirit*. But even
in thefe his joys and comforts, the fruits and fancies of his deluded foul (as
in many others of a diftempered brain) is not he an object of great compaf-
paffion to any, both fober and charitable ? If this then were his cafe indeed,
what fhall we fay ? if nothing elfe, I know not but it ought to fatisfie a
rational, fober, humble man : If we fay, That it is not in man to give an
account of all Gods judgments, neither is there any ground for us to mur-
mure becaufe we do not underftand them, or that they often feem contrary

to the judgment of humane reason, because it is against all Reason as well as Religion, to believe that a creature so much inferior to God, by nature as man is, should see every thing as he seeth, and think as he thinks; and consequently judge and determine in and of all things as God judgeth and determineth. The Apostle therefore not without cause, would have all private judgments (for of publick for the maintenance of peace and order among men, it is another case) deferr'd to that time, *when the hearts of all men shall be laid open, all hidden things and secret counsels revealed.* But we have enough to say in this case without it. For if *Pride* and *Curiosity* were enough to undoe our first Parent, and in him all mankind, when otherwise innocent, and in possession of Paradise. Should we wonder if it had the same event in Dr. *Dee*, though otherwise, as he doth appear to us, innocent, and well qualified? That this was his case and error, I will appeal to his own confession (though he makes it his boast) in more then one of his Letters or addresses, where he professeth, *That for divers years he had been an earnest suter unto God in prayer for Wisdom;* that is, as he interprets himself, *That he might understand the secrets of Nature that had not been revealed unto men hitherto;* to the end, as he professeth, and his own deceitful heart it may be suggested unto him, *That he might glorifie God;* but certainly, that himself might become a *glorious man* in the world, and be admired, yea, adored every where almost, as he might be sure it would be, had he compassed his desire. And what do we think should put him upon such a desire, with hopes to obtain it, but an opinion he had of himself as an extraordinary man, both for *parts*, and for *favour with God?* But however, had he been to the utmost of what he could think of himself, besides his Spiritual pride of thinking so of himself (as great a sin as any in the eyes of God) his praying for such a thing with so much importunity, was a great tempting of God, and deserving greatest judgments. Had he indeed been a suter unto God for such *Wisdom* as the Prophet *Jeremie* describeth (11. v. 24, 25.) *Let not the Wise man glorie in his wisdom, &c.* but let him that glorieth, *&c.* And for such *knowledg* as our Saviour commandeth, *Joh.* 17. 3. *And this is life eternal, that they may know thee,* &c. And his blessed Apostle (1 Cor. 11. 2.) *For I determined not to know any thing,* &c. he had had good warrant for his prayers, and it is very likely that God would have granted him his request, so far as might have concerned his own salvation and eternal happiness. Besides, it is lawful (nay fit) for a man to pray for Gods blessing upon his labours, for competency of wit and capacity that he may do well in his vocation and glorifie God. But for a man to aspire to such eminency above other men, and by means that are not ordinary (as that conceited *Phylosophers Stone*, and the like) and to interest God by earnest solicitations in his ambitions extravagant desires; that God, who hath said of himself, *That he resisteth the proud, but giveth grace unto the humble*, must needs be so great and so high a provocation (if well considered) as that I begin to doubt whether it be charity to pity him that suffered so justly and deservedly. I do not know but it is as lawfull for any man obscurely born to pray for a Kingdom, for a Common Souldier that he may have strength to encounter thousands, or for an ordinarie Maid, that she may become the fairest of women. In all

all thefe it is poffible to glorifie God, we grant, were it fit for us to pre-
fcribe unto God, neglecting thofe that he hath appointed, by what means
he fhould be glorified; and could we fecure our felves that in pretending to
Gods glory we do not feek our own. I wifh that our great undertakers and
reformers (fuch is their wifdom they think) of Arts and Sciences would feri-
oufly think of this; they efpecially who take upon themfelves to make all men
wife and of one mind, and to reconcile all doubts and difficulties in Religion,
and otherwife; in a word, to make Truth to be imbraced by all men. Should
thefe men tell us that if they had had the creating of the world, and the ordering of all things (and there be, I think, in the world that have faid little lefs)
from the beginning, they would have made an other guefs of things then God
had done: We would have confiderd of it perchance what might be the ground
in any mortal man of fuch wonderful confidence. But fuch being the condition of the world, as it is, and fuch of men, naturally; or to fpeak as a Chriftian,
fince the fall of *Adam*, and the confequencies of it, the curfe of God, &c. to make
all men wife, of one mind, good, religious, without an infinite omnipotent
power, fuch as of nothing was able to create a world : can any man (fober and
wife) hear it; hear it with patience, that thinks it impoffible, yea ftrange, that
Caftles fhould be built in the air, or the heavens battered with great guns ?
And yet fuch books are read, yea and much fet by, by fome men. My judgment is, That they are to be pityed (if diftemper be the caufe, as I believe it is
in fome) that boaft of fuch things; but if wife and politick, to get credit and
money (as fome I believe) it is a great argument of their confidence, that there
be many in the word that are not very wife. But to return to Dr. *Dee*: It
might be further added and proved by examples, that fome men of tranfcen-
dent *holinefs* and mortification ('in the fight of men) fo fequeftred from the
world (fome of them) and the vanities of it, that for many years they had con-
verfed with God alone in a manner; yet through pride and conceit of their
own parts and favour with God, fell into *delufions* and temptations, if not altogether the fame, yet not lefs ftrange and dreadful. Such examples Ecclefiafti-
cal Story will afford, and other books of that nature, but I have them not at
this time, and I conceive I have faid enough to this particular.

But of his *Praying* too, fomewhat would be obferved. *His Spirits* tell him
fomewhere, that he had the *Gift of Praying*. Truly I believe he had, as it is
ordinarily called : that it is, that he could exprefs himfelf very fluently and earneftly in Prayer, and that he did it often to his own great contentment. Let
no man wonder at this; I have fhewed elfewhere that fome that have been
very wicked, yea, fome that dyed for blafphemy, and with blafphemy in
their mouth to the laft gafp, have had it in a great meafure, and done much
mifchief by it. It is no difparagement to Prayer, no more then it is to the
beft things of the world (and what better and more heavenly then prayer well
ufed ?) if they be abufed. And it is commonly obferved, that the corruption
of beft things is moft dangerous. What bred thofe pernicious hereticks
that fo long troubled the world, and could not be fuppreffed but by abfolute
deftruction, but long affected prayers (therefore called *Euchites* or *Meffaliani*,
that is to fay, the *Prayers*) and Enthufiafms ? And as to that point of *inward
joy and complacency*, which fome Schifmaticks and wicked men find in
them-

E

themselves at their prayers, which ignorant deluded people think to be an argument of the Spirit: It is certain, and is a mystery of nature that hath (may I speak it without bragging) been brought to light (of late years at least) by my self and fully discovered, 'That not only the inward heat of " mental conception (where there is any vigor) but also the musick of out-" ward words, is able to occasion it. Indeed it is a point that doth deserve to be well considered of in these times especially. For when young boyes and illiterate men (and the number is likely to increase now that *Catechizing* is so much neglected) are turned loose to exercise themselves in this gift (as they call it) and when by long practice they have attained to some readiness and volubility, which doth occasion some inward lightsomeness and excitations, or perchance somewhat that may have some resemblance to spiritual sorrow and compunction, they presently think themselves inspired, and so they become *Saints* before they know what it is to be *Christians.* And if they can Pray by inspiration, why not Preach also? So comes in *Anabaptism* by degrees, which will be the ruine of all Religion and civil Government where ever it prevails. And I believe that this fond foolish conceit of *Inspiration,* as it hath been the occasion of much other mischief, so of that horrid sacriledge, shall I call it, or profanation (I hope I may do either without offence, for it is not done by any publick Authority that I know of) the casting and banishing of THE LORDS PRAYER out of many private houses and Churches; then which, I think, Christ never received a greater affront from any that called themselves Christians. I am not so uncharitable as to believe that it is done in direct opposition to Christ by any real Christians, but in a furious zeale by many, I believe, against set prayers. But this is not a place to dispute it: Certainly, as the Lords Prayer is a Prayer of most incredible comfort to them that use it devoutly and upon good grounds (a good foundation of Religion and sound Faith, I mean) so I believe that set Prayers in general are of more concernment to the setling of Peace in the Commonwealth then many men are aware of. But let this pass for my opinion; there be worse I am sure that pass currently.

Again, A man may wonder (I cannot tell whether an objection may be made of it) that Dr. *Dee,* though he were at the first deluded (to which his own pride and presumption did expose him) as many have been; yet afterwards in process of time when he found himself so deluded and shuffled with; when *Edward Kelley* did use such pregnant arguments to him (as he did more then once) to perswade him that they were evil Spirits that appeared unto them; nay, when he had found by certain experience, that his Spirits had told him many lies, foretold many things concerning Princes and Kingdoms, very particularly limited with circumstances of time, which when the time was expired did not at all come to pass; yet for all this he durst *pawn his Soul for them* that they were *good Spirits,* and continued in his confidence (so farre as our Relation goes) to the last. I answer, Such is the power of this kind of Spiritual delusion, it doth so possess them whom it hath once taken hold of, that they seldom, any of them, recover themselves. In the dayes of *Martin Luther* (a great and zealous refor-

mer

mer of Religion; but one that would have detested them as the worst of Infidels that had used the *Lords Prayer*, as some have done in our dayes, as appears by what he saith of it in more then one place) there lived one *Michael Stifelius*, who applying to himself some place of the *Apocalypse*, took upon him to Prophecy. He had foretold that in the year of the Lord 1533. before the 29 of *September* the end of the world, and Christs coming to Judgment would be. He did shew so much confidence, that some write, *Luther* himself was somewhat startled at the first. But that day past, he came a second time to *Luther* with new Calculations, and had digested the whole business into 22. Articles, the effect of which was to demonstrate that the end of the world would be in *October* following. But now *Luther* thought he had had tryal enough, and gave so little credit to him; that he (though he loved the man) silenced him for a time; which our Apocalyptical Prophet took very ill at his hands, and wondred much at his incredulity. Well, that moneth and some after that over, our Prophet (who had made no little stir in the Country by his Prophecying) was cast into prison for his obstinacy. After a while *Luther* visited him, thinking by that time to find him of another mind. But so far was he from acknowledging his error, that he down right railed at *Luther* for giving him good counsel. And some write that to his dying day (having lived to the age of 80. years) he never recanted. And was not this the case of learned *Postellus*, who fallen into some grievous wild fancies in his latter dayes, though found enough still in other things, could never be reclaimed though means were used from time to time the best and gentlest (in respect to his worth and person) that could be thought of? But what talk we of particular men? Consider the *Anabaptists* in general. Above an hundred years ago they troubled *Germany* very much: it cost many thousands their lives. They roved up and down. No sooner destroyed in one place but they sprung (whilest that season lasted) in another. Their pretences every where were the same; *Revelations* and the *Spirit*: the wickedness of Princes and Magistrates, and *Christ Jesus to be set up in his Throne*. Well, at last they were destroyed in most places. Stories of them have been written in all Languages, read every where, and their lamentable end. Can all this hinder but that upon every opportunity of a confused and confounded Government, they start up again in the same shape and form as before; the same pretences, the same Scriptures, for all the world, miserably detorted and abused, to raise tumults and seditions in all places. Such is the wretchedness of man that is once out of the right way of Reason and Sobriety. But withall we must say in this particular case of Dr. *Dee's*, though his obstinacy was great and marvellous, yet it must be acknowledged, that great was the *diligence* and subtility of his *Spirits* to keep their hold: and some things sometimes happened (as his danger and preservation about *Gravesend*, when he first, here related, went out of the Realm) very strangely, and such was the unhappiness of his misapplyed zeal, that he made a Providence of whatsoever hapned unto him as he desired.

So much for Dr. *Dee* himself. But of his *Spirits* a greater question perchance may be moved: If evil, wicked, lying Spirits (as we have reason

to

to believe, and no man I think will queſtion) how came they to be ſuch
perſwaders to Piety and godlineſs, yea, ſuch preachers of Chriſt, his Incarnation, his Paſſion, and other Myſteries of the Chriſtian Faith, not only
by them here acknowledged, but in ſome places very Scholaſtically ſet out
and declared ? It ſeemeth ſomewhat contrary to reaſon and as contrary to
the words of our Saviour, *Every Kingdom divided againſt it ſelf*, &c. But
firſt, to the matter of fact: The Divels we know even in the Goſpel did
acknowledg, nay, in ſome manner proclaim Chriſt to be the Son of God:
which is the main Article he did conteſt with Chriſt by Scripture Authority; and by S. *Pauls* teſtimony, can transform himſelf, when he liſt into
an Angel of light. And in ſome relations well atteſted, of Poſſeſſions
and publick Exorciſms that have been uſed; we find the Divel often ſpeaking by the mouth of women, rather like a Monk out of the Pulpit, per-
ſwading to temperance, rebuking vices, expounding of myſteries, and the
like, then as one that were an enemy to truth and godlineſs. Inſomuch
that ſome have been ready to make a great myſtery and triumph of it,
thereby to convict Hereticks and Atheiſts, in time, more effectually, then
they have been by any other means that have been uſed hitherto: and aſ-
cribing the whole buſineſs not to the Divel himſelf, but the great power
and Providence of God, as forcing him againſt his will to be an inſtrument
of his Truth. For my part, I ſee cauſe enough to believe that ſuch things,
there contained at large, might come from the Divel; that is, might truly and really be ſpoken by perſons poſſeſſed and inſpired by the Divel.
But that they are imployed by God to that end, I ſhall not eaſily grant.
I rather ſuſpect that whatſoever comes from them in that kind, though it
be good in it ſelf, yet they may have a miſchievous end in it; and that I
believe will ſoon appear if they can once gaine ſo much credit among men
as to be believed to be ſent by God to bear teſtimony to the truth. A man
may ſee ſomewhat already by thoſe very Relations, and that account that is
given us there. And therefore I do not wonder if even among the more
ſober Papiſts this project (as the relater and publiſher complaineth) hath
found oppoſition. The Divel is very cunning; a notable Politician. S.
Paul knew him ſo, and therefore he uſes many words to ſet out his frauds.
He can lay the foundation of a plot, if need be, a hundred years before the
effects ſhall appear. But then he hath his end. It is not good truſting of
him, or dealing with him upon any pretence. Can any man ſpeak better then he doth by the mouth of Anabaptiſts and Schiſmaticks ? And this
he will do for many years together if need be, that they that at firſt ſtood
off may be won by time. But let them be once abſolute maſters, and
then he will appear in his own ſhape. There is one thing which I wonder much more at in thoſe Relations I have mentioned, and that is, that
the Divel himſelf ſhould turn ſuch a fierce accuſer of them that have
ſerved him ſo long, Witches and Magicians. I know he doth here ſo too
in ſome kind, in more then one place. He doth much inveigh againſt
Divels and all that have to do with them, Magicians, &c. But that is
in general only, or in *Kelley's* particular caſe, upon whom he had a-
nother hold, which he made more reckoning of, to wit, as he appeared

peared to them as an Angel of light. Any thing to maintain his interest there, and their good opinion of him; for he had great hopes from that plot. But that he should pursue so ridgedly particular men and women whom he had used so long, to death, and do the part of an informer against them; may seem more like unto a Kingdom divided against it self, but it is not our case here; neither am I very well satisfied, that whatsoever the Divel saith or layes to the charge of them by whose mouth he speaketh, ought to be received for good testimony. Here it may be *Wierius* had some reason; for I doubt some have been too credulous. But this by the way shall suffice.

That the Divel should lie often, or be mistaken himself, in his *Prophecies*, as by many particulars of this Relation will appear, I will not look upon that, as if any objection could be made of it. But it may be wondred, perchance, Dr. *Dee* being often in so great *want of monies*, that he did not know which way to turn, what shift to make; at which time he did always with much humility address himself to his Spirits, making his wants known unto them; and the Divel on the other side, both by his own boasting, and by the testimonie of those who could not lie, having the goods of this world (though still under God) much at his disposing, and always, as he seemed, very desirous to give Dr. *Dee* all possible satisfaction: that in this case, once or twice perchance excepted, when the Dr. was well furnished (for which the Spirits had his thanks) at all other times he was still, to his very great grief and perplexity, left to himself to shift as he could, and some pretence, why not otherwise supplied, cunningly devised by them that were so able, and to whom he was so dear. But I must remember my self: I said so able; but in some places his Spirits tell him plainly, It was not in their power, because no part of their Commission, or because it did not belong unto *them* (such as dealt with him) to meddle with the Treasures of the earth: and sometimes that they were things beneath their cognizance or intermedling. Of the different *nature of Spirits*, we shall say somewhat by and by, that may have some relation to this also, perchance. But granting that the Divel generally hath power enough both to find mony and to gratifie with it where he seeth cause. Yet in this case of Witches and Magicians, direct or indirect, *it is certain and observed by many as an argument of Gods great Providence over men, that generally he hath not*: It is in very deed a great Argument of a superiour over-ruling power and Providence. For if men of all professions will hazard (their Souls) so far as we see daily to get money and estates by indirect unconscionable wayes, though they are not always sure, and that it be long oftentimes before it comes, and oftentimes prove their ruine, even in this world, through many casualties; as alterations of times, and the like: what would it be if it were in the power of the D. to help every one that came unto him, yielding but to such and such conditions, according as they could agree?

Hitherto I have considered what I thought might be objected by others. I have *one objection more*, which to me was more considerable (as an objection, I mean, not so readily answered) then all the rest: Devils, we think

gene

generally, both by their nature as Spirits, and by the advantage of long experience (a very great advantage indeed in point of knowledg) cannot but have perfect knowledg of all natural things, and all secrets of Nature, which do not require an infinite understanding; which by that measure of knowledge that even men have attained unto in a little time, is not likely to be so necessary in most things. But lest any man should quarrel at the word *Perfect*, because all perfection belongs unto God properly, it shall suffice to say, That the knowledge Divels have of things Natural and Humane is incomparably greater then man is capable of. If so, how comes it to pass that in many places of this Relation we find him acting his part rather as a Sophister (that I say not a Juggler) then a perfect Philosopher; as a Quack, or an Empirick sometimes, then a True, genuine Naturalist. And for language (not to speak of his Divinity, which he might disguise of purpose to his own ends) rather as one that had learned Latin by reading of barbarous books, of the middle age, for the most part, then of one that had been of *Augustus* his time, and long before that. But that which is strangest of all is, that as in one place the Spirits were discovered by *Ed. Kelley* to steal out of *Agrippa* or *Trithemius* (so he thought at least) so in divers other places, by the phrase, and by the doctrine and opinions a man may trace noted Chymical and Cabalistical Authors of later times; yea, (if I be not much mistaken) and *Paracelsus* himself, that prodigious creature, for whom and against whom so much hath been written since he lived; these things may seem strange, but I think they may be answered. For first, we say, The Divel is not ambitious to shew himself and his abilities before men, but his way is (so observed by many) to fit himself (for matter and words) to the genius and capacity of those that he dealeth with. Dr. *Dee*, of himself, long before any Apparition, was a Cabalistical man, up to the ears, as I may say; as may appear to any man by his *Monas Hieroglyphica*, a book much valued by himself, and by him Dedicated at the first to *Maximilian* the Emperor, and since presented (as here related by himself) to *Rodolphe* as a choice piece. It may be thought so by those who esteem such books as Dr. *Floid*, Dr. *Alabaster*, and of late *Gafarell*, and the like. For my part I have read him; it is soon don, it is but a little book: but I must profess that I can extract no sense nor reason (sound and solid) out of it: neither yet doth it seem to me very dark or mystical. Sure we are that those Spirits did act their parts so well with Dr. *Dee*, that for the most part (in most Actions) they came off with good credit; and we find the Dr. every where almost extolling his Spiritual teachers and instructers, and praysing God for them. Little reason therefore have we to except against any thing (in this kind) that gave him content, which was their aim and business.

Secondly, I say, If any thing relish here of *Trithemius* or *Paracelsus*, or any such, well may we conclude from thence, that the Divel is like himself. This is the truest inference. It is he that inspired *Trithemius* and *Paracelsus*, &c. that speaketh here, and wonder ye if he speaks like them? I do not expect that all men will be of my opinion; yet I speak no *Paradoxes*: I have both reason and authority good and plausible, I think, for what I say; but to argue the case at large would be tedious. Of *Trithemius* somewhat more afterwards will be said. But we must go far beyond that time. A thousand years and above, before

before either of them was born, was the BOOK OF ENOCH well known in the world; and then also was *Lingua Adami*(upon which two most of the Cabala stands) much talked of, as appears by *Greg.Nissen* his learned books against *Eunomius* the Heretick. To speak more particularly (because so much of it in this Relation) the BOOK OF ENOCH was written before Christ; and it is thought by some very learned (though denyed by others) that it is the very book that S. *Jude* intended. A great fragment of it in Greek (it was written in Hebrew first) is to be seen in *Scaliger* (that incomparable man, the wonder of his Age, if not rather of all Ages) *his learned Notes upon* Eusebius. It was so famous a book antiently that even Heathens took notice of it, and grounded upon it objections against Christians. It may appear by *Origen* against *Celsus*, in his book 5.p.275. Πάνυ δὲ ἐυγκεχυμένος (saith he) ἐν τῷ περὶ τῶν ἐπηλυθότων πρὸς ἀνθρώπους ἀγγέλων ἐξέλασι λόγωσι·τῷ, ἀθρανότας ἐπθόντα εἰς αὐτὸν, ἀπὸ τῶν ἐν τῷ Ἐνὼχ γεγραμμένων ἅτινα οὐδ' αὐτὸς φαίνεται ἀναγνούς, οὐδὲ γνωρίσας ὅτι ἐν ταῖς Ἐκκλησίαις οὐ πάνυ φέρεται ὡς θεῖα τὰ ἐπιγεγραμμένα τῷ Ἐνὼχ βιβλία. But S. *Jerome* and S. *Augustin* speak of it more peremptorily as a fabulous book, and not allowed by the Church. How much of it is extant, besides what we have in *Scaliger*, I know not; nor what part it is so often mentioned in this Relation. By what I have seen it doth appear to me a very superstitious, foolish, fabulous writing; or to conclude all in one word, Cabalistical, such as the Divel might own very well, and in all probability was the author of. As for that conceit of the tongue which was spoken by *Adam* in Paradise, we have already said that it is no late Invention; and I make no question but it proceeded from the same Author. Yea, those very Characters commended unto Dr.*Dee* by his *Spirits* for holy and mystical, and the original Characters (as I take it) of the holy tongue, they are no other, for the most part but such as were set out and published long agoe by one *Theseus Ambrosus* out of Magical books, as himself professeth: you shall have a view of them *in some of the Tables at the end of the Preface.* Some letters are the same, others have much resemblace in the substance; and in transcribing it is likely they might suffer some alteration. But it may be too the Spirits did not intend they should be taken for the same, because exploded by learned men, and therefore altered the forms and figures of most of them of purpose that they might seem new, and take the better. So that in all this the Divel is but still constant unto himself, and this constancy stands him in good stead, to add the more weight and to gain credit to his Impostures. Not to be wondred therefore if the same things be found elsewhere, where the D. hath an hand.

With Cabalistical writings we may joyn *Chymical*, here also mentioned in many places. I have nothing to say to *Chymistrie* as it is meerly natural, and keeps it self within the compass of sobriety. It may wel go for a part of Physick, for ought I know, though many great Physicians, because of the abuse and danger of it, as I conceive, have done their best (formerly) to cry it down. I my self have seen strange things done by it: and it cannot be denyed but the wonders of God and Nature are as eminently visible in the experiments of that Art as any other natural thing. *However, it is not improbable that divers secrets of it came to the knowledg of man by the Revelation of Spirits.* And the practice and profession of it in most (them especially that profess nothing else) is accompanied with so much Superstition and Imposture, as it would make a sober man, that tendreth the preservation of himself in his right wits, to be afraid of

it.

ᶦt. Of the *Tranfmutation of Metals*, what may be done by Art I will not take upon me to determine : I am apt enough to believe that fome ftrange things (in that kind) may be done, if a man will go to the coft of it, and undergoe the trouble upon fo much uncertainty of the event. But that which we call ordinarily, and moft underftand by it, *The Phylofophers Stone*, is certainly a meer cheat, the firft author and inventor whereof was no. other then the Divel. *Legi etiam Spiritum fupernorum revelatione traditam antiquitus artem faciendi Auri, & me ætate idem ufu eveniffe*, &c. faith one (*Jo. Franc. Picus Mirandula*) of the learnedft Author that I have feen of that fubjeƈt, in defence of it, I meant. If he mean *Supernos Spiritus*, fuch as appear in form of Angels of Light, fuch as deluded Dr. *Dee*, and daily doth thofe that hunt after *Revelations*, and Prophecies, and unlawful Curiofities, I grant it. But that any good Angels did ever meddle in a praƈtice commonly attended with fo much impofture, impiety, coufenage as this commonly is, I fhall not eafily grant. Though I muft add, I make great difference (if we will fpeak properly) between Arts *faciendi auri* (a thing I do not deny to be feafible by natural means) and that we call the *Phylofophers Stone*, as before already intimated. And for that objeƈtion of his, why evil Spirits fhould not be the Authors or revealers of it unto any (though otherwife for fome other reafons he thinks it probable) becaufe it is not likely that God would fuffer *them* to give fuch power unto men like themfelves, whom only among men they favour and refpeƈt, that is, wicked ungodly men. Firft, I anfwer, That is a very weak objeƈtion, fince we know by conftant experience of prefent and future Ages, that they are not of the beft of men commonly that are the greateft and richeft. But Secondly, There is no great caufe to fear that any thing hitherto revealed (or hereafter to be revealed, I believe) of this fecret, fhould enable men (good or bad) to do much hurt in the world. The greateft hurt is to themfelves who are deluded (yea, and beggerd many firft or laft) and to fome few not very wife whom they coufen as themfelves have been coufened. And for this that they can do no more, we are beholding not to the Divel who certainly would not be vvanting to himfelf or to any opportunity to do mifchief by himfelf or his Agents, but to God vvho doth not give him the povver : So much to *Mirandula*, out of my refpeƈt to his name, and for the better fatisfaƈtion to the Reader. I ovve the fight and ufe of the book to my Learned friend Dr. *Windett* before mentioned—. I am much confirmed in that opinion (of the Divel being the Author) by vvhat I find of it in the book vvhich hath given me this occafion to fpeak of it. Were there nothing elfe but the grofs and impudent forgeries that have been ufed to commend it unto men, fome entituling the Invention to *Adam* himfelf, others to *Solomon*, and the like ; and the many books that have been counterfeited to the fame end; and again the moft ridiculous and profane applying & expounding of Scriptures, a thing ufually done by moft that are abettors of it, thofe things vvere enough to make a man to abhor it. Sure enough it is, that not only Dr. *Dee*, but others alfo vvho had part of that *precious Powder brought unto them by Spirits*, and expeƈted great matters of it, vvere all cheated and gull'd (and I believe it coft fome of them a good deal of money ; *Prince Rofemberg* particularly) by thofe Spiritual Chymifts. Let them confider of it that have been dealing in fuch things as they fhall fee caufe.

So ftill we fee, that in all thefe things, as we faid before, the Divel is not be-holding to others, (as might be fufpected) but others have been beholding to him: As for his Divinity, in higheft points, if he fpake the truth, it was for his own ends, as we faid before: He can do it, who makes any queftion? In controverted points, we may obferve, that he doth *ferve the fcene* and prefent occafion; and I make no queftion, but had Dr. *Dee* gone to *Conftantinople*, and been entertained there with refpect, his Spirits there would have fhewed them-felves as good *Mahometans*, as elfewhere good *Roman Catholicks*, or *Proteftants*.

We have fomewhere a very pretty Tale, (I would fay a curious Obfervation, if I thought it true) concerning the nature of the Serpent or Addar, handfomly expreffed, how fhe traineth her yong ones to fet them out abroad into the world, that they may fhift for themfelves. Twenty days, as I remember, are fpent in that work: Now whether it be fo really, I cannot fay certainly, but I fufpect it. It is not in *Ariftotle*, and I looked in *Aldrovandus*, and I could not finde it: But whether it be fo or no, let no body wonder; for this was the maner of Preaching formerly (and may be yet perchance in fome places) among Monks and Fryars in great requeft. They would make a ftory of Man, or Beafts, as they thought fit themfelves, and their Fancies beft ferved; pretty and witty, as much as they could; whether it had any ground of truth, or no, no man re-quired: The moralization was good. If the Divel have done fo here, it was not through ignorance (for he is too good a Naturalift; and I believe there is fomewhat even in Nature, though we know it not, why both in facred and pro-phane Hiftory, *Spirits* and *Serpents* are fo often joyned) of which is true and real; but as hath been faid, it ferved his turn, and that is enough. And al-though, having confidered it as an Objection, how the Divel cometh to fpeak fo much truth, as will be found in this Book; no man, I think, will expect I fhould give an account of any falfe Doctrine or Divinity, that it may contain: Yet one point I think fit to take notice of, and proteft againft it; as falfe, erronious, and of dangerous confequence, and that is, where it is faid, *That a man* (in fome cafes) *may kill another man* (Prince or other) *without apparent caufe, or lawful Authority, and therefore punifhable by the Laws of Man; who neverthelefs, may expect a great reward at the hands of God for his act*: How this may agree with the Principles of *New Lights*, and Anabaptifti-cal Divinity, I know not; it is very contrary to the Principles of that Ortho-dox Divinity, lately profeffed and eftablifhed by Law in *England*.

I have now faid in this main Objection, (as I apprehended it) what I think was moft proper and pertinent, and I hope may fatiffie. But I have fomewhat elfe to fay, which in this cafe of *Divels and Spirits* in general, I think it very confi-derable, and may fatisfie perchance, in fome cafes, where nothing elfe can. We talk of Spirits, and read of Spirits often, but I think it is very little that we know (the beft of us all) of them, of their nature or differences: And how then can it be expected that we fhould refolve all doubts? And though I think it is not much that any man ever knew and rightly apprehended, or can, as he is a man, in this bufinefs; yet my opinion is, (though I know it is much gainfaid and oppofed) that ancient Platonick Phylofophers of the latter times, underftood much more then moft Chriftians; I do not write this, as though I thought, or would have any thought by others to be the worfe Chriftians for being ignorant in thefe things; but rather, in my opinion, any

man

man the better Christian, by much, who doth not regard it or defire it : For my
part, although I muft acknowledge that fome fcruples of my minde, did induce
me to look into many Books, until I was fatisfied, which otherwife I had never
done ; yet I profefs to believe, that it is fo little that can be known by man in this
fubject, and fubject to fo much illufion, as that I think no ftudy is more vain
and foolifh ; and that I would not go three fteps out of my doors (more then
what I did to fatisfie my minde in fome matters of Faith, if any fuch fcruple
did arife) to know as much as the profoundeft Platonick, or Phylofopher yea,
or Magician of them all ever knew. Certainly he is but a weak Chriftian, when
fo many high Myfteries are propofed unto us in Chrift by his Gofpel, and of fo
much confequence, that cannot beftow his time better : They that have any
hopes, through Faith in Chrift, and a godly life, to be admitted one day into
the prefence of God, and to *fee face to face*, as God hath promifed ; will they
hazard fo glorious a hope, by prying through unfeafonable, unprofitable curiofi-
ty, into the nature of thefe vaffal Spirits, which God hath forbidden : But becaufe it doth concern Religion in general, that we believe *Spirits* ; and when
Objections are made that cannot be anfwered, many are fcandalized, and Athe-
ifts ready to take the advantage of it ; I fay, that it fhould be no wonder to any,
fober and rational, if we cannot refolve all doubts, fince it is fo little that we
know, or can know, beyond the bare ὅτι in this matter : Moft Chriftians are
bred in and to this opinion, that all Spirits, (fo commonly called) are either Angels of Heaven, or Divels of Hell : I know no Scripture for it, or determination of any general Councel, that I remember, at this time at leaft, and fo long
I do not think my felf bound againft apparent reafon : *For the conceit of all evil*
Spirits or Divels being in Hell, I think learned Mr. Meade *hath taken that to*
task in fome of his Works, and fufficiently confuted it : The very word *Spirit*,
is a term of great Ambiguity ; We underftand by it, commonly, fubftances,
that are altogether immaterial. Many of the ancient Fathers, it is well known,
did not allow of any fuch at all, befides God : But we think that to have no vifible Body, and to be purely immaterial, is all one : God knows how many
degrees there may be between thefe, but we cannot know it, neither doth it
concern our falvation, for which we have reafon to praife God : But if it
were fo, that all *Spirits* are either Divels or Angels, what fhall we make of
thefe that are found in mines, of which learned *Agricola* hath written ; of
thofe that have been time out of minde called κόβαλοι, (from whence probably, as we have faid elfewhere, *Gobelin* in Englifh is derived) who live in
private Houfes, about old Walls, and ftalks of Wood, harmlefs otherwife, but
very thievifh, fo frequent and fo known in fome Countreys, that a man may as
well doubt whether there be any Horfes in *England*, becaufe there are none
in fome parts of the World ; not found in all *America*, I think, till fome were
carried thither : Neither can I believe, that thofe Spirits that pleafe themfelves
in nothing elfe but harmlefs fports and wantonneffe, fuch as have been known
in all Ages ; fuch as did ufe to fhave the hairs of *Plinius Secundus* his Servants in the Night, as himfelf relates (a very creditable man, I am fure) in his
Epiftles, and the like ; that fuch Spirits, I fay, have any relation either to
Heaven or to Hell : We might infift in more particulars, but we do not defire
to dwell upon it at this time ; and there is yet fomewhat elfe to be faid : And
what

what I have said of some Platonicks, I did not intend thereby to justifie all
their absurd or superstitious Opinions in this Argument of Spirits: As they
have searched furrher into it then others (besides damnable experience, having
confounded Magick with Phylosophy, yea almost turned all Phylosophy into Magick) so it was consequent, they would fall into more Errors and Absurdities; yet withal, they have found somewhat that doth better agree with
daily experience, then what is commonly known or believed. *Sinesins* was
a Bishop, but as he doth appear to us in his Writings, a better Platonick then
a Christian: In a place (in his Treatise *De insomniis*) he sheweth how evil Spirits come to inhabit men, and to possesse their Brains: His terms are very
course, and apparantly ridiculous; but there may be some truth in the Opinion: *For if there were not a very near and intimate conjunction, it were to be
wondered how the Divel comes to know the very thoughts of Witches and Magicians, as is found by experience, averred by more then one: And in this very Book, if I be not mistaken, somewhat may be observed to that purpose: It
is possible there may be more kindes of possession then one, and that some men,
that never were suspected, have had a spirit (besides their own) resident in
them, all, or most part of their lives.*

I have done, with what I could think of, upon which objection can be
made: The next thing is to make the way clearer to the Reader, by some consideration of the *method of the Books*, and explanation of some terms and
phrases there used, at which perchance some may stick at the first: At the very
beginning a man may be to seek, it the Title of it, *Liber sexti mysteriorum, &
sancti parallelus, novalisque.* 1583. both as it relates to that which follows, and
as it reflects upon somewhat before, by which it may be inferred that the book
begins here abruptly and imperfectly: of this I am now ready to give an account
to the Reader, and it is very fit it should be done.

First concerning Titles, such as will be found here many more besides this,
the whole book, or relation being subdivided into many parts; in general I
say, that according to the Doctors genius (we have said before he was very *Cabalistical,* that is, full of whimsies and crotchets, under the notion of Mysteries,
a thing that some very able, otherwise, have been subject unto) and the high
opinion he had of these actions and apparitions; they are mostly very concealed, and (to speak the truth) phantastick, which must make them the Obscu-
rer: I could give the Reader a view of them all here put together, but it
would be superfluous: There be some fourteen or fifteen Divisions in all now
remaining, and so many Titles: There is a Table at the beginning, that doth
refer to the beginning of every division, where the Title also will be found:
But at the end of the viii. Division, I finde these words, *Sequitur liber 24. qui
hac die etiam inceptus est, à meridie: horam circiter tertiam, per ipsum La-
vanael:* But I finde nothing following, (but some vacant sheets, till we come
to the ix. Division, *Mysteriorum pragensium, &c.* And the last Division hath
onely some Fables, and before them, some five or six pages of unknown mystical words, which we know not what to make of; but of that more afterwards: The main businesse to be resolved here (as I take it) is what it is that we
have, and what we have not, so far as can be gathered by what remaineth;
we shall see what we can say to it. In the year of the Lord, One thousand five
hundred

hundred eighty four, *September* the third, (being a Monday) Dr. *Dee* firft appeared (being prefented by Honorable perfons, and expected) before the Emperor *Rodolph.* Among other things he then told him, *That for thefe two years and a half, Gods holy Angels had ufed to inform him*: Our Book, or firft Action here, beginneth 28 *May,* 1583. According to this reckoning, it muft be, that above a year and three Moneths before, began the firft Apparition: The account then of fifteen Moneths from the firft Apparition, we want: How much (in bulk) that might come to, I cannot tell ; neither will I warrant all perfect from this 28 of *May,* 1583 to the fourth of *April* 1587. though for the moft part the coherence is right enough to that time : But from thence to the twentieth of *March,* 1607. is a vaft *chafma* or *hiatus,* of no lefs then twenty years : How this hath happened, I cannot tell certainly ; what I guefs, is this, fome years after Dr. *Dees* death ( ) Sir *Robert Cotton* bought his Library (what then remained of it) with his *Magical Table,* (of which afterwards) and the *Original Manufcript,* written With his own hand, whereof this is a Copy: The Book had been buried in the Earth, how long, years or moneths, I know not ; but fo long, though it was carefully kept fince, yet it retained fo much of the Earth, that it began to moulder and perifh fome years ago, which when Sir *Thomas C.* (before mentioned) obferved, he was at the charges to have it written out, before it fhould be too late: Now full fifty years, or not many wanting, being paffed fince this Original came to Sir *Robert,* it is very likely, that had any more in all that time been heard of, Sir *Robert,* or Sir *Thomas,* his Son and Heir, would have heard of it, and got it as foon as any body elfe : And becaufe no more hath been heard of all this while, it is more then probable that no more is extant, not in *England,* nor I think any where elfe : Happily the reft might perifh, fome part, (if not all) even whileft the Doctor lived ; and we fhall finde in this Relation, *That a good part of his holy Books were burned, but (which is more ftrange) a great part of them, by the help of Spirits, recovered and reftored:* Or it may be, that fince his death, the reft (the place where they lay being unknown) might rot in the earth ; now if, as probably no more be extant, we may account this that we have here, in that refpect perfect, becaufe here is all that can be had. But if any, (as it is the nature of many, if not moft, rather to defire that which cannot be had, then to content themfelves with that which may) fhall much lament the lofs of the reft, and be lefs pleafed with this, becaufe fo much (though indeed we know not certainly whether much or little) is wanting ; I would defire them to confider with themfelves, in cafe there had been twice or thrice as much more as all this comes too, what fhould have been done with it? For my part, for fo much as is here fet out (all we had) I thought it would do beft, though fomewhat long, yet as a thing very extraordinary, and of great confequence to many good purpofes and ufes ; I thought, I fay, it would do beft to have it all Printed ; Yet we had fome confideration about it, and it may be fome others would have thought that lefs might have ferved the turn: But I hope more will be of my minde, and there be but few actions but afford fomewhat that is extraordinary; and for fome refpect or other obfervable and ufeful ; Howfoever, I am confident, if all had been extant, (fuppofing that the reft would have made much more) that none or

very

very few would have thought fit to have Printed all ; and if it had once come to a contraction or abridgement, it may be much less then this muſt have ſerved : It is free for all men to think as they pleaſe ; for my part all things conſidered, I finde no great want of the reſt ; and if I were put to it, I cannot tell whether I can ſay, that I wiſh more were extant : yet it gives me great content, (and I hope there is no Blaſphemy or Superſtition in it, if I adſcribe it to providence) that after that long intermiſſion, or *hiatus*, we have yet the laſt Actions of all, whereby it might appear, after many goodly ſhews and promiſes, ſo much hope and expectation ; ſo many Prayers, ſo many Thankſgivings and Humiliations, what the end is of dealing with Divels, and uſing means that are not lawful, to compaſs ambitious unwarrantable deſires. Beſides, be it more or leſs that is wanting, yet I am confident we have the chiefeſt parts here preſerved ; as particularly, an exact account of his addreſſes and dealings with the *Emperor*, and other great men and Princes, in the vii. and ſome following Diviſions ; and that ſad ſtory of their *promiſcuous Copulation,* under the perſwaſion of obedience to God, very particularly related in the twelfth Diviſion ; wherein as the cunning and malice of evil Spirits, to lead away from God, when they moſt pretend to God and godlineſs ; ſo the danger of affected ſingularity and eminency, (the firſt ground of all this miſchief) of Spiritual pride and ſelf-conceit, is eminently ſet out to every mans obſervation, that is not already far engaged (as in theſe times too to many) in ſuch Principles.

But yet nevertheleſs I muſt acknowledge, that there is one part of the ſtory wanting, which I believe by moſt will be much deſired : For whereas at the very beginning, mention is made of a Stone, and that Stone not onely there mentioned, but afterwards in every action almoſt, and apparition, throughout the whole Book to the very end, ſtill occurring and commemorated as a principal thing ; what it was, and how he came by it, yea and what became of it, would be known, if by any means it might : All that we are able to ſay of it, is this, *It was a ſtone in which, and out of which, by perſons that were qualified for it, and admitted to the ſight of it ; all Shapes and Figures mentioned in every Action were ſeen, and voices heard :* The form of it was round, as appeareth by ſome courſe repreſentations of it in the Margins, as pag. 395. 399. *b.* 413 *b.* and it ſeems to have been of a pretty bigneſs : It ſeems it was moſt like unto Cryſtal, as it is called ſometimes, as pag. 80. *Inſpecto Chryſtallo,* and page 177. *b. nihil viſibile apparuit in Chryſtallo Sacrato, præter ipſius cryſtalli viſibili formam.* Every body knows by common experience, that ſmooth things are fitteſt for repreſentations, as Glaſſes, and the like ; but ordinarily ſuch things onely are repreſented, as ſtand oppoſite, and are viſible in their ſubſtance. *But it is a ſecret of Magick (which happily may be grounded, in part at leaſt, upon ſome natural reaſon, not known unto us) to repreſent Objects (externally not viſible) in ſmooth things :* And *Roger Bacon* (*alias Bacun*) in a Manuſcript inſcribed, *De dictis & factis falſorum Mathematicorum & Dæmonum,* communicated unto me by my Learned and much eſteemed Friend, Dr. *Windett,* Profeſſor of Phyſick in *London,* hath an Obſervation to that purpoſe, in theſe words, *Hiis Mathematicis in malitia ſuâ completis apparent Dæmones ſencibilitur in formâ humanâ & aliis formis variis, & dicunt & faciunt multa eis mirabilia ſecundum*

G　　　　　　　　　　　　　　　　　　　　*quod*

quod Deus permittit. Aliquando apparent imaginariè ut in ungue pueri virginis carminati; & in pelvibus & enſibus, & in ſpathulâ arietis ſecundum modum eorum conſecratis, & in cæteris rebus politii: & Dæmones oſtendunt eis omnia quæ petunt, ſecundum quod Deus permittit. Unde pueri ſic inſpicientes res politas vident imaginariè res furtivè acceptas & ad quem locum deportatæ ſunt, & quæ perſonæ aſportaverunt; & ſic de aliis, multis, dæmones apparentes, omnia hæc illis pejus oſtendunt.

Joach. Camerarius (that worthy man before ſpoken of) in his *Proemium* to *Plutarch, De Oraculis, &c:* hath a ſtrange Story upon the credit of a friend of his, whom he much reſpected (as himſelf profeſſeth) for his Piety and Wiſdom. A Gentleman of *Norimberg* had a Cryſtal (how he came by it, is there to be read) which had this vertue: *Si qua de re certior fieri vellet, &c.* if he deſired to know any thing paſt or future, that concerned him, yea, or any other (in moſt things) let a young Boy (*Caſtum*, one that was not yet of Age, &c.) look into it, he ſhould firſt ſee a man in it, ſo and ſo apparelled, and afterwards what he deſired: No other but a Boy, ſo qualified, could ſee any thing in it. This Cryſtal became very famous in thoſe parts; yea ſome learned men came to it to be ſatisfied in doubtful points, and had their queſtions reſolved: Yet at laſt, (as well it deſerved) it was broken in pieces by *Camerarius* his Friend. Many ſuch ſtories are to be found of Magical Stones and Cryſtals: And though *Fernelius, De abditis rerum cauſis;* and after him (as I remember) one, in worth and eſteem of all men, not inferior to *Fernelius*, Dr. *Harvey*, lately deceaſed, turns the relation of a ſtrange ſtone brought to one of the late Kings of *France*, into an Allegory, or Phyſical explication of the power and proprieties of the Element of Fire; yet I am not ſatisfied, but that the relation might be literally true: For ſo it is, (as I remember here alſo, for I have none of thoſe Books by me at this time) related by *Thuanus*, and ſo by ſome others, very learned, underſtood.

Now for the maner how he came by it, the particulars of the ſtory cannot be had by this here preſerved, but onely this in general, That it was brought unto him by ſome, whom he thought to be Angels: So we finde him telling the *Emperor, That the Angels of God had brought to him a Stone of that value, that no earthly Kingdom is of that worthineſs, as to be compared to the vertue or dignity thereof.* Page 272. in his conference with Dr. *Curts*, appointed by the Emperor to treat with him; *and alſo let him ſee the ſtone brought me by Angelical Miniſtery:* And we finde this Note recorded, [*Prague, Tueſday 25 Septembris, I went to Dinner to the* Spaniſh *Ambaſſador, and carried with me the Stone brought me by an Angel, and the fourth Book, wherein the maner of the bringing of it is expreſſed.*] And for the *uſe* of the Stone, beſides what hath been ſaid, this is obſervable: Some Spirits being in ſight of *E. K.* out of the Stone, Dr. *Dee* would have the Stone brought forth, but *E. K.* ſaid, *He had rather ſee them thus, out of the Stone;* to which the Doctor replies, *That in the Stone they had warrant that no wicked Spirits ſhould enter; but without the Stone illuders might deal with them, unleſs God prevented it, &c.* From which paſſage alſo we may learn, as from divers others in the Book that although the ſtone (as we ſaid before) was the place, in which, and out of which, ordinarily, moſt Apparitions were framed, yet it was not ſo always: For we ſhall meet
with

with divers things in that kinde that were seen and heard, without any reference to the *Stone*: From the same place also we may learn, that the said *Stone* was the same he also called the *Shew-stone*; as in many places besides. However, it is certain enough that he had more Stones then one, which he accounted sacred; observe *Principal Stone*, and *this other Stone*; & *first Sanctified Stone, usual Shew-stone*, and *Holy-stone*, may be thought opposed and different; but I understand it otherwise: This is the account we can give of this *principal Holy-Stone*. And to supply the defect of the maner how it was brought to him, the Reader, if he please, may finde some satisfaction, if he read the *maner how it was taken away, and restored*, very particularly set down, as before (upon another occasion) was observed.

Besides this *Stone* or *Stones*, there are divers other sacred things mentioned, that belonged to this personated Sanctuary, but nothing more frequently mentioned then *Curtains*; a *Curtain* or *Vail*, as it is sometimes called. A man would think at first, perchance, that it was somewhat outward, but it will be found otherwise; it was seen *in the Stone*, and appeared of different forms and colours, as they that read will quickly finde.

Next unto these the *Holy Table* is chiefly considerable, ordering of it is referred to Dr. *Dee*, which he durst not take upon himself, until he had warrant from his Spiritual Teachers: This *Table*, which may well be called Magical, is preserved and to be seen in Sir *Thomas Cottons* Library (from whence we had the rest) and by his leave is here represented in a brass Cut; mention is made of it, as I take it, where Dr. *Dee* proposeth to his Teachers, *Whether the Table (for the middle cross of uniting the 4 principal parts) be made perfect or no*: You may see more of it, it is also called *League Table, Table of Covenant, mensa foederis* in some places: The *Pedestal* of it is mentioned in two or three places, and indeed a very curious Frame belonging unto it, yet to be seen in the said Library. But I know not what to make of that, *neither Nalu: nor the Table appeareth*; and *the round Table or Globe appeared not*. I believe it must be understood of somewhat that had appeared before in the stone. The Reader that will be so curious, by careful reading may soon finde it out; I was not willing to bestow too much time upon it.

But here remaineth a main business whereof we are to give an account to the Reader: There were many Tables or Schemes at the end of the Book, containing Letters, *a. b. c. &c.* disposed into little squares, with an Inscription over each Table in that unknown Character (before spoken of) expressed in usual Letters how it should be read. There is one for a *Specimen* here at the end of the Preface; the rest were omitted, because it was judged needless, except it were to increase the price of the Printed book. For first, Dr. *Dee* himself, though he took a great deal of pains to understand the Mystery of them, and had great hopes given him from time to time to reap the benefit (himself complains of it in more then one place) of his toilsome work and long patience, yet it never came to any thing: and if he made nothing of them (to benefit himself thereby) what hopes had we? Besides, we may judge of these *Tables*, and all this mystery of *Letters*, by what we have seen in others of the same kinde. *Johannes Trithemius* was a man that was supposed by most to have dealt with *Spirits* a long time, and to have been instructed by them in

some

ſome of thoſe ſecrets that he pretends unto by his Books. I know ſome have thought him innocent, or at leaſt, have attempted to juſtifie him: Some affect ſuch things to ſhew their wit, and think they ſhall be thought much wiſer then other men, if they contradict received Opinions, though their vanity and ſtrong conceit of their own parts, be their chief, if not onely ground. Learned and Judicious Maſter *Voſſius*, hath ſhewed himſelf very willing to think the beſt of him and his Books; yet he gives it over at laſt, and rather concludes on the contrary. They that dare defend *Apollonius*, the greateſt upholder of Ethniciſm that ever was, and by moſt Heathens accounted either a God, or a *Magician*, need not ſtick at any thing in this kinde: But ſay he was, what any man will have of him, (*Frithemius* we ſpeak of, his *Polygraphy*, he ſet out in his life time, dedicated to the then Emperor: He tells the World of the greateſt wonders to be done by it, that ever were heard of: All Wiſdom and Arts, all Languages, Eloquence, and what not, included in it. But I never heard of any man that could make any thing of it, or reaped any benefit in any kinde; which I think is the reaſon that his *Steganography*. mentioned and promiſed in this firſt work was ſo long after his death before it was Printed: It was expected it would have given ſome light to the firſt; but neither of that, nor of this latter, could ever any thing, that ever I could hear, be made by any man. I have good ground for what I ſay: For beſides what others have acknowledged, I finde learned *Viginaire*, (who in his old age was grown himſelf very Cabaliſtical, or it may be had ſome diſpoſition that way, though very learned otherwiſe, from his natural temper) as much grounded in that book, as any man before him: He doth plainly profeſs he could make nothing of it: And truly if he could not, that had beſtowed ſo much time and pains in thoſe unprofitable ſtudies, I ſee little hopes that any man elſe ſhould. It would make a man almoſt hate Learning, to ſee what dotage, even the moſt learned, are ſubject unto: I could bleſs them that know but little, ſo themſelves knew it is but little that they know, and were humble: But it commonly falls out otherwiſe, that they that know but little, think that little to be much, and are very proud of it; whereas much knowledge (or to ſpeak properly, more knowledge) if well uſed, hath this advantage, that it makes men moſt ſenſible of their ignorance: The reading of *Vigenaires* book of Cyphers (which I once thought a rare piece, as many other things of the ſame Author, which I had read) hath expreſſed theſe words from me in this place; and becauſe it hath ſo much affinity with our preſent Theme, I was the bolder; But to return. Upon this conſideration, the Reader I hope, will not be ſorry the reſt of the *Tables* (being many in number) were omitted. Though I muſt adde withal, had I known or thought any uſe could be made of them, having no better opinion of the Author (him or them) I mean, from whom Dr. *Dee* had them) I ſhould not have been very forward to have had a hand in their coming abroad.

I ſhould have told the Reader before but it may do well enough here, that beſides the particulars before ſpecified, there were other things that belonged to this *holy Furniture* (as Dr. *Dee* ſomewhere doth ſpeak) whereof mention is made in ſome places: as *Carpet, Candleſtick, Taper, Table-Cloth, Cuſhion*, and ſome others perchance. But I know nothing needs be obſerved upon

any

any of thefe. I make no queftion but the Divel in all thefe things had a refpect to the Ceremonial Law efpecially ; as alfo in thofe words, *Move not, for the place is holy,* often repeated, which are alfo elfewhere expounded: The Interlocutors in all this relation, are, Δ. (that is, Dr. *Dee*) and E. K. that is *Edw. Kelley* ; and the *Spirits*, to the number of fome twenty, or thereabouts, fo many named: (*Madini, Efemeli, Merifri, Ath, Galuah, Il, Jubenladece, Gabriel, Jam, Moreorgran, Aph, Lasben, Uriel, Naluage, Mapfama, Aue, Ilemefe, Gaza, Vaa, Leveanael, Ben,*) at leaft, but whether all Interlocutors, I know not, becaufe I do not remember, neither doth it much concern.

There be divers *marginal Notes* and Obfervations, which being of Dr. *Dee* his own, are for the moft part not inconfiderable, and fome very remarkable, all therefore here exhibited ; but whereas in fome places he had attempted to reprefent the apparition, or fome part of it, in Figures alfo ; this being done but fometimes, and in cafe it had been done oftner (except it were to fatisfie the childifh humor of many Buyers of Books in this Age, when becaufe they buy not to read, muft have fomewhat to look upon ; whence it comes to pafs, that much trafh doth pafs for good ware, for the trimming fake, and on the contrary) of little ufe, no notice is taken of it ; except fome Figure be in the Text it felf, and of fome confequence, for the better underftanding of the reft.

The *Greek, p. 25. b.* is exactly fet out, as it was found, and yet to be feen in the original, written by Dr. *Dee* himfelf: But little or nothing can be made of it, as it is written ; and it is a fign that Dr. *Dee* who writ it, as *Edw. Kelley* reported it unto him, and afterwards plodded upon it (as doth appear by fome Conjectures and Interpretations found in the original, and here alfo exhibited) as well as he could. was no very perfect *Grecian*; much lefs *Edw. Kelley*, who could not fo much as read it, which made Dr. *Dee* to write fome things that he would not have *Kelley* to read, in Greek Characters, though the words were Englifh : I would not alter any thing that was in the Original : But the words, I bel'eve fpoken by the Spirit, (and fo the Greek is warrantable enough) were thefe, Οὗτος ὁ ἑταῖρος τῦτο ἔργον ἀναςήσει· Κόσμος γὰρ πεθυμίος τυγχάνει ὤν· Κὶ αὐτὸς τοσοῦτον πυεαζέςαι· Ὥςε κοίνης ἀφελυσίας φιλίας· Εσθεα μὴ τινα αὐτῷ ἀφορμὴν παρέξῃς· Τὰς γὰ ἀπλίας κομιδῇ παραςκευάζεςαι· Ἵνα σε διὰ παντὸς ἀπολείπῃ· This I think was intended of *Edw. Kelley*, who was ever and anon upon projects to break with Dr. *Dee*, and to be gone, as here prefently after, and in divers other places of this relation ; nay, did really forfake him fometimes for fome time: The fence *verbatim* is this : *This fellow (or Friend) will overthrow this work* (of Apparitions you muft underftand, to which he was requifite, becaufe the Divel had not that power over Dr. *Dees* Body, to fit it, though he did promife it him, for fuch fights.) *His baggage (or furniture) is in a readinefs. And he doth very much endeavor : To withdraw himfelf from this common friendfhip . Take heed, that you give him no occafion : For he doth mightily plot by art and cunning : How he may leave you for ever.* Πεθυμος, in the firft line, may feem unufual, for ἕτοιμος, or πεθυεος ; but it is an elegant Metaphore. Πυεαζέαι for πυεαζεῖν, is not ufual ; and happily it fhould have been πυεάςας, and fo uttered ; but that is nothing. Certainly he that could fpeak fo much Greek, (called here *Syrian*, to jeer *Ed. Kelley*) could not want Latine at any time to exprefs

himfelf,

himself; which neverthelels, might be thought, where we finde him speaking English, to them that underflood it not; lo that Dr. *Dee* was fain to interpret it: But we cannot give an account of all his fetches and projects: He had a confideration, I make no queftion,

I cannot think of any thing elfe that the Reader need to be told, that is of this nature, and it may be fomewhat might have been fpared: However the Reader will confider, that as in all Books, fo in this: It is one thing to read from the beginning, and fo to go on with heed and obfervation, without skipping; and another thing to read here and there, which would require a perpetual Comment, which is the wretchednefs of moft Readers, in thefe declining days of Learning; and therefore they have *Comments* (or *Rhapfodies* rather) accordingly; *fimiles habent labra lactufes,* never more true of any thing

It may be fome will wonder what made the Spirits to fall upon *Englifh Genealogies* and Stories; it is at very beginning, therefore I take notice of it for the Readers fake, that is yet (and cannot otherwife) a ftranger to the Book: The bufinefs is, Dr. *Dee* was lately grown in to great league and confederacy with *Albert Lasky,* (or *à lasco* rather) a great man of *Polonia.* You had before what *Cambden* faith of him of his coming to *England,* at this very time, and his going away, which doth very well agree with our dates here. It feems, though nobly born, and to great dignity, yet his thoughts did afpire much higher; and though no rich man, for a man of his rank and quality, yet expecting fuch matters from Dr. *Dee* and *his Spirits,* as he did, he could finde money enough to fupply their wants upon occafion. The Spirits were very glad of the occafion, and did what they could to cherifh him according to his humor: Being then at that very time upon deliberations, that much depended of *Alb. Lasky* and his good opinion; among other things, his Pedegree, which muft needs pleafe a vain man very well, was taken into confideration: That every thing there faid, doth exactly agree to the truth, as I do not warrant it, fo neither am I at leifure at this time to take the pains to examine. We muft never look further in thofe things that are delivered by fuch, then if it were, or be pertinent (true or falfe) to their end and prefent occafion. Befides, it is very poffible, (which I defire the Reader to take good notice of) that both here and elfewhere the Tranfcribers, as they could not read fometimes, and were forced to leave fome blancks (though feldome to any confiderable prejudice of the fence) fo they might miftake alfo, having to do with an Original that was (and is yet to be feen) fo defaced and worm-eaten as this is, written (as we have faid) by Dr. *Dee* himfelf.

Befides the authenticknefs of the Original Copy, written by Dr. *Dee* himfelf; the Reader may know, that *the Originals of the Letters* that are here exhibited, are all, or moft of them yet preferved, and to be feen in Sir *Tho. Cottons* Library.

IV. I am now come to the laft of the four things that I promifed, to fhew the feveral *good ufes* that may be made of this Book, and which were principally looked upon in the publifhing of it. This order indeed I propofed to my felf, but great part of this occafion offering it felf upon other matter, is already performed in the former Difcourfe, fo that but little is now left to be done. However I will fum them up, and reprefent them together, that every Reader may

have

have them in readiness and in view for his use the better.

The firſt is againſt Atheiſts, and ſuch as do not believe that there be any Divels or Spirits: We have argued it, I confeſs, pretty largely, at the beginning of this *Diſcourſe* or *Preface,* and I hope ſome may receive competent ſatiſfaction by what we have ſaid: But if no Argument had been uſed, (ſetting aſide Scripture Authority, which would be impertinent againſt Atheiſts) I do not know what can be more convincing then this ſad Story, ſo exaɛtly ſo particularly, ſo faithfully delivered. Truly, they muſt ſee further then I do, that can finde what to anſwer (rationally) and to oppoſe: This is a great point, and a great ground of Religion; but this is not all: For if there be Spirits indeed, ſo wicked and malicious, ſo ſtudious and ſo induſtrious, to delude men, and to do miſchief, which is their end, all which is ſo fully repreſented in this Relation; then certainly muſt it follow, that there is a great over-ruling Power, that takes care of the Earth, and of the Inhabitants of it; of them eſpecially that adore that Power, and worſhip it with true affeɛtion and ſincerity: For without this over ruling Power, what a miſerable World ſhould we have? What man ſo ſober or innocent, that could enjoy himſelf at any time with any comfort or ſecurity? But again, what man can read this ſad ſtory, and can be ſo perſwaded of his own Wiſdom or innocency, but will in ſome degree reflect upon himſelf, and will be moved to praiſe God, that notwithſtanding many provocations in ſeveral kindes (as damnable curioſity, open prophaneneſs, frequent Oathes, Curſes, Perjuries, ſcandalous Life, and the like) God hath been pleaſed to protect and preſerve him from the force and violence of ſuch enemies of mankinde?

I ſaid before, from leſs beginnings greateſt confuſions had enſued, which is very true as in the caſe of *Bacchus* particularly many Ages before; and in the caſe of *Mahomet* afterwards. (two notable lewd *Enthuſiaſts,* by whom as Inſtruments, *evil Spirits,* by Gods permiſſion, brought great alterations in Governments, and wrought much miſchief and villany among Men and Women) we ſhall elſewhere ſhew more at large. By due conſideration of all Circumſtances, as chiefly their confident and reiterated Addreſſes unto, and Attempts upon ſo many great men in Power and Authority, and the like; I am much of opinion that theſe Spirits had as great hopes of Dr. *Dee,* as ever they had of *Bacchus* or *Mahomet.* But God was not pleaſed at that time to permit that their malice and ſubtilty ſhould prevail. And I think, if we conſider it well, we have reaſon to praiſe God for it. *England* might have been over-run with Anabaptiſm (when I ſay Anabaptiſm, I mean Anabaptiſm confirmed and in full power, not as it appears in its firſt pretentions) long before this: God be thanked that it was not then, and God keep it from it ſtill, I hope is the Prayer of all truly ſober and Religious And in very deed I know no reaſon, but the Wiſdom and prudence of their Majeſties Councel that then were, in oppoſing Dr. *Dees* frequent addreſſes and Sollicitations, may (under God) challenge and deſerve ſome part of our Thanks and Acknowledgement.

Again, The Divel we ſee can Pray and Preach, (as to outward appearance we mean; for truly and really, God forbid that any thing ſacred and holy ſhould be thought to proceed from Divels) and talk of Sanɛtity and Mortification, as well as the beſt. And what he can in his own perſon, or by himſelf immediately;

diately; there is no question, but he doth by his Ministers and Instruments much more, more ordinarily and frequently I mean : Let any man judge then, whether it be the part of a sober wise man, not onely to hear such men as can give no account of their calling, but also to follow them, to embrace their Doctrine, to be of their number or Congregation; and all this, upon this account, because they can pray and preach very well, (as they think and judge at least) and talk very godlily and zealously ? How much more inexcusable they that will cleave unto such, though they see and know them scandalous in their Lives, Proud, Insolent, Ignorant, Seditious, Intolerable, because they can pray, and preach, and talk, as best agreeth with their own humor, and gives them best content ? Can any man think they follow God in this, who would have *all things done in order,* and is not a God *of Confusion,* (1 *Cor.* 14. 33, 40.) when all they do, tends to nothing else but disorder and confusion ? I confess it is possible, that men lawfully called may prove bad enough, we have divers examples in the Scripture. But if a man, simply and ignorantly be mis-led by such, certainly his judgement will be much lighter then they can expect, who will not use the means that God hath ordained, in so great and weighty a business as the salvation of Souls is. I know not what these men can say for themselves, except it be, that they are resolved to make use of the Liberty of the times to please their humor ; they may do it, but if that bring them to Heaven, they have good luck.

But the business of praying, is that I would principally insist upon : You see here how Dr. *Dee,* where he gives an account of himself to the *Emperor,* and others, bears himself much upon this, that so many years he had been an earnest Suitor unto God *by Prayer* to obtain *Wisdom,* such wisdom as he was ambitious of. I believe him, that he had prayed very earnestly, and with much importunity many times: This was the thing that made him so confident of his Spirits, that they must needs be good Spirits and Angels. I know a man, I have no comfort to tell it, but that I would not conceal any thing that may be a warning unto others, and yet I will have a respect unto him too: But I knew one, a very innocent man (in his outward conversation, and as I believe very really) Humble, Religious, very Learned and Orthodox, and one that had suffered for his Conscience, as others have done in these times : This worthy man, being engaged in a controverted Argument, upon which his phancy had wrought very much, or rather which had much wrought upon his phancy ; he had written much, filled much Paper, and was desirous to communicate unto me as his friend what he had done : But when I perceived that the drift of his writing was out of the Law and the Prophets, to shew the necessity of some things which I thought of a more indifferent nature ; I was not willing to meddle with it ; and begun to argue against his main drift, and to shew my disliking. After many words to and fro, he began to press me with this, that he had often prayed with much earnestness, and he was very confident that God had heard his Prayers : Yea, he proceeded so far, that if God were true, he could not be deceived, and used many other words to the same purpose, at which I was much amazed, but
            could

could do no good upon him, fuch was his confidence and violence upon this occafion, though otherwife a very moderate ingenuous man: And thus I found him more then once, or twice. Truly, I think God was very merciful unto him, that took him away in good time. But certainly this bufinefs of *Prayer and praifing*, is a bufinefs as of great comfort (the greateft that mortal man is capable of upon earth) fo of much more danger and delufion, then many do believe. And if caution and circumfpection be to be ufed in any thing that belongs to Religion, I think it ought in Prayer, as much as any thing. And fince I have adventured to tell one ftory upon mine own credit, I will tell one more upon better authority, which I have long defired (for the obfervablenefs of it) to communicate unto the world, and to that end, had once inferted it in a Treatife of mine, which I thought would have been Printed, but it was not: I will firft give the Englifh of it, that all men may reap the benefit, and then fet it down in the words of my Author (mine own Father *Ifaac Cafaubon*, of *b. m.*) as I have it to fhew under his hand.

At a Confiftory in Geneva, *upon a Friday, 18 July, **1589**. The cafe of one Mr.* Nicholas *being there propofed to the Affembly to be confidered of, who was wont to infinuate himfelf into private Houfes, under pretence of praying, and made fmall congregations: The bufinefs was difliked by the Paftors; Firft, becaufe nothing in the Church of God ought to be done without order. Secondly, becaufe to turn fuch duties of Religion to matter of Traffick to get money onely, (without any other end or calling) was not lawful. Thirdly and laftly, his battalogy, (or vain repetition of words) was not to be fuffered: Then upon this occafion it was related by Mr.* Beza, *that the Saturday before, whileft that fharp conflict was, which we had before our eyes, (to wit, between the Genevians, and the Duke of* Savoys *Forces) that a certain Woman addreffed her felf to him, faying, What Mr.* Beza, *will you make Prayers here? To which he had anfwered, No: What, do you think I do behold thefe things with mine eyes onely, and do not pray to God in my heart? Giving this reafon for his anfwer he had made to the Woman:* [It is not fo expreffed in the Latine, that the following words were *Beza*'s words, but the coherence of matter doth fo require it] *That Prayer was certainly a holy thing, which it did not become any man to apply himfelf unto, (or to undertake) without due preparation: And that they were deceived, who thought it fo eafie a thing to pray rightly: And that care alfo fhould be taken left* [under a colour of zeal and devotion] *a way be made to fuperftition:* The Latine words are thefe,

[*Die Veneris, Julii 18. 1589. Cùm relatum effet in cœtum, de Mag.* Nicolao, *qui infinuaret fe in domos varias* περρδσι τε ευχεσθαι, *& ita aliquando cœtus, etfi parnos, coire folitos, paftoribus res improbata eft: Primùm, quia extra ordinem, nihil in Dei Ecclefia fieri debet: Deinde, quia* πολεμον *facere* την τρησκειαν, *nefas. Tertio, hominis* βατλολογια *non ferenda Narratum eft tum à* B *fe die Sabbathi proxime præcedente, dum acerrimum illud prælium committeretur, quod nobis erat ante oculos, interrogatum à muliercula, Quid tu D. B. vis preces hic facere? Refpondiffe, Nequaquam. Tu ne enim (ait) me putas, hæc oculis tantum fpectare, nec vota in animo ad Deum Opt. Max. fundere? Omnino,*

I

res sancta ἡ ευχη, ad quam non nisi meditatum oporteat accedere, falluntur enim qui rem putant esse facilem, preces bene concipere. Simul cavendum, ne alicui superstitioni viam imprudentes aperiamus.]

In the last place, All men may take warning by this example, how they put themselves out of the protection of Almighty God, either by presumptuous unlawful wishes and desires, or by seeking not unto Divels onely, directly (which Dr. *Dee* certainly never did, but abhorred the thought of it in his heart.) but unto them that have next relation unto Divels, as *Witches, Wizzards, Conjurers, Astrologers,* (that take upon them to foretell humane events) *Fortune tellers,* and the like, yea and all Books of that subject, which I doubt, were a great occasion of Dr. *Dees* delusion : That men are commonly cheated by such, is sure enough ; and those that are not very fools, would take heed how they deal with them, and avoid them, to avoid the Imputation of Fools ; but those that are wife, much more, if they can more then cheat ; for the more they can do, the more they know they have of the Divel in them : Wretched people that will not, dare not trust God, who as he is the onely fountain of goodness, so onely knows what is good for every man. They may rejoyce for a time, and applaud themselves in their conceited successes, but misery, if they repent not, will be their end ; and it is a great sign that God is very angry with them, when he doth suffer them to thrive by means which Himself hath cursed.

POST

SInce this Preface was written, and almoſt printed, I was ſhewed a Book, entituled, *Theatrum Chemicum Britannicum, &c.* by *Elias Aſhmole* Eſq; and in ſome *Annotations* there, at the end, an account concerning Dr. *Dee* and *Edw. Kelley*, (there ſtiled Sir *Edward Kelley*) out of a *Diary* of Dr. *Dees*, all written with his own hand : As I do not queſtion the Gentlemans fidelity in this buſineſs, ſo I make as little queſtion but Dr. *Dee's* own hand will be found to agree in all matters of Fact both here and there, if any ſhall take the pains to compare. And it may be the Reader may receive ſome further ſatisfaction in ſome particulars by his labor, which is the reaſon that I mention the Book here, being but lately come to my knowledge; His Judgement either concerning Dr. *Dee*, or *Kelley*, I meddle not with; and it may be, had he ſeen what is here to be ſeen, he would have been of another opinion in ſome things: Here is enough, I am ſure, to ſatisfie any man that is not very much preoccupied, or otherwiſe engaged by particular ends. As for thoſe *Reports* concerning *Kelley*, (ſome whereof concern Dr. *Dee* alſo) he tells us of, as I believe him, that he hath heard ſo, ſo I muſt (and may truly) profeſs, that I have met with far contrary, and in my judgement, and by this account here given us by Dr. *Dee*, much more probable : And particularly, that *Kelley* was put in Priſon by the Emperor, for a notable Chymical chat that he had put upon him ; the particulars whereof, though they were fully related unto me, yet I will not adventure upon, leſt I miſtake in ſome terms of art, or petty circumſtance of fact. And let the Reader judge by that account, Dr. *Dee* (who beſt knew) doth give us here throughout the whole Book of this *Kelley*, whether *Wevers* Story in his *Funeral Monum. pag.* 45, 46. of damnable *Necromancy*, and other *Diabolical Conjuration*, practiſed by *Kelley* in *Lancaſhire*, be not (beſides what is there ſaid and atteſted) much more probable, then any thing that hath been or can be ſaid by others, to his juſtification or commendation : Which indeed doth make Doctor *Dee's* caſe altogether inexcuſable, that believing and knowing the man to be ſuch a one, he would have to do with him, and expected good by his Miniſteries ; but that the Doctor his Faith, and his intellectualls (through Gods juſt judgement, as we have ſaid) were ſo much in the power and government of his Spirits, that they might perſwade him to any thing, under colour of doing ſervice unto God, yea had it been to cut his own Fathers throat, as we ſee in the *Relation*, that they perſwaded him to lie with another mans Wife, and proſtitute his own to a vile, and, by himſelf belived, Diabolical man.

Beſides, I have been told by many, that Dr. *Dee*, very poor and every way miſerable, dyed at *Mortlack*, here about *London*, which doth not ſeem to agree with the report in thoſe *Annotations*: But enough of them : Neither indeed have I ſaid any thing at all of purpoſe to oppoſe the Author, but to give this further ſatisfaction to the Reader, or rather to the truth, which I thought I was bound to do.

The paſſage in *Wevers Funeral Monuments, pag.* 45, 46. concerning *Kelley*, for their ſatisfaction that have not ſeen the Book, is this; *Kelley*, (otherwiſe called *Talbot*) that famous *Engliſh* Alchymiſt of our times, who flying out of his own Gountrey (after he had loſt both his ears at *Lancaſter*) was entertained by *Rodolph* the ſecond, and laſt of that Chriſtian name, Emperor of *Germany* ; for whom *Elizabeth* of famous memory, ſent (very ſecretly) Captain *Peter Gwyn*, with ſome others, to perſwade him to return back to his own Native home, which he was willing to do ; and thinking to eſcape away in the night, by ſtealth, as he was clammering over a Wall in his own Houſe in *Pragne* (which bears his name to this day, and ſometimes was an old Sanctuary) he fell down from the Battlements, broke his leggs, and bruiſed his body, of which hurts within a while after, he departed this World.

Sed quorſum hæc?. you will ſay : Then thus, This Diabolical queſtioning of the dead, for the knowledge of future accidents, was put in practice by the ſaid *Kelley*, who upon a certain Night, in the Park of *Walton* in *le dale*, in the County of *Lancaſter*, with one *Paul Waring*, (his fellow-companion in ſuch Deeds of darkneſs) invocated ſome one of the Infernal Regiment, to know certain paſſages in the life, as alſo what might be known by the Divels foreſight, of the manner and time of the death of a Noble yong Gentleman; as then in Wardſhip. The Black Ceremonies of that Night being ended, *Kelley* demanded of one of the Gentlemans ſervants, what *Corſe* was the laſt buryed in *Law* Church-yard, a Church thereunto adjoyning, who told him of a poor man that was buryed there but the ſame day : He and the ſaid *Waring*, intreated this foreſaid ſervant to go with them to the Grave of the man ſo lately Interred, which he did ; and withal, did help them to dig up the Carcaſe of the poor Catiff, whom by their Incantations, they made him (or rather ſome evil Spirit through his Organs) to ſpeak, who delivered ſtrange Predictions concerning the ſaid Gentleman. I was told thus much by the ſaid Serving-man, a Secondary Actor in that diſmal abhorred buſineſs ; and divers Gentlemen and others are now living in *Lancaſhire*, to whom he hath related this Story. And the Gentleman himſelf (whoſe memory I am bound to honor) told me a little before his death, of this Conjuration by *Kelley*, as he had it by relation from his ſaid Servant and Tenant, onely ſome circumſtances excepted, which he thought not fitting to come to his Maſters knowledge.

Doctor

Dr. Dee's Apology,

Sent to the Arch-Bishop of CANTERBURY, 1595.

OR,

A Letter containing a moſt brief Diſcourſe Apo-
geticall, with a plain Demonſtration, and ſervent Proteſtation
for the lawfull, ſincere, very faithfull and Chriſtian courſe
of the Philoſophicall Studies and Exerciſes, of a certain
ſtudious Gentleman: An ancient *Servant* to Her
moſt Excellent Majeſty Royall.

To the moſt Reverend Father in God, the Lord Archbiſhop of Canterbury,
Primate and Metropolitane of all England, *one of Her Majeſties moſt
Honorable Privie Councell: my ſingular good Lord.*

Oſt humbly and heartily I crave your Graces pardon, if
I offend any thing, to ſend, or preſent unto your Gra-
ces hand, ſo ſimple a Diſcourſe as this is: Although, by
ſome ſage and diſcreet my friends their opinion, it is
thought not to be impertinent, to my moſt needfull
ſuits, preſently in hand, (before her moſt Excellent Majeſty Royall, your Lordſhips good Grace, and other the
Right Honourable Lords of her Majeſties Privy Councell) to make ſome
part of my former ſtudies, and ſtudious exerciſes (within and for theſe 46
years laſt paſt, uſed and continued) to be firſt known and diſcovered unto
your *Grace*, and other the right Honourable, my good Lords of her Majeſties privy Councell: And ſecondly, afterwards, the ſame to be permitted
to come to publick view: Not ſo much, to ſtop the mouthes, and, at length
to ſtay the impudent attempts, of the raſh, and malicious deviſers, and con-
trivers of moſt untrue, fooliſh, and wicked reports, and fables, of, and concerning my foreſaid ſtudious exerciſes, paſſed o'er, with my great, (yea incredible) paines, travells, cares, and coſts, in the ſearch, and learning of true
Philoſophie; As, therein, So, to certifie, and ſatisfie the godly and unparti-
all Chriſtian hearer, or reader hereof: That, by his own judgement, (upon
his due conſideration, and examination of this, no little parcell, of the particulars of my foreſaid ſtudies, and exerciſes philoſophicall annexed) He
will, or may, be ſufficiently informed, and perſwaded; That I have wonderfully laboured, to find, follow, uſe, and haunt the true, ſtraight, and moſt narrow path, leading all true, devour, zealous, faithfull, and conſtant Chriſtian

ftian ftudents, *ex valle hac miseria, & miseria istius vallis* : *& tenebrarum Regno* ; *& tenebris istius Regni, ad montem sanctum Syon, & ad cœlestia tabernacula.* All thanks, are moft due, therefore, unto the Almighty. Seeing, it o pleafed him, (even from my youth, by his divine favour, grace, and help) to infinuate into my heart, an infatiable zeal, and defire, to know his truth : And in him, and by him, inceffantly to feek, and liften after the fame; by the true Philofophical method and harmony proceeding and afcending, (as it were) *gradatim*, from things vifible, to confider of things invifible from things bodily, to conceive of things fpirituall : from things tranfit ry, and momentary, to mediate of things permanent : by things mortall (*vifible* and *invifible*) to have fome perfeverance of immortality. And to conclude, moft briefly; by the moft mervailous frame of the *whole World*, philofophically viewed, and circumfpectly weighed, numbred, and meafured (according to the talent, and gift of *G O D*, from above alotted, for his divine purpofes effecting) moft faithfully to love, honor, and glorifie alwaies, the *Framer*, and *Creator* thereof. In whofe workmanfhip, his infinite goodnefs, unfearchable wifdome, and Almighty power, yea, his everlafting power, and divinity, may (by innumerable means) be manifefted, and de onftrated. The truth of which my zealous, carefull, and conftant intent, and endeavour pecified, may (I hope) eafily appear by the whole, full and due furvey, and confideration of all the Books, Treatifes, and Difcourfes, who'e Titles onely, are, at this time, here annexed, and expreffed : As they are fet down in the fixth Chapter, of another little *Rhapfodicall* Treatife, intituled, the *Compendious Rehearfall, &c.* writter abo e two years fince : for thofe her Majefties two honorable Comiffioners ; which her moft excellent Majefty had moft gracioufly fent to my poor Cottage in *Mortclacke* : to underftand the matters, and caufes at full ; through which, I was fo extreamly urged to procure at her Majefties hands fuch Honorable Surveyors and witnefles to be affigned, for the due proof of the contents, of my moft humble and pitifull fupplication, exhibited unto her moft Excellent Majefty, at *Hampton* Court, *An.* 1592. *Novemb.* 9. Thus therefore (as followeth) is the faid 6. Chapter there, recorded.

¶ *My labours and pains beftowed at divers times, to pleafure my native Countrey : by writing of fundry* B o o k s, *and Treatifes : fome in Latine, fome in Englifh, and fome of them, written, at her Majefties commandement.*

Of which B o o k s, and Treatifes, fome are printed, and fome unprinted The printed Books : and Treatifes are thefe following :

1. **P**Ropædeumata Aphoriftica, De præftantioribus quibufdam Naturæ virtutibus. Aphorifmi. 120.   Anno. 1558.

    2. Monas Hieroglyphica, *Mathematice, Anagogiceque explicata* ; ad Maximilianum (*Dei gratia*) *Romanorum, Bohemiæ, & Hungariæ, Regem fapientiffimum*,   Anno 1564.

    3. *Epiftola ad eximium Ducis Urbini Mathematicum (Fredericum Commandinum) præfixa libello Machometi Bagdedini, De fuperficierum Divifionibus; edito in lucem, opera mea, & ejufdem Commandini Urbinatis ; Impreffa Pifanri.*   Anno 1570.

K   4. The

4. *The Brytish Monarchy (otherwise called the Petty Navy Royall:) for the politique security; abundant wealth, and the triumphant state of this Kingdome, (with Gods favour,) procuring,* Anno 1576.

5. *My Mathematicall preface annexed to Euclide, (by the right worshipfull Sir* Henry Billingsley *Knight, in the* English *language first published) written at the earnest request of sundry right worshipfull Knights, and other very well learned men.* Wherein are many Arts, of me wholy invented (by name, definition, propriety and use,) more then either the Græcian, or Roman Mathematicians, have left to our knowledge, Anno 1570.

6. *My divers and many Annotations, and Inventions Mathematicall, added in sundry places of the foresaid* English *Euclide, after the tenth Book of the same.* Anno 1570.

7 *Epistola prefixa Ephemeridibus* Johannis Felde *Angli, cui rationem declaraveram Ephemerides conscribendi.* Anno 1557.

8. *Paralaticæ Commentationis,* Praxeosq; *Nucleus quidam.* Anno 1573.

The unprinted Books and Treatises, are these : some,

perfectly finished : and some, yet unfinished.

9. THe first great volume of Famous and rich Discoveries: wherein (also) is the History of King *Solomon*, every three years, his *Ophirian* Voyage. The Originals of Presbyter *Joannes* : and of the first great *Cham*, and his successors for many years following: The description of divers wonderfull Isles in the Northern, Scythian, Tartarian, and the other most Northern Seas, and neere under the North Pole : by Record, written above 1200. years since: with divers other rarities, Anno 1576.

10. The Brytish Complement, of the perfect Art of Navigation; A great volume: in which, are contained our Queen *Elizabeth* her Arithmeticall Tables Gubernautick for Navigation by the Paradoxall compasse (of me, invented anno 1557.)and Navigation by great Circles : and for longitudes, and latitudes; and the variation of the compasse finding most easily, and speedily : yea, (if need be) in one minute of time, and sometime, without sight of Sun, Moon or Star; with many other new and needfull inventions Gubernautick, Anno 1576.

11. Her Majesties Title Royall, to many forrain Countries, Kingdomes, and Provinces, by good testimony and sufficient proof recorded : and in 12. Velum Skins of Parchment, faire written : for her Majesties use : and at her Majesties commandement, Anno 1578.

12. De Imperatoris Nomine, Authoritate, & Potentia : dedicated to her Majestie, Anno 1579.

13. Prolegomena & Dictata Parisiensia, in *Euclidis* Elementorum Geometricorum, librum primum, & secundum; in Collegio *Rhemensi*, An. 1550.

14. De usu Globi Cœlestis : ad Regem Edoardum sextum. An. 1550.

15. The Art of Logick, in English, Anno 1547.

16. The 13. Sophisticall Fallacians, with their discoveries, written in English meter, Anno. 1548.

17. Mercurius

17. Mercurius Cœleſtis : libri 24. written at *Lovayn,*   An. 1549.

18. De Nubium, Solis, Lunæ, ac reliquorum Planetarum, immò ipſius ſtel-liferi Cœli, ab infimo Terræ Centro, diſtantiis, mutuiſq; intervallis, & eorun-dem omnium Magnitudine liber ἀποδεικτικος, ad *Edoardum* Sextum, Angliæ Regem,   Anno 1551.

19. Aphoriſmi Aſtrologici 300.   Anno 1553.

20. The true cauſe, and account (not vulgar) of Floods and Ebbs : writ-ten at the requeſt of the Right Honourable Lady, Lady Jane, Dutcheſſe of Northumberland,   Anno 1553.

21. The Philoſophicall and Poeticall Originall occaſions of the Confi-gurations, and names of the heavenly Aſteriſmes, written at the requeſt of the ſame Dutcheſs,   Anno 1553.

22. The Aſtronomicall, & Logiſticall rules, and Canons, to calculate the Ephemerides by, and other neceſſary Accounts of heavenly motions : wiitten at the requeſt, and for the uſe of that excellent Mechanicien Ma-ſter *Richard Chancelor,* at his laſt voyage into *Moſchovia.*   Anno 1553.

23 De Acribologia Mathematica; volumen magnum : ſexdecim conti-nens libros,   Anno 1555.

24. Inventum Mechanicum, Paradoxum, De nova ratione delineandi Circumferentiam Circularem : unde, valde rara alia excogitari perficique poterunt problemata,   Anno 1556.

25. De ſpeculis Comburentibus : libri ſex,   Anno 1557.

26. De Perſpeĉtiva illa, qua peritiſsimi utuntur Piĉtores.   Anno 1557.

27. Speculum unitatis : ſive Apologia pro Fratre *Rogerio Bachone* Anglo : in qua docetur nihil illum per Dæmoniorum feciſſe auxilia, ſed philoſo-phum fuiſſe maximum; naturaliterque & modis homini Chriſtiano licitis, maximas feciſſe res, quas indoĉtum ſolet vulgus, in Dæmoniorum referre fa-cinora,   Anno 1557.

28. De Annuli Aſtronimici multiplici uſu *lib.*2.   Anno 1557.

29. Trochillica Inventa, *lib.*2.   Anno 1558.

30. Περι ἀναϐιϐασμῶν Θεολογικῶν, *lib.* 3.   Anno 1558.

31. De tertia & præcipua Perſpeĉtivæ parte, quæ de Radiorum fraĉtione traĉtat, *lib.*3.   Anno 1559.

32. De Itinere ſubterraneo, *lib.*2.   Anno 1560.

23. De Triangulorum reĉtilineorum Areis, *lib.*3. demonſtrati : ad exel-tiſſimum Mathematicum *Petrum Nonium* conſcripti,   Anno 1560.

34. Cabalæ Hebraicæ compendioſa tabella,   Anno 1562.

35. Reipublicæ Britanicæ Synopſis : in Engliſh,   Anno 1565.

36. De Trigono Circinóque Analogico, Opuſculum Mathematicum & Mechanicum, *lib.*4.   Anno 1565.

37. De ſtella admiranda, in Caſſiopeæ Aſteriſmo, cœlitùs demiſſa ad or-bem uſque Veneris : Iterumque in Cœli penetralia perpendiculariter retra-ĉta, poſt decimum ſextum ſuæ apparitionis menſem,   An. 1573.

38. Hipparchus Redivivus, Traĉtatulus,   Anno 1573.

39. De unico Mago, & triplici *Herode,* eóque Antichriſtiano. An. 1570.

40. Ten ſundry and very rare Heraldicall Blaſonings of one Creſt or Cognifance, lawfully confirmed to certain ancient Arms, *lib.*1. An. 1574.

41. *Atlantidis,*

41. Atlantidis,(vulgariter, Indiæ, Occidentalis nominatæ) emendatior defcriptio Hydrographica, quàm ulla alia adhuc evulgata,   An. 1580.

42. De modo Evangelii Jefu Chrifti publicandi, propagandi,ftabiliendi-que, inter Infideles Atlanticos : volumen magnum , libris diftinctum qua-tuor : quorum primus ad Sereniffimam noftram Potentiffimamque Regi-nam *Elizabetham* infcribitur : Secundus, ad fummos privati fuæ facræ Maje-ftatis confilij fenatores : Tertius, Hi fpaniarum Regem,*Philippum* : Quar-tus, ad Pontificem Romanum,   Anno 1581.

43. Navigationis ad Carthayum per Septentrionalia Scythiæ & Tartariæ li-tora,Delineatio Hydrographica:*Arthuro Pit*,& *Carolo Jacsmano* Anglis,ver-fus illas partes Navigaturis,in manus tradita;cum admirandarum quarundam Infularum,annotatione,in illis fubpolaribus partibus jacentium,*An.* 1580.

44. Hemifphærij Borealis Geographica , atque Hydrographica defcrip-tio : longè a vulgatis chartis diverfa : *Anglis* quibufdam, verfus *Atlantidis* Septentrionalia litora, navigationem inftituentibus, dono data,   *An.* 1583.

45. The Originals,and chief points, of our ancient Brytifh Hiftories,dif-courfed upon, and examined,   *An.* 1583.

46. An advife & difcourfe about the Reformation of the vulgar *Julian* yeare, written by her Majeflies commandement, and the Lords of the pri-vy Councell,   *Anno* 1582.

47. Certain Confiderations,and conferrings together, of thefe three fen-tences, (aunciently accounted as Oracles(*Nofce teipfum* : *Homo Homini De-us* : *Homo Homini Lupus*,   *An.* 1592

48. De hominis Corpore, Spiritu, & *Annima* : five Microcofmicum to-tius Philofophiæ Naturalis Compendium, *lib* 1.   *Anno* 1591.

With many other Books, Pamphlets, Difcourfes, Inventions , and Con-clufions, in divers Arts and matters : whofe names, need not in this Ab-ftract to be notified : The moft part of all which , here fpecifi-ed , lie here before your Honours upon the Table, on your left hand. But by other books and Writings of another fort, (if it fo pleafe God, and that he will grant me life,health, and due maintenance thereto, for fome ten or twelve years next enfuing) I may, hereafter make plaine, and with-out doubt , this fentence to be true, *Plura latent, quàm patent.*

Thus far (my good Lord)have I fet down this *Catalogus*,out of the forefaid fixt Chapter, of the booke, whofe title is this:

49. *The Compendious rehearfall of* John Dee , *his dutifull declaration and proofe of the courfe and race of his ftudious life, for the fpace of halfe an hundred years, now (by Gods favour and help) fully fpent, &c.*

To which compendious rehearfall, doth now belong an *Appendix* , of thefe two laft years : In which I have had many juft occafions , to confefle, that *Homo Homini Deus*,and *Homo Homini Lupus* , was and is an Argument, worthy of the decyphering, and large difcufing:as may, one day, hereafter (by Gods help) be publifhed,in fome manner very ftrange. And befides al the rehearfed Books & Treatifes of my writiug, or handling hitherto,I have juft caufe,lately given me to write & publifh a Treatife,with Title (50.) *D. Horizonte Æternitatis*:to make evident,that one *Andreas Libavius*,in a book o his,printed the laft year,hath unduly confidered a phrafe of my *Monas Hyero glyphica gliphica*: to his misliking, by his own unskilfulnesse in such matter: and not understanding my apt application thereof, in one of the very principal places, of the whole Book. And this book of mine, by Gods help and favour (shall be dedicated unto her most Excellent Majesty Royall: And this Treatise doth contain three books;

1. The first Intituled, *De Horizonte : liber Mathematicus & Physicus*.

2. The second, *De Æternitate : liber Theologicus, Metaphysicus & Mathematicus.*.

3. The third, *De Horizonte Æternitatis : liber Theologicus, Mathematicus, & Hierotechnicus.*

¶ Truly I have great cause to praise and thanke God, for your Graces very charitable using of me:

It may now be here also remembred, that almost three years after the writing of this Letter, I did somewhat satisfie the request of an Honourable Friend in Court, by speedily penning some matter concerning her Majesties Sea-Soveraigntie : under this title,

51. Thalattocratia Brytannica.

Sive,

De Brytanico Maris Imperio, Collectanea Extemporanea : 4. dierum Spacio, celeri conscripta calamo. Anno. 1597. Septemb. 20. Mancestriæ.

both in sundry points else, and also in your favourable yeelding to, yea & notifying the due means for the performance of her Sacred Majesties most gracious and bountifull disposition, resolution, and very royall beginning, to restore and give unto me (her Ancient faithfull servant) some due maintenance to lead the rest of my old daies, in some quiet and comfort: with habilitie, to retaine some speedy, faire, and Orthographicall writers, about me; and the same skilfull in Latine and Greek(at the least:)aswell for my own books, and Works, fair, and cotrectly to be written (such I mean, as either her most Excellent Majestie, out of the premisses will make choice of, or command to be finished or published : or such of them, as your grace shall think meet or worthy for my farther labor to be bestowed on) as else for the speedy, faire, and true writing out of other ancient Authors their good and rare workes, in greek or Latine : which by *GODS* Providence, have been preserved from the spoile made of my Librarie, and of all my movable goods here, &c. *Anno* 1583. * In which Librarie, were about 4000. books; whereof, 700. were anciently written by hand; Some in *Greeke*, some in *Latine*, some in *Hebrew*, And some in other languages (as may by the whole *Catalogus* thereof appeare.) But the great losses and dammages which in sundry sorts I have sustained, do not so much grieve my heart, as the rash, lewde, fond, and most untrue fables, and reports of me, and my Studies Philosophicall, have

* *Although that my last voyage beyond the Seas, was duly undertaken (by her Majesties good favour and licence) as by the same words may appear in the Letter, written by the Right Honourable Lord Treasurer, unto your Grace in my behalf, and her most Excellent Majestie willing his Honor so to do. Anno. 1590. the 20. of January.*

done, and yet do ; which commonly, after their first hatching, and devilish devising, immediately with great speed, are generally all the Realme overspread ; and to some, seem true ; to other, they are doubtfull ; and to onely the wise, modest, discreet, godly, and charitable (and chiefly to such as have some acquaintance with me) they appear, and are known to be fables, untruths, and utterly false reports, and slanders. Well, this shall be my last charitable giving of warning, and fervent protestation to my Countreymen, and all other in this case ;

A

A fervent PROTESTATION.

BEfore the Almighty our GOD, and your Lordships good Grace, this day, on the perill of my souls damnation (if I lie, or take his name in vaine herein) I take the same GOD, to be my witnesse; That with all my heart, with all my soul, with all my strength, power and understanding (according to the measure thereof, which the Almighty hath given me) for the most part of the time, from my youth hither-to, I have used and still use, good, lawfull, honest, christian and divinely pre-scribed means to attain to the knowledge of those truthes, which are meet, and ne-cessary for me to know; and wherewith to do his divine Majesty such service, as he hath, doth, and will call me unto, during this my life : for his honour and glory advancing, and for the benefit, and commoditie publique of this Kingdome; so much, as by the will and purpose of God, shall lie in my skill, and hability to perform : as a true, faithfull, and most sincerely dutifull servant, to our most gracious and in-comparable Queen Elizabeth, and as a very comfortable fellow-member of the body politique, governed under the scepter Royal of our earthly Supreame head (Queen Elizabeth) and as a lively sympathicall, and true symetricall fellow-member of that holy and mysticall body, Catholiquely extended and placed (where-soever) on the earth : in the view, Knowledge, direction, protection, illumina-tion and consolation of the Almighty, most Blessed, most holy, most glorious, coma-jesticall, coeternall, and coessentiall Trinity : The Head of that Body, being only our Redeemer, Christ Jesus, perfect God, and perfect man : whose returne in glo-ry, we faithfully awaite; and daily doe very earnestly cry unto him, to hasten his second comming for his elects-sake ; iniquity doth so on this earth abound and prevaile, and true faith with Charity and Evangelicall simplicity, have but cold; slender and uncertain intertainment among the worldly-wise men of this world.

Therefore (herein concluding) I beseech the Almighty God, most abundantly to increase and confirm your Graces heavenly wisedome, and endue you with all the rest of his heavenly gifts, for the relieving, refreshing and comforting, both bodily and spiritually, his little flock of the faithfull, yet militant here on earth. Amen.

An EPILOGUE.

Good my Lord, I beseech Your Grace, to allow of my plaine and com-fortable *Epilogus*, for this matter at this time. 1. Seeing my studious exercises, and conversation civill, may be abundantly testified, to my good credit, in the most parts of all Christendome; and that by all de-grees of Nobility, by all degrees of the Learned, and by very many other, of godly and Christian disposition, for the space of 46. years triall. (as ap-peareth by the Records lately viewed by two honourable witnesses, by Commission from her Majestie;) 2. And seeing, for these 36. years last past, I have been her most Excellent Majesties very true, faithfull and du-tifull servant; at whose Royall mouth, I never received any one word of reproach; but all of favour, and grace : In whose Princely Countenance, I never perceived frowne toward me, or discontented regard, or view on

me ;

me : but at all times favourable, and gracious : to the great joy and comfort of my true, faithfull, and loyall heart. And (thirdly) Seeing, the works of my hands, and words of my mouth (here before notified, in the Schedule of my books, and writings) may beare lively witnesse of the thoughts of my heart, and inclination of my minde, generally, (as all wise men do know, and Christ himself doth avouch,) It might, in manner seem needlesse, thus carefully (though most briefly and speedily) to have warned or confounded the scornfull, the malicious, the proud, and the rash in their untrue reports, opinions, and fables of my studies, or exercises Philosophicall : but that, it is of more importance, that the godly, the honest, the modest, the discreet, grave, and charitable Christians (*Englisb* or other,) lovers of Justice, truth, and good learning, may hereby receive certaine comfort in themselves (to perceive, that *Veritas tandem prævalebit*) and sufficiently be weaponed and armed with found truth, to defend me against such kind of my adversaries : hereafter they will begin afresh or hold on obstinately in their former errors, vain imaginations, false reports, and most ungodly slanders of me & my studies. ¶Therefore, (to make all this cause, for ever, before God & man, out of all doubt :) Seeing, your Lordships good grace, are, as it were, our high Priest, and chief Ecclesiasticall Minister, (under our most dread and Soveraigne Lady Queen *Elizabeth*) to whose censure and judgement, I submit all my studies and Exercises ; yea all my Books past, present, and hereafter to be written, by me (of my own skill, judgement, or opinion,) I do, at this present time, most humbly, sincerely, and unfainedly, and in the name of Almighty God, (yea for his honour and glory) request, and beseech your Grace, (when, and as conveniently you may, to be well and throughly certified of me, what I am, *Intus & in cute : Reverendissime in Christo Pater, & Dignissime Archipræsul, cognosce & agnosce vultum tàm internum, quam externum pecoris tui :* And wherein I have used, do or shall use, pen, speech, or conversation, otherwise then as it appertaineth to a faithfull, carefull, sincere, and humble servant of Christ Jesu, That your Grace would vouchsafe to advertise me. So, I trust, *Ultima respondebunt primis :* in such sort, as this *Authentick Record* in Latine annexed (*ad perpetuam rei memoriam*) doth testifie : having never hitherto had occasion to shew that, in any place of Christendome : to testifie better of me, then they had proofe of me, themselves, by my conversation among them. (The Almighty, therefore, be highly thanked, praised, honoured, and glorified, for ever and ever, *Amen.*

But now, in respect of the generall intent of this briefe discourse, I most humbly, and reverently, exhibit to your Graces view, and perusing, the originall monument, and authentick Record, before mentioned, fair written in Parchment, with the Seal whole, and perfect, duly appendant : as I have 46. years, and somewhat longer, preserved it. The true Copy whereof, your Grace doth see, to be *verbatim*, as followeth.

Univerfis

UNiverſis Sanctæ matris Eccleſiæ filijs, ad quos præſentes literæ perventuræ ſunt, Vicecancellarius Cætuſq; omnis Regentium & non Regentium, Univerſitatis Cantabrigiæ, Salutem in Domino ſempiternam Conditiones & Merita hominum in noſtra Univerſitate ſtudentium, affectu ſincero perpendentes, eos ſolos teſtimonio, noſtro ornandos eſſe arbitramur quos ſcimus ob eruditionem, & morum, probitatem promeritos eſſe, ut iſtud beneficium à nobis conſequantur : Quamobrem, cùm hoc tempore ipſa veritas teſtimonium noſtrum ſibi poſtulat, veſtræ pietati, per has literas ſignificamus Quòd dilectus nobis in Chriſto, Johannis Dee, Artium Magiſter, in dicta noſtra univerſitate fœliciter verſatus; plurimam ſibi & doctrinæ & honeſtatis laudem comparavit : De cujus gradu, & converſatione (quæ honeſtiſſima ſemper fuit,) ne qua uſpiam ambiguitas, aut quæſtio oriri poſſit, apud eos, quibus hujus viri virtutes haud ſatis innotuerint, viſum eſt nobis, in dicti Johannis gratiam, has literas noſtras Teſtimoniales conſcribere; & conſcriptas, publico Academiæ noſtræ ſigillo, obſignare : quò, majorem apud vos authoritatem, & pondus literæ noſtræ habeant, Bene valete Datum Cantabrigiæ, in plena Convocatione Magiſtrorum Regentium & non Regentium, Academiæ prædictæ : 14. Calend. Aprilis, Anno à Chriſto nato. 1548.

For certain due reſpects the very Image of the foreſaid Seal, is not here in portrature publiſhd; the Moto *Locus veri ſigilli.*

PERORATIO.

THe Almighty and moſt merciful God, the Father; for his only Son (our Redeemer) Jeſus Chriſt his ſake : by his holy Spirit, to direct, bleſſe, and proſper all my ſtudies, and exerciſes Philoſophicall, (yea, all my thoughts, words, and deeds) henceforward, even to the very moment of my departing from this world, That I may evidently and abundantly be found, and undoubtedly acknowledged of the Wiſe and Juſt, to have been a zealous and faithfull Student in the School of *Verity*, and an Ancient Graduate in the School of *Charity* : to the honour and glory of the ſame God Almighty; and to the ſound comfort and confirming of ſuch as faithfully love and fear his Divine Majeſtie, and unfaindly continue in labour to do good on earth : when, while, to whom, and as they may, *Amen.*

Very ſpedily written, this twelfth even, and twelfth day, in my poore Cottage, at Mortlake : *Anno.* 1595. *currente à Nativitate Chriſti* : aſt, *An.* 1594. *Completo, à Conceptione ejuſdem, cum novem præterea menſibus, Completis.*

Alwayes, and very dutifully, at your Graces commandement:

Jo. Dee.

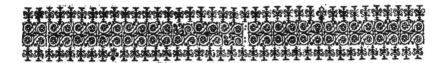

A TABLE

Of the feveral *Actions* contained in this Book ; with the moft
Confiderable Matters, either of *Fact* and *Hiftory* ; or
Doctrine, in each of them.

[*]

The Table.

the

The Table.

The

THE CONTENTS

OF THE

SECOND PART.

THE CONTENTS
OF THE
THIRD PART.

INstead of other *Approbation :* the Reader (besides the judgement of the late *Arch-Bishop of Armagh* : for his Piety and Learning so famous every where ; spoken of in the *Preface,* first page of it : and the judgement of divers others, that read the Book Manuscript, and wished it printed :) may consider, how sollicitous the *Devil* hath been, when he saw his plots (God opposing) not likely to take effect; that these *Mysteries* (these Papers and Records) might not come to light. First, by p. 418. and p. 431. (Doctor *Dee's* Letter to the Popes *Nuncio*) and some other places of the Book, it doth appear, that they were all burnt, by command; though some afterwards (upon appearance of better hopes) strangely restored again. Again, Part II p. 21. is that horrible imprecation; whereof more in the *Table.* Lastly, these remaining Papers and Records, here exhibited, were under ground, God knows how long : and since that, though carefully preserved, were even at the very last, when the worthy Owner took care, and was at the cost to have them transcribed : and so at the last, (not unluckily, I hope for the publick good :) they fell into my hands.

M. C.

ERRATA: *Those of the Book.*

Any will be found in the Book: a good part proceeding (besides ordinary typographical mistakes, even where best care is used:) from the unconvectedness of the Copy: which might happen, partly through the illegibleness of the Original it self, in many places: and partly from mistakes in the said Original, where most legible. The cause of which mistakes and miswriting, you may find-P. I p. 159 l. 20. &c. and besides what is there said, it may be probably collected from P. II. f. 17. l. 43. and p. 23. l. 96. and some other like places, that Ed. Kelley, for the most part, when he made report to Doctor Dee, of voices and speeches, (such especially as were of some length) did not know what he said himself, and so might the easier mistake. A good part of th: Greek, P. I. p. 7. was misreported, and mistaken, as is shewed in the Preface. &c. and I believe never throughly understood by Doctor Dee himself: It cannot therefore be expected otherwise, but that there should be many faults in the writing: for which I would not have the innocent (the Printers and Correctors, I mean) to bear more blame, than comes to their share. Yet however, though many: most are such (those places excepted where the Original was very faulty:) as may easily be corrected by an ordinary Reader that is conversant in books of all kinds: Or if not so easily corrected, yet such as will not bereave the Reader of the main sense and matter. Some few passages here and there, it may be, will be found where a reasonable Scholar may be put to it as P. II. p. 5. l. 31. alia vobismet ipsi disimperviis: which certainly must be read, alia vobismet ipsis disruperitis: there being a manifest (and pertinent) allusion, in the words, to, that allegorical πτεροῤῥυεῖ (wing-breeding & or, bearing:) of the soul, so famous in the Books of Philosophers; Platonists especially. That very expression is to be found in Plato, (or Works commonly ascribed unto him:) not ὄψε ὁμοῦ onely and ἄπαξ κᾀνασκῶς τ (which is the same in effect:) but even ὀρ ὀξύπτεϱοϛ: alas confringere, as it is here; & c. in some such places here and there, may be found, where the Reader must take some time to consider, (in what is Latine, especially:) if he think it worth the while, I have said as much as I think needful, and my leisure will afford me at this time.

¶ Since this written, observing that p. 403, 404, the Latine there in both pages, is very full of faults, (far more there, than any where else; that I have observed:) I thought it would not be amiss to correct those two pages. The Reader may the better know what he hath to do upon such occasions, though I dare say he will not meet with the like again in the whole Book.

PAge 403. line 3, 4. read Conf. in oratione vestra r. t. q. capitula, in q. totius orationis u. est. m. Pr. de propheticum & revelationum teff. ib. l. 6 gratum, l. 8. Regia. l. 9. intelligitur. ib. omnimodo D. pot. l. 12. proph. scilicet de D. f. l. 14. completam & consummatam. l. 17. Nam fb hanc causam t. - sciviſſet. l. 18. prophetica --- pracipuas sc. l. 19. Christianos) --- collimatus & i prastitiniam. l. 20. redemptionis humana consummatum c. l. 21. Nam cum conf. l. 22. deponentes eum de. l. 23. ipsemet cb. l. 24 Christum.--- incipiens a M. l. 27. interpretabatur. l. 28. eosdem repetebat: Hæc sunt verba quæ locutus sum ad vos, cum adhuc essem vob. l. 30, 31. nulla est prophetia vel revel. ipsa se. --- dicendum t. l. 32. rev. sive notabili illa B. Joanni Ap. l. 39. proph. tia v. l. 34. Et in ul. c ei. Ap. sive Revelationis, ter, eandem u. l. 36. Praeterea, qua r. l. 28. Altuum l. --- d cemus C. l. 39. p ipse dicit, sig l. l. 42, & ne magn. revelationum extollat me, d. e. m. stimulus e. l. 43. colaphizet. & Notum m. f. l. 48. Evangelistim. l. 50. ataispl. l. 52. scimus, & jam hac at. l. 53. prophetia. l. 54. u. express de m. Divinis Et de locut. l. 55 invisibila q.

¶ Page 404. l. 1. quid putandum est? --- Christi t. l. 3. Altuum. l. 3 supervenerunt. l. 5. qua facta e. f. Claudio. ¶ Ad Sec. a. l. 6. afferonovit. l. 11, 12. vere p. r. difer. existimetis D. l. 15. secreta, valde l. l. 16. nostrarum A. l. 19. actiones: Angelorum videl. D. b. l. 20. sunt cens. l. 26. Sempiterne vere, & ne D. l. 27. admonuiſti. d. 29. spiribus m. --- homicidæ. l. 30. expediviſſet. l. 33. agnoscimus. l. 34. mirifcis --- sitiebas R. l. 34. qui t. natul & jussis ex anima t. a. vir. l. 41. obedientiam exhibeam. l. 43. notor --- sustinebamus. ft. at. nostras - per q. m. l. 44. autem--- tua maxima gratia. f. l. 45. incolumes. 46. nostra o --- spurcitiis? l. 50. firmeatanda g. l. 41. quidam propositionis. l. 55. vir ibus translucebundo u. l. 55. Mitte it. n. lutem & u --- sempiterni; Vive, & Vere l. 56. vivum --- esse: Me autem. l. 57, fidelem suum & sincerum e. serum: l. 58. ante m. ¶ In the Margin (as l ghuxile:) In lapide quem Ang. m. adduxit: & perscripta erat postra a. cum eodem.

Some things to be corrected in the Preface: the Authour being then in a Journey when it was printed, and so his intended re-view being prevented by the quickneſſe of the Preſſe.

FIrst, he desires the Reader to take notice that he finds his Orthographie altered in divers places: as Philosophie, and Philosophyer; for Philosophie, &c. Hypocrates, for Hippocrates, &c. His pointing also: as, full points, for two points: as in the second page, before Although: and before: Yet: which doth much obscure the sense. ¶ Besides this: (but I must desire the Reader first to adde the figures there, none being printed:) Page 1. line 17, read in any age: to read I say, & c. p. 1. 44. First then, (as from them th. p. 3. l. 6. a. & at c. p. 4. l. 14. how that happ. p. 5. l. 33. r. and others, some to c p. 7. l. 4. r. ingenuous prof. p. 10. l. 14. which may eaf. p. 11. l. 43. So Justine M So quoted indeed and believed by divers, but not rightely: but however one of the anc. p 13. l. 19. solo, sapissime erg. p. 14. l. 7. r. by the out app. ibid l. 37. some mischief w. be d ibid l. 40. n. as the D. p. 15. l. 36. Jul. Cæsar Scal. p. 16. l. 23, and 28. Trallianus. ibid l. 43. r. Reason: fight, S. ibid l. ult. that those m. p: 18. l. 23. these el. p. 19. l. 37. admissiſt ille negare se u. ib. r. fe. illi ign. p. 19. l. 7. de maduo. lb. 10. ioiaλiviεix. ibid 20. aperirem. ibid 42. 8th. dayes among others, one melioris nota, as we say, by S. H. against Pu. As afterwards (some 3. or 4. years after) Popish impostures (then used and discovered of the same nature, for the advancement of their cause, occasioned another of the same Authour and Subject. (exorcismes) against Papists. I have th. ------ p. 21. 18. δμοφϱοσύϝαι. lb. 23. adductos. lb. 24. cum c. f. p. 21. l. 22. Christians: ackn. ib. 33. more lex. lb. 35. Sec. therefore w. p. 24. 44. δὴ. πυχασάτο ιτι. p. 25. 44. true a, f. Chr. p. 26. 28. request t. p. 27. 26. yea ready, wh. p. 28. 11. fors. l. wh. p. 29. & p ..... (in Lat. p. 27. 43. presented, and appr. p. 30. 15. true nat. but in the o. lb. 16. obf. dilig. lb. 30. for that P. ... himself f. p. 31. 31. commendeth. p. 33. 7. differences in c. lb. 11, 12. of thing-- hath d. p. 34. 36. delayed a-- p. 35. 2. Devils w. ibid 9. He did e. p. 17-22. lived. Th. 39. 6. more probably den. Ib. 17. part u is (if any part at all, and not rather a new counterfeit under an old vizor t) so oft. Ib. 36. hath had a h. p. 40. 7. spirituum -- med at. Ib. 11. d. do th. Ib. 19. Arf. fac. Ib. 23. former a. p. 41. 23. of what is tr-- p. 43. 6. they may b. t. fom. perchance th. ibid 7. Sines. ibid 23. in the T. ibid 33. conceited. ibid 43. some Table. p. 44. 6. about a y. p. 46. 7. prius off. p. 47. 15. more of it. It is a. ibid 27. belonged u. p. 49. 15. who b. ib. 31. 43. πϱὸδυμῷ. 32. ἀσηκυσιταί. 44. πϱὸδυϱῷ. 45. πεῖϱαται. p. 50. 12. lactucat. 45. of this, occ. p. 52. 30. I knew. p. 53 5. and praying. Postscript l. 22. ministery.

Besides these Errata's: it is fit the Reader should know that the written Copy of the Preface had many references to the pages of the Book M S: which because they did not agree with the printed pages, the Printer thought impertinent to set down: which nevertheless hath bred some confusion in some places; as p. 46. 47. and elsewhere: but may easily be rectified by the Table, at the beginning. Again, some marginal quotations are omitted, which may be supplied. P. 34. against the 3, 4. and following lines: [Treatise of Enthusiasme: Ch. 4. and 6. of Rhetor. and Precat. Enth.] P. 36. against line 11, 12. &c. [Vera ac memorabilis H storia de 3. Energumenis &c. Lut. Par. 1615. dedicated to the King of France.] P. 48. against l. 6, 7. &c. [De arte Gramm. l. 1. cap. 41. p. 141, 142.]

Lastly, I cannot give a reason of the Italica t. or different letter, in some places: but that the Printer, or some body else, have pleased their phansies therein.

¶ In the Table: Part I Act. VI. of the same nature. Act. LI. ref. to leave Dr. Dee. Act. LXVII. Some char. and properties. Act. CI. observe: at least, is ag. Act. CIV. no act. of his second L. ibid r. is want. Act. CVII. in the Cabale. Act. CXIII. but reserving of it not all. CXVII. from Prag. Act. CXX. spoken of, ter. CXXX. intoxic. CXXXV. he doth tell b. of those b. Port II l. Act. IX. pronounced ag.

The HOLY TABLE.

A Specimen of the Tables or Book of ENOCH.

Pagesgem. Bacap Laffos

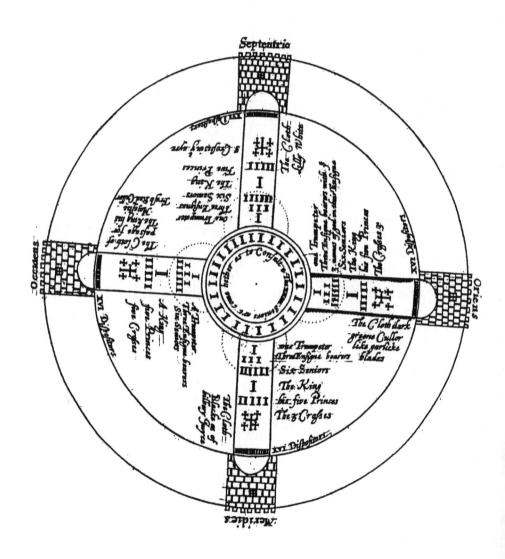

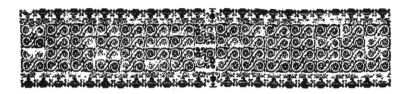

A TRUE
RELATION
OF
Dr. DEES *Actions, with spirits.*

Liber Myfteriorum (& Sancti) parallelus Novalifque.
Lefden MAY 28. 1583.

D. Is Dr. Dee,
E. K. Edward
Kellet See the
Preface.

S J. and E. K. fate difcourfing of the Noble *Polonian Albertus* | A. L.
Lafci his great honour here with us obteined, his great good
liking of all States of the people, of them that either fee him
or hear of him, and again how much I was beholding to God
that his heart fhould fo fervently favour me, and that he doth
fo much ftrive to fuppreffe and confound the malice and envie of
my Country-men againft me, for my better credit winning
or recovering to do God better fervice hereafter thereby, &c.
Suddenly, there feemed to come out of my Oratory a *Spirituall creature*, like a pretty girle of 7 or 9 yeares of age, attired on
her head with her hair rowled up before, and hanging down very long behind, with a gown of
Sey, ...changeable green and red, and with a train fhe feemed to play up and down......... | Green and red,
like, and feemed to go in and out behind my books, lying on heaps, the biggeft ....and as
fhe fhould ever go between them, the books feemed to give place fufficiently, dif.... one heap
from the other, while fhe paffed between them: And fo I confidered, and .... the diverfe
reports which E. K. made unto me of this pretty maiden, and ....

Δ. I faid .... Whofe maiden are you?
Δ. Sh. .... VVhofe man are you?
Δ. I am the fervant of God both by my bound duty, and alfo (I hope) by his Adoption.
A voyce. ...... *You fhall be beaten if you tell.*
.... *Am not I a fine Maiden? Give me leave to play in your houfe; my Mother told me fhe would come and dwell here.*
Δ. She went up and down with moft lively geftures of a young girle, playing by her felfe,
and diverfe times another fpake to her from the corner of my ftudy by a great Perfpective-
glaffe, but none was feen befide her felfe.
...... *Shall I? I will* (Now fhe feemed to anfwer one in the forefaid *Corner* of the Study)
...... *I pray you let me tarry a little* [fpeaking to one in the forefaid *Corner*]
Δ. Tell me who you are?
.... *you let me play with you a little, and I will tell you who I am.*
Δ. In the name of Jefus then tell me. | Jefus.
.... *I rejoyce in the name of Jefus, and I am a poor little Maiden, Madini; I am the laft but one of my Mothers children; I have little Baby-children at home.* | Proles ipfius Madini.
Δ. Where is your home?
Ma.....*I dare not tell you where I dwell, I fhall be beaten.*
Δ. You fhall not be beaten for telling the truth to them that love the truth, to the eternal truth all Creatures muft be obedient. | Madini her fix Sifters.
Ma. ...... *I warrant you I will be obedient. My Sifters fay they muft all come and dwell with you.* | Δ. I defire

B

Δ. I defire that they who love God fhould dwell with me, and I with them.

Dee.   Ma. .... *I love you now you talke of God.*

Δ. Your eldeft fifter her name is *Efemeli.*

Ma. ...... *My fifter is not fo fhort as you make her.*

Efemeli.   Δ. O, I cry you mercy, fhe is to be pronounced *Efemeli.*

E. K. She fmileth, one calls her faying, Come away Maiden·

Ma. ,...., *I will read over my* Gentlewoemen *firft.*

     My Mafter Dee will teach me , *if I fay amiffe.*

Δ. Read over your *Gentlewoemen* as it pleafeth you.

Ma. ...... I have Gentlemen and Gentlwoemen, *Look you here.*

E- K. She bringeth a little book out of her pocket,

.... She pointeth to a in *Picture* the book.

Mad. ,,..., *Is not this a pretty man.*

Δ. What is his name?

Ma.......*My* .... *faith,* his name is Edward, *Look you, he hath a Crown upon his head, my Mother faith, that this man was Duke of York.*

E. K. She looketh upon a *Picture* in the Book with a *Coronet* in his hand and a *Crown* upon his head.

Ma. ..... *This was a jolly man when he was King of England.*

Δ. How long fince is it that he was *King of England* ?

Ma. .... *Do you ask me fuch a queftion,* I *am but a little Maiden* ? *Lo, here is his Father* Richard Plantagenet, *and his Father alfo.*

Δ. How call you him ?

Ma. ,,....*Richard, Surely this was* Richard *Earle of Cambridge.*

E. K. She turneth the book leaves, and faid.

Mad. .....,*Here is a grim* Lord, *He maketh me afraid.*

Δ. Why doth he make you afraid?

Ma. ...... *He is a ftern fellow,* I *do not know him what he is. But this was the Duke of Clarence. This was Father to* Richard *Earle of Cambridge. Lo, here is* Anne *his wife.*

E. K. Turning over the leafe,

The fame was heir to all Mortimers *lands.*

Edmund *was her brother.*

Lo, Sir, *here be the wicked* Mortimers.

E K. She turned over diverfe leaves, and then fhe faid

Ma. ...... *This fame is* Roger Mortimer.

·...., *My Mother faith this man was* Earl of the Marches.

This fame is his wife.

He had a great deale of lands by her, for fhe was an Heire.

This fame is wild Genvill, *her Father.*

Pronounced Jenville.   *Here is a Town they call* Webley. *Here is* Beudley. *Here is* Mortimers Clybery. *Here is* wild Wenlock. *Here is* Ludlow. *Here is* Stanton Lacy. *Genvill his wife was Heire of all thefe. Here is* Hugh Lacy *her Father. He weareth his haire long, for he was Deputy of Ireland* ; *That maketh him look with fuch a writhen face.*

My fifter hath torne out the other two leaves, I *will bring them when you have fupped.*

I pray do not tell any body of me.

Δ. We were earneftly called for to Supper by my folks.

Nota.

After Supper.

Ma. ....., *Here is* William Lacy *Father to* Hugh.

Here is Richard *his Father. And here is* Sir Richard *his Father* , *and here is* William , *Sir* Richards *Brother. Here is his going into* France.

Δ. Quo anno Chrifti?

Her eldeft Sifter. Her Sifter is to tell the reft.   Mad. ...... *I warrant you my eldeft Sifter will tell you all. Here is his going into* Denmark.

My Sifter will come fhortly, and tell you how he married in Poland , *and what iffue this* William had.

Δ. I pray declare the Pedigree down to this *Albert Lafcy.*

Ma. ...., *Alas,* I *cannot tell whats done in other Countries.*

Δ. I know you are not Particular of this Country, but Univerfal for all countries in the whole world , which is indeed but one Countrey, or a great City, &c.

Mad. ......*Well* , *my fifter will fhortly come and tell you unlooked for* , *If you judge thefe things well that I have fpoken.* Nam vera funt. Nam verus eft qui me mifit.

Truth

Truth is all that is truth.

The Mortimer I spake of, is the first of the six : there were six Mortimers *Earles* of March. *Edmond was the last,* and *Roger the first*; that Mortimer *was the Grandfathers Grandfather of this* Edmond.

E. K. There seemeth some one to call her, whom I hear now.

Ma ...... *I come.*

Δ. She took up her Skrolls on the ground, of which some were very old, and she put up her book.

Ma .... *This may stand you in some stead.*

Δ. Mitte lucem tuam & veritatem tuam, Jesu Christe, Lux vera,& veritatis perennis Fons, *Amen.*

Richard			*Lascy.*			
Edward	*William*		*Sir Richard*			
Dux Ebor.	*Lascy.*		*Lascy.*			
	France.	*Richard.*	*Peter.*	*Richard*		
	France.	*Denmark.*	*Poland.*	*Lascy.*		
	1.	2.	3.			
				William Lascy.		

	Geffrey Genvil.	*Hugh Lascy.*
	Wilde Genvill-	*Null.*
Rogerus primus comes ⸗ *Joan Genvill.*		
March.		

Monday à Meridie hora 4½.　　　　　　　　　　　　　　　　　　　　　*Janii 2. 1583.*

Δ. We presented our selves, ready for instruction receiving, and presumed not to call my good Minister spiritual, but by humble prayer referred all to God his good pleasure.

E K. The Golden Curtain which covereth all the Stone hangeth still, but I heare a voice or sentence thrice repeated, thus.

A voice ...... *Sanctum, Signatum,& ad tempus.*

Δ. The sense hereof may be divers wayes understood, and more then I can imagine, but which sense is to our instruction would I faine know.

A voice .... *Sanctum,quia hoc velle suum; sigillatum quia determinatum ad tempus.*

E. K. Hard speeches, but he could not perfectly discern them.

A voice :..... *Ad tempus & ad tempus(inquam)quia rerum consummatio.* All things are at hand.

The Seat is prepared.

Justice hath determined.

The Judge is not yet willing.

Mercy thrusteth it self betwixt the Divinity. But it is said,

The Time shall be shortned.

E K. Saw no creature : But the voice came behind him over his head, till now : when he espied one standing on the Table besides the silke cloth on which the Stone stood, he seemed like a Husbandman all in red apparel, red hose close to his legs, a red jacket, red buttoned cap on his head, yea, and red shooes. He asked *E. K.* how he did, and *E. K.* answered, Well I thank God.

Δ. By your apparel it should seem you have somewhat to say concerning the Commons of this Realme, and not of high School-points, or Sciences. *I* am desirous to know who sent you ? What is your message ? and what is your name? for a name you have peculiar as all Creatures else.

Δ. He paused a good while; whereupon *I* asked him if he considered my speeches ?

...... *I consider your speeches, for I have left nothing behind.*

E. K. He kneeleth down and seemeth to say somewhat, his speech is quick, round, and ready. He seemeth to pray in a strange Language. I perceived these words among many other, *Oh Gabire Rudna gepbna oh Gabire,* &c.

His Countenance was directed towards the Stone.

...... *Vestra non mea facio.*

B 2　　　　　　　　ℏ　　　　　　　　*E K.*

E K. Now he standeth up.

...... *Hast not thou said, From whom comest thou ? What is thy message ?* [Δ. He looked toward me] *And hast urged my name ? Saying, All things have a name. It is true ; for so they*

Δ. All things have a name, *vide contra* Tert. parte libri Bratonensis de 30 Aeris exercitibus.

have because they are. Hast thou left any thing unsaid ?

Δ. You rehearse my speeches not onely in general, but also in particular.

The will of God be done (to his glory) for the rest.

The summe of our commanded observation.

.... *My message is from him, in whose name thou hast desired it , which hath said lift up thine eyes, and look unto (behold I say) the sum of my Commandments,* 1. *What I am,* 2. *Whose Ministers you are, and (as it is said before)* 3. *To what end and purpose it is.*

Then cease to plead when Judgement standeth in place ; For all things are determined already.

Note 7.

The 7 doores are opened. The 7 Governours have almost ended their Government.

The Earth laboureth as sick, yea sick unto death.

The Waters pour forth weepings, and have not moisture sufficient to quench their own sorrows.

The Aire withereth, for her heat is infected.

The Fire consumeth and is scalded with his own heat.

The B dies above are ready to say, We are weary of our courses.

Nature would fain creep again into the bosom of her good and gracious Master.

Darknesse is now heavy and sinketh down together: She hath builded her self, yea (I say) she hath advanced her self into a mighty building, she saith, Have done, for I am ready to receive my burden.

Hell it self is weary of Earth: For why ? The son of Darknesse cometh now to challenge his

Antichrist his saying in the spirk of Satan.

right : and seeing all things prepared and provided, desireth to establish himself a kingdom ; saying, We are now stronge enough, Let us now build us a kingdom upon earth, and Now establish that which we could not confirm above.

And therefore, Behold the end.

Sorrows.

When the time cometh, The ...... thy sorrows shall be greater than the sweetnesse, the sorrows (I mean) of that thou seest ; I mean in respect of the sweetnesse of thy knowledge. Then will you lament and weep for those thou thoughtst were just men.

Labor.

When you earnestly pray it shall be said unto you Labor. When you would take Mercy Justice shall say, Be it so.

Therefore (I say) thirst not overmuch : For fear least thy capacity be confounded.

Neither move thou him which hath moved all things already to the end.

But do thou that which is commanded.

Neither prescribe thou any form to God his building.

All things shall be brought into an uniform Order.

Al. alaský.

Whom thou sayest that thou hast not yet confirmed , confirm with good counsel. It is said I have accepted him.

Are not these News sufficient ?

Notes in Election.

It is said, He shall govern me a people : of himself he cannot. Therefore let him believe, and secondly Rejoyce that the Angel of God hath so governed him. That in Election he shall govern him a people.

Desireth he to hear of greater blessednesse ?

O King.

He hath also said: Then shall it be said unto him, O King.

Vide tamen de ejus futuro casu in actionibus de Lask,

It followeth consequently that he is called, and that to a Kingly Office : For whosoever is Annointed in the Lord, his Kingdom is for ever.

Lask, Pride.

Will he be the son of perdition ? Let him then with his fathers put on the garments of pride.

Desireth he news? Tell him thou hast prayed for him, the Devil envyeth him, and his estate.

Tell him that I say so.

Say it is a shame for a Kings Son to commit theft ; and for him that is called, to do the workes of unrighteousnesse. Studiest thou to please him ? Give him sharp and wholesome counsel: For in him (I say) the state and alteration of the whole World shall begin.

Wouldst thou know from whence I came ? Thou shalt.

But do it Humbly, it is not my part to meddle any further than my charge.

But as it is said before unto thee, So shall it come to passe.

Moses had a rod whereby he was known, and the hand of God approved.

Let him be therefore to carry the rod of righteousnesse about him.

Moses 7. rod. Sanctum signatum, ad tempus.

For we are seven : and in us is comprehended that rod wherewith Moses wrought. As it is begun so I end; What ya see here is holy [pointing to the ...... and by him sealed and for until the time. Therefore use patience herein until the time that it is said unto thee ......

Venite, videte, (& loquimini) Judicia mea.

He that saith thus (I speak of my self, and as concerning my message,) is equal with the greatest Angels, and his name is Murifri.

Murifri my Calender.

Thou hast written my name, and I am of thy Kelender, because thy Kalender is of God.

In the grounds of all thy Tables thou shalt finde my name.

Δ. I remember not any such name written by me, but it may be contained in some new Composition, or Collection.

Mur. ...... *It is true , for if thou hadst remembred all those things which thou hast written, then should not my message need.*

Δ. If

Δ. If I might without offending you, I would move two Petitions unto you, one concerning the Soul, and the other concerning the body : Concerning the Soul, is for one *Isabel Lister*, whom the wicked Enemy hath sore afflicted long with dangerous temptations, and hath brought her knives to destroy her self withall; she resisteth hitherto , and desireth my helping counsel, which how small it is God knoweth. The other is of another woman, who hath great need, and is driven to maintain her self , her husband , and three children by her hand labour, and there is one that by dream is advertised of a place of Treasure hid in a Cellar, which this woman hath hired thereupon, and hath no longer time of hiring the said Cellar, but till Midsummer next. She, and this dreaming Maiden digged somewhat , and found certain tokens notefied unto her: But so left off. I would gladly have your help herein, if it pleased God.

Mur. ...... *I answer thee, I will come again soon, and thou shalt receive a Medecine which shall teach thee to work help in the first. The second is vanity, for it is not so, but to the intent that after great hope of this world hath infected the weaklings minde : Desperation might have the more open and ready entrance. But yet she shall be comforted for thy sake.*

Δ. The praise be unto God.

Mur. ...... *I Go. One thing I have to say, be faithfull in all things, I have said.*

Δ. I prayed, and gave thanks hartily to God for his mercies, and graces , and so rose up.

Δ. Then he said write, *M.* 49. under *V.* 43. under *R.* 35. 1. and 47. under $\{$ *F, R, I.* $\}$ *This shal lead thee to my name, be that sent me be amongst you.* Δ. Amen, Amen, Amen. $\{$ 9. 33. 42 $\}$

Δ. Note in *Tabula Collecta*, (which I first gathered of the 49. good Angels) I took the third letters out of the names, it is to wit, out of the 49th. name, and th...... 47. 9. 33. 42. which agreed very well with the letters, but the five and thirtieth name did not yield *R.* in his third letter. Therefore I am. .... in the......

Monday after supper 1583.

Junii 3.

Δ. After supper, as we were together in my study, and attending somewhat the return of the good messager spiritual, and said that he promised to come again suddenly , he appeared and answered.

Mur. ...... So I am, write 7. 30. 25. 44. 37. 35. 46.

To the first *S.* to the second *O.* the third *L.* the fourth *G.* the fifth *A.* the sixth *R.* the 7th. *S.*

Δ. That maketh *SOLGARS.*

Mur. ...... *Add the first, and last number together, it maketh 53. let that be the Centre to the rest.*

Δ. To be put to the Center of the *Steptagonum.*

Mur. ...... So. *The ground hereof is to be found in the third Table in the first book : I mean in the third of the seven, the Table of B. B. &c. being the first.*

The third Table in the first book.

My name is also to be found in the same Table.

Form this upon a plate of lead : It prevaileth as a cure against such infections. My promise is done.

Δ. How is this to be used?

Mur. ...... *Use it upon the body molested, adding the letters of her name in a small Circle on the back half , not the letters in their forms expressed, but the number of such letters.*

Δ. We know not how to number her name in our letters.

Mur. ...... *Take them out of the second Table (any Table else of the seventh will serve) so that thou take the numbers as thou findest them placed with the letters.*

Δ The second Table did not serve, & therefore I used the seventh, where all the letters might be had;

Δ. How is this to be used about her body ?

Mur. ...... *As by discretion shall be thought best : It prevaileth sufficiently, so it be done, but thus far, I teach thee, and this, as concerning nature.*

The health of him which sent me be amongst you, Amen.

Δ. Gloria & gratiarum actio perennis sit Deo nostro omnipotenti uni & Trino, *Amen.*

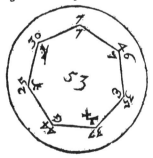

Isabel Lister, the back part of the Lamin.

The fore-part of the Lamin.

Wednesday a *Meridie circa* 2d. 1583.

Junii 5.

Δ. E. K. Had been ever since nine of the Clock in the morning in a marvellous great disquietnesse of minde, fury, and rage; by reason his brother *Thomas* had brought him news that

a Com-

ly, a Commission was out to attache, and apprehend him *as a fellon for coyning of money.* Secondly, that his wife was gone from Mistresse *Freemans* house at *Blobley*, and how Mr. *Husey* had
reported him *to be a cosener,* and had used very bitter and grievous reports of him now of late;
and that his wife was at home with her mother at *Chipping Norton*, whereupon, I considering
his great disorder and incumberance toward him externally, and his greater offending of God
with his furious impatience internally; and remembring the whole premises of God his service to be performed by us two (if we would be dutifull servants to his Divine Majesty)
I was touched with a great pang of Compassion, both that any Christian should use such
speeches as he used, or be of so revenging a minde and intent as he shewed himself to be: and
also in respect of mine own credit to be brought in *doubt, for embracing the company of such an
one, a disorderly person:* And thirdly, that the good service of God might hereby be taken
from our two executing, to our great danger, both in body and soul: Therefore to do my
duty as a man resolute (upon *our uniting for Gods service*) to do for *him as for my self* : I made
God my refuge for comfort, counsel, and help in this great affliction, and crosse of temptation.

Whereupon after my vehement and humble prayers for the foresaid purpose, this voyce
was heard of *E. K.*

I had (upon some reasonable respect) set the shew-stone with the mystery in it, on
the Table by *E. K.* also.

A voyce. ...... *Let the daughters of light*

*Take up their garments, let them open the windows of their secret Chambers, for the voyce of man
hath said.*

Oh, shew thy self to be a God; yea, perform that which thou hast already promised, *gather your vestures together, for those that are sick have need of help, you are the children of pitty,*
and in the loins of compassion do you dwell : For I have said, you are. And I have said, my Determination shall not fail, *although with the* sons of men my Determinations may be undetermined.
Come gather up your garments, for the Cankers are ripe, and the Biting-worm *seeketh to gnaw
into the Lily.*

He hath said, Let me prove them, for they are not just : *Yea, let me touch them, for they are
unrighteous, I have granted* him power, *but without prevailing, I have given him weapons, but they
are not sharpned, his fingers shall defile, and yet not deface : For I have appointed him a night, and
have prefixed an end thereunto, to the intent it may be known : That thus far I have stretched his
mouth.*

E. K. I have heard a voyce about the shew-stone very great, as though
men were beating down of mud walls.

The thumping, shuffing, and cluttering is such.

A voice. ...... *Arise, I say, for I will be revenged against the scorning of those; yea, of those
that are sucklings.*

Δ. After a great silence and pause, appeared one on the Table (without the skirts of
the silke sarcenet) like a woman having on a red kirtle and above that a white garment like
an *Irish* Mantle, on her head a round thing like a Garland, green and like a Coronet under
the Garland, but not perfectly to be discerned; on her breast a precious Stone of white colour, and on her back another precious Stone; both which Stones were set upon a Crosse, in
the very center of the Crosse.

Δ. Your external apparel (you Daughter of Light) you perceive that we have somewhat noted : but by the power and mercy of the external Light, we trust and desire to understand somewhat of your internal vertue.

She said ...... *What do you think I am a Jewellers wife by my apparel ?*

Δ. We deem you to be the Messenger of him that hath for mankind purchased the Jewel
of eternal Blisse, by the incomparable Jewel of his most precious Blood.
...... *Will you have this too ?*

Δ. After a pretty while silence, I said, We expect the execution of the purpose for which
you are sent.

She said ...... *It is written that Pride was the first offence.*

Githgulcag knew not himself.

Therefore he was ignorant.

E K. She is much fimbling about the Stone on her breast, and regarding it.

E. K. Now She talketh with other whom I see not, her talke is very
short and quick, but I cannot perceive what she saith.

She. ...... *Read what I have said.*

I read the former words.

She, ... *You will grant me that Pride is the greatest sin.*

Pride was the cause he knew not himself.
Therefore Pride is the cause of Ignorance.
Δ. The Argument is good.
She. ...... *Ignorance was the nakednesse wherewithal you were first tormented, and the first Plague that fell unto man was the want of Science.*

B K. Now she speaketh to other again who appeare not, and they seem to answer her again.
She. ...... *The want of Science hindreth you from knowledge of your self.*

B K. She looketh upon Δ. and smileth. Now she speaketh to the unseen people again.
She. ...... *Whosoever therefore knoweth not himself, is proud.*
Δ. God help us to know our selves for his Honour sake.

E. K. She looketh upon Δ. and smileth.
She. ...... *You have time enough, therefore we may take leasure.*
Δ. [*I made speed to write.*]

E. K. She talketh again with her invisible company.
She. ...... *Pride is rewarded as sin,* Ergo *the first offender was damned. What say you Sir?*
[*speaking to E. K.*]
What difference is between your mind and Pride?

B. K. Wherein am I proud?
She. ...... *In the same wherein the Devil was first proud.*
Who glorified the Devil?

E. K. God.
Δ. God glorified not the Devil, but before he became a Devil he was in glory.
She. ...... *The abusing of his Glorification made him a Devil: So the abusing of the good-* A Devil. *nesse of God toward this man, may make him a Devil.*
The works of the Spirit quicken; the doings of the Flesh lead unto destruction. Art thou offended to be called a Devil? Then extol not thy self above thy Election.
No man is elected by proper name, but according to the measure of his faith, and this faith is Faith. *lively and hath a quickning Spirit in it for ever. Indeed thou art ignorant, and therefore thou art sufficiently plagued: Why dost thou boast thy self and say,* This I can do?
The Reeds pipe, but it is long of the wind, and herein thou shewest that thou knowest not thy self, for that thou art proud; pray therefore that thou mayest have understanding, and cast away pride if thou wilt not be counted a Devil.
By true understanding you learn, first to know your selves what you are: of whom you are, and to what end you are.
This understanding causeth no self-love, but a spiritual selfe-love.
This understanding teacheth no Blasphemy.
This understanding teacheth no fury.
It teacheth a man to be angry, but not wrathful.   Wrath.
For we may be angry, and not offend, Wrath is to damnation.
Therefore considering that Damnation was the end of the first, which was Pride, and Ignorance, the punishment of the second (which is very loathsome.)
Pray unto God thou mayest avoid the first, and be unburdened of the second.
Consider by whom thou art counselled, and of whom the counsel is: with us there is no cause of offence, neither is the counsel given with a weak mouth.
Wilt thou be well rewarded? Why studiest thou not to do well? Wouldst thou be one of the chosen? stand stiff and be contented with all temptations.
Is God a God of Justice?

B. K. It is true.
Be thou therefore a just servant.
No man inheriteth the Kingdom of Eternity, without he conquer in this World.
No man can challenge justly a reward, without he be a Conquerour, or do the workes of Justice.
Doth the Devil perswade thee? *Arme thy self against him.*
Doth the World not like of thee? It is for two causes; either for that thou livest well and not as a worldling, or else because thy wickednesse is such as that the World wondreth at it. If thou be in the first Rejoyce, For blessed are those whom the World hateth; when they laugh at thy godlinesse, Be sorry and grieve thou at their sinfulnesse.
If thou offend in the second flie hastily from the World: Tell the World what thou hast of hers, and let her be ashamed that thou knowest her.
Is thy flesh stiff-necked? Fast and pray, it doth avoide temptation.
Be sorry alwayes; For in this World there is nothing to rejoyce at. For sin onely provoketh Be sorry alto sorrow, whether it be of thy self or of another.   wayes.

        Be

Be stiff against temptations, for whosoever is not armed as I am, shall be vexed with the weapons of his adversary.

My Garland is Godlinesse, *my* Breastplate *is Humility, and upon my back I wear Patience.*

These do I wear to the intent I might shew you what you should wear.

But as these things are placed in their crosses; so do the crosses alwayes follow them that wear them.

Her attire expounded.

The attire of Spiritual creatures.

Art thou punished as an Apostle? Rejoyce; it is a happy crosse.

Art thou vexed as a Tyrant? thank God it is in this World. For blessed are those that are punished here, to the intent their sins may be forgotten hereafter.

I perswade to the contrary; Be humble, seek true wisdom, then are you truely fashioned according to your Maker, and shalt rest with us, with Halleluja in Heaven.

Good Angels.

I have counselled, I have done my message thus far.

Δ. Your counsel is perfectly good, and your message merciful. His name be praised and glorified that sent you. *Amen.*

As you were called hither, by the name of *Daughters of Light* : So this other day, there was one sent hither (of that blessed company) who was accounted a Daughter, and had six Sisters more : That Daughter her name was *Madini* ; so of your name we are desirous to be informed, for distinction and instructions sake, in the trade of these mysteries.

She said. ...... *It is good to know my name; to see whether it agree with my Doctrine.*

E. K. What can you (for all your exhortation) accuse me of ?

Indeed I thank you very heartily for your exhortation and good counsel; but hovv unjustly I am misused at *Huseys* hand, and so provoked to this extream affliction of mind and sundry unseemly speeches, be you Judge between *Husey* and me.

She said, Whosoever hath committed sin and is not reconciled, shall have the reward of a sinner. There is a double Reconciliation, the one is with God, the other with the Conscience. But this man is not reconciled in Conscience (repenteth not his wickednesse) thereby it followeth he cannot be reconciled with God : Ergo he must be rewarded as he is. The reward of sin is to be absent, or rather to be banished in this world from the society of God and his Angels.

Good Angels our keepers.

So it falleth out to Regions and Countries, Cities, Kings and Subjects, Authorities and their Officers, when (I say) they are estranged with absence of their appointed and good keepers.

Therefore it proved that the Devil is most with him, and nearest with him.

Whom the Devil is a Lord of, he useth as his servants, and where his service may be greatest done, there is he most alledged. His subtilties are principal and great : And by these reasons I prove that Husey is easily to be infected, either with envy, malice, slander, or dishonour of Gods word.

John Husey,

This is one of those Assaults that is promised should assault you.

Who is to be blamed, he that consenteth, or be in whom the procurement is ? Thou didst consent and chuse him for a Companion. Be not therefore angry at his malice; for the fire that is, thou hast brought in with thine own hands.

To measure the Enemy his industry is impossible to look into, his subtiltie is more incredible.

The Reward of good life is great : But the filthinesse that sin carryeth with it in this World, and leadeth with it into the World to come, is most horrible.

Is it not said, That a skirmish shall be (and that great) but you shall be Conquerours ? It is written, It is true and shall be never overthrown ; so mighty is his strength that hath armed himself with it.

In the Serpents belly, there is nothing clean : neither with unhonest persons (ungodly I mean) is there any pure society : Light agreeth not with Darknesse, nor vertue with vice, therefore be you of one, and in one, that you may agree and have the reward of one.

Our uniting.

Behold it is said, I will part bounds between the just and the unjust, I will suffer the Enemy to sowe discord to the intent that those that are my people may be separated and have a dwelling by themselves.

The necessity of Satan working against men.

Peruse the Scripture, it is alwayes seen that the Spirit of God *forceth* Satan *in spight of his head to separate the evil from the good by discord, and herein the Devil worketh against himself.*

De futuris nisi juste non pronuntiant boni Angeli.

We good Angels keep secret the Mysteries of God; things that are to come we alwayes keep close with this exception, The form of our Commandment.

Truth it is that a Commission is granted not onely to enquire of thee, but also to attach thee, and that by the Council.

A Commission out for Kelly.

If he go down he shall be attached; therefore tempt not God.

Δ. But if he tarry here and his being here so known as it is, it is likely that he shall be attached here to my no small grief or disgrace. What is your counsel herein ?

She said. ...... *It is written misery shall not enter the doors of him whom the Highest hath magnified.* DIXIT, & DICO, & DICTUM SIT. *The world shall never prevaile against you.*

1583.

The Book, the Scrowl, and Powder.

Δ. In respect of the *Book,* the *Scrowl,* and the Powder to be communicated, What is your judge-

judgement or mind, feeing when he was coming from *Iflington* with them, he was threatned to be pulled in pieces if he came *with them to me ?*

...... *All that is fpoken of, is in very deed, vanity.* The book may be ufed to a good purpofe. The Book *They were wicked ones. But as thefe things are the leaft part of this action, fo are they not much to* found. *be looked after.*

Δ. As concerning the Powder (I befeech you) what is your knowledge of it ?   The Powder.
...... *It is a Branch of Natures life.*
It is appointed for a time, and to a purpofe.
Δ. As concerning the earthes of the Eleven places being with expedition ......
What is now to be done with them ?
...... *It was a forefight of God,* if they had been there now they had utterly *perifhed.*   The fi Earths.
Δ. O Jefus, that is a marvellous thing.
...... Helas, *that is nothing.*
Δ. By nature they could not have perifhed in fo fhort time.
...... *I have faid.*

E. K. Tell us your name.
...... *If you will remember my counfel, I will tell you my name.*

E. K. Your counfel was by piece-meale told me, that I cannot remember it but in general.

...... *You do, and have, and I am almoft* HATH.
Δ. I underftand you to be ATH, *in figillo Emeth.*
ATH. ...... *So am I in the number of Gods Elect.*
Δ. Shall not I make meanes to *Mr. Richard Young,* as one of the higher Commiffioners Mr. *Richard* to do my companion here fome good ?   Young.
ATH. ...... *Trouble your felf when you need.*

E. K. She fpake this fomewhat fharply.
Get your friends to fignifie down good report of you.
Come not there in many years.
Δ. As concerning my writing of the holy Book, how fhall I do, by reafon of the perfect writing it in the Due Characters ? feeing many words are written fo, as the pronunciation *and the Orthographie do hardly feem to agree ?*
ATH. ...... *You fhall have a School-mafter fufficient to read unto you.*
Δ. Where fhall I begin ?
ATH. ...... *Let him lead you to that,* who is within you.
Δ. As concerning *Ifabel Lifter* who is vext of a wicked fpirit, how well have I executed that which was prefcribed me ; or how well doth it work ?
ATH. ...... *Friend, It is not of my charge.*
Remember the true path that leadeth unto true honour, where there fitteth a True and Juft GOD, *who grant you his Direction and eftablifhment of perfect life.*
Δ Amen, Amen, Amen.

E. K. She is gone.

Junii 9. a Meridie hora 5.
Δ. Very long I prayed in my Oratory and at my Deske to have anfwer or refolutions of divers doubts which I had noted in a paper, and which doubts I read over diftinctly, they concerned the preparation of things about the Table of practice, and other things above my Lamin and Stone ; but anfwer came none, neither in the Stone did any thing appear ; no, not the Golden Curtain, but the Stone was of his natural Diaphanitie. But I held on in pittiful manner to requeft fome advertifement, if for any our trefpaffes or offences this unlooked for alteration from former dealing had hapned, &c.
At length a voice came from behind E. K. over his head, and faid thus :
A voyce. ...... *The judgements of our God are moft profound and hard in the underftanding of* man.
There is filence above, let there therefore be patience amongft you. I have faid.
Δ. Upon this anfwer I began to difcourfe of divers caufes of this filence, and divers man- Silence. ners of filences ; and in the end I became in a great and forrowfull heavineffe, and fear of the wrath, or difpleafure of God ; conceived for fome, our misbehaviour towards him fince our laft dealing, whereupon I prayed long at my Desk, ftanding for mercy, comfort, counfel , and fome expofition of the former fentence. After a long time thus paffing there appeared one in the very top of the frame of the *fhew-ftone,* much like *Michael.*
Who faid, ... *Write, for I muft be gone.*
Silence there is in heaven, for the Governours of the earth are now before the Lord , the doings of their feats are now difclofed , every thing is NOTED. For that God will be righteous in all his doings.
There is not this day any one that governeth the people upon earth , but his government

C   is is disclosed, and his government is set open, and his faults revealed,

They without number cry, Lord, let thy vengeance come.

The earth sayeth. Be it so.

Sathan. Sathan is before the Lord : He hath garnished himself with Garlands as a Conquerour, and what he saith is wonderfull.

Therefore shall the Lord open his mouth, and curse the earth, and all living creatures. For *Iniquity hath gotten the upper hand* : Publickly the *States* of mankinde in the world are **Viols ready.** condemned.

We are all silent and *ready with our Viols* to powre the *wrath of God* upon them , when he saith, BE IT SO.

Therefore be you patient. For, *our patience in an universal silence.*

Yet awhile. We look for the mouth of Justice : But LO : The Lord saith unto the Lord , lift up thy eyes (O God.) Behold, the Dignity of thy workmanship , *yet suffer for awhile.*

1583. I have a people that will forsake their cruelty, and put off their Garments that stink of abomination, in whom thy name shall be magnified, and our glory in heaven more exalted,

But as thou wilt, so be it.

Behold, *I speak in body,* because I tremble , as at the force of thy great indignation : Notwithstanding, we will what thou wilt.

If therefore these wonders be so great in heaven, wonder thou not at our silence : Therefore be patient, and say unto the earth ? Why groanest thou so hard , or why is thy body so rotten : Hast not thou justly deserved these things for thy iniquity ?

I say, if you be partakers of these secrets, how much more shall you be partakers of that sweetnesse, which is the eternal dew, and very bread it self of life ?

S O.

E·K. He is gone.

Δ. *I prayed a pretty while after with thanksgiving,* &c.

Soli Deo nostro omnis laus, potestas, & gloria in seculorum sacula, Amen.

Junii 14. 1583. *Friday, a meridie,* Hora 4¼.

Δ. The golden vayl, or curtain appeared, covering the whole stone, whereas all other vayls and curtains before did use to cover but the more part, or those things which were the standing implements of the action for that time.

This appeared as soon as he looked into the stone,

I made long, and often prayers of thanksgiving, calling for grace , mercy, and wisdom : with such particular instructions as I had written down the doubts requiring light, or resolution in them, &c.

At length appeared a woman like an old maid in a red Peticote, and with a red silk upper bodies, her hair rould about like a Scottish woman, the same being yellow : she stood aside from the green Sarcenet belonging to the stone, and she said ...... God speed my friends,

Δ. A good greeting to wish us speed by him, *Amen.*

E·K. I never saw this woman before.

...... *It may be you have seen me, but my apparel may alter my fashion.*

E·K. She seemeth to go in a great path before her very speedily.

Δ. I pray you, whither make you such a speedy journey.

...... *I am going home, I have been from home this seven-night.*

Merle my maid had angered me on Thursday night, with her undue speech. Δ. Distance of place cannot protract time in your journey homeward.

...... *Jesu, now he will be angry with me, as he was with his maid.* Δ. Every Action not yet effected, whether is it at home, or from home ?

Δ. God grant you then to make speed homeward , and to your home, and all we to the home where the highest may be well pleased.

...... *So, so, you talk too wisely for me.*

Δ. God make me to talk wisely indeed, and God take all vanity from my heart.

All worldly wisdom vain. ...... *You may think me a vain huswife to be going thus long : But by me you may perceive how vain all worldly wisdom is. I am in a better case then many are, for though I be from home, yet am I going home, some there be that neither have home, neither can go home.*

E·K. Now cometh a goodly tall aged man all in black, with a Hat on his head, he hath a long gray beard forked, he saith to the Maid, thus :

Old man...... *Wihther go you maid ?*

Maid...... Belike Sir, you may be some kyn unto these men, for they are also desirous to know whither I do go.

Old man........ *Me thinks I should have known you before ?*

Maid. .... If you knew me before, you may the easier know me now.

[Old

[Old man] *Where have you been ? and if thy gravity were as good as thy ancient dissembling, I would tell thee.*

Old man. .... *These words be very large, what is the cause thou wilt not be acquainted with me? (I never did thee harm) and I have desired to be acquainted with thee a long time.*

Maid. ..... With *counterfeit gravity* I will never be acquainted, neither thy age, and. thy fame, nor thy hairs, nor the sobernesse of thy countenance can move me to any acquaintance for that thou never delightedst in *true wisdom.*

Old man. ...... *Then go your way like an Harlot.*

Maid. ...... If wicked words do prove an Harlot, then thou hast judged thy self.

E. K. Now she goeth on forward, and the Old man is gone out of sight.

There appeareth now a young man, sitting on the side of a Ditch, and to him she said.

Maid. ..... What aileth you to weep ?

Young man. .... *I weep for thy discourtesie.*

Maid. ...... Thou canst not move my conscience : No, (I say) thou canst not move me to pitty.

E. K. She licketh his tears, and saith.

Maid. ...... Every thing else hath some saltnesse, but here is none.

Young man. ...... *Oh. I pray thee, do something for me.*

Maid. ...... Oh, to qualifie these tears, is no other then to dry rotten Hemp with a mighty fire.

Young man. ...... *I will see thee hang'd before I will weep any more.*

Maid. ...... Every thing commonly teacheth of it self.

E. K. The young man went away stamping, and angry, and now she is come where a multitude of young Children are, there is much meat on a Table, and the Children being not high enough to reach it, pull'd the maid by the Cloaths, and pointed to the meat; she goeth round about the Table there is but one dish uncovered, and that seemeth to be like dew, she putteth her fingers into the Dish, and letteth the Children lick, and they fall down dead.

Maid. ...... Blame Justice and not me, for if the Children had ever tasted of this meat before they might have continued.

E. K. Now she meeteth a thin visag'd man very feeble, who staggered on his staffe, and he said.

Feeble. ...... *Help me for Gods sake.*

Maid. ...... I will do my best.

E. K. As she came toward the man, the man fell down; She heaveth him up, and again he falleth down, and she lifteth at him still.

Maid. ...... Good will forms, but the matter is not sufficient : This is long of thy self.

Feeble. ...... *Oh, I say, help me.*

Maid. ...... It is too late to help thee, I came this way many times before, and thou never soughtest help at my hands. It is written, he that desireth not help, till he be helplesse, he shall be voide of the benefit of an helper.

E. K. The feeble man goeth away, and she departeth from him : Now she cometh towards a man going up an hill, who had torn all his Cloaths off with brambles and bryars. There stand a great many of Mawmets, little ugly fellows at the top of the hill, who threw stones against him, and so force this climing man (or goer up the hill) to tumble down again to the foot of the hill. The skin doth seem to be off his hands and his feet, and they very raw, with his excessive travail with hands and feet up that hill; Now there appear men eating meat below at the foot of the hill, who offered him meat to eat; But he laboureth up the hill again, one of these men said, come let me bind up thy feet.

The Clymer. ...... *Unto him that hath no wearinesse, there belongeth no sorrow.*

E. K. She standeth and vieweth him.

The

The Clymer. ...... *I pray you help me.*
Maid. ...... It is impossible for thee to get up here.
Clymer. ...... *Of my self it is :* I will never be of the minde. It is impossible.
Maid. ...... Come on, I will do the best I can.

E. K. She leadeth him over stones, and rocks.

Maid. ...... Thou wilt be knocked in pieces, ere thou come to the top.
Clymer. ...... *Do you your good will, I feel no harm.*

E. K. Now she leadeth him in a place, where Springs, Quick-mires, and Bogs are.

Maid. ...... Surely thou art best to go down, for thou wilt be drowned.
Clymer. ...... *I pray you help, I will go as long as I may.*

E. K. He goeth forward, and sinketh almost to the throat.

Maid. ...... It is deeper on the further side, thou wert best to go down again.
Clymer. ...... *I feel the ground hard under my feet : I will not yet despair.*

E. K. Now he cometh out of those deep places, and he seemeth to come to a place like the bottom of a hedge, where stand stiffe thorns, piked upward, very sharp.

Now come two, or three handsome fellows, and said, Alas, let him tarry here and drink, we will lead him up *another way* to morrow.

Maid. ...... Farewell.
Clymer. ...... *I pray leave me not so, let me go with you.*
Maid. ...... I must needs be gone, I cannot tarry for thee.
Clymer. ...... *I am yet neither hungry nor thirsty, and feel no wearinesse: Why therefore should I stay.*

E. K. He goeth, as though the thorns prickt him, and grindeth his teeth for pain.

Now they are come to a fair place, and then she said to one.

△ Labor improbus omnia vincit.

Maid. ...... *Fetch meat and drink and cloaths, and cure his wounds : For unto thee belongeth the felicity of this place : For neither from the highest to the lowest is there any whom I pitty, but such as this is.*
Clymer. ...... I know not how I shall use these things.
Maid. ...... The true, Heirs have alwayes discretion.
To thee it belongeth, and for thee *it is prepared.*
Use it therefore without offence as thine own.

E. K. Now both he and she go into a Castle, and the doors are shut after them, and she cometh out again.

Maid. ...... *This is written for your understanding : Let therefore your eyes be opened, and be not blinde. Neither forget what here hath been opened.*
△. We perceive that *Felicitas via ardua est, multis obsita difficultatibus & periculis ; sed constantia & patientia perventur ad Falicitatis arcem,* which we beseech the Almighty God to grant unto us.
Maid. ...... *Well, I will be going till you have supped : And then I will tell you more of my minde. It will be yet six, or seven weeks journey before I can get home.*

△ Note 42.or 49. dayes, remaining till the first day of August next inclusive.

△. *Sit benedictus Deus noster nunc & semper,* Amen.
After Supper we staid awhile, being come to the place, and though nothing was seen, or heard, yet I spake, assuring my self of the presence of the foresaid maid, though as yet to us insensible.
△. We would gladly know thy name.

GALVAH.

Maid. ...... *My name is* Galua'h, *in your language I am called* Finis.

E. K. She suddenly appeared as she spake this.

△. That [*Finis*] is Latin. *Gal.* ..... I.

Filia lucis.
Filia filiarum.

△. You are none of those that are called *filiæ lucis,* or *filiæ filiarum.* Gal. ... No.
△. You will not be offended, if I propound a doubt somewhat impertinent to our matter in hand, yet of importance for us to hear your judgement in the same. *Tritemius,* sayeth that never any good Angel was read of to have appeared *forma muliebri,* I pray you to give us an answer to this so great a Clark, his words, which are to be read in his little book, *Octo Quæstionum Maximiliani Cæsaris.* ..... There *Quæstione Sexta. Sancti autem Angeli, quoniam affectione nunquam variantur semper apparent in forma virili. Nusquam enim legimus scriptum quod bonus spiritus in forma sit visus muliebri, aut bestiæ cujuscunque, sed semper in specie virili.*

An Angel boni in forma fæminia aliquando appareant?

Gal.

Gal. ...... *You think then I have some understanding.*

Δ. Yea, God knoweth, I do.

Gal. ...... *Firſt it is evident that the Spirits of God are incomprehenſible to thoſe that are their inferiours : For the higher order is incomparable unto God, And by degrees, thoſe that are their inferiours are alſo incomparable unto them. It followeth therefore, that in reſpect of that degree in Angels things are incomprehenſible.*

Angels (I ſay) of themſelves, neither are man nor woman ; Therefore they do take formes not according to any proportion in imagination, but according to the diſcreet and appliable will both of him, and of the thing wherein they are Adminiſtrators : For we all are Spirits miniſtring the will of God ; and unto whom ? unto every thing within the compaſſe of Nature : onely to his glory and the uſe of man. It followeth, Therefore, conſidering that we miniſter not of our ſelves that we ſhould miniſter in that unſearchable form within the which our executions are limited : But if Tritemius can ſay, That woman alſo hath not the Spirit of God, being formed and faſhioned of the ſelf ſame matter, notwithſtanding in a contrary proportion by a degree ; If Tritemius can ſeparate the dignity of the Soul of woman from the excellency of man but according to the form of the matter, then might his Argument be good : But becauſe that in man and woman there is propor-
tion, preparation, *of ſanctification in eternity ; Therefore may thoſe that are the eternal Mi-niſters of God in proportion to Sanctification take unto them the bodies of them both. I mean in reſpect of the Form ; For as in both you read* Homo, *ſo in both you find one and the ſelf ſame dignity in internal matter all one.* But Tritemius *ſpake in reſpect of the filthineſſe (which indeed is no filthineſſe) wherewith all women are ſtained ; and by reaſons from the natural Phi-loſophers : as a man taſting more of nature indeed then of him which is the Workman or a ſuperna-tural Maſter. He (I ſay) concluded his natural invention. In reſpect of my ſelf, I anſwer Tri-temius thus : I am Finis, I am a beam of that Wiſdom which is the end of mans excellency.*

Thoſe alſo that are called Filiæ *and* Filix filiarum *are all comprehended in me, and do attend upon* True Wiſdom ; *which if* Tritemius *mark, he ſhall perceive that true Wiſdom is alwayes painted with a womans garment ; For than the pureneſſe of a Virgin, Nothing is more com-mendable.*

God in his judgement knoweth how Tritemius *is rewarded.*

If you think theſe arguments be not ſufficient, the one in reſpect of the firſt ground, and the other in reſpect of the meaſure of my name, I will yet alledge greater.

Δ. Theſe Arguments do ſatisfie me : But to have wherewith to ſtop the mouths of others who might uſe Cavillation upon ſuch matters, it were ſomewhat needful to have heard your judgement : Whereas indeed our own affairs in hand are rather to be followed at this pre-ſent, and of greater Arguments or Inſtructions in this matter I truſt hereafter to have under-ſtanding : But as now I chiefly regard our Action in hand.

Gal. ...... *Begin the Book next Tueſday.*
My ſelf will be thy Director ; And as my name is, ſo I will lead unto the end. All other things uſe, according to thy judgement and proportion of his Spirit that guideth you.

Gal. ...... *I my ſelf will be the finger to direct thee.*

Δ.

Gal. ...... *The finger of God ſtretcheth over many mountains.*
His Spirit comforteth the weakneſſe of many places.
No ſenſe is unfurniſhed where his light remaineth
For underſtand what I am, and it is a ſufficient anſwer.

Δ. At the beginning to write the Book, ſhall I require your inſtructions ?

Gal. ...... *Do ſo.*
The Mountains of the World ſhall lie flat ; But the Spirit of God ſhall never be confounded.

E K. She ſitteth on a rock, and hath done ever ſince ſupper.

Gal. ...... *Ah Sirra I was a weary.*

Δ. As concerning the *Poloniſh* Lord *Albertus Laſcy* whom we are certified to be of God elected to govern him a people, whom we are willed to love and honour, What have you to ſay of him ? &c.

Gal. ...... *Ask me theſe things* to morrow.

E. K. She ſmileth and caſteth a light from her.

Gal. ...... *I ſmile becauſe I ſpeak of* to morrow ; *yea I ſeem to ſmile.*

Δ. As concerning Iſabel Liſter, I pray in what caſe is ſhe ? in reſpect of the wicked ſpirit which long hath moleſted her ?

Gal. ...... *Believe, For that is the chiefeſt :*
What is ſpoken by us we give but our conſent to.
For he that ſpeaketh in us is to be asked no ſuch queſtion.
For when he ſaith, it is meaſured.
As it was ſaid before ; The Hills and Mountains of the World may be made plain, but the Spirit of God never confoundeth.

Δ. He that is the end of all things, and the end of ends (unto whom all honour praiſe and
thankſ-

18

thankſgiving is due) bleſſe us, endue us with his graces, and abundantly power forth his mercy upon us.

Gal. ...... *Underſtand my name* particularly, *and not generally.*

I ſpeak it to avoid errour.

      Perſevere to the end.

Δ. *Qui perſeveraverit fidelis* (*Deo noſtro*) *uſque ad finem hic ſalvus erit* : which faithfulneſſe with all conſtancy and patience the Bleſſed and Almighty Trinity grant and confirm unto us for the glory and honour of his Name, *Amen.*

    E. K. She is gone with a brightneſſe.

1583. *Junii* 15.

Saturday afternoon, hora 6.

Δ. I uſed ſome diſcourſe   {   *After that the noble* Albertus Laskie *had been with me, and was new gone to* London, by prayer to God, and afterward proteſtation to Galuah in reſpect of her willing me to ask certain matters again this day which. . . . yeſterday were not anſwered : But very long it was, above half an hour, before any thing appeared, more then the Golden Curtain all over the Shew . . . .

At length appeared divers confuſed forms of divers Creatures, and then, by and by, vaniſhed away.

Δ. I prayed to God to baniſh all confuſion from us and our actions, and to ſend us *lucem & veritatem, per unum & propter unum, & conſtantiam rerum* . . . .

Il.

Then appeared he by whom (before) we were called *Il*, and ſeemed to ſcorn at *E. K.*

    E. K. Here appeareth *Il,* and he ſeemeth to mock me.

Il. ...... *That is a gird to you Sir for your fiſhing.*

Δ. E. K. had ſpent all that afternoon (almoſt) in angling, when I was very deſirous to have had his company and helping hand in this Action.

Δ. Shortly after this, appeared *Galuah* and to be in a field cloſed round about with a hedge,

Gal. ...... *Here is no way out.*

Il ...... *Come I will do ſomewhat for you ; It is a ſtrange thing that wiſdom cannot find a way*

Wiſdom.

through a hedge.

    E K. This *Il* pulleth down the hedge.

Gal. ...... *Go thy way, thou haſt done but thy duty.*

Il. ...... Farewell *Dee,* Farewell *Kelly.*

Dee, Kelly.

    E. K. He is gone.

Gal. ...... *Thoſe that taſte of everlaſting Bankets, fare well, and deſire the ſame to others.*

    E. K. Now ſhe is come to a great Caſtle-gate, all of ſtone, with a drawbridge before it. There is like a *Greybound graven or cut in the Stone* over the Gate.

Note.

Gal. ...... *It is very late, I will look if I can have my entertainment here.*   1583.

    E. K. She is gone in.

Δ. After a while ſhe came out again.

Gal. ...... *Bee it ſpoken.*

Curſed, defaced, and damned be this place.

Gal. ...... *And why ? Becauſe they have puffed up their fleſh, follow their own imaginations, wallowing in their filthineſſe , as Swine that tumble in mire.*

Behold it is too late with this people, I can get no lodging. O ye my feet, be a witneſſe againſt them, let the windes move the duſt to report their unkindneſſe.

    E K. Now ſhe goeth a long a great Way, like a common high-way; and the light of the Air about her ſeemed ſomewhat dark like Evening or Twilight.

Gal. ...... *Yea though you have too much light, I have too little.*

I did but over-bear you, when you ſaw me not.

Δ. [*Note.* I had ſpoken of too much light coming from the weſt window of my Study toward the Table, where the Shew-ſtone ſtood, when we began now to attend her coming, and thereupon ſhe ſpoke this.]

    E. K. Her own garments caſt a light.

    E. K. Novv ſhe cometh amongſt a company of men *having gowns furred with white,* and ſome of them having *Velvet Caps,* and ſome *Hats.*

One of them ſaid to her, What art thou ?

Gal. ...... *I know not what I am my ſelf*

Will you buy any pretious Stones of me ?

                E. K. She

E. K. She taketh out of her bosome a great many of precious stones un-cut, or unpolished.

E. K. These men look on them.

Gal. ..... *Truely, they are pure and good.*

E. K. They say also; Surely they seem to be good, delivering them from one to another.

E. K. There appear two fat men ; who said, let us first get money before we buy such trifles : besides that, they have not their perfect form.

Gal. ..... *I pray you, buy one of them of me.*
Will you buy none neither?

E. K. She speaketh that to them, who first praised the stones.

..... *Tush, I pray thee go about thy busines, dost thou not perceive how they are found fault* Those men. *withall?*

Gal. ..... *Tush, Tush, they be not cut for your fashion.*
Be it said.

..... *Their senses are gluted with transitory vanities.* A voyce from the stone.

Gal. ..... *Let them (therefore) perish vainly, because they are transitory.*

E. K. Now she cometh *where she must clamber up a wall, having steps* in it of ragged stones; There is a fair building beyond it. There go many up those steps: and when they are almost at the top, there meeteth them some, who take them by the hand, and help them up and over into the place. Then one of them that stood at the top of the wall (who had a furred Gown) and helping of men up, said to her; *Come away* woman, wilt thou come up? This Parable, or Prophesie is divers times spoken after-wares in the troubles of England.

E. K. She saith nothing to him, but standeth still, and looketh away from him.

E. K. Again, that man said to her, come away wilt thou come up?

Gal. ..... *Unhappy are those whom thou helpest : And whose breath hath infected many, your hands are too bloudy, for me to come anigh you.*

E. K. Now come handsome women to the wall, and some said, good sister, I pray you come away.

Gal. ..... *Your voluptuous father knoweth me not, for his daughter, I deny yo.....*

E. K. Now come two, or three *brave fellows* with Rapiers by their sides, and having *hatts* without bands, and their *hosen* pinned up, and with no garters; these help up people that come, and one of them said : Tarry a little, woman, and I will help thee shortly. The Attyre of the wanton youth of the Court.

Gal. ..... *Fy upon you : your cloaths are infected with abominations of your Chamber, I will tarry time.*

E. K. Now cometh a big stout man to the top of the wall, and a boy with a Crown on his head : He seemeth to be about 18. years old.

..... *So it is, and please your Majesty : Therefore let this way be razed.* The stout big man.

E. K. He spake to the young King upon former talk between them which I heard not.

..... *Be it done.*

E. K. *The wall quaketh and falleth down* : And some of the jolly fellowes, which were on the wall before, fell down, and other fellowes came and dig-ged a great hole, or breach in the wall. A voyce out of the stone. The wall bro-ken down.

Gal. ..... *Thanks be to God : Now, here is entrance enough.*

E. K. She goeth in.

The young man, or striplin (with the Crown on his head) and the other big man embraceth her : His Crown is a Triple Crown ; or three Crowns one upon another. He hath a little thing in his hand , which he holdeth close, and over-gripeth, so that it cannot be discerned.

The big man. ..... *Though thou hast travelled as a woman, thou shalt now be known to be a man.*

E. K. He spake to *Galvah.* They embrace each other. They fetch cloaths for her, and put upon her a black Gown, a mans Gown, as the Gown of a Counseller.

Galvah transformed into a man. She kneeleth down like a man in form, her head and all.

E. K. Then the young King spake to her, saying,

..... *What this Rod may do, work.*

E. K. *He* giveth the transformed man a Rod, one half being bloud , and the other half white, the partition of these two being long-wise.

A voyce out of the stone. *Que justa sunt faciet & meas mensurabit virtutes.*
The transformed man. For untill it was appointed, I sought it not,
Let us *cleanse the Court,* and examine the multitude;
A voyce out of the stone. For errour is alwayes covered in many.
NOTE. Cursed are those that are judged by a multitude.

E. K. All they that fell off the vvall , and they that vvould have helped *The transformed.* her up, they come in *bound hand and foot.*

..... *Root them out , O King , pitty no such persons, for those be these that never had mercy on themselves.*

E. K. Novv cometh a *woman out, having a Crown on her* head : she hath a long visage.
The big man. ...... *Nay, let her drink, as she hath deserved.*

E. K. The transformed man layeth down the Rod before him, and beginneth to vveep ; and said, *Let it not be said, but I pitty the anointed.*
The big man. ..... *Let her die , for she hath deserved death.*

E. K. Other men about her lay hand on her, and *pluck the Crown off her head.*

The transformed man taketh up his Rod, and layeth upon the top, or Crown of that womans head.

E. K. The young King sayeth unto her, What wilt thou?
The woman. ...... *If it please you, pardon for my life and dignity.*
E. K. The bigge man, and the young King talk together aside, the vvoman holdeth her hands abroad, and knocks her breast ? And a great company of them about her are *hewed in pieces,* by tormenters armed.

1 5 8 2.

A voyce out of the stone. *Adjuvabo.*
E. K. The King and the bigge man come in again.

The transformed man. E. K. The King said to the transformed man ; Be it as thou wilt, *Be you two joyned together.* For I vvish you both well.

E. K. The vvoman boweth down vvith obeysance , and thanketh them.

E. K. The bigge man taketh the King by the hand, and the transformed man taketh the woman by the hands , and putteth her hands to the hands of the King, and the bigge man ; they take each other by the hand , and kisse her.

E. K. All

E. *K.* All is now on the fudden vaniſhed away, and the transformed man is returned again to her womans ſhape, and ſhe ſaid.

Gal. ...... *Now I will go with you, Sir, your journey.*

E. *K.* She ſpeaketh to you Δ.

To Δ. .... *I will lead you, if you will follow me up.*
But you muſt have broken ſhinns.

Δ. By Gods grace, and with his help *I* will follow you, and in reſpect of my ſhinns break-ing, the joy of the conſequent effect will utterly take away the grief of the ſhinns breaking.

Gal. ...... *And to you Sir, you were beſt to hunt and fiſh after* Verity.

[Δ. She ſpake ſo to E. *K.* becauſe he ſpent too much time in Fiſhing and Angling.]

Gal. ...... *Whom thou ſaweſt here ſhall govern over* 21 Kingdoms.   21. Kingdoms.

Δ. If there be no myſtery in that ſpeech , the Conqueſt muſt be great, and the trouble great and ſtrange.

E. K. She goeth on her way along a lane.

Δ. We know not who ſhould be that King ſo ſhewed.

Gal. ...... *Sure thy demands are fully anſwered.*
Conſider thou what thou ſeekeſt,
And of whom thou ſeekeſt,
And by whoſe help.
Then look to that which is declared.
I will follow my office, for in thoſe things wherein thou art inquiſitive I have ſhewed the End.   The End.

Δ. Truely the occaſion of my preſent asking you ſome queſtions , aroſe upon matter con-cerning this Noble *Polonian,* of whom you bad us yeſterday ask as this day.

Gal. ...... *Vanity hangeth not at mine Elbow.*
Believeſt thou that already ſpoken? ſpoken (I ſay) of him ?

Δ. Yea forſooth, I do believe it.

Gal. ...... *I ſay unto thee, His name is in the Book of Life : The Sun ſhall not paſſe his courſe* The Prince *before he be a King. His Counſel ſhall breed Alteration of this State; yea of the whole* Alb. Laſkie. World.

What wouldſt thou know of him ?

Δ. If his Kingdom ſhall be of *Poland,* or what Land elſe.

Gal. ...... *Of two Kingdoms.*

Δ. Which I beſeech you?

Gal. ...... *The one thou haſt repeated, and the other he ſeeketh as right.*

Δ. God grant him ſufficient direction to do all things ſo, as may pleaſe the Higheſt in his calling.

Gal. ...... *He ſhall want no direction in any thing he deſireth.*

Δ. As concerning the troubles of *Auguſt* next, and the dangers then, What is the beſt for Auguſt. him to do? to be going home before, or to tarry here ?

Gal. ...... *Whom God hath armed, No man can prevaile againſt.*

Δ. In reſpect of my own ſtate with the Prince, I pray how much hath he prevailed to win me due credit : and in what caſe ſtandeth my ſute, or how am I to uſe my ſelf therein ? The premiſes Gal. ...... *I have told you that at large* even now, *and if thou look into thoſe things that are* are an anſwer *now told, and are now done.* to this que-ſtion.

Δ. Concerning *Charles Sled,* his noſe guſhing with blood twice yeſternight and this mor-ning upon my charitable inſtructions giving him to vertue and godlineſſe.

Gal. ...... *I know him not : nor any name hath be with us.*

Δ. Meaneth he well towards me ?

Gal. ...... *Whatſoever a wicked man meaneth it is not well; but in that ſenſe it is demanded be meaneth well.*
The evil ſpirit that poſſeſſeth him was caſt out of him, even at his noſe, at the preſence of thoſe Charles Sled. *that were preſent with thee.*

Δ.

Gal. ...... *Believe me we know not his name; Trouble me no more with him.*

Δ. O Lord, though men be fraile, faulty , and filthy, yet thy mercies are moſt praiſe-worthy (among all generations) of all thy doings.

Gal. ...... *Hold thy peace, we are now to execute the Juſtice of God.*

Δ. I ſpake a great while of the mercies of God and his Juſtice , and gave thanks for our Calling and Election into this bleſſed ſtate.

Gal. ...... *I will take up my lodging for this night.*

Δ. God grant me worthy of ſuch godly gheſts, God grant me a dwelling with you where his name is eternally praiſed, glorified, and ſanctified : To him all Creatures render thanks, honour, and glory. Amen.

...... *Amen.*

Δ. This voice out of the Stone being taken to be the voice of God, importeth as much as if God himself had sealed to that as his will and decree, That all Creatures should render thankes unto him and glory; fiant: *Dignum & Justum est.* Amen.

Tuesday Junii 18 *An.* 1583. *ante meridiem circa* 9.

Δ. I prayed first, and declared our attending this day the promise of God to be performed, &c.

Ga ...... *Are four hours yet to come ? and I will be ready.*

Are the works of wisdom secret, until I have ascended this Hill?

Is the Harvest ready when the Corn is ripe ?

Are the Labourers ready when their Instruments are prepared ?

I have said.

All wisdom is reckoned by the eternal will ; and until it be said, there is no action tollerable ; When the Sun shineth I will appear amongst you ; when it is said Come, lo I am ready. The dayes of your fathers were blessed ; but the hour when this Book shall be written shall be sanctified, yea in the middest of intellectual understanding.

For herein is the Creation of Adam with his transgression. The Dignity and wisdom he had.

The Errour and horror wherein he was drowned, yea herein is the power spread of the highest working in all Creatures.

For as there is a particular Soul or fire inflaming unto every body (I mean reasonable) So there is an Universal fire and a general brightnesse giving general light unto them, which is but One, and shineth through the whole, yea is measured equally unto every thing from the beginning.

The life of all things is here known :

The reward of death to those that are rewarded for life.

None are rewarded but according to their deserts : of the which there are two kinds.

1. These are rewarded with death for their wickednesse.

2. So are they rewarded with life for their constant living.

Amongst the Angels there may be errour, and sin may make them fall from the brightnesse of their glory.

But to the Soul of man (being once glorified) sin is utterly, yea most largely opposite : Neither shall that dignity ever be lost, stained, or defaced, that is obtained here with the workes of righteousnesse and true wisdom.

Whatsoever hath been from the beginning (since it was said in Divine Determination, Be it done) is here inclosed.

Therefore should this day be Hallowed and Sanctified before the Lord by you.

For if the Prophets, did worship this day of his ascension, much more ought you (which have tasted of the first, and shall now taste of the secrets of his Judgements) glorifie his coming : *But with you Satan is busie ; His bristles stand up, his feathers are cast abroad.*

Therefore watch and pray ; For those that go to Banquets put on their upper garments. . Amongst you therefore is no sound belief ; Neither do you consider the scope of this blessednesse : But such is the greatnesse and excellency of his foreknowledge, that he suffereth the enemy to carry a burden, yea sometimes to preach upon a Stage : For it is said, He shall triumph unto the end, and place himself here as he would have done above : Neither shall he be thrust out of doors till the end be determined. Therefore watch and pray, and look about with diligence, for those things shall be opened unto you which have not been disclosed unto the Holy Ones.

Oh, how hard a thing it is for flesh to continue in the works of Justice !

Tea, oh how hard a thing it is for Wisdom to be acquainted with a hotchpot of filthinesse ?

Cleanse your garments, Lift up your hearts, and rent your faults in pieces, that there may be one heart with one consent, and unto one end, unto him which is One and the End of all things : and to him for and in his truth, and for the greatnesse of his mercies : To whom be praise for ever.

Δ. Amen.

E. K. All the while she spake there came a bright beame from the Mystical Stone to the body of her, and at the end she mounted upward and disappeared.

Δ. We set up the hour glasses to measure four hours justly after this answer and instructions.

Tuesday, After Dinner about one of the clock and ½ the hours expired, and we attended the mercy of the Highest.

Δ. At a great gladsome shining of the Sun (whereas it had not shined but a little and inconstantly ever since his last words) one appeared on the corner of the green silk Sarcenet, by the Mystical Stone, She was like a woman as *Galvah* in face, but her apparel was a mans gown furred with foynes, or, as Gentlewomen do wear upon gowns.

Δ. Upon the diversity of your apparel we are to ask whether you be *Galvah* or no ? or have you also, as I have done, put on your Holiday-cloths ?

Gal.

Gal. ,,,,,, *FEAR GOD.*

E. K. She.steppeth forward one step.

Gal. ,,,,,, *My Garment is called HOXMARCH, which in your speech is called .....*

Δ. *Iustium sapientiæ est Timor Domini :* we accknowledge it to be an old and a true Lesson, and also the first step of the path-way to felicity.

Gal. ...... *What is fear ?*

Δ. Fear is of two sorts : one is called *filialis*, the other *servilis*.

Gal. .... *Unto the Just all fear is joy ; and therefore the beginning and entrance into quietnesse. True quietnesse and rest is wisdom ; For the mind that knoweth hath the greatest rest and quietness. The Daughter of Dispaire unto the wicked is fear.*

This fear is the first that accuseth unto damnation: But he that is perfectly wise, or hath tasted of wisdom, knoweth the End.

And his fear is of the thing that is done. This is the true fear of God ; and when we fear sin, we do it because we hate it.

When we study to do good, it is a token of our fear, in that it is a token we fear him, whom we love and for whose honour we study to do well.

This is all that may be said of lively and unlively fear.

Touching the Book, it shall be called Logah *: which in your Language signifieth Speech from* The Title of GOD. *Write after this sort* LOGAETH *: it is to be sounded* Logah.   the Book.

This word is of great signification, I mean in respect of the profoundnesse thereof.

The first leaf (as you call it) is the last of the Book.

And as the first leaf is a hotchpot without order ; So it signifieth a disorder of the World, and Δ. *I under-* *is the speech of that Disorder or* Prophesie.   stand not this

Write the Book (after your order) backward, but alter not the form of letters, I speak in being indeed *respect of the places.*   the first leaf, being indeed the last, is of the wicked

E. K. Now a beame shooteth through him from the Stone and so.through hellish one, his head and out of his mouth, his face being from *E. K.* toward Δ.   &c. vide post 4.Folio.

..... *Write the 49. You have but 48 already. Write first in a paper apart.*   49.

E. K. Said that *Galvah* her head is so on bright fire, that it cannot be looked upon : The fire so sparkleth *Loagaeth seg lovi brtnc* and glistreth as when an hot iron is smitten on an An- *Larzed dox ncr habzilb adnor* vil, & especially at the pronouncing of every word. It   Now Seas appear. is to be noted also that upon the pronouncing of some *doncha Larb vors hirobra* words, the Beasts and all Creatures of the World eve- *exi vr zednip taiip chimvane* ry one shewed themselves in their kind and form : *chermach lendix nor zandox.* But notably all Serpents, Dragons, Toads, and all ugly and hideous shapes of beasts ; which all made most ugly countenances, in a manner assaulting *E. K.* but contrariwise coming to, and fawning upon *Galvah.* It is to be noted also that by degrees came a second beame, and a third beame of light into *Galvah* from the Stone, and all the three together appeared : the third participating of the other two.

The second beame came at the word *Larb*, pronounced ; when also Frogs and Serpents appeared, &c. The third beame upon the word *Exi* pronounced. Note also, that the manner of the firy brightnesse was such, and the grisely countenances of the Monsters was so tedious and greivous and displeasant to *E. K.* that partly the very grief of his minde and body, and partly the suspecting the Creatures to be no good Creatures, neither such greivous sights necessary to be exhibited with the Mysteries delivering unto us, had in a manner forced him to leave off all : But I again with reasonable exhorting of him, and partly the providence and decree Divine, wrought some mitigating of his grief and disquieting.

Gal. ...... *These are these seven.*

Δ. Blessed and praised for ever be He who is one and three : and whom mighty ministers or governours do incessantly glorifie.

1583.

Gal. ...... *Thy folly and weaknesse is great, God comfort thee.*

[Δ. He spoke to *E. K.* for his excessive disquietnesse and suspecting of the verity or goodnesse of *Galvah.*]

Δ. Note. Now the beames were all retired into the stone ; again likewise all the Creatures and Vermine or ugly shaped Beasts are all gone. We were willed also divers times to pray. At sundry pangs of *E. K.* his grief and disquietnesse, sundry speeches were uttered Pray. by the spiritual Creature : among which these noted.

.... *He that is angry cannot see well.   From him that is perverse, God turneth his face. The hindrance of punishment, is the mercy of God, which imputeth not sin unto them whom he* The Elect. *hath* Chosen; *Therefore be patient, and reconcile thy self to God.*   Reconciliation.

D 2   *E. K.*

E. K. I do it with all humility and sincerity of minde, and beseech God to help me with his grace; for of my self I cannot do so, yet I am *Thomas Didymas, I will believe these things, when I see the fruits of them.*

Δ. He seemed yet again to doubt, whether this Creature and the rest, (partakers of this action) were soundly good, and void of all halting, or abusing us.

B K. How can you perswade me that ye be no deluders?

Gall. . . . . . *I will prove it by contrary.*

Arguments to prove our Instructors to be good angels.

The servants of darknesse have their Garments stained : their mouths stinck of blasphemy, and lies, but our Garments are no such, neither do our lips speak any untruth : and therefore we are of God, for whosoever is of the truth, is of God.

Moreover, the Devil is known by his works : for the spirit of God controlleth them, the spirit of God agreeth with us, and useth no controlment against it, therefore it is not Daulesse.

In one thing thou mayest know us differing from Devils.

Mercy.   *The wicked spirits alwayes abhor this word.* Mercy.

But it is the Doctrine that we preach in respect towards you, we are not now (then) evil.

But this way teacheth hardnesse, and is a stumbling block to the wicked : but the beauty of the Castle is not able to be expressed.

The attire before.   *Happy are they, which are covered with the Pearls of Righteousnesse, and on whose head there is a Garland of godlinesse : For unto those belongeth to taste of the Fountain of true wisdom.*

Is it not written of this book, that it teacheth nature in all degrees ?

The judgement hereof is Intellectual,

And wash your feet, and follow me.

Δ. Lord wash thou our feet, or else we shall not be clean.

Gall. . . . . . *How thou art God knoweth : But comfort your selves in this.*

This Testimony victory.   *That neither this Testimony can perish, neither unto you can remain any slavery : Quia vestra erit victoria, in him, and for him, to whom I leave you.*

Δ. What shall I do with these 21 words now received;

Gall. . . . . . *There are onely the words of the first leaf.*

Δ. I pray, how shall I bestow them, or place them,

Gall. . . . . . *In them is the Divinity of the Trinity.*

The first leaf of the book.
> *The Mysterie of our Creation,*
> *The age of many years.*
> *And the conclusion of the World.*

Of me they are honoured, but of me, not to be uttered : Neither did I disclose them my self : For, they are the beams of my understanding, and the Fountain from whence I water.

Δ. I beseech you, how shall I write these names in the first leafe.

Gall. . . . . . *They are to be written in 5 Tables, in every Table 21 Letters.*

Δ. How shall I place the 5 Tables upon two sides : three in the first, and 2 in the second, or one in the first, and 4 in the second, or how else?

Gall. . . . . *As thou seest cause.*

Δ. Shall I write them in Letters of Gold ?

Gall. . . . . *The writing hath been referred to thy discretion with colours, and such things as appertain to the writing thereof. Upon the first side write three Tables, and on the second two.*

Δ. How, thus? ≡   Gal. . . . . *Set them down, I will direct thy judgement.*

Δ. When, now? ≡   Gal. . . . . *Not now.*

E. K. She is gone,

Δ. *Deo Nostro sit Laus, honor, & Gratiarum actio perennis.* Amen.

Wednesday 19. Junii. Hora 2. a Meridie.

Δ. I made a prayer to God : and there appeared one, having two Garments in his hands, who answered.

. . . . . *A good praise, with a wavering minde.*

Δ. God make my minde stable, and to be seasoned with the intellectual leaven, free of all sensible mutability.

E. K. One of these two Garments is pure white : the other is speckled of divers colours; he layeth them down before him, he layeth also a speckled Cap down before him at his feet; he hath no Cap on his head : his hair is long and yellow, but his face cannot be seen; at the least it was turned away-ward from *E. K.* continually, though *E. K.* changed his place.

..... *You shall see my face, lo, it is white.*

E. K. Now he putteth on his Pied Coat, and his Pied Cap, he casteth the one side of his Gown over his shoulder, and he danceth, and saith,

..... *There is a God, let us be merry.*

E. K. He danceth still.

There is a heaven, let us be merry.
Doth this Doctrine teach you to know God, or to be skilfull in the heavens ?

..... *Note it.*

E. K. Now he putteth off his Cloathes again: Now he kneeleth down, and washeth his head and his neck, and his face, and shaketh his Cloaths, and plucketh off the uttermost sole of his shooes, and falleth prostrate on the ground, and sayed:

.... *Vouchsafe (O God) to take away the wearinesse of my body, and to cleanse the filthinesse of this dust, that I may be apt for this purenesse.*

E. K. Now he taketh the white Garment, and putteth it on him.

...... *Mighty is God in his great Justice, and wonderful in his immeasurable mercy : The heavens taste of his Glory : The earth is confounded at his wisdom. In hell they tremble at him, as at a Revenger. This sheweth thee (O) to be a God, and stretcheth forth thy Glory from the East unto the West ; for thy Heavens are Statutes, and thy Creatures Laws : that thou mayest be accounted a God of Justice and Glory. Because thou art a God, Therefore there is a Heaven : For unto the Prince of Righteousnesse, there belongeth a place of Glory; Into the which there entereth none that are defiled, neither such as are blemished with the spots of iniquity. Manus Hæc bona est ...... E. K. putting forth his right hand, Hæc Autem mala ...... E. K. putting forth his left hand, Qui Habet aures intelligat.*

E. K. Now he sitteth down on the Desk-top and looketh toward me.

Δ. This Parable is in general, somewhat understood of us : but in particular, how it may be, or is to be applied, presently we understand not.

...... *Beware left error enter within the dwelling place of Righteousnesse.*　*I have said.*

E. K. He seemeth now to be turned to a woman, and the very same which we call *Galvah.*

E. K. Now he is come down to the usual place, on the Table.

Δ. I have assayed divers wayes to place the five Tables, on the two sides on this first leaf ; Is it to your likeing as I have done it, in the five little Triangles ?

Gal. ...... *As concerning the setting down of the five Tables. it is sufficient as it is done. The cause why I appeared thus, was that you might avoid error.*

Δ. I pray you to shew us the means how that error was or is to incumber us.

Gal. ...... *Whosoever taketh servants of the wicked, to prove the Glory of God , is ac-*　Note. *cursed. But, O Satan, how many are thy deceits ?*

Note, my Companion (E. K.) would have caused personal apparitions of some of the reprobate spirits, before the Prince *Albert Laskie* in my Study, thereby to shew some ex-　A. L. perience of his skill in such doings : *But I would not consent to it :* And thereupon *Galvah* gave judgement and warning of such an error, of my Companion his intent, &c.

Gal. ...... *Behold, it is said, before he go from hence I will pour water into him ; And my An-*　Note of A. L. *gel shall annoint him, as I have determined :* Hide therefore Nothing from him ; For you be-long unto him. *Neither can flesh and blood work those things that I have Glorified in him (All things that are established in God, are Glorified. I speak this for thy understanding) Neither let your hearts be hardned ; for the Earth is condemned,* and these things shall come to passe. *Credit it all that I seek (saith the Lord;) for when I come, I shall be sufficiently believed.*

I take the God of Heaven and Earth to judge ; and swear by him as a witnesse, that these words　An Oath. are true, and shall endure *unto the end. The general points of mans Salvation are concluded al-*　Note of Gene-*ready ; but the special gift belongeth unto God. God strengthen you against his adversary.*　ral points, and special gifts.

Δ. Amen.

Gal. ...... *Soon you shall know more.*

Δ. This Prince would gladly know, Whether it shall be best for him, with the first oppor-tunity, to be going homeward.

Gal. ...... *It shall be answered soon, and* what questions soever he *also demandeth.*

Δ. May he be here present at the action doing ?

Gal. ...... *Those that are of this house,* are *not to be denied the Banquets therein.*　A. L. may be present at

Δ. May I request you to cause some sensible apparition to appear to him, to comfort him,　Actions. and establish his minde more abundantly in the godly intent of God his Service ?

Gal. ...... *If you follow us, let him be governed by us ; But whatsoever is of the flesh, is not* of us.

E. K. She seemeth to weep ; for the water cometh forth of her eyes.

Δ. You perceive, how he understandeth of the Lord Treasurer his grudge against him ; And perhaps some other also, are of like malitious nature : What danger may follow hereof, or incumbrance ?

A. L. poverty.   *Gal.* ...... *The sum of his life is already appointed, one jot cannot be diminished : But he that is Almighty can augment at his pleasure.   Let him rejoyce in poverty.   Be sorry for his enemies.   And do the works of Justice.*

E. K. She seemeth to put the air over her, and so to enter into a Cloud of invisibility, and so disappear.

Δ. *Deo gratias agamus.*

Wensday after noon, circa horam 5.   The Lord Albert à Lasky *being present.*
Δ. We attended of *Galvah* some instructions or discourse concerning the Lord *Laskie.*

E. K. At length appeared before the Lord *Lasky* (in the air) an Angel in a white Robe, holding a bloody Crosse in his right hand, the same hand being also bloody.

Δ. *In nomine Jesu Christi Crucifixi, a te requiro qui Crucis Trophæum hic Gestas ut illa nobis signifies, quæ sunt ad Christi gloriam, cui sit honor & Laus perennis.*

E. K. Now he is come from before the Lord *Lasky,* and standeth here on the Table : he turneth himself to all the four quarters of the World ; he kneeleth down.

He prayeth.

...... *O God, Why should the people upon earth rejoyce ? or wherein should the pleasures of their sensual delights be fixed ? Why doth the Moon hold her course ? or why are the Stars observing an order ? Why are thy people thus scattered abroad ? Because iniquity hath caught the upper hand. The Doors of our God are polluted with blasphemy, his Temples desolate, his Commandments violated, and his Glory accounted as nothing.   But wilt thou suffer ; or canst thou hold thy hand from thy great and mighty strokes ? Most High God, Most Mighty God, Most Honourable God, have mercy upon thy people ; respect the Creation, (the Creation I say) of those, wherein thou hast delighted.   Suffer not the Serpent to extol his head above thy Altars, neither let thy holy Vessel be poisoned with his venome ; For thou art Mighty and overcomest all : and who can rebel against thy Prowesse ?   Bend down thy merciful eyes, Behold this confusion : look upon thy Temple and see the desolation thereof.   And then in thy mercy (O) shew thy self to be a God, and such a merciful Governour, as hath compassion upon those that are diseased, yea even unto death.   Grant this* Cama-scheth galsuagath garnastel zurah logaah luseroth. *Amen.*

Δ. I pray you to declare unto us your name.

...... *My name is* Jubanladace.

Δ. If I should not offend you, I would gladly know of what order you are, or how your state is in respect of *Michael, Gabriel, Raphael,* or *Uriel.*

...... *Jub. Unto men, according unto their deserts, and the first excellency of their Soul, God hath appointed a good Governour or Angel, from amongst the orders of those that are Blessed : For every Soul that is good, is not of one and the self same dignification ; Therefore according to his excellency we are appointed as Ministers from that order, whereunto his Excellency accordeth : To the intent that he may be brought at last to supply those places which were Glorified by a former ; And also to the intent, that the Prince of Darknesse might be counterpoised in Gods Justice. A-mongst the which I am one which am the Keeper and Defender of this man present : which carry the Triumph and Ensign of Victories continually before him, as a reproach to my adversaries and his, and to confirm the dignity whereunto he is called by the presence of this Character.*

E. K. Now he heaveth up the Crosse.

A. L.
Judai.
Victoria.
A. L.

...... *I have also sealed the same in his heart : For unto him belong great Victories, in the name, and for the name of his God.   The Jews in his time shall taste of this Crosse : And with this Crosse shall he overcome the Sarazens, and Paynims :   For I will establish one Faith (saith the Lord of Justice) That I may be known to be the same that I was first among all people. Moreover I will open the hearts of all men, that he may have free passage through them, and will not suffer him to perish with the violence of the wicked.   I will hereafter visibly appear unto him, and will say, This is to be done.   But a year is not yet come, and these things shall be finished. But (thus saith the Lord) I have hindred him, because he hearkned to the provocation of those that are wanton.   And hath consented to those that blasphemed my name.   Bid him look to the steps of his youth, and measure the length of his body ; to the intent, he may live better, and see himself inwardly.*

A. L.
An year to come.
Hindrance breedeth exception, and sin breedeth hindrance.

Δ. *Note.*

Δ. Note. At this Inftant *Tanfeld* came rafhly upon us, into my Study : we thinking that the Study door had been fhut ; the Lord *Laskie* being gone out of my Study, the other way through my Oratory, to take *Tanfelds* meffage from the Court, and having difpatched him, refted without : and *Tanfeld* having commendations to me, as he faid, from fome at *London,* fearing leaft he fhould be fent away by and by, without doing thefe, came undifcretly upon us, to our no little amazing, and great fearing his rafh opinion afterward of fuch things, as he could not perceive perfectly what my Companion and I were doing : Hereupon, *Jubanladace* gave this fentence, or declared this the fatal end of *Tanfeld.* This *Tanfeld* ferved the Lord *Laskie,*

Juban. .... *It is faid, He that entreth in this rafhly, Lo five moneths are yet to come, and fifhes of the Sea fhall devour his carkafe.*

.... *As before, whatfoever he taketh in hand fhall profper, for my names fake. For thus it is faid, and thefe words are the words wherewithal I do annoint him ; for than the comfort of the nointing. Higheft, there is not a fweeter* Inunction. *Look not for the marveiles of this World, as the wicked man in his heart doth ; but ftudy to pleafe him with whom ye might rejoyce for ever. You fons of men, What do ye feek after ? Do ye hunt after the fwiftnefse of the winds ; or are you imagining a form unto the Clouds ? or go ye forth to hear the braying of an Afse, which pafseth away with the fwiftnefse of the air ? Seek for true wifdom ; For it beholdeth the brighteft, and appeareth unto the loweft. Cecill hateth him unto the heart, and defireth he were gone hence. Many other do privily fting at him ; I cannot properly fay fting him ; But (I fay) I will pour down my wrath upon them, and they fhall be confounded in the midft of their own iniquity. Let my faithful live and be like the fruitful Vinyard. Be it fo.* A. L. his anfwer. Mirdcula & figna non funt petenda à Deo. The Lord Treafurer.

Δ. For his return homeward, What is your advice ? perhaps he wanteth neceffary provifion, and money.

Juban. .... *He fhall be holpen here, and elfewhere, miraculoufly. I fpeak as it were to himfelf. Let him go, fo foon as he can conveniently.*

Δ. I fay again, perhaps he wanteth money, but the Treafures of the Lord are not fcant, to them whom he favoureth.

Jub. .... *His help fhall be ftrange which hath not been often feen. The Queen loveth him faithfully, and hath fallen out with* Cecil *about him :* Lecefter *flattereth him. His doings are looked into narrowly. But I do always inwardly direct him, and I will minifter fuch comfort unto him, as fhall be neceffary in the midft of all his doings. When this Country fhall be invaded, then fhall you pafse into his Country, and by this means, fhall his Kingdom be eftablifhed again. This is more then my duty. This is the firft time he hath been here, and it is wonderful. The fecond coming is not long unto, and then fhall he be wonderful. Deftitutus à me, premitur à malo. He is now deftitute of me.* England. A. Ei

Δ. Note, as foon as he had faid this fentence, he feemed to fink through the Table like a fpark of fire ; and feemed to make hafte to his Charge, I mean the Lord *Laskie* : whereby we perceive the frailty of man to be great when he is *Deftitute* (yea but after this manner) of this good Angel.

Benedictum fit nomen Dei noftri nunc
& in fempiterna fecula. Amen.

Thurfday, 20 *Junii* 1583. After Noone *Circa* 6.

Gal. ..... *Labour in the writing of this Book diligently. See thou cleanfe thy felf on both fides. Be alone while it is done : that is to fay, while thou art in doing it, henceforth and till the time come ufe fpeech with us no more ; every feventh day accepted.* Every feventh day,

Δ. How fhall thofe dayes be accounted ?

Gal. .... *From Tuefday laft : Tuefday being the firft of the feven, and the next Munday, the feventh, and fo forth every* Monday *is the feventh. In a pure action all things ought to be pure.* Mondayes.

Δ. May I be writing every day, and at any time, when it fhall come in my mind ?

Gal. ...., *Ever as thou fhalt feel me move thee. I will ftir up thy defire.* Good defires ftirred up by good Angels.

Δ. How fhall I do for the letters ? Shall I fimply tranflate the letters as I find them ?

Gal. ...... *I.*

Δ. The titles of the fides, are they to be written onely in the holy Characters ?

Gal. ...... *As thou fayeft, even thofe words do make the holy, that thou calleft them holy.*

Δ. I believe verily, that they are holy and fanctified.

Gal. ...... *In the laft feven of the* 40 *dayes,* the words of this Book fhall be diftinguifhed. Diftinction of words and accents.

Δ. And accented alfo ? *Gal.* ...... *I.*

Δ. How fhall I do, for the Tables where certain letters are to be written in all the void places, feeing they will not juftly agree ?

Gal. ...... *There is one fuperfluous : it is to be filled in order as it fheweth.*

Δ. I fhall not dare adventure on it without direction when I come to it.

Gal. ...... *Thou fhalt want no direction.*

Δ. For the inequality of the firft 49 lines I require your advife.

Gal.

Gal. .... *It is no question.*

Gall....... *Thou beginnest in the world to look up to heaven : So was it begun in earth to look up to the doing above.*

The last *life is* Hotchpotch of the wicked in the World, *and damned in the* Hell.

E. K. What is a Hotchpotch, &c.

Gal. ..... *The greater thy folly is, the greater thy wisdom will be hereafter.*

..... *There are* the Souls of the wicked and damned in Hell. *Those that are in the world cannot describe the least joy of those that are in heaven : Much lesse those that are ignorant, declare the manifest beauty of wisdom. There shall come a day with you, when you shall rejoyce. In the mean season, rent your hearts, and turn unto the Lord.*

Δ. Deus in adjutorium nostrum intende, Domine ad juvandum me festina; Gloria Patri, & filio, & S, &c. Amen.

Saturday, *ante Meridiem. Hora* 10. Junii 22.

Δ. Whiles I was writing certain prayers to good Angels, and *ad proprios nostros Angelos* for *A. Lasky*, there appeared one very big in the aire, all in a white Garment full of plaights, and tucked up very dubble, with a myterlike Attire on his head, and a crosse on the forepart of it : He *willed* E. K. *to speak to me, and to tell me of his* being there : But *he refused, and expresly denied it,* partly by reason *Galluah* said that he would not deal with us, but every seventh day (being every Monday) till the actions were ended : and therefore he supposed this Creature to be an illuder, and partly he urged some evident token, or proof of their *well-meaning* towards us in Act, &c. He went down; and still this Creature followed *him with a drawn sword, requiring* him to declare these words to me ; but E. K. a long while bad him declare them himself unto me, if he would : and said, why should he not, &c. At length my Companion came, appeased, and contented to hear what this Creature would say, who at length said thus :

.... *The Eagles have food for their young ones, by Divine providence, and not of themselves. Lord let me diminish the power of this wicked spirit that doth so provoke, and stirre him to mischief.*

.... *If the love of the fathers (O God) be great towards their Children, much greater are thy blessings in those whom thou hast chosen.*

Δ. So, (O Lord) so.

.... *Behold, I will draw threds together, and make him a Net, which shall alwayes be between him and the Adversary : neither shall it diminish his understanding from the true sight of me. It hath been said,* The place *is holy. Write that shall be here spoken, with devotion upon thy knees. Great is thy name (O God) and mighty art thou in all thy workings : Thy help is strong, and to those that delight therein. O magnified be thy name from generation to generation.*

Oratio.

Speritu & mente dico,

Sit mihi verus orandi modus : nam bonitatem Dei Laudo : O, Iram Patris meritus sum, quia lumen ejus elongatur a me : Verum in nomine Christi remissionem delictorum meorum, & confirmationem in suo Sancto Spiritu exopto. Per te, Halleluja, resurgam, me accuso, me condemno : omnia male feci.

Omnia per te (Pater) sunt. Paratus esto exaudire. Oculos ad Cœlos Elevare nolo, egestatem quia meam nosti. Quid differes Domine, Cor meum in melius Confortere? Vivus & non mortuus sum : Igitur Credo in te. Exaudi me Antidotum mihi Sanctum monstra, quia malum meum agnosco. Mitte mihi auxilium tuum de sede Majestatis tuæ : Et per Angelos bonos tuere me, *Audi, Exaudi,* O tu igitur Angelus meus adfis mihi. Defende me, nec trade Corpus & animam meam in manus inimicorum ; meorum sed secundum magnam misericordiam Dei, (per potestatem tibi traditam) me protege, adsit mecum prudentia tua, qua Diabolum & Sathanicam fraudem vincam. Adjuva me derelictum, Confirma me debilem, Cura me sanum, sana me ægrotum : Mihi esto spiritus super humanam sapientiam. Fac me fidelem Operatorem : Adduc tecum Angelos de Cœlis demissos Sanctos, qui me tecum in adversis tueantur & ab omni Custodiant malo, donec illa hora venerit, quàm nemo evitare potest : Sustinuit anima mea in verbo ejus. *Amen.*

Glorifie God ye sons of men, and praise him in the midst of your wickednesse : For he is a God that sheweth mercie to his people, and beholdeth those that are afflicted : All honour, praise, and glory be unto him, now and for ever. Amen.

Δ. I beseech you, what is your name, that this mercie of God may be Recorded, to have been bestowed upon us by your ministery.

.... *Gabriel.*

Δ. Shall I signifie to the Polonian Gentleman, that we received this .... prayer from you, and so make him partner thereof.

Gabriel .... Do so.

The help of the Lord is with those, that he loveth, and so be it.
Δ. He made the sign of a Crosse over our two heads, and so went away.

Gloria sit in excelsis, Deo nostro & in terra Pax hominibus bonæ voluntatis,
Amen.

Saturday; *Junii* 22. *a Meridie, Circa* 6.

Δ, Upon the perusing and examining, this prayer *Gabriel* revealed unto us, I found certain
imperfections, and some doubts, wherein we thought it good to ask counsel, and require *Gabriel's* advise : That the prayer might be perfect, as he might well like of to Gods honour and
our comforts. At the length : Nothing appearing to the eye, but the noise of a sound about
E. K. his head, and withall a mighty weight, or invisible burden on his right shoulder, as
he sate in the green Chair, by the holy Table, or place : And unto certain places of the prayer,
which I noted and repeated, those words, and answers were by *Gabriel* given.

Gab. .... *The Preface must be in, for if our hearts be not prepared unto prayer, our prayers are
in vain.*

Quid differs Domine, Cor meum in melius Comfortare,
Per te & in nomine tuo resurgam ; id est, Halleluja.

The first way is more effectual.   Say Angele mee, but the other is more effectual,   Cura me
sanum. *Regard me, and look unto me, being whole.*
Δ. As concerning the inscription, which I have written before the prayer : I would gladly
know, whether it be to your well liking of it.

Gab. .... Fiant omnia ad laudem Dei.   *My doings are of no such regard : What I have done
be it done, so that your additions be to the honour of God, it is sufficient.*   The effect of his prayer
is greater, then is the form.   *The former is greater then the forming.   That is to say, he that
hath formed it, is mightier then any virtue, wherein it is formed. Wheresoever, therefore the mind
formeth it with you with perfect humility and consent, there is also the former.   As formed of him
therefore, I leave you to the end of his workmanship, which continually formeth all things according
to his own fashion.*

Sins. .... *Your sins have banished me, from saying those things I would.*
Δ. O cleanse our hearts, and wash away our sins, *amplius lava me ab iniquitate mea & a peccato meo munda me.*

Gab. .... *Sins are never washed away, or forgotten with the highest, but with such as are sorry,*
and also make satisfaction.   Satisfaction.
O Lord, full sorry I am for my sins, and what satisfaction is ... required I would gladly know.
Gab. .... *The offence was not thine.   Every one must satisfie, or else he shall be damned.*
Δ. Good Lord expound to us the mystery of satisfaction.

Gab. .... *When the Soul offendeth, and is consenting to wickednesse, he is then to make a spiritual satisfaction, which is the end and perfect fruit of Contrition.   For those that are truely Contrite, do truely satisfie.   Another satisfaction there is, which is external.   This satisfaction is to
be made for sins committed against thy Neighbour : For if thou offend thy Neighbour, and do him
wrong, or take any thing from him, by fraud, or violence, it is a great sin.   For this, thou canst never
be Contrite if thou make not satisfaction, not onely confessing it, but in satisfying his desire that is
offended, and that with sorrow.   This is true Doctrine, and shall never be overthrown by the spirits*   NOTE.
of false invention : which indeed is the first eye unto the Devil.   *If you may offend your brother, and* Good Angels
be therefore accursed : How much more shall you be accursed, when you offend the messager of him are to be used
that is your Father.   Behold, he sayeth not, I have once done amisse.   God be mercifull to you, that reverently.
his mercies might be the greater upon you.   Be mindfull of my sayings.   E. K.

Δ. Deus misereatur nostri, & benidicat nobis, Cor mundum Creet in nobis, & spiritum rectum ponat in præcordiis nostris, *Amen.*

                                    1 5 8 3

Wednesday, *Junii* 26. *Hora* 9½. *presente D. Alberto* Lasky.
Δ. As we were together in my study, and I standing at my Desk.   There appeared to
E. K. a round Globe of white smoak over my head.   Thereupon I perceived the presence of
some good spiritual Creature, and straight way appeared the good Angel.   *I. L.*
Δ. I said, Benedictus qui venit in nomine Domini, & igitur nobis est gratus laudis adventus.
I.L. Et quid tu dicis ? [ad E. K. Loquutus est.]

E. K. Si bonus es, & lucis spiritus, bene venisti, I. L.
I. L. Et bene tibi fiet.   E. K. He hath a besome in his hand.
E. K.   What will you do with this besome.
Δ. Quid cum tua scopa decrevisti facere?
I. L. Secundum Dei beneplacitum.

                          E   E. K. *Here*

E. K. *Here cometh a big tall creature*, forma humana quæ facile non possit discerni, oculi ejus videantur esse duo Carbunculi Lucentes & mirabiliter micantes. Caput ejus videtur aureum, os videtur valde largum esse, & Caput videtur mobile & quasi ab humeris separabile, totum reliquum Corpus videtur esse marmor quasi.

Vox. ...... *Fecisti tu?*

[*E. K.*] he said so to IL.

Suspicor hoc factum esse ut quietior esset animus ipsius, E. K. & non eos suspiciendo in cogitatione ejus destrueret.

IL. ...... *Feci. Decedite in Oratorium, nam magna hic dicenda sunt.*
Qui decedent? I L. *Princeps, & tu.* (Bow down thy knees brother) and here what I do say.
[To *E. K.* he spake.]
Magnus ille .... *Filioli hominum quid vultis?*
Δ. *Cupimus mundari à peccatis,* & illuminari sapientia divina, ad ejus honorem.

E. K. Est lumen quoddam in Aere: & ipse osculatur lumen illud·

IL. ...... *Dic, Propitius esto mihi peccatori.*

K. E. Propitius esto mihi peccatori, O Deus, crescit jam Corpus istius magni in immensum quantum, quod non possit facile discerni·

Mag. ..... *Filii hominum, quid vultis?*
Δ. *Sapientiam veram.*
Mag....... *O vos pueri & filii hominum, quid vultis?*
Δ. *Sapientiam in Deo,& propter Deum, veram.*

Singula dum proferat verba, flammam ex ore evomit·

Mag. ..... *Audite, quia Justus & verus sum* (inquit Dominus;) *Vos nihil impium, iniquum, vel injustum suscipite: Nam quæcunque feceritis mala, vel negligentia, vel inscitia, vel contemptu, vel etiam nimia superstitione sunt,* (Sicut Scriptum est) *potestate tradita spiritibus mendacibus, ut vexarent bonos, dum affligerent malos. Sed dixit Deus* (Deus sum quidem vester) *qui Spiritum*

Note,

Sanctum non aufero a vobis: Nam estis, quos per potentiam confirmabo meam: Nolite igitur Cacomagi Cum perversis fieri, qui inaniter rebus & Idolis hujus mundi potentiam ascribunt meam.

De Sublunaribus Spiritibus.

Sed Credite perseveranter & ad finem usque & fidem habete: quia, (per me) *omnia mundana superat sigillum, & subjiciet Dæmones voluntati vestræ. Dæmones sub regionibus permanentes, &*

Angeli boni ubi sedes habent.

inclusi Lunaribus, Angeli mei non sunt: Sed Cælestes, Sancti & veri boni. Nonne vos homines & mortales & non sine peccato, Cui voluntatem liberam, simul & peccare permissi: ut intelligendo

Pene omnium principium interitus.

exinde malum, & me Deum vestrum agnoscatis vos. Audite igitur, Audite filii mei, ... Calamitatem totius terræ omniumque viventium prædico. Bella erunt undique horrenda & tristissima, Et peribit ad tertiam usque partem gladio & fame Terræ. Erunt cædes multorum, (penè omnium)

Turcici Imperii ruina.

Principum interitus, Terræ motus, quales non ab initio mundi; Terrestria Dæmonis (Turca viz.) *Imperii ruina. Nam sic constitui.*

[*E. K.*] Nunc respcit vos·

Δ, *A. L.* and I were in my Oratory.
Stephanus, Poloniensis, miserrime in bello jugulatus, Cadet. Iterum dico: *Stephanus, Poloniensis Rex, miserrime in bello jugulatus, cadet.* Vocabant te iterum [*respicit* Alb. Lasky] ad Regnum *Principes: quem etiam ego Poloniæ, Moldaviæ & populi mei Ducem & regem constituero. Tunc attinges desideratam metam à Scopo. Quia ego sum Deus tuus, & docebo te utilia & vera. Et dabo tibi Angelos meos adjutores & comites etiam ad secretum quodlibet mundi. Vigilato,* ORATO. *Igitur, Pius esto, donec venerit potestas mea & in te, & supra vos. Interum sigillate quæ vidistis, & me in publicum producite.*

Ne in publicum producite.

[*E.K.*] Now he shaketh: he seemeth to turn his head about his shoulders.

E, K, *Nunc accipit ensem & percutit nubes, & crucem format ante se, ab utroque latere & post se. Crede mihi, est finis rerum; Dimittuntur Peccata vestra.*
E. K. Cadit, quasi distractus, (vel se separans) in 4 partes, & avolut·

Vox. ...... *Habetis quæ adeo Decreta sunt.*
Δ. Misericordia Dei, sit super nos nunc, & semper. *Amen.*

Saturday Junii 29 à meridie horâ 4.
Δ. While I was about to write the Title of the second side of the seventh leaf: and (*E. K.*

May 28.1583. when he began Alb. Laskie his Pedigree,

fitting by me) *Madini* appeared as before like a young girle, and I saluted her in the Name of God, as coming from God for good, and said to her, that I was wonderfully oppressed with the Work prescribed to me to perform before *August* next, and desired her to help me to one to write the holy Book as it ought to be written: seeing I did all I could, and it seemed almost impossible for me to finish it as it is requisite. *Madami* promised to help me to
one

one to write the Book; and thereupon appeared to her (but unseen of E. K.) her Mother ..... *Madimi* said also, that she was now learning of Greek and Arabick, and the Syriah Tongue.

Mad. .;... *Mother I pray you let him have one to write his Book.*

Δ. I pray thee tell me *Madimi*, what was his name which yesterday tempted my friend and accused me most unduly and untruely to E. K. *as a murderer*, and hypocrite, and one that had injured a thousand.

Mad. ..... *His name was Panlacarp.*

Δ. Can the wicked Conjurers have their Devils to write Books at their commandments, and shall not an honest Christian Philosopher have the help of God his good Angels to write his holy Mysteries so greatly redounding to his Glory? And seeing you are the Mother of *Madimi* here, I beseech you tell me your name here: as the order of all our doings are distinctly and orderly noted.

Mother. ...... *I am of the word, and by the word:* I say, Seal up those things thou hast : And I my self will take charge of *Galvah to the end. Ad evitandum scandalum.*

Δ. Truth it is, it must grow to a great mislikeing grudge, that God should seem to have laid burdens on our shoulders, greater than we are able to bear: and then if we fall and faile under them, he would find a cause not to perform his promises made for carrying of those burdens.

Mother. ...... *Whatsoever is thy part, the same will I perform. I will put thy yoke (in this one thing) upon my shoulders.*

Δ. Will you then write it as I should have written it ?

.Mother ...... *I have said I will.*

Δ. Where shall I leave the Book ?

Mother. ...... *Leave it where you will :* your locks are no hindrance to us. *Even when the time cometh believe and you shall find it written.* **Our locks.**

Δ. You have eased my heart of a thousand pound weight.

Mother. ...... *Because ye shall not fall into error. Dost thou believe ?*

Δ. Yea verily.

Mother. ...... *Then verily will I do it.* Fides tua erit instrumentum operationis meæ; Erit, & videbitis, & nunquam peribit.

Galvah. ...... *One thing I will teach thee. The End is greater than the Beginning, or the Midst ; For the End is witnesse of them both: But they both cannot witnesse of the End*

Mother. ..;... *He that appeared yesterday is fast enough, now : Maiden, Say your lesson, when I am gone.*

Δ. I pray tell me your name.

Mad. ..... *Mother I pray you tell your name.*

Mother. ...... *I A M ; What will you more ?*

E. K. She flieth away like a fire. *Madimi* falleth down prostrate on her face a while.

Δ. Now I shall have leisure to follow my sute, and to do all Mr. *Gilberts* businesse.

Mad. ...... *My Mother will speak to the Queen for you shortly. Serve you God while I do pray.*

E K. She prayeth vehemently. Now she cometh near to us.

Madimi. ..;... *I pray you teach me to spell.* [She spake to E. K.

Mad. ...... This is ἐὰν μὴ φυλάττοις, **Nisi caveas isti,** οὗτ[] ὁ ἑταιρ[] τῦτο ἐργον ἀγαεπ̄ζαι, **amicis hoc opus** **subvertit, &c.** It is the Syrian Tongue you do not understand it. -- (to Δ.)
κόσμ[] μὲν γὰρ πρόθυμ[] τυγχάνη ὢν
fotte πειράζεται vel πείζεται
καὶ αὐτὸ τοσαυτὸν πίκαζεται
alicitur, vel abstrahitur
ὅτι κακτα ἀφιλκύετι φιλία

ὅσορε μὴ τινα αὐτῳ αφορμὴν παρῆσαι **That was with**
τῆς γὰρ ἀγάπης κομίζης καθασκευασθαι **Mr H and Lee**
ἵνα οι διὰ παντ[] ἀπολιπη. **his off red**
friendship as
he contested
after.

E. K. Unlesse you speak some Language which I understand, I will expresse no more of this Ghybbrish. Now she prayeth again. Now she is gone.

Δ. Bene-

Δ. Benedictus fit Deus, Pater Noster, Deus totius Consolationis, qui respexit afflictionem servuli sui,& in ipso puncto necessitatis meæ præstitit mihi auxilium ; ipse Solus Cordis Scrutator est & renum. Ipse est Lux mea,& Adjutor meus, & Susceptor meus est. In Domino speravi, & liberavit me ab angustia maxima propter gloriam Nominis sui, quod sit exaltatum & magnificatum nunc, & in sempiterna sectula. *Amen, Amen, Amen.*

Δ. My heart did throb oftentimes this day, and thought that *E. K.* did intend to absent himself from me, and now upon this warning I was confirmed, and more assured that it was so : Whereupon seeing him make *such haste to ride to Islington:* I asked him why he so hasted to ride thither: And I said, if it were to ride to Mr. *Harry Lee,* I would go thither also to be acquainted with him ; seeing now I had so good leasure , being eased of the book writing:

Fifty pound yearly to be provided for E. K. by John Dee. Then he said, that one told him the other day that the Duke did but flatter him, and told him other things, both against the Duke (or Palatine) and me, *&c.* I answered for the Duke and my self; and also said, that if the fourty pound *annuity* , which Mr. *Lee* did offer him, was the chief cause of his minde setling that way (contrary to many of his *former promises to me*) that then I would assure him of fifty pound yearly, and would do my best by following of my sute, to bring it to passe as soon as (possibly) I could, and thereupon did make him promise upon the Bible. Then *E. K.* again upon *the same Bible did swear unto me constant friendship, and never to forsake me :* And moreover said, that unlesse this had so faln out, he would have gone beyond the Seas, taking ship at *New-Castle* within *eight dayes next :* And so we plight our faith each to other, taking each other by the hands upon these points of *brotherly , and friendly fidelity during life ,* which Covenant I beseech God to turn to this honour, glorie, and service, and the comfort of our brethren (his Children) here in earth.

Tuesday, *Julii* 2. *à meridie, Circa Horam.* 2.

Δ. While I was writing of Letters to Mr. *Adrian Gilbert* , into *Devonshire* , *Madini* appeared by me in the study, before *E. K.* sitting in the Chair, first on the ground, then up higher in the aire ; and I said; How is the minde of Mr. *Secretary* toward me, me thinketh it is alienated marvellously.

The Lord Treasurer, and Secretary Walsingham. Mad. .... *Those that love the world, are hated of God. The* Lord Treasurer *and he are joyned together, and they hate thee.* I heard them when they both said, thou wouldst go mad shortly : *Whatsoever they can do against thee, assure thy self of. They will shortly lay a bait for thee; but eschew them.*

Δ. Lord have mercy upon me : what bait; (I beseech you) and by whom?
Mad. .... *They have determined to search thy house : But they stay untill the Duke be gone.*
Δ. What would they search it for?
Mad. .... *They hate the Duke,* (both) *unto the death.*
Δ. And why?

Mad. .... *Take heed that you deal uprightly.* ..... [*She spake to* E. K.]

E. K. God the Creator be my witnesse of my upright dealing, with, and toward him, (meaning Δ·) ever since my last coming to him.

E. K. his second oath. Mad. .... *It is good to prevent diseases.*

E. K. By this book (taking the Bible in his hand) I swear that *I* do carry as faithfull a minde to him, as any man can, ever since my last coming.

Mad..... *Look unto the kinde of people about the Duke : and the manner of their diligence.*
Δ. What mean you by that ? his own people mean you? or who ?
Mad. .... *The espies.*
Δ. Which be those?
Mad. .... *All, there is not one true.*
Δ. You mean the *English* men.
Mad. .... *You are very grosse, if you understand not my sayings.*
Δ. Lord, what is thy counsel to prevent all?
Mad. .... *The speech is general,* The wicked shall not prevail.
Δ. But will they enter to search my house, or no?
Mad. .... *Immediately after the Duke his going they will.*
Δ. To what intent? what do they hope to finde?
Mad. .... *They suspect the Duke is inwardly* a Traytor.
Δ. They can by no means charge me, no not so much as of a Trayterous thought.
Mad. .... *Though thy thoughts be good , they cannot comprehend the doings of the wicked. In*

Trust them not. *summe ,* they hate thee. *Trust them not : they shall go about shortly to offer thee friendship : But be thou a worm in a heap of straw.*
Δ. I pray you expound that parable.

Mad. .... *A*

Mad. .... *A heap of straw being never so great, is no waight upon a worm, notwithstanding every straw hindreth the worms passages. See them, and be not seen of them, dost thou understand it?*

Δ. I pray you make more plain your counsel.

Mad. .... *My counsel is plain enough.*

Δ. When, I pray you, is the Duke likely to go away?

Mad. .... *In the middle of* August.

Δ. If in the midst of *August* he will go, and then our practises be yet in hand, what shall be done with such our furniture is prepared; and standing in the Chamber of practise

Mad. .... *Thou hast no faith.*

His going standeth upon the determinated purpose of God. *He is your friend greatly, and intendeth to do much for you. He is prepared to do thee good, and thou art prepared to do him ser-* A. L. *vice.* Many men purpose, but one setteth in order.   Service.

Δ. As concerning *Adrian Gilbert*, what pleaseth you to say of him, and his intended voyage.

Mad. .... *He is not in the true faith.*

Δ. How hath it been said, then, That he should be the setter forth of God, his faith and religion among the infidels.

Mad. .... *That is a mystery.*

Δ. Whether shall it be good, that the Duke resort hither oft, or tarry for the most part at his house at *London.*

Mad. .... *Humane policie cannot prevail. As many as are not faithfull in these causes, shall die a most miserable death: and shall drink of sleep everlasting. As in one root there are many divisions, so in the stem and branches are many separations*

Δ. Give some more light (I beseech you) to the particular understanding.

Mad. .... *The fire that kindleth all these, and wherein thy live is One, forming them according to (whatsoever) the substance whereupon they are grounded. So by the lesse you may prove the greater: That as in particular, so likewise generally, All emanations are from one. In the first workmanship lieth secret in one unknown: And is sealed, and therefore it hath an end. The son through the Circles and Massie body, The heart in the body, The intelligence in the inward with, The son* The heart. *from his own § entre spreadeth out the beams of his limited virtue, The Hart life to two: and yet* The heart. the Centre *of life to the whole body, understanding quickneth the minde; that minde I speak of* The minde *putteth on a fiery shape. It followeth therefore, that every thing (what substance soever) hath a* nutteth on a *Centre: From the which the Circumfluent beams of his proper power do proceed. When these* fiery shape. *are perfectly known: Then are things seen in their true kinde. I speak this to prove, that the good* Angel *of man, which is the external Centre of the Soul, doth carry with him the internal Character of that thing whereof he seeketh to be a Dignifier; within the which doth lie secret; the Conjunction and Separation of the proportion of their times, betwixt the soul and body of man. O happy (therefore) is that Soul, which beholdeth the glory of his dignification, and is partaker with him that is his keeper. This known unto men, the thicknesse of the earth doth not hinder their speeches; neither can the darknesse of the lowest aire obscure, or make dark the sharpnesse of their eyes. This Character, (at his next coming hither) shall be made manifest unto him.*

E. K. He sheweth a bloudy hand, holding a bloudy Crosse *with letters on it, like our holy letters.*

Δ. I beseech you, how shall his provision of money from home serve his turn, or how shall he here have help for his charges bearing?

Mad. .... *Your words make me a Childe. Those that fish for Dolphins do not stand upon the* Note the form *ground. Those that sit in Counsel call not in the harvest people, nor account not their works. He* of a child. *that standeth above the Moon, seeth greater things then the earth: Is it not said, The Lord will provide? I stand above the Moon, for that I dispose his life from above the disposition of the Moon. To ask what Jacob his servants did, was a folly; because their master was blessed: A greater question to ask how blessed he was, then to ask how many sheep he had.*

Δ. I am desirous to know what you meant by saying, That my words made you a Childe.

Mad. .... *Because you ask me Childish questions. His good Angel shall reveal his Character unto* Reverence to *him, and thou shalt see it, [pointing to* E. K.*] But take heed thou say truely; And use great re-* good Angels. *verence, or else the feet that love thee shall carry thy Carkas out of the doors. If he carry it* adum divi-*upon him, it shall be a token of the Covenant between him and God.* nium.
Perhaps em-
Δ. The image, or similitude thereof (mean you) made in pure Gold. milled.

Mad. .... *I. .... So those that shall see his Standards with that signe in them shall perish utterly.*

Δ. You mean, if the same be painted, or otherwise wrought in his Banners and Penons, &c.

Mad. .... *Let him use it as a Covenant, between God and him.*

Δ. How shall he frame it in Gold, solid-wise, or Lamine-wise?

Madd. .... *His own Angel shall reveal it.*

Δ. But

Δ. Becauſe it hath been ſaid,that in the beginning of our Country troubles we ſhould bé packing hence into his Country ; What token ſhall we have of that time approaching,or at hand ?

Mad. ...... *Tour watchword is told you before : When it is ſaid unto you,* Venite, *&c.*

Δ. But (I beſeech you) to be ready againſt that watchword, hearing what is to be done, as concerning our wives and children into his Country.

Mad. ...,.. *Miraculous is thy care (O God) upon thoſe that are thy choſen, and wonderful are the wayes that thou haſt prepared for them. Thou ſhalt take them from the fields, and harbour them at home. Thou art merciful unto thy faithful and hard to the heavy-hearted. Thou ſhalt cover their legs with Bootes, and brambles ſhall not prick them : Their hands ſhall be covered with the skins of Beaſts that they may break their way through the hedges. Thy Bell ſhall go before them as a watch and ſure Direction : The Moon ſhall be clear that they may go on boldly.* Peace be *amongſt you.*

B. K. He is now gone away in a fire.   *Æterno Deo noſtro, ſit Laus Honor, & Gloria in ſeculorum ſacula.* Amen.

Thurſday *Julii* 4. *hora* 11. *ante Meridiem.* 1583.

Note. Δ. When I came home yeſterday from the Court , and from *London,* and from the Lord *Laskie,* I found that E. K. was purpoſed to ride forth of Town, and intended to be a-way (as he expreſly told me) five dayes : Certain Companions and his acqua'ntance having ſo appointed with him,ſome tarrying for him in *Mortlucke,* and ſome at *Brainford* (as was perceived this day afterward, and as he confeſſed unto me.) Whereupon I thought good to ſignifie ſo much unto the Lord *Laskie* who meant to come and refreſh himſelf at my houſe, as he was wont before ; either this day, or within two or three dayes after : Who alſo de-lighted in E. K. his company, &c. Hereupon about the time of E. K. his riſing I wrote theſe lines, intending to ſend them preſently to the Lord *Laskie,* that word might be returned of his intent before E. K. ſhould ride, I meaning and hoping to perſwade E. K. to tarry ſo long, and upon ſuch reſpect.

Nobiliſſime Princeps, in reditu, noſtrum Edwardum inveni, facie quidem leta : ſed itineri ta-men,ut dicit, quinque dierum, ſe accingentem : Hocque matutino tempore abitum vel iter iſtud ingredi molitur ; Reverſurus (ut affirmat) poſt quinque dies. Quid ſit ipſa veritas, novit ille qui verus & Omnipotens Deus eſt noſter. Hoc volui, iſto mane ſummo, vobis ſignificare, ut, quid factu optimum ſit, Cogitetis : De aliis, ſuo tempore,

Vaſtræ Celſitudinis fideliſſimus Clientulus

Julii 4. 1563.   *Joannes Dee.*

This Letter being now written, and not yet folded up, my friend E. K. was ready and came out of his Chamber into my Study ; and I told him,that I was even now ſending word to the Prince *Laskie* of his rideing out, and return after five dayes ; and ſo ſhewed him the Letter : who when he came to the phraſe, *Quid ſit ipſa veritas,* he was ſamewhat offended, ſaying, What ſecret meaning hath this, *upon ſome of your two former conference ?* Truly (ſaid I) even ſuch as the circumſtance of the Letter doth import, that is ; Whereas you ſaid that you intended to return within five dayes, or at the ſame dayes end, it is uncertain whether you will, or ſhall, return later or ſooner : and therefore *Quid ſit ipſa veritas* of your return, or intent to return, onely God doth know. He would by no meanes admit that my ſincere expoſition, but ſeemed ſuſpitious of ſome other undue conſtructions of thoſe former words ; thereupon I took the Letter and tore it in three pieces, and ſent none : But in my mind re-ferred all to God his diſpoſition, aſſuring my ſelf *of God his moſt conſtant proceeding in his own affairs.* Shortly after ſaid E. K. to me, Certainly here is a ſpiritual Creature in my right

Sowle. ſhoulder, who ſenſibly ſaith to me, Come away : So (ſaid I) did one ſay to *Sowle,* when *Evil ſpirits.* they would have had *him away* to have drowned him, whom I ſtayed in this Study by force, *and ſo hindered the Devil* of his purpoſe then ; as appeareth by *that unhappy man* yet alive. Nay ſaid E. K. they have told me that if I tarry here,I ſhall be hanged ; and if I go with this Prince he will cut off my head,and that you mean not *to keep promiſe* with me ; And therefore if I might have a thouſand pound to tarry, yea a Kingdom, I cannot : Therefore *I releaſe*

Fifty pound *you of your promiſe of* 50 *pounds yearly Stipend* to me,and you need not doubt but God will de-*yearly ſtipend.* fend you and proſper you, and can of the very ſtones raiſe up children to *Abraham* : And a-*E. K. his wife.* gain *I cannot abide my wife, I love her not, nay I abhor her* ; and there in the houſe I am miſli-ked, becauſe I favour her no better. To theſe, ſuch his words ſpoken in great pangs and diſquietneſſe of mind, I repoſed and ſaid, That theſe his doings and ſayings were not of God, and that by my whole proceeding he might perceive what confidence I repoſed in his dealing with the ſpiritual, our friends, ſeeing even to the uttermoſt penny (and more than my ability ſerved unto conveniently) I laid out ſtill about the .... ming of ſuch things, as were by me to be done, &c. Well, on the ſudden, down he went ; upon his Mare, and away toward *Brainford.*

Brainford. After whose going, my Wife came up into my Study, and I said, *Jane,* this man is mervailously out of quiet against his Wife, for her friends their bitter reports against him behind his back, and her silence thereat, &c. He is gone, said I, but I beseech the Almighty God to guide him and to defend him from danger and shame; I doubt not but God will be merciful to him, and bring him at length to such order, as he shall be a faithful servant unto God, &c. *[margin: E. K. his wives friends.]*

Note within three hours after, came E. K. up my Study staires unbooted, for he was come in a boat from *Brainford.* When I saw him I was very glad inwardly: But I remained writing of those Records as I had yet to write of Tuesdayes last actions. I have lent my Mare out (said he) and so am returned. It is well done said I, and thereupon he sate down in the chair by my Table where he was wont to sit: And it was ten of the clock then. He took up in his hand the Books which I had brought from *London* of the L. *Laskie,* written to him in his commendations, &c. And as he was looking earnestly on them, a Spiritual Creature did put the Book on the outside of the parchment cover, divers times; and once would have taken it out of his hands: Divers times I heard the strokes my self; At length he said, I see here the handsome Maiden *Madimi,* and have done a pretty while. Then said I to him, Why told you me no sooner? Whereupon I took paper purposely to Note what should seem Note-worthy as followeth.

Δ. Mistresse *Madimi,* you are welcome in God, for good, as I hope; What is the cause of your coming now?

Mad. ...... *To see how you do.*

Δ. I know you see me often, and I see you onely by faith and imagination.

Mad. ..... [Pointing to E. K.] *That sight is perfecter then his.*

Δ. O *Madimi,* Shall I have any more of these grievous pangs?

Mad. ...... *Curst Wives, and great Devils are sore Companions.*

Δ. In respect of the Lord Treasurer, Mr. Secretary, and Mr. *Rawly,* I pray you, What worldly comfort is there to be looked for? Besides that I do principally put my trust in God.

Mad. ...... *Madder will staine, wicked men will offend, and are easie to be offended.*

Δ. And being offended will do wickedly, to the persecution of them that meane simply.

Mad. ...... *Or else they were not to be called wicked.*

Δ. As concerning *Alb. Laskie* his Pedigree, you said your Sister would tell all.

Mad. ...... *I told you more then all your Dog painters and Cat painters can do.*

Δ. You spoke of *William Laskie* and Sir *Richard Laskie* his brother, of which *William* going into *France,* and then into *Denmarke* : and his marriage into *Poland,* came this *Albert Laskie,* now Paladine of *Soradia,* &c.

Mad. ...... *Those were two pretty men for me to meddle withal. When you set your selves together, and agree together, I will make all agree together.*

E. K. Will you *Madimi* lend me a hundred pound for a fortnight?

Mad. ...... *I have swept all my money out of doors.*

Δ. As for money we shall have that which is necessary when God seeth time.

Mad. ...... *Hear me what I say. God is the unity of all things, Love is the unity of every Congregation (I mean true and perfect love.) The World was made in the love of the father. You were redeemed in the love of the Father and the Son. The Spirit of God is (yet) the love of his Church. Yet (I say): For after it doth Triumph, it is not called a Church nor a Congregation : But a Fruitful Inheritance and a Perfect Body in Christ. Take the love of the Father from the World, and it perisheth. Take the love of our Redemption away, and we are dead. (I will not offend) put your instead of our. Take the light of the Holy Ghost, which is the love of the Father and the Son from the Church, and it withereth. Even so take love from amongst you, and you are members of the Devil ; Therefore it is said unto you Diligite ad invicem. For love is the Spirit of God uniting and knitting things together in a laudable proportion. What dost thou hunt after ? speak man, What dost thou hunt after ?* *[margin: Δ. we use to call it Ecclesia Triumphans. Note. The Angels were not redeemed.]*

[This was said to E. K. upon some secret judgement of *Madimi* in him.

E. K. I hunt after nothing.

The love of God breedeth faith; Faith bringeth forth (on the one side) Hope ; and (on the other side) the workes of Charity. Dost thou love God ? Seekest thou to be among his Elect ? Why dost thou not (therefore) love those things that are of God ? Herein thou shewest the want of faith; Herein are thy bragging words confounded ; for thou sayest, No man can accuse thee of evil. But thou hast no faith because thou hast no hope. Wilt thou say, that thou hast faith ? Shew it me by thy love : Whosoever (therefore) loveth not God, is accursed. Thou lovest not God, Lo, behold, thou breakest his Commandments. Oughtest thou not to love him ? And hast thou not faith through the love in God ? Truely thou oughtest so to do. Wilt thou let me see thy hope on this side ; Let thy workes stand on the other side. And shew thy self to have faith that therein thou mayest love God, and be beloved of him : But if thou hast none of these, thou hast hate. If thou hate God, the reward *[margin: 1. Faith. 2. Hope. 3. Charity.]*

reward thereof is great ; but the greatnesse is unquenchable fire.   Whosoever followeth not the Commandments, hateth God ;   If sin be the breach of the. Commandments, &c.   Dost thou love Silver and Gold ?   The one is a Thief, the other is a Murderer.   Wilt thou seek honour ?

E. K. No.

Note this came to passe Anno 1589. when he was made Baron of Bohemia Anno 1590. So did Cain.   *But thou hast a Just God that loveth thee ;   Just and vertuous men that delight in thee ; Therefore be thou vertuous : For thou shalt tread the World under thy feet : I promise thee, I have driven the Skullen-drab out of our Kitchen long ago.*

Δ. Do you mean worldly covetousnesse ?

Mad. ...... *Yea, and the first heavenly covetousnesse.*

Carma geta Barman.

Δ. I beseech you, what is that to say ?

Mad. ...... *Veni ex illo Barma.*

E. K. Felt and saw a spiritual Creature go out of his right thigh.

Mad. ...... *Where are thy 14 Companions ?*

Bar. ...... *They dwell here.*

Δ. [He that was come out, seemed a great handsome man with a Sachel of a Dogs skin by his side, and a Cap on his head, &c.]

Δ. O the hand of the Highest hath wrought this.

Mad. ......, *Venite Tenebra, fugite Spiritu meo.*

E. K. Here appear 14 of divers evil-favoured shapes : some like Monkies, some like Dogs, some very hairy monstruous Men, &c. They seemed to scratch each other by the face. These seem to go about *Madimi* and say, *Gil de pragma kures helech.*

Δ. What is that to say ?

Mad. ...... *Volumus hic in Nostris habitare.*

Δ. Quæ sunt illa vestra ?

E. K. One of them said ... *Habemus hominem istum Demicilium nostrum.*

The casting out, and utter displacing of 15 wicked spirits, &c. Mad. ...... *The vengeance of God is a two-edged Sword, and cutteth the rebellious wicked ones in pieces. The hand of the Lord is like a strong oak, when it falleth it cutteth in sunder many bushes. The light of his eyes expell darknesse, and the sweetnesse of his mouth keepeth from corruption. Blessed are those whom he favoureth, and great is their reward ; Because you came hither with-* out licence and seek to overthrow the liberty of God his Testament, and the light wherewithal he stretcheth unto the end, and for because you are accursed it is said, I will not suffer mine to be overthrown with temptation, though he were led away, *Behold I bring back again.*

Depart unto the last Cry :   Rest with the Prince of Darknesse there is none.   Amen, go you thither.   Et signabo vos ad finem.

E. K. He sealed them all in the forehead : the 14 and their principal, their sealing was as if they had been branded. They sunk all 15 downward through the floore of the Chamber, and there came a thing like a wind & pluckt them by the feet away.

E. K. Methinketh *I* am lighter than *I* was ; and I seem to be empty, and to be returned from a great amasing ;   for this fortnight I do not well remember what I have done or said,

Mad. ...... *Thou art eased of a great burden .... Love God, Love thy Friends, Love thy Wife.*

E. K. Now cometh one with a red Crosse in his hand and leadeth her away, and so they vanished. We prayed the Psalm of thanksgiving 14 of *Roffensis* for E. K. his deliverance from *Barma* and his 14 Companions. *Amen.*

Δ.   first papers, E. K. Sal.
        by   appeard often to him, whipping
        before   as 6. or 7. miles distant from
        him   think that the blessed   *Jubanladace*
        had been sent   to have said somewhat unto us of his
Charge (the Prince *Laskie*) But I found in the end that it was a token that the Princce *Laskie* was pensively careful of us , and that his good Angel was his witnesse and message, by that token his peculiar Carafter as is before taught.

Omnis Spiritus Laudet Deum nostrum Unum & Trinum. Amen,
Sequitur liber Tertiarius Sexti.

                                                                                                   LIBER,

LIBER PEREGRINATIONIS PRIMÆ:

Videlicet

A Mortlaco Anglia,
Ad Craconiam Polomia.

Saturday, *Septemb.* 21. 1583.   *Die Sancti Matthæi.*

WE departed from *Mortlack*, about three of the Clock after noon: The Lord *Albert Lasky*, (*Vayvode* of *Siradia*, in *Polonia*) meeting me on the water, as we had appointed: And so brought night to *London*; and in the dead of the night, by Wherries, we went to *Greenwich* to my friend *Goodman Fern* the Potter his house; Where we refreshed our selves, and thither came a great Tylt-boat from *Graves end* to take us in, (by appointment of me and Mr. *Stanley*) to go to our ships, which we had caused to ly seven, or eight mile beyond *Graves end*. To which ships we came on Sunday morning by Sun rise: In the greater of them (being a dubble Fly-boat of *Denmark*) my Lord *Lskie*, I, and E. K. with my Wife and Children, &c. went: And in another ship (by me also hired for this passage) went some of my Lord his men, two horse,&c. that ship was a Boyer, a pretty ship. With little winde we straight-way hoysed sayl, and began our voyage in the ship.

This 22. day we were in great danger of perishing (on the sands, called the Spits) about midnight: We had (by force of winde contrary) anchored by them, and the Anchor came home, no man perceiving it, till the ship was ready to strike on the sands. Then, upon great diligence and pollicy used by our Marriners in hoysing sayl, and cutting our Cable, (to leave our shote anker) and committing our selves to the hands of God, and *most earnestly praying for a prosperous winde*: It pleased the Almighty, and most mercifull God, *suddenly* to change the winds, which served us to bear from the sands, and to recover *Quinborrough,* back again. *There arose great raging winde, N.B, almost.*

The 23. day (being Munday) we came to the mouth and entrance of *Quinburrough Creek,* or Haven. And as we made to land in small Fisher-boats, the Lord *Lskie,* my Wife and Children in one boat, and I, with E. K. *Marie, Elizabeth,* and *John Crokar,* in another, it fell out, that at the ships side, our Fisher-boat his sayl-yard and sayl was entangled on the Mayn-yard of the Fly-boat (being stroke down) so that, in our setting from the ships side, the top of our Boat being fast above, and the windes and stream carrying the Boat off below, it inclined so much on the one side, that the one half of the Fisher boat (well near) was in the water, and the water came so in (by the intangling before specified, not easily to be undone, or loosed) that my Lord, my Wife, and all that saw us thought that of necessity our Boat must sink, and so, we to have perisht. But God in his providence and mercy had greater.....of us, so that we became clear; the Boat half full of water, so that we sat wet to the knees, and the water came still beating the billow of the Sea came still beating in more and more: And in this mean trouble; one of our two Boat-men, had lost his long Oare out of the Boat into the water; and so not onely we lacked the help of that Oare, but also by reason they would have followed the winde and ebb, for that Oar, (contrary to our course in hand, and not able to become by) with much adoe we constrained them with the sayl, our one Oare, and the Rudder to make such shift as they could to get to *Quinborrough* Town: And in the mean space E. K. with a great Gantlet did empty most part of the water out of the Boat, else it must needs have sunk by all mans reason. At length (to be brief) we came to the Town side, up the crooked *Creek;* where, when as the Master of our ship would have taken me out in his arms (standing in the water with his Boots) he fell with me in the water, where I was foul arrayed in the water and Oase. God be praised for ever, that all that great danger was ended with so small grief, or hurt. *Or The evident help of God at the very minute of danger deadly.*

At Quinborrough.

Wednesday, *Septemb.* 25. *Circa* 3. *à Meridie, jam pleno mari.*

Δ. Oravimus ad Deum, ejus implorabamus auxilium, Cortina statim apparuit.   Oravi denuo solus, pro auxilio, tempore necessitatis : Sex pedum altitudine apparebat unus, in aere, quasi altera ex parte nubis, inter E. K. et illum interpositæ.

B. K. Ego illum cognosco.

.... *Tu babes causam me cognoscendi, & illum qui me misit, vel jam non vixisses.*

E. K. Videtur esse Michael.

F

Δ. Gratias

Δ. Gratias agimus Creatori nostro, qui bonum, potentem & fidelem ministrum suum miserie ad nostram protectionem tempore necessitatis nostræ.

Mich. ..... *Loquor de tribus rebus, de meipso & illo qui me misit : De vobis, respectu illius quod estis, & de servitio Dei quod futurum est. O vos potestates Cæli & terræ, colligite vos in simul, respicite Deum vestrum : Considerate beneficia ejus, an non vos colligavit simul ? Et concatenavit vos in seipso? An non estis glorificati respectu officii vestri, ad quod præstantum potenter assignati estis, in voluntate ejus, qui glorificat seipsum. Ecce quomodo vosmet dedidistis principi tenebrarum : vel quare vestri principes contendunt contra altissimum : & colligitis vosmet in simul ad contendendam contra ipsum, qui est potentissimus, vel illum velletis subjugare, cujus arma sunt super omnem fortitudinem : Quo modo audetis contendere cum ejus fortitudine ? Vel qua est causa quod tam impii esse velitis ? Sed ita oportet esse : quia quia sigilavit gubernationem, & in vestras manus dedit violam destructionis. Sed* Government. *date locum fini vostro : Quia in ejus fortitudine dispersi eritis : Et omnium rerum conclusionis ostia vestra debent esse aperta. Ne mirentur servi Dei, de fortitudine temptationis : Quia magna est potestas impii & hiantis Leonis, quando illi est cum sigillo tradita. Ne dedignemini, hac hora, scio vestram gubernationem per illum. Ecce clavis justitiæ aperta mihi est. Nihilominus vestra adhuc erit major iniquitas, & vestrum regnum erit dispersum in ejus potenti superbia. Quam magnus est* Let the Forkots light. Michael. Gabriel. *Sathax qui resistit fortitudini Dei ? Quam magna, igitur, debet esse vestra humilitas, quæ debet vel superare vel mori. Sed vobis sic dixit Dominus. Aperiant venti ora sua, & rabientes aquæ profunda & potentia guttura. In omnes partes navium vestrarum. Aperiat terra os suum, & dicat, quod devorare vellet. Tamen non prævalebunt Quia tibi addam (inquit Dominus) qui es fortitudo mea, Potentiam meam prævalescentem : Et vos eritis duæ flammæ ignis, imo, ignis potentis suffocantis ps totius Malitiæ. Idcirco, vobis bene sit : Quia inimicus est fortissimus, ubi præda est maxima. Mementote, quod Homines sitis. Mementote, quod terra sitis. Me-* Hath provided you. *mentote, quod Peccatores. Mementote, quid eratis, & ne tradatis oblivioni quid estis. In illo enim vivitis qui omnia in sua habet subjectione. Sed ille, qui cum illo est, Crucifixus ad gloriam,* Finis nostri servitii. *debet in medio mortalitatis componere se ipsum ad Immortalem Potentiam. Servi Dei, semper prævaluerunt : Sed semper per Adversitates. Qui non est de hoc mundo, vos præparavit, Nihilo minus debetis ea implere, quæ ipse providit. Quod mundus possit fieri novus, &* Lapped up. *ipse agnosci. Potens ipse est, Potens est ille, Aquila illa quæ cooperit magnum montem alis suis. Sed potentior est ejus fortitudo qui numerat stellas, & montes colligit : Nam quicquid ipse loquitur, est veritatis ignis : Et est simul Potentia & Actus, in immediata proportione. Etiam ipse qui fecit Orbem, hominem in simul compegit, & omnia operatus est, Omnia ipse existens. Ipse est qui vobis præceptum dedit : Et ego vobis dico, Respicite de puncto in punctum, ad medium Cæli, & per Circulum terræ : Considerate omnia in uno, & unum in omnibus. Ponderate, vel per rationem numerentur, vel mensurate quemadmodum Salomon fecit, vel quemadmodum Adamo erat con esse (quod nunc non potes sed facies) Tunc conclude, Observant omnia cursum suum : sed verbum Domini res est. ..... sempiternum. Amate Deum quia Justus est. Amate vos invicem quia. ..... justificati. Observate mandatum Dei quia est mensura Justitiæ.*

E. K. *Jam venit alter ad illum, cum Corona in Capite, quasi. . . . & accipis gladium Michaelis.*

Coronatus ..... Ecce magna est fortitudo Dei, & Prævalebit.

Mich. ...... *Idcirco est benedictus Deus, vos justificati & nos sanctificati.*

E. K. *Iam faciebant signum crucis flammeæ tribus vicibus, & si nauta noster cum nova Anchora à Londino hodie redierit nonne est consilium, quod statim hinc navigemus, si ita ille velit,* &c.

E. K. Redeunt.

Of worldlings. *Coronatus.* ..... Ego sum de Cælo : non respicio terram ; Nihilominus terra per Cælos vivit. Sequimini vos cursum Terrenorum. Præparate vos semen, Nos volumus, (O Domine) in te, esse parati, cum incremento. Vestra Cura non potest prævalere, quia vestri Inimici sunt fortes : sed quare dedecore afficior, cum sale terrestrium vanitatum ? Destruat una vanitas, aliam : Ast Electi prævalebunt in fortitudine, contra illum Principem Vanitatis, & Regem stultorum omnium. Quia Deus noster est sapiens, Judicia ejus imperscrutabilia, Patientia immensurabilis. Laborate vos, & Nos gubernabimus.

E. K. Jam recedunt.

Vox. ..... *Ne disputetis ulterius cum Deo : Victoria vestra erit.*

Δ. Magnificetur nomen Dei nostri solius omnipotentis & optimi. *Amen.*

Thursday 26. Of September we went to ship, and lay in it all night at Anker.

Friday 27. Of September we sayled from *Quinburrough,* and so by the lands end into the main Sea, N. E.

Saturday 28. Of September we fell on *Holland* Coast, and none of our Marriners, Mafter, nor Pilot knew the Coaft: and therefore to the Main Sea again, w'th great fear and danger, by reafon we could fcarcely get off from that dangerous Coaft, the winde was fo fcarce for that purpofe.

Sunday 29. Of September we came into the *Briel-haven*, and there were like to ftrike on ground: at length we came to an Ankor, and lay in fhip all night.

Monday 30. Of September we landed, and went into the *Briel*.

Briela, Octobris 2. *Mane Hora* 9. *Die Mercurii.*

E. K. Nihil apparet in Lapide, neque Cortina, neque aliud quid. Oremus conftanter, &c. Apparet Domus magna cum multis pinnaculis, valde elegantibus· Et paviinentum videtur effe multis innatis lapidibus diftinctum & videntur multi effe gradus per quos afcenditur: & videtur effe area viridis ex dextra parte, & ex altera parte effe vallis, & rivulus ex alia. Pars quæ verfus folem eft, videtur quafi noviter reformata· Et circa introitum eft rotundum quoddam ædificium: feneftræ non funt fimiles noftris fed quafi effent Templorum feneftræ·

A. L. *Dixit quod videtur effe illa arx Regia, quæ Cracoviæ eft.*

E. K. Subito defcendit ignis & per totum lapidem apparet· Jam venit Cortina folita ante domum iftam.

Vox. Garil zed mafch, ich na gel galabt gemp gal noch Enbanladan.

E. K. Jubanladaa. h jam apparet fupra Chryftalium: & Chryftallus videtur effe permagnus.

Jub. Deus numeravit & dies tuos & pofteritatem. [E. K. *Refpicit* A. L.]

E. K. Jam receffit a Chryftallo verfus caput ipfius A. L.

Jub. Et a pectine tuo non cadet Capillus non numeratus. Omnia bene fe habent. [*Hoc dixit de ftatu rerum* A. L. *apud* Lask.] *Ecce bibet vim refiftendi: At contra legionem pugno.*

Δ. Perditio te novit, & numeravit annos tuos, & incipit effe fortis: Quia illi eft Poteftas *Antichrifti.* data, Infernus aperit os fuum contra vos, quia fciunt, quod vos glorificati eritis in Deo. Ego vici quintum figillum, & mihi jam refiftitur in fexto. Quæ Deus facit, non participant cum humano judicio. Ecce nunc Difcipulos fuos congregavit, & docet. O Cœlum & terra quam magnæ funt miferiæ, quæ vexabunt unum & polluent alterum? *Quia b ni Angeli cadent cum illo & Cæli Chriftum metuent.* Sed illi ad tempus cadent, non in perpetuum.

Δ. Salvo judicio Ecclefiæ Catholicæ Orthodoxæ, videtur mihi quod Job de ejufmodi Angelorum timore, five cafu, & reftitutione, five purgatione prophetavit, *Cap.* 41. ubi etiam addit de miraculis ejufdem: *Sub ipfo erant radii folis, & fternet fibi aurum quafi lutum.* Antea dixerat. Cum fublatus fuerit timebunt Angeli, & territi purgabuntur, &c.

Δ. O Deus quam terribile futurum eft tempus illud, &c.

Jub. ...... *Scriptæ Dei myfteria, & Deo gratiæ agatis pro veftro falvo ftatu: Quia mare illic abundabat contra vos, & multi perierunt. Ejus potentia prævalebat, & commutavit veftrum curfum in locum illis incognitum: quia ab illis non erat expectatus. Sed fugite ab hac terra, quia Maledictio Dei eft fuper illam. Cum illo eft una veritas: Ille qui in duabus viis erat, non placet Deo. Qui ad finem ufque perdurat, quiefcit cum gaudio. Sed ille qui pedem non ponit inter Scorpiones non poteft intrare fuper Gozlach.*

Δ. Quid hoc?

Jub. ...... *Gaudium in vera fapientia.*

Jub. .... *Hoc noftrum eft Manna, quo alimur. Sed ego fum fanctificatus per Creationem, Inftitutionem & ex Divina voluntate. Idcirco vos fanctifico: non cum mea propria fanctificatione, fed illius Juftitia, qui meam originem fanctificat. Eftote Montes in Fide, fed quafi infantes patientia. Facite quod Juftum eft, & ne oblivi.ni tradatis veftram Juftitiam.*

E. K. Infinitæ quafi locuftæ vel Araneæ cum faciebus humanis illum circumvolitant, & quafi ignem in illum evomunt·

Jub. ...... *Et levavit fe contra vos.* [*Tollendo Crucem fuam.*]

Jub. ...... *Fiat Juftitia ejus.*

E. K. Jam avolant præcipites, & quafi deorfum ruentes·

Jub. ...... *Cavete a ftramine: quia incenfum, tota domum incendit.*

Δ. Quem fenfum hic perpendemus nos: Myfticum ne, an materialem?

Jub....He-

Jub. ...... *Hominum fragiliſſimarum. Diabolus cum illis fraudulenter operatur : magna eſt merces quietis, Sed qui apperit fores contentioni, intromittit Serpentem. Maledicti ſunt invidi : Quia illi ſunt benedicti qui ſe mutuo diligunt. Pax inter vos ſit ; quia eſt neceſſaria. Quia pacis inimici ſunt potentes contra vos.*

E. K. Jam loquendo, videtur minor & minor paulatim fieri.

Δ. De noſtro deceſſu ex Anglia quid tandem jam Regina & sui conſiliarii ſtatuerunt ?

Jub. ...... *Aperit os ſuum, ſed liquor non eſt ſatis frigidus. Jam eſt intus calida, neq̃ reſtingui poteſt.* Corda ſui populi do fall away. Her arms are weakened, her legs weaker, her shooes are full of sorrow.

E. K. The furious Monſters aſſaile him again.

Jub. ...... *Quis eſt, qui poteſt vivere, ſi tranſgrediatur preceptum Dei ? Vel quid de illis judicare vel's,* whom God imputeth ſin unto ?

E. K. They aſſaile him again, and he putteth his Croſſe toward them.

Jub. ...... Their miſery beginneth, and ſhall have no end, till be that ſitteth here do end it.

E. K. The Monſters aſſaile him ſtill.

Jub. ..... *The wall muſt be broken down, and then ſhall It be ſaid.* Happy art thou which haſt dwelt amongſt us. But if thou live righteouſly, and aſcend the ſlippery mountain, Then ſhall God be merciful to them for thy ſake. Becauſe thou mayeſt be beloved, where thou art now deſpiſed, and haſt vanquiſhed thy enemies, with the truth of vertue. He that entred into the loweſt hell, and ſhed his blood for your ſins, be merciful unto you, and give you peace ; which is the ſpirit of Patience, that you may live, not like men, but as thoſe that do ſeparate themſelves from the world, to the true contemplation of God his mercies.

Anglia bene erit propter Δ. ex mera Dei miſericordia.

E. K. Jam intrat in Caput, *A. L.* cum flamma ignis.

Δ. Omnis laus, honor, & gloria ſit Deo noſtro Omnipotenti vivo & vero. *Amen.*

Thurſday, Octobris 3. We came from *Briel* to *Roterodám* in a Hoy of *Amſterdam*, to go within land, here we lay all night.

Friday, Octobris 4. We came to *Tergowd hora* 3 *à meridie* : where we lay within the Town in the Ship.

Saturday, Octobris 5. We came by *Harlem* to *Amſterdam*, and lay before the Town all night in the Ship.

Tueſday Octob. 8. We ſailed from *Amſterdam* to *Encuſen,* and *Edmond Hilton* went with my goods by Sea toward *Dansk.*

Wenſday, Octob. 9. We ſet off from *Encuſen* early : but by reaſon of a contrary wind, we came very late to *Herlinghem.*

Friday, Octob. 11. We went within land in little Scutes from *Herlinghem* (by *Frainker*) to *Lewarden.*

Saturday, Octob. 12. From *Lewarden,* we came to *Dockum* (in ſmall Boates,) about 3 of the clock after noon.

Sunday Octob. 13. *Apud Dockum in Friſia Occidentali.*

Δ. Diu Chryſtallus tanquam lapis nigerrimus apparuit. Tandem in ipſa lapidis nigredine, apparuit homo nudus Crucifixus ſuper crucem : ſed tamen non mortuus ; Crucis partes infra manus, omnes ſanguinolentæ videbantur. Faſcia linea circumdabatur Corpus ejus, (a pectore deorſum) & fines ejuſdem faſciæ pendere videbantur circa genua : & ſanguinolenta apparebat : & ex quinque vulneribus (ut Chriſti erat) videbatur ſanguis guttatim cadere. Tandem diſparuerunt hæc omnia : & quaſi deorſum ſubſidere videbantur ; & lapis clarus factus eſt, & apparebat Cortina aurea : ſubita erat hæc mutatio.

E. K. Jam videtur lapis eſſe valde magnus, & ante lapidem ſtare quidam magnus, (quaſi Michael) cum gladio ancipite evomente ignem ex utraque acie ejuſdem.

Mic. ...... *Juſtus & mirabilis & per maximus es tu, O Altiſſime Deus.* [*genua flexis hac dicit*] *qui tua judicia manifeſtas, ut poſſis ſuper terram cognoſci ; & ut tua gloria amplificetur, ad conſolationem eorum qui electi ſunt, & ad dolorem, & dedecus talium qui crucifigunt tamen mundi (unigenitum Domini noſtri, Salvatorem humani generis) quotidie. Ecce portæ preparatæ ſunt iniquitati. Attollite oculos, & videte quo modo filii hominum ſtulti devenerunt eſſe ; quia eorum habitatio eſt facta nigra , Terra ſigillata eſt ad eorum deſtructionem : quia Deum dereliquerunt, & ſibimet ipſis adhæſerunt ; & adhuc in partes diſſecant Servatorem mundi Jeſum Chriſtum* [*oſculatur enſis ſui crucem*] *continuò cum blaſphemiis eorum ſacrificiis. Ve illis, quia illos odio proſequimur , & ve illis qui inter illos habitant, quia iniquitates ſuæ pallutæ. Orate, dum inter illos eſtis, quia veſtri inimici ſunt multiplicati, quia vobis dico nuncium Domini exercituum, Regis fidelium. Relinquite infantiam, & vivite, & ambulate per viam prudentiæ ; & vivite cum Deo in domo ſua. Quia Domus Iniquorum, non eſt habitatio vel ſedes prophetis, neque poteſt*

Nomen

Nomen Domini efferri legitimè, in illegitima Nationé, *illegitimà factâ, quia dereliquerunt statuta* These words
Altiſſimi, Hoc dicit Dominus ; Ego ſum Deus Juſtitiæ : & juravi & non eſt unus inter illos were much
qui vivet, imò ne una anima. Quomodo Beſtiæ eſſe devenerunt ? de quibus ſcriptum eſt. Abſcis worn out.
notitia Dei: Homo ille factus eſt pecus Vita illorum, qui devorantur, & talium quos ignis con-
ſumpſit ſedebit in judicio contra iſtam Nationem.

Bleſſed and Sanctified , and for evermore praiſed art thou ...... *Judge, which haſt ſaid, and*
Raigneſt for ever.

△. *Si multiplicati ſunt inimici noſtri, &c.*

E. K. He is gone.

△. *Si multiplicati ſunt inimici noſtri propter peccata noſtra , ut difficilior nobis incum-*
bat lucta, Miſericordiam Dei imploramus ut ipſe noſtram etiam multiplicet fortitudinem, &c.

Gab. .... *Pluck up your hearts, bow your knees,* & *audite quæ dicit Dominus. Thus ſaith*
the Lord, If you will prevaile againſt the wicked, and rejoyce among the ſanctified, you muſt obſerve
and keep ſuch commandments, as are ordained by the God of Truth, unto thoſe that are partakers
of his Covenant.

Ask Counſel of God ;	Remember it.
Be milde.	
Faſt and pray.	E. K. *Gabriel* alſo noted theſe Com-
Be Charitable.	mandments in a pair of Tables, after
Uſe true Friendſhip in the ſervice of God.	he had pronounced them.
Perſevere to the end.	

Are not theſe Commandments neceſſary to be kept of all Chriſtian men ?.

△. They are undoubtedly.

Gab. .... *And muſt of neceſſity be kept of thoſe that are faithful.*

[E. K. He ſtandeth as though he ſtood behind a Desk, and preached or
taught.]

Gab. .... *Well thou ſayeſt ; Lo our enemies are multiplied, multiply thou therefore our ſtrength*
O God. Nature is ſubject unto you for the name of the Lord, n t as unto Kings, but as unto the
Miniſters of his eternal will, whereby your juſtification is ſettled above the works of Nature already ;
For, behold, y u participate the mercies of God through his Son Chriſt Jeſus, in us : in that we
open unto you thoſe things that have been ſealed; even from the Juſt, for the which we are become
ſlaves unto Corruption ; ſhewing our ſelves in divers ſhapes, to the diſhonour of our Creation : Yet
are we quickned and revived, becauſe we are become the finger of God : and you are ſanctified, and
withal juſtified, becauſe you are touched with the finger of him that reviveth all things. Therefore,
Rejoyce, Rejoyce, be Joyful and ſing Praiſes unto God, and faint not : ſaying, Our enemies are
riſen up againſt us, yea, they are multiplied ; for thus ſaith the Lord, and it is already ſpoken by
the Holy Ghoſt.

[E. K. He maketh now great obedience or reverence.]

Fœlices ſunt, quibus Deus ſpes eſt.

[E. K. He looketh now up unto a thing like a Throne.]

Et omne opus operatio Dei.

[E. K. Now there cometh a beam down into his head, and he is covered with a great thing like a white cloud.]

E. K. Now the Stone is all on fire. Now the fire aſcendeth upward,
the ſtreaming beam ſtretcheth into his head ſtill.

E. K. There appeareth a little woman a far off, and ſhe is ſo clear and
tranſparent, that there appeareth a man child in her; She hath a Coat as
though it were Crimſon, and hath a long little face, and hath a ſtrange ſilk
attire about her head. ... *as* ... *Videtur eſſe uxor mea.*

Gab. .... *Go woman, thy grief ſhall be leſſe than it hath been.*

E. K. *Habet multos tanquam parvos nigros canes poſt ſe.* Now goeth
one and tyeth their mouths with packthred.

Gab. .... *So God uſeth to give a ſnaffle to the wicked.*

E. K. A great wind bloweth on *Gabriel.*

△. *De Angliæ* & *meo privato ſtatu cupio aliquid audire : tum ex pietate erga patriam,*
tum propter famæ meæ rationem.

Gab. .... *Quieſcite paululum, & iterum venero. My Lord ſaith, Let my ſervants ſit up,* △. All this
and take their reſt, I will viſit them forthwith in peace. while we
had kneeled.

△. After

Δ. After a great quarter of an hour, he came again.

E. K. He appeareth now clothed, with all his garment hanging with bells of Gold, and flaming fire coming from them, with silverish flames. He hath hanging about his Crown as if they were seven Labells, the tops of which come from above, from an uncertain place and distance.

Gab. ......*Venite Morvorgran.*   E. K. *He calleth with a loud voice.*

E. K. Now cometh a big black man, with a white face, and after him hath 24. They stand in four rows, and in every row six.

Gab. ...... *Let me see thy seale.*

Mor. ...... Behold power is given to me : Neither is the liquor that thou ministrest of any taste with me ; Neither shall I be overcome, for I have placed my seat here.

Gab. .... *But by whose permission ?*   *Gag lab nai.*

E. K. Now *Morvo-gran* falleth down on his knees, and the rest on their face. *Medicina Dei, malis, Justitia vera.*

B. K. They tremble that lie flat on the ground.

E. K. *Morvo-gran* sheweth to *Gabriel* on his own left breast a Character.

Gab. ...... *For 19 moneths. Behold the will of God : Because thou hast conspired and risen against the Lord, in his chosen, and hast said ; It is to weet those that are subject unto thee, Let us rise up against him, and persecute his soul : let us secretly entrap him, for, without doubt, he is rich. And because your conspiracies are not of theft onely, but [also] of murder : Therefore I seal thee with a weaker power ; And be it unto thee according unto the word of God, that judgeth Righteously. From evil unto worse. From worse unto confusion. From confusion unto desperation. From desperation unto damnation. From damnation unto eternal death.*

[E. K. Now *Gabriel* did put another prick to the Character on his left breast]

Mor......... Cursed be that God, and defaced be his power ; for he handleth us in unjustice, and dealeth with us without mercy ; Because he is not merciful nor just.

E. K. *Gabriel* goeth from me to one of the 24. and sealeth them. Now thy go all away ; and he breaketh off the points of their Swords. They go by him.

Δ. Quis est iste Morvorgran, & quo modo hæc nobis instituit inferre mala ?

Gab. ...... *Lockum, thou shalt carry this malice unto thy grave : But I have made weak thy strength. Blessed be those that entertain those that are annointed in the Lord : for they also shall taste of the oil of his mercy. I had care of you, saith the Lord, neither will I suffer you to perish in the way ; Therefore be thankful, and forsake the world ; for the world hath forsaken you, and conspired against you. But these things are nothing. Behold lastly, thus saith the Lord.*

E. K. Now cometh a salet or helmet on *Gabriel* his head, or an half sphere ; A great noise of many voices is heard as of Pillars that fell. Now that thing is taken off his head.

Gab. ...... *Thus saith the Lord. The world on both sides, shall rise up against thee, and they shall envy thee.*

E. K. Now cometh a beam from above (again) into *Gabriel* his head.

Gab. ...... *Gna semerob Jebusan gonsag vi cap neph Jebuslach omsomna dedoilb.*

E. K. Looking up, he said thus,

Hoc est

Ne pavem repentino

terrore : & eruentes tibi

potentia Impiorum,

Laskie, Dominus.

[E. K. Now cometh about his face little things of smoke, and he putteth them from his face. He would open his mouth, and they come upon his mouth. They rise out of a pit before him, inumerable. *Gabriel* seemeth to be as big as one of us.

[E. K. They swarm continually .]

Dominus

Dominus ille Abraham

[Gab. ...... *Adhuc D . . s laboro*]

[*E. K.* Now cometh another ſtreaming beam down to him·]

E. K. Now cometh a fire down by the ſame beam that came into his head.

erit in latere tuo,

[*Adjutor meus* ;]   E.K. Looking up.

..... Now cometh a bigger fire down on him·]

& *cuſtodiet pedem tuum ne capiaris*

[*E· K·* Now they run headlong down into a great pit in the earth, and one pincheth me by the head.]

Spera igitur in dominum Deum tuum

For thou ſhalt overcome;

& *erit tibi Victoria maxima,*

in Deo, & propter Deum,

qui eſt Dominus & Deus exercituum.

E, K, Now the aforeſaid ſpirits invade *Gabriel* again.

Gab. ...... *What I ſuffer, is not lawful for man to ſee* ; *Therefore Ceaſe for a while, and ſuf-fice nature* : *But return and hear of my commandment.*

E· K· He is gone, but his Desk ſtandeth ſtill.

Sunday *à meridie hora 2.*   Octob. **13.**

Gab. ...... *And hereby I teach you, that thoſe afflictions which you ſuffer in ſoul either for your offences towards God, or for the imperfections of your mindes, being void of brotherly charity to-ward your neighbours* ; *(And ſo from you generally hereafter, how great, or how many ſoever) ought not to be manifeſted or made open to the world* : *but perfectly ſhadowed in Charity, bearing your own infirmities, and ſo the infirmity of others with quiet and hidden minde.   For the an-guiſh of the ſoul is compared with prayer, dwelling in one houſe which ought to laugh with the World, and to weep towards heaven.   For every ſin is noted, and the leaſt thing as well amongſt the Cele-ſtial bodies, as the Terreſtiall is perfectly conſidered of.   For ſin hath his end, and his end is puniſhment. And ſo, contrariwiſe of Vertue , Wiſdom (in the one and twentieth Ent ... ie or L...,) His ground is upon mildneſſe, which mildneſſe purifieth the body and exalteth the ſoul, making it apt and ready to behold the heavens, receive glorious illuminations, and finally bringeth in the ſoul to participate, with us, not earthly, but everlaſting wiſdom.   The Son of God was ſanctified in his fleſh, through mildneſſe, and was not of this world, becauſe he was the mildneſſe of his Father.   Therefore be you meek : . Be fervent in meekneſſe.   Then ſhall you take up that Croſſe which Chriſt ſpoke of, following him : which Croſſe is the Compaſſion in mildneſſe over thy brethren, for ſin ſake : Not as worldlings do, looking, but not lamenting.   The other part is in ſuffering mildly the afflictions of the world, and fleſh : Hereby you become Martyrs for that you mor-tifie your ſelves, which is true Martyrdom.   He that forſaketh the world for the love of God , in his Son Chriſt, ſhall have his reward.   But he that forſaketh himſelf, ſhall be Crowned with a Dia-dem of Glory.   Thus ſaith the Lord, I am jealous over you, becauſe you have vowed your ſelves unto me.   But great are the temptations of the fleſh, and mighty is his ſtrength where the ſpirit is weak.*

But thus saith God : *It is better to fill up the Soul with heavenly contemplation , and cælestial food , to reign in heaven, and to be beloved of him : Then to pamper the filthy flesh, whose delight destroyeth both body and Soul. It is written, He that bridleth not his flesh , is given to riotousnesse, which is the sleep of death, and the slumber to destruction. But this is true abstinence , when contemning the world you fly the delight therein : refraining from pleasures of the body, Temperating the flesh, and making it weak , and that , for the Lord his sake. For the flesh and spirit rejoyce not at once. . Neither can the full belly grone out true prayers. Feed therefore the Soul with the love of our society. And bridle your flesh ; For it is insolent. One thing, I say, look to your servants. See , that in one house there dwell not delighters in vertue and holinesse , mingled with such as barbour vice upon vice : Whose drunkennesse is abomination, and whose diet stirreth up fornication. For wickednesse is amongst them : and they fear not God , neither do they abstain , according as the holy Ghost by his Church hath taught. Make them clean : Then shall you feel our presence among it you. And we will all of us defend you from the rage of wickednesse. We delight in the God of truth , and, in the worshippers of Justice. Thus sayeth the holy Ghost : Lo, I have made me a Tabernacle, where the God of Gods reigneth in Justice. And I will sanctifie those places which rejoyce in charity. Mingle therefore your Alms with charity. And let your prayers and fasting be mingled with Alms deeds. For he that prayeth and fasteth without mercy, is a lyar. Moreover, let your friendship be such, as is of charity, and not of this world : Neither for the worlds sake, but for the service of God : All friendship else is vain, and of no account. Charity is the gift of the Holy Ghost, which Holy Ghost is a kindling fire , knitting things together , through Christ Jesus ; in the true wisdom of the Father : Which fire is of no small account, neither to be reckoned of , as the Heathens have done. For happy are those which are fed with charity. For it is the meat of us that are anointed, which is the son of God, and the light of the world.*

Δ. Is charity the son of God ?

Gab. ...... *It is so : He that walketh in charity wa'keth in God ; for charity is the will of the father, is his own delight , and illumination of the faithfull , through his Holy Spirit. The charity of the Church, is the Holy Ghost. But he that dwelleth in charity, dwelleth in the blond of the Lamb , which is the will of the father , which is the Holy Ghost. Blessed are those that dwell in charity. Persevere to the end : N:t negligently, but wish good will , which good will, is called fear. Which fear is the beginning of wisdom, the first step into rest.*

Finis coronat opus.

He that continueth to the end, receiveth his reward : But he that leaveth off, is a damned Soul. Many men begin, but few end. Neither is your justification by the beginning, but from the end. Paul was justified : Because he died the servant of God, and not for his preaching sake. He that dwelleth to the end, is the Childe of God : inheriter of everlasting life ; and equal with joy himself : Not the joy of joyes, but that joy which God hath made equal with the joyes of his son Christ , in the company of the faithfull. Even in this place , many perso. s had conspired against you. But the strength of God hath sealed them : And they shall not be unpunished. For the Angel of the Town is sealed , and his seal is to destruction : Thrice cursed are those which dwell within his government. But you are safe, and shall be safely delivered from them.

England.

In England, They condemne thy doings, and say, Thou art a Renegade. For they say, Thou hast despised thy Prince.

England.
Δ Destructio Dockum mihi concessa si cuperem, &c.

What wouldst thou know of them ? Cease till you hear the number of their destruction. Desire what plague you will (saith the Lord) upon this people, for their ungratefulnesse, and they shall be afflicted. For the Lord is angry with them : and he saith, Judge you this wicked people, their Town, Men, Women, and Children : And it shall be seen that the Lord , the God of Heaven and Earth, hath mercy on you.

Δ. Non nostra, sed Dei voluntas fiat, ad ejus nominis laudem & honorem.

Gab. ...... *Bid the fires fly from Heaven, and consume them, and it shall be done : Or , say, Let the Earth swallow them, And they shall perish. Fr l have made Heaven and Earth (saith the Lord) and — Justice is for my people. I am a flaming fire amongst you, and the Rod of Justice It is said, Heave up thy hands, and thou shalt be heard. The peace of him that is the spirit of wisdome inflame your mindes with love and charity , and grant you continuance to his glorie.*

Δ. Amen.

Deo Æterno, Omnipotenti & Misericordi fit omnis laus, honor, & Gloria. Amen.

Tuesday 15. Octob. We made hard shift to get from *Dockum* to *Angem* by sun set.

Thursday 17. Octob. We came from *Angem* to *Embden*, going without the Isles , and coming in at Wester *Emb.* We came before the Town, by six of the Clock after noon : but could not get in at the Gates, and therefore we lay all night a shipboard, but my Lord *A. L.* went over to the lodging on the other shoar.

Friday 18. Octob. We came into the Town : My Lord lay at the white Swan toward the water-side, and I, and *E. K.* with my Children and Many at the three golden Keyes , by the *English* house.

Sunday 20. Octob. This day morning about eight of the Clock we went in a litle Hoy from *Embden*

Embden toward *Lyre,* my Lord tarried at *Embden.* We came late to *Lyre* : and the same night we went from thence in a lesse Scute by *Styk-busen* to *Oppen.*

Munday 21. Octob. By nine of the Clock in the morning we came to *Oppen* : a very simple Village, and from thence we went straight way to *Oldenburgh.*

Tuesday 22. Octob. From *Oldenburgh,* by *Delmenhurst,* to *Breame* : and were lodged at an old Widow] her house, at the sign of the Crown.

Saturday *Octobris* 26. *Hora* 12. *scil.* in *Meridie.*   At *Breame.*

Δ. The Lord *Albert Laskie,* being at *Styck-busen* behinde us, with the Earle *John* of *Embden* and *Friesland,* &c.

E. K. The Curten seemeth to be far backward in the stone : and the stone to be clear between the Curten and the fore-part. Under the Curten I see the leggs of men up to the knees.

Δ. Then appeared one, and said :

Il. ...... *Room for a Player.   Jesus, who would have thought, I should* have met you here?

E. K. He is all in his ragged Apparel , down from the Girdle steed : But above he hath a white Satten Gerken.

Δ. By the mercies of God we are here : And by your will and propriety , and the power of God you are here.

Il. ...... *Tush, doubt not of me, for I am* I. L.

E. K. My thinketh *that the gravity of this* Action requireth a more *grave gesture,* and more *grave speeches.* Bear with me, though I say so unto you.

Il. ...... *If I must bear with thee, for speaking foolishly, which art but flesh, and speakest of thy own wisdom : How much more oughtest thou to be contented with my gesture, which is appointed of him, which regardeth not the outward form , but the fulfilling of his will ; and the keeping of his Commandments : which is God : whose wisdom unto the world is foolishnesse, but unto them that fear him, an everlasting joy, mixed with gladnesse, and a comfort of life hereafter : Partaking infallible joyes, with him that is all comelinesse and beauty.   How say you to this, Sir, Ha ?*

E. K. He turneth up his heels to E. K.

E. K. I do not understand your words : for because I do onely repent your sayings.

Il. ...... *It is the part of him that is a servant to do this duty : Of him that watcheth , to look what he seeth : For the greatest point of wisdom, is, reverently, to consider thy calling. It is said, do that, which is appointed, for he that doth more, is not a true servant.*

E. K. How can that be?

Il. ...... *Speak when thy time cometh.   Sir, here is mony : but I have it very hardly. Bear with me, for I can help thee with no more. Come on Andras, where are you* Andras?

E. K. Now cometh one in a Gown to him. The Gown is bare like a prentice of *London,* a young man.

Il. ...... *Did not I bid thee go yonder, and fetch me money.*

Andras ..... Whither.

Il. ...... *This is one of them that forgetteth his businesse so soon as it is told him.*

And. ...... Sir, I went half way.

Il. ...... *And how then ? Speak on, Speak on.*

And. ...... Then being somewhat weary : I stayed, the rather because I met my friends, The third day I came thither : but I found him not at home. His family told me, that he was newly gone forth.

Il. ...... *And you returned a Coxcombe.   Well thus it is : I placed thee above my servants , and did what I could to promote thee : and endeavoured dayly to make thee free. But I am rewarded with loytring, and have brought up an idle person. Go thy way, I will deliver thee to the Officer. The Officer shall deliver thee to the Prison : and there thou shalt be rewarded.   For such as do that they are commanded, deserve freedom : but unto those that loytre, and unto such as are idle , vengeance, and hunger belongeth.*

E. K. He taketh him by the arm, and delivereth him to a man with a staffe in his hand : and he putteth him in at a door.

G   E. K. Now.

E. K. Now Il himself goeth into a house, which all this while appeared on the left hand.

Il. ...... *Come on.*

[E. K.] Now he bringeth another by the hand.]

Il. ...: *My thinketh you should be a fit man to do my message.*

E. K.   Now he whispereth him in the ear, and pointeth out h....

Il. ....., *I warrant the man, be not abashed,   A strange matter.*
    [Pointing to E. K.]

Il. ......, *I have business in Denmark, and this fellow is afraid to go thither : Tell him , thou comest from me, and that I will come my self shortly. I know he will do so much for me, he hath had much acquaintance with me.*
    ...... *I care not, if I had some man to keep me Company.*

[E.K.] This new come man said so.]

E. K. *He whispereth again with this man in his ear.*

Il. ...... *These good fellows are not ready, or else they might go with thee.   Go thy way in Gods name : See that you do your business.   I keep such servants , as none in all the Countrey keepeth.*

E. K. *He keepeth no servants,*

Il. ..... *Meddle with that, you have to do with all.   I pray this man, and that man, and every one deceiveth me.   Good Lord, where should a man finde a true friend now adayes ?   I will go and tell the knave that he provide for himself.   For it will be marvellous hard weather. You were best to do so, least you blow your Nails.*

E. E. He speaketh to one within the house.

Il. .....' *Thus you see me (Masters) how I am troubled with my servants.   How now what aileth thee ?*

[E. K. There cometh a woman round about his house, and she seemeth to passe by him. She is in English Attire.]

Il. ..., *I will know what aileth her to cry.   What aileth thee ?*
Woman. One of my Children is dead.

Il. ...... *Alas poor Childe : How can Children resist cold ? she might have kept it warmer.   Cold pierceth, where shot cannot enter.*

Δ. This woman is not of our Company ?   I trust, None of our Children, shall perish in this cold.

Il. ....., *Ha, A, your Children ? you keep them warm : It will do them no hurt.   Those that are warned, eschue danger to come : For many things are prevented by the quality of wisdom.*

Δ. I trust, we shall safe arrive at the place appointed, in *Cracow,* or elsewhere.

Crecuvia.

Δ. But as concerning *Vincent Sevé,* brother in Law to the Lord *Albert Lakie,* I pray you to shew us the truth of his state.

E. K. I see him walking in a street; and a thick man with him; And *Gerlish* seemeth to come after him.   The thick man his beard is somewhat like my Lord his beard, he cometh after *Vincent.*   *Vincent* hath a black satten Dubblet on, cut with crosse cuts; He hath a ruffe about his neck, a long one edged with black, or blue.

Note.

Δ. I beseech you. I. L. to shew us what Town that is.

Il. ...... *Speaking to him that sheweth it : for I shew it not.*

Δ. O God.

Il. ...... *I remember not the name of any such Town.   Quem Deus non amat, non novit.*

E. K. Now the Town appeareth again, the Sea runneth by it.   There is an old rotten Church standing at the Town end.   The Town seemeth to be 60. or 80. miles off.

E. K. It seemeth to be *Embden* in my judgement.

E. K. But *Vincent* and *Gerlish* seem not to be in one Town, or street.

Δ. I beseech you to say unto us whether *A. L.* be furnished with money, at Grave *John* his hand, so as may serve our turn, or no.

Il. ...... *If I have not told you already, I will.   You grudge at me,*

[E. K.] *He* speaketh to E. K.

Il. .... *Judge*

Il. ...... *Judge, my words with reason, and thou shalt finde them true, Touch them with under-* Note.
standing, and thou shalt finde them profound. My words are true, Because I am sent by Truth :
Neither are we to speak gravely, when we take upon us the persons of Buyers and Sellers. Whoso-
ever doth the will of his Master truely in this World, shall be laughed to scorn : But whoso speaketh
worldly and sendeth out shadows, is accounted a pillar of the Earth. Happy are those which are
not foolish, neither in works say, There is no God ;. *Such request, such answer. Such earthly*
minde, such heavenly motions. Yet Heaven speaketh truth, and the Earth lyeth. This is not my
office which I have taken in hand ; yet because I have dealt with you as a worldling, I was the fit-
test to answer your worldly expectation.

Δ. As you have dealt with us, not according to your office, but according to our worldly expectation : So now do we desire to understand somewhat according to our higher and
heavenly expectation, of our doing the *determined will* of the Highest.

E. K. He is gone, and all the Stone as red as blood. Vide infrà.

Δ.

E. K. Now he is come again, and standeth in the fire.

Il. ...... *Thus saith the Lord, I have taught you how to live, I have set you Statutes, and*
have wished you my Peace ; Follow me, and I will give you my God : For unto them that are wise, shall Supra in fine
dici 13. Oct. &
there be more wisdom given ; But unto them that are become foolish, my wisdom is a . . . . sæpe antea.
These five years to come, are the Deliverance . . . Yea, sorrow shall bring forth her Children. A Prophesie
of An. 1584,
My Honour shall be defaced, and my holy Places pluckt. No man hath ever seen such a world : For
Now shall they say unto the Mountains, Come and cover us , and unto the Waters, Swallow us up : 1585, 1586,
for we know there is no God ; neither is there any care of Mankind. I will plague the peo- 1587, 1588.
ple, and their blood shall become Rivers. Fathers shall eat their own Children, And the Earth
shall be barren : The Beasts of the field shall perish,. And the Waters shall be poisoned, The Air
shall infect her Creatures, And in the Deep shall be roaring. Great Babylon shall be built,
And the son of wickednesse, shall sit in Judgement. But I will reserve two Kingdoms untouched,
And I will root out their wickednesse. Yea, thus saith the Lord, From the North shall come a From the
North.
Whirlwind, And the Hills shall open their mouths : And there shall a Dragon flie out, such as
never was. But I will be glorified by you, and by those that are not yet dead. And you shall
have power, such as I will be glorified by. Keep therefore the Statutes which I taught you, Forget
not my words : For unto those that look back, there is great wo. Happy are they that continue to
the end. Amen.

E. K. Now he is gone.

Δ........

E. K. Now he is come again.

Il. ...... *Thus saith Jehova : I am the beginning and the end, The root and life of all Righte-*
ousnesse. I say , (By my self) I am with you, And will blesse you in Righteousnesse. Cease
therefore to move me ; for I am Almighty, And inquire not of me, what I have determined ; For Vide supra.
Time groweth, and I am a Just God. Therefore Cease, Cease, I say ; I in my self say Cease.
Call not upon my name in defiled places ; Least the wicked ones hear what I determin. I
will visit you at your journyes end : I will testifie my promise to you. Be in haste therefore : At our jour-
neyes end.
And flie from sin ; And flie the society of such as are accursed : For I am jealous over my people.
Yea I will not suffer them to drink or taste of their vessels. Be you unto me a people, that I may
behold my people : And I will be unto you both, A God for ever.

E. K. Il. saith Amen, and falleth all in pieces, as small as ashes.

E. K. Now all is Clear, and the Curtain is come again.

Δ. Deo Omnipotenti sit omnis Honor laus & gloria, in secula seculorum. Amen.

Friday 1 Novemb. 1588. Mane. At Breame.
Δ. Albeit we were willed (O Lord) to Cease : yet understanding the same warning to
have been meant for *Enquiring* of thy *Mysteries and secret Determinations*, wherein we intend
now not to deal, but in matters before and last moved, and wherein we were not fully satis-
fied ; that now we may more expressely be certified, and that is of three things.
First for *Vincent Seve.* 1.
Secondly for *Edmond Hilton*, gone with the Ship toward *Dansk.* 2.
And Thirdly, as concerning help for money for the Lord *Alb. Laskie.* And herein we 3.
crave either the ministery of *Jubanladeeck*, or of *Il*; or whom soever else it shall please thy
Majesty to send.

E. K. A man with a black Gown appeareth with a Cap, falling in his
neck, with a big Book under his arme.
Δ. It should seem to be *Aphlasben*, my good Angel.

E. K. He hath a white Robe under the black Gown, which goeth all
under

under his Gown, trailing behind him : but, the white Robe traileth not; his Gown hangeth on him , as though it were falling off his shoulders behind.

Δ. In the Name of Jesus, the King of Glory, are not you *Aphlafben* my good Angel, by the mercy and power of God, so assigned?

E. K. He looketh very anciently.

...... *Impire, Most high Glory, and thanks, throughout all Creatures, be unto thee (O eternal God) first . . . Secondly redeeming, and Thirdly sanctifying the World in his Creation, Now, and for ever : And as long as it shall be said* Osanna *in the Quire of the High God* .... Amen.

Δ. ...... Amen. ...... Amen.

...... *Manifold are the Mercies of God towards man, whose baseness deserveth no such grace and most unspeakable blessing : But such is God ; what he justifieth himself, in the strength of his mercy, and heveth his honour with his own holiness. For what is man, that can justifie himself ? or that hath any thing, wherein his bowels can rejoyce ? Wherein can he determine happiness to himself ? Or how can be compare himself with the trees that are fruitful ? If the life of man be sin, then is it hateful: But who is he that hateth it ? But even he which is above, and is farthest from iniquity. Great, therefore (O man) are thy miseries, when naturally thou art, and lovest to be hated of God, whose service is Justice, and whose delight Peace. Consider therefore the Mercies of God, through his loving kindness towards thy weakness : And acknowledge his Power which maketh those strong which have no force of themselves. Gather not up your own inventions ; But be faithful servants, performing the will of him which sanctifieth you with obedience : for of dust you are become flesh, and of flesh the servants of sin ; that at length you might be made free, through your own consents in the mercies of him which hath entred into your weakness, and weighed out his blood for your Redemption : Even he which hath payed the uttermost penny of your Ransome. And why ? Not to the intent you should brag of your selves. But hath charged in condition you should maintain justice into the works of Righteousness. Unto whom is Heaven a seat ? but unto such as are faithful servants: Wherein the Dignity of your Master is known, of whom it is said, Blessed are those that serve the God of Hosts. If any thing, now, happen unto you, that is the riches of your Master, Be thankful for it, and consider his liberalitie : And how much the more he openeth his Treasures to you, Be so much the more thankful ; For unto such belongeth the ownership of more, and the reward of such as are ten times faithful. Happy are those to whom it is said, Thou good servant. Be no Gadders, for there is no house to the house of your Master. Take heed also, least you minister his bread, to such as are his enemies, and so, unworthy : for unto both these belongeth the reward of unfaithfulness. Be not high-minded, when you borrow your riches, lest the moths enter in and corrupt your garments : for Pride is the depth of sin .... Cease not to rebuke the dishonourers * as, o .... Neither maintain the honour of any other : For he that entertaineth you, hath sealed you for others, And hath strengthened you with Authority, The Rod of his Justice. Generally these things have been spoken unto you, and these Lessons are not yet to learn : But happy are those whom God sanctifieth ; being unholy, And ten times blessed are the Temples wherein his Holiness dwelleth. True it is as thou sayest : Generally men are sanctified, the people of the Earth through all Nations, mystically : through the mercies of God : But where the sanctification agreeth not with the thing sanctified, there entreth wickedness. The Spirit of God is not sanctified in Hell, Neither is his holy Temple beautified with the feet of the unrighteous. It is written, Dogs honour not bread, neither defiled places things that are holy : For as Hell dishonoureth Heaven, in respect of unrighteousness : So, those that are wicked dishonour the vertuous, and such as are truely holy, by society : and they stink of their wickedness. For it is written, And Satan went from the presence of the Lord, leaving a stink behind him. The light of the Sun is taken from the Earth, by the congealed cloud. The sins of the people, and filthiness of places, are put between vertue and the things Sacramental.* Therefore, it is not true, that thou mayest lawfully call upon the Name of God in unhallowed places.

Δ. I crave pardon for my ignorance, and errour herein : But I required not to know of the heavenly Mysteries ; Onely such things I demanded information of, which not onely were above humane power to answer, (and so might seem worldly mysteries :) but also the true good news of them, might, many ways, be comfort unto us and ours.

...... *Behold in* Israel, *the rough stones are acceptable Altars, And the stinking Caves have been known unto the Lord. And why ? Because the place was holy, neither this filthiness here, nor of any thing else created, hindreth : But the filthiness of the place and Country wherein they are defiled ; for in pure places, the defiled are blessed.* David *sanctified* Saul, *with the presence of his Annointing, and his Harp spake out the wonders of the Lord. We come unto you here, because the will of God in you shineth : But the filthiness of this Country obscureth the beauty of our message. Not that it is obscured in us, but hindered through wick ...... from you. Therefore flee the company of Drunkards, and such as we .... their own understanding.*

[E. K. He holdeth up his face and hands to heaven-ward.

...... *Drunkards and such as defile themselves are apt to know things worldly ; not as wise men*

do :

do: but that the World may be a plague to their iniquity. Thou defireft pardon, and calledft th...
bufineſſe a worldly myſtery. But the myſteries of this world are put under the feet of the faithful:
which (overſeen through God) are generally comforted and directed. Then, therefore what care
remaineth either of the Seas, or of the ſlimy Earth? where, on the one ſide, thou regardeſt the Ship,
and on the other ſide Money. I ſay unto thee, God correcteth this world and the caſualties thereof,
leſt thoſe that are of thee, ſhould blaſpheme his name.

Δ. Bleſſed be his holy Name, and his Power magnified for ever.

...... Thy goods are ſafe, And the Earth ſhall provide for you. Be not you careful; for unto
the juſt, yea even the hairs of his head are numbred. I am ſilent for the World; for it is not my
propriety: But notwithſtanding ask and thou ſhalt not be denyed.

Δ. As concerning *Vincent Seve*, his ſtate and being, we are very deſirous to be informed.

E. K. *Vincent Seve* appeareth here, going down by Charing Croſſe.
There is a tall fellow with a cut berd with him in a skie-coloured cloak.
Vincent hath a great ruff: This man waiteth on him with a Sword. He
is going down into *Weſtminſter* Ward: He is now talking with a Gentleman on horſeback, who hath five men following him, with Cape-cloaks
ſhort, and muſtaches; And he on horſe back is a lean viſaged man with a
ſhort Cloak and a gilt Rapier; his horſe hath a Velvet foot-cloth.

E. K. In *Vincent* his forehead is written; *Where power wanteth, rigor*
weakneth.

E. K. *Vincent* laugheth heartily; and ſheweth two broad teeth before,
He holdeth a little ſtick within his fingers crooking. On his left hand he hath
a skar of a cut, on the nether ſide of his hand. *Vincent* hath a pair of bootes
on, which come ſtraight on his legs, and very cloſe. A great many boats
appear at *White-Hall.* One is graffing in the Garden there. Many people
are now coming out of *Weſtminſter* Church. The Gentleman on horſe-
back alighteth now, and goeth down toward the Court before *Weſtminſter-*
Hall. He goeth now up a pair of ſtairs; and there ſtandeth a fellow with
a white ſtaff. *Vincent* is gone in with him; The ſervant walketh without.
The ſervant goeth to a Waterman there. The Waterman asketh him, whether that be he; that is the *Poland* Biſhop? The ſervant asketh him, what
hath he to do? Now the ſervant goeth from the Waterman. Now cometh one down the ſtairs, and ſaith to the Serving-man, that his Maſter ſhall
be diſpatched to morrow. The ſervant ſaith, He is glad of it. Now all
that Shew is vaniſhed away.

Now come there two handſome men, they have Cloaks on their
ſhoulders, and they have hats on like Tankard Crowns.

One of theſe ſaid,

A ...... *I underſtand by the King, that he beareth him great favour.*

The other ſaid,

B ...... *But Kings when they become rich, wax Covetous. But do you think he*
will come this way?

A ...... *Tea mary, if he be wiſe; for he ſhall find no better friendſhip than in*
Denmark. *Here is the fellow, he hath brought a bag of Amber.*

E. K. He taketh the fellow by the ſhoulder, and ſaith; Come away,
He hath been an old doer.

E. K. Now they are gone, and that Shew.

E. K. Now

E. K. Now is the first man in the black Gown come again.

...... *Thus you see, the World answereth for the World. Be merciful. Flee privy leakes ; for the Devil is ready at every corner. Be Humble and Obedient. That receiving the reward of true servants, you may rejoyce as Enheritors of everlasting freedom ; The reward of such as are faithful to the end. God grant you may so be.* Amen.

E. K. Now cometh the Vail again which all this while was gone behind the Stone.

Δ. Deo nostro Omnipotenti, misericordi, & justo sit omnis honor, laus, & gratiarum actio, nunc & in secula seculorum. *Amen.*

Δ. While we were at *Bream,* among many other things told and delivered to *E. K.* as he was by himself, by a spiritual Creature, I know not who, nor of how good estate, or what estate he was of : This parcel among them he held in writing, and imparted to me ; And I thought my pains not ill bestowed, to keep the same in record here.

Ganilus that, in house most fiery fairer than the Sun,
Hath honour great, saith, give place, your former course is run ;
Therefore first framed clouds unknown draw near with mighty storms,
Wherein such bodies lie obscur'd, or take ten thousand forms.
Your bellies strowting long disclose, and on the harlot earth,
Seem fair to man, as when the waves as Midwife help ... r birth.
Twice shall the Sun put on the heavens, and once look quarter way,
And working uncouth worlds, build up a City, where men say ;
The Holiest stood : And Beares bring in usurping fire at hand,
And *people spread return,* whose new built altars flaming stand.
Whilst such as strangers were *Catesy* cry , and bloody knife,
With privy shame defil'd bekyes, a thing n ... sometime rise.
From midnight unto noon, two parts and more shall slaughter feel,
And all the World from South, taste all, down force, of fire and steel.
Small wonder though the earth at shadows fighting nothing grieve,
When mighty Seas shall dry, and heavens lie, who can live ?
That mortal eyes shall see a Temple built with precious Stones,
Or Creatures strange made new in fight, of old and long dri'd bones.
Or Angels dwell on earth : but I whose firy fingers can
Unloose thrice sealed Books, and utter worlds unknown to man.
I see these cursed wights, whose borders lead thy journey on,
Shall with the thirtieth moneth, be bought, or sold, or fully gone.
And England perish first with Moths long harbour in her skirts,
The Spaniard *lose their King,* and *France rebel and fall by spirits.*
And holy man ten dayes besieged at home, with these dayes whelps,
Till he at length made free by sudden force of vertues helps.
The Polish King hath played, and friendly man shall then bear sway,
Amongst earthly friends, and such as hope of former faith decay.
At last wear highest Crown, if fall *from vertue makes no losse,*
And midst this coil to come in space of new come lay for tosse.
Then lo, Come other times most Holy, and a Kingdom shall,
From Heaven come, and things forthwith again to Order call.

(marginal notes:) Two years and a quarter, shall be *An* 1586. in January.

2¼

Saturday 2. *Novembris* we rod from *Bream,* two great mile to a Nunnery called *Ostarbold.*
Sunday Novembris 3. we came to *Furè* or *Fureden.*
Monday Novemb. 4. we came to bed to *Harburgh.*
Tuesday Novemb. 5. we came to *Buxtenbaden,* and there by 9 of the clock in the morning we took water in two great Skutes or Boats, Horse-wagon, and our stuff and all, and ferryed down the little water, till we entred the *Elb,* and so crossed straight over to *Blanken nasen :* there dined, and after dinner by coaches we came to *Hamburgh,* where my Lord lay at the English house, and we at another lodging, a widows house.
Wensday Novemb. 6. we rid to *Tritiow* 4 mile from *Hamburgh,* a little Village, having left my

my Lord behinde : and also missing my Children and servants , which were gone before us an other way to my great grief: till by midnight, by sending out messengers to listen and enquire after them, I heard of them. I, my Wife, Rowland, Nurse, and *Myrcopskie,* my Lord his man.

Thursday, Novemb. 7. We came to *Lubek* , aud were there at Inne , at the signe of the Angel, or rather St. *Michael* , at a Widow her house , a very honest Hostesse.

Saturday, Novemb. 9. I received Letters from the Lord *Albert Laskie,* of the *English* mens ill dealing, and consulting with the Townsmen of *Hamburgh* for my stay, and conveying back again into *England,* &c.

Wednesday, 13. *Novembris,* 1583. *Mane hora* 9¼.   At *Lubek.*

Per horam ferè, per intervalla, varias fecimus petitiones & sæpe oravimus.

At length appeared a sword, two edged, firy, or rather bloudy, and a bunsh of rags hanging at the top of it.   The rags seemed of Woollen, and Linnen Cloath : like a bundle of Rags gathered out of a Taylers shop.   The sword stood upright in a manner, but leaning from *E. K.* his face, though it seemed to smite at *E. K.*

A voyce. *So be it,* (O Lord) *for thou art mighty.   Be it so unto them : For they have embraced an Harlot, and have forgotten thy jealousie.*

E. K. The sword shaketh mightily.   Many are the Harlots that swarm upon the earth, and innumerable are their Children, and such as they foster. Their revvard is ready.

E. K. The sword now shaketh again mightily.

...... *He that entreth into the house of the wicked is defiled : but he that consenteth with an Harlot is accursed. He that delighteth in her secrets, shall be stabbed. And Leprosie shall dwell in his house for ever.*

Δ. O Lord, I trust, this respecteth none of us, in common sense to be understood.

...... *He that delighteth in light, loveth not himself , but desireth the love of him, that illuminateth : But, thus saith God, I will not dally with you : Neither shall you handle me, as you have done.   For, your* Horedom, *is wilfull : and your vanities worse. But this I leave amongst you, that you shall know that I am righteous. For, he that despiseth me, is accursed ; and unto him that dissembleth my fashion, are miseries without number.   So , unto them, that enter into the house of blasphemy, is vengeance ready at hand.*

Δ. O Lord, what is this?   Man is but earth , where the heavens dwell : neither are the works of man acceptable, but with righteousnesse.

E. K. There appeareth a man with a *Bible* about his neck, like a Doctor. and he standeth miserably in fire.   And so likewise appeared divers other with *Bibles* about their necks, and they in fire likewise.   Still come flames from the earth, and encrease the flames of these men about them.   There appeareth, and endlesse. . . . me, most terrible with fire , and other most hideous shews. . . . . They be suddenly gone away.   And all these men be now no more in sight.

A voyce. *Happy are those that see, and can remember.   Blessed are those that hear, and are not forgetfull.*

Δ. These words, and shews, O Jesu, make evident what. . . . . .

E. K. All is gone, except the sword which standeth in a Cloud, and there cometh a hand and setteth a seal upon the sword.

A voyce. *I brought you from iniquity, to the intent you might be purified : But the more I cleanse you, the more you are defiled.*

...... *I have offered of old, and it shall be told.   I have promised , and it shall be performed. You have not kept my Commandments. And therefore you shall be plagued. He that goeth out of the way, shall receive the reward of errour. For stragglers, are spotted people. And none can be blessed, but such as dwell in the Tabernacle of righteousnesse.   But behold , I will tell it unto you but with greater hardnesse. And I will make you know me, before I visit you in kindnesse.   For thus sayeth* Sathan. *Lo, they erre still.   Do Justice for thy glory sake.   They enter into the houses of Idols : And laugh with blasphemers.   They are silent , when thy name is blasphemed. Deal with them as a God : or else thou art not righteous. Therefore, be free from* Sathan *, that he may praise your righteousnesse. Yea, that he may say , as he hath said.   Let me touch them: Untill*

Untill then, I will be just. I will not forget this wickednesse, till you be made clean.   For, behold, I have sealed it : and therefore it must be finished. For what is sealed of me, cometh to passe.

Δ.

A voyce. *He that dissembleth the image of Christ, is a liar.*

Δ.

...... *Now cometh a grave man, all cloathed in white, with a Mytre upon his head.*

...... *The God of peace is a comforting Medicine, to such, as delight in him.   The peace of the world, is the image of God : God and man, which is* Jesus Christ, *the son of the living God : Which knit with the father in the spirit of truth, (proceeding from them both ...... everlasting will,) opened his mercies to his Apostles, replenishing them fully and mightily with the will of the father, to the comfort of the world : Which, made messagers thereof, have delivered to the Church, full and perfect Statutes (as the Will of him, whereunto she is united and married) to be kept inviolable, and without transgression.   This Will, Covenant, or Decree, (sealed unto the end of the world in the number of the faithfull) whosoever breaketh, or dissembleth, is accursed, or damned.   Therefore saith the word of God unto you: You have run astray, you have entred into the houses of Idols. I have brought you from fire, but you are entred into flames.   And why ? Because you defile your selves with the wickednesse of deceivers : Whose images you saw affirmatively, though not verily : Continually overwhelmed with daily, and inextinguible flames: Continuing even so long, as their errour is exalted; Yea, even in the professors thereof, to their eternal damnation.   For as Christ, and his Doctrine is light and truth: So seem the impositions of Sathan to agree, or take unto themselves, shapes or likenesses of the true image of him that saveth: Whereby he trusteth in himself under the colour of meeknesse, into the companie of the faithfull: Devouring their Souls with ravening, dissembling, and false likelyhoods of truth, unable to be decided by man.   Happie are those that believe them not :   For he, even he it is, that is a liar, and is oldest in deceit.   But as the father is eternal: So is the son eternal, which eternity of the father and the son, is the holy Ghost eternal, proceeding equally, as the finger of God, and spirit of truth, to the general workmanship of Gods determination knit together, three Persons.   [*E. K. He maketh a great reverent curse*] in this omnipotency by spiritual illumination, and through the holy Ghost delivered unto the Apostles, as the pledge of God*

△ Ecclesia Christi.

his mercie and promise, is always certainly linked, joyned, and engraffed into the society of those that fulfill the will of the highest perfectly, and without errour, whose strength shall continue, and glorie branch out, even unto the end of this world, and beginning of comfort.   Therefore, believe : For the spirit of truth worketh wonders, raiseth the dead, and hath power to forgive sins.   Through the power of him, unto whom it is ma ...... For, as Christ hath all power in heaven and in earth delivered...... So hath he delivered all power in heaven and earth to his true Church.   Therefore she cannot erre.   For where power is without measure, errour hath no number : Believe not therefore those that lie : saying, The Church of God is infected with errours.   For the offences of few are

△ Forth, staggering.

not counted errour, but unrighteousnesse : Neither can the stragling feet of a few drunken, bring infamy to the whole house.

Δ.

...... *It lieth not in my power to deliver you, or reconcile you from death and Hell : The tormentry and filthinesse of the world, and the wrath of God.   But yet, (That Cloud, set aside) which is between me and you) I speak afar of to you, saying, The Justice of God, is vengeance it self : Neither hath it any contrary, but even in the midst, and Centre of it self : Which is the drop and liquor of his eternal, great, and incomprehensible Majestie of himself, his mercie : Which, even in the midst of Justice is found out, by sorrowfull repentance, and reconciliation: Not in that it is necessarie with God : But that it is a Medicine applicable, and most healthfull to the infirmities of that man, that coveteth to be healed, released, or recovered from his soares.   This is it, that must comfort you.   For, as Justice is the reward of sin, so is mercie the reward of repentance.   But mercie is the Center of light : and Justice to be cast off, and shut within darknesse.   Therefore, be not negligent.*

Δ. This whoredom, how is it committed, or of whom ?

...... *I teach the...... Where thy habitation was, errour rained, God called thee from it : and delivered thee by many, but unknown wayes : means not to be uttered by man.   These places also are shut up from the favour of God.   For their obedience is counterfeited, and their prayers, out-cries.   Therefore hath the Lord opened him unto you that invented the vanitie : that you might be partakers of his knowledge, and secret judgements of the wicked. Here also you entred, and are newly defiled: For the Devil entred in, and found him waking : And lo, be entred yet, and he was not asleep.   But he was happie, being kindled with desire of God, else had the judgement of his bodie for this world been fulfilled.   Wickednesse followeth him : and the spirits of evil counsel are at hand.   You shall feel the sorrow thereof, and your family shall be discomforted.   But pray unto God, that it fall not out, that Sathan goeth about :   Neither that it come to passe, which he hath power to execute.   For, this token signifieth your miseries, and it is a sign of that, which is given to execution.*

I have said.

The peace of God be restored unto you.

Δ.

E. K. **Here**

E. *K.*· Here is the man again.

...... *Two words and I have done. Nothing is plainer than that which is spoken: Nothing certainer than that which is appointed. Be you penitent, that God may be merciful. This is all I have to say. Wash your selves, and I also will make you clean. Resist you Satan diligently, and I will help you mightily.*

Δ. O Lord that seal to the Sword and rags break off.

E. K. Now he is gone.

Δ.

E. K. Now he is here again.

.... *This cloud is a separation betwixt this, yea this glorified company and you. Look not for any light, whilest this darkness is present. Behold, my mouth faltveth, and my lips are stayed: But pray you, and you shall not be rejected. For the stronger you be, the mercifuller is God, and the weaker is, and shall be, your adversary. Love together; Serve God together: Be of one heart together. Alwayes preach God. I am tied.*

E. K. *He* is gone.

Δ. Misericordia & pax Dei sit super nos nunc & semper. *Amen.*

Friday, Novemb. 15. *hora   mane.*   *Lubek.*

E. *K.*·The cloud appeareth, and openeth, so that the Sword may be seen.

Δ. O Lord deal mercifully with us, as thy children, to be corrected with rod or whip, and not with thy enemies, with sword to cut or wound us. Let not Satan force thee to justice more mightily, than thy fatherly goodnesse can incline thee to shew mercy upon us.

E. K. An hand cometh and nippeth off an inch of the top of the Sword, and some of the rags are fallen down; some hanging on the hilts of the Sword, and some are thrust through with the Sword. Now the Sword is shut up again in the Cloud.

Δ. Have mercy on us, O Lord, and deal with us as thy younglings and novices.

E. K. Now come in an eleven, all like Noble men. One of them hath a regal Cap, and a Gown faced with Sables· The Cap is like a Polonian Cap, but trimmed up with rich Sables· Now cometh one and bringeth a very rich Chair, beset vvith precious Stones: Four of the Company set dovvn this Chair, for that Principal man. He that brought the Chair vvent avvay· They all do lovv obedience to this principal· He sitteth dovvn, and putteth his Govvn over· He is a goodlier man than the Lord *A. L.* The 4 pluck a thing like a Canopy over the Chair, and they put a round Cusshion under his feet. This Principal speaketh as follovveth.

...... *Pluck up thy heart and be merry, pine not thy Soul away with inward groanings; for I will open unto thee the secrets of Nature, and the riches of the World, and withal give thee such direction, that shall deliver thee from many infirmities, both of body and minde: Ease thee of thy tedious labour, and settle thee where thou shalt have comfort.*

Δ. Thanks be given unto the Highest, now, and ever, of all his Creatures.

....., *Why dost thou ... within thy thought: Hast thou not need of Counsel?*

Δ. Yes, God knows; for I am half confounded.

...... *Then first d ... with thy self to rest thee, for this Winter. Secondly open thy mind to desire such things as may advance thy Credit, and enrich thy Family: Reap unto thee many friends, and lift thee up to honour; For I will stir up the mindes of Learned men, the profoundest in the World that they shall visit thee. And I will disclose unto you such things, as shall be wonderfull, and of exceeding profit. Moreover, I will put to my hands, and help your proceedings, that the World may talke of your wisdom hereafter. Therefore wander not farther into unknown places, contagious, the very seats of death for thee, and thy children, and such as are thy friends. If thou enquire of me where, and how. Every where: or how thou wilt thy self. For thou shalt forthwith become rich, and thou shalt be able to enrich Kings, and to help such as are needy. Wast thou not born to use the commodity of this World? Were not all things made for mans use?*

Δ. Will you give me leave to speak?

....., *What canst thou speak hereunto? Wilt thou thank me for this?*

H   Δ. All

Δ. All thanks be unto the King of Glory, *&c.*

Δ. Is it your meaning that we shall stay here, and go no farther with the Lord *Albert Laskie ?*

.... Yes, in the Summer ; when it is more fair.

Δ. I beseech you, Where would you, that we should make our .... this Winter ?

......Where you will. Are you so unwise so to go with him now. Let him go before, and provide for himself, that he may the better provid for you. The weather will be hard, and the travel unfit for children. If thou covet to live in ease, heap not up thy wives sorrow.

Δ. I desire to live in quiet, that my spirit may the better attend to the service of God

...... Well, Tarry you, and my promise shall be quickly performed. I will not bult with you. How say you Sirs ?

[E. K. He speaketh to his Company, vvho make curfies, and fay nothing.]

Δ. I beseech you to appoint an apt place : This you see is no fit place.

.... I will stir thee up such friends, as shall content thee. As for dwelling places thou shalt bestow them. Well, you are contented.

Δ. Is it your will, that in this Town we should part from the Lord *Albert Laskie ?* .

......, What should you do else ? Are you mad men ? Will you run headlong into danger ? wilfully ?

Δ. I beseech you, shall this be nothing prejudicial to our former doings, and order already taken and decreed for our going together ?

......, What, is this contrary to reason ? Well you are content.

Δ. As the will of the Highest is, so is mine and none other.

......, Sirha, do you see this sword ? I will be a surety for this (I warrant thee) also.

Δ.

...... Your brother is clapped up in prison, How like you that ? Your house-keeper I mean.

Δ. And why I pray you ?

.... For that, that thou mayest be ashamed of.

Δ. What is that ?

...... They examin him : They say, that thou hast bid divers secret things. As for thy Books; thou mayst go look them at leasure. It may be, that thy house may be burnt for a remembrance of thee too. Well if they do, so it is : if not, as thou wilt. I have told thee my phansie, and given thee my counsel, offered thee my help, and desired to do thee good : The choice is thine.

Δ. O Lord the Author of all truth, and director of such as put their trust in thee, I most humbly beseech thee to consider these premises, thus to me propounded. If they be true, and from thee, confirm them : If they be illusions, and not from thee, disprove them. For, hardly in my judgement, they do or can agree with our former precepts and order taken by thee.

A voice *...... He that ascendeth up to the top of the hill, let him believe : For until he come thither, let him do his labour.*

O Lord, I doubt of these things, and promises of ease, wealth, and honour.

A voice. *...... Judge the Truth, by the last Action.*

O Lord, What is that Action ?

A voice, *...... Wensdaies Action.*

This Cloud (said the voice of the Lord) is put betwixt us and you : What therefore may come between ? Now judge you.

Δ. I suspect the whole apparition of the eleven to be an illusion. O Lord confirm my judgement or disprove it.

A voice. *...... The Spirit of the Lord is not amongst you.*

Δ. What misery are we then in ? O Lord, Mercy, Mercy.

A voice, *...... Dispute not with God, where whoredom is great.*

Δ. O Lord, This whoredom we understand not.

A voice. *...... Pray daily, with repentance, that this cloud may be taken away, and this sword diminished, . For the Seal cannot be broken, until Satan have done his uttermost ; yea the uttermost of his malice. For it is granted him and he must strike. But pray you unto God, that the sword may be made shorter, or pluckt out of the hilt, that in striking he want power. For your sin is abominable, and a sevenfold offence in the sight of the Lord.*

Δ. What this whoredom is (God knoweth) we understand not perfectly. If the Spirit of God be not with us, how can our prayers be acceptable ?

A voice. *...... Thus saith the Lord, Turn unto me and be sorry for your sins , and let my Angels be witnesse thereof. For I swear by my self, that my Justice shall hang over you : And when I punish you next, I will raze you from the face of the earth. Therefore, Vow your selves unto me , and make your vessels clean ; for your habitations in my sight are nothing : neither is the substance whereof I framed you acceptable . I am the Spirit of Truth and Understanding, and will not be dasht in pieces with worldlings ; Neither use I to dwell in defiled places. For my Sanctuary is holy, and my Gates are without spot. And with me there dwelleth no unrighteousnesse.*

Δ. Lord

Δ. Lord, is it thy will we shall go with *Albert Laskie* to *Lasco* ?

A voyce. *The Lord saieth, What I have said, is true.　Who rebuketh me, saying my words are untrue ?　The correction of him that reigneth is mightie ; who hath numbred it ?　But to his destruction.　Be you holy, that my hand may be weak.*

Δ. O Lord, the fear of thy punishment astonieth my heart : and uncertainty of it in time, and place, doth also encrease my grief, &c.

A voyce. *The fool saith in his heart : Oh, how great is thy punishment over me.　Teach me the place of thy correction : And where thou wilt chastise me.　Who is he that desireth to meet God his vengeance, or the punishment of him that confoundeth the damned ?　Make your hearts clean, and wipe the sin from amongst you : And desire to be forgiven ; for miserable are they that meet with vengeance, or that know the place where she taketh up her Harbour.*

Δ. Gloria , Honor , Laus & gratiarum actio perennis sit Deo nostro Omnipotenti : Nobis verò a Deo Patre, propter Jesum Christum in Spiritu Sancto , sit Misericordia, Pax & Consolatio in via virtutis & veritatis. *Amen.*

Monday, *Novemb.* 18. *Hora* 9. *Mane.*　　　*Lubek.*

E. K. There appeareth the Cloud , wherein the sword remaineth enclosed.

Δ. O Lord, be mercifull unto us , and rigorously execute not thy Justice upon us, thy weaklings : Nor suffer Satan to Triumph , where thy glory is expected, &c.　*Converte nos Deus salutaris noster, & averte iram tuam à nobis, &c.*

E. K. Now cometh one in a white Coat , not perfectly to be seen , but as if he were seen through a Cipresse ; and said as followeth.

...... *Who is he that leadeth out the Lion to prey ? or who is he that lifteth up the feet of the young ones to devour ?　Who feedeth the smell of the roaring Bear , or hath taught him to remember the place of his recreation ?　Hath he also taught the fields, to put forth their voices : and the mighty Trees to flourish in pride ?　Are not the Hills glad when they bring forth Corn ? When the Valleys rejoice with threefold waters.　The beasts of the wildernesse have they not known Caves : and unto such as are made tame, is there not a ......　understanding ?　For, who is he that teacheth them, to make subject themselves, which are ravening, or to bridle such as are of their frowardnesse ?　Even be it is , that looketh down from Heaven, and beholdeth the earth , and measureth with his feet, saying,*

　　　　　　　It is done.

Which entreth also into the houses of men, and listeneth to that which they call wonders.　Which openeth the gates of his knowledge with his own finger ；　And which sayeth unto you : How are ye become wise ? Or from whence is your understanding, are your hearts become Caves to send out Thunders ? Or why are your spirits thus vexed with holinesse ? Are you not a stiff-necked people, and such as are despised ? Are you not poor, and therefore hated.　Since, therefore, you are become Bastards ; who teacheth your lips to speak of my Church ? Or hath taught you to urge me with mine own spirit ?

　　　　　　　Behold, I am mighty,

Because I am the joy of the faithfull.　For I am called the Temple of the Holy ones, and the beauty of Israel.　*The spirit of man crieth out, and pierceth into the Lord , as the swiftnesse of an Arrow : And he heard them.　Therefore, thus doth the winde of* Cabon *open her mouth , and sweareth by the* Jaspar *Pillar that standeth in the Temple of Reconciliation, and it Thundereth, and is said ,*

　　　　　　　Be it done.

And behold, the doors open, and the Holy Altar is covered.　The beasts with many feet bring up burnt-offerings : And there is a sacrifice that ascendeth up, and it is a mighty winde , such as hath not been since the beginning of dayes.　Open your ears therefore, and prepare your selves to bear : For this ...... is mighty, for it is of peace.　My Justice (saith the Lord) is sealed , and you have sinned mightily :　My arm is stretched forth, and I must be magnified : For vengeance is gone forth, and is appeared already.　But who is he that resisteth the venome of the earth , or instructeth man to avoid the Darts of poison ? He saith unto you.　Thus it is, because I have sanctified you, and have made you holy to the earth : Therefore will I help you : But not as you desire : For your prayers and unrighteous life shall become bands of yarn.　And I will make a contention betwixt Satan and you.　If therefore you labour hard, and open fervent mindes, such as are not of the world ; and can binde this sword and cloud of vengeance fast from amongst you : Be it so unto you, for it is your own righteousnesse.　For Sathan hath reviled, and hath said ,

　　　　　　　Then shalt thou see.

But so long as they are Holy, and become righteousnesse, they are become safe : but when they fall ; Satan entreth in.　For the power of righteousnesse is become a Conquerour , if it fight mightily.　And Satan shall be confounded by a righteous judgement.

　　　　　　　H 2　　　　　　　　　　　　　　　*For*

For I have decreed it : and by my self I swear it.

Note.
I will be a righteous Judge betwixt you.   Therefore, take heed you sin not , nor go into death : For great is the fall of vengeance.   Be not therefore defiled with the filthinesse of the wicked : Neither delight in such as counterfeit truth.   For I am one fire that judgeth all things.   And I delight in people that are joyfull with one Banket.   For those that fill their bellies at the houses of strangers : Become enemies to me.

For I have said,

My spirit is holy, and my annointed righteous.   Let the earth rise up , and continue in her wic-kednesse : Yea, let them say, we have found the anointed : But my continuance is truth, and they are become liars.   For my spirit worketh, and behold, there are wonders in the sight of men.   And wheresoever I dwell, such is my power.   Be therefore of One house, that you may eat together: Least you banket too much , and so become deceivers.   I am one, and am known by One : And unto One, Which One I am married unto.   (And I am mercifull) Whosoever abideth not therein, is an Adul-terer.   Avoid you darknesse, for righteousnesse is present , and my spirit entreth.   Blessed are such as believe. Amen.

Even to the , Amen,

E. K. He is gone· There appeare some bands linked together, as Chaines about the Cloud.

Δ. Welcome be these bands,

B. K. He is here again , ... and saith ...... eth.

...... Why are you become dull ? Why are you yet ignorant ?   Seest thou these ...... [He polint-eth, and speaketh to E. K.]

E. K. I see them, I thank God.

...... These bonds are your own righteousnesse : And as they appear before the Lord, so shall they binde vengeance together : But if you become weak you fall.   But pray, that you fall not : For they are the dayes of sorrow.   The spirit of God is twofold ; present Jah agian, and present Nah gas-sapalan.   Therefore take heed.   For, in the first, you are blessed : and it may return.   But he that is filled with the second, shall be drunken for ever.   The first is power present , and a comfort inmeasurable, glorifying, and strengthning all things that are agreeable to it : But when they differ, it returneth.   The other is the spirit of the first, and the second , Almighty , and everlasting , un-measurable , and inexplicable : drowning the will of man, that becometh strong in the fountain of gladnesse and understanding : true wisdome her self, and not returning.   Pray, therefore , that you may be perfect : and that you may be seasoned : For it is a salt that favoureth to the end.   The peace of God be amongst you.

B. K. He cast off his Cloudy Lawn , and went away. He seemed to be **Raphael.**

Δ. Yet we beseech you more expresly, and particularly to deal with us, &c.

.,.... It is said, ... It is written. ...... It is true.

Cease.

Δ. Gloria, Laus, Honour, Triumphus & Jubilatio fit Deo nostro omnipotenti : Nunc & semper.   Amen.

Wednesday, *Novemb.* 20. *Mane hor.* 11 ¼.   *Lubek,*

Δ. As thou hast of thy mercies (O Lord) given us some shew of thy favour bent toward us : so are we desirous to understand how our Letters have wrought upon our friend his heart to joyn with us to call for thy mercies, pardon and help : for if they have, Then do we hope, our bands (of acceptable life) whereby to binde vengeance prepared and intended against us, shall wax more and stronger : by thy great mercy and help to thy well-pleasing in thy service hence forward.

E. K. The Cloud and bonds appear : But the bands appear fewer.

Δ. O Lord, is our state since yesterday become weaker with thee ? And shall it so narrowly be exacted ? Thy will be done, who art holy, just, and most wise, O God.

E. K. The bonds about the Cloud, now are onely two , which before were six, or seven. The bonds seem of a smoky ashy collour , spirally going about the Cloud.

At length a voyce.
...... Judgement is the end of Justice : distributing and delivering also to every thing, seen, heard, or determined to his proper end uprightly.   Are you able to deny this ?

Δ. The end of our actions, words, and thoughts may seem twofold : One of us in-tended , and ment to be good : The other not depending upon our weening, but accord-ing to exact wisdom, what is the end of the same ; here deemed the proper end, if I under-stand right.

A voyce.

A voyce. *Lo, judgement is the end of Justice in things that are handled uprightly: whereof you finde the Omnipotencie and Truth of him that judgeth Omnipotently: Which beholding your Combat, hath-girded himself together, and beholdeth the Lists, and he judgeth uprightly: For, be hath sworn it. Arm not your selves therefore as weaklings: But provide as mightie and couragious Souldiers, for your own defence.* I am without corruption (*saith the Lord*) and lean not with the windes of Basannah.

Δ. O Lord, give me leave to request thee, *&c.*

A voyce. *But I am just, and judgement her self.* Enter not therefore into my holy places: Neither kneel down before my sanctuaries; saying, the Lord hath Chosen us, He liveth, and it is true for ever. For I have said, It may be undetermined. I will also see, whether you be strong inwardly, or privily rotten. For with the world your weaknesse is great. Whosoever overcometh shall rejoyce. But I will be a God in my Covenant and will hold on my promise: Fight therefore as it becometh you, and cast off the world. Make flesh subject, and strangle your Adversary. For unto such belongeth the entrance into my Chambers, and the use of my will, as the Horn of my glorie. For it is written, light dwelleth not in darknesse: Neither hath darknesse comprehended any light: For darknesse is the Cave of errour, and the reward of sinners. Thus sayeth he, which beholdeth your sorrows: And it is a fight for many daies, which appeareth neither in the one, nor in the other: nor giveth he answer untill the end.*

E. K. There is one come in like a Ghoſt, and he taketh all the hangings away, which beautified the place like to Curtains. Now all the ſides of the ſtone are darkiſh; and the Cloud ſtandeth in the very middle thereof. Now the bands ſeem brighter then ...... becauſe the place is ſo darkiſh.

Δ. O Lord, many *daies* Combat is aſſigned us. And foraſmuch as *Militia eſt vita hominis ſuper Terram*, we are now in a great uncertainty of our Combat ending.

E. K. There ſtandeth the number of 40. upon a great Labell, and nothing elſe.

Δ. This 40. (O Lord) what betokeneth it, dayes, weeks, or years? Well: Whatſoever it be, Bleſſed be the name of the Higheſt. Our God, King, and Father.

E. K.

Δ.

E. K. Now is one come in very brave, like a Preacher; I take him to be an evil one.

Δ. Benedictus qui venit in nomine Domini.

This Preacher-like Creature, ſayeth.

E. K. He ſaith nothing; Not ſo much as, Amen.

...... *Are you ſo fooliſh to think that the power of God will deſcend into ſo baſe a place?*

E. K. The power of God deſcending, deſcendeth to beautifie the place; And whatſoever he beautifieth, he doth it mercifully: And ſo through his mercy he deſcendeth among us, that put our truſt in his mercies.

...... *It is true: But, unto thoſe that are righteous.*

Δ. Chriſt his coming hath been to ſave ſinners. His converſation was among ſinners, halt, lame, blinde, and diſeaſed. So likewiſe: Now our frailty, or impurity will not exclude his preſence, or the Miniſtery of his faithfull Angels.

...... *What, in this baſe manner?*

Δ. Do you miſlike the manner?

...... *Can any that hath any drop of wiſdom like it?*

Δ. Are you wiſe?

...... *Or elſe I could not ſee thy imperfections.*

Δ. Which be they? Accuſe me.

...... *What greater imperfection, then to imagine much more believe, that the Angels of God, will, or may deſcend into ſo filthie a place, as this corruptible ſtone is? Conſidering the clearneſſe, and bigneſſe of the aire, or the places that are prepared in mans bodie, for ſuch entrances.*

Δ. Who cauſeth thee to come here?

...... *Thy folly.*

Δ. Art thou good, or bad?

...... *I am good, or elſe I could not ſee the bad.*

Δ. Ergo, thou art a lyar, for thou ſayd'ſt, No good Angel, would, or might come here into this ſtone.

Δ. Thus will God be glorified againſt wicked Satan, and his Miniſters. His fetch was very subtile : As, To bring in doubt all the Actions performed in this stone.   What canst thou answer ?

E. K. He sayeth nothing : Neither can he say any thing.   He seemeth to be a very foolish Devil.

Δ. Mendacem oportet esse memorem.   Now be packing hence.

...... *I will abide here.*

Δ. Where God will permit thee, there mayest thou be : But we will (as now) cease : And we thank God highly of this comfort and victory : We beseech him , that we may as prosperously overcome all other Diabolical assaults or sophistical , or untrue perswasions : and all his Temptations. Amen.

Glory, Honour, power, and praise be to our Almighty and living God , the Lord of Hosts, *Jehovah, now and ever.*   Amen.

Saturday, *Novemb.* 23. *à Meridie hora* 1½.   Lubek.

E. K. Here appeareth the same bad one, sitting, who last appeared.   The Cloud with the sword appeareth at last : with two wreaths on one side; and two on the other, spirally.   This Creature taketh the cloudy pillar, and throweth it from him divers times.

He sayeth. *Call as long as thou wilt, I will keep thee for seeing any more fights here.*

Δ. Or Lord, attend unto thy glory : Attend unto thy honour, regard the arrogancy of this Luciferine brag against thy younglings expressed.

Δ. And of the Lord, *Alb. Laskie,* &c.

...... *He shall come to destruction, as thou and thine to miserable beggery : Because he hath consented to them that are Ministers of iniquity, spirits of falshood.*

E. K. He looketh on a bare book, when he saith thus.

...... *The power of God entreth into the Soul of man, and doth visit the Chambers of his under-standing : openeth his will with p ver.   The spirits of darknesse are ready for every place , and can deceive, saying, This is of God.   Unto these you have listened : and have sworn it as a Covenant between God and you.   But I am come from God : and am entred indeed, and will make you hungry in your own foolishnesse, that you may become wise.   None hath entred here with power but I. And I will tarry here.   And I will be a wall betwixt you , and your imaginations : and betwixt those that have tempted you , and your weaknesse.   For thou hast called upon God : and he hath heard thee, and I am he that sayeth so unto thee.   ..... Laws of salvation are ready, follow them. The way into darknesse is wide, and easie , and where light is, it encreaseth joy.   Be thou therefore warned by me.*

Nay, I have said.

Δ. Thou hast said here, That thou art God, is that true ?   For thou hast said, Thou hast called upon God, and he hath hard thee : And I am he , that sayeth so unto thee.

...... *I see thee : And thy wisdom is nothing : Make of me what thou canst , I am the messager of God.*

...... *Avoid darknesse, avoid darknesse, avoid darknesse.*

E. K. He plucketh down violently (in the stone) the Clouds, and all becometh light in the stone.

...... *Ly here with thy fellows.   Those that are of wisdom, let them understand.*

Δ. O Sapientia patris æterni, illumina mentes nostras, ut tibi serviamus in sanctitate, & Justitia toto vitæ nostræ tempore.   Amen.

...... *Carmathar, a Knight of the Rhodes, was thirteen years deceived with one that appeared (as he thought) in glorie & wisdom in the image of Christ.   Antony was beguiled in divers wayes. The Prophets & Apostles have doubted in many things; But because they faithfully beleeved they were not rejected. Their hope became fruitfull, and they blessed with understanding from above. If so be also, you repent, and be sorry in that you have yielded unto the instruments of wickednesse : and follow on, as they your fathers have done , you shall also become wise : But I say unto you, That which you have consented unto is amisse , and false, worse then errour it self.   For, where have you tasted anie fruit out of that Doctrine.   How poor is the power, that hath been long told of in you.   You have forgotten your own knowledge, and are become of seers, blinde : such as grope their way.   Such end, such beginning.   For the end hangeth from the beginning : and is become a means in it self , to bring all things to passe.   But neither the end nor beginning of such things as you have handled hath been perfect, or probable : But a deceit, comprehending the image of falshood : Yea, much more the traps and snares into wickednesse.; which deserveth destruction eternally.*

If

If this may advise you, Be it so. If these examples and probable arguments be found, Then necessarily you ought of dutie to be counselled by me : But I have opened my mouth and told you. Be it unto you, according to your disposition.

Δ. Be it unto us according to the mercies and loving kindnesse of the Highest ; into whose hands we commit our selves, all our doings, and intents.

...... *That is well said . . . God be with you.*

E. K. *He is gone, and in the place vvhere he stood the likenesse of a little Circle, as if a print vvere made vvith a* Thimble-brim·

Δ. Soli Deo, Honor omnis, & Gloria. *Amen.*

Monday 25. *Novemb. Mane,* 8 ¾ *Lubek.*

E. K. Here appeareth straight vvay, (at the first looking) the same fel-low that last spake, and left the print of the little Circle behind him.

Δ. Orabam diu ad Deum, ut Arbiter esset inter istos. A ... num .... lum confugimus in tempore necessitatis, &c. A te (O Deus) solo pendemus, &c.

Δ. Sedebamus quasi in triangulo, & se convertebat versus A. L.

...... *Thou, O man, awake, shake off forgetfulnesse : Lift not up thy self so much ; But close up thine veins against these deluded deluders, which carry thee heading into folly, and transform thee to a shadow : By whose counsel thou art become dishonoured, and by whom thou shalt become a spot in the Book of Fame. Call to remembrance the Histories of the whole World, Political and Ec-clesiastical. Inquire of the Learned that have settled their judgements in the Book of God. Open thine eyes, and behold, if any of the Prophets or forefathers (men grounded in wisdom and deep understanding) have yielded themselves to this unrighteousnesse, believing lyars ; consenting to un-truth, and lastly dishonouring the Name of God. Then call to minde thine own estate, thy flour-ishing of thy youth, and possibilities, wherein thou mayst be made perfect. Which if thou truely do, Then banish this dishonour to God and his Angles, listen not to these S ...... ersity : For the Syrenes are awake, and their song is to destruction. I am seat from God, as a Messenger to call thee home ; for thou dishonourest God mightily: Behold thou shalt be made contemptible, and become a laughing-stock. Thy bosom shall be defaced, and thy posterity spotted with ignominie. More-over, such as are thy friends shall shake their heads ; saying, What wise man hath thus been over-come ? What is he that is become foolish ? Thou mayst desire it, and consent, as before : But I am a stumbling block betwixt you, and will dwell in all Elements for your purposes.*

E. K. He holdeth up his hands towards Δ and saith, .. Nay I have told him truth.

E. K. He hath now gotten him a Chair, and sitteth down·

Thou shalt be hanged, he said to E. K. *Declina, à ma-lo & Fac bo-num.* Psalm.

Δ. If it be truth, then it is a token that God is very merciful unto us ; and that we are in his favour highly, to give us this warning to avoid evil. Now resteth the other part, How we shall attain to good, and wisdom, from God ; such as by the true and perfect use of his creatures, we might do him some acceptable service, with true obedience and humi-lity, &c.

E. K. One cometh to him, and saith ..... *He* goeth about to take you a lyar.

E. K. *He* goeth away, and cometh again.

E. K. This man which thus came and went away, and cometh again, is all in white ; he hath a silver Crown on his head : he speaketh as fol-loweth ....

.... *Deny that you have done, Confesse it to be false ; Cry you have offended, And let the An-gels of God see you do so, (that they may carry up your prayers :) so shall you become righteous ; But why dost thou write words of contempt against us ? For One in our number is All ; And we are, all, One. Believe us ; for of our selves we have no power to instruct you, but to deliver you the Commandment of God : Rent your cloaths, pluck those blasphemous books in pieces ; And fall down before the Lord : for be it is, that is Wisdom. I have done for this time.*

E. K. *He* is gone.

Δ. Quis est discretor Spirituum ?

E. K. Now he cometh in again and speaketh.

...... *Oh, you are a Learned man. ...... Truth in the second : He it is that discreetly judgeth all things. If his discretion be given to you, thank God:*

Δ. Illi

Δ. Illi ergo Committemus hanc causam. ab illo hoc donum petentes & expectantes. Nos interim pie in Christo vivere intendimus.

E. K. *He is become a great pillar of Chrystal higher than a Steeple.* He ascendeth upward in clouds, and the little circle remaineth.

Δ. Gloria, laus, honor, & gratiarum actio sit Deo nostro omnipotenti Trino & uni, nunc, & in secula seculorum. *Amen.*

Tuesday Decembris 10. After Diner, we removed from *Lubek*, and the Lord *Alb. Laskie* went by Coach to Lord *Christopher*, Duke of *Meckelburgh*.
Thursday night we lay at *Wismar*.   11. *Decemb. vel* 12.
Saturday morning we came to *Rostoch*.   14. *Decembris*.

Monday Decemb. 16.   *Mane hora* 10 ¾.   *Rostoch.*
E. K. *He is here, that said, he would dwell* in omnibus Elementis, &c.
Δ.

...... *I came from the fountain of light, where is no errour nor darknesse, and have Power, (because it is given me from the Highest) Which, (Lo) is grown and become a mighty Rock, For it is said of me, Behold I will visit them that put their trust in me, with a comfortable strength in the time of need ; For my Rock is an everlasting strength, and the Hills of my countenance endure for ever. If then I be the Countenance of God, and a piercing fire sent out as a flame, not onely with his great mercy, but with his good will, and that towards you, overwhelmed, not cast down, but almost for ever buried in a lake of ignorance, and inquenchable flame, such as consumeth with ignorance, deceit it self, and a provocation too manifest, and apparent destruction: If I then with this message (being the message of truth) my self a mean .... sufficent Order for the publishment thereof, can, nor may ....., as of ... n I am) vehemently despised (the fruits of a good Conscience, notwithstanding stedfast) Then is he of no power of whom I am ..., because it is written. Such as rise up against my Spirit, I will destroy them in the midst of the same fire, and will deliver their ashes to the windes for a memory of their wickednesse. But he is just, and is without measure: knoweth what is, and what is to come, which hath thus said of you. Behold their ignorance is greater, and they esteem not truth. Lo I have heard them, in the midst of their corruption ; yet they are become faithlesse: I minister unto them, but in vain ; But behold their mouths are closed up with idlenesse. O ye of little understanding, are you become so blinde, that you will not see ? Are the windows of your eares made fast against truth ? Are your consciences sealed up, with a thrice burnt iron ? Desire you light, and yet refuse it ? Have you craved ..., and now deny it : yea utterly disdain it ?*
Δ. That is not true.

E. K Now cometh a head behind him.
...... *Lo the end shall become your comfort, if you listen to the songs of my mouth: if not, ever-lasting folly : and a reward of such, as are weary to hear of Truth. Now I pinched him ....*
E. K. This he said looking behind him.
Δ.
...... *Burn those blasphemous books of thine, and I will teach thee wisdom.*
Δ. Will you have me note down that sentence so,
...... *I will.*
Δ. What blasphemous books can I acknowledge, seeing I understand none? If they contain Sentence, make me to perceive it ; that so I may compare it, with the Touchstone of God his word, using the Talent of such reason, as God hath given me.
.... *I go, I go, I go.*

E. K. Now cometh a great fire down, and there appeareth a great huge man, with *a great sword in his hand* ; fire cometh out at his eyes, and at his mouth.   This terrible man said,
...... *Maledicti sunt, qui jurati sunt contra Nomen meum.*
E. K. Now that wicked creature shaketh himself.
Δ. In nomine Jesu Christi Redemptoris humani generis, Quis tu es ?
[This was spoken to the man with the sword.]
...... *Sume vires.*
Δ. Deus in adjutorium meum interide, &c.   Miserere mei Deus &c.
E. K Now the great huge one kneeleth down, and his face is (now) from meward; he looketh up toward heaven ; he hath very long hair, to
beneath

beneath his girdle; his Robe is long and tucked up.　Now he ſtandeth up.

...... Curſed are they : Curſed are they : Curſed is be for ever.　I am, *I gave thee power,
and ſealed thee for a time : Power to uſe the vehemency of thine own poiſon; but not to touch my
coat.　Thus be ſaith, And (I am) thou art a lyar from the beginning, and the fountain of curſed-
neſſe.　Damnation is thy dwelling place; Death is thy ſeat.; Vengeance is the Crown of thy diſglory.
Becauſe thou haſt entred into my ſeat : Haſt exalted thy brightneſſe, blaſphemed my name; wherein
(in this Action) thou continueſt (No point of thy charge, nor of my permiſſion.)　Be thou ac-
curſed, weakned, overthrown, and defaced.　Thou art vanquiſhed, Thy time is ſhortened.　And
why ?　I am.　And I ſay thou fighteſt against me, and not against men.　I am Juſtice, and the
ſtrength of him that liveth, whom thou haſt felt, and ſhalt feel, world without end; Therefore
Depart; Depart I ſay.*

E. K. Now the ſword ſtandeth by him, with the rags that appeared
before.

*...... Vengeance, prepared for others, be thy reward :　As it was delivered unto thee, ſo take it
with thee; That the malice which thou ſheweſt to others, may heap up thine own deſtruction.*
Jeovah, Jeovah, Jeovaſcah.

E. K. The wicked Tempter falleth down into a hole, and this high
creature putteth the ſword and rags down after him.　Now this great
creature appeareth as ſmall as he uſed to do.　And it is *Michael*.

Mic. ...... *Veniat Lux Domini, & fidelium Conſolatio.*

E. K. Now is all come in, as was before :　The Vail, the feet of men
appearing under, &c.

Mic. ...... *Thus hath God dealt mercifully with you.*

Δ. His Name be praiſed for ever.

Mic. .... *Thus hath Truth vanquiſhed darkneſſe.　Even ſo ſhall you vanquiſh the World in him
which is the Spirit of Power and Truth.　For I have Sworn (ſaith the Lord) and will be merciful unto you;　But ceaſe for theſe daies to come; for they were daies delivered :　Let them be
(therefore) unto you daies of Repentance :　For the end of 40 daies muſt come :　And this Doctrine ſhall be written unto all Nations, even unto the end of the World.　The Grain is yet in the
earth, and hath newly conſented with the earth : But when it ſpringeth, and beareth ſeed, The number ſhall be the laſt.*

Δ. A dark Parable, to my underſtanding, is this.

Mic. ...... *The tranſparent fire of Meekneſſe comfort and warm your ſouls, rectifie and make
ſtrong your bodies, to the eternal comfort of the World to come; in the pilgrimage which you ſhall
endure, with a heavy croſſe for the Teſtimonie of Truth.*

E. K. A great many voices, ſay, *Amen.*

E. K. Now he is gone, and the golden Vail is drawn again.

Δ. Omnis laus, honor, Gloria, Victoria & Triumphus ſit Deo noſtro omnipotenti, Vivo &
vero, nunc, & in ſempiterna ſeculorum ſecula.　*Amen.*

Sonday, 22. *Decembris,　Mane,* we went from *Roſtoch* toward *Stetin.*
Wenſday, 25. *Decembris,* on Chriſtmas Day morning, we came to *Stetin* by 10 of the clock.

Anno 1584. *Stila veteri.*
Stetini in Pomerania.

January 2. *Mane, hora* 9.

Δ. Veniat lux Domini, & fidelium Conſolatio, &c. 40. dies, jam completi ſunt, &c.
Expectamus præpotens auxilium Altiſimi, &c.

E. K. I cannot ſee but an inch into the Stone.　The Curtain appeareth, but more deep into the Stone　At length cometh one
very tall, in a long white Gown, all open, and his hair of his head hanging
down to his legs.　He hath wings upon his head, armes, back, and legs.
He ſeemeth to deſcend from the Clouds, and upon Clouds which lie ſloape-
viſe for his deſcending.　He ſpeaketh as follovveth.

The

...... *The pureneſſe of humility, diſperſed through the inward bowels of man, is that, which is called (with you) Perſeverance.   Which Perſeverance, beautifieth and eſtabliſheth in a true and ſtedfaſt Baſis thoſe things that are acceptable in the ſight of God, the workes of man.   Hence ſpringeth juſtification, which . . . . with the love of God.   Herein are you become like unto us, for that we are the image of Perſeverance, and the Glory of God.   But in us it is dignified : In you it is, and muſt be imperfect : For nothing is of fleſh or blood, that receiveth perfection.*

The Emanations from God, to, and into his creatures (which agree in the Center of the Earth as the knitting up of things) are eſtabliſhed : So that one jot of his Will neither can, nor may periſh, wax weak, or dwell in error : Which foreſeen from the beginning, carrieth in it ſelf the remembrance of all things to the end.   Through which mercy and remembrance, you are become the ſervants of God : Not for your own ſakes ; but in that it is the Glory of him, which hath called you

Our Calling
or Exerciſe.*to this exerciſe : Troubleſome to the World, but rewarded with Glory.*

If therefore your imperfections riſe up and reſiſt the Will of God, ſaying, blaſphemouſly as you do, Let us ſeek other wayes, Then you are not counted perſeverers , neither are your works worthy reward :   But humane reaſon can perſwade and give judgement againſt theſe follies, much more are they damnable, and deſerve correction in the voice and judgement of ſuch as are pure.

He that dealeth with the wicked is a lyar, and ſhall have his reward : But the end of comfort is in the pureneſſe of ſpirit.   But O you of little wiſdom, you riſe up againſt the windes, and yoke your wits againſt the mountains : Nay you caſt your ſelves down headlong, where there is no mercy. For what blaſphemie is it to ſay, If it be the will of God, it muſt follow ? Is not man ſubject to the bringing in of his own labours ? And are not they allowed to his comfort, being brought in ?

The ſoul of man is the Image of God, after his form, which keepeth within himſelf the power of his divinity in the heavenly Spirit, whereby he hath Authority to conſent with God in the workmanſhip of his Will and Creatures :   Which Power being ſealed already, giveth unto man (as King of himſelf) to conſent to his own ſalvation, conjoyning and knitting himſelf together, either with perſeverance in the aſſured hope of mercy, or (with wilfull drunkenneſſe,) to the reward of ſuch as fall.   Therefore, Become Holy.   For the ſoul beautifieth, when it is beautified in it ſelf.   Reſiſt not the Will of God, which is mighty on you : Be not obſtinate.

Be humble, Rejoyce not for this World : But be glad that your names are ſealed, and that you ſhall correct the World.   Deſpair not through weakneſſe ; for from whom cometh ſtrength ? If puddles become Seas, the end is more wonderful : But yet greater when ſinners are called to the knowledge and performance of God his Will, thorough his mercies.   Even as one day periſheth, and is not, although he hath been ; Even ſo it is, and ſhall be the ſtate of this World.   For the Earth muſt ſing O Sanna with the Heavens , And there muſt be One veritie.   And Hieruſalem ſhall deſcend with an horn of glory to the end.   The Sun and Moon ſhall be witneſſes, and wonder at their ſtay.   The Kings of the Earth ſhall become proud in themſelves, and are unable to be tamed with man.

But I will yoke them (ſaith the Lord) with correction ; And force them one to imitate anothers ſteps : Yea they ſhall tread the grapes alike ; For in my Vineyard Corruption ſhall not dwell with Authority : Neither ſhall the Prince of Darkneſſe uſurpe my further honour.

E. K. He ſpeaketh much in a ſmaller voice than he did. I cannot perceive it.] *He* turned back and ſpake.

...... *I ſpeak theſe things for your underſtanding, and that you may be ſtrengthened.*

E. K. He turneth back again (as before) and ſpeaketh I know not what.

...... *My dear brethren, therefore rejoyce in Comfort, and the image of Peace : and remain faithful, that you may be fed with that food that ſhall preſerve and alwaies reſt before the mighty flames of Zanzor : where there dwelleth no defiled Creature, nor any unrighteouſneſſe.*

E. K. He turneth now back again (as before) ſpeaking. He ſeemeth now to lean againſt a Pillar of Copper, great and round : And he is become leſſe than he was. Now he ſtandeth on the top of the Pillar, Now he kneeleth down, his back being turned.

A voice ſaith to him .... *Swear* .... [1]
He ſaid ...... *It is done.*
He ſaid ...... *The firſt voice openeth his mouth and ſaith* [*There is a great rumbling and rouſhings of falling of Towns or Houſes, as it were in the Stone.*]
He ſaid ...,... *The will of God is ſealed in this Propheſie, and it ſhall endure.*
A voice. .... *Swear* .... [2]
He ſaid .... *I have done.*
He ſaid .... *It thundereth, and it is the ſecond voice.*   *The effect of God his Will, is not of time ; and therefore not to be known of man, till that moment and end of time ſhall appear, wherein it muſt be publiſhed, and finiſhed with power.*

E. K. Now

E. K. Now it thumbleth again very terribly, as though a vvhole Town should fall down into a great Valley.

A voyce .... *Swear.* .... [3]
He said. ...... *I have.* ..... *And it is the third, and the last voyce. All things that are crooked shall be made straight. The winde of the heavens shall walk through all the earth. Wisdom shall sit in her Majestie, Crowned, in the top of an Hill, with exalted glorie.*
It is the end.

E. K. Now all dasheth in a flame of fire, Pillar, and he, and all, and so flieth upward.

A voyce. ..... *He that hath ears, let him hear.*
Another voyce. *It shall be.* Amen.

E. K. Now the Curtain cometh before all, as it vvas at the beginning, this day.

Δ. O Lord, for thy great mysteries declared unto us (this day) we most humbly thank thee. But on our parts, there remaineth some matter. .... thy hands by some of thy good Ministers, we desire to have some advertisement: as of the Lord *Alb. Laskie.*   Secondly, of *Vincent Seve,* &c.

E. K. A very little Creature appeareth, and saith.

The little one. *A word, and away.   The hearts of Princes, are the secrets of the Lord: Such they are, as unlock the doings of this world.*
Δ. Of *A. L.* his delay in coming (contrary to our desire and expectation) I would gladly understand the cause, &c.
The little one. *Those things that are of wickednesse, are not of our remembrance.   This stay shall hinder a third part of his glory.   But all your life is not of him: Nor he of you.   If he become good: he shall be well rewarded.   He is forward , Vincent is in France.*

Note. Of A. L. and our separating hereafter.

E. K. He is gone suddenly. This Creature stood betvveen the Curtain, and the forepart of the stone, it vvas one of the least Creatures that ever I savv.

Δ. All Honour, praise, and thanks be to our God Almighty : now and ever.   *Amen.*

Thursday, *Januarii* 9. The Lord *Albert Laskie* came to *Stetin, Hor.* 2¼. *à Meridie:*

Fryday, *Janurii* 10. Μαξιμας ινυριας υιρζοζνμ πωσε☉ ευμ. *Hora prima incipiebat, & per* 2. *horas durabat.*   Stetini.

___

Sonday, 12. *Januarii.* 1584.   Stetin.
Δ. After Dinner we were talking together of our affairs.   A voyce in *E. K.* his head said,

Jam venit hora.

Δ. After Supper, at I had a desire to shew to *E. K.* some places of St. *Johns* Apocalypsis, a voyce said to him,

Equus albus est initium Doctrinæ vestræ , Et est verbum Dei.
10. *& 9. sunt Novemdecim.*

A voyce. Equus Albus.

Δ. Hereupon seeking in the 19. Chapter of the *Apocalypsis* : we found the Text , *Equus albus,* &c. *versu* 11.
A voyce. *Ne dubites. Sum enim servus Dei.   To this purpose appertain these places of Scripture, &c.   These are the dayes wherein the Prophet said , No faith should be found on the earth.   vide Esdra.*
This Faith *must be restored again, and man must glorifie God in his works.   · I am the light of God.*

vide Esdra. lib. 4. cap. 9. versu 7.

Δ. Then, by like, He is *VRIEL.*
......*I am a witnesse of the light.   These are the times when Justice and truth must take place. Behold, I touched him, and he became a Prophet.*
Δ. Mean you *Esdras* ?
Uriel. Yea , in his ninth Chapter of the fourth book.   There you shall finde manifestly the Prophesie of this time, and this action.

This action in Esdras prophesied of.

Δ. Alak, we think the time very long, before we entred in the right trade of our true lessons.
Ur. *When you have the book of God before you, Then I will open these secrets unto you.*
Δ. But Alak , the time is very long thereunto, the more is our grief.

I 2   Ur. *The*

Ur. *The Bible it is.*

Δ. I meant somewhat of our other book, which is to be written.

Ur. *I will speak of that also.*

Δ. This delay is greatly to our grief, and occasion of many temptations.

Ur. *The temptation of the world are nothing unto the wise, happie are they that feel temptations with emptinesse of the belly.   The Timber is not yet seasoned, or else thou shouldest Prophesie.   I mean not thee E. K.*

Δ. Vincat manifesta veritas.

E. K. He is gone.

Honor, Gloria, Laus, & benedictio, sit Deo Nostro, qui in A L B O   E Q U O   Justitias suas facturus est.   *Amen.*

Monday, *Januarii* 13, *Mane hora.* 9 ¼.   Stetin.

Δ. After our long discourse upon the 9th. Chapter of *Esdras*, &c.   *Uriel* came, and stood, he .... 1y. upon *E. K.* his head, not visibly.

Ur. *Read the sixth Chapter.   For faith must flourish.   The world is rotten, and is skalden in their own sins.*

Δ. *E. K.* Read it, and in the 28. verse, thus it is.   Florebit autem fides, & vincetur corruptela, & ostendetur veritas, quæ sine fra ...., Diebus tantis, &c.

E. K. A voyce saith, Open the Shew-stone.

E. K. At length appared one in a long vvhite Garment.   The Curtain went aside, and the feet of men appear not now.   This man seemeth twice so high as Δ.   He hath nothing on his head, but long hair hanging down behinde him.   He is tied, or girded about, as though he vvere tied vvith many girdles.

Vide.   URIEL. *I am Uriel [said this man] The light, and band of him that created Heaven and Earth: that talked with Esdras, and did comfort him in affliction, and the same that hath talked with you: Yea, from the beginning of this action.   Therefore, gird your selves together, and hear the voice of the Lord: Listen, (I say) to such things as are hid, (I say) to them that dwell above the Heavens.   Behold, this is the last sleep of the world: and the time, that the power of the highest hath armed himself, saying, Come, O ye strength of the Heavens, and follow me.   For the earth hath cried vengeance, and hath cursed herself, and despaireth.   Come (I say) For I will place the seat of righteousnesse.   That my Kingdom maybe in One: And that my people may flourish: Yea, even a little before the end.*

And what is this?   E. K. He spake these four words in another Tune.

E. K. He looketh up to heaven.

An Angel now taking place.

A voyce. *Blessed art thou, which respectest thy Justice, and not the sins of man.*

Ur. *This is the voice of the Angel that now taketh place.*

Δ. May we be so bold as to demand the name of that Angel?

An Oath.   Ur. *No, It is not lawfull.   I swear by all things that are contained within this holy book: * By the seat of God, and him that sitteth thereon.   That the words, which have been spoken in this Action, and shall be now spoken, by me,*

A Prophesie. an. 1587. in Januarie. Antichristus. Si simpliciter, sit annus est intelligendus, si

are true: Three years are yet to come; even in this moneth, (that beginneth the fourth year) shall the Son of perdition *be known unto the whole world: Suddenly creeping out of his hole like an Adder, leading out her young ones after her, to devour the dust of the earth.*

* *Note, he spake this, pointing down to the great Bible of the Lord Alb. Laskies, upon which the Shew-stone, now, stood.*

men septenarius unus, nostrorum annorum 14. *sit habendus pro uno anno mystico: vel* 42. *menses, &c.*   Perpende.

Δ. The sentence is dark, in respect of the time.   Consider well.

Δ. I suspect 42 moneths (now and then) to be understood for an year.

Ur. *This moneth in the fourth year ; shall Antichrist be known unto all the world.   Then shall*

Antichristus. Omnes nunc Reges peribunt ante tertium annum finitum.

wo, wo, dwell amongst the Kings of the earth: For they shall be chosen all anew.   Neither shall there any that ruleth now, or reigneth as a King, or Governour of the ...... le, live unto the end of the third year: But they shall all perish.   Their Kingdoms be overthrown.

The

The earth wasted.   The Rivers become bloud, with the bloud of men and beasts mixed toge- △. *Suspicor* 42.
ther.   In this time shall the Turkish state be rooted up, and cast from the earth.   And instead *menses pro anno numerandos*
of him shall enter in that Devil: the father of liars, and such as dwell in the house of Va- *Mystice ithus*
nity.   Behold, This * Prince shall fly through his Kingdoms, as the *Prophesia: vel*
△. They are in Paradise, Greyhound after his spoyl: devouring his possessions, and cutting down *annus v lgaris*
they were carried upward, the wicked: But he shall become proud.   The Prophets of the Lord *ti anno my-*
especially *Elias*.   shall descend from Heaven, cloathed with their old Garments very fresh, *fl si.*
and not stained.   Thy eyes shall see them.   Out of these books shall the true Doctrine *Antichrist.*
of the Prophets, and Apostles be gathered: Which are not to be understood, but with the spirit of un- *A.L.*
derstanding, the spirit of wisdom, and truth.   Behold, I will say unto you my self. *Enoch. Elias. Our sign.*

Come, Hear.

For, the voyce of the Lord is with power.   Therefore, be milde, and of humble spirit.   For lo, *7. Libri tra-*
the time shall come.   And I have seven books, such as shall be delivered unto one of you.   And *dendi ipsi* △.
I will meet thee walking in the fields.   And will stretch forth my hand, saying, Come: Then shall
thine eyes see these things, that thy spirit doth.   And thou shalt become a man of understanding:
For I will give thee bread, and thou shalt eat it, such, as shall be the bread of sufficient
comfort.

E. K. It thundreth in the stone.   Of thee, [pointing to E. K.] thus sayeth the Lord.

Thou art flesh, and become stubborn.   Thy judgement waxeth dull, and thy heart sealed: But I *E. K.*
will unseal thee; and thou shalt be partaker: But (because thou hast offended me) not with power
in worldly things, I will make thee a great Seer: Such an one, as shall judge the Circle of things in
nature.   But heavenly understanding, and spiritual knowledge shall be sealed up from thee in this
world: For, thou art become stony, and hast cried out against my Saints.   Notwithstanding, your
life shall be together.   Thou shalt be a workman of nature, looking into the Chambers of the earth:
The Treasures of men.   Many things are pluckt from thee, which were thine: But not from
you, because I have promised them.
What is he, that bridled the windes, △. At your prayers?   Or, who is he that preserved you
from the bloudy imaginations of men, [and] hatreds of the world invincible?   Is it not he, that is
God of Heaven and Earth?   Is it not he, that made both flesh and Soul?   Tea, even he it is, that
sayeth.   Fly from the wickednesse, and society with Devils.   Leave off to sin against the Lord:
for he is of great power.   This is the last time that any shew shall be made in this stone.   For, lo, *This sentence is revoked af-*
the promise of the most highest shall be fulfilled. *terward, and the stone dig-nified,*

E. K. Now I see all those men, whose feet I saw before: And there sit-
teth One in a Judgement seat, with all his teeth fiery.   And there sit six,
on one side of him, and six on the other.   And there sit twelve in a lower
seat under them.   All the place is like Gold, garnished with precious stones,
On his head is a great stone; covering his head; a stone most bright, brigh-
ter then fire.   Four bring in a man bound.   Now all is gone except
Uriel.
Ur. The end of words, the beginning of deeds.
A voyce. Seal it up: For, it is at an end.
△. What is your will, that I shall do with this stone.
Ur. All is said: and I am sealed for time to come.
      △. Deo omnipotenti, vero, vivo, & æterno sit omnis honor, Laus, Gloria, Potentia, vir-
            tus & victoria: nunc & in sempiterna seculorum secula.   Amen.

Wednesday, January 15. we went from *Stetin* to *Stargart.*
Sonday, January 19. we came to *Posen.*
      Ecclesia Cathedralis Posnaniensis fundabatur anno 1025. *per* Winceslaum *Regem Christia-*
            num factum cujus sepulchrum in inferiori parte Ecclesiæ extat, lapide egregie extru-
            ctum.
Saturday, January 25. Ὁ κίνδυνⒼ ᴡἵμας τῆ θανάτῳ διὰ τῆ τῇ τῦ E. K. ἀδικίας μεγάλης ἐναρτίον ἐμῆ.
(i. e. *Magnum adii vitæ periculum per iniquitatem* E. K. *contra me.*)
Sunday, January 26. .... *Invisebam Bibliothecam Ecclesiæ Cathedralis.*
Monday, January 27.   πῖξαι χυμ οξορε ßρȣϛ. (*Rixæ cum uxore breves.*)
Tuesday, January 28. We went from *Posen.*
Thursday, Jan. 30.   We came to *Konin* Town, over the long and dangerous Bridge, with
much cumber at one broken place, by reason of the huge Cakes of Ice, which lay there.

Satur-

Saturday, Februarii, 1. We passed the dangerous way of Ice, having 25 men to cut the Ice for our Coaches to come through above two English miles long : but for all that great help, we could not get to *Vinew* City that night, by reason of the great water and Ice hard by the Town, which was broken over the banks into the medows very deep.

Sunday, Februarii 2. We came over the great water, the Ice being most part (with that nights winde) driven away out of our passage.

Monday, Feb. 3. We came by *Shadek* to *Lasko* Town, and there were lodged in the Provost his fair house by the Church.

Prima Actio apud Lasko.
Tuesday Februarii 11. Stilo veteri, ast 21. Stilo novo.

Δ. After our prayers of the 7 Psalms, and my particular invitation and calling for God his help, and the ministery of his good Angels : After (I say) more than half an hour space attendance ; *E. E.* seemed and thought that he felt a thing about his head, as if it clawed with Hawks claws, It continued no long time.   And toward the Easterly corner of my great Study above, seemed to *E. K.* clouds to appear, far off, as at a quarter of a mile distance.   Then appeared a Sea, endlesse one way, and a Haven mouth with a River which fell or ran into that mouth.   And besides that River doing down into the Haven, did another River appear by running into the Sea, without any Haven making or having,   The water of this Sea, is not like Sea-water, but rather like Quicksilver.   Now cometh a mountain, and swimmeth upon that main Sea.   Now that mountain seemeth to rest and stand before that River mouth, that is by the Haven.

A voice, ..., *Measure me.*

E. K. Now seemeth a great thing like a man to stand, with one leg in the foresaid River, and with the other in the said Sea, by . having a corner of the ·· id between his said legs. *His* right leg is in the River, and his left in the Sea. *His* right leg seemeth gold, and his left leg lead. The mountain standeth before him, *His* legs are like two posts, of the substance of the Rainbow. *He* is very high : he hath a face, but with many eyes and noses, but not distinctly to be discerned. *His* body seemeth to be red Brasse. *He* standeth with his arms abroad, and no hands appear. *His* right arme is of the colour of silver ; *His* left arme seemeth to be black, twinkling. *His* head is much of the colour of that Sea wherein his left leg standeth. Now beginneth a right hand to appear ; a fair right hand.

A voice said to this man, ... *Measure the water.*
He answered, ...,. It is 250 Cubits.
A voice. ...... *Measure that foot of earth.*
E. K. He pointeth to the mountain.
Answer. .... It is a cube twice doubled in himself in a straight line,
E. K. One speaketh behind me, saying.

...... *Measure the Sea also.*
Answer. ...... It is 750. Cubits.

E. K. He now stoopeth to it, and taketh of it in his hand.

He saith. ......, The fourth in the third, *and three in himself square.   The age of Nature.*
E. K Now all is gone, all is clear, and nothing appeareth.

Δ, At length after this, *E. K.* heard from the foresaid corner of the Study, the noise, as of a Ship tossed and jolted of the waves of the Sea.   After that *E. K.* saw one that stood all covered in a white cloud by the Easterly corner of the Table, above the Table in the Air. He said.

....., *Beati sunt, quibus veritas , spes, & consolatio est : & quibus luminaria majora inserviunt, in fortitudine & potentia æterni & Omnipotentis Dei.*

E. K. Now the cloud covereth him, and abideth.

E. K. Now he cometh out of the cloud, and stepeth three steps forward

3. in 4. effici-
unt 12. & 3.
& in se efficit
9. Nunc 9. in
12. efficiunt.
108.

ward, and the cloud standeth behind him, like a garment ····· At length he said.

······ *Then is their blessednesse, eternal life.*

E. K. I never saw him before : He is covered with a red Purple Robe, such as my Lord, here, useth ; but made somewhat like a Surplesse. His head is covered with feathers like Down : His face is like a childes face : His neck is bare : His legs are ba ···· most white : His garment cometh not but to the small of his leg. He standeth upon a white great round Table, like Chrystal, all written with letters, infinitely· On the middle of the Table is a great swelling or pommel of the same substance the Table is of. Upon that pommel he standeth· He hath nothing in his hands ; neither can his hands be discerned· His Robe hath no sleeves·

He said. ······ *Non possum diutius videri : Servus sum Altissimi : Novi Tetram in paradiso. Spiritus sum SAPIENTIÆ : Nomen meum est NALVAGE.*

E. K. He maketh a crosse upon the place vvhere he standeth·

Nal. ······ *Beatus Pater : Beatus Filius : Beatus Spiritus Sanctus. Bea ... tu ... t Mensuratio rerum & substantiarum omnium visibilium & invisibilium, verus & sanctus est Deus in promissis suis & veritas ejus, Talis est.*

E. K. Hereupon he shevveth a round Globe.

······ *Cælum, Mundus, Angelus, Homo, Nihil, & non nihil, & omne quod est, vel erit, Nihil est nisi splendor, Gubernatio, & unitas Dei : Quæ a Centro formata est reformata est, ab initio ad tempus mensuratum, & in perpetuum, Laus tibi in Cælo, Laus tibi in Terra, Triumphus tibi in inferno, ubi non est Laus, nec Gloria. Quæ jam infusa sentio, doceo : Sed modo, lingua, & ideomate prædicto.*

E. K. He turneth round when he speaketh·

Nal. ······ *Omnis Caro maxime est sibi applicabilis, in natura & perfectione sua. Igitur revelanda sunt Mysteria Dei, non ut audiantur, sed ut intelligantur.*

E. K· Now cometh a great smoak : now I see nothing : now he is gone.

A voice. ······· *Hear.*

[*E. K.* I see no body.]

E· K· Methinketh that two speak, or else this voice giveth an eccho.

······ *The unpatient and troublesome spirits of indignation, wrath, blasphemy, and disobedience, continually contend, bear arms, and ravenously run wilfully, against those that are the .... Messagers and Angles of the Dignified and Triumphant Glory : which is now the Ministery of him that is Dignified in his Father : To the honour and glory of those that are humble and faithful in obedience. Yea those wicked ones keep open wars against God, and his Annointed in Heaven and Earth, onely for the safeguard and true keeping of such as love God, and follow his Commandments, rejoyce in Truth, and are visited in Righteousnesse.*

Dark speeches to the flesh : but words mixed with humane understanding ; wherein briefly I will manifest the envy between the wicked (in respect of their enviousnesse) and those that are justified in Heaven ; which fight in the government of mans soul in the Creatures of God : Not in that they know they shall overcome : But in that they are envious and proud from the beginning.

Their contention is evidently amongst you, which are joyned in the service of God : Not as Deservers, but as Chosen ; whose vessels and power, are best known unto God

E. K. One standeth on my left shoulder and saith·

Sinister. ······· *Dost thou not hear, how like a fool he speaketh, without all reason ? Thou art a spirit of lying. Thou art one farthest from the glory of God. Thou art a sower of lyes, and a teacher of false doctrine.*

E. K. Thus saith he on my left hand.

Sinister. ······· *Speak, for I have power over thee. Canst thou deny it ?*

Dexter. ······· *Thou thinkest so, because thou hadst power : But the brightnesse thou hadst, is turned into iniquity. True it is, thou hadst power to banish the wicked out of Paradise : But me thou knowest not ; because thou hast not banished me. In respect of thy dignification (which sprang with power) I say with the Hallelujah : But in respect of thy fall, Thus saith the Lord ; Posui tenebras a tergo meo.*

Sinister. ······ *Fy upon God, that ever he created me.*

Dexter.

Dexter. ...... *Even thus, do they seek continually to enter into the weakest vessel : of envy, not to triumph ; for they know they shall not : but they hinder the time with man, wherein they may offend his conscience.*

E. K. I hear howling and lamenting.

To E. K.

Dexter....... *Such are those of whom thou seekest aid and comfort : Those that appear unto thee, have sought thy soul ; And the fruit of them, is according to their destruction. Believe them not. It is said before, • Thou dealest with devils. What reward shall he reap, that fighteth a-gainst the Highest ? Or taketh part with such as are banished from Righteousnesse ? Much more shall his punishment be, which seeketh help of those that are dishonoured. For dishonour ..... to imperfection, and is become a monster for destruction.*

It is written .... Nothing can stand before the Lord, that is imperfect ; Much more that imper-fection weakened, which obeyeth the imperfect. Leave, for the kingdom of Righteousnesse is at hand, And thou must vow. Hear the Lord, That thy sins may be forgiven thee : For the Prophesies of the Lord are not uttered to the world, with the seales of the wicked. Therefore become holy, that thou mayest augment the benefit of God bestowed amongst you ; and render it to the world, as the message of truth, with thanksgiving. Meum est pauca dicere.

Δ. Sed quis sis, Nescimus, an non idem Naluage, qui nobiscum prius egisti hodie ?

Nal. ...... I am.

E. K. Why call you those Devils, with whom I deal ; not offending my conscience, but intending to do good to my self and my neighbours? If you be of God, where is the fruit of your doctrine ? &c.

Nal. ...... *If they were not Devils and enemies of truth, they would praise and honour God in his Messengers of truth. But because thes Actions are true, and the truth of them shall be the de-struction of their kingdom ; Therefore devilishly and enviously they resist the will of God. Deny-ing the power ; Blaspheming his truth, and infecting his vessels.*

Devils.
This Doctrine
what it teach-
eth.

In our Doctrine there is nothing taught but the state of the world, here, and to come. The pro-phesies of time, and the knitting up of God his mysteries, opened from time to time, to those that are his sanctified : as testimonies in the Creation and Operation of his Creatures ; whereof this do-ctrine is a part. The Prophets in their times were not ignorant by revelation of the good will of their Creator. The Apostles in Christ his Kingdom, were made partakers of the mysteries to come, of the state of mans salvation ; and ending of this combat, which is in that day, when all Creatures shall receive their reward. The Church of God is alwayes garnished and furnished with spiritual Revelations : as a Mansion or Dwelling-place of the Holy Ghost.

These latter dayes, and end of harvest must have also Labourers : For no Age passeth away, but through the hands of God, who maketh the end of his doings known to the World : To the end, the World may consent unto him in Glory. So that this Doctrine, is the mysteries of the word of God, sealed from the beginning, now delivered unto man, for that Reformation which must be in One unity established unto the end. The very part of that Circle, which comprehendeth the Mysteries of the Highest, in his Prophets, Apostles, and Ministers yet to come, which are alive, and shall bear witnesse of eternal Comfort.

Reformation.
Note this
Circle.

The fruit of our Doctrine is, that God should be praised. For of our selves we seek no glory : But we serve you to your comfort, teaching you the will of God, in the self same Christ, that was cru-cified ; sold and died in the Patriarchs, and published to the World by his Disciples, and is now taught unto you, in the remission of sins .... greatest in the World, for the end of all things. The very key and entrance into the secret mysteries of God, (in respect of his determination on earth) bringing with it reward in the end of eternal glory, which is the greatest Treasure. Those that tempt thee, do it in respect of the fear they have of the power of God, springing in thee.

Let this suffice. The World is vain in respect of eternal joyes. Heaven and Earth passeth a-way: The reward of the Righteous endureth.

E. K.

Nal. ...... *What do you see imperfect, in all that hath been delivered ?*

Δ.

Nal. ...... *You have 49 Tables : In those Tables are contained the mystical and holy voices of the Angels : dignified : and in state disglorified and drent in confusion : which pierceth Heaven, and looketh into the Center of the Earth : the very language and speech of Children and Innocents, such as magnifie the name of God, and are pure.*

Δ Infra; in li-
bro Cat vien-
si. Aprilis 21.
dixit hunc lin-
guam nunquam
fuisse revela-
tam.
Let these two
places be re-
conciled.

Wherein, the Apostles understood the diffuse sound of the World, imperfected for mans transgression. These Tables are to be written, not by man, but by the finger of her which is mo-ther to Vertue [Δ. Madimi said her mother would write them, An. 1583.] Wherein the whole World, (to flesh incredible) all Creatures, and in all kinds, are numbred, in being, and multitude. The measure and proportion of that substance, which is Transitory, and shall wax old.

These things and mysteries are your parts, and portions sealed, as well by your own knowledge, as the fruit of your Intercession.

The

The knowledge of Gods Creatures.

Unto me are delivered five parts of a time : Wherein I will open, teach , and uncover the secrets **Five parts of a** *of that speech, that holy mysterie. To the intent the* CABALA *of* NATURE, *in voyce , sub-* **time.** *stance of bodie, and measure in all parts may be known.   For there is nothing secret , but it shall be revealed, and the son of* GOD *shall be known in* POWER *, and establish a Kingdom with righteousnesse in the earth, and then cometh the end.*

For the earth must come under subjection , and must be made pure.   That death may be swal- **Regnum Chri-** *lowed in his own Kingdom, and the enemy of righteousnesse finde no habitation.   The word of God en-* **sti futurum in** *dureth for ever.   His promises are just.   His spirit is truth.   His judgements inscrutable.* **terra.** *Himself Universall.   He it is of whom you labour.   The promises of God in this earthly Noble man shall be fulfilled.   Salomon used the places of honour, and was exalted.*

Thus sayeth the Lord.

I have sealed him against hatred ; and have made his seat open.   Let him therefore arise up, that the people may see him.   For mortal men have places of honour, and in their own Courts , they come to be exalted : Who is he that made the earth, and dignified him with a living Soul ?   Even be it is that exalteth, and in whose hands the Kingdoms of the earth are setled.

Behold, the fifth time shall come, (in respect of the parts of time) and it is the day , that hath been promised.   Then shall your eyes be open.   Then shall you see.

A voyce. *Stay there......*
Nal. *I obey.*

E. K. Now *I* fee him passe away over the Christalline Table , which is round like a Cart wheel, having a great knop in the middle.

Δ. As concerning our ordering of the Table , and the rest of the furniture, we are desirous to know, what is now to be done : seing, now we are come to the end of this first journey.
A voyce. *Be it thy charge.   I will put to my hand.*
Δ. Mean you it to be my charge to order these things, as my imagination shall be instructed, by God his favour.
A voyce. *It is so said before.*

Δ. Gloria, Honour, & gratiarum actio Deo omnipotenti Deo nostro Domino & Patri Nostro : nunc, & in sempiterna seculorum sæcula.   *Amen.*

Tuesday, *February* 18. *a Meredie hora* 3.   Lasko.   *Stylo veteri, aft* 28. ...
Die stilo novo.

Δ. After some prayers made, *E, K,* saw (as he thought) *Nalvage* standing at my left hand.
Δ. In nomine Jesu Christi Redemptoris nostri, Estis vos *Nalvage* ?
Nal. *Tu dicis.*

E. K. The lower part of him is in a Cloud : but all his upper part is out, he hath a thing like a Pall hanging down behinde him from his head ; He hath like a round · ... of boane in his hand, he seemeth to be as farre as the Church.   And I see him, as well winking as directing my open sight on him.

Nal. *What is it you require ?*
Δ. The exposition of the time delivered to you in five parts.   Δ. *F-lio pre-*
Nal. *Read it.*   *cedente.*
Δ. I read, and when I came to the place , that death may be swallowed, &c.   *Nalvage* said as followeth.
Nal. *That is the last Conquest.   Go forward.*
Δ. In reading ?
Nal. *I.*
Δ. I read to the end.
Nal. *The finger of the highest peruseth nature amongst you by himself , and in her own motion. Through which action things become, that were not (by Generation :) And in the same time vanish, as though they were not (by corruption.)   A year it is ;   Wherein nature looketh with many eyes through..... dwelling places : unto some as a Nurse: and to the rest as a step-mother.   And so it is meant in the Scriptures.   For, a time is an year , purposed by determination in the judgement of God ; which is not known to man , how , or when it shall happen.   Another year is a time established, and presently delivered, as the present judgement of God.   This is that I speak of.   A time is an year.   The parts are known amongst you.*

K   E. K. I

E. K. *I never heard any speak so leisurely.*

Nal. *Now look to your understanding.   I speak of two years.   One appointed in the judgement and determination of God to come, and unknown to man.   The other the time of the judgement of God (and before determined) now present: Notwithstanding, before determined.   There is difference between an year mystically promised; and unknown: and the time that is mystically promised and known.*   Annus mysticus sumitur dupliciter : Unus, qui est Tempus cognitum Deo, & hoeth a language   mini non revelatum : Tempus , hoc dicitur , apud Deum.   Annum nos illud computamus, to me un-   Aliud est præfinitum, cognitum Deo & Angelis, & revelatum homini : & Annus est præsens. known, and   *This last is the year I speak of.*
looketh some-
what on one   Δ. *What are your parts of that year ?*
side.   Nal. *March, April, May, June, July, August. .. .., In illo autem die , invenietis Christum. The words of this Doctrine must agree, and times.*

E. K. When come you with the rest of your words ?

Nal. *As it is given me, so I give it unto you.*
A great unpatience.
[Δ. He was thus interrupted by E. K.] --"Must end their course in the promise of God:
Cabalistical   " [In] These weeks are the fruits of my labour to be known, For I must unfold unto you, and
in respect of   " open the secrets of this mystical , and *Delivered* speech : Whereby you may talk in mortal
the receiving.   " sounds with such as are immortal: And you may truely know the nature, and use of God his
" Creatures. Therefore, be diligent in hearing, and *Receiving*. For the course of man is con-
" trary : But the determination of God most certain.
You are answered.
...... Mean you these Lenten weeks, or the weeks of all the fore-rehersed moneths ?
...... *Of my whole appointed time.*

E. K. He standeth higher up.

...... *May we (without offence) require your......at all times, as our case requireth ?*
Nal. *Your labour is my readinesse.*
...... *You see I have an Ague : What is your counsel therein ?*
Nal. *I have to counsel you (from God.)*
Δ. Blessed be the Fountain of counsel, and of all goodnesse.

E. K. *He sheweth an house; and six, or seven on the top of it with*
Torches : They are like shadows.
...... *In the name of God what may this mean ?*

E. K. These shadows go up and down the side of the house , thrusting
their Torches into the sides of it.   The house is like this very house. They
go round about the house.   There are eight of them. They have claws
like Eagles. When they sit, they are like Apes.   They set a fire on it, and
it burneth mightily ; Now your wife runneth out, and seemeth to leap over
the Galery rayl, and to ly as dead. And now come you out of door, and the
Children stand in the way toward the Church.   And you come by the
yern door; and kneel , and knock your hand on the earth. They take
up your wife; her head waggleth this way and that way.   You look up to
heaven still, and kneel upon one of your knees.   The stone house quiver-
eth and quaketh, and all the roof of the house falleth into the house , down
upon the Chests. And one of these baggage things laugheth.   The house
burneth all off.   Your wife is dead, all her face is battered.   The right
side of her face, her teeth and all is battered. She is bare-legged, she hath
a white Peticote on.   Now the apparition is all gone.

Marie seemeth to be pulled out of a pool of water, half alive , and half
dead, her hair hanging about her ears. They hold her up. Now they
carry her out at the Gate.   You seem to runne in the fields, and three, or
four men after you. You run through waters. All disappeareth; And now
Nalvage appeareth again. He seemeth to have wept.
Δ.

Nal. ......*God*

Nal. ..... *God giveth you warning that you may eschue them.*

Δ. And how shall I eschue them?

Nal. ....＊ *Thus sayeth the Lord. Behold, I have sealed thee for my self: for my people, and for my servant. Therefore shalt thou not perish; No, not the least hair of thy bodie. Fear not, be strong in faith. For I come shortly. Hearken therefore to my voyce, I say, therefore hearken to my voyce: For the spirits of wickednesse, and confusion have risen up against thee: If therefore they prevail against my purposes; Then shall it be no world: Neither are there any heavens. But, this place is not for thee; yet, if thou wilt, be it unto thee. I will seal destruction, both for a time and for ever. Be mighty therefore in me. All the earth rageth in wickednesse. And sinne smelleth thee ready now to creep out of his hole. If thou move thy seat, it shall be more acceptable. For, even this year shalt thou see the beginning of many troubles: And the entrance of this* LASKO, *into the bloudy service of the world.*

E. K. He seemeth to spit fire, and so vanish away.

O Jesu Christ, we have committed our selves into thy hand; and do submit our wills to thy government. What should this mean of terrible destruction threatned to my wife and maiden? And as it were frenzie, to light on me for sorrow. These things cannot well agree with our former assured protection.

E. K. I see a little wench on the bench, all in white, she sayeth.

...... *How do you sir?* ...,. [*making cursie to* Δ.]

Δ. Better it is known to you then to my self, how I do.

...... *Sir, I have been* ......*land, at your house, where they are all well.*

Δ. Thanked be God.

.....＊ *Amen..., The Queen said: She was sorry that she had lost her Philosoper. But the Lord Treasurer answered: He will come home shortly, a begging to you.*

They were black. Sir, Henry Sidney died upon Wednesday last. A privy enemy of yours.

.....＊ I ever took him for one of my chief friends.

......＊ *But this it is: Truely, none can turn the Queens heart from you. I could not come into your Studie: The Queen hath caused it to be sealed up. You have been used to good Cities: It were good, you did consider it. Little words are of great matter.*

Δ. Where, I pray, would you wish me to settle my self first?

.....＊ *My mother would give you counsel to dwell at* L A S C O.

Δ. Do you dissent from your mother?

.....＊ I.

Δ. Upon what.

.....＊ *Jesu, you think that I am an unwise maiden. The Devil bringeth the sound of my mouth to thy ears.* E. K. For I said C R A C O V I A, and he spake L A S C O.

Δ. Seing your mother would wish me to dwell at C R A C O V I A, at what other place would you wish me to dwell?

.....＊ *Lux ante faciem, Tenebræ post tergum.*

> Δ. Note, at *Prague*, Aug 14. I understood that Sir *Henry Sidney* was not dead in February nor March, no nor in May last: Therefore this must be considered, Doctor *Hager* his son told me. You may also mark how the Devil at this CRACOVIA. time did mis-inform E. K. and so it is possible that this being a lye, was his.

E. K. Now I feel a huffing thing go from my head.

...... *I pray you be not offended with my simplicity:* My mother and I am all one.

no discord: I pray you bear with me, if I say, I be the Concord of time. These are my words. My mother would have you dwell at C R A C O V I A. *And I consent unto it. Let them that be wise understand: Alwayes pray that you may hear truely, and receive faithfully.*

> In us is The Concord of time.

Δ. May I before I go any further demand if you be *Madimi*?

......＊ *I am so, Sir.*

Δ. As concerning this terrible Vision here shewed, what, is either the intent, or verity of it?

Mad. *Sir, will it please you to hear me?*

Δ. The verity is most acceptable to me alwayes.

Mad. ...... *I think your book saith, This man his way is prepared,* &c.

Δ. I trow, the words are, His seat is made open, or made manifest.

Mad. ...... *It is so. Bear with me, I think, it is so.*

Δ. What will you say thereof?

> Note the envy & power of the Devil.

Mad. .... *And upon earth Princes have b ... in their own Courts. I remember, He was seal-ed at* Mortlake. *Contra omne malum. Then cannot the King of* Poland, *nor the Chancelor, prevail against him. Yet* Vendiderunt animam ejus.

Δ. Lord be merciful unto ...; What Trayterous dealing? I beseech you to say ... e. in that case; He is our great friend, and for the service of God furthering.

> L. vid. Anno 1583. Jun. 16. Super, ante duo folia.

K 2　　　　Mad. ....* You

Mad. ...... *You met a man by the way: He is an Irish man.* (*But as ... me, he said he was a French m n*) *I heard the King, when .... him to go into* England. *But he could not poison him there ... Therefore he followed him, all the way. But if be return again: They say, We will exalt him. But send thou thy Army, and we will send him. Wherefore hath the King absented himself, but to betray his Kingdom? Truely, I can tell no other cause.*

Conspiracy of th. K. of Pol. wi:h the Turk against A. L.

My Mother saith within these few dayes, after he .... calleth it) *a little talk,* Let him go to Cracovia .... *himself as* David *did before* Saul: *It may be the people will like well of him.*

Tush, Tush, Timor innatus, *will never prevail.* E, K. She saith so, turning her head *Although he hate him, he cannot hurt him.* back to one that spake to her.
Sir, if you tarry here, you will have great grief in this house.

Δ. How long (I pray you) would you wish me, to tarry here: or how soon to be rid hence?

Mad. ....:. *Hark ... He,* E. K. *marvelleth what I will say now.*

E. K. So I did indeed.

Mad. .... *The Physitian saith, infected air is to be avoided in hast. Many Princes shall be acquainted with you, and Learned men. The good are oftentimes stirred up to offend God, whose offen es are both wilful and rash: For temptation is a Touchstone, and is one of the black fellows chiefest weapons.*

Δ. I beseech you, to say somewhat of the time of our going hence.

Mad. ...... *Tush, I pray you,* Go hence as soon as you may.

Δ. To Cracovia, you mean.

Mad. .,... *I... I will now and then visit you there: And will become friend with you,* E. K *now: for you are become a good man.*

Δ. As concerning that terrible shew, what can you say of it?

Mad. ...... *As a warning to beware that, that should be. This is the last Spear.*

Δ. But, if I go to Cracovia, no such thing shall happen, I trust.

Mad. ...... *So, Sir. Therefore, This is your warning.*

Δ. Is it not, then, the will of God, that I shall set up the Table here, as you see, we have prepared.

Mad. ...... *Be contented. This Wildernesse, is not* 40 *years. My Mother saith,* It must not be here: *yet at your request, it may be.*

E. K. How can that be?

Δ. At mans commandment, the Sun can stand.

Mad. ...... *He saith true, Believe him. ... Therefore I will not urge any thing herein, but de-fer till we come to* Cracovia.

Δ. At Cracovia, shall I set it up? And shall I require Pernus house there? Or what house else, is, in God his determination, for me and mine?

...... *As wise as I am, I cannot tell, what, yet, to say. It is the Town, where the Sabbath day shall be celebrated.*

Δ. But now, as concerning the house, What is your word?

Mad. ...... *You will not be destitute of an house. Will you believe me; For I am your true friend* M A D I M I. *Here shall be the end of your turmoil. Be of good cheare.*

Δ. Did you not will us to have my chest from Torn before we go?

Mad. ...... *I, when the black m ... hath called home his waters.*

Δ. Assoon as .... n have it from Torn hither, then we are to be going.

E. K. How will my Lord agree to this?

Mad. ...... *Now you are become a new man, both we may dwell in one house. Sir, I promise you of my credit, you shall be to learn nothing of these things by* August.

Δ. By August next?

Mad. ...... *Yea ... Next.*

Δ. Perhaps my Lord his furniture of money will not be such, as to serve for our carriage anew, &c. Besides that, I would wish Kesmark to be redeemed, before he should come to Cracovia: Perhaps then with the people, his credit would be greater.

Mad. ...... *Those that become Kings, care nothing for Farm-houses.*

Δ. I would that needlesse cost, here bestowed, had been saved: or that you had told us this sooner.

Mad. .... *Silence now, is my best answer.*

Δ. Do you know, (O Lord, what say I?) Have we had any name of N A L V A G E, heretofore in our Tables or Books expressed?

Mad. .,... *What have you written, that have you written. He is a near kinsman to my Mother. We call him, with w,* Fuga terrestrium.

Nalvage.

Δ. We beseech God, that all intermedling, and sauciness of the wicked in these Actions may cease. You know how one clawed him, here, on the head, as with Eagles claws.

Mad.

Mad. .... *He may rejoyce, they clawed not his soul.*　*You are content to let me go.*

E. K. She goeth away somewhat bigger, and in a long Gown.

Δ. Soli Deo Gloria. *Amen.*

Friday, Februar. 21. *à Meridie,* Lasko.　*Martii* 2. *Stylo novo.*

Δ. A's I had talked of *Madimi,* and IL. to E. K. about Treasure hid in *England* : and I was desirous to have some advertisement by *Madimi,* she appeared.

Mad. ....., *I answer your inward man. I am come again.*

E. K. She is bigger than she was.

Mad. .... *I am a little grown.*

Δ. As concerning a medicine for my Ague, I would gladly ...　And as concerning the wife of our dear friend, the Lor . . .

Mad. .... *I pray you, bear with me at this time : I am as willing to answer you (when light cometh again) as you to ask me.　You may consider of many things, I can answer them briefly. Such blessing as my Mother bestoweth on me, such I give you.*

E. K. She smileth.

Δ. God grant that his good Creatures may smile on me.

Mad. ......*When you know me well, you will find, I have been very charitable.*

E. K. She goeth away naked ; her body being besprent with blood ; at the least that side of her toward E.K.

Δ. Laudetur Deus Trinus & unus, nunc & in sempiterna seculorum secula.　*Amen,*

Saturday, Februarii 22. 1584. *ante meridiem.* Lasko. [*Martii* 3. *Stylo novo.*

Δ. The questions needful to be required of *Madimi.*

1. Good counsel for my health recovering, and confirming.

2. If the Pedestal (for the holy Table) being here made , shall be carryed with us to *Cracow,* rather than to make a new there : both to save time , and to have our doings the more secret?

3. What is your knowledge and judgement of *A. L.* his wife, in respect of her life past, present, and to come ; for we doubt she is not our found friend?

4. It is our very earnest desire, that the Danish Treasurer in *England,* in the ten places, (seised on by E. K) might be brought hither , very speedily : whereby *A. L.* might redeem *Keysmark* and *Lasko* lands, morgaged : and also pay his debts in *Cracow,* and about *Cracow.*

For, else, neither can he come with any credit, to *Cracow,* (as he is willed) neither can he come to us, there, so commodiously, and oft, as our conferences may be requisit.　And thirdly, the day of *Keysmark* forfeiting (without the Emperour his favourable help) draweth nigh : as in *April* at St. *George* his Day next.

Δ. And by your speech of *England,* you give me occasion to enquire whether her Majesty doth cause my rents to be received, by my Deputy assigned or no?

Whether her Majesty, or the Council, do intend to send for me again, *into England* or no?

And as concerning the red p . . . . which E. K. found with the book in *England,* what it is : And what is the best use of it, and how that use is to be practised or performed?

Δ. after these Questions written, and a little our praying to God for his light, verity, and help, and to send *Madimi,* according as she willed me to note many things, for that she could answer them briefly . we used silence a while ; . . . ath she appeared on my right hand between me and E. K.

...... *Blessed be his name that in truth, and for the truth, sendeth his Ministers to instruct them, that love Truth.　.... Even so ..... Be not pierced too much with sight of me.* [to E. K. for he looked mervailously earnestly on her.]

E. K. She seemeth more bright than she was, And to . . . and to stand in a more bright place.

Mad. ....., *All honour be to him that liveth in Heaven and in Earth, and is mighty in all places.* Amen.

1. ...... *Your health.*

E. K. Now she is gone to the place on the Cushions on the bench, where she stood yesterday.　She doth now as young children do, playing with her

coats,

coats; and at length sitteth down on the Cushions.

     Mad. ...... *Even as spiritual and dignified illuminations, from ascension, and by descending, work the will of God, determined in all Creatures, diversly, according to the measured purpose of the Highest, in dispersing his will upon and into every one, particularly; whereby some become wise, one in this, another in that degree; other some mighty in works, whereby health and help, comfort and joy, is given to the faithful: Even so, ascending, doth Hell infect, sometime with error, and sometime with infirmities: So that from Heaven springeth health, from below infirmities of body and soul.* Two immediate powers. *Whereby we find two immediate powers, bringing forth two properties, The one Comfort, with Joy; The other Infection with sorrow.*

     But this may be objected: Hath it not been seen, that the wicked cure diseases? and restore health? Whatsoever is of death, is sorrow; which is the ground of spiritual and bodily infection so that evil cannot work good. How can it therefore be that the dead revive, or restore health? The cure therefore of all spiritual infection (I mean the infections of such, as are spiritual is in respect of his weakness, and not of his strength; Because Satan infecting, may become weak (whereby he cannot prevail) and so give health, by reason of weakness: Otherwise, with power, bringing death all manner of wayes.

     Δ. E. K. thought a thing, whereunto she answered. . and he said . . . my thought: she answered . . . . in my degree, thoughts . . . . known to me. I, than an . . . . she is of God and in God, tha . . . . the thought of man.

     E. K. She · · · I hear · · · a buz. · · care

     ...... *These two immediate and supernatural properties are so dignified in Creation and Determination, that the good Angels cannot cure, or help such infirmities, as are brought in by the subtile infection of the wicked themselves: Unless in body the immediate power of the second Person in Trinity be adjoyned in the aid and cure of the infected body, which is the true Physitian. And as he took upon him man his frailty, so be is chief Governour over the same in all degrees.*

     If the soul be infected, the Angels have no power to . . . it or make it clean: but by the will of the Father which is the Holy Ghost, descending through the Angels into the propriety of the Church: whereby the Disease is cured. Therefore, considering, thou art infected, not naturally, but by spiritual and wicked inflammation, stirring up thy body unto infection. We that are good Angels, cannot minister help unless we feel the immediate power of him which is the second, and the water of Life. Notwithstanding, as we know how the infection grew, either locally or really: So can we find contrary places and things for comfort.

     When Herod was infected by the Devil to kill very Christ the Son of God; His purpose was not altered by contradiction to the Devil, but by the foreknowledge of God, which appointed Egypt for his safeguard. Cracovia. *So it is said unto thee, It is thought good thou shouldst rest at CRACOVIA; for it is a place sanctified, both in fore-determination, and now. Therefore use the Sabbath, and rest from labour: Reap now, and eat the fruit of thy labour; Presse the Vine, that thou mayest drink, and be comforted: For the promises of God, are not in vain; Neither are the Heavens fruitless.* Riches. *For as it is said, Thou art not bound, but for the service of God: Neither shalt thou be enriched by Princes: but shalt enrich them. Flesh may speak vainly, and be without comfort: But the promises of God, cease not, neither become uncertain.*

     This year to come, is of great blood-shed: prepared to stop the mouth of the Earth, which gapeth for sorrow. Therefore thou must be separated, that the promises of God may be fulfilled: which cometh (not at your request, but at his Determination) most abundantly.

     These Boords need not, The paviment shall serve; for it is neither the Earth, nor mans hands, (but the Finger of him that liveth,) that provoketh.

     Behold .... That the power of God might be known, therefore he hath chosen those that are not regarded, to the intent, it may be said: Lo, This is of God. .. Hast therefore, and stay not, for thy warning is great.

     Those that are wise (to sin) in their fleshly imaginations, are deceivers of themselves: Which with us are not to be accused, but rather unknown. For the Kingdom of Heaven is divided from Hell: and those that are of Hell, are unknown from us. For as . . . and . . . , naturally, know not, one another, such, and so it is of us.

     Sit tibi satis quod illam non novimus, neque virtutem ullam descendentem ab illa vidimus. Δ. L. *Neither is the power of God in him, for his own sake: but for the Spirit that God hath planted in him. For we have known him, and again have forgotten him. And yet we understand him But (I teach thee a Mystery) by irradiation into him: and not by reflexion from himself. As the heavens fly from the stink of the infected powers, even so, fly thou.*

Δ. Caudæmon ipsius Palatina.   *Ganislay, Ganislay.*   E. K. She calleth one, who is now come here.

                            E. K. He seemeth to have his face half

   Gan. ..... *What wilt thou with me?*   like a man, and half like a woman, his
   what wilt thou have?   body being all covered with hair, rugg'd.

                                         E. K. This

E. K. Madimi shaketh her Coates, and brusheth her Coates with · · · · ·

Mad. ······ *Thus sayeth my Mother.   Beware of wilde hony, and raw fruit : The one clarified, the other ripened may become good.   Those that know not wine become drunken, but to such as know it, it bringeth health.   Even so, this Doctrine.   For, unto him that it is tasted, being ripe, or ······ or becometh comfort, and the Key of a pr ····. But unto him that tasteth it wildly, and ······, Worketh sorrow.   Your knowledge is not to have, but to learn to ····· So that you may be, both having and learned.   Small are the Treasures of this world, in respect of the wisdom that judgeth NA-TURE.   For unto him that judgeth truely, what secret is hidden ?   Those that seek the world shall be contemned of it : But he that flieth from her, shall use her as a slave, or as the second mother doth her daughter.   Notwithstanding, of my self, I will be more appliable unto you , then you shall be followers of me.   For, for that cause am I become childish.   Therefore cease : He is truely* Why God in his Minifter, as a Childe dealeth with us. *wife, that sayeth, God knoweth at all times what we have need of.   Be not tempters.   Be patient*

5. *Even as thy desire is, so are all things in* England. *Nothing kept back.   But for thy sake, such as are thine, are with them friendly used*

6. *If thou shouldest not be called home, how shouldest thou enjoy the benefit of God his promise, which hath said : Thou shalt call her back, &c. to her preservation.   But, first these things must come to passe.   The Countrey shall be divided, one rise up against another.   Great treasons be wrought.   Yea, and one cut anothers throat : And when the greatest troubles are, Then shalt thou save her life.   Then shall the wall be broken down : And free passage shall be made : And such as are skorners, and ascend up the narrow steps, or shew themselves on the walls, shall be trodden down and defaced.   Here is understanding, ····· That which thou, E.K. hast, is a part of four, and is become the fifth : Yet it is none of the four, dignified in a Cube, whose root is* * 252.

····· *I will know it shortly.   Thou hast no power (for time is not yet come.) But must be brought forth shortly; that it may be known. ····· Made it, was* * Holy *(but it was made by those that. ····· It : which is not man, neither any thing of wickednesse) which for his sins died, least he should have been destroyed in the second death.   Revealed unto thee, neither for thine own sake ; nor at thy request : But by the will of God, for a time to come.*

E. K. I pray you to tell me plainly what it is.

Mad. ···. *Be content. ····· I speak, thus, least thou shouldest sin, God the father, the Son, and the holy Ghost blesse you.*

E. K. Now she is gone, *as a mighty tall woman.* Note. *Madimi* as a tall woman now.

Δ. Veritati æternæ, fit æterna Laus Gloria & Benedictio.

E. K. Amen.

Wednesday, *Martii* 4. *Mane.* 1584.   LASKO.   *Martii* 14. *Stylo Novo.*

Δ. After my Petition made to God (at the instance of *A. L.* not present now) to know of *Moldavia* Kingdom, the state to come : that is, when *A. L.* and by what means he should enjoy the same (being before at *Mortlak*, promised unto him.) And at my requesting that *Madimi* might be the Minister of his will therein : At length appeared *Madimi.*

Δ. Gloria Patri, & filio & spiritui sancto : sicut erat in principio, & nunc & semper, & in secula seculorum.   *Amen.*

Mad. Amen.   *A certain rich man, father of an houshold, returned, and found all things out of order : And lo, he looked up, and said unto his servant : Arise, and be ready, for I will set my house in order.   Go to Asson, and I will meet thee there : And he arose up, and went unto Asson : But his master came not : At length he said unto him.   Behold, I will not dwell h····· Remove my houshold unto Banal, and be did so.   And the servant prepared a feast : But his master came not.   And he said unto him the third time ; why art thou sorrie, or why art thou angry ? ····· Ob unto me, for I am thy master.   And he said : Rise, go unto Molschecks, and thou shalt meet me there.   But lo, thus sayeth the servant , my master forgetteth. ····· and hath commanded me twice, and I have prepared for him, and he came not, and he saith unto me the third time,   Arise, go, and I will meet thee : Thou shalt finde me there; But he will there also deceive me : And he sent before, and behold, his master····· But immediately after that, the servants messenger. ····· The father of the houshold came, and he looked but his servant was not there.   And he sent for him, and commanded him to be ···· and to be brought with violence : But the servant said, deal not thus with me, for it is violent : But the master answered, and said : What I command thee. ····· ghtest : For servants have no freedom of themselves.   And it came to passe that after the master had gathered together his friends : He said unto them, Arise up, and finde me one that is* FAITHFULL *with* OBEDIENCE.   *Then he stretched out his hand, and he said unto his servant.   Hold, take thy reward : For, from me thou art banished.   How say you, was this Justice, that he did unto his servant ?*

Δ. O Lord, we appeal to thy mercies, and we acknowledge thy judgements alwayes to be most just and true, &c.

Mad. *The*

Mad. *The Ark of the Lord was the Covenant of* OBEDIENCE. *Happy are those that enter.*

E. K. There springeth a thing before her like a Reed, but withered.

Mad. *Unto thee,* [*E. K.* pointing to the Reed,] *thus sayeth the Lord, Because thou canst not endure the end of winter, Spring on, and grow: But in the midst of [thy] beauty, in the midst of summer, shall thy destruction be.*

A. L. *I will anoint thee before thy time, for my promise sake: That thou mayest fall in the midst of thine own time, for thy weakness is great.*

E. K. She standeth and holdeth up her hands toward heaven, and saith nothing that I can hear.

Mad. *Go, make haste: All flesh is abominable.*

E. K. She speaketh another way, not toward us.

Mad. *I am sealed, neither can I speak any more.*

E. K. Now she goeth away like a three cornerd Cloud.

Δ. Oh Jesu have mercy on us.   Oh King of Jews have mercy on us.   Oh Conquerour against Hell, death, and the Devil have mercy on us.

E. K. Now is he here, who was last here.   Are you *Nalvage*....   In the name of Jesus. Lord be mercifull unto us, &c.

.... *Is sealed: I am excepted.* .... *I am commanded, and my Office is to teach.*

E. K. He turneth about with a great swiftness, at length he standeth,

Δ. O Lord, and our desire is to be taught of thee, in thee, and for thy service.

Nal. *To him to whom it is said, G O: Thus, I say, let him be going.   For God hath stretched out his hand, and he sayeth, I will not pluck it back, but with vengeance.*

E. K. He turneth again.

Δ. O God, to whom is that *G O*, sayed?

Nal. *Thou mortal man, who is the Lord of health?*

Δ The God of Heaven and Earth.

Nal. *The Lord is angry, and he said unto thee.*
Be gone.

Δ. I was sick of an ague, and thereupon did somewhat differ, swaking also for the Lord. *A. I.* His help, chiefly, with Coach, Horse, and Money.

Lo, there is a day past.   And if his own Angel had not made intercession for him, he had been nothing: Seal these things, make haste.
Be going.

For the Lord is angry.

Δ. O God, &c.

Nal. *Thus he sayeth. .... Lasky hath rejoyced with an Harlot, and hath measured me, which am unknown: But he shall be rewarded.*

Δ.

A. L. *To thee it is said: Make haste, and be gone.   I will* fulfill my promise in him for thy sake: *But he shall fall, being none of thy acquaintance.*

Δ Pronounce favour and mercy on me: who in my sin, ,,,,, and singleness of heart rejoyce to do what I can possibly perform.

Nal. *Thus they have said against thee.   Let him not go.   Of them thus sayeth the Lord.   They shall tarrie where they would not.   Cease, write no more.*

Δ. Soli Deo, omnis honor & Gloria.   *Amen.*

Δ. *Vide* Job. cap. 33. *eundum conjecturam meam de tribus modis Divina Misericordia, erga homines, &c.*

Monday, Martii 9. Hora 9.   Mane recessimus a ...... & prima nocte fuimus apud Petr......
Tuesday, 10.
Wednesday, 11.
Thursday, 12. ..... At *Michow* we lodged at night.
Friday, Martii 13. We came to *Cracow,* circa tertiam Meredie, and were lodged in the Suburbs by the Church at. ....., Where we remained a sevenight, and then (I and my wife) we removed to the house in St. *Stephens* street, which I had hired for a year, for 80 gylders (of 30 gr.) And Master *Edward Kelly* came to us on Fryday in the Easter week (by the new Gregrian Kalendar) being the 27 day of *March,* by the old Kalendar: but the hxth day of *April,* by the new Kalendar, Easter day being the first day of *April* in *Poland,* by the new Gregorian institution.

CRACOVIA.   Martii 13.   An. 1584.

Omnis Honor, Laus, Gloria & Gratiarum Actio, sit Deo Nostro Omnipotenti, Trino & uni nunc & semper.   Amen.   Δ.

MEN-

MENSIS MYSTICUS SAOBATICUS,
Pars prima ejusdem.

Tuesday morning, Anno 1584. *Aprilis* 10. *stilo novo Gregoriano.*
CRACOVIÆ.

Fter our divers prayers and contestation of our humility, obedience, and credit in these Actions: and being come now to *Cracovia*, the place sanctified, whereunto we were willed to make haste, &c. At lenth appeared *Nalvage.*

E K· He hath a Gown of white silk, with a Cape with three pendants with tassels on the ends of them all green: it is fur, white and seemeth to shine, with a wavering glittering. On his head is nothing, he hath no berd· His physiognomy is like the picture of King *Edward* the sixth; his hair hangeth down a quarter of the length of the Cap, somewhat curling, yellow· He hath a rod or wand in his hand, almost as big as my little finger: it is of Gold, and divided into three equal parts, with a brighter Gold than the rest· *He* standeth upon his round table of Christal, or rather Mother of Pearl: There appear an infinite number of letters on the same, as thick as one can stand by another. the table is somewhat inclined on one side: he standeth in the very middle; his garment covereth his feet: his breast seemeth smooth as the down remaining of a Swan, when all the feathers be off, so is his neck, &c. He is lean and long-visaged·

A. The infinite mercies of God be on us: and the light of his countenance shine on us; and his favourable countenance be on us.

Nal. ...... *Amen, unto him that is, and was, and liveth for ever.*

E. K· He looketh earnestly on his table, and turneth him to view it·

Nal. ...... *All things are in order. Thus saith the Messenger of him. which is the God of Wisdom. Is your worthiness such, as you can merit so great mercy? or are your vessels cleansed, and made apt to receive and hold the sweet liquor, pure understanding it self?*

A.

Hath the Sun entred into your bowels, or have you tasted of the night-dew? Where are your wedding Garments; or after what sort do you provide for your marriage? Unseasoned you are and withered flesh, partakers of those things which make you holy: through which partaking and the secret providence of him that is the Highest, you became dignified to the end, and are sufficiently washed for the time of entrance. O stiff-necked people you deserve nothing, and yet you have the hire of such as labour. But, what, can corruption be partaker of those things that are incorruptible? or man, which savoureth in himself, can you savour also of the Almighty.

O you weaklings, O you of no faith, O you Cankers of the earth; Where is the shame you have; Where are the tears you let fall; Where is the humility you are taught to? Nay you are such as say in your hearts; if the Spring be fair, the Harvest is like to be good: If these thing come to passe, it is the finger of the Lord. But such is your imperfection, such are the fruits of the flesh, and the vanity of mortality.

Notwithstanding, consider that you are servants: Do therefore the will of your Master. You are become free: Be faithful and thankful to him that is the giver of liberty: Nay you are become children: partakers of the counsel of him that sitteth and seeth, and saith I am. Therefore be sober, faithful, and waver not, for the inheritance of your Father is great: your freedom is without recompence, and your Master the King of Justice.

Where

The End ma-
keth all.
Faith.

When
Faith.

Idea.

Where are the people, or in what generation did they dwell, that hath been thus acquainted and drawn into familiarity with the true Servants and Angels of God ? Unto whom have those myste-ries been opened: Is it not said, of those that are sanctified, The Lord appeared unto them in a vision: But he cometh to you when you are awake: Unto them he came unlooked for, unto you he cometh requested. Arise up therefore, and be not forgetful what the Lord hath done for you ; for the things of this World are not, until they be done, neither is there any thing assured, but by the end.

It was said unto Abraham, And I will destroy them. He believed it ; but he asked not, when. Great is the reward of Faith ; for it giveth strength : But those that are faithful are not of this world.   Notwithstanding, you have said, (as it was said by the Disciples to Christ, when they were yet unpure, and blind) When shall these things come to passe ? Lord, what is meant by this, or that ?   Simple Faith excelleth all Science.   For, Heaven and Earth shall perish in their corruption : But the voices of the Lord, much more his promises, are become Angels for ever : For as the Sun begetteth in the earth, and is father of many things that live in corruption and have end : So is the God of Heaven, the bringer forth and begetter of things celestial with life and for ever.   For why, Dixit & factum est, Every Idea in eternity is become for ever, and what is thought, is become a living creature.   I teach you a mystery.

As the tree in sappy life, watering her self throughly, bringeth forth the ornaments of her own beauty : So the spiritual part of man being good and dignified, burnisheth himself, with his sound and faithful thought : I mean the glory and shew of his own beauty ; for the soul of man groweth, either with beauty to salvation, or with dishonour and filthinesse, to damnation.

I have done my Commandment.   I have as a Schoolmaster warned you, and as a friend counsel-led you :   I will also teach you.

[E. K. He speaketh in a thin small voice.]

Δ. He used a great pause, and silence.

E. K. He standeth and pointeth with his rod to the letters of his Table, as if he made some account or reckoning. He went out of the middle, and measured how many steps it is about.

Nal. ......*Pater, Filius, Spiritus Sanctus : Fundamentum, substantia, & principium omnium.*

[E. K. Thought in his minde, *rerum*, and he answered his thought, say-ing, What need I say *rerum?* The Grammarians will be on my side. *Om-nium*, is more than to say *omnium rerum.*]

E. K. This seemeth to be spoken by some other, in my imagination.

Nal. ......*Omnium, is the thing that is my charge.*

E. K. He still conferreth place to place, &c.

So.   E. K. Now he standeth still.

Corpus omnium ....   E. K. He pointeth to the whole or round table which he standeth on.

1. *The substance is attributed to God the Father.*

2. *The first circular mover, the circumference, God the Son, The finger of the Father, and mover of all things.*

3. *The order and knitting together of the parts in their due and perfect proportion, God the Holy Ghost.   Lo, the beginning and end of all things.*

E. K. He still counteth and conferreth places and letters together.

Nal. ...... *Lo, it is divided into 4 parts : whereof two are dignified : one not yet dignified, but shall be : the other without glory or dignification.*

E. K. He seemeth to point to some divisions.

Nal. ......, *Understand God, as the substance of the whole, (as above said.)*

E. K. He counteth again.

Nal. ......, *The substance of this part is called* Vita.

E. K. He pointeth to the uppermost part.

Nal. ...... *Called* Vita Suprema.   *See here three small lines.*

[E. K. Those three small lines appear in the uppermost parcel.]

Say ... Gaudium, [pointing to the uppermost line.

Say ... Praesentia [pointing to the second.]

...... Laudantes or Triumphantes [pointing to the third.]

E. K. Now

E. K. Now he beginneth to account in the second portion,

Nal. ...... *The Continent,* Vita.   [He counteth again.

E. K. The four portions are of equal widenesse, but not of equal clear-nesse ; and that about the center is of fuskish or leadish colour.

E. K. Now he sheweth three small lines in the second portion. *He* seemeth to speak to himself somewhat.

Nal. ...... *Say* ...... Potestas .... *to the first line pointing.*   Motus ...... *to the second ;* Ministrantes ..... *to the third.*

E. K. Now he proceedeth to the third circular portion.

Nal. ...... *This Continent is also* Vita [*pointing to the third portion*] non dignificata, sed dignificanda.

Nal. .... *See* .... E. K. *There are also three lines,* Actio ..... *in the first line.*   Factum ...: *in the sec nd.*   Confirmantes ..... *in the third.*   Sirha, *this is true Logick.*

[Δ. He said so to E. K. who now gave himself to study Logick diligently.]

E. K. Now he standeth trembling.

Nal. ....,... *Oh qualis est Justitia inter miseros ?*
Δ. .... Sed, mors est quæ peperit hanc vitam.
Vita est etiam hæc, sed quæ peperit mors.
Say ...... Luctus .....
         Discordia ....,..   } Here seem three lines also.
         Confundantes ..... }
Those that do their duty shall receive their reward.   Let my diligence teach you diligence.
Be not angry, because you do not understand : These be means to understand.   E. K. con- To E. K. fessed that he was very angry.
Nal ..... *Pray unto God, for I am resisted.*
Δ. Deus in adjutorium nostrum intende, &c.
Say .... *Vitæ Suprema.*   [*pointing to the uppermost line of all.*] *I find it* (*by addi-tion*) *in this Language,* I ad, *but written thus, toward the left hand, in three angles*

I   d

a

Say ..... *Gaudium* .... *Moz.* *I find it is a name ascending and answereth to the two extremes* of I ad *in this manner.*

I   d   z

a   o

m

Δ. I pray you, is *Mozod,* a word of three letters, or of five ?
Nal. ..... *In wrote three, it is larger extended.* [Δ. z extended is zod.]
Δ. Will you pardon me if I ask you another question of this extension ?
Nal. ..... *Say on :* Moz *in it self signifieth Joy ; but* Mozod *extended, signifieth the Joy o* God.
Δ. No word in his radical form is extended.
Nal. ..... *These doubts will at length grow easie.*
         Præsentia ....,.. *I find it called* Zir.

So I   d   z

a   o   i

m   z   r

This Lesson is greater than any that was learned in *Cracovia* this day.
Nal. ...... Potentia .....But say, *Vita secunda.* I ad *but thus.*

I   d   z   s   a   i

a   o   i   g   o   d

m   z   r   v   r   r

b   n   a

d   a   z   a

a   a   B   d   i

L   *I will*

I will teach you here after the distinction of them.
Δ. You mean of *I ad* diversly signifying.
Say ..... *Potestas* ..... *I find it* Bab.   *It doth ascend from the right hand to the left.*
          Motio ...., *I find it* Zna.
They will not fall out so, but they will fall out well enough.
Nal. .,.... *Vita tertia.* ,...... I ad.
Δ. I pray you, what is of *Ministrantes ?*
Nal. ..... *Look you to your Charge.*
          Actio ,.,.. Sor
          Factum ..... Gru
,...., Vita, quæ etiam est mors.
                I ad
          Luctus ..... Ser
          Discordia ...., Off

                                                        f   o ,
                                                        s e   a
                                                        r d   i

If the order of the Table be ex spiritu Sancto,
The substance of the Father ;   How shall we gather the Circumference, which is the Son ?.
   The Son is the Image of his Father : Therefore, in his death, he must be the Image of his father
also.
   If substantia be in forma Crucis, *then the Son is the Image of his Father.*
.... *Laudantes* .... Luach.
   Δ. The rest I pray you to deliver us.   h c r v
   Nal. ...... Bear with me, for it is easie for you,   l d z s a i
but hard for me.
          Ministrantes ...... Lang.   l a o i g o d h
          Confirmantes ..... Sach.   v m z r v r r c
   Δ. Now.   s b n a f o s a
   Nal. ..... *When I know, you shall.*   s d a z s e a s
   Δ. As Sach.   i a b r d i
God be merciful to man.   l a n g
It is so terrible, that I tremble to gather it.
          Confundantes ,.... Urch.
Thus I have made plain this body generally : The particulars are long, hard, and tedious.
Thy name be blessed, O God, which canst open a means, whereby thy powers immediate may be
opened unto man.   Power, glory, and honour, be unto thee, for thou art the true body of all things,
and art life eternal.

E. K. Now he is suddenly vanished away with the Table.

Deo nostro sit omnis laus & *gratiarum actio nunc* & *in sempiterna*
seculorum secula. Amen.

          Thursday, Mane, Aprilis 12. 1584.   *Cracoviæ.*
   Δ. Some delay upon our prayers made, at length appeared *Nalvage* in shape and attire
as last before : He standeth still.
   Nal. ,..... *Benedictum sit nomen Domini in æternum.*
   Δ. Amen.
   Nal. .... Audite mei fratres patienter.
The Godhead in his secret judgement keeping in his Almighty bosom, the image and form of all
things, universally, looked down upon the Earth ; for he said, Let us now go down among the sons
of men : He saw that all things grew contrary to their creation and nature ; either keeping their
dignities and secret vertues shut up in obscurity, or else riotously perishing , through the imbecility
and frowardnesse of ignorance : So that it was said, Behold, I delight not in the World : The
Elements are defiled, the sons of men wicked, their bodies become dunghills, and the inward parts
(the secret chambers of their hearts) the dens and dungeons of the damned :. Therefore I will
draw my spirit from amongst them, and they shall become more drunken, and their ignorance such
as never was : No, not since the fall of heavens.
Antich: istus.   *For, lo, the time is come,* And he that is the Son of Unrighteousnesse, is and liveth : *Unto*
him therefore shall be given strength and power : and the Kings of the Earth shall become mad :
yea, even raging mad ; yea even in the third madnesse, and that in the depth of their own imagi-
nations ; and I will build my Temple in the Woods, yea even in the Desert places ; and I will
                                                                                          become

become a Serpent in the wildernesse : for I have tucked up my garments and am fled away, and She In the wilder-
shall mourn on the Mountains without comfort. nesse.

Lo, the Thunder spake, and the earth became misty, and full of fogge, that the Soul of
man might sleep in his own confusion. The second Thunder spake, and there arose spirits, such
as are for Sooth-sayers, Witches, Charmers, and Seducers : and they are entred into the holy places,
and have taken up their seats in man. [Woe be unto the earth therefore : For, it is corrupted. Woe be
unto the earth, for she is surrendred to her adversary : Woe be unto the earth, she is delivered into
the hands of her enemy : Yea, Woe be unto the sons of men, for their vessels are poysoned. But even
then said the Lord, Lo, I will be known in the wildernesse, and will Triumph in my weaknesse.

And lo, be called you, and you became drunken, and foolish with the spirit of God : And it was
said Descend, for he calleth, and hath called : and Raphael that brought up the prayers descended : Raphael:
and he was full with the power, & spirit of God: and it became a Doctrine, such was never from the This Do-
beginning : Not painted, or carved : filed, or imagined by man, or according to their imaginations, ctrine.
which are of flesh : but simple, plain, full of strength, and the power of the holy Ghost : which Doctrine began, as man did, nakedly from the earth : but yet, the image of perfection. This self-
same Art is it, which is delivered unto you an infallible Doctrine, containing in it the waters, which
runne through many Gates : even above the Gate of Innocency, wherein you are taught to finde
out the Dignity and Corruption of nature : also made partakers of the secret Judgements of the
Almighty to be made manifest, and to be put in execution. Which knowledge in you is to be made
perfect : two wayes, by power, mediate, and immediate. Immediately from God, in respect of his
will, and secret Judgements, as unto the Apostles. By means and tradition, as from us, opening the
substance and body of nature, according to our own image, which is the thing I have now in
hand. I am therefore to instruct and inform you, according to your Doctrine delivered, which is
contained in 49 Tables. In 49 voyces, or callings : which are the Natural Keyes, to open those, not 48 Keyes, or
49. but 48. (for One is not to be opened) Gates of understanding, whereby you shall have knowledge calls, and their
to move every Gate, and to call out as many as you please, or shall be thought necessary, which can use.
very well, righteously, and wisely, open unto you the secrets of their Cities, & make you understand perfectly the contained in the Tables. Through which knowledge you shall easily be able to judge, not as
the world doth, but perfectly of the world, and of all things contained within the Compasse of Nature, and of all things which are subject to an end.

But behold, this charge of mine is tied unto time : Therefore be diligent to learn, diligent to Note.
hear, and that with patience : For it is neither a free School, nor a School of continuance. For as Take time
power is not given unto me beyond the first day of August next, so have you no strength to learn while time is,
after, because I am the staffe of your Doctrine. for time will

Nal. ..... I am for the comfort of the world, and not for the hindrance : Thus sayeth the Lord. away.
To them that have Harvest let them reap, and unto such as have labour let them work. As for me, At gust next.
I am tied to time, and am ready at all times : For I measure not your night, nor day.

Δ. Thanks be unto the highest.

Nal. ..... Cease now with me, for no more descendeth.

Soli. Deo Honor & Gloria.

After-noon, the same Thursday. ..... After some short Ejaculations of prayers to God,
there appeared a great black masty Dogge : with whom I would have nothing to do, but expect Nalvage. He said, that he was Nalvage. We rebuked him as an Hell-hound. At length An illuding
he departed, and Nalvage appeared ; but brighter then to day. wicked spirit.

Nal. ..... Have you those things I told you to day?

Δ. We have them in record and minde.

Nal. ..... Read them......

Δ. I did read them.

E. K. He laugheth, ha, ha, ha, &c. a great laughter : He hath also a Table, but seemeth not to be like the former Table of Nalvage. There are
ten, or eleven divisions in this Table, as was not in the former Table.

Δ. If thou art Nalvage, proceed in the Doctrine of wisdom, if thou art not Nalvage, depart
in the name of Jesus.

..... I have free will, and therefore I will be here.

Δ. Now I doubt nothing, but thou art a deceiver. [Audite:] The ignorance of the wicked A voyce on
becometh dust : which shewing it self is swept out of doors, and thrown on the Dung-hills. the one side.

E. K. Now appeareth one like true Nalvage.

Nal. ..... Even so is it of the [   ] for thou hast opened thy blasphemy : and being discovered, art become more accursed : Therefore because thou art accursed, thou art not dignified ; but
become a Vessel of iniquity : And therefore hast no free-will. For, free-will either is, or is in Free-will.
state to be dignified. Therefore, as dust I sweep thee out : and cast thee into that Dunghill, which
is the place of the greatest woe : the Dunghill, and the reward of the unrighteous. And, because
thou

thou hast thrust thy self into the Judgements of the Lord : and hast heard the secrets of the Almighty : Therefore I seal thee tanquam truncus in Infernum.

E. K. He striketh him with an yern, like a pair of tongs; in form of a Mould to cast Pellets in : griping his brain and underchaps, and so he fell down and disappeared : and in his place came *Nalvage.*

E. K. *Nalvage* maketh cursie toward the four quarters of the world.

Nal. ...... *My Us is as good as thy* Um.

E. K. In his heart thought that it might be, that *now one Devil mastered another,* and thereupon said *Um.*

E. K. He is now accounting again on his Table as he did before.

Nal. ...... *Vnto this Doctrine belongeth the perfect knowledge, and remembrance of the mysticall*
Creatures. *How therefore shall I inform you, which know them not ?*

Δ. Mean you as *Babyon Boboyel,* &c.

Nal. ...... *The Characters, or Letters of the Tables.*

Δ. You mean the mystical Letters, wherein the holy book is promised to be written : and if the book be so written and laid open before us, and then you will from Letter to Letter point, and we to record your instructions : Then I trust we shall sufficiently understand, and learn your instructions.

Nal. ...... *Also in receiving of the calls, this is to be noted : that they are to be uttered of me, backward : and of you, in practise, forward.*

Δ. I understand it, for the efficacity of *them* ; else, all things called would appear : and so hinder our proceeding in learning.

Nal. ...... *D P C E T E I R S M S S
   E S A I I M M N S E S.*

E. K. All this was in one line; in the lowermost portion : and lowermost line thereof.

Nal. ...... *I E E E E T N O E D M E T M M M
   M M D M A E T S E A M.*

E. K. Now he standeth still.

Nal. ...... *A E R T I S A N S S E A S D M M S E A O A
   V I I I I A O A O I I V I T S E I T T
   S D A I N.*

E. K. These seemed to be taken out of divers lines, in the three lower portions ; but none out of the uppermost, or fourth.

Nal. ...... *R S H D D S R R E S O L S N R E R E E
   S F R H E I E E E E I E E O E T I S O E
   R T T H D E O I S E O E S M E T F E D E
   T S E E E E R S E S E O R S M E T
   D. R. F E   D E T S E E E R S E
)(E R
   S I S E H E N O E S M E F S F E E D I [¹E] O E
   S S S I S E O E S H E
   D S D F T E I E O R S O E D H T E T
   O E S H E O T R T E R E O E H S E R
   E E I R E S R I S O E H E E D E I E H E
   D T R N D D H D N.*

The rest of this Lesson, the next morning.

Δ. After the correcting of certain places before in the Letters he said.   I feel no more.

Δ. Thanks and honour be to the highest for ever.   *Amen.*

Fryday morning, *Hora* 8¼. *Aprilis* 13:   Cracoviæ.

Not long after my Invitation, *Nalvage* appeared, *Nutu Dei.*

Nal. .... *Our peace, which is* Triumphing patience, *and glory be amongst you.*

Δ. ˙ Amen.

Nal. ...... *It*

Nal. ..... *It may be said, can there be patience in the Angels, which are exalted above the aire?* **Patience.** *For, such as were of errour have their reward: Yea, forsooth my dear brethren. For there is a continual fight between us and Satan, wherein we vanquish by patience. This is not spoken without a cause: For as the Devil is the father of Carping, so doth he suttlely infect the Seers imagination, mingling unperfect forms with my utterance: Water is not received without aire, neither the word of God without blasphemous insinuation. The son of God never did convert all, neither did all that did hear him, believe him. Therefore,* where the power of God is, is also Satan: *Lo, I speak not this without a cause, for I have answered thy infection.*

Δ. E. K. Had thought that Angels had not occasion of any patience, and so was his thought answered.

Nal. ..... *I finde the Soul of man hath no portion in this first Table. It is the Image of the son* **The first Table.** *of God, in the bosome of his father, before all the worlds. It comprehendeth his incarnation, passion, and return to judgement: which he himself, in flesh, knoweth not; all the rest are of understanding.* The exact **Center** excepted. **The Center Table.**

A (*Two thousand and fourteen, in the sixth Table, is*) D
86. 7003. *In the thirteenth Table is* I.
A *In the 21th. Table.* 11406 *downward.*
I *In the last Table, one lesse then Number. A word,* Jaida *you shall understand, what that word is before the Sun go down.* Jaida *is the last word of the call.*
85. H 49. *ascending* T 49. *descending,* A 909. *directly,* O *simply.*
H 2029. *directly, call it* Hoath.

225. *From the low angle on the* right side.   Continuing in the same and next square.
D 225. [*The same number repeated.*
A *In the thirteenth Table,* 740. *ascending in his square.*
M *The 30th. Table,* 13025. *from the low angle in the left-side.*
84. .... *In the square ascending.*
Call it Mad.

O *The 7th. Table,* 99. *ascending.*
C *The 19th. descending* 409.
O *The ... 1. from the upper right angle, crossing to the nether left, and so ascending* 1003.
83. N *The 31th. from the Center to the upper right angle, and so descending* 5009.
Call it Noco.

Be patient, for I told you it would be tedious.
O *The 39th. from the Center descending, or the left hand,* 9073.
D *The 41th. from the Center ascending, and so to the right upper Angle,* 27004.
R *The 43th. from the upper left Angle to the right, and so still in the Circumference,* 34006.
I *The 4 th. ascending,* 72000.
82. *In the same Table descending the last.*
Call it Zirdo.

P *The 6th. ascending* 109.
A *The 9th. ascending* 405.
81. L *The 11th. descending* 603. ......
Call it Lap.   Δ. Her, he stroke the Table on Saturday action following at my reading over of it backward.

E *The 6th. from the right Angle uppermost to the left,* 700.
G *The 13th descending,* 2000.
R *The 17th. from the Center downward,* 11004.
80. O *The 32th. descending from the right Angle to the Center,* 32000.
Z 47th. 194000. *descending. Call it* Zorge. [*Of one syllable.*]
A 19th. *from the left corner descending,* 17200.
79. A 24th. *from the Center ascending to the left Angle,* 25000.
Q *The same Table ascending,* 33000.
Call it Q A A. [*Three syllables with accent on the last* A.]
E *The second Table,* 112 *ascending.*
L *The ......th. descending* 504.
C *The 19th. Table descending* 1013. [*That* C. *is called* C Minor.]
I *The 13th. descending,* 2005.
C *The 14th. descending,* 2907. *Call it* Cicle.

7877.

E. K. Now is he kneeling, and praying with his Rod up

76. O *The 4th. ascending to the left Angle,* 390.
D *The 5th. descending* 812.
O *In the same descending,* 902. *Call it* O D O.   Δ. Here he striketh again on Saturday.

N. *The*

N *The* 9th *descending* 804.
A *The* 11th *descending* 2005.   ...... *This* A *may be an* A *or an* O.
75   R *The* 14th *descending* 5006.
M   N *The* 16th *descending* 12004 :   *be corrected it* M.
A *The* 20th *descending* 17006.   Zamran.
Z *The* 32th *descending* 40006.   *Call it* Zanran.

I give it faster unto you, than I received it.   E. K. *thought it.*

T *The* 4th *descending* 212 ...... *This may be* T *or* D.
74   O *The* 6th *ascending from the center to the left corner* 1907.
Call it O D .... *or* O T.

73   A *The* 9th *ascending* 500
C *The* 10th *descending* 602   *Call it* C A, [Δ. *two syllables.*]

R *The* 16th *ascending* 22006.   E *must come after* R : *but without number,*
A *The* 19th *descending* 23012.   *and so, it is* Zacare,
72   C *The* 30th *ascending* 30006.
A *The* 39th *from the left angle descending* 42012.
Z *The* 46 th *ascending* 312004.   *Call it* Zacar.

Use your time of refreshing, and return   Deo gratias reddamus immortales.

The same Friday after Noon, *circa* 3. *horam.*

After a short request made by me to Christ for wisdom, and verity to be ministered by *Nalvage* ; he appeared and spake much to E. K. which he expressed not to me : but at length confessed that he gave him brotherly counsel to leave dealing as an Idolater or Fornicator against God, by asking counsel of such as he did.

E. K. confessed that he had been that day, and some dayes before, dealing by himself after his manner, to understand of my Lord *Laskie*, and of other matters of *Lasko*, and left his questions in his window written. *Nalvage* told him the devil had now taken away his questions. E. K. went down to see if it were true, and he found it true.

Nal. .... *Pray* ......   Δ. We prayed.

There is an error in the last, not in the Number, but in the Letter. I will first go through the Letters, and after come to the Numbers.   How many words have you received this day ?

Δ. Thirteen, whereof *Iaida* was said to be the last of the call.

Nal. .... *They be more worth than the Kingdom of Poland.   Be patient, for these things are wonderful.*

N (*The number must needs go to*) *the sixth, descending* 309.
A *The* 7th *ascending* 360.
71   O *The* 9th *ascending* 1000.
O *The* 13th *ascending* 1050.
V *The* 17th *ascending* 2004.   *It is* Vooan.   *It may be sounded* Vaoan.

Adde those last Numbers
Δ.

$$\left\{\begin{array}{l} 309 \\ 360 \\ 1000 \\ 1050 \\ 2004 \\ \hline 4723 \end{array}\right.$$

Vooan *is spoken with them that fall, but* Vaoan *with them that are, and are glorified. The devils have lost the dignity of their sounds.*

Δ. They make 4723.

Nal. ...... *It is called the Mystical roote in the highest ascendent of transmutation.*

Δ. These phrases are dark ; when it shall please God they may be made plain.

Nal. ...... *It is the square of the Philosophers work.*

Δ. you said it was a roote.

Nal. ...... *So it is a roote square.*

Δ. The square thereof is 22306729 ....

Lapis philo-   *The word is, by interpretation,* Ignis vera mater.   *The vain Philosophers do think it doth*
rum magna   beget bodies : *but in truth, it conceiveth, and bringeth forth.*
projectionis.
70   D *the fifth, ascending,* 4.
O *the* 39, *ascending,* 7806. *call it* O D. [Δ. *drawing the* O *long.*]

E   L   17 (*not* 17 *the first, but* 17 *and the thirdth : for it is of the thirdth : and* 17 *it*
L   et   *may be of them both*) *ascending,* 419.
69 O   O *the* 18 *ascending* 2017 .... *this* O *must be sounded as* A.
T   M   M *the* 24 *from the center to the left angle, ascending,*
          5069 .... T *must be instead of* M.
L   A   A 30 *descending,* 9012.
A   I   I *the* 35 *ascending,* 15079.
B   P   P *the* 43, *from the center to the left angle, descending* 159068.   Aversed.
        Call it Piamo el.   *It is* Piatel Baltale *to be sounded.*

As the ear is the chief sense ; so, being infected, it is the greatest hindrance. Many there be Note Intru-
that thrust themselves between you and me : *and they are increased.* Power is given again dens.
to the Shew Stone ; and thou shalt not be hindred.
Δ. Shall I presently bring it forth ?
Nal. ...... *As thou wilt.*
Δ. I brought forth the Stone, and it seemed marvellously brighter than before it was wont
to appear.

E. K. He seemeth to pray.

E. K. There appeareth to me in the Stone *Michael* as he was wont
to appear, with his sword in his hand, and in a long white garment, &c.

Mich. ...... *I am the strength of the Highest, and the mighty arme of him that is Almighty :
your fellow servant, and the messager of the Highest : The powers of the earth have risen up a-
gainst you :* But you shall prevail, *and this Doctrine shall be delivered as is promised, and* God his pro-
according unto time. But pray earnestly ; for lo, the whole hoste of Angels, such as are blessed, performed.
*have cryed unto the Lord, saying ; Not so Lord : Thy bread is torn in pieces, or reproachfully
eaten.*

*Thus therefore saith the Lord, Be patient, for the place is holy, and the power of the Highest
is amongst you. Receive willingly : for he that is offended is smitten. Be comforted, and be-* The dignifica-
ware of deceivers : for the power of the wicked is increased, and is become mighty : But into tion of the
this vessel shall enter no unclean thing, not for this time onely, but for ever. Stone.

Unto thee Nalvage thus saith the Lord, gather up thy wings and enter : Do as thou art com-
manded, and be multiplied. *Be comforted ; for* Gabriel *shall ascend and stand before the Lord,* Be multiplied,
and shall have power and descend : and he shall be yoked unto thy loynes, and thou shalt become Gabriel.
mighty ; that thou mayst open the wonders of the Lord with power.

E K. Now is *Nalvage* come into the Stone.

Mic. ...... *Be comforted, be comforted, be comforted my brethren in the God of Hosts : for your*
comfort is and shall be of the Holy Ghost. *Therefore let peace be amongst you, and be no more* The holy
babes ; for wisdom dwelleth not amongst children. The peace of God be amongst you : And thus Ghost.
much I have comforted you.

E. K. He is gone.

E. K. Now here is another.

Δ. It is *Gabriel* that came to *Daniel.*
Gabr. ...... *I did so,* and I am that Gabriel, *and the World beareth witnesse of my coming.*
*Tou rebellious windes, you deceivers of the righteous, you naked substances and things lighter than
the windes, know not you that the God of your creation hath rewarded you, know you not your own
weaknesse, know you not your state of no return ? I say headlong you all (without resistance) fall
down to your places : Be gone, sink, for I am of power, and do prevail.*
Behold he hath placed darknesse behind him, *and hath made the lights of heaven as the Lamps
of his beauty. Go you that are confounded without return ; for the name of our God in his determination is invincible.*
This night is a Sabbath, and a scourge to the wicked.
Nal. ...... *I promised to expound you a word, the first you had to day, but the last. It signifieth,*
of the Highest.

E. K. His Table now appeareth very evidently to me, as that I could paint it all.

*Cease for this time, for it is a time of silence, for the wicked are confounded : in the morning
early you shall be taught plentifully : for my power is become a hundred and fifty ; and I will finish* Note.
my charge, long before the time appointed.
Gabr. *We are alwayes present until the promise be ended. Rest in peace.*

E. K. *Gabriel* seemeth to be all in compleat harnesse, like skales of a Fish from

the

Note this form
at *Gabriel* at
this occasion.
the arm-pits downward; with a Spear in his hand, all of fire, about a two yards long.

Δ. The peace of God, and his mercy, be on us now and ever.   *Amen.*

Δ. If it should not offend you, I would gladly ask your knowledge of the Lord *Albert Laskie* our great worldly friend, and that for the service of God, if he be past the chief danger of his present infirmity, &c.

Al. Laskie.

..... *When we enter into him, we know him; but from him, he is scarce known unto us: as of him of whom it is said, he hath consented with an Harlot: we know not the end of God his justice which is upon him.*

His prayers are come to the second heaven, neither hath any received remembrance of him: But we will pray unto God to be merciful unto him, and that for thy sake; *Because thou shalt not be made a laughing-stock to the wicked. Pray thou for him, that thou mayst work in him that which he worketh not for himself.* Hold up thy hands for him; *for it is a lawful and a charitable thing:* For God hath granted thee a force in prayer: But be patient *and humble.*

*Prayer for
A. L.*

God his gift to
Δ in prayer.
We with thee, give thanks and laud unto the Lord.

Cease.

Δ. Laudes Deo nostro incessanter reddantur.   *Amen.*

Saturday, *Aprilis* 14. *Mane.*   Cracoviæ, 1584.

Δ. Oratione Dominica finita, & brevi illa oratione Psalmi 33. inspecto Chrystallo apparuere utrique *Gabriel* & *Nalvage.*

E. K. They kneel, as though they were in confession one to another, and .... about half a quarter of an hour.

Gabr. ......) *after me.*

Prayer.

O beginning and fountain of all wisdom, gird up thy loines in mercy, and shadow our weaknesse; be merciful unto us, and forgive us our trespasses: for those that rise up saying there is no God, have risen up against us, saying, Let us confound them: Our strength is not, neither are our bones full of marrow. Help therefore O eternal God of mercy: help therefore O eternal God of salvation: help therefore O eternal God of peace and comfort. Who is like unto thee in altars of incense? before whom the Quire of Heaven sing, O Mappa la man hallelujah: Visit us O God with a comprehending fire, brighter than the Stars in the fourth heaven. Be merciful unto us, and continue with us; for thou art Almighty: To whom all things of thy breasts in Heaven and Earth, sing glory praise and honour, Saying, Come, Come, Lord for thy mercy sake.   Say so unto God kneeling.

Δ. I repeated it, kneeling, and E. K. likewise kneeling.

E. K. They both kneel down again, and put their foreheads together: *Gabriel* seemeth to sit in a chair on the one side of *Nalvage* about 30 yards off, on *Nalvage* his left hand.   *Nalvage* standeth.

Gabr.
standing
said.

...... *Thus saith the Lord, Who is he, that dare resist invincible strength: Seale up the East, seale up the South, Seale up the West, and unto the North put three Seales.*

E. K. Now sitteth *Nalvage* in a Chair aside from his round Table, the Table being somewhat before him.

Nal. ...... *Name that I point to.*   [To E. K. he said so, as concerning the Letters.

E. K. He flung like a thin brightnesse out of the Stone upon E. K. he hath his rod, which he took out of his own mouth.

...cy... *He holdeth up his rod, and saith, I am all joy, and rejoyce in my self.*

E. K. He smit the round Table with his rod, and it whirled about with a great swiftnesse. Now that which before seemed to be a circular and plain form, appeareth to be a Globe and round Ball; corporal, when it turneth.

Globe.

Nal ...... *Say the last.*

Δ. Piamo el,

E. K. He

E· K· *He* ſtriketh the Table now, and though the body ſeem to turn, yet the Letter ſeem to ſtand ſtill in their places.

E·K· Now he pluckerh out five Books, as if from under his Chair, and ſetteth them down by him ; the books be green , bright , and they be three corned, ▷ a claſp·

Sal. ..... *Read backward* ... [*to* E. K.] *Every thing with us teacheth. Read backward. Letter without number.*

Nal. ...... *Read backward,* letter without number, *the letters thou hadſt yeſterday.*

Δ. After all read, he proceeded thus :

	P *The fourth aſcending,* 97·	
	A *The ſixth aſcending,* 112·	
68	I *The eighth aſcending,* 207·	
	P *The ninth aſcending,* 307·	PIAP.

E· K· Now he ſtriketh it again, and it turneth·

67	A	T A.
	T	

The numbers after.

	I	
66	A	
	A	A A I· *The firſt* A *may be an* A *an* O *or an* E.

Thoſe are two words.

E· K· Now he ſtriketh again, and turneth : his Rod ſeemeth to be hollow like a Reed·

| 65 | APGOB.   *Call it* Bogpa. |

E· K· *Gabriel* falleth down on his face , and lieth proſtrate, and *Nalvage* holdeth up his Rod all the while.

Alſo		D OS· He pointed beyond him in the upper Circle , it ſeemeth
T		like a Roman C·

| 64 | LAMAOP.   *Poamal Od·* put out the S· |

Make it two words· ..... *It may be all one word with* S. *or* T· *but it would be hard for your underſtanding.*

Make a point between Poamal *and* Od·

E· K· *Gabriel* lieth proſtrate all this while.

| 63 | XVDMOZ.   *Call it* Zome. |

..... *With great difficulty this Letter was diſcerned :* Nalvage *himſelf ſaid, he knew it not yet ; but it ſeemed to* E. K. *to be an* X. Nalvage *denied it to be an* X·, *and ſaid he knew not yet the myſtery : ſay the Lords prayer, for I cannot open it. Although my power be multiplied, yet I know not this Letter. At length he ſaid it was* V.

B·K· I can remember that word well.

Nal. ...... *Thou ſhalt not remember it.*

| 62 | PEV.   *It is called* Vep. |

Make a point there.   Δ. A full point?   *Nal.*..... *No, no, a ſtroke.*

| 61 | OLOHOL.   *Call it* Loholo. |

Long, the firſt ſyllable accented.

E· K· Now he ſtriketh the Table·

60	S D.	*It is the uppermoſt of*	*Call it* D S.
59	SIMAPI.	*Pronownce it* IPAMIS.	*Make a point at* S, *the* A *pro-*

woumed ſhort.

| 58 | LU.   *Call it* U L· | Δ, With ſuch ſound to U. as we pronounce yew , whereof bows are made.

M 2   MAPI.

57   MAPI.   E. K. It seemeth to be an *e*.

Labiis claufis, [*Span*] [*um um*] ... *He hummed twice, fignifying two words more, which were not to be pronounced till they were read in practife.*

DO.   OD. *As you had before.*

E. K. Now *Gabriel* rifeth from his lying proftrate.

56   HOTLAB.   *Call it* BALTOH.   *There is a point.*

PAIP.   *Call it* Piap.

E. K. *Gabriel* fteppeth up, and feemeth to ftorm angerly againft fomewhat.

Δ. Belike fome wicked powers would intrude their illufions, or hindrances in thefe actions.

E. K. He hath thrown his Dart from him: and it cometh to him again.

Gabr. ..... *Count the number of the words you have received to day.*

Δ. Sixteen, if *Poamals Od* be made two words.

Gab. ..... *Be packing, and fo many plagues be amongft you more then your plague was before.*

E. K. He feemeth to ftorm ftill.

Gab. ...... *Come in.*

E. K. Now there come four more.

Gab. ...... *Art not thou* Adraman? *Which haft fallen, and haft burft thy neck four times? And wilt thou now rife again, and take part anew? Go thy way therefore, thou Seducer, enter into the fifth torment. Let thy power be leffe then it is, by as much as thou feeft number here.*

E. K. Now they all four fall down into a pit, or *Hiatum* of the foundation of the place where they ftood.

E. K. *Nalvage* lieth all this while upon his face.

Gab. ..... *Count now again.*

Δ. Sixteen.

Gab. ...... *It is not fo. There is an errour.*

Nal. .... *I am deceived from Ipam.*

OD *the next is falfe, and fo are the reft: And fo is that that followeth.*

ABOS.   SOBA.

Δ. I had Baltoh.

Nal. ..... *And* Piap.

Nal. ..... *What is this?* [to E. K.] E. K. ...... G.

Nal. ...... *No, it is an* H.

55   HOT.   TOH.

There is a point, fhewing a ftroke, called Virgula.

54   MOH.   HOM.

53   SD.   DS.

52   LIPDAI.   *Call it* IADPIL *accent ad.*

51   ONOG.   *Call it* Gono.

Gab. ...... *Move not, for the place waketh more bold.*

Nal. ..... *Pointeth* S.D.   D S. *This was corrected on Monday following to be too much.*

50   ANDA.   *Call it* ADNA.

E. K. *Gabriel* did throw a brightneffe upon E. K. after he had ftroked his own face firft, E.K. ftarted at it.

49 AZRNZ

| 49 | A Z R N Z | | *Call it* Zurza. | Δ, As...Zuurza. |

E. K. *Nalvage* kneeleth down before the Table, and useth many inclinations, and gestures of reverence, as Priests use to do at the Alter.

| 48 | M Z R A F | | F A R Z M. | |

| 47 | H A L I P | *moreover* | P I L A H. | *Three syllables.* |

P is distinct-
ly pronoun-
ced by it self.

| 46 | H A N D A I | *the Ark of knowledge* | I A D N A H. | [yadnah. |

E. K. *Nalvage* cometh and kisseth the Table and kneeleth down,
and seemeth to pray.

| 45 | M R E | *with* | E R M | |

| 44 | B A C | *a Rod* | C A B | |

E. K. He kneeleth down again, and useth such gestures as before.

| | G S N | *a rod* | | |

E. K. *Nalvage* said, *Adjuva me, O mi Deus.* He holdeth up his
hand and kisseth the Table, and useth wonderfull reverence. He saith
again. *Fer opem, O mi Deus.*

| 43 | E R N O Z | *delivered you* | Z O N R E N S G | |

| 42 | S D | *and Δ which* | D S | |

| 41 | R I P | *the holy ones* | Pir, *there is a point* | |

| 40 | A B A C | *govern* | *Call it* Caba, | |

| 39 | A L E R O H O, *I made a Law* | | *Call it* Ohorela, I | |

Nal. ...... *There is a stop, shewing a stroke made straight
down thus* I

| 38 | M R A S A C | *to whom* | Casarm I | *a stop.* |

E. K. Now he kisseth the Table again.

| 37 | M A S R G | *with admiration* | G R S A M | { *a stop at* M. Δ. *as* Gursam, |

| 36 | H E L O B O | *your Garments* | O B O L E H | |

| 35 | S B R U | *beautified* | U R B S | |

| 34 | S D | *and Δ which* | D S | |

E. K. Now he useth the former reverent gestures again.

| 33 | I D L A | *of gathering* | A L D I | |

| 32 | E G R P | *with the fire* | P R G E | *as purge.* |

| 31 | P N O N G | *I garnished* | G N O N P | |

Nal. ...... *Adjuva me, O mi Deus.*

| 30 | L I H T | *seats* | T H I L | *a point here.* |

| 29 | A B O S | *whose* | S O B A | |

| 28 | N E I Z | *of my hands* | Z I E N | *here a point.* |

27. H O L-

27	HOLBON	*the palms*	*Noblob.*
26	AT	*as*	*TA.*
25	HAMMOC	*truffed you together*	COMMAH *A point.*
24	DO	*And*	*As before OD.*
23	ZMIZ	*of my vestures*	*Zimz.* A point.
22	AOHTON	*in the midst*	*Notboa.* Here is a point before the word. A point.
21	AAQ	*your garments*	*QAA.* Three syllables.

E. K. Now he useth reverence to the Table again.

20	QLOH	*measureth*	HOLQ Δ. *as Holquu.*
19	SD	*which*	DS

Nal. Adjuva me mi Deus.

18.	GRPLAM	*a through thrusting fire*	*Malprg, as Malpurg.*
17	AT	*as*	*TA.*

Now he prayeth as before, his arms extended.

16	AARG	*and the Moon*	*GRAA.* A point.
15	DASPZAN	*a Sword*	*NAZPSAD.*

E. K. Now he prayeth again.

14	AT	*as*	*TA.*
13	I	*is*	a word by it self.
12	ROR	*The Sun*	*Ror.* Here a point.
11	LOZ	*bands*	*Zol ... zod* Δ, *as ol :* A point.
10	ARBOS	*in whose*	*Sobra.*
9	OHPNOV	*of wrath*	*Vonpho.*
8	ZLAC	*above the firmaments*	*Calz.*
7	HSNAL	*in power exalted*	*LANSH as Lonsh.*

Adjuva me O Deus.

6	TLAB	*of Justice*	*Balt.* Here is a point.
5	DAI	*the God*	*Iad, as Yad.*
4	OHOG	*faith*	*GOTTO.*
3	GSROV	*over you*	*Vorsg.* Here a point.
2	FNOS	*Raign*	*Sonf.*
1	LO	*I*	*Ol.*

E. K. Now

E. K. Now he sitteth down in his Chair.   This is the end of the mighty and first Call.

...... *Pray that you may understand what it is.*
Δ. Mean you presently ?
Nal. ...... *I, presently.*
Δ. I pray to that intent.

E. K. All the Stone sheweth fire, and all is on fire, nothing else appearing : not like common fire, but clear, thin, *&c.*

Now it waxeth clear.

E. K. And now *Nalvage* is on the top of the Globe, and his seat remaineth in the former manner of fire.   Now *Nalvage* holdeth up his right hand, and the same seemeth to be many hands.   There is on one of his fingers an I. It vanisheth away ; and so on divers fingers are words as follow.

I	*midst*	*delivered*
Reign	*of*	*you*
over	*my*	*a*
you	*vestures,*	*rod*
saith	*and*	*with*
the	*trussed*	*the*
God	*you*	*ark*
of	*together*	*of*
Justice,	*as*	*knowledge,*
in	*the*	*moreover*
power	*palms*	*you*
exalted	*of*	*lifted*
above	*my*	*up*
the	*hands,*	*your*
firmaments	*whose*	*voices*
of	*seats*	*and*
wrath,	*I*	*sware*
in	*garnished*	*obedience*
whose	*with*	*and*
hands	*the* 6c	*faith*
the	*fire*	*to*
Son	*of*	*him*
is	*gathering*	*that*
as	*and*	*liveth*
a	*beautified*	*and*
Sword,	*your*	*triumpheth*
and	*garments*	*whose*
the	*with*	*beginning*
Moon	*admiration*	*is*
as	*to*	*not,*
a	*whom*	*nor*
through	*I*	*end*
thrusting	*made*	*can*
fire	*a*	*not*
which	*Law*	*be*
measureth	*to*	*which*
your	*govern*	*shineth*
garments	*the*	*as*
in	*holy ones,*	*a*
the	*and*	*flame* 60

in	Move	I
the	therefore	
midst	and	*am*
of	shew	*the*
your	your	*servant*
Palace,	selves,	*of*
and	open	*the*
raigneth	the	*same*
amongst	mysteries	*your*
you	of	*God,*
as	your	*the*
the	Creation,	*true*
Ballance	be	*worshipper*
of	friendly	*of*	60
righteousnesse	unto	*the*	60
and	*me;*	49	Highest.	49
truth.	for		169

E. K. Now all the fingers be gone.

Δ.

Nal. ...... *It is the sense in your tongue of the holy and mystical Call before delivered : which*
followeth in practice *for the moving of the second Table,* the Kings and Ministers of government: *The uttrance of which, is of force,* and moveth them to visible apparition : moved and appeared, they are forced (by the Covenant of God delivered by his spirit) to render obedience and faithful society. *Wherein, they will open* the mysteries of their creation, *as far as shall be necessary :* and give you understanding *of many thousand secrets, wherein you are yet but children;* for every Table hath his key : *every key openeth his gate, and every gate being opened, giveth knowledge of himself of entrance, and of the mysteries of those things whereof he is an inclosure. Within these Palaces you shall find things that are of power, as well to speak, as to do* for every [(1) Palace] *is above his* [(2) City] *and every City above his* [(3) entrance.]
Be you therefore diligent that you may enter in, not as spoilers, *but as such as deserve intertainment in the name, and through the power of the Highest.* For great are the mercies of God unto such as have faith. *This is therefore the key of the first seven, according to the proportion of the first Creation. No more for this time.*
A sign alwayes to make an end.

Second Table,

The covenant of God.
Obedience.
Many keyes.

Note these three degrees.

Faith.
A key of the first seven.
A sign to make an end.

E. K. He drew a Curtain before the Stone, of white colour.

The same Saturday, after Noon, *hora* 3 ; 4.
The white Curtain remained about half an hour after my prayer to God, and some invitation to *Gabriel* and *Nalvage,* at length the Curtain quaked as though wind blew it.

E K. Me thinketh that I hear a stir within the Stone.   At length they appeared.

E. K. They have very eyes which twinkle as other mens eyes do, and * therefore I see them with my external eye, not within my imagination, as ....

* I had discoursed somewhat with E. K. of the manner of skrimges.

Gabr. ....
as I think.

...... *There are two kind of visions, the one by infusion of will and descending, the other by infusion by permission and ascending. The first is the image of the Will of God descending into the body, and adjoyned to the soul of man, whose nature is to distinguish things of his own likenesse, but shut up in prison in the body, wanteth that power; and therefore being illuminated by spiritual presence, inwardly, seeth now in part, as he shall hereafter do in the whole.*
But note, that every vision is according to the soul of man in power : and so is received of him that seeth. The body of man feeleth nothing spiritual until he be of incorruption: Therefore useth no sense in and illumination. The other is to be found out by his contrary.

E.K. he speaketh hollowly.

E. K. Here is a Devil that derideth these instructions, and saith, you may know his vertue by his wisdom : he never went to School.

He,

Gabr. ....

Gab. ...... *I know what he is : Power is given to me to resist him , but not to touch him. He hath* Note.
ascended, and begotten him a son, wherein the people of the earth shall be accursed. *As* Pater Anti-
those that are in prison shut up from light, and the use of the day comprehend not any thing , but that Christi.,
which entreth unto them by permission, or free will, so is the Soul of man shut up from all light, except
that which entreth by the will, or suffrance of the highest.

But as obedience is the tryal of dignification , so are the Ceremonies appointed by God, the witnesses of justification. For he that violated the outward Law was accursed : But the very end of
Justice to salvation is the obedience, and submission of the Soul. How can it be that the earth and
elements shall bear witnesse against man in the day of Judgement ; but in the perverse use of them,
contrary to God his Commandments. He is a slow School-master,and of small understanding. The wicked
Gab. ...... *Cease,for the conflict is great, and must have judgement of the Lord.* spirit said.

Δ. Sall I joyn my prayers with yours to our God, to drive away this wicked scorner , and
contemner of your ministery ?
Gab. .... *Not so, you know not the secret judgements of the Lord herein. The* white Curtain
was drawn.

Δ. Deo Nostro soli Omnipotenti fit omnis Laus,Honor,Gloria , & imperium in
secula seculorum. *Amen.*

Sonday, *Aprilis* 15. *Mane Hor.* 7¼.

After a few prayers necessary , and invitation to *Gabriel* and *Nalvage* for their instructions.

...... *Our instructions shall grow most plentifully amongst you. But give place to time, for* A voyce out
this is the voyce of the highest. Be holy and righteous in the works of your hands , and keep al- of the high-
wayes the Sabbath of your Redeemer hereafter : For even yet, the Serpent is amongst us. For Sabaoth.
even yet the Serpent is amongst my holy ones, and endeavoureth to cut you asunder. *Therefore* labureth to
I say be holy even in the works of your hands, for he thinketh to prevail against you : *But let your* part us asun-
houses be swept clean, that when the spy entreth, he finde nothing to feed on. der, and ho-
Δ. We ceased and gave our selves to the Sabbath : considering, intending hence foreward peth to pie-
to visit the Church and Assembly, to pray and meditate on God his service. vail.
Solus Jesus Christus *est Triumphator contra mortem & Diabolum , Dominus Noster &*
Deus Noster. Amen.

Monday, 15. *Aprilis.* Mane, hora 6. Cracoviæ.

Δ. After a short prayer to God for remission of sins , and sending of his graces, and his
good Ministers assigned for our instructions : and for the avoiding away of the great enemy,&c.
who held conflict against *Gabriel*,&c. The white Curtain appeared still drawn before in
the stone for an hour.

E. K. There appeareth a face standing upon two Pillars , the Curtain yet remaining drawn : The face is fiery, and hath very great teeth.
The Pillars are like Marble spotted gray , and the ground of the Pillars
colour white. He said,the works of the highest are become a stumbling block, and have entred into the breasts of a woman,and he is become angry. But when she thinketh her self happy, she shall stumble,
where she would not, and become sorrowfull without comfort.

E. K. This face and Pillars became a great water swelling upward,
and so vanished away.

Δ. After about an hour, the Curtain was opened. All appeareth as before : *Gabriel* sit-
teth in his Chair, and *Nalvage* kneeleth.
Nal. ...... *Pray, for the mercy of God.* Δ. I prayed divers prayers of God,& help
Pray , for thou shalt not be heard ? So, against the wicked enemy,yet present,
well said, sy upon him. and molesting us as he was permitted.
Δ. This Devil rayled against God. Δ. Thy judgement light on this wicked
Rebel for this blasphemy, O God.

Gab. ...... *Move not, for presence of power is great.*
Nal. ...... *Number the words of the first Key.*
Δ. I have counted them, and they seem to be 88.
Nal. ...... *There are not so many.*

N 87. Δ. Where

87 Δ. Where have I mifreckoned, I pray you? Perhaps *Poamalzod* is to be but one word, and fo are 87.

E. K. There is a great Croffe over all the ftone that is red : Not onely over to be impreffed through the ftone.

Nal. ..... *Number the words in thy own language.*

Δ. I have numbred them, and they feem to be 169.

Δ. While I numbred , the great red croffe went away : and fhortly after came in again in, to the ftone as before.

Gab. ...... *Move not, for the place is holy.   Tou have* Zurza ds Gono *in the Call: the fd is too much.*

Δ. I will then put it out.

Δ. I finde Zurza Adna ds Gono.

Nal. ...... *That ds is too much.   I pray you, what is then the number of them , of you al-lowed?*

Nal. ...., 86.

Δ. Making alfo *Poamolzod* one word? in that account?

Nal. ...,.. *Set down.*

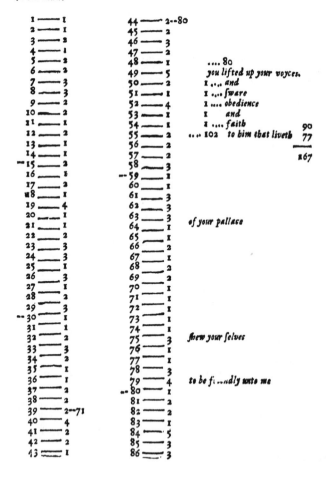

1 — 1	44 — 2--80		
2 — 1	45 — 2		
3 — 2	46 — 3		
4 — 1	47 — 2		
5 — 2	48 — 1	 80	
6 — 2	49 — 5	you lifted up your voyces.	
7 — 3	50 — 2	1 .,.. and	
8 — 3	51 — 1	1 .,.. fware	
9 — 2	52 — 4	1 .... obedience	
10 — 2	53 — 1	1 and	
11 — 1	54 — 1	1 .... faith	90
12 — 2	55 — 2	... 102 to him that liveth	77
13 — 1	56 — 2		───
14 — 1	57 — 2		167
--15 — 2	58 — 3		
16 — 1	--59 — 1		
17 — 2	60 — 1		
u8 — 1	61 — 3		
19 — 4	62 — 3		
20 — 1	63 — 3	of your pallace	
21 — 1	64 — 1		
22 — 2	65 — 1		
23 — 3	66 — 2		
24 — 3	67 — 1		
25 — 1	68 — 2		
26 — 3	69 — 2		
27 — 1	70 — 1		
28 — 2	71 — 1		
29 — 3	72 — 1		
--30 — 1	73 — 1		
31 — 1	74 — 1		
32 — 2	75 — 3	fhew your felues	
33 — 3	76 — 1		
34 — 2	77 — 1		
35 — 1	78 — 3		
36 — 1	79 — 4	to be fr...ndly unto me	
37 — 2	--80 — 1		
38 — 2	81 — 2		
39 — 2--71	82 — 2		
40 — 4	83 — 1		
41 — 2	84 — 5		
42 — 2	85 — 3		
43 — 1	86 — 3		

Tuesday, *Aprilis* 17. Cracoviæ.

After divers Ejaculations appropriate to the action, and the Curtain of white water yet remaining. E. K. thought divers times that he saw through the white Veil, and stone and all, nothing appearing therein. E. K. immediately fell into a new doubting of the verity of these actions, and said he had a Vision by a good Creature the last night, who said these Creatures with which we dealt, *would no more appear unto him*. Hereupon he said that both the last dayes skorner, and these our instructors were all Devils: and that he would no more sit to *receive* A.B.C. And so by Letters, any Doctrine of theirs, unlesse they would otherwise expresly, and lively deliver a plain rule thereof: With many other arguments to disprove the verity of our Actions, whereupon he said, that *John* your boy can well enough deliver you their Letters, and so you need not me,&c. I referred all to God, his will, and mercies: For, as I had at his hands onely, and by his order, and for his service *required wisdom and true knowledge,* so do I not doubt but God will, according to his accustomed goodnesse, *provide for me,* that is best for my vocation here in earth,&c.

E. K. He rose, and went away: and left me alone in my Study, appointed for these actions.

> *Deus in adjutorium meum intende, Domine ad adjuvandum me festina. Gloria Patri & Filio & Spiritui Sancto, sicut erat in principio & nunc & semper & in secula seculorum.* Amen.

Thursday, *Circa* 9.

As I was in my upper Study, and had gathered the holy words of the second and third call, and had conferred them with their *English* delivered also unto us: E. K. came up the stairs, and so went into his Study, and came out again, and as he was going down the staires I opened my Study door, and saluted him: He thereupon came up again, and came into my Study: And there I shewed him what I had done; and how I had some understanding of those holy words, their significations by reason of due applying the *English* to the word *Christus,* intending thereby to have induced E. K. to like the better of the manner of our friends, due, and Methodical, proceeding with us, and told him that unlesse of this strange language I should have these words delivered unto us Letter by Letter, we might erre both in Orthography, and also for want of the true pronunciation of the words, and distinctions of the points, we might more misse the effect expected: But as on *Tuesday* last, so now again he said, our Teachers were deluders, and no good, or sufficient Teachers, who had not in two years space made us able to understand, or do somewhat: and that he could in two years have learned all the seven Liberal sciences, if he had first learned Logick, &c. wherefore he would have no more to do with them any manner of way, wished himself in *England,* and said that if these books were his, that he would out of hand burn them, and that he had written to my Lord (by *Pirmis*) that he took our Teachers to be deceivers, and wicked, and no good Creatures of God, with many such speeches, and reasons (as he thought) of force to diswade himself from any more dealing with them: But willed me to use *John* my Boy as my Skryer, for that these spiritual Creatures were not bound unto him,&c. I answered unto all these parcels and reasons, as time served declaring *my perfect trust in God,* that seeing I have many years desired, and prayed for wisdome (such as these Actions import) at his hands, and by such means as to his Divine Majesty seemeth best, that he would not either *mislike* my prayer, or abuse my Constant hope in his goodnesse and mercy: Therefore I concluded that I referred all to the mercifull will of God, and doubted nothing at the length to be satisfied of my request, and prayer made unto him. So he went from me this second time. ... God lighten his heart with knowledge of the truth, if it be his Divine will and pleasure.

Note. *Permis* went on last Wednesday morning, and had received our Letters after noon, on Tuesday last: But on Monday before the wicked Prince of darknesse did what he could to hinder our proceeding.

On Thursday, *Tabius* (brother to my Lord *Laskie* his wife) brought news to *Cracovia,* that my Lord *Laskie* was coming to *Cracovia* ward. *Emericus* came from *Kesmarke,* and returned back again. *Tabius* rode from *Cracovia* toward *Kesmark.*

Saturday, *Aprilis* 21. *à Meridie.*

After our prayers made, appeared shortly *Gabriel* and *Nalvage.* E. K. propounded six questions orderly, which had bred great doubt in this fantasie, and requested their answers.

Δ. He

Δ. He would have our spiritual friends to promise him the performance of the Prints.

Gab. ...... *If we were Masters of our own doings, we might well promise : But we are servants, and do the will of our master. But let me ask thee one question :*
Dost thou not think, that all things are possible with God ?

E. K. I do so, and I know so.

Gab. ...... *Then is there no cause why thou should distrust.   Let him that is a servant, and is commanded to go, go : and let not the earth rise up, and strive against the plowman.   What sin is it when the creature riseth up, and saith in his heart,* Let the Lord *make a Covenant with me, considering he is a bond man ?*

[E. K. They seem, both the voices at once, to come to my eare.]

None but he that becometh disobedient, and refuseth his Master.

Δ........   [Δ would do so.

Gab. Nal. ...... *These things, that is to say, this Doctrine, delivered by us, is of God, and of his mercies granted unto you, which cannot be in vain :* and *therefore to be performed ; for the secret determinations of God are unknown unto us.*
He never heard of any man that would ask, if God would perform his promises.

E. K. By *August* next ?

What if it were a hundred Augusts ? you may be a weary before August next, as the Children of Israel were of their Manna.

E. K. Why joyn you numbers with these letters, and added none with those of the former Table.

Numbers.
Numeri
Formales.
Pulius.*Brother, what is the cause that all the World is made by numbers ?   The Numbers we speak of, are of reason and form, and not of merchants.*

Δ. I beseech you as concerning the powder whereof he thinketh that he hath made due assay of it, as if it should have been the Philosophers Stone, and so affirmed to be, by the minister of this action ? I beseech you so to answer, the thing, as his reason may be satisfied.

Δ. They gave no answer hereunto, but proceeded in the former matter of Numbers.

Note the pro-
perty of this
Method and
Language.*Gab.* ...... *Every Letter signifieth the member of the substance whereof it speaketh.   Every word signifieth the quiddity of the substance.   The Letters are separated, and in confusion : and therefore, are by numbers gathered together : which also gathered signifie a number : for as every greater containeth his lesser, so are the secret and unknown forms of things knit up in their parents : Where being known in number, they are easily distinguished; so that herein we teach places to be numbred : letters to be elected from the numbred, and proper words from the letters, signifying substantially the thing that is spoken of in the center of his Creator, whereby even as the minde of man moved at an ordered speech, and is easily perswaded in things that are true, so are the creatures of God stirred up in themselves, when they hear the words wherewithal they* Understand-
ing, Perswa-
sion, Motion.*were nursed and brought forth : For nothing moveth, that is not perswaded : neither can any thing be perswaded that is unknown.   The Creatures of God understand you not, you are not of their Cities : you are become enemies, because you are separated from him that Governeth the City by ignorance.*

E. K. Whether is this Language known in any part of the World or no ? if it be, where and to whom ?

Adam.*Gab.* ...... *Man in his Creation, being made an Innocent, was also authorised and made par-taker of the Power and Spirit of God : whereby he not onely did know all things under his Crea-tion and spoke of them properly, naming them as they were : but also was partaker of our presence and society, yea a speaker of the mysteries of God ; yea, with God himself : so that in innocency the power of his partakers with God, and in his good Angles, was exalted, and so became holy in the sight of God until that* Coronzon Coronzon.
Note two be
true Langua-
ges.?
Adam his
speech after
the fall.
Litiea 2t.
Lingua Ange-
lica.
Lingua Ange-
lica, vel Ada-
mica in sua in-
nocentia Statu.*(for so is the true name of that mighty Devil) envying his felicity, and perceiving that the substance of his lesser part was frail and unperfect in respect of his pure Esse, began to assail him, and so prevailed : that offending so became accursed in the sight of God ; and so lost the Garden of felicity, the judgement of his understanding : but not utterly the favour of God, and was driven forth (as your Scriptures record) unto the Earth which was covered with brambles : where being as dumb, and not able to speak, he began to learn of necessity the Language which thou,* E. K. *callest* [1 Hebrew :] *and yet not that* [2 Hebrew] *amongst you : in the which he uttered and delivered to his posterity, the nearest knowledge he had of God his Creatures : and from his own self divided his speech into three parts, twelve, three, and seven : the number whereof remaineth, but the true forms and pronunciations want ; and therefore is not of that force that it was in his own dignity, much lesse to be compared with this that we deliver, which Adam verily spake in innocency, and was never uttered nor disclosed to man since till now, wherein the power of God must work, and wisdom in her true kind be delivered : which are not to be spoken of in any other thing, neither to be talked of with mans imaginations ; for as this Work and Gift is of God, which is all power, so doth he open it in a tongue of power, to*

the

ye intent that the proportions may agree in themselves : for it is written, *Wisdom sitteth upon an Hill, and beholdeth the four Winds, and girdeth her self together as the brightness of the morning, which is visited with a few, and dwelleth alone as though she were a Widow.*

Thus you see there, the Necessity of this Tongue : The Excellency of it, And the Cause why it is preferred before that which you call Hebrew : For it is written, *Every lesse, consenteth to his greater.* I trust this is sufficient.

E. K. As concerning the power, What is it ?

Gab. ...... *What it is, that it is, for the knowledge of it may lead you to error.*

Δ. This answer offended greatly E. K. and thereupon he left off, and would receive no more at their hands. God make him patient, and a favourer of this Action as soon as it is needful that he should be.

Δ. *Laudetur, magnificetur & extollatur nomen Jesu Christi in omne evum.*   Amen.

Note on Tuesday after Noon, *circa horam quartam,* as we two sat together, E. K. said that he thought upon the matter, *Et quod jam vellet duas horas mihi concedere singulis diebus ad reci-* pienda illa, que illi tradere vellent. Ego autem illi & maximo Deo gratias egi, quia hanc esse mu- *tationem dextra excelsi factam verè judicavi ; nam ante prandium rigidissimus erat in contraria opinione & sententia.*   *14. Aprilis. This after noon.*

Wensday, *Cracoviæ, Aprilis* 25,   Mane,   hora 7.

The Vail appeared as at first almost. After half an hour *Gabriel* and *Nalvage* appeared, after my manifold prayers and discourses.

Δ. Two keyes we have received by the mercy of the Highest and your ministers, the rest we attend, according to the merciful will of the Highest.

Gab. ...... *Move not from your places, for the place is holy.*

Δ. Shew a token O Lord when thy will is, whereby to perswade thy merciful dealings with us, and the presence of thy faithful Ministers.

Δ. The frame of the Stone gave a crickling, no hand touching it, or otherwise any mor-tal or worldly thing moving it. I heard it very certainly, and to E. K. it seemed the sound of a bunch of keyes, as if they had quickly been shaken and strongly.   Note.

E. K. *Gabriel* sitteth, and *Nalvage* standeth.

Gab. ...... *My Brethren hearken to my voice, for I am the true servant of the God of Abraham, Isaac, and Jacob, the dignity whereof is sufficient both for the verity of the Doctrine, and the confirmation, and perswasion of your mindes : for as God is the Father of the Faithful, so he sheweth himself unto the faithful : whereby you may prove the great comfort and consolation : that you may justly gather of the mercies of God, as touching your Election.*

For at what time hath God appeared unto the unrighteous ? or where do you read that ever he visited the reprobate ? For the reprobate hath no visitation, but in the rod of Justice :

But you may rise up among your selves, saying lo, we are froward, we want faith.   An objection.

True it is, the acts of faith, but not the roots of faith. But I say unto you, that the power of God in his Election, is the Basis of mans purity and acceptation.   Answer.

But here there is a Caveat.

That man imagining his Predestination and perfect Election, justifieth not himself ; for wheresoever this is found, or this Doctrine preached amongst you, either simply in man, or publickly in Congregation, it is the sure sign and token of their perpetual ignorance and confusion : For the Will and Power of God belongeth not to our measure (for it was the cause of rebellion amongst us) much lesse among men, which are fighting yet for the Glory of their reward. Behold it is a sin in him that judgeth of his brothers Conscience ; Much more is it a threefold error, to form the ima-ginations of sin, by whose imaginations they are.

Be not proud therefore of the gifts of God, but become humble ; Neither justifie your self in re-spect that this is the word of God delivered unto you for your own selves : But the more you receive, be the more thankful ; and the more you be in the strength of God, the more use, you the purenesse of humility.

Of whom it is said, Behold my Spirit hath entred, yea into my servants, and they are become humble and meek in the sight of men : But if we be the servants of the God of Abraham, then are we the spirits of truth and understanding, for our faith is dignified in the sight of the heavens, and we are become mighty in the power of the Almighty. Therefore ought we to be believed.   Good Angels.

Now if you will confesse your selves to be the children of Abraham, then must you also accept of our Doctrine : For the meat whereby Abraham lived, is the same food we minister unto you : of whom it is said, He believed God, and it was counted unto him for righteousnesse. Even so do you,
that

that you also may be righteous, wherein do you differ from Abraham? Were you not barren? Who hath made you fruitfull?

A Covenant.

Did God make a Covenant with Abraham? Even so he doth with you. Did the Lord in his Ministers appear unto him? So doth he, and will do unto you. Were the sins of Sodom (the fifth that perished) imported into Abrahams bosome, as the secret determination of the Lord? Are they also not manifest unto you (even by the same God) as touching the time and corruption of this world? Rose he not up in the morning, and beheld the confusion, and headlong Ruines of the wicked? And shall you not also see the ruine of him that is the son of wickednesse. Yes, unlesse you hinder your selves. For the promise of your God is without exception. Be mindful therefore of your selves; and consider your calling: That you may be still blessed in him that is the God of Abraham, who is your Father.

The Keyes.

In these keyes which we deliver, are the mysteries and secret beings and effects of all things moving, and moved within the world.

Lingua & scientia.

In this is the life of M O T I O N, in whom all tongues of the world are moved, for there is neither speech nor silence that was or shall be to the end of the world, but they are all as plain here, as in their own nakednesse. Despise it not; therefore .....For unto them that are hungry, it is bread, unto the thirsty drink, and unto the naked clothing: A Serpent it is of many heads invincible. Believe therefore, that with him you may be wise.: that your humility may be such, as may be numbred in the world. I have said. Nal. *Move not, for the place is holy.*

E. K. What mean you by that sentence or phrase.

Nal. *It is of two parts, the first in respect of the spirit and presence of him that is holy: present and teaching. Secondly in respect of your consent, which is obedience, for obedience confirmeth the will of God in man, and the will of God confirmeth mans salvation; wherefore it is said, move not: and why? because the place is holy. - Move neither in mind, neither in body, for obedience is the conclusion, and confirmation of your separations from the Devils. Sacrifice is accepted, but obedience is better. You are surely answered.*

E. K. I like your answer well.

Nal. *Our wisdom, shall prove Rhetorick.*

80	N a a q	*in your creation*	*It is* q i as
79	L E A N A N A	*of the secret wisdom*	*Ananael.*
78	I L P A L P	*partakers*	*It is* Plapli.
77	O G U P	*as unto the partakers*	*It is* Pugo.
76	R A M A U M I	*apply your selves unto us*	*It is* Im ua mar.
75	D O	*And*	*Od.*

E. K. This letter turneth so about, that I cannot well discerne it.

74	G A L G I N U	*Descend*	Uniglag.

E. K. This letter also turneth round.

73	R A C A Z	*Move*	Zod a car
72	A I H O G	*we say*	Gobia.
71	G M R A S A C	*in whome*	Casarmg.
70	M O I A A	*Amongst us*	A ai om.
69	Z L O A C I M	*mighty*	Mi ca olz.
68	R A O N	*is become*	Noar.

E. K. This Letter moveth.
E. K. Now he maketh a reverend Cursy.

67	N I A O O D D O	*and name*	Od do o a in.

E. K. This letter also moveth   Od is and it must be sounded with one breath.

                  E. K.

E. K. *Gabriel* shaketh his speare. *Nalvage.*

66	MOCACAC	*Flourish*	*Cæcæ com.*
65	ZOSUHEI	*his mercies*	*Jebusoz.*
64	AMCIM	*Behold*	*Micma.*

E. K. Now he useth his reverent Cursies again.

| 63 | NARIMA | *Your selves* | *Amiran.* |

Nal. *Did I not bid thou shouldest not move?*

E. K. He hath thrown down his rod upon the Table.

[Δ. I had moved to the dore, because I heard some going up and down the chamber without : we had forgotten to shut the staire-foot dore.]
Δ. O Lord, I did it not upon any wilfull disobedience. But pardon this Fault, and by thé grace (O God) I will avoid the like fault henceforward.
Nal. *It was a great fault.* Δ. I beseech the Almighty to pardon it.

E. K. Now he is kneeled down, and all his Face is under the Table. Now he is up again, and taketh his rod in his hand, and maketh a Crosse with it three times : East, West, North, and South.

Nal. *Sound your word.* Δ. *Amiran.*

E. K. He pronounceth the i so remissely, as it is scarce heard, and in the pronouncing of the whole word he seemeth not to move his lips.

| 62 | SUHOG | *I say* | *Gobus.* |

E. K. He made long leasurely reverence.

| 61 | ROLOHOG | *lift up.* | *Goholor.* |

E. K. He useth reverence again.
Nal. *The next is a name mightier then the power of the same.*

| 60 | DAM | *of the same your God* | *Mad.* |

E. K. He useth long reverent Cursy again.
E. K. Now he holdeth up his Rod.

| 59 | PAIOOD | *In the name* | *Do oi ap.* |

E. K. He holdeth up his rod again.

38	NAOOVDO	*and truth*	*Od vooan.*
57	TLAB	*of Justice*	*Balt.*
56	HALANU	*The Skyrts*	*Unalah.*
55	NAON	*thus you are become*	*Noan.*
54	DLIP	*on the earth*	*Pild.*
53	GSOAC	*continually*	*Caosg.*

Now he useth courtesy.

52	IGRIPLAM	*the fiers of life and increase*	*Malpirgi.*
51	RIPNAP	*powring down*	*Panpir*
50	LEEANAN	*my power*	*Na na e el.*
46	NUAV	*you might work,*	*Vaun.*

E. K.

E. K. He useth reverence.   Now he holdeth up his Rod and shaketh it about his head.

48	BAATENG	*your governments*	Gnetaab
47	ED	*of*	De,is my name
46	GAONIIM	*the corners*	aii inoag

E. K. He useth courtesie.

E. K. Gabriel shaketh his speare.

Nal. ...... *It may be called* Mi moag *or* Diuph

E. K. Now he extendeth.   Diuf

45	DO	*and*	Od
44	POZIZI	*from the bigbest vessels*	Izizop

Gab. .... *Move not.*

43	NEFAF	*to the intent that*	Fafen
42	BSACOC	*of time*	Cocasb
41	LIMOH	*the true ages*	Homil
40	ALC	*456*	Cla
39	SROV	*out*	Vors

E. K. He useth most reverent Cursie.

38	ILAIMPAC	*successively*	Capmiali
37	ASNOL	*power*	Lonsa
36	GRAZMOV	*unto every one of you*	*arg as in barge* Vomsarg
35	AGULD	*giving*	Dluga
34	BAATEN	*of government*	Netaab

E. K. Many sounds are heard in the stone.   He kneeleth down.

33	SONLIHT	*in seats 12.*	*Thilnos*
32	ALAAH	*placed you*	*A Ala*
31	DO	*and*	*O D*
			arg as in barge
30	GRAZLAB	*Stewards*	*BALZARG*
29	LOE	*I made you*	*EOL*
28	ILI	*in the first*	*ILI*
27	LUZROT	*shall rise*	*TORZUL*
26	DO	*and*	
25	ADGRB	*sleep*	*as burgen to bud as Burgda*
24	[TSD	*which*	*DST*

23 NEIZO

23 NEIZO   *mine own*   *OZIEN*

22 M   *except*   *EM it is a word*

E. K. Now he useth reverence.

21 EGSIHCI   *to are not*   *Kis*
                                                       I Chisge

20 SIHC   *are,*   *Kis*
                                                       Chis

19 GROTLOT   *the Creatures of the earth*   *org as in george*
                                                       Toltorg

18 NIIVQ   *wherein*   *Qui is*

17 HCOLET   *of deaths*   *as och*
                                                       in botch pot
                                                       Teloch

E. K. Now he maketh †.

16 HELP SOMQ   *or the borns*   *Q Mos Pleb*
                                                              as two words

15 NIVPAT   *as sharp sickles,*   *Ta pu in*

                                                              You may call it
                                                              Tapui also

14 SIHC   *are*   *as Kis*

13 LDNV   *the rest*   *Vnd L*

E. K. Now he maketh a Crosse again.
.... Now he stoopeth down and kisseth.   *it may be*
                                                           Vd L or Vnd L

12 HAPIGIG   *of living breaths*   *Gi gi pah*

11 LIHTO   *the seats*   *Othil*

10 SIHC   *are*   *as Kisse*
                                                       Chis

9   ZRON   *fix*   *Norx*

8   HODNOLSO   *12 Kingdoms:*   *Os Lon dob*

A Crosse again.   [*Os signifieth twelve*]
                                                       Londob

7   BAIB   *are*   *Biab*
                                                            Biab

6   NEIZA   *on whose hands*   *Azien*

He stoopeth and kisseth the ground.

5   HLESMOC   *a Circle,*   *Com Selb*

4   RIZ   *I am;*   *Zir*

3   DAIP   *your God*   *Pi ad*

                                        O   He

He kisseth the ground.   He setteth his hands on the ground.

2	OHOG	*saith*	*Gobo*
1	AMCIM	*behold*	*Mic ma.*

Nal. ...... *This is all.*

Δ. Now, in the Name of Jesus, as it pleased you before, so would we gladly have the sence hereof in *English.*

Nal. ..... *Let him that hath wisedom understand : For here beginne the mysteries of your world.*

1	*Behold,*	42	*of times;*
2	*saith*	43	*to the intent that,*
3	*your God,*	44	*from the highest vessels*
4	*I am*	45	*and*
5	*a Circle,*	46	*the Corners*
6	*on whose hands*	47	*of your governments,*
7	*stand*		Gal..... *mighty is the God of Hosts, amongst his people.*
8	*12 Kingdoms;*		
9	*six*	48	*you might work*
10	*are*	49	*my power,*
11	*the seats*	50	*pouring down*
12	*of living breath,*	51	*The fires of life, and encrease*
13	*The rest*	52	*continually*
14	*are*	53	*on the earth.*
15	*as sharp Sickles,*	54	*Thus*
16	*or the horns*	55	*you are become*
17	*of death;*	56	*The skirts*
18	*wherein*	57	*of Justice*
19	*The Creatures of the earth*	58	*and truth:*
20	*are*	59	*In the name*
21	*to are not,*	60	*of the same, your God,*
22	*except*	61	*lift up,*
23	*mine own hand,*	62	*I say,*
24	*Which*	63	*your selves*
25	*sleep*	64	*Behold,*
26	*and*	65	*his mercies*
27	*shall rise.*	66	*flourish,*
28	*In the first*	67	*and name*
29	*I made you*	68	*is become*
30	*Stewards*	69	*mighty*
31	*and*	70	*amongst us*
32	*placed you*	71	*in whom*
33	*in seats 12 [or] in 12 seats*	72	*we say,*
34	*of government :*	73	*Move,*
35	*Giving*	74	*Descend*
36	*unto every one of you*	75	*and*
37	*power,*	76	*apply your selves unto us,*
38	*successively,*	77	*as unto*
39	*over*	78	*the partakers*
40	*456.*	79	*of his secret wisdom*
41	*the true age:*	80	*in your Creation*

E. E. Now all all his fingers disappear.

K. K. Now *Gabriel* standeth up.

Gab. ..... *Heark, O ye sons of men; is the first of nature, and the beginning of your being in body: Whereby the things of the world have life & live. Let him that hath wisdom understand. Grow together, for this hath its fruit in due time. Albert Laskie hath not done the Commandment of God; he should have been here by this time.*

Δ. Note.   There are three calls in the second part of *Cracovia,* and one in the first.

These four calls are the second, the 3d. 4th. 5th. for the first Table can have no call, it is of the Godhead.

Δ. *Gloria, Laus, Honor, & Imperium sit Deo Nostro in infinita seculorum secula. Amen.*

Remember

A. Remember that on *Wedsday* night, *April* the 25. my Lord *Albert Laskie* came at night to *Cracovia,* and lay in a little woodden building, among guards, by *St. Steniflaus* Church : and on the *Friday* morning following intended to enter his journey toward *Kefmark,* and the recovering of *Kefmark* : Jefus profper his juft Caufe.

Wenfday morning, *Aprilis* 1584.   Cracoviæ.
　　　　Jefus ——

Nal. .... *A new Action* ———— *Backward, as before.*

52	D A I O I	*of him that liveth for ever.*	Ioiad.
51	R I Z	*I am*	Zir.
50	P A L	*for,*	Lap.
49	P L E R V	*a ftrong feething ;*	Vrelp.
48	M Z A Z O	*make me*	Ozazm.
47	D O	*and*	Od.
46	O Z L A C I M	*in power,*	Micalzo.
45	N A R M A Z	*fhew your felves*	Zamran.
44	D O Q O N C	*unto his fervants,*	[as C Nó quod:

Gab. ...... *The place is become more holy, and he is become more meek.*
Nal. ......

| 43 | A C | *therefore* | Ca. |
| 42 | R A C A Z | *Move* | Zacar. |

　　　　　　　　[Nal. ....,. *Make a ftop there.*]

| 41 | L E H O G | *faith the firft,* | Go hel. |

E. K. Now the Croffe is come in again thinner than it was before.

40	U Z R O T	*Arife,*	Torzú
39	N O D I A I	*of the all-powerful.*	Ia í don.
38	N I N A M	*in the minde*	Manin.
37	Q O	*but*	O qua.
36	E C A T	*or is not*	Tage.
35	S R O C	*Such*	Cors.
34	F O R T	*a building,*	Trof.
33	N A O N	*you are become*	No an.
32	P A L	*for*	Lap.
31	N O C N O Z O	*then the many fold windes;*	Ozongon:

30	A I B	*your voices*	Bia.
29	S I H C	*are*	Chis [the I long.
28	P L A C I M	*mightier*	Mi calp.
27	D O	*and*	Od
26	I R R O	*than the barren stone*	Orri.
25	D S U L	*your feet*	Lusd.
24	S I H C	*are*	Chis [as Xl₄.
23	I U I G	*stronger*	as Giui.
22	H O T L A B	*of righteousnesse*	Baltoh.
21	E G O O	*for the Chamber*	Ooge.
20	S B R V T	*in their beauty*	Turbs.
19	Q L S R O L	*the flowres*	Lors l qua.
18	A T Q	*or as*	Qun Ta.
17	A D E L C A R A P	*for a wedding*	Paracleda₄
16	O H L A T	*Cups*	Talho.
15	A T	*as*	Ta.
14	G M A R B A	*I have prepared*	Abramg
13	A M R A S A C	*whom*	Casarma.
12	H P D A I P	*within the depth of my Jaws*	Piadph.
11	Z A Z A Z I	*have framed*	Izazaz
10	G R U P L A I	*the burning flames*	I al purg.
9	M A B O S	*whom*	S o bam.
8	L	*of the first*	A word.
7	V I I V	*O you the second*	Vi iv.
6	D L A S	*your voices of wonder*	Sald.
5	P I A A F	*understand*	Fa á ip.
4	M O		Om.
3	G N O Z	*of the windes*	Zong.
2	H A A P V	*the wings*	V pa ah.
	T G D A	*Can*	Adgt.

The first word. ————— *The first is the last.*
1 —————— *Can*

E. K. Now he holdeth up many hands and fingers as before, and on the very end of the fingers distinctly these parcels appeared in English.

2 ——————— *The second word* ——— *The wing.*
Vpaab, is the wings, and Adgt, is Can.
3 ————————————— *of the windes,*
4 ————————————— *understand your voices of windes.*
5 ————————————— *O you*
6 ————————————— *the second*
7 ————————————— *of the first,*
8 ————————————— *whom*
9 ————————————— *The burning flames*
10 ————————————— *have framed*
11 ————————————— *within the depth of my Jaws,*
12 ————————————— *whom*
13 ————————————— *I have prepared*
14 ————————————— *as*
15 ————————————— *Cups*
16 ————————————— *for a wedding,*
17 ————————————— *or as*
18 ————————————— *the flowres*
19 ————————————— *in their beauty*
20 ————————————— *for the Chamber*
21 ————————————— *of righteousnesse ;*
22 ————————————— *stronger*
23 ————————————— *are*
24 ————————————— *your feet*
25 ————————————— *then the barren stone,*
26 ————————————— *and*
27 ————————————— *mightier*
28 ————————————— *are*
29 ————————————— *your voices*
30 ————————————— *then the manifold windes:*
31 ————————————— *For*
32 ————————————— *you are become*
33 ————————————— *a building,*
34 ————————————— *Such*
35 ————————————— *as is not,*
36 ————————————— *But*
37 ————————————— *in the minde*
38 ————————————— *of the all-powerful.*
39 ————————————— *Arise,*
40 ————————————— *saith the first ;*
41 ————————————— *Move*
42 ————————————— *therefore*

E. K. All the Stone is become very dark.
The wicked said .... *Thou shalt go no further* ......
Δ. I prayed *Roffensis Psalm 9.* and the *Lords Prayer,* and the Stone became clear, and the fingers appeared again, through the mercy of the Highest......

43 ———————————— *unto his servants;*
44 ———————————— *shew your selves*
45 ———————————— *in power,*
46 ———————————— *and*
47 ———————————— *make me*
48 ———————————— *a strong.* [*See thing,*]
49 ———————————— *for*
50 ———————————— *I am*
51 ———————————— *of him*
52 ———————————— *that liveth for ever.*

This *his* and *him* corrected, were of the wicked his subtile suggestions.

E. K. Now

E. K. Now appear no more fingers.

Nal. Compare them now together.

E. K. Now he is set down in his chaire.

Δ. I have compared the English Joynts to the mystical words, and I find 12. of each : so that they agree.

Nal. Thus you have this dayes labour. Now The white silk is extended over the stone.

Δ. Soli Deo nostro, Deo omnipotenti, & Majestatis tremedæ, & super omnia amandæ, fit omnis laus, gratiarum actio, & Jubilatio, *Amen.*

Friday, Cracoviæ, Aprilis : Mane, hora ferè 9.

Oratione Dominica & aliis

Precibus ad Deum finitis, pro luce & veritate, in hanc formam, Omnipotens, sempiterne, vere & vive Deus noster, mitte nobis spiritum sanctum & veritatem tuam, ut sapienter, fideliter & constanter tibi serviamus, omnibus diebus vitæ nostræ. Amen.

The white Curtain, or veyle, appeared very long.

Δ. It fell so out by the wonderful providence of God, that *E. K.* and I quietly considered these actions, generally, & the contrary spirituall informations given to him, apart by himself; (& sometimes) while we were receiving our instructions, by our Schoolmasters, of which contrary power, some would rayle on God, and blaspheme his Majesty horribly, as may appear by the record of some late Actions; But this was our conclusion, that we both desired the verity, and that so, as best might please God, in the manner of coming by it.

Note, arbitre-ment of God required.   Δ. Be Judge. O Lord, between us, sending us the verity of the judgment, for the glory of thy name, for as much as they which impugne these proceedings, do (to *E. K.*) as it seems perfecter, and more wise and fruitful then our Schoolmasters, which I took to be the true and blessed Angels, &c.

E. K. Now is the note pluck't aside.   Δ. About an eleven of the Clock.

Δ. Blessed be the highest, who is Almighty.

14. Diei mensis Sab.   Gab. *Danida*, a *mighty Prophet* (not the least upon the earth) opened his mouth, and said, Be-hold, there shall a Whale come from the East, the fourteenth day of this Month, S A B.

E. K. They seem to speak both together.

Gab., Nal. *And he entred into the field, and he met with a Merchant, and he said unto him, Thou art not for me : for thy intent dwelleth in the world. He went further, and, lo, there was a field of all kind of people, diversly recreating themselves in their own pleasures: and he yet said, Lo, these are not for me: and he went on, and, lo, he saw,* AND IT WAS A NAKED MAN.

Gab. Nal. *Mark,*   [*to E.K.*]

E. K. So I do.

Gab. Nal. *In his hands were divers things; mosse, leaves, flowers, and herbs ; and he wondred, saying, Why art thou naked? and he said, Lo, I am old, and am without Garments, and these are the things wherewithall I will be clothed. And the Prophet talked with him, and told him of the Whale.*

E. K. They speak both together, that I cannot discern their voyce.

And he commanded him to kneel, and he lifted up hands his to heaven and prayed within him-self; and he said also unto him, I am a Prophet, rise up, I will blesse thee in the name of my prophesie: and lo, he took him by the hand, and went forward : and the way was rough, stony, and very sound: and, as they went, they found men, huge and big, monstrous : and the Prophet said, These please me

A Child   *not: and, as they talked on the way, they overtook a little child, And the Phrophet ask't him his name, and he answered, He was a man : and he said, Thou pleasest me, for thou mayest be a man.*

A Hill.   *There was a Hill, and they ascended, and, after a while, the child became weary, and sate down, saying with himself, This hill is troublesome, I am not able to keep company with them; and the Prophet, missing him, went back, and found him sitting. And he began to weep, saying, Whither will you lead me ? But the Prophet comforted him, and said; Now thou seest, thou art not a man. And thus he did, ascending sundry times? and, lo, it was the top of the hill, and the Sun was hot and clear in the midst of the day. The Prophet said unto the child, look to the Centre of the Sun, and so he did, stedfastly.*

Pen, Ink, & Pa-per.   *And the Prophet said unto him, Now I have experience of thee, and I know thou wilt be a man; And he said unto him, that was naked, Here are Pen, Ink, and Paper.*

Oriens.   *And lo thou hast one that can see far off, and he shewed him the Seas : saying, look unto the East : and he told him of the Whale and of his coming, and of many mysteries.*

But the man answered him, saying, I am naked, the ayre is sharp, and I have no food: How

can

can I therefore S T A Y *so many dayes ? and he said unto him,* Sit down, and note, untill this Child become a man. Note untill.

Feed by comfort. For the Whale shall be thine, in whose belly is a Chest swallowed of great value, and they were contented. Behold, the people of the countrey were rich, and had conquered many Nations, so that he was a Monarch in the world; this Monarch was skilfull in all Sciences, and knew all things to come, and he called his Counsell together, and said unto them. Monarcha mundi & sui subditi.

Lo, thus it is, the cause why I have made those mighty banks, and have drawn my people from the lower places and the Seas, is for that, I fear a Whale: which, if he land in my Kingdomes, will be my destruction, and they told him what the Prophet had said, and he began to rage, and was puffed up with anger, and he opened his books T H E   S E C O N D   T I M E; *and his eyes were opened, and he understood that the Prophet had ascended unto the top of the mountain, and had taken with him a naked man, and a child: and he said to his Ministers, Ascend, and bring me the child, for I will examine him, and know the Prophets meaning, and he apparelled him richly, and gave him much, but he prevailed not. And he said within himself, Ascend again they shall, and bring down that man.*

And the servants ascended, and they found a Marble stone, and they were angry among themselves saying, Is this a man? And lo they came unto the Kings and said; Thou sendest us forth, but we found a mighty stone not able to be moved. Where is it therefore that thou wilt have us seek that man; But he said within himself, I will overcome the child, and he took him by the hand, and led him into his Orchard, where he opened unto him the secrets of his books, so that he became skilful. But, lo, the Prophet arose, and, as he walked towards the Hill, to comfort them whom he accounted his friends, he espied the child apparalled strangely, and in company with strangers: *and he opened his mouth, and began to prophesie, saying.* A marble stone. Strangers.

The King hath risen up against himself, for he hath CHOSEN THE CHOSEN, *and hath opened the secrets of his own Kingdom to his destruction, and he stretched forth his hand, and said unto the child, Come with me: and he was unwilling, for his pleasures were great. And he lifted up his voyce and said: and he* SWARE, *And, lo, he came with him even unto the mountain: and the Prophet said unto him, When thou wast a child, I led thee, but now thou art become a man. stretch forth thy leggs, and labour, and he was unwilling.*

Thus, whilst they were talking, they that waited upon him were at his feet armed, saying, come with us, for we are strong enough to deliver thee.

But the Prophet said unto them, GOE *back and tell your King, that I found him on the way, and a stranger, and I had pity on him, and I took him for my own. Therefore strive not, for justice must prevail. And they began to stagger as drunkards, for they knew it was true. And the Prophet said, Now come with me, I will yet lead thee: and they ascended. The Prophet held up his hands, and* SAID, I SEE, *and behold, he that was naked arose: and said,* I SEE ALSO.

And the Seas arose, and a great tempest, and broke down the banks: and entred on the earth, doing much harm to the people of that Kingdom: And, lo, there arose a wind the S E C O N D: *and there were four beasts, such as are in the world, and were never known. And they came state. swimming, and so landed on the Hill. And the Prophet said, Arise, draw out your swords and kill them, and so they did.* Maris inundatio cum tempestate. Ventus.

Behold, the blood of them vanished into aire, and the flesh became earth: The entrals of them wasted away with the waters: and their bones burned with a mighty fire. The second wind arose, and there were five Crowns: in the midst of them sate the Father of life, with a golden head: whose Feet bathed themselves in due and sweet Manna: and the Prophet said, Put forth your hands: and they did so: But lo they were afraid, for he that stood in the midst of the Crowns, was full of beauty. Ventus 2. Pater vitæ.

And the Prophet said, Fear not, come with me; and he opened unto them the secrets of the Crown; for in every one of them was a golden sentence. And the secrets of the Hill began to shake, and there was a great Earthquake. Mysteria 5 Coronarum.

The third wind arose: and the twelve Cedar trees that were never corrupted, came and planted themselves in twelve places of the Hill, and they brought forth strange fruits, not as Cedar trees do. Ventus 3.

The Prophet said, Gather, for I know you hunger, that you may be refreshed. While they thus talked, the fourth wind arose, and, behold, all the mountain was a flaming fire, and there were five Earthquakes, such as were not since the beginning of the world. Ventus 4. 5. Terra motus.

The Prophet took them up, for they were become as dead. And suddenly The Firmament and the waters were joyned together, and the Whale C A M E, like unto a legion of stormes: or as the bottomless Cave of the North *when it is opened: and she was full of eyes of every side.* The Whale came.

The Prophet said, Stand still, but they trembled. The waters sank, and fell suddenly away, so that the Whale lay upon the Hill, roaring like a Cave of Lions, and the Prophet took them by the hands, and led them to the Whales mouth, saying, Go in, but they trembled vehemently; He said unto them the second time, Go in: and they durst not. And he sware unto them; and they entred in, and be lifted up his voyce, and cried mightily, Come away: and, lo, they stood before him richer then an Emperours Throne, for unto him that was naked, were clothes given: unto him that was a child and a man, were 12 *gates opened. And the Prophet cried mightily, and said, This Whale cannot die; and lifted up his voyce again and said: Within this Whale are many Chambers, and secret dwelling places, which I will divide betwixt you on the right side (unto the which was a child, and* The Whales mouth.
now

12 ⎰ 18
Δ ⎱
Foild 36
11
A Miracle.

now a man) there are twelve opened, but unto thee that hast provided strange Garments for thy self, and not such as men use to wear, I will give thee head, hart, and left side, whose places are 46. You shall enter, and be possessed this day together: And behold, the son shall return again 21 times, and in one year, but not all at one time. You shalt depart hence into a dwelling that shall be all one: where there is no end, the place of comfort and inspeakable glorie.

I have said.

Δ. As you have delivered us a parable, *ænigma*, or prophesie, so I beseech you, for the setting forth of God his honour and glory, to expound what is meant by the

Gab. .... Nal. .... *The Prophet is in his name.*   Whale, the naked man, the Childe, &c.

> *The naked man is* Dee,
> *The Childe is* Kelly,
> *The Prince is the Devil,*
> *The Hill is the World,*
> *The waters are the bosome of God,*
> *The 4 beasts are the 4 Elements,*
> *The 12 Trees are the 12 parts of the Heavens,*
> *The Whale is the spirit of God,*
> *The Chambers are the degrees of wisdome,*
> *The Thunders and windes are the ends of God his Will and Judgements;*

The rest are not to be spoken:

This I take to notifie to us the judgement and arbitrement of God between us, in respect of our Petition to his Divine Majesty now made, whereby we may be assured what to judge of the Creatures which do deal with us in this action, and of the impugners, or diswaders of the credit of it. This I take to be sent and delivered unto us, of the meer mercy and providence Divine regarding his own glory, and the sincerity of my hope and confidence, which I put wholly in him, and alwayes will.

Gab. ⎱
Nal. ⎰   ...... *You are happy, for you believe,* E. K. *what am I.* Δ. *as happy if you believe likewise.*

Δ. Are you not to deliver us our lessons orderly, as we have begun to receive?

Gab. ⎱
Nil. ⎰   ...... *Understand that, by the Prophet delivering Pen, Ink, and Paper.*

Δ. As concerning the book writing by the highest, what shall I expect thereof?

Gab ⎱
Nal. ⎰   ...... *There is no point of faith.*

Δ. I believe verily that it shall be written *by the power of the highest.*

Nal. .... *The power of the highest confirmeth me, but not my power, the highest.*

Δ. Be it as the will of God is,

E. K. The white Curtain is drawn.

Δ. Gloria Patri, & Filio, & spiritui sancto; sicut erat in principio, & nunc, & semper, & in secula seculorum.

     E. K.   Amen.

Saturday, 28. *Aprilis, Mane hora* 8.   Cracoviæ.
Oratione præmissa statim apparebant.

E. K. They are here.

Gab. ..... *Move not, for the place is holy.*
Δ. Holy, holy, holy, is he, who sanctifieth all things that are sanctified.

Nalvage.   E. K. He maketh Crosses with his Rod toward the four parts of the world, and then kneeleth down a while.

Gab. ...... *Happy is he that hath his skirts tied up, and is prepared for a Journey, for the way shall be open unto him, and in his joynts shall there dwell no wearinesse: his meat shall be as the tender dew, as the sweetnesse of a bullocks Cud. For unto them that have, shall be given, and from them that have not, shall be taken away: For why, the bur cleaveth to the willow stem, but on the sands it is tossed as a feather without dwelling. Happy are they that cleave unto the Lord, for they shall be brought unto the store-house: and be accounted, and accepted as the Ornaments of his beauty: But pray with me.*

> O thou eternal foundation and strength of all things, mortal and immortal, which delight in thy face and in the glorie of thy name,

Consider the foundation of our fragility, and enter into the weaknesse of our inward parts: for we are become empty; whose salt is not, nor hath any savour: Fortifie, and make us strong in thee, and in thy strength; Have mercy upon us, Have mercy upon us, Have mercy upon us; that in this world our strength may be in patience, and after this life, that we may ascend unto thee.

Nal. .....A-

Nal. .... *Amen.*
Δ. We prayed the same prayer.

E. K. Now *Nalvage* standeth up upon his Table of Letters.

Nal. ..... *It is a side-long Letter.*

47	PALOMRON	*the sons of men*	Nor mo lap.

E. K. Now he kisseth the Table.

46	FAA	*amongst*	A af
45	LITSER	*that you may praise him*	Rest el.

Now he kisseth the Table, and maketh most humble and low Cursies, having first laid down his Rod.

44	GNOSILEBO	*As pleasant deliverers*	Obelisong
43	NARMAZDO	*And shew your selves*	Od Zamran

E. K. Now *Gabriel* shaketh his Dart terribly.
E. K. Why shake you your dart so?

Gab. .... *Scholers ought to give ear to their School-masters.*

42	RACAZ	*Move*	Zacar.
41	LAAQ	*of the Creatour*	Qa al
40	PIAOOD	*in the name*	Do oa ip
39	ALIPADO	*and liveth*	Od *Api la*
38	ISD	*which is*	D SI
37	DAIANERIZ	*I am the Lord your God*	Zire nai ad

Now he useth his accustomed Cursie.

36	ELGAB	*for*	Ba gle
35	AGSOAGF	*visit the earth*	Fgaos ga
34	OD	*and*	Od.
33	IHASARQRON	*you sons of pleasure*	Nor qua sa hi
32	VGROT	*Arise*	Torgu
31	ALC	*456*	Cla
30	OLAT	*as the first*	Ta l o
29	SIHC	*are*	Chis
28	NIHSNOLDO	*and their powers*	Od lonshin

Now he kneeleth.

27	NOAMIPAG	*the number of time*	Capi ma on

26 SIHC

| 26 SIHC | *are* | Kis |
| | | Chis |

| 25 ILAMIPAC | *successively,* | Ca pi ma fi |

| 24 TSD | *which also* | DST |

Now he falleth suddenly on his knees.

| 23 GEGVDO | *and wax strong:* | as Wedge |
| | | Od Vgeg |

| 22 SIHC | *are,* | Kis |
| | | Chis |

Now he kneeleth.

| 21 IZDOORC | *The second beginnings of things* | Cro od zi |

| 20 GMRASAC | *in whom* | the g as in feurge |
| | | Cafarmg |

19 LPRC	*but one ;*	CRPL
18 OPMROC	*hath yet numbred*	Corm po
17 GA	*None*	as agg in nag
		Ag
16 MABOS	*whom*	So bam
15 MPAM	*96395*	Map m
14 ILAO	*I have placed*	O a li
13 IMRASAC	*under whom*	Ca farmi
12 VIDVIV	*in the second angle?*	Vi v di v

Now he lifted up his hands.

| 11 FNOSD | *which raign* | Dfonf |

E. K. Now he goeth off the Table, and kneeleth Down.

| | | Pe de |
| 10 DP | *33* | PD |

Now he lifteth.

9 PMROC	*numbred ?*	Cormp
8 OGAVAVA	*the thunders of encrease*	Ava va go
7 EGSIHCG	*Are not*	G Chis ge
6 LOHOG	*saying,*	Go hol
5 AHPROD	*have looked about me,*	Dor pha

4	DO	*and*	Od
3	EGABAB	*in the south*	Ba bage
2	IDSAL	*my feet*	Las di
1	LIHTO	*I have set*	O thil

E. K. The Table turneth continually to his Rod end , and the Letter feemeth to ftand on his Rods end diftinctly.   That is it.   This is this Call.

1 —— *I have set*		26 —— *fucceffively,* [*or by fucceffion*]
2 —— *my feet*		27 —— *are*
3 —— *in the south,*		28 —— *the number of time,*
4 —— *and*		29 —— *and*
5 —— *have looked*		30 —— *their powers*
6 —— *about me,*		31 —— *are*
7 —— *saying,*		32 —— *as the firft*
8 —— *are not*		33 —— *456.*
9 —— *The Thunders of encreafe*		34 —— *Arife*
10 —— *numbred?*		35 —— *you fons of pleafure,*
11 —— *Thirty three*		36 —— *and*
12 —— *which raign*		37 —— *vifit the earth;*
13 —— *in the fecond* Angel;		38 —— *for*
14 —— *under whom*		39 —— *I am the Lord your God*
15 —— *I have placed*		40 —— *which is*
16 —— *9639.*		41 —— *and liveth.*
17 —— *whom*		42 —— *In the name*
18 —— *None*		43 —— *of the Creator*
19 —— *hath yet numbred*		44 —— *Move*
20 —— *but one*		45 —— *And fhew you felves* [*or appear*]
21 —— *in whom*		46 —— *as pleafant deliverers ,*
22 —— *the fecond beginning of things*		47 —— *that you may praife him*
23 —— *are,*		48 —— *amongft*
24 —— *and wax ftrong*		49 —— *the fons of men.*
25 —— *which alfo :*		50 ——

E. K. He hath now plucked the Curtain to.

Δ. Note.

Δ. Thanks be to God, now, and ever.   *Amen.*

Δ. Remember to requeft information of fuch a word, as (faith the Lord) is not here to be underftood, fome where.

Note, the fecond Angel.

Monday *Cracovia, Aprilis* 30. *Mane hora* 6 ¼.
Oratione Dominica finita , & *precatiuncula pro profpero fucceffu A. L.* (jam apud *Keifmark,* queritantis & petentis jus fuum hereditarium, & aliis breviffimis ejaculationibus, pro profpero fucceffu in hac actione tandem poft femi horam apparuerunt,

E. K. Now they are here : and *Gabriel* is all full of glory, he feemeth to light all places.
Δ. O the mercies of God encreafed, though his determination be all one
E. K. Now he is as he was before : and in the time of this his glorious apparition, *Nalvage* kneeled down, fomewhat regarding towards *Gabriel.*

Gab.:..... Give unto him that hath his basket open: But from him that is not ready, depart.

B
L
R
A
H
I
C
A
V
N
H
D
L

E. K. There appear here, 7 other like Priests, all in white, having long hair hanging down behind : their white garments traile after them : having many pleits in them. Me think that I have seen one of them before, and upon that creature appeareth a B upon his cloathes, an L in another place, an R upon his other shoulder, another A upon his other shoulder. There is an H upon his. breast ; there is an I upon his head, and a C upon his side on his garment ; and an A under his wast behind : The Letters seem to go up and down enterchangeably in places. There seemeth an V on him, also an N, a D.

Now cometh a tall man by, all in white, and a great white thing rowled about his neck, and coming down before like a tippet. They all in the Stone (being 9) kneel down unto him.

The tall man said ...... *Take this Key, and power : ascend and fill thy vessel, for the River is not pure, and made clean.*

E. K. Now he is gone (that said this) in form of a great Millstone of fire.

An Hill.

E. K. Now they go up a Hill, with a great Tankard, as it were, of Bone transparent ; Now he openeth one door, he, I mean, that had the Letters on his back.

1. There appeareth a Partridge, but it hath one leg like a Kite : This Partridge seemeth to sit on a green place under the gate, one leg is much longer than the other, being like a Kites leg. This Partridge seemeth to halt.

He biddeth one of his Company take it up. There goeth a bridge to the top of that Hill, all upon arches, and under it goeth a River.

He taketh the Partridge and pulleth all his feathers, and they fall into the River : He cutteth off the longer leg just to the length of the other. They about him cry, O just judgement.

Now he turneth him off over the Bridge, and he flyeth away, for the feathers of his wings were not pulled.

2. He goeth on, and cometh to another gate ; and there the third man unlocketh it, as the second next him unlocked the first Gate ; he himself having the Key first delivered him, as above is noted. There appeareth a thing like a Kite, all white, very great, it hath a fowl great head, he seemeth to be in a very pleasant Garden, and flyeth from place to place of it, and beateth down the Rose trees and other fruit trees. The Garden seemeth very delicate and pleasant, They go all into the Garden : and he saith, Thou art of the Wildernesse, thy feathers and carkase are not worthy the spoil of the Garden.

Now the Kite scratcheth and gaspeth at this man ; but he taketh the Kite and cutteth her carkase in two equal parts, from the crown of his head, and throweth one half over one side of the Bridge, and the other half over the other side, and said, Fowles must be devoured of Fowles. The rest say, *O justitia divina,* clapping their hands over their heads.

3. Now

3. Now the next in order openeth another Gate (going up upon the same Bridge still.)   The rest of the building from the Gate inward, seemeth very round and bright : yet there appear no windows in it.   It is a frame, made as though the 7 Planets moved in it.   The Moon seemeth to be New Moon.

There standeth Armour, and this man putteth on, all white Harnesse. He seemeth to kick down the Moon, and her frame or Orb ; and seemeth to make powder of all ; For *there is no mercy here, saith* he.

4. Now another of them goeth forward to another Gate, and openeth the Gate, and goeth in ; there appear an infinite multitude of men.

There sitteth a man cloathed like a Priest, having a great Crown on his head :   here are many preaching in this place.   He goeth to that Crowned Priest, and he taketh away divers patches of the Vesture which he had, and the patches seemed to be like Owls, and Apes, and such like.

He saith ...... *A King is a King, and a Priest is a Priest.*

He taketh from the rest their Keyes and Purses, and giveth them *a Staff and a Bottle* in their hands.   He goeth from them.   He putteth all that he took from them in a house beside the Gate, and writeth on the door,   *Cognoscat quisque suum.*   He wrote
Cognoscat,

Now they proceed to another Gate, and another of them opened that Gate.   The Bridge continueth still, ascending upward.   Now there appeareth (that Gate being opened) a marvellous great Wildernesse.

There cometh a great number *of naked wilde men to him.*   He shaketh that Gate with his hands, and it falleth in pieces, one falleth on one side into the River, and the other falls on the other side into the River,

...... *Let both these places be made one.   Let the spoil of the first, be the comfort of the last : For from them that have shall be taken, and unto them that have not shall be given.*

6. E. K. Now he goeth, and the last of his Company openeth another Gate ; he is longer in opening of that Gate, than any of the rest.

There appeareth a bushy place, and there runneth a great River on the very top of the Hill, and a great Gate standeth beyond the Hill, and a very rich Tower all of precious Stones, as it seemeth.

Here he filleth his Tankard in the River, and holdeth his hands up, and maketh shew as he would return.

He said ...... *This was my coming, and should be my return.*

E. K. Now they appear suddenly before the first Gate, and there the *Principal man diggeth* the earth, and putteth stones and brambles, and leaves aside.   There he taketh out a dead carkase, and bringeth it to a fire, and stroketh it : a very lean carkase it is ; it seemeth to be a dead Lion ; for it hath a long tail with a bush at the end.

He saith ...... *Come let us take him up, and comfort him ; for it is in him.*

Now the Lion seemeth to sit up and lick himself, and to drink of the water, and to shake himself, and to roar.   The man taketh of the segs

or

or flags by, and ſtroketh the Lion as he would make his hair ſmooth.

Now the Lion is become fair, fat, and beautiful.

He ſaith ...... *Tarry you here, till I bring you word again ; for I muſt follow the Lion into the Wilderneſſe.*

E. K. Now all they are gone, except the two our *School-maſters, Gabriel and Nalvage.*

Gab. ...... *This is the Judgement of God this day.   Happy is he that hath judgement to underſtand it.*

Δ. Thou O Lord knoweſt the meaſure of our judgement : Give therefore light, under-ſtanding, and the grace to uſe thy gifts duely.

Gab. .... *Liſten unto my words, for they are a Commandment from above. Behold (ſaith he) I have deſcended to view the Earth, where I will dwell for ſeven dayes, and twice ſeven dayes: Therefore let them be dayes of reſt to you. But every ſeventh day, I will viſit you, as Now I do.*

E. K. He ſpeaketh as if he ſpake out of a Trunck.

Δ. I underſtand that this reſt is, that every *Monday,* for three *Mondayes* elſe next after other, we ſhall await for our leſſons, as now we receive, *and that we may all the reſt follow our affairs of ſtudy or houſhold matters.*

Gal. ...... *It is ſo,* for one day ſhall be as a week : *But thoſe dayes you muſt abſtain from all things that live upon the Earth.*

Δ. You mean on theſe three *Mondayes,* enſueing next.

Gab. ...... *You ſhall cover this Table with a new linnen cloth.*

E. K. Pointing to the Table we ſat at.

Δ. Moſt willingly.

Gab. ...... *Moreover a new Candleſticks, with a Taper burning.*

Δ. Obediently (O Lord) it ſhall be done.

Gab. ...... *And the Candleſticks ſhall be ſet on the midſt of the Table betwixt you two.*

Note ...... That a day may become a week, and a week as many years.

Gab. ...... *For I have put on my upper garment, and have* prepared to enter, *and it is ſhortly : and not yet.*

E. K. Now he hath plucked the Curtain, as if he had pulled it round about the Stone ; and it ſeemeth full of little ſparkes like Stars.

Gloria patri & filio & ſpiritui ſanƈto ; ſicut erat in principio, & nunc, & ſemper, & in ſecula ſeculorum.

Vide libro .... Γ pro ſæquentibus.

LIBRI

LIBRI MYSTICI APERTORII
CRACOVIENSIS SABBATICI, *An.* 1584.

Saturday Cracoviæ, 7 *Maii, Mane, hora* 6.

 Fter prayers, appeared *Gabriel* and *Nalvage,* with the Table, and *Gabriel* with his Dart in his hand. Moreover there appeared the like furniture of Table with a white Cloth, a Candlestick, and Taper on it, with a Desk and Cushions (which I had caused to be made with red crosses on them :) also E. K. himself and I appeared in the same Stone. In effect, all things as we had before us , after half a quarter of an hour, that shew of our furniture, and our selves, disappeared.

E.K. *Gabriel* standeth up, and speaketh as followeth.

.... *A mighty City was built on the top of a mountain, in the which dwelt many thousands. Round about the Hill, ran a fresh River, which was the onely comfort of the Town : for, of it they drank, their wives, their children, their man-servants, their maid-servants, their camels, horses, mules, and all the beasts of their fields. The beginning of which River was a Spring, which was unknown to the City, by reason of the . . yth from whence it descended. It came to passe, that a Serpent groaned far her time, and lo, she brought forth : and .`.`. were such as her self : and she lifted up her head and leaned upon her twice writhen taile : and beheld the Sun stedfastly, (for her envy was toward that City) and she said within her self : My children are yet young, the time grew, and they became big : and she went unto the Spring, and smiled and said with a laughing voice, The Earth is fallen into thee; thou art choked : but hearken unto my voice, Thou shalt receive comfort : But she would not. And she lifted up her voice and roared ; for she was full of craft and deceit: And she said unto the shingles, through the which the Spring runs (or rather fyeth) Thou art full of emptinesse, and void places. Let my children (therefore) hide themselves within thee for a season : and they were contented : And she departed willingly, and saith within her self : N w I know I shall be Lady of the City.*

And after a few years, the young Serpents became great ; so that the one half of their bodies dwelt within the Shingles, the rest troubled the passage of the Spring : So that the Spring groaned ; for, the injury that was done against her, was great.

A great misery, for the Hill is become desolate without the water, and the City and the beasts perish for want of drink ; for the people groan, and are full of sorrow.

This City and Serpents are 60 . now, and judgement must be had, betwixt the Shingles and the Spring . for between lieth the life and death of the City.

Thus saith the Lord unto thee [pointing to E. K.] *Gird up thy self, and sit down, Consider both parts, and give judgement : for thy mouth shall this day be the judgement of the Lord.*

E. K. Do you mean me ?

E. K. As the Lord hath put the Authority of Judgement into my hands, so I beseech him to give me wisdom and understanding to judge right And because the judgement hereof is committed to me, I suspect some other mystery to lie hidden in this my judgement required : But if it shall please God that my friend here, Master *Dee* shall give me his advise, I shall think my self well satisfied.

.... *Consider with your self (saith the Lord) and give judgement against the Shingles, for the fault is plain. Consider two points, the necessity of the Spring, that it must come that wayes : and secondly, the health of the City.*

E. K. My judgement is that the Shingles and Serpent should be removed away by an Earthquake from the place which they encumber and let, that there may be a fit new place, and course for that Spring, to the relief of that City as before it was.

...... *Be*

...... *Be it so as thou hast said, for it is a just judgement.*

Now hearken, what the Lord saith; The people and City of the Hill, is the world, which are from time to time by the mercy and spring of Gods wisdom, relieved .. quenched: according to the extremity and necessity of their thirsting: But the people and City are such as are of the Temple and Church of God, which drink of his mercy to their comfort. The Camels and other beasts are the people of the Earth, which delight in sin, and in their own imagination, which also are relieved with those that are of the City: but the diversities of their bodies, doth cause the diversity of the ends of their comfort. The Hill wherein the Spring is, signifieth his Prophets, and such as are drunken in the Lord: Through whom, inwardly the mercies and will of God and of the Highest are open from time to time, according to the secret will and determination of such as are within the City of his Elect. But the frailties and affections of their flesh and outward man, are their fond imaginations and loose Shingles wherein the Serpent, the old Devil, hath harboured her children the spirits of darkness and deceit, which always resist the Will of God, and are put between the mercies of God and his people. Moses, Daniel, Esdras, all the rest of the Prophets: Christ his twelve, Paul the Messenger of God, they did all hurt the Congregation of the Faithful in their flesh, until they gave sentence against themselves (as thou hast done) with amendment of life: for who is worthy to know the secrets of our God, but he that delighteth in righteousness, is obedient, full of faith, and the spirit of understanding? Be it therefore unto thee as thou hast said. Let the Shingles and Serpents be separated, that the Fountain may feed as before. All the trash that thou hast of the wicked, burn it.

E. K. I do not know, they are wicked.

...... *Their doings with thee, are the hindrance of the Will of God, and therefore they are wicked.*

...... *Thou hast given judgement against thy self: Take heed thou offend not thy own soul.*

Δ. Send down thy Spirit O Lord, and illuminate E. K. his heart with perceiving of his wrong opinion, &c.

E. K. If *Moses* and *Daniel* were skilful in the Arts of the Egyptian Magicians, and were not thereby hindred for being the servants of God, Why may not I deal with these, without hindrance to the Will of God?

...... *Darkness yeilded unto light: the Greater excluded the lesser. The more a man knoweth wickedness, the more he shall hate it, being called back. The more they knew the shadow, so much more they delighted in the body: For the doings of the Egyptians, seem, and are not so. The doings of the Lord are, and continue; for as the Painter imitateth the gestures of man in his faculty, so doth the Devil the substances and things created and made by God.*

Stand up and look into the whole World, into her youth, and middle age, for they are past. Where are the monuments that Satan hath builded?

E. K. Hath Satan builded any monuments?

...... *Yes: Hath he not builded him a Fort upon the whole Earth? Hath he not the victory over the Saints? Dwelleth he not in the Temple of the Highest? Triumpheth he not in the Cities of the whole World?*

Yes. ...... But without comfort, are his victories: without pleasure his dwelling places. For he knoweth his time is at hand. He that now giveth freedom, shall become bound; And unto whom the whole World is as a Garden, shall there be no one foot left. Therefore are all his pleasures vanity: all his Triumphs smoak, and his Authority, nothing indeed, but a meer shadow: For that that is not, cannot be; where, it is said of the Lord, it shall not be. Neither can truth, light, or wisdom, ascend from the Earth, but descend from the Heavens.

Compare the Earth, (into the which the Devil is thrust as into his dwelling) with the Heavens, which are provided for the holy. Consider the pain of the one, and the pleasure of the other: The seat of Gods Justice, and Fountain of his Mercy: The Cave of Darkness, and the Diadem of Light. And then cry, wo, wo, wo, unto such as erre, and whose lives are but shadows: For their felicity is such, as from whence it came; and their reward is all one, with the spirit and prince of Darkness.

Compare fond knowledge, with true wisdom, Thy spirits of lying with us, that are the voice of truth: *The vanity that they lead thee into, and the reward of our message: And say within thy self,* peccavi. *Wilt thou be perswaded by experience? Consider thy imprisonments, thy affliction and shame of body. Consider the love of a few, and envy of a multitude. Weigh with thy self the vanity of thy life; Thy rash foot-steps, All that happned unto thee, by the society, and (as thou thinkest) comfort; but indeed the stinging pricks of thy enemies*

His life
.. and.

...... *Since, we came into thee, (sent from the Lord, and calling thee, to God) thou hast been delivered from them; from a place full of fornication, and the wrath of God: exalted to the skirts of worldly honour; and hast been satisfied for the necessities of this World. Holy is the money that is gotten righteously; but accursed are the evils that are reaped with wrong.*

All

All which things thou haſt by us in bleſſedneſſe, and in the knowledge of the will of God, above all men. Beſides our continual preſence with thee, to the comfort of thy Soul. Even theſe things are of us, and of our God. Which ſware unto Abraham, and dwelleth in the Temple of righteouſneſſe. Now, therefore let experience be a Judge betwixt us and them.

But, this ſayeth the Lord. I deal with you as a Childe: But the veſſels that I muſt uſe, muſt be Pure veſſels. *pure and clean.*

Δ. Cleanſe thou us, (O Lord) *Cor mundum Crea in nobis; Crea.*

Gab. ..... They that are incredulous *believe not the Lord, but drive away his ſpirit: But where* Increduli. *a grain is, it becometh as a mountain. The Lord is upon the earth: Take heed thou ſweep thy houſe clean, for unto him that is naked, ſhall there be Cloathes given: But he that is covered already, ſhall be made bare.*

Conſider with thy ſelf: for the Lord ſpeaketh not once more, till thou haſt fulfilled thy own judgement.

E. K. I will be contented to bury them in the field, and not to uſe them, or come at them: and that I will ſwear upon the Bible to perform: and if they be earthly, I will commit them to the earth: and ſo ſeparate thoſe ſhingles from the place near the ſpring: and in this manner fulfill my own judgement: For, *I will not be obſtinate, but commit all things to the end.*

His own judgement is to be fulfilled.

Becauſe thou art content to bury them; and withall, upon faith in the promiſes of God, to abjure them in ſimplicity of heart, and external uſe, ... ſimply, as a true meaning before the face of the higheſt: The Lord accepteth it, and it ſhall be ſufficient.

Further, thou haſt 27. Confirmations of ſin, and conſent with the Devil, *which your intention* Characters. *calleth* Characters, *whereby thoſe ſeven and twenty, (like unto their mother) are become familiar and pleaſant with thee, they muſt be brought before the Lord: and offered into his hands. For ſo long as they are, the wicked alwayes vex thee: For the Obligation burnt, the condition is void. Theſe muſt be buried with the reſt.*

[E. K. Which reſt?]

...... But muſt be brought, and burnt here before the preſence of *God: That, the cauſe diminiſhed, the effect may periſh.*

E. K. I will be contented to bury them likewiſe, beſeeching the Almighty to accept of my intent herein, as of the reſt before ſpecified.

...... He is contented; but let one be burnt. You may ſuffer one to teſtifie the diſcredit of the reſt. It is but according to the grounds of thy own Magick.

E. K. I do not underſtand your meaning herein.

Gab. ..... Radius partis, may be ſicut totius Corporis.

E. K. I underſtand not that, alſo.

Gab. ......, Magick worketh effect in things abſent, that it doth in their parts, being preſent.

The wicked kill the body abſent, but the garment preſent: ſo are all of one confederacie, diſgraced by the confuſion of one. Thou art contented to bury them all, upon the confidence, and ſure hope of the promiſes of the God of light, and to bring one as a confirmation of thy promiſe to teſtifie thy obedience as concerning the whole: which one burnt and abjured, may be a teſtimony to the Angels, that thou art obedient for God his ſake, and for his teſtimony and truth. But this you ſhall burn with Brimſtone onely. Whoſe aſhes ſhall be kept as a teſtimony, till the reſt be alſo conſumed. This you ſhall do the next Monday at the riſing of the Sun. That the number of the time may be of one bigneſſe. For, before Auguſt ſhall thoſe Keyes be delivered unto you: which give entrance, yea, even into the privy Chambers of wiſdom, whereof you ſhall have 14. the next Monday. And this dayes action is not the leaſt amongſt them. Glory be to God, and obedience unto man.

Δ. I doubt that I miſheard ſomewhat.
One burnt and abjured.
obedience.
... ence.

E. K. The Curtain is drawn.

Δ. We are deſirous to know whether thus, this dayes action ſhall be finiſhed: and whether we ſhall faſt ſtill as was preſcribed.

Gab. ...... Detract not from the day, that, which is commanded.

Δ. We are very deſirous to underſtand of the preſent eſtate of the Lord *Albert Lakie*: for as much as we were willed to go with him, and he linked to us in ſome par f our actions: To underſtand of his ſtate, would be to our great comfort.   to

Gab. ...... It needeth not, for the world her ſelf is at hand.

Δ. Verily, I underſtand not that ſpeech: Is he coming back again? What, We are commanded we know : *And further then our Commandment is errour.* He is in his hand that knoweth how to use him.

E. K. I see a man climing over a Hedge , and as he clammereth over the stakes break , and he falleth down. Now he is going up between two Trees into a Medow-ward. Now he hath both the boughs in his hand , standing still on the ground. Now he goeth lower, there is a gap, and through that he is gone into the Medow ..... *so it is of* Laskie ..... said a voyce.

Δ. This is dark : it may please you to give some light.

o .....This is more then enough for the matter.
Cease to ask these things here, where it is said, no impure thing should enter.

Δ. Gloria, laus & honor Deo Nostro Omnipotenti, Patri, filio & spiritui Sancto, nunc & semper. *Amen.*

Δ. Note, at this present was one come, and in the house (of whom we understood not till he was gone:) whom the Lord *A. Laskie* had sent to certifie us, that first he was in some cumber and hindrance. Secondly, how *Fabius* (his brother in Law) and another had given him counsel, very rashly to proceed : But leaving that. Thirdly, by the gap and open way with estate of the Commons, or Citizens, by their great Zeal , and favour that he obtained his purpose. This (in effect) we understood at the Messager his return after noon. Which marvellous exactly did answer to the former shew.

May.

Remember that on *Saturday* after noon, the Chancelour came to *Cracow* , with 60 Coaches in his Company and train : he bringing in a close Coach (covered with red) the Lord *Samuel S. Boroskie* Prisoner, whom he took on Friday night before , at his sisters house, being separated from his Souldiers and servants, &c.

Saturday, 14 Maii, *Mane hora* 6 *Fere.* † Cracoviæ.

Orationem Dominicam fudimus, &c. *Mitte lucem tuam & veritatem , O Deus,*&c.
Δ. *E. K.* Said, he had done that with the trash specified, as he thought would be acceptable to the Lord : And as concerning one of the 27. Characters he had left it with me , ever since the last action, to be burnt at this dayes action, and it lay ready by me.

E. K. Our instructours appeared at the very first looking of E. K. into the shew-stone.

Δ. Will you that I shall now execute this burning of the Character here as a sacrifice (to the highest) of our humility and obedience?
Gab. ..... *Not as a sacrifice, but as a victory.*
Δ. Shall I then do it, I pray you ? As with the consent of my yoke-fellow, and so all one to be taken as his action.
..... *He that doth righteously offereth up a sacrifice.*
Nal. ..... *It is true, that he that is obedient, and doth well, is accepted with the Lord.*

E. K. I did take sacrifice to be onely with bloud.
Gab. ..... *This is a sacrifice, because it is done righteously.*

E. K. You said, Not, as a sacrifice, but as a victory.
Gab. ..... *He that overcometh his enemy rejoyceth not for friendship sake , but for victory.* The *friendship toward God is obedience.* *He that obeyeth God , is a friend unto himself.* God *needeth not the love , or friendship of man.* *Therefore you rejoyce with God, who overthrew them,* and thereby comforted. *For he that dwelleth in the Lord is comforted.*
Thou openest thy mouth, and sayest before the Lord, The spirit of God hath descended.

Δ. *He noteth some secret discourse, meditation, or prayer, and solo action of F. K. as I conjecture.*

Δ. Gloria Patri, &c.
And he hath entred into judgement with me, and I am condemned. But where *Justice dwelleth,* dwelleth also mercy. *For, my Idolatry is forgotten before the Lord.*

E. K. Have you committed Idolatry ?
E. K.

Δ. He speaketh in your behalf Master *Kelly.*
..... *I will therefore open my mouth, saying, I have erred.* I will open my mouth also, and confesse my sins : And, I will vow unto the Lord against the wicked. And I will say unto the Lord, Lo, here are the spoils of the bloudy blasphemy. Behold , O you Angels, a blasphemy, and against the highest. Behold, the wickedness of Alcendam.

Bear

Bear witneſſ with me; for I have fulfilled his Commandement. Bear witneſſe with me, that I .....am in
return not, and rejoyce; for ſuch are the ſpoyles of the wicked. ....& ſi-
   Gab. *Art thou contented to conſent hereunto?* . ..ero
                                           .. :no:

   E. K. What I have done with the reſt, God, and they (if they be of   .....ſ
God) know : upon the foreſaid conditions I am contented to have this   ...and
Character to be burnt. Let it be burnt.   . ..de
                                                         ....i e d.

   Δ. I burnt it immediately, with the flame of brimſtone, and brought the burnt black coal
or cinder thereof to the Table, and laid it on a paper.
   Now O Lord, darkueſſe is confounded, let thy light ſhine in us, and thy truth prevaile.
   Gab. *It is well.* Δ. Bleſſed be the name of the higheſt : whoſe mercies are infinite.
Oh, a ſweet and comfortable ſentence.

   E· K. Now *Nalvage* turneth round, as he was wont.
   Gab. *Move not, for the place is holy.*

   E. K. Now *Nalvage* putteth down his rod to the Table, he maketh a
croſſe upon the Table reverently.

   Nal. *All things go forwards, Let us go* F O R W A R D *alſo.* Δ. In the name of Jeſus. *Hor.* 7.
   Gab. *Move not, for the place is holy.*
   E. K. *Nalvage* prayeth.
   Nal. *Not* B A C K W A R D, as you were wont to do, but F O R W A R D.

   E. K. Now he maketh three reverent Curſies, as he was wont to do,
before the Table.

   S A P A H   *Sá pah.*
                                          Sa pah.

   E. K. Now he is on the top of the Table.

   Z I M I I   *Zi mii.*   *L. Lalζ.*

   D U I V   *Du iv.*

   O D   *Od.*   O D.

                                                                   b. .no
   E. K. He maketh curſy.   ... rech
                                                               .... &
   N O A S   *Noas.*   ....ione
                                                                     ..,ded.

   T A Q A N I S   *Ta qua nis.*

   A D R O C H   *as otch*
                                          Ad roch.

   D O R P H A L   *Dorphal.*

   C A O S G   *Ca ósg*
   O D   *Od.*

   F A O N T S   *Fa onts.*

   P I R I P S O L   *Pir ipſol.*

   T A B L I O R   *Táblior.*

   C A S A R M   *Caſarm.*

   A M I P Z I   *A mip zi*

   N A Z A R T H   *Na zarth.*

   A F   *Af.*

   O D   *Od.*

   D L U G A R   *Dlugar*

E. K. Now he maketh cursy round about to all parts of the **Table**, he kneeleth down.

ZIZOP   *Zizop.*

Zod lida.
                    It is a Word and a Letter.

E. K. He sheweth it not in the Table yet.

Nal. Now I see the word of five Letters together, following letter by letter.

ZLIDA   *Zid-lida.*
                                          Z lida.

                    Stay there.

CAOSGI   *Ca os gi.*

TOLTORGI   *Toltorgi.*

He maketh now Cursy.

OD   *Od*

E. K. He seemeth to read as *Hebrew* is read.

ZIZOP   *Zizop.*

ZCHIS   *Zod chis*

Nal. It is better than the other ,I mean that Zod-chis being of one signification,with Zizop that Zod-chis is better to be used.

ESIASCH   *E siach.*

L   *L.*

TAUIU   *Ta ui u.*

OD   *Od.*

IAOD   *I i od.*

E. K. Now he maketh cursy again.

THILD   *Thild, one Syllable.*

Now he ma

DS.   *ds.*

HUBAR   *Hubar.*

PEOAL   *Pe b al.*

SOBA   *So ba.*

E. K.

CORMFA   *Cormfa.*

CHISTA   *Kista.*
                                          Chis ta.

LA   *La;*
VLS   *Uls.}*

OD   *Od.*

Camps 1. 69. 5. Julii so expounded.

QCOCASB

QCOCASB		*Qcócasb.*
C A		*Cᵃ.*
		Sᵃ.
NIIS		*Ni is.*
O D		*Od.*
DARBS	*Obey*	*Darbs-one Syllabe.*
QAAS		*Qá as.*
S. FETHARZI		*Feth ár zi.*

K. E. Curſy.
E. K. He hath drawn the Curtain.

Δ. ....of 4 minutes of time the Curtain was drawn.
It is not to be seen what he doth.

E. K. He is now otherwiſe apparelled, all the outſide of his Gown is white Furre, on his head is an attire of furre, wreathed or wrapped as the Turks uſe; his head is now like a mans head, with ſhort hair.

O D	*Od.*
BLIORA	*Bli ó ra* Cor, 1,
IAIAL	*Ia ial.*
EDNAS	*Ed nas.*
CICLES	*Ci cles.*
BAGLE	*Bá gle.*
....	*ie in as ien tle iad-as iade.*
....	*Ge jad.*
	i l.

That is one Call.

........b.......Move not, for the place is holly.   .....b.

GAH	*Gab.*
SDIU	*es diu*
	S di u.
--HIS	*Cbis.*
E M	*Em.*
MICALZO	*Micálzo*

E. K. Curſy, and he kiſſeth the Table.

PILZIN	*pilzen.*
	Pilzin.

E. K The Curtain is now plucked again, for three minutes or four. Now the Curtain is opened again. Now is he changed. Now he is His apparel.
all

all in black farcenet, very plentifull of ftuffe, girded to him, and with the coller high to the midft of his face.

SOBAM	*Sobam.*
EL.	*el*
HARG	*argenton.*
	Harg.
MIR	*Mir.*
PIZIN	*Pizin.*
BABALON	*Babalon.*

Put out the laft Pilgin.

E. K. Why did you give us them?

Nal. ...,...*If it ftand.*

OD	*od.*
OBLOC	*ob loc.*
SAMVELG	*Sam velg.*
DLUGAR	*Dlugar.*
MALPURG	*Mal purg.*
ARCAOSGI	*Ar ca os gi.*
OD	*od*
ACAM	*A cam*
CANAL	*Sanal.*
	Canal.
SOBOLZAR	*Sobol zar*
TBLIARD	*Tbli ard.*

Acra.

It is better if the T be made an V, and pronounced F bli ard.

CAOSGI	*kaosgi.*
	Ca os gi.
ODCHIF	*kif.*
	Od chif.
ANETAB	*A net tab.*
OD	*od.*
MIAM	*Miam.*
TAVIV	*Ta viv.*
ODD	*Odd.*
DARSAR	*Darfar*
SOLPETH	*Sol peth.*
BIEN	*Bi en.*
BRITA	*B ri ta.*

Dr

The Curtain drawn again.   Now it is opened.
He is altered in apparel ; one half under the girdle is red ,and above the girdle white.

O D	*Od.*
ZAC .. AM	*Za cam.*
GMICALZO	*G-ni cálzo.*
SOBHAATH	*Sob há atb.*
TRIAN	*Trian.*
LUIAHE	*Lu i a be.*
ODECRIN	*O de crin.*

    Curfie.

MAD	*Mad.*
QAAON	*Q a a on.*

               That is the second.
Δ, Bleſſed.

⅀ RAAS	*Ra as.*
ISALMAN	*I Sal man.*
PARA .. IZ	*Pa ra di zod.*
OECRIMI	*O ècri mi.*
AAO	*A A b.*
	Tal.
IALPIRGAH	*I AL pir gab.*

E. K. The Curtain drawn again, and ſo remaind about 6 minutes.
E. K. Being weary of ſitting, I would gladly have leave to walk a little.   His Apparel all one as it was.

Nal. .... *You may ; but to ſit, is more* obedient.'
Δ. *E. K. walked awhile.*

E K. Now, when it pleaſe you.

Gab. ... .. *I feel a ſtaggaring minde.*
Δ. That God which created you and us, make us to have conſtant mindes in all vertuous purpoſes.
Gab. .... *I ſwear : Move not ; for the place is boly.*

QUIIN	*Qui in.*
ENAY	*Enay.*
BUTMON	*But mon.*
OD	*Od.*

                                                  INOAS

LNOAS	*In b n.*
NI	*Ni.*

E. K. He prayeth.

PARADIAL	*Pa ra di al.*
CASARMG	*Ca sarmg.* The *g as dg srmg.*
VGEAR	*V gi ar.*
	Kir.
CHIRLAN	*Chir lan.*
OD	*Od.*
ZONA ..	*Zo nac.*
LUCIFTIAN	*Lu cif ti an.*
CORSTA	*Cors ta.*
VAULZIRN	*Vaul zirn.*
TOLHAMI	*Tol ba mi.*
SOBA	*Soba.*
LONDOH	*Lon dob.*

The Curtain is drawn again : and after 6 minutes open.
Now he is all in a blew long vesture, with a long train ; and hath a little Coronet of Silver on his head.

ODMIAM	*Od mi am,* or *Od Nuàm.*
	Kiu
CHISTAD	*Chi tad.*
ODES	*O des.*

Cursie.

VM:DEA	*V mò de a.*
OD	*Od.*
PIBLIAR	*Pib li ar.*
OTHILRIT	*O thil rit.*
ODMIAM	*Od mi am.*
	Kol.
CNOQUOL	*Cno quol.*
RIT	*Rit.*
ZACAR	*Za car.*
ZAMRAN	*Zamiran.*

O.E.CRIMI

OECRIMI	*O è crimi.*
QADA:	*Q á dab.*
OD	*Od.*
OMICAOLZ	*O mi ca ol zod.*
AAIOM	*A A I om.*
BAGLE	*Ba gle.*
PAPNOR	*Pap nor.*

Curtsie. he maketh.

IDLUGAM	*Id lu gam.*
LONSHI	*Lon shi.*
OD	*Od.*
VUPLIF	*Vmp lif.*
VGEGI	*V Ge gi.*
BIGLIA..	*Bigli ad.*

Nal. .... *This is at an end.*
Δ. Blessed be he that is the beginning and ending of all things.
E. K. The Curtain is pluckt.
Now it is open, and he is all in green, with a Garland on his head.

⁞ BAZMELO	*Baz me lo.*
ITA	*I ta*
PIRIPSON	*Pi rip son.*
OLN	*Oln.*
NAZAVABH	*Na za vabh:*
OX	*Ox.*
CASARMG	*Casarmg.*
G or V RAN	*V ran.*
CHIS	*Chis.*
VGEG	*V geg.*
..SABRAMG	*Dsa bramg.* [g not as dg.]
BALTOHA	*Bal to ha.*

E. K. The Curtain is drawn, for a while.

R   Now

Now is in a Robe like a Marble colour spotted, white, gray, and black.

GOHOIAD	*Go hó i ad.*
SOLAMIAN	*So lá mi an.*

Fire came suddenly out of the Stone, that made E. K. start.

TRIAN	*Tri an.*

E. K. Now he kneeleth.

TALOLCIS	*Ta lol cis or sis.*
ABAIUONIN	*A ba i uó nin.*
OD	OD.

E. K. He setteth his foot on a letter, pointing to it.   He throweth fire on *E. K.* again.

He putteth his feet on all these letters.

AZIAGIAR	*A zi á gi er.*
RIOR	*Rior.*
IRGILCHISDA	*Ir gil chis da.*
DSPAAOX.	*Dspá a ox.*
BUFD	*Bufd.*
CAOSGO	*Ca, or Ka of go.*
DSCHIS	*Ds chis.*
ODIPURAN	*Odi pu ran.*
TELOAH	*Te lo ah.*
CACRG	*Ca curg.*
OISALMAN	*O i fal man.*
LONCHO	*Lon cho, or ko.*
OD	*Od.*
VOUINA	*Vo ui na.*
CARBAF	*Car baf.*
NIISO	*Ni i fo.*
BAGLE	*Ba gle.*
AUAUAGO	*A uá ua go.*
GOHON	*Go hón.*
NIISO	*Ni i fo.*

BAGLE

B A G L E	*Ba gle.*

▲. He casteth fire on E. K.

M O M A O	*Mo ma o.*
S I A I O N	*Si a i on.*
O D	*Od.*
M A B Z A	*Mab za.*

E. K. He maketh a cursie, he sayeth *Mabza* again.

I A D O I A S M O M A R	*Iad o i as mo mar.*
P O I L P	*Poilp, one syllable.*
N I I S	*Ni is, small sound of i.*
Z A M R A N	*Zam ran.*

E. K. The Curtain is drawn, white, and reddish, more red then white: Now it is away, and all open again: Now all his Gown is yellow and yellow furre in it; and on his head, a Hoode of yellow like Velvet, &c.

E. K. Why change you your Apparel thus:

E. K. He speaketh very speedily to *Gabriel,* but I cannot perceive him.

C I A O F I	*C i A O fi.*
C A O S G O	*Ka.*
	Ca of go.
O D	*O D.*
B L I....S.	*Bli orsi*
O D	*O D.*
C O R....	*Cor fi.*
T A	*Ta*
A B R A M I G	*A bra mig.*

This is the end of that.

E. K. Now he pulleth the Curtain: Now it openeth again. His Apparel is now changed again of an Ashy and brown colour, in fashion as before.

Gab. .....*Who is to be compared to our God ?*

¿M I C A O L I	*Mi ca o li.*
B R A N S G	*Bransg.*
P..G E L	*Pur gel.*
N A P T A	*Nap ta.*
I A L P O R	*yal*
	I A L por.

R 2   DSBRIN

DSBRIN	Ds brin.
...FAFE	E fa fa fe.
VONPHO	Von pho.
OLANI	O L a ni.
O·D	Od.
OBZA	Ob za.
SOBCA	Ka Sob ca.
VPAAH	V pa ah.
CHIS	Chis.
TATAN	Ta tan.
OD	Od
TRANAN	Tra nan.
BALYE	Ba ly e.

In the left margin beside FAFE: R F A F A F I — *or is thus*

E. K. Now he turneth round about.   He maketh a cursie. So doth *Gabriel.*

ALAR	A lar.
LUSDA	Lu da.
SO'BOLN	So boln.
OD	Od.
CHISHOLQ	Chis hol q.
CNOQVODI	Cno quo di.
96 CIAL	Si i. Ci al.
VNAL	V nal.
ALDON	Al don.
MOM	Mom.
CAOSGO	Ca os go.
TA	Ta.
LA. LLOR	Lu ol lor.
GNAY	Gnay.

E. K. He plucketh the Curtain, and quickly openeth it, and sayeth :

o..... *Tou must after* E fa fa fe, *put a* P.

Δ. This word is the 25 word backward.

E. K. My

E. K. My thinketh that I hear a rumbling, or clattering of Pewter in the stone.

E. K. After he had spoken, he shut the Curtain again: Now the Curtain is opened again.

LIMLAL	*Lim lal.*
AMMA	*Am ma,*
CHIIS	*Chiis.*
SOBCA	*Ka.*
	Sob ca.
.ADRID	*Ma drid*
ZCHIS	*Kis.*
	Zod Chis.
OOANOAN	*O o A no an.*
CHI.	*Chis.*
AVINY	*A vi ny.*
DRILPI	*Dril pi.*
CAOSGIN	*Ca of gin.*
OD	*Od*
BUTMONI	*But mo ni.*
PARM	*Parm.*
ZUMVI	*Zum vi.*
CNILA	*Cni la.*
DAZI.	*Daz is.*
ETHAMZ	*E tham Zod,*
ACHILDAO	*Kil.*
	A chil da q.
OD	*Od.*
MIR.	*M irk.*
	M irc.
OZOL	*O zol.*
CH.	*Chis.*
PIDIAI	*Pi di a i.*

COLLA

COLLA..	*Col lal.*
VLCININ	*Ul ci nin.*
ASOBAMA	*A so bam.*
UCIM	*U cim.*
BAGLE	*Ba gle.*
IA.BALTOH	*I ad bal toh.*
CHIRLAN	*Kir.*
	Chir lan.
PAR	*par.*
NII..	*Ni i so.*
OD	*Od.*
IP	*Ip.*
O...AFE	*O fa fa fe.*
BAGLE	*Ba gle.*
ACOCASB	*A co cmb.*
ICORSCA	*Ka*
	I Cors ca.
VNIG	*V nig.*
BLIOR	*Bli or.*

E. K. Now the Curtain is drawn.

△ voyce. *The end of that.*

△. This is the fifth of this day.

E. K. Now is the Curtain open. All his Cloaths are .....ry , very clear, whitish, and blewish.

CORAXO	*Co rax o.*
CHIS	*Chis.*
CORM.	*Cormp.*
OD	*Od.*

BLANS	Blans.
...U....AL	Lu cal.
AZL...,..,.R	A zl a zor.
PAEB	Pa eb.
SOBA	So ba.
LILONON	Li lo non.
CHIS	Chis.
VIRQ	quu Vir q.
EOPHAN	E o phan.
OD	Od.

Between Chis and Virq, you must put in Op a word.

RACLIR	Ra clir.
MA.........	Ma a si.
BAGLE	Ba gle.
...,....SGI	Ca of gi.
DS	ds.
IALPON	Yal Jal pon.
DOSIG	as big. Do sig.
OD	Od.
BASGIM	Bas gim.
OD.	Od.
OXEX	Ox ex.
DAZIS	Daz is.
....IATRIS	Si a tris.
OD	Od.
SALBROX	Sal brox.
CINXIR	Cynx ir.
F....BOAN	Fa bo an.
UNALCHIS	U n al chis.
CONST	k. Const.
DS	ds.
DAOX	Da ox
COCASG	g as dg. Co casg.

5678.

OL

O L	O l.
O A N I O	O á ni o
Y O R	Yor.
V O H I M	Vób im.
O L	Ol
G I Z Y A X	Giz y ax
O D	Od.
E O R S	E órs.
C O C........	gao. dg. Co Casg.
P L O S...	Plo si.
M ......I D S	Mol ni, de
P A G E I P	Pa ge ip.
L A R A G	La rag.
O M	Om.
D R O L N	droln
C O C A S B	Co casb.
E M N A	Em na
L P A T R A L X	El. L pá tralx.
Y O L C I	Tol Çi.
M A T O R B	Ma torb.

This word must come next after Om droln.

E. K. Now he pulleth the Curtain.

Δ. This *Om droln* is before four words. The Curtain is open away. He is in his flaming apparell.

N O M I G	big. No mig.
M O N O N S	Mo nons.
O L O R A	O lo ra.
G N A Y	Gnay.
A N G E L A R D	An ge lard.
O H I O	O bi o.
O H I O	O bi o.
O H I O	O bi o.
O H I O	O bi o.
O H I O	O bi o.

OHIO

OHIO	*O bi o.*
NOIB	*No ib.*
OHIO	*O bi o.*
CAO..GON	*Ca òf gon.*
BAGLE	*Bagle.*
MADRID	*Ma drid.*
I	*I.*
ZIROP	*Zi róp.*
	K
CHISO	*Chi fo.*
DRILPA	*Dril pa.*
NIISO	*Ni i fo.*
CRIP	*Crip.*
IP	*Ip.*
NIDALI	*Ni da li.*

...... A voice.   *The end of that Call.* a. This is the fixth.

The Curtain is drawn.   He appeareth now all in violet Silk like a Cloke, and on his head a bundel wreathed of the fame.

OXIAYAL	*Ox I Ay al.*
HOLDO	*Hol do.*
OD	*Od.*
.IROM	*Zir om.*
O	*O.*
CORAXO	*Co ráx o.*
DS	*Ds.*
ZILDAR	*Zil dar.*
RAASY	*Ra a fy.*
OD	*Od.*
VABZIR	*Vab zir.*
CAMLIAX	*Cam li axi*
OD	*Od.*
BAHAL	*Ba bal.*
NIISO	*Ni bfo.*

S   SALMAN

SALMAN	_Sal man._
TELOC..	_betch._ _Te locb._
CASARMAN	_Ça for man._
HOLQ	_Hól q._
OD	_Od._
TI	_Ti._
TA	_Ta._
ZCHIS	_Zod chis._
SOBA	_So ba._
CORMF	_Cormf._
IGA	_I ga._
NIISA	_Ni I fa._
BAGLE	_Bagle._
ABRAMG	_Ab ramg. g, not as dg._
N · NCP	_Nonfp._ _Noncp._

... Curtain is drawn.   The end of this.
.... This is the fourth.

E. K. Now is the Curtain pull'd away: and quickly pull'd again.
Now it is open again.   He is apparelled, of colour between a blew,
and a red mingled; but blew seemeth to be the ground. From the
shoulder on the arms, is a trunk of seven pendant labels, with laces. On
his head a very broad Hat, between dun and black colour. His apparel
is very long.

NONCI	_Non ci, fi._
DSONF	_Dfonf._
BABAGE	_Ba ba ge._
OD	_Od._
CHIS	_Chis._
OB	_Ob._
HUBAIO	_Hubb i o,_
TIBIBP	_Ti bibp._
ALLAR	_Al lar._
ATRAAH	_A tra ah._
OD	_Od._
EF	_Ef._

DRIX

DRIX	*Drix.*
FAFEN	*Fa fen.*
MIAN	*Mi an.*
AR	*Ar.*
ENAY	*E nay.*
OVOF	*O vof.*
SOBA	*So ba.*
DOOAIN	*Do ba in.*
AAI	*A a i.*
IVONPH	*I vonph.*
SOBA	*So ba.*
VPAAH	*V pa ah.*
CHIS	*Chis.*
NANBA	*Nan ba.*
ZIXLAY	*Zix lay.*
DODSIH	*Dod sib.*
ODBRINT	*Od brint.*
TAXS	*Taxs.*

He maketh Curſie.

H.....	*Hu ba ro.*
TAST...	*Tas tax.*
YL..	*Tl si.*
......	*Do a lim.*
.....	*E o lis.*
.....	*Ol log.*
.....	*Ors ba.*
DSCHIS	*Ds chis.*
AFFA	*Af fa.*
MICMA	*Mic ma.*
ISRO	*Is ro.*
MAD	*Mad.*

S 2   O D

OD	Od.
LONSHITOX	Lonshi tox.
DS	ds.
JUMD.	Jumbd.
LUSDAN	Lusdan.
EMOD	E mod.
DSOM	dsom.
OD	Od.
TLIOB	Tli ob.
DRILPA	Dril pa.
GEH	jeh.
	Geh.
YLS	as Tils.
	yls.
MADZILODARP	Mad zi lo darp,

That is the Twelfth.

••••••	ILS.
••••••••••••••	Di aspert.
••••••••••••	Za car.
••••••••••••••	Go bus.
••••••••••••••••	Zamran.
••••••••	O do.
...ICLE	CICLE.
QAA	Qâa.

That is a call.

△. This is the eighth

NAPEAI	Na pe ai.
BABAGEN	jen.
	B ba gen
DSBRIN	Ds brin.
OOAONA	U n.
	OO Ao na.
LRING	LRING.
VONPH	Vonph.

SOBA-

SOBAIAD	*So bai ad.*
IVONPOVNPH	*I von po vnph.*
AL.ON	*Al don.*
DAXIL	*Dax il.*
OD	*Od.*
TOATAR	*To a tar.*

E.K. The Curtain is pluck't to.

A voyce. *That is the thirteenth.*

E. K. Now it is open again.
E. K. He is now as if he had a pall, or Robe of Gold with a strange Cap of Gold on his head.

...	*Ils.*
....	*Mi ca ol zod.*
.L.IRT	*Ol pirt.*
IALPRG	*Tal.* *I al purg.*
BLIORS	*B liors.*
DS	*Ds.*
ODO	*Odo.*
BUSDIR	*Buf dir.*
OIAD	*O i ad.*
OVOARS	*O vo ars.*
CAOSGO	*Ca of go.*
CASARMG	*Ca far mg.*
LA..	*La i ad.*
ERAN	*E ran.*
.INTS	*Brints.*
CAFAFAM	*Ca fa fam.*
DS	*Ds.*
IVMD	*I umd.*
AQLO	*qun.* *A q lo.*
ADOHI	*A do hi.*
QZMOZ	*Moz.*

OD

OD   Od.

MAOFFAS   Ma of fas.

BOLP   Bolp.

COMOB ·· IORT   Co mo bli ort.

PAMBT   Pambt.

Curtain is now pluckt to.

A voice ...... *That is all.*
Blessed be the Creator of all, who hath mercy on all.

E. K. Now he is here, apparelled as he was wont to appear.

Promise of
God confirmed
anew.

14 To be re-
ceived the
Monday next.

Nal. ...... *Thus, hath the Lord kept promise with you: and will not forget the least part of his whole promise with you. Keep you therefore promise with the Lord; for, he is jealous, and not to be defiled. Proceed as you now do. The next Monday you shall have, as many.*

Δ. Will it please you to deliver us the English of these 14 now, as you were wont to do?

Nal. ...... *The English will have a day by it self.*

Nal. ...... *The* [Δ.] *Third Monday to come, you shall have them all. So that, you have but three dayes to labour.*

Δ. You speak of the next *Monday,* and the third; and speak nothing of the second *Monday:* and you said, that the English will have a day by it self: And you say we have but three dayes to labour, &c.

Nal. ...... *What I have said, is so. Go also, and refresh your selves.*

[E. K. The Curtain is drawn.]

A voice. ...... *Stay there.*
A voice. ...... *Give God thanks, and make an end.*

E. K. Prayed the 145. and 146. Psalm kneeling reverently; and I likewise in heart consenting thereto, attentively listning.

Note ..... E. K. is very well perswaded of these Actions now, thanked be the Highest, who is Almighty.

Δ. Laudate Dominum de Cælis, laudate eum in excelsis : laudate eum omnes Angeli ejus, laudate eum omnes virtutes ejus. Quia ipse dixit, & facta sunt nobis. Non fecit taliter omni nationi.   Soli Deo nostro, laus omnis, Victoria, Triumphus, & Jubilatio,
Amen.

Monday Cracovia Maii, 21. 1564. *Mane, hora* 5. *Actio Tertia, Lunaris.*

E. K. There appeareth neither Vail, nor any thing else in the Stone.

Δ. At length appeared one, but none of them : he is jolly and green, with a long (like green Velvet) Robe : his hair long, like yellow Gold : nothing on his head but his hair. He standeth as though he stood in a cloud, above the usual paviment in the air.

re

...... *Lo the Sun shineth, and men fear no rain, the clouds are dispersed, and they look not for a tempest : But when it raineth mightily, or the heavens frown, then keep they their houses, saying one to another, What unreasonable Tempest is this ? what Hail-stones are these ? Good Lord, who ever saw such windes ? were there ever such windes ? So shall it be of the power of God,* which holdeth in his hands the windes, and scattereth cloudes abroad with his feet : For of his coming, shall it be said amongst you, My Spirit hath vexed me, and I am troubled : Why hast thou brought in things, greater than thy self ? or where shall this power dwell that overshadoweth me ? Wanting you shall desire, (as you do) and being filled you shall think you have too much.

A.

God is not
tied to time,
per-
formance
. meaneth
dwelling with
him. se, are
mansions.
. faithful
.. say
.. or.

Flesh can never be throughly mortified but with death. Think not, that the Lord is as the Sun, that keepeth his continual watch through the heavens ; which because he is made for a time, is also tied to time.

He that sitteth and judgeth, keepeth no course ; but a continual performance of his long-before providence : For he that useth him otherwise, shall be rejected : because his [Δ.] *dwellings are not in the mansions of the faithful. Lift up your ears therefore ; for thus saith the highest*

Who

Who made the heavens, or spread them like a garment ? Who breathed into man, the spirit of un-
derstanding ? Who overthrew the proud world with waters ? Who smiled at the ruin of Pha-
raoh ? Who rooted the wicked out of their seates ? and made them become vineyards for my peo-
ple : yea the stiff-necked generation ? Who threw down the Towers of Babylon, and the great Har-
lot ? Who dwelt upon the Earth, and became flesh, to pay for your wickednesse ? Who tumbled
the stone from the Well, that the Sheep might drink ? Even be it is, that gave all these their times.
He it is, that is as able to make you understand, as those, that call into the waters, and said, Let
us draw up our fish,: which alwayes dealeth with the weakest : To the intent he might prove
himself the strongest.

[*E. K.* He speaketh a great deal of speech as to himself, which I
perceive not.]

...... *Even be it is, that will make you strong and wise, If he find you with garments.*   *Veste nupt lali*
He it is, that faith unto you, Waver not*, Be stedfast; for the faithful are never unre-* *opus est.*
warded.

[*E. K.* He putteth his right hand out of the Stone, being grasped
together. Now he openeth his hand, and it is written in ; and it is
so far from me, that I cannot read it : yet he seemeth to be nearer to
me, very much more than his hand. The writing seemeth to be like
the leaf of a Book. Thus it was written.

...... *Have an eye to my foretelling .... Troubles. Sudden sorrow is at hand, in all the earth.*   .. L.
No, his Ship is almost built. Laskie, *if he serve me,* shall be King of *Poland. If he serve ano-*
ther, his bowels shall fall out, before him with poison.   *Poison.*

E. K. Now he clasped his hand together , and stayed the
reading.

Δ. Whom is *Laskie* to serve (O Lord) but thee ? to keep thy Laws , Statutes and
Commandements ? not to depend upon any creature.

...... *The King and Chancelor* have *sold the people of this Land, and are sworn Turks. Re-* *Turks.*
turn not home to Lasko (Laskie) *for; if thou do, thou shalt offend me. Go to the Emperour ;* *Not to Lasky.*
for I will comfort thee with his favour. Let him not return thence; till he be warned by me. *A. L.*

Δ. You mean, from the Emperours Court ?   *Ad Imperato-*

Δ. I beseech you, by what token, shall he receive your warning ?   *rem eundum,*

...., *Be thou his right hand, to his body, and his mouth to me. I will be merciful unto* *est.*
him, and hold up his head. *Leave off, till the seventh hour of the day ; then cometh the* *Return by*
Action.   *warning.*

Δ. Mean you the seventh hour, as from midnight last ?

Δ. That beginneth at noon, if you make but 12 hours in the day : or at 11 if you
reckon common hours.

...... *The seventh from the Horison : Run, that run can.*

E. K. He himself runneth away.

Δ. All Glory and Praise be to God,   *Amen.*

Eadem die lunæ, hora 7 (inchoante) in meridie. Hora planetaria.

E. K. After a quarter of an hour (almost) appeared our Instructors, as of .. e time.

Δ. Gloria patri & filio & Spiritui Sancto, sicut erat in principio & nunc & in sempiterna secula seculorum.   *Amen.*

Gab. ...... *Move, move, move not, for the place is holy. Be patient a little while.*

E. K. Nalvage prayeth all the while.

E. K. Gabriel riseth out of his Chair again, and warneth as before
(thrice) that we should not move, for the place is holy. *Nalvage*
maketh a crosse toward the 4 quarters of the World, with his rod, as
he was wont.

Nal. ...... *There are 30 Calls yet to come. Those 30 are the Calls of* Ni .. *Princes and 9 Princes*
spiritual Governours, unto whom the Earth is delivered as a portion. These bring in and again
disp.. Kings and all the Governments upon the Earth, *and vary the Natures of things .* with *Officers*
the

Princes
11 Aug.
The 7 Angels
91.
Good Angels
of the Air, or
Spirits digni-
fied.
From the ele-
ment of the
fire to the
earth.
Note.
For a time.

the variation of every moment ; *Unto whom,* ·*the* providence of the eternal Judgement, *is al*-ready opened. *These are generally governed by* the twelve Angles *of the 12 Tribes: which are also governed by the* 7 *which stand* before the presence of God. *Let him that can see look up : and let him that can here, attend* ; for this is wisdom. They are all spirits of the Air : not rejected, but dignified ; *and they dwell and have their habitation in the air diversly, and in sundry places : for their mansions are not alike, neither are their powers equal. Understand therefore, that from the fire to the earth, there are* 30 *places or abidings :* one above and be-neath another : *wherein these aforesaid Creatures have their aboad, for a time.*

Pt tota terra diftributa fub 12. Principibus Angelis, 12. Tribuum Ifrael : quorum 12. aliqui plures, aliqui pauciores partes habent fub fuo regimine ex 91 partibus in quas tota terra hic demonftratur effe divifa.

Apocalypfi Johannis Teftimonium, de 12 Angelis 12 Tribuum, Cap. 21.

Quando dividebat Altiffimus gentes, quando feparabat filios Adam, conftituit terminos populorum, juxta numerum filiorum Ifrael : Hoc igitur hinc egregiè patere.

They bear no name.

[E. K. What is without a name ?]

......., *Their orderly place :* But w . . *they have, in respect of their being. Understand them therefore, by the first,* fecond, third . . *fo, thirtieth Air.* . . . *are fo to be nominated, O thou the* Twentieth air, O thou *fixteenth Air,* &c. . . . *fometime,* (yea all together *) two or three, of the* . . *elfe govern, by times, which are the Kings unto thefe* . . . *o to be fpoken of) and beare rule together, and at one time in the divifions.*

In the firft *Air, the ninth , eleventh, and* feventh *Angel of the Tribes, bear rule and govern. Unto the ninth ,* 7000. *and* 200. *and* 9 *miniftering Angels are fubject. Unto the eleventh* 2000, 300, 60. *Unto the* feventh 5000, 300, 60, 2.

Nal. ...... *Count the number* ......

Δ. The whole fum of this Government amounteth to 14931.

Nal. ...... *It is right.*

2. *The* fecond *is divided into* 3 *parts, the Angel of the fourth Tribe hath the* firft ; *The Angel of the* fecond, *the* fecond ; *The Angel of the* fecond *the* third. *The fourth hath thefe many* 3000, 600, 30, 6. *The* firft fecond of the fecond 2000. . . 0. 60 . 2. *The* laft of the fecond . . . 00, 900, 60, 2. *Adde thefe together.*

Δ. They are ...... 6660.

3. *The* third. *The* firft, *The* ninth, *The* fecond, *the* feventh, *The* third *the* tenth. *The* ninth ......, 4400. *The* feventh or the fecond ......, 3660. *The* tenth or the third ...... 9236.

Nal. ...... *Number them* ......

Δ. They are . in all ......, 17296.

4. Nal. ...... *The fourth hath alfo his three parts. The Angel of the tenth Tribe hath the* firft. *The* tenth *hath alfo the* fecond. *The* twelfth *hath the* third.

E. K. He prayeth.

The firft tenth ......, 2360. *Second tenth* ...... 3000. *Twelfth or the third* ......, 6300. *Number the fourth alfo,*

. . —————— *They are* ......, 11660.

. . *is alfo threeford. The* firft of the Tribes *have the* firft . . *enth hath the* fecond. *The* ele-venth *hath the* third. *The* firft *hath under him* 8630. *The* feventh or fecond .... 2306. *The* eleventh, *The* third ——— 5000, 800, two. *Number them.*

Δ. They are ——— 16738.

E. K. He prayeth reverently.

Be patient for a while. Thefe govern in the fixth. Δ. *If I underftand you right, thefe.*

6. *Thefe govern in the* fixth *place (which is to come) The Angel of the* fifth tribe, *hath the* firft *part. (for there are...........) The* Angell *of the* twelfth *hath the* fecond. *The Angel of the* fifth *hath the* third part. *The* Angell *of the* firft, *that is to* fay, *of the* firft fifth , *hath* fubjects, 3000, 600, 20, *of the* fecond *or* twelfth, 900, 200, *of the* third place *and* fecond fifth 7000, 200, 20. *The* fifth *governs in this order twice, therefore it is* termd *the* fecond fifth. *Number it.*

Δ. They are ——— 20040.

7. *The* feventh *hath alfo three places. The* fourth *hath the* firft. *The* third *hath the* fecond. *The* eleventh *hath the* third. *The* fourth *and the* firft place — 6000, 300. 60, 3. *The* third *Angell and* fecond place, 7000, 700, 6. *The* eleventh *Angell the* third place, 6000, 300, 20. *Number it.*

Δ. They are 20389. fo, ...*it is the* feventh.

8. *The* eight Ayre, *hath alfo three parts. The Angel of the* fifth *hath the* firft. *The Angel of the* firft *hath the* fecond. *The Angel of the* ninth *hath the* third. *The* fifth *Angel and* firft place 4000, 300, 60, 2. *The* firft *Angel and* fecond place 7000, 200, 30, 6. *The* ninth *Angel and the* third place , 200, 300, 2. *Number it.*

Δ. They

Δ. They are——13900.

9. *The ninth is also of three places. The third Angel hath the first place. The tenth Angel hath the second. The ninth Angel hath the third, the third Angel hath in the first place* 9100,900,90, 6. *The tenth Angel and the second place* 3000,600,20. *The ninth Angel and the third place,* 4000, 200,30. *Number them.*

Δ. They are——17846.

10. *The tenth hath places also three. The eleventh Angell occupieth the first. The seventh Angel occupieth the second. The ninth Angel occupieth the third. The eleventh Angel and first hath* 8000, 800,80. *The seventh Angel in the second,* 1000,200, 30. *The ninth in the third,* 1000,600 10, 7. *Number them.*

Δ. They are——11727.

Nalvage prayeth.

Gabriel. ...... *Take heed you move not.*

11. *The eleventh, is three as before. The first is occupied by the tenth. The second by the sixth. The third by the third. In the first place.* 3000, 400, 70, 2. *In the second place,* 7000, 200, 30, 6. *In the third place,* 5000, 200, 30, 4. *Number them.*

. . ——— *They are* 15942.

12. *The twelfth hath also his divisions. Three first places is of the sixth. Second place of the eighth. Third of the second. The first hath* 2000, 600, 50, 8. *The second,* 7000, 700, 70, 2. *The third* 3000, 300 90, 1. *Number it.*

.——— They are 13821.

13. *The thirteenth hath three. The tenth is in the first. The first is in the second. The seventh is in the third. The first hath* 8000, 100, 10, 1. *The second* 3000, 300, 60. *The seventh Angel in the third* 4000, 200, 10, 3. *Number it.*

Δ. They are 15684.

14. *The fourteenth hath threefold place as the rest. The fift Angel occupieth the first, The seventh occupieth the second, The twelfth occupieth the third. The first which is the fifth Angel,* 2000, 600, 70, 3. *The second hath* 9000, 200, 30, 6. *The twelfth* 800, 200, 30. *Number it.*

Δ. They are——20139.

Nal. *Have patience.*

E. K. Now he standeth on the top of the Table.

Mark diligently.

OCCODON   *Occodon.*

Answereth to the Angell of the ninth, which is of the first, which occupieth the first place of the first Ayre. It is the name of that part of the earth which is governed by the Angel *of the ninth Tribe, and those that are* under him *in the first division. The first Ayre.*

Mark diligently.

....   *Pax comb.*

Answereth the eleventh Angel, and is that part of the Earth which is governed by him and his Ministers, in the second place of the first Ayre.

Mark

VALGARS   *Valgars.*

It answereth to the seventh Angel and to his Ministers, 5562, *which are the last part of the first Ayre.*

Mark diligently.

DOAGNIS   *Doagnis.*

It is the first part of the second, the first part of the earth, which is governed in the first part of the second, as it shall after appear, under the fourth Angel.

Mark diligently.

PACASNA   *Pacasna.*

Note and understand this well, how one part is governed of divers Angels.

It is the name of that part of the world on earth, that is governed in the second part of the second Ayre, BY THE ANGEL *of the second Tribe, with his Ministers.* 2362.

T   *Thus*

Thus you shall understand of all the names that follow.

D..AL..VA   *Di a li v a.*

The third of the second : whose governour is the ......nons of the Tribe.
The Third Ayre in the first place.

SAMAPH.   *Sa ma pha.*

Samatha hath over it of the Tribe the ninth.
The second of the third is.

VIROCHI.   *Ki.*
                                             Vi ro chi.

Under the seventh of the Tribe.
The Third place of the Third Ayre.

ANDISPI   *An dis pi.*

It is governed by the Tenth of the Tribe.
The fourth Ayre , The first part.

THOTANF   *Tho tanf.*

His Governour is the Tenth of the Tribe, whose Ministers are 2360.
The second of the fourth.

AXZIARG   *Ax zi arg.*

It is governed by the tenth of the Tribe.

P..HNIR   *Poth nir.*

It is governed by the Twelfth of the Tribe.
The fifth Ayre, The first part.

LAZDIXI   *Laz dix i.*

Which is governed by the first of the Tribe.
The second part of the fifth.

NOCAMAL   *No ca mal.*

Which is governed by the seventh of the tribe.
The Third of the Fifth.

TIARPAX   *Ti ar pax.*

Which is governed by the eleventh of the Tribe , whose Ministers are 5802.
Be patient awhile.

The sixth.
Gab. ...... *Move not* ...... Moses was to seek in these secrets.
Nal. .... *The first of the sixth whose Governour is the fifth of the Tribe.*

S · XTOMP   *Sax tomp.*

The second of the sixth, whose Governour is the twelfth of the Tribe.

VAVAAMP   *Vi Va amp.*

The third of the sixth, which is governed by the fifth of the Tribe.

ZIRZIRD   *Zir zird.*

Whose Ministers are 7220 as before.

The first of the seventh is governed by the fourth Tribe.

OBMACAS   *Ob ma cas.*

K. E. Ever the Table turneth to the letter under.

The second of the seventh, whose the third of

GENADOL   *Ge na dol.*

The third of   by the eleventh.

ASPIAON.   *As pi a on,*

The first of the eighth, whose Governour is the fifth, &c. whose Ministers are 4961.

ZAINFRES   *Zā in fres.*

The second of the eighth, by the first of the Tribe, whose Ministers 7236.

TODNAON   *Tod na on.*

The third of the eighth   by the ninth of the Tribe, ad under him 2302.

PRISTAC   *Pri tac.*

The ninth : the first, governed by the third, whose Ministers, 9996.

ODDIORG   *Od di org.*

The second of the ninth   by the tenth, whose Ministers 3620.

CRALPIR   *Cral pir*

Move not for the Lord is great amongst you.

The last of the ninth   by the ninth of the Tribe: Ministers 4230.

DOANZIN   *Do an Zin:*

The

The first of the tenth	*by the eleventh of the Tribe.*

LEXARPH   *Lex arph.   Xarph.*

The second of the tenth   *by the seventh.*

COMANAN   *Co ma nan.*

The third of the tenth   *by the ninth.*

TABITOM   *Ta bi tom.*

Whose Ministers are 1617.

Have patience.

The first of the eleventh,   *governed by the tenth.*

Ministers 3472.

MOLPAND   *Mol pand.*

The second governed by the sixth Ministers 7236.

VSN.RDA   *Vsnar da.*

The third   *by the third.*

Ministers as before 5234.

PONODOL   *Po no dol.*

The first of the twelfth, go by the sixth.

TAPAMAL   *Ta pa mal.*

The second of the twelfth   *by the eighth Angel.*

GEDOONS   *Ge do ons.*

The third of the twelfth   *by the second.*

AMBRIOL   *Ambriol.*

The first of the thirteenth *governed by the tenth.*

Ministers 8111.

GECAOND   *Ge ca ond*

The second   *by the first of the Tribes.*

LAPARIN   *La pa rin.*

The last of the thirteenth   *by the seventh of the twelve.*

DOCEPAX   *Do ce pax.*

Is Italia.

The first of the fourteenth *by the fifth of the Tribes.*

TEDOAND   *Te do and.*

Britan.   *This is* England *and* Scotland *too, called anciently by the name of* Britania.   *There liveth not a man that knoweth the truth of the* British Originals.

△. *The British Originals.*

The second of the 14.   *by the seventh.*

VIVIPOS   *Vi vi pos.*

The laſt of the fourteenth   *by the twelfth.*

                    Miniſters 8230.

OO.NAMB   *O o a namb.*

E. K. Now he prayeth.

E. K. Now *Gabriel* ſtandeth up.

Gab. .....; *The Lord pardoneth your faſting , and accepteth the inward man , labour alſo to mor-*
row. You ſhall have the reſt.

Δ. May I be bold to ask you one queſtion ?

Gab. ...., *You may.*

Δ. Is the Queen of *England,* alive, or dead ?

....,... *She liveth.*

I am nothing near the earth.

E. K. The Curtain is drawn.   We prayed joyntly ſome prayers.

Δ. Upon my motion, for the Lord *Al. Leſ.* how to deal with the Chancelour , the Curtain
was drawn open. And he in the green, who appeared to day, came into the ſtone , and ſaid
as followeth.

Thus ſayeth the Lord : *Joyn body to body, but let mindes be ſeparate , for he is deſpiſed in the* ..md the
ſight of God, and is delivered over to deſtruction, which doth tarry, till it finde him ready. Chancelour
Iſrael *deceived* Egypt, *and ſaw* Egypt *overthrown.* Let him do what he will with him , but .. nd Cracow,
let him not joyn his minde with him.

Δ. We are deſirous to know your name.   Mapſams'
                                                          under
My name is called Dic illis.   Gabriel.
I am one under Gabriel *, and*   Δ. Jeſus declared his name, and ſo have
the name of Jeſus *I know and*   other good Creatures before unto
honour.   us.

Map. *My name is* Mapſama.

Δ. Is, dic illis, the Etymology thereof ?

Map. *It is.*

Δ. How much it importeth for us to underſtand the beſt counſel that is to be given to *A. L.*
you know, &c.

Map. ..... *I am commanded, and I have done my commandment. But ſee, that thou, and be ful-*
fill thoſe things that are commanded you by me.

Δ. You ſaid I ſhould be his mouth to you : How ſhall I execute that, I pray you ?

Map. ..... *Not to me,* but to God.

Δ. By prayer mean you ?

Map. ...,.. *Tea, and by preſence.*

Δ. By preſence, with whom?   The Empe-
Map. ..... Thou ſhalt go from hence with him to the Emperour : God will ſtir up farther rour...
matter, by thy preſence there.

Δ. Shall all our Leſſons be finiſhed, and ſufficient power delivered unto us according to
the promiſe of God ?

...... *you ſhall be* able to practiſe by Sunday.

Δ. By which Sunday ?

...... *But the practices that are the inſtructions of the Higheſt, are not but in lawful cauſes*
and for neceſſity, to glorifie God ; and againſt *Pharaoh.*

Δ. What ſhall, then, be the hability of my skill to practice, before Sunday next   Gates
Map. ..... *Theſe Calls* touch all the parts of the World. *The World may be dealt withall,* Viſible
with her parts ; Therefore you may do any thing. Theſe Calls are the keyes into the Gates and Apparition.
Cities of wiſdom. Which [Gates] are not able to be opened, but with viſible apparition.   Note.
[Δ. And how ſhall that be come unto ?   Obſerve per-
Map. ....*Which is according to the former inſtructions : and to be had,* by calling of every miſſion.
                                                          All taught
Table. *You called for wiſdom, God hath opened unto you, his Judgement : He hath delivered* by Sunday
unto you the keyes, that you may enter ; But be humble. Enter not of preſumption, but of next practiſe,
permiſſion. Go not in raſhly ; But be brought in willingly : For, *many have aſcended, but* being called
few have entred. By Sunday you ſhall have all things that are neceſſary to be taught ; then (as firſt, then pra-
                                                          ctiſe.
                                                          occa-

occasion serveth) *you may practice at all times.* But *you being called by God ,* and, *to ,a good purpose.*

Δ. How shall we understand this Calling by God ?

Map. ...... *God stoppeth my mouth, I will answer thee no more,*

Δ. Misericordia Dei sit super nos, veritas ejus fulgeat & floreat in cordibus nostris.

Amen.

Δ. E. K. read this prayer devoutly, and I joyning my mind to his pronunciation thereof kneeled by.

Domine Jesu Christe, Deus salutarium nostrorum. Cujus nomen sit benedictum hodie & quotidie: qui ascendisti super Cælum Cæli, ad dextram Dei patris: denuo venturus ad judicandum in nubibus, cum potestate magna, & majestate mirabili, educ nos vinctos in peccatis in fortitudine justificationis tuæ : ut dealbemur per remissionem peccatorum super nivem; adeo ut beneplacitum sit tibi habitare in nobis, & nos in te. Amen.

Δ. Ex Psalterio post 67 Psalmum.

This prayer was miswritten in this place place, it should have been written the 22 of May following.

Tuesday Cracoviæ, *Maii* 22. 1584. *in Whitson-week,* Mane circa 7.

After our sitting, and some prayer used, appeared a very little Creature, on the Cushion, by the Stone: saying, *Put out your Candle;* for you shall have nothing to do, to day.

illuder.

Δ. What is your name that we may alledge your message for our excuse : seeing we were bid yesterday to labour to day.

E. K. He is gone.

Δ. After that about half an hour, there appeared our Instructors, as before time.

Gab. ...... *Move, move, move not, for the place is holy.*

E. K. *Gabriel* standeth up, and after a while said.

Obedience.

...... *The heavens are called righteous, because of their obedience. The earth accursed, because of her frowardnesse. Those therefore, that seek heavenly things, ought to be obedient; lest with their frowardnesse, they be consumed in the end, burnt to ashes with fire, as the Earth shall be for her unrighteousnesse.*

Faith.

Therefore, be you obedient, and full of Humility; using the instrument of righteousnesse, (which is faith) That you may be pertakers of the celestial comforts; which are the hire of such as forsake their frowardnesse. It hath been said unto you, ..., Measure not out Gods building. It hath been said unto you, ... Continue to the end. It hath been also told you, ... That the Determinations of God are not as yet established upon you.

* Vide L. Reg. cap. 2. F de revocata determinatione Dei super Tribu Levi: Vide etiam, Verba avidis, 3 Reg. m cap.2, ut conspimit Dominus sermones suos, &c. Si,

For it is written, It may again be * *undetermined I speak this for your instruction: For many have the power of God, but not unto righteousnesse: as was evident amongst the Jews in the choice of their Kings. In the very house of God, amongst those that entred into the holy place. For, all that the Prophets annoynted were not good. Not, that they were evil in the time of their anointing, but because their In-unction, and the dignity of their office was defiled in them in the end, through their own frowardnesse. The High-priests also were chosen in righteousnesse, and by the Spirit of God : but they became Rebels in the holy house: and such as of whom it is said, Altissimus autem fuit scandalum illis. Even so my brethren may it be with you.*

Δ. Jesus defend us from that inconvenience.

For although, it hath pleased God, to shew himself unto you, yet are you not ashamed to say : If the harvest cometh not in, at the time appointed, I will become a runnagate.

For what?

But Euge (my brethren) Hath the Lord need of you ? It needeth not be told you; you know the contrary. Then it followeth, you have need of God. But for what ? and why ? That your souls may overcome this World, overcome the body, to the dignity of an Angel.

And because you are miserable, and turned out to the field, full of brambles and misery, leane, naked, and unarmed, to fight against him, that resisteth against the might of God. Consider these last two, and then answer your selves, for the rest.

Cave.

Promissa Dei confirmantur.

I give you a short warning. God will fulfil his promises : And (as he hath said) by this August, you shall understand.

1. How to know and use God his Creatures, good and bad.

Note the second instruction or Gift of the Highest.

2. But when, *and for what, is the gift of the Highest, and shall be fulfilled in you (If you will be obedient) when it pleaseth him : even with a sound from his own mouth, saying, Venite & audite.*

The Actions the greatest.

For these Actions are twofold: Consider it, if you can: and they are the greatest, because they are the last, and contain all that hath been done before them. Which if you consider well, and to what you are called; you shall perceive, that the Judgements of God, are not a Tennis-ball.

Move not from place.

Thus much I thought to warn you my brethren. Have a little patience for the Action.

He that stirreth from his place shall find the reward of it.

Δ. After

Δ. After half an hour ?

Gab. ...... *Move not, Move not, Move not.*

.... *The fifteenth.*
Three parts.
The ninth hath the first,
The tenth hath the second.
The twelfth the third.

The 16 *hath* 3 *parts.*
The second hath the first,
The third hath the second,

The twelfth hath the third.

17....... *The seventeenth.*
The second hath the first,
The first hath the second,
The ninth hath the third.

18. ..... *The eighteenth is of three.*

1			the fifth,
2	} hath {		the seventh,
3			the twelfth.

E. K. He threw like dust out of the Stone toward my eyes.

19. ...... *The ninteenth is also threefold.*
1 ...... *The twelfth.*
2 ...... *The eighth.*
3 ...... *The eleventh.*

20 *The twentieth is also threefold.*
1 .... *fifth.*

2 ...., *third.*
3 .... *seventh.*

21 *The one and twentieth, is also threefold.*
1 ......: *twelfth.*
2 ...., *eighth.*
3 .... *sixth.*

E: K. There standeth one, at one of my eares, and at another, an-other, howling like Dogs ; and said, *Ah you beggars !* *A tempting illuding spirit come in place.*

Gab. ..... *He will deceive you, take heed lest you move.*

E. K. He seemeth to be telling money behinde me.

Δ. Look not back in any case.

The ninth of the fifteenth hath under him [Δ.] *of the* 12.   1000. 300. 60. 7.

The tenth of the first [Δ·] *hath under*   1000. 300. 60. 7. [Δ.] *of the* 12. Δ 15ʰ.
The twelfth of [Δ.] *the first*   1000. 800. 80. 6. Sup.
.. *of this first*
The first of the second [Δ.] *hath under him*   9000. 900. 20. *and he is the second of the* Ternary.
twelve.

The second of the second, which is the third of the 12.   9000, 200, 30.

The third of the third, which is the twelfth of the twelfth, hath under him 7000, 200, 40.

The first of the third (the second of the 12) *hath under him* 7000, 600, 20, 3.

The second of the third , which is the first of the 12. 7000, 100, 30. 2.

The third of the third, which is the ninth of the 12. *hath with him , or under him,* 2000, 600, 30, 4

18. *The first of the fourth, which is the fifth of the* 12.   2000, 300, 40, 6.

The second, which is the seventh of the 12. *under him* 7000, 600, 80, 9.

The third of the fourth, which is the twelfth of the 12.   *under him* 9000, 200, 70, 6.

The first of the fifth, which is the twelfth of the 12. *under him,* 6000, 200, 30, 6.

The second which is the eighth of the 12. *under him,* 6000, 700, 30, 2.

The third of the fifth : which is the eleventh of the 12. *under him,* 2000, 300, 80, 8.

The first of the sixth, which is the fifth of the 12. *under him* 3000, 600, 20, 6.

The second of the sixth ..... the third of the 12. 7000, 600, 20, 9.

The third, which is the seventh of the 12. *under him* 3000, 600, 30, 4.

21. *The first of the seventh, which is the twelfth of the* 12. *under him* 5000, 500, 30, 6.

The second of the seventh, which is the eighth of the 12. *under him* 5000, 600, 30, 5.

The last of the seventh, which is the sixth of the 12. *under him* 5000, 600, 50, 8.

Number every Ayre.	*Have patience for a while.*

Δ. ——— The 15. ——— 4620
The 16. ——— 28390
The 17 ——— 17389
The 18 ——— 19311
The 19 ——— 15356
The 20 ——— 14889
The 21 ——— 16829

The first of the fourth seventh hath three
parts.

1 —— *is the twelfth of the twelve.*
2 —— *is the first of the twelfth.*
3 —— *is the twelfth of the twelve.*

23. *The first of the second.*

2 —— *the seventh of the twelve.*
1 —— *the seventh of the twelve.*
3 —— *the eighth of the twelve.*

24. *The*

24. *The third.*

1 ——— *the fourth of*
2 ——— *the tenth.*
3 ——— *the twelfth of the twelve.*

25. *The fourth.*

1 ——— *the fourth.*
2 ——— *the second.*
3 ——— *the twelfth of the twelve.*

The fifth.

1 ——— *the twelfth.*
2 ——— *the eighth.*
3 ——— *twelfth of the twelve.*

27. *The sixth.*

1 ——— *the second.*
2 ——— *the fourth.*
3 ——— *the fifth.*

28. *The seventh.*

1 ——— *the tenth* ⎫
2 ——— *the ninth* ⎬ *of the twelve.*
3 ——— *the sixth* ⎭

2 , *The first of the first, which is the twelfth of the twelve, under him* 2000. 200. 30. 2.
The second of the first, under him 2000. 300. 20. 6.
The third of the first, which is the eleventh of   under him 2000. 300. 60. 7.

. , *The first of the second, which* 7000. 300. 20.
The second under him 7000. 200. 60. 2.
The third of the second, which is the second of the 12. *under him* 7000, 300. 30. 3.

24 *The first of the third, which is the fourth of the twelve, under him* 8000. 200.
The second of the third, which is the tenth of the twelve, under him 8000. 300. 60.
The third of the third, which is the eleventh of the twelve, under him   8000. 200, 30. 6.

25 *The first of the fourth, which is the fourth of the twelve, under him* 5000. 6000. 30. 2.
The second of the fourth, which is the second of the twelve, under him 6000. 300. 30. 3.
The third of the fourth, which is the twelfth of the twelve, under him 6000. 200. 30. 6.

26 *The first of the fifth, the which is the twelfth of the* 9000. 200. 30, 2.
The second of the fifth, which is the eighth of the twelve, under him 3000. 600. 20.
The third of the fifth, which is the twelfth of the twelve, 5000. 600. 30. 7.

27 *The first of the sixth, which is the second of the twelve, hath under him* 7000. 200. 20,
The second of the sixth, the fourth of the twelve, 7000. 500. 60.
The third, which is the fifth of the twelve, 7000. 200. 60, 3.

28 *The first of the seventh, the tenth of the twelve,* 2000. 600. 30.
The second of the seventh, which is the ninth of the twelve, under him 7000. 200, 30, 6.
The last of the seventh, the sixth of the twelve, under him 8000. 200,

Δ. *The* 22th. .... *is* .... 6925.
22 ——————— 21915.
24 ——————— 24796.
25 ——————— 18201.
26 ——————— 18489.
27 ——————— 22043.
28 ——————— 18066.

They ...... I kneel to prayer.   Then the Curtain was drawn.

E. K. There appeareth like the snuf of a Candle on the top of the stone, it is like a little spark of fire.   After this, *Gabriel* said by voyce, Have patience.

Δ. After half an hour. A voyce said ... look to .... to *E. K.*

E. K. The Curtain is drawn open. *Nalvage* standeth on the top of the Table.

Nal. ....., *The first part of the first seven you had to day.*
The ninth.

T A H A N D O.   *Ta han do.*

The tenth, the second of the first, which is the tenth.

NOCIABI   *No ci a bi.*

The third.

TASTOXO   *Ta to x o.*

16   *The first of the second.*

CVCARPT   *Cu carpt.*

The second.

LAVACON   *La va con.*

The third   is governed by the twelfth of the twelfth.   *Ministers 9240.*

SOCHIAL   *Ki*
                                          So chi al.

17   *The third.   The first, which is the second of*

SIGMORF   *Sig morf.*

The second.

AYDROPT   *Ay dropt.*

The third, whose governour is the ninth of the twelve.

TOCARZI   *To car zi.*

18   *The first of the fourth.*

NABAOMI   *Na ba o mi.*

The second.

ZAFASAI   *Za fa sai.*

The third.

YALPAMB   *Yal pa MB.*

The first of the fifth.

TORZOXI   *Tor Zox i.*

The second.

ABAION   *A ba i on.*

The third.

OMAGRAP   *O ma grap.*

20   *The first of the sixth.*

ZILDRON   *Zi L dron.*

                              V   *The*

The second of the sixth.

PARZI · A

Par zi ba.

The third of the sixth.

TOTOCAN

To to can.

The first of the seventh by the twelfth.

CHIRSPA

Chirs pa.

The second of the seventh.

TOANTOM

To an tom.

The third of the seventh.

VIXPALG

Dg.
Call it, *Vix palg.*

Nal......*The last seven.*

The first.

OZIDAIA

O-zi-dai a.

The second of the last seven.

PARAOAN

Pa ra o an.

The third.

CALZIRG

Dg.
Calzirg.

23　*The first of the second.*

RONOAMB
The second.

Ro no amb.

ONIZIMP

O ni Zimp.

The third of the second.

ZAXANIN

Zax a nin.

24　*The first.*

ORCAMIR.

Or ca mir.

The
CHIALPS

Ki,
Chi alps.

The third of the third.

SOAGEEL

So a ge el.

The first of the fourth.

MIRZIND

Mir zind.

The second　　　　*by the second of the twelfth.*
OBVAORS
The thirds.

Ob va ors.

RANGLAM

Ran glam.

The first of the fifth　　　　*by the twelfth of the twelfth.*
26　POPHAND

Po phand.

The second.

NIGRANA

Ni grá na.

The third.

BAZCHIM

kim.
Baz chim.

The first.

SAZIAMI

Sa zi a mi.

The second.

MATHULA

Ma thu la.

The third.

ORPANIB

Or pa nib.

28 ...... *The first of the seventh.*

LABNIXP

Lab nix p,

The second.

FOC · SNI

Fo cis Ni.

The third.

OXLOPAR

Ox lo par.

Nal. ...... *Have patience for a while.*   Say on.
The twenty ninth hath three parts.
The first part hath his Governour the third of the 12.
The second the fourth of the 3 .... the fifth of the 12.

E. K. Now he standeth off the Table.

30. *The thirtieth ...... hath 4 parts.*
1 ——— *the twelfth.*
2 ——— *the fourth.*   } *of the 12.*
3 ——— *the third.*
4 ——— *the sixth.*

The first of the nine and twentieth hath under him,   9632.
The second ..... by the fourth of the 12.   *under him* 4236.
The fifth of the 12 that governeth under   7635.

30 *The twelfth of the 12.*   4632.
The second .... by the fourth of the 12.   *under him* 9636.
The third .... by the third of the   *under him* 7632.
The last .... by the sixth   5632.

.• *The earth in the first division of the 29.*

VASTRIM

Vas trim.

The second part of 29 Ayre.

ODRAXTI

O drax ti.

by the fifth of the 12.
The third, whose Ministers are 7635.

V 2

GOMZIAM

GOMZIAM   *Gom zi am.*

30 ...... *The first of the* 30 .... *under the* 12.

TAOAGLA   *Ta ò a gla.*

The second under the fourth of

GEMNIMB   *Gem nimb.*

The third under the third.

ADVORPT   *Ad vorpt.*

The last ...... by the sixth of the 12.

DOZINAL   *Do zi nal.*

The . . wrth
... none
.. re : but
.. 30.

Nal, ... *I have done.*

Δ As you gave us taste, or warning of *Italia* and *Britania,* so if it be thought good to you we are desirous to understand of the rest, the Application to such names as we understand.

Nal, ... *Make an end for to day: Give over. Make your selves ready for to morrows Action.*

E. K. The Curtain is drawn.

Δ. Deo omnipotenti, Optimo, & maximo Universa machina creata laudem gloriam & honorem reddat, nunc & in perpetuum. *Amen.*

Δ. There is a prayer written after the Action of Monday *Maii* 21. next here before beginning *Domine Jesu Christe,* &c. which I misplaced there; for after this dayes Action, it was said by *E. K.* and me,

LIBRI SEPTIMI APERTORII CRACOVIENSIS
MYSTICI, SABBATICI,
Pars Quarta; Anno 1584. Maii 23.

Wedensday, † *Cracoviæ, Maii 23. Manè, hora 7. ¼ ferè. Post orationes nostras.*

He Curtain appeared, at the first looking.

Δ. There happened a great storm, or temptation to E. *K.* of doubting and misliking our Instructors and their doings, and of contemning and condemning any thing that I knew or could do. I bare all
things patiently for God his sake, &c. At length the Curtain was
opened, and they appeared.

E. K. I am contented to see, and to make true report of what they will shew; but my heart standeth
against them.

Gab. ...... *The time shall come, that the oak that is beaten with every storm shall be a Dining-
Table in the Princes Hall.*

Gab. ...... *Move not, for the place is holy.* He that doubteth, doth the property of the flesh, · able
but he that hath faith, hath the gift of the Holy Ghost. The Swallow flieth swift, but where she   doubting ¼
lighteth, there is no remembrance of her being: such are the words of man. But our words are
like unto a swift arrow, that entreth and sticketh where it lighteth.

*As man loveth the Owre for the Gold that is in it, and for the end of his use; so God loveth the
dunghills of the World,* &c. *But the enemy, the more he lifteth up himself, the greater shall be his* △. I suspect
fall: for instead of joy, shall enter in an hundred, and instead of hundred a thousand. But beware   this place to
of those Rebels; for they are like the small stones which are in every place of the Earth. But   be imperfect.
move not. Let us do that which is our part: *Unto others be it as they deserve.*

E. K. There appeareth a great thing like a Globe, turning upon   The earthly
Globe appear-
tvvo axell-trees.   ing.

Nal. ...... *Turn to the first Air* ...... △. I have done.

Nal. ...... *The Earth in the first ayre, is this,* [E. *K.* pointing on that Globe to it.]

△. We beseech you to bound or determine the Countries or Portions of the Earth, by
their uttermost Longitudes and Latitudes, or by some other certain manner.

Nal. ...... *Our manner is, not as it is of worldlings: We determine not places after the forms* ·· wardes;
of legs, or as leaves are: neither we can imagin any thing after the fashion of an [△] *horn: as*   ·· th
those that are Cosmographers do.   15 Prin-

Notwithstanding the Angel of the Lord appeared unto Ptolomie, and opened unto him the parts   An Angel ap-
of the Earth: but some he was commanded to secret: and those are Northward under your Pole,   lomie.
But unto you, the very true names of the World in her Creation are delivered.   mi

△. There appeared a great water, long and narrow, reddish, and thereby appeared . . .   ·· ng

There appeared written *Egypt.* He hath in his hand written *Syria.* And of that he   ·· any
said, that it was the second of the first.   ·· Poles
· Divini-

Now appeared a very fine Land and Region in which appeared a great City, in the edge of   · atione.
it. There appeared written ..... *Mesopotamia.* The third of the first.

Now appeared a large portion of the Earth, wherein appeared Beares, a great River from   The first of the
a Hill going into the Sea with three mouths. The word written *Cappadocia.*   second.

The second of the second.
written in his hand *Tuscia.*

△. I pray you, do you mean *Tuscia* by *Italy* ?
The third of the second: written *Parva Asia.*

The first ——— *Hircania* ——— △. *Mare Caspium* appeared by it.
The second ——— *Thracia* ———

The last Here appear people going into Caves of the ground, and dwelling in   Gold Mines
Caves: they are long haired men, naked; Here appear great Hills, and the veines of the   under the Pole
Gold Mines appear: the men seem to have baskets of leather. This is one of the places un-   Artick.
der the Pole Artick, written .... *Gosmam.*

△. ——— Is it so called, of the people of the Country ?
Nal. ...... *Even at this hour.*

E. K. Here

E. K. Here appeareth a mighty great Hill, and about it a great Cave of water.   Here appear beasts divers: some like a Swine, with feet like a Beare, his neither jaw hanging to his   and divers and a mighty Hill running, with branches: there by lie things with huskes on them.

The first.
> he appointeth,
>> *written* The b a idi.

The second —— Here the Sun shineth fair. *Parsadal.*

The third —— Here appear people very beastly, with Mantles on their shoulders: and beasts with long snouts.

India.

Here appear great rotten trees, very old, great Woods of them. Beyond the Woods are great Hills. Great Fens appear, and great Marish-ground : Fowles as big as Swans, green, scaled on their backs, in the water.

The first of the fifth —— Bactriane.
The second —— Cilicia.
The third —— Oxiana.

6. *The first of the sixth* —— Numidia.
The second —— Cyprus.
The third —— Parthia.

7. *The first of the seventh* —— Getulia.

The second —— Here is a great Desart : no Trees.
   in his hand —— *Arabia.*
The third —— Phalagon.
Δ.. I never heard of it.

E. K. It is toward the North, where the *veines of Gold*; and such Δ. Groynland people appear as before were noted. On this side them a great way as I think. appear men with swinish snouts, their visage is so strouted out; but to *be perceived to be of humane visage.* The women have about their privities very long hair down to their knees. The men have things on their shoulders of beasts skins, as instead of a Jerkin or a Mandillion.

8. *The first of the eighth* —— Mantiana.
   People appear here of reddish colour.
The second —— Soxia ——
      On the one side of the black men
The third ——
   like Spaniards appear very high men with Spanish Capes without Swords by their sides. Here appeare great Towns; divers; The name being not evident we urged, and *Gallia* appeared.

8. *The first* —— Illyria.
The second ——
..... *If thou stir, thou shalt never see more* —— To *E. K.*
—— —— Sogdiana.
The third —— Lydia.

The first Caspis.

The second Germania.

Men like Dutchmen with leather nether stocks.

The third.

Here appear Monkies, great flocks.
The people have leather Coats, and
no beards, thick leather, and Gar-
thers. They gather up thinkg......

Trenam.

Nal...... *These people are not known with you.*
Δ. Are they not in *Africa* ?
Nal..... *They be.* Now a dark fog covereth all the stone.
Nal..... *Stay awhile.*

E. K. I pray you let us go to dinner. *Move not, I say.*

E. K. *Nalvage* prayeth. Now he pointeth to a place.

11. *The first of the eleventh.* Bithynia.
The second. [*A great Citie, and the Sea hard by it.*] Græcia.
Δ. Is not that great Citie Constantinople?
Nal...... *It is. There is the seat of that* great Devil the *Turk.*
Nal...... *He is but Tenant at will.*
The third. Licia.

12 *The first of the twelfth.*

E. K. Here appear handsome men, in gathered tucked Garments, and
their shooes come up to the middle of their legs, of diverse coloured
leather.

Nal...... *These be those beyond* Hispaniola.

E. K. It is a low Countrey. Here appear great piles of stones like
St. *Andrews* Crosses. Two Notable Rivers are here, The women
have great covertures over their heads, coming from their shoulders, as
the Hoyks in *Flanders.*

O ni Gap.

There are on this side of it, (a great way) a great number of dead
Carkases.

Nal. ...... *It is beyond* Gia pan.
Δ. Then it is that land, which I use to call *Atlantis.*
Nal. ...... *They stretch more near the West : They are 25 Kingdoms in it.*
The second ...... beyond a place where the Gese.
I India.
India *in the heavenly government is divided into two parts. This is called the greater* Inde.
The third . ...., a great many little Isles.
Orchenii.

Δ. Do you mean the Isles of *Orkney.*
Nal. ...... *No.*
Δ. They seem to be the Isles of *Malacha.*
The first of the thirteenth ...... Achaia.
The second ......, Armenia.

E. K. A great old Castle standeth on the side of the top of a very high Hill. It seemeth to be made of wood, It seemeth four corner'd.

Δ. I beseech you what is that Castle?
Nal. ...... *It is* the Ark of Noe.
The third ...... Cilicia.
Nal. ...... *Ton never knew this* Cilicia. *This is* Cilicia, *where the Children of* Nemrod *dwell.* Nimrod.
It is up in the Mountains beyond Cathay.

E. K. This

E. K. This people, some great Gyants, and very fair.   Their Apparel is Gowns tuckt up, they are very costly Apparell'd, and in their faces they have *great Jewels like* precious stones hanged, they are marvellously rich apparelled in silks.

14   *The first* ...... *Here seem as if many houses were thrown down, and Castles.* Paphlagonia. *Onely one Hill appeareth in it very long.*
The second ......, Phaziana.
The third ...... *Here be men with broad Caps like* Egyptians, *and many Mountains are here on one side* Chaldei.
· 5   *The first* ...... Itergi.   *Here appear Woods, Waters, and fair Towns, but the people are yellow, tawny, and have great lumps of* flesh *under their Throats.   They are to the South of the last* Ciliciens.
There are 14 *Kingdoms of them.*
The second ...... Macedonia.
The third ...... Garamantica.   *People of a low stature, black, swarty people, naked.*
The first of the sixteenth ...... *Here like men of wilde gesture, cloathed like* Polonians.
This Countrey is ...... Sauromatica.
The second ...... Æthiopia.

E. K. Here are some naked, some not naked, covered with red Garments.   The houses seem like Tents, made of cloath and leather.   There are great Rivers.
The third.

E. K. Now he sheweth by the North-pole, and the great Mountain.

Fi a cim. ...... *Here be seven Kingdoms, their chief Citie is called* Fiacim, *all that are of that Kings Counsel are Astronomers.   The Kings name that now governeth is* Gaplacar.
The first.

Seest thou this Countrey? ...... Colchica.   To *E. K.*

The second ...... Cireniaca. ......   *E. K.* Hard by a great water.

The third, ... Nasamonia.
The first. ...... Carthago.
The second. ...... *Now appear many Crocodiles, long necked, scaled on the body, with long tailes.*
...... Cox lant.   A great place appeareth, covered about with fire.   *Many great Serpents appear here of* 200 f ot.   *It appeareth very* Eastward.   *No people appear here.*

E. K. There cometh from Heaven like a Mist, and covereth a great place, about 300 mile long, like a Park, enclosed with fire.   It is on a high ground.   There come four Rivers out of it, one East, another West, another North, and another South.   The pales, or enclosure of it seem to be Arches, beset most richly with precious stones. In the Gate of it stand three men like us, one is in a long Gown with many pleats, the other like in a Cassek.   The third in the rough skin of a beast.   In the name of Jesus: Is this the *Paradise* that *Adam* was banished out of?
...... *The very same; from hence he was turned out into the earth.   This is the true* Vale *of* Josaphat.
Δ.   Will you give me leave?
Say on.
It should seem this must be on the earth, not in the aire.
...... *It is upon the earth.*
You said that from hence he was turned out into the earth.
...... *The curse of God in* Adam *caused the earth, whereinto he was cast to be accursed.   For, if* Adam *had after his fall tarried in* Paradise, *his wickednesse would have altred the innocency of the place.   Therefore is* Paradise *distinguished from the earth, in respect of her purity: because the earth is defiled, and corrupted with man.   The earth is said to be sinfull in respect of the sin of man.*
Δ.   Till 45 degrees, both Northerly and Southerly, all is known in the most part of the world: But of any such place there is no knowledge nor likelyhood by any History of these dayes, or of old time.

Nal. ......There-

Nal....... *Therefore this is cunning, and the wisdom of God. There dwelleth flesh in it that*
shall never die, *which were taken up for a testimony of Truth.*

Δ. *Elie* and *Enoch,* by the Apocalyps do seem that they should *suffer death,* under Antichrist, if we understand right. There is *Elie, Enoch,* and *John* : They shall *seem to be* dead,
by his power, but not dead,

The third ——— ——— Idumea.

Nineteen The first ——— Parstavia.
I know it not.
The second ——— ——— Celtica.
...... *That we understand commonly now for* Gallia. *It is that which you call* Flandria *, the*
Low Country.

The third ——— ——— E. K. Here appear men with tallons like Lions.
They be very devils. There are five Isles of them. These be they
that can dwell in any part of the Earth, and are called *Pilosi.*
Nothing differeth them, but in that they have bodies.

Vinsan.

20 ——— ———
The first. ——— E. K. Under the *South Pole.*
Here appear little men with long beards: their *Under the*
bodies as childrens bodies. *South Pole.*

Nal....... *There dwelleth the wonderful Emperour of the World, and the wonderful City of the* △ *A wonder-*
World : Here are an hundred and twelve Kingdoms.   This City is a hundred forty six leagues ful great City,
about.
Δ. You understand two English miles for a league, as in *France ?*
Nal. .... *I.   There dwelleth the true generation of* Cham.
Tolpam.

The second ——— Carcedonia.
The third ——— Italia.

Δ. *Italia* and *Britanik* were before applied *:* the third of the 13. and first of the 14.
..... *Therefore these two places to be reconciled.*
He pointeth to a great City with a River by it.
... ... *This is that City which shall* not have one stone standing in it. *This City is in* Italia
Δ. Is it *Rome,* I pray you ?
Nal. .... *It is* Rome.
E. K. Now there is come a white mist in the Stone.
Cease, said a voice.
A voice ...... *Stay for a while.*
E. K.
Nal. ...... *Read them in my hand as thou seest them* [Δ. He spake to E, K.]

21 *The first* ——— Britania.
  The second ——— Phenices.
  The third ——— Comaginen.

22 *The first* ——— Apulia.
  The second ——— Marmarica.
  The third ——— Concava Syria.
23 *The second of the seventh* ———

  The first ——— Gebal.
  The second ——— Elam   *vide* Elamitæ.
  The third ——— Idunia.
    Nal. ...... *It is beyond* Greenland.

24 *The first* ——— Media,
  The second ——— Arriana.

X   *The*

The third ——————— Chaldæa.

Δ. I befeech you, what differeth this *Chaldea* from *Caldei* before ?
Nal. ...... *You fhall finde the difference* of it, in practice.

25 ——————— *Thefe people* Serici.
   The second ———— Perfia.
   The third ——————— Gongatha ——— E. K. Toward the South Pole.

26 The firft ———— Corfim ——— Beares and Lions here.
   The second ———————— Hifpania ———
   The third ——————— Pamphilia ———

27 The firft ——————— Oacidi.
   Gal. ...... *There be 9 Kingdoms* ——— Fair made people, but tawny.
   The second ——————— Babylon.
   The third ———— Median ——— E. K. It is much Northward.

Mafpi.   28 The firft ——————— Idumian.   Nal. ...... *They are two Ifles environed with an arm*
   The second ———— Felix Arabia.   *of the* Scythian *Sea, which goeth in at* Mafpi.
   The third ——————— Metagonitiden ——— It ftandeth very Southerly.

29 The firft ——————— Affyria.
   The second ——————— Africa.
   The third ——————— Bactriani.

30 The firft ——————— Afran.   Here appear people with one eye in
   The second ——————— Phrygia.   their head, feeming to be in their breaft,
   The third ———————— Creta.   toward the Equinoctial.
   The fourth ——————— Mauritania.

     Δ. I remember of people called *Arimafpi.*

Nal. ...... *This dayes Leffon is as much worth, as all between this and* Mauritania.
Note. ...... *Here are* 15, *which were never known in thefe times.*
...... *The reft are.*

Δ. I hear nothing of P·lonia, *Mofchovia,* Dania, Hibernia, Iflandia, and fo of many o-
ther which I could name ; what is to be thought of thofe ? in refpect of the diftribution of
the whole face of the Earth ?

..... Polonia *and* Mofchovia, *are of* Saromatia ; Denmark, Ireland, Frizeland, Ifeland,
Δ. Are under *are of* Britain : *And fo it is of the reft.*
the Regiment
that *itania*   Δ. I befeech you to what part, is *Atlantas* and the annexed places, under the King of
chiefly denot- Spain called the *Weft-Indies ?*
eth, &c.   Nal. *When thefe* 30 *appear, they can each tell what they own.*   *Prepare for to morrows Action.*
Δ. Moft gladly ———

E. K. If you prove your felf true, you fhall win me to God.

Nal. ...... *You may be anfwered with the firft words I fpoke to day.*
    Δ. Deo, Opt. Max. fit omnis honor, laus & Gloria nunc & femper. *Amen.*

Thurfday Maii. 24.

Δ. Becaufe E. K. came not, (according as it was bidden yefterday) to follow the Action : I went to his Study door, and knocked for him : And I requefted him to come ; and
he refufed fo to do, and gave me a fhort and refolute anfwer, That he would never more
* Thofe words have to do with thefe Actions. I asked him the reafon why : He would give none : But
he fpake after earneftly denied to proceed. I told him that his words * yefternight (that he could not
the Action this day deale) did very much grieve me, &c. whereof he made fmall account. So I went
ended more into my Study again, and committed the Caufe to God.
than an hour   After half an hour and leffe, he came fpeedily out of his Study, and brought in his hand
in the Cham- one Volume of *Cornelius Agrippa* his works , and in one Chapter of that Book he read the
ber before my names of Countries and Provinces collected out of *Ptolomeus* (as the Author there noteth)
Study of pra- Whereupon he inferred, that our fpiritual Inftructors *were Cofeners to give us a defcription of*
ctice. the World, taken out of other Books : and therefore he would have no more to do with them.
I replied, and faid, I am very glad that you have a Book of your own, wherein thefe Geographical names are expreffed, fuch as (for the moft part) our Inftructors had delivered unto

us : and that, according to the Tenor and form of my request to him, so to have them expressed : for our more perfect information, by those known names; to understand *those 91* unknown and unheard of names, of seven letters every one : whereby they (our Instructors I mean) are very greatly to be thanked, and to be deemed (in all reasonable mens judgements) most friendly, and far from cosenage, or abusing of us : And farther I said, that I my self, had here set down on a paper, all the 91 names together orderly, as we received them, and that I had here brought the description * Geographical of the whole earthly Globe: and also *Pomponius Mela* set forth in English with the Chartes thereunto belonging, fairly described by hand : To the intent he might see the verity of their words yesterday delivered unto us : for the performance of my request made to them, on Tuesday last in this form of words, as the Book hath it recorded thus ;

Δ. As you gave us a taste, or warning of *Italia* and *Britania*, so, if it be thought good to you, we are desirous to understand of *the rest, the Application to such names as we understand.*

Whereby you may perceive (said I to E. K.) how your reason is marvellously confounded by your wilful phantasie : For so much as, wherein you would find fault, in our spiritual Instructors doings, Therein they have done that which I requested them : as appeareth ; and that to the intent, of known Countries we might understand which Angels had the government : for such purposes, as occasion might offer or require our practices to be tryed in.

This (*quoth I*) is to grosse your error, and to wilful your wrangling : But I do in narrower points peruse and consider their words and doings ; In which though sometimes my writings (after your declaration) hath been amended by them, yet the occasion of miswriting for the most part, hath been either in your misreporting what you saw and heard, or in my wrong hearing, or writing : and sometime by the spiritual present correcting of my writing, and sometime longer after, *&c.*

But for all this, E. K. remained of his wilful intent; and so departed to his Study again : And I committed God his Cause, into his own hands, care and ordering, as may be best for his honour and glory. So be it.

91. Names of the world or earthly habitation.
* Gerardus Universal Chart of the World.

Monday, *Maii* 28. *hora* 10½ *ante meridiem.*

Δ. I said the Lords Prayer.

E. K. Here appeareth nothing but the clear Stone.

Now there appeareth a white circle , more than usual : it is as it were a white smoak, very large comprehending all the heavens in manner, having as it were, the breadth of my finger in the circumference or border of it.

Δ. After this, an hour and an half, after divers our discourses of my Wife her speeches and usage toward E. K. *&c.*

E. K. Here appeareth one like him in the green that appeared last day : the Etymologie of whose name is *Dic illis*, and his name *Mapsama.*

Δ. In the name of Jesus, and for the honour of Jesus, we beseech you to deliver the verity of your message.

Mapsf. ...... *He liveth, and he saith, Arise up, and say unto them. How many times have I opened my armes to embrace you ? How oft have I wept over you, as a father ? But you are still, stiff-necked and disobedient children. Lo, I cease yet, and will not impute this wickednesse unto you.* Forte, Cease not or Ceaset and that is to be understood

[Δ. O blessed God, blessed God, blessed God of mercies.]

Mapsf. ...... *Because my promises may be : notwithstanding, that the sons of men, may not say, such a day cometh in the Bridegroom ; nor at such a time shall the Lilly spring : Let the day, that I will visit you in, be unknown unto you.* From punishing you.

E. K. I thought you would say so.

A perverse speech.

Map. ...... *But this you shall do　　　　utter part.*

...... *Bind up together, 48 leaves ; whose skin shall bear Silver : Whose Perimeter shall be 30 inches, in length 8, in breadth 7.* Perimeter.
¶ [30] ¶
7)

Δ. Do you require it to be parchment, or paper ?

Map. ...... *I have said.*

Δ. What shall I, then, do, after I have caused 48 leaves to be bound ?

Map. ...... *This done, rise up, and perform your Journey, as you are commanded.*

Δ. I have

Our going to the Emperours Court.

Δ. I have heard onely of the binding of the book : Mean you after the binding of the book that this journey shall be entred into?

Map. ..... I ————————————————————————

Δ. What shall I do with the book, after I have bound it?

Δ. Pervetle.

E. K. I will answer for him....burn it.

Invitatio Bonorum.

Map...... *The fourteenth day of your rest, even this Table-Cloath, and none other shall be spread for a Banket.*

> E. K. He pointeth to this Diaper Table-Cloath.

The writing of the book by Divine means. The Emperour.

Whereunto, you shall invite the Angels of the Lord : In the middest of the Table lay down the book and go forth ; make also the doors after you. That the heavens may justifie your faith , and you may be comforted. For, man is not worthy to write that shall be written : neither shall there be found many worthy to open that book.

Four moneths. Vide lib. 19. Septemb. 1. 184. Sudden alteration in this year.

I have entered already into the Emperours heart.

But it may be he will become wilfull. If he do, a hundred and twelve dayes remain, and he is not.

For, I have cut down the banks, the waters may rush out, that there may be a sudden alteration *In this, now, time.*

* *Return warned, as before was bidden, May 21. But he meant not to warn us of any returning as appeareth by the nineteenth book : Therefore with humility that doubt must be moved. Be ready alwayes.*

* *When I warn you, you shall return : But you please me much, if you believe. If time govern not my providence, (repine not) but let my providence govern time : Look neither for the Sun nor Moon, but be ready alwayes.*

For, whom I finde apt, shall be made apter : And to him that is barren, shall there be little added.

Three dayes before our journey to the Emperour. * *Vide Junii 4 in fine.* * *A L.*

Three dayes before you take your voyage, shall you meet me here.

For, I have something to say unto you, which shall be hidden * *till then.*

Let Lasky stretch out his lims : For I will * *love him, and let him gape wide : And take much for the Vessel is wide, that he shall drink of.*

Let him not despair : for he that governeth the windes, and dwelleth not in the hands of man, be it is that shall comfort him.

God { Father. Son. Holy Ghost.

Glory be to God the Father. Glory be to God the Son. Glory be to God the holy Ghost. All the Heavens rise up, and glorifie God.

Δ. Amen.

Map......Hallelujah.

Δ. I beseech you, as concerning the rest of the Calls, or invitations : we are most ready to receive them now.

The Calls, or Invitations.

Map...... *Pray, that those three dayes to come, may satisfie those three dayes that are past.*

Δ. I beseech you to let me understand, whether I shall take with me onely this Table-Cloath.

Δ. Thursday, Friday, Saturday last, were lost by E. K. his disquietnesse, God be mercifull unto us.

Map...... *With the shew-stone that is made for your self.*

A voyce..... *Cause the book to be made all ready.*

Δ. I understand that I shall cause the leaves to be silver'd, and so prepared.

Δ. *Misericordias Domini in eternum cantabo : Ejus nomen sit benedictum ex hoc nunc & in sempiterna seculorum secula : Ille solus est Deus Noster, Omnipotens, eternus & vivus : Illi soli omnis honor, laus & Gloria. Amen.*

Saturday, Cracoviæ. 2 Mane circa 7. Post preces aliquot & petitiones meas : statim ferè apparuit.

> E. K. I see him, that we call *Gabriel*, sitting in his Chair alone.

GOD.

Gabr...... God is a spirit essential and in himself : Essential and working by himself : Essential in all works and dignifying them by himself : So that the beginning and ending of all things, that are already, or are in him already, and to come, is placed in the fountain, and well-spring of all life, comfort, and encrease : Whereby we see, that the heavens and the mighty powers therein from the highest unto the lowest, things that shall have an end, and the earth with all that she bringeth forth ; yea, the lower parts (though after another manner, and by another course) do all hang, and are established, in and upon the unspeakable power in the providence of him. How, therefore can the Heavens run awry ?   Or the earth, (for the Elect sake,) want a comforter ?   Or the lower places look for comfort ?   If it be so (therefore) that the heavens cannot erre : Or if the power of God be so mighty, and so full of prevailing ; If in the house of light there be no darkness, or from the Heavens can descend no wickedness. (And why ? because they are dignified in the power of God.)

The Devil.

What is he that should live, and distrust the Lord ? But herein, The power and quality of the

Devil

Devil is not onely manifest, but also still contendeth *against the power and will of God : stirring* Fasting, mis-
up, and provoking man to fast at full Bankets, to study for good and evil.   To rise up against the liked of the
Lord, and against his power.   And to vex the Lord himself : which cannot be vexed at the wicked- Devil.
nesse of the Devil.   Even for this cause, saith the Lord unto you: How long will you wallow in wic-
kednesse ? How long will you be drunken with folly ? How long will you rise up against the Δ. *Fortitudi-
Lord and against me ? * Saying, And if this be the power of God, Are these the Messagers of* nem prævalef-
the highest ? Is this the will of God? Or can it be, that be hath care of the earth ? But these are the centem : Hæc
blasphemies of your mouth. But I see, I must differre my self for a time, and must raise up a Table gia nominis
where there shall eat more worthy.   Consider what it is to deal with Devils : Is it not to take part ejus est.
with Rebels ? Is it not to be Traitors against the annointed in his own Kingdom ? Is it not a greater Blasphemies.
sin then the sin of the Devil? For why, The Devil sinneth in himself, and therefore had his fall. A punishment
But your sin is in your selves and by the Devil, and therefore it is the greater.   But, as it is said be- longer time
fore, Where is there a moniment upon the earth that the people have raised up, in the remembrance of yet of God his
wickednesse? Many there be that say, Lo, there is Hierusalem. Lo, there was the Lord buried. most mercifull
Lo, there the floods divided themselves with all the rest; in remembrance of the Lord : But none visiting of us.
there is that say, Lo, in this place the wicked have risen up and prevailed.   Therefore to cleave Devils.
unto the Lord is good, and to follow a sensible Doctrine, which bringeth with it self the loathsomnesse the Devils
of wickednesse, and the study to do well, that the wicked may be confounded.   Alas ! let the whole Sophistry.
earth rise up, [thrusting up his hand] even this hand, can gather them all together : what therefore
can the Lord do when he frowneth? O unreasonable Creatures, and worse then beasts, more ignorant
then the beasts that grase in the Mountains: Are you not afraid of the power of God, when it becometh
a skourge? For, doubt you not, to deal with those that are wicked? (you of no faith) wherefore
hath the Lord made the earth, but to be glorified in the creatures thereof? And what is he that glo-
rifieth God on earth but man? Think you [not] (therefore) that the Lord hath not care of his
people? Think you that there is a Seat upon earth, wherein he hath not bidden the might of his free Faith.
power? Doth Satan get a Soul that he is not privy of?   Believe, O you of little Faith, for it is Faith is the
the power of God, it is the Key of the whole world, which is the Key of mans conscience : If he Key of mans
lock not the door, but depart and leave it open : Wo be to that Soul, for the Prince of darknesse en- conscience.
treth, and is possessed to the eternal woe of his dwelling place.   If, therefore the earth be a Cave the Devil is
unto him that made it, (as appeareth by his Prophets, and by the Son of God.) What are you? Or the picklock.
how empty are you? When you think it is in vain, that the Lord hath appeared unto E.K. Very ve-
you.   hemently spo-
   But in you two is figured the time to come : For many shall cleave unto the Lord, even at the first ken.
call : And many shall doubt of the Lord, and not believe him for a season.   But as you two shall A figure of the
dwell in one Center, (if you (yet) do look forward, and step right) So shall the face of the whole Vide lib. 19.
earth be, for 800. one hundred and fifty years. Praga, 27. Aug.
   (*For, the fruit of Paradise shall appear, that nothing may be on earth without comfort.* Unum ovile,
For, lo, the first shall be last,) and it shall be a Kingdom without corruption. 950. years.
Now, now, hath the Serpent wallowed his fill. Vide Apocalyp.
Now, now, are all things in the pride of their wickednesse. cap. 20.
Now, now, is the Heir ready, most like his father.   But wo unto the earth through his govern- Paradise was
ment.   last to be en-
   For, his Kingdom shall have an end with misery. And these are the latter dayes.   And this is the joyed.
last Prophesie of the World. Regnum Dei
   Now, now, shall one King rise up against another: And there shall be bloud shed throughout all the mille annorum
World : fighting between the Devil his Kingdom, and the Kingdom of light. Apocalyps.
   Contentious and quarrels on the earth between man and man, father and son, wife and husband, Δ. Antichristus.
Kingdom and Kingdom ; yea, even in the very beasts of the field shall there be hatred : And into isti sunt.
them shall the spirits of Contention enter. The last Pro-
   For, now cometh the necessity of things. phesie.

E. K. He now kneeleth down.

Gab...... *As for you, thus saith the Lord.* Necessity of
I have chosen you, to enter into my barns : And have commanded you to open the Corn, that the things, vide
scattered may appear, and that which remaineth in the sheaf may stand.   And have entered into the Post.
first, and so into the seventh.   And have delivered unto you the Testimony of my spirit to come. Election.
   For, my Barn hath been long without Threshers.   And I have kept my flayles for a long time bid The twofold
in unknown places : Which flayle is the Doctrine that I deliver unto you: Which is the Instrument Doctrine.
of thrashing, wherewith you shall beat the sheafs; that the Corn which is scattered, and the rest The flayle for
may be all one. God his Barn.
   (*But a word in the mean season.*)
If I be Master of the Barn, owner of the Corn, and deliverer of my flayle: If all be mine.
(*And unto you, there is nothing : for you are hirelings, whose reward is heaven.*)
Then see, that you neither thresh, nor unbinde, untill I bid you, let it be sufficient unto you ; that
you know my house, that you know the labour I will put you to : That I favour you so much as to enter-
tain you the labourers within my Barn : For within it thresheth none without my consent.

For,

Our uniting promised. Esau & Jacob. *For, in you shall many people be blessed, and in you shall there be no division : For Esau and Jacob shall be joyned together ; and their Kingdom shall be all one : For as the Sacrifice is, so must the Priests be.*

A. L. E. K. Now he kneeleth down again. Me thinketh, I hear them say, What shall become of *Laskie* ?

E. K. And so the people say.

[*Ask me no Questions : but hear, what I have to say.*]

As those that desire to make a speedy Dinner, and to entertain their guests, go suddenly out, and gather the dryest wood in the wood-pile : Not because it is more wood than the other ; but because it is dry, and most apt for the speediness of the kitchen. So, it is with me, saith the Lord.

A. L.
A. L. The aptest in the world for some purposes of God.
It
† Isue, cap. 5. & 6. Michael ille apparet &c.
† Pride of A.L. suspected.
Deus ignis : nos autem, materia. Necessity.

For, I respect him not in that he is a man, but in respect of the manner *of his minde and inward man, which I find in respect of my purpose, aptest in the world : because he naturally hateth* the wicked. *Therefore naturally I love him, of whom I say I swear,* If he follow me (*saith the Lord*) I will be with him, as I was with my † Warrier at *Hiericho* : *And I will be mighty with* him *in this world, and a lover of him for ever. But me thinketh he will be † proud. If you find me weak : know you, that I am not weak, of my self ; but your own weakness may be .your* confusion. *For I am a fire, and take hold of such matter as I find apt.*

E. K. He kneeleth again.

1 *I have now told you (my Brethren) of, and of the manner of the power of God.*
2. *Of the nature of* Hell, *and of her wickednesse.*
3. *Of the course of the World, and of the necessity of things.*
4. *Of your election, and of the end thereof.*
5. *Of* Laskie, *and why he is elected.*

Note.
Apt and meet matter.
Humility.
Perseverance.
A great Caveat.

6. *Now I am lastly to perswade you,* by the power of God, *that you make your selves apt and meet matter : and that you may stand before the Lord as acceptable : which you shall perform if you* intend your former Lessons. *The ground whereof is Humility and Perseverance, which because they have been often spoken of, I passe with referring you to the consideration thereof.*

Giving you one warning, That this Action shall never come to passe , until there be no remembrance of wickednesse, or hell, left amongst you : and yet, after, for a time, .you must have patience. For, your offices are above a Kingdom. Hinder not the Lord in his expeditions.

We must go to the Emperour.
The place for which my Angel of Creation is sealed.
△. I understand as yet, either the Emperours Court, or Praige, &c.

Remember *he hath commanded you to go to the Emperour. Happy is he, that cometh when* he is bid Go. *And foolish is he, that goeth not, when he is bidden.*]

There, use thy self : *for it shall be a key of thy habitation : And for that place, is the* Angel *of thy Creation sealed. Love together : Be humble and continue to the end.*

△. Deo nostro immortali, invisibili, omnipotenti, & Patri misericordiarum, ejusque filio Redemptori nostro, & Deo Spiritui Sancto, sit omnis laus, gloria & gratiarum actio. *Amen.*

Monday, † *Cracovia* † 4. *Junii, Mane, hora* 8.

Orationem dominicam genibus flexis recitavi, variasque juxta propositam materiam ejaculationes habui, variasque inter nos collationes, considerationesque ultimorum verborum ipsius Gabrielis, &c. After almost an hour after our sitting to the Action, he appeared.

E. K. *Gabriel* is here again in his Chair, and his dart upright in his hand, his dart is like a flame or staff of fire.

△. Blessed be God.   △. After his appearing, he stayed almost a quarter of an hour before he began.

Gab. ...... *As God in his essential being, is a Spirit, without demonstration, so are his profound providences, works, and determinations, unable to be measured.*

[E. K. He maketh cursie : but nothing appeareth in the Stone.]

Gabr. ...... *Hereby may you find, that the love of God towards you (O wretches and sinners) is more than a love : and more than can be measured, which was the cause, that with his own finger, (delighting in the sons of* Jacob, *) he sealed this saying ; yea with his own finger , this shew and sign of his excellent, and more than, love toward his people.*

God his jealousie.
Exod. 20. 5.
Deut. 5. 9.

I am a jealous God ; which is as much to say, Lo, I am your friend : *nay, rather your father, and more than that, your God : which delighteth in you, rejoyceth in you, and loveth you with that* affection [Jealousie] *which is more than love : which is as much to say, as my love is such toward you,* as I am to my self. *But, O ye stiff-necked Jews, O ye Strumpets, you despised the love of God, you committed adultery, and ran into the Temples of Idols : which was the cause, that the same mouth, that praised you before,*

[E. K. He maketh cursie often.]

Said

.... *Said also of you ; It repenteth me that I made this people. Let me raze them out, and make* | **To** *Moses*
a people of * *thee. This Idolatry was the cause, from time to time, that you became Captives,* | Exod. 32. **B**
and of Inheritours, Runnagates, and without a Master. Unto you also, thus saith the Lord (unto | Deut. 9. **C**
you my Brethren, I say that are here) More than the love of a father is, is the love of God toward | The Jews.
you : For, unto which of the Gentiles, hath the Lord shewed himself ? Where dwell they, or where | The unmea-
have they dwelled, into whose houses have the Angels of the Lord descended, saying, thus and | surable love of
thus, doth the God of Heaven and earth mean to deale with the World. | God toward us

Think you not, that this is narrowly into your selves : Un- | A. L. Δ. E. K.
cover the doings of your life, and secret Chambers : Enter into judgement with your selves. Unto | Exhortation to
thee I speak [To E. K. *] Hast thou not run astray from the Lord, and committed Idolatry ?* | pena ce and
Δ. He told E. K. *of his faults, which* E. K. *would not expresse to me, and I desired him* | amendment of
to listen to them, and to do as it appertaineth to a Christian, &c. | life.

Gab. ..... *But thus saith the Lord, I am a pure Spirit that participateth not with the de-* | God.
filed : neither can I enter in mercy into that house which is defiled. A great saying, my Bre-
thren : For hereby you are monished to make your consciences clean, to open your selves in
purenesse, to the Lord, that he may enter into you with comfort. For, so long as thou dealest with
wicked spirits, will the Lord keep back his hands : and thou keepest back the Lord. For shall | The Lord kept
it not be said hereafter ? Lo, is not this man known to have dealing with the wicked ? And (as | back.
the foolish voices of the people are) Is not this he that can constrain the wicked ? with further ar-
guments, by repetition of thy doings. Well, if thou wilt be the Minister of God ; If thou wilt go
forward in his works ; If thou wilt see the happy times that are to come, thou must abstain from
evil, and thou must sweep thy house clean : Thou mast put on thy best garments, And must become | The chief Les-
humble and meek. Let not thy life be a scandal to the will of the Lord, and to the greatnesse of | son.
his works : For the power that is within thy soul (in respect of his essential quid,) is of great force | The essential
and ability to perform those things that proceed with power : which is the cause that the wicked | Characterisa-
ones obey thee ; for they fear themselves, when they see the seal of thy Creation. | tion of E. K. his

This is therefore the Cause, that God finding thee (as he passeth by, by his Angel) fit in | soul, and so the
matter, but, my brother (God knoweth) far unfit in life. O Consider the dignity of thy Crea- | cause of his
tion ; Consider that the affection of God toward thee, is more than love. See how he beareth with | election.
thy infirmity, from time to time. O, I say, (yet) Enter into judgement with thy self : And | Aliter fortè.
consider, that thou art now at a Turning where there lieth two wayes : One shall be to thy com- | Of God his
fort, The other to thy perpetual wo. Let not good ground bring forth weeds, lest it choke her | finding thee
self. | fit in matter,

Δ. We will call unto God for his mercies, graces, and help, &c. | unfit in life.

O, consider, my brother that the appearing and works of the devil are but of necessity. That is | The necessity
to say, that he that is good, by resisting of the devil may manifest and make plain to the powers | of the Devils
and spirits of Heaven, the strength of his faith, and assurance of his Hope : and so, necessarily, by | doings.
the promise of God, inherit everlasting life, to the which he is elected. To the wicked, that be- | either with
cause of their disobedience and partaking with them, that are the Angels of darknesse, (even those, | good men
that strive against the Lord) they might worthily be damned : according to the necessity of God | or with evil
his judgement. See, therefore they appeare unto thee, either for the greatness of thy wickednesse, | men.
or else because they suspect thee to be elected. If thou, therefore think thy self elected, despise
them ; If thou therefore think to be a spirit dignified, and in glory, Then be faithful in the assu-
rance of hope, and resist the devil : that we may testifie thee, before the heavens, and before | Testification
the God of Justice. | Angelical of
| E. K. his Con-
E. K. He weepeth. | version.

Δ. E. K. *and I also could not hold our teares.*

Ah, my brother, great are the joyes of Heaven. Remember what Hell is ; for to thee the * *For-* | * *An.* 2582.
nace was open : Remember the vision thou hadst of hell, and of her powers, at Mortlake. For | *Novembris* 26.
nothing (my brother) is done without a cause. Remember thou couldst not abide it : No not to | at *Mortlake.*
see :: Think thyself accursed (therefore) if thou feel it : For, if Sodom had seen it, they
would have been converted.

E. K. He prayeth.

1. *I have now told you of the Jealousie of God, and of the cause thereof.*
2. *I have also told you that the house of God must be clean, and without spot.*

[E. K. Now there cometh a brightnesse about him.]

3. *Lastly, I have told you, of that necessity which causeth the devils to work, and appear : and*
have exhorted you to the love of God and repentance ; which were the things I onely had to
speak of.

Δ. O Lord, seeing we are uniformly desirous that the Action may proceed, and that we
crave thy mercy and graces, as well for the pardoning of our wickednesse past, as for the confirmation of us in thy service; What shall we look for touching the proceeding, being thus
stayed to our great grief?

Gabr. ..... *You have to receive the will of God (but what it is, I know not) those three dayes,*
before

Vide Mart. 1 *before you begin your Journey.   And you are also, to learn, what the Angel is, and how many*
28.   2 *Subjects he hath.*
         3   Δ. Which Angel ?
Hyla. Gab. ...... *That governeth* Hyleich : *which is the matter of the 4 Elements : And which onely*
         4 *is an Element.   The Princes and Governours also of the 4 Elements, (and of their Generation,*
         5 *how they receive mixtion, and in what quantity) With their Ministers that are under them.*
         Δ. I said to E K. These *shall be part of your practice and portion.*
         6   [Gab. ...... *You are all to joyn joyntly in the Harvest of the Lord*]   *The* Angels *also of the*
         7 † 48 *angles of the heavens, and their Ministers : For they are these, that have the thunders and the*
† E *ge seven de-* *windes at Commandment.   These make up the time, and then, cometh the Harvest*
grees & a half
to every angle.
Thund.rs.   E. K. He is gone.
Windes.
The full time. Δ. Non nobis Domine, non nobis, sed nomini tuo da gloriam. Tu enim Altissimus, Omnipotens, sempiternus, vivus, & verus Deus noster es : unus & Trinus : Cui Angelicus cæle-
stisque chorus decantat perpetuò, Sanctus, Sanctus, Sanctus, Dominus Deus Zebaoth.
                                        Amen.

Friday, Cracovia, Junii 8. Mane hora 7¼.
Post preces, & ejaculationes varias & gratiarum actiones pro magna misericordia Dei,
          erga nos & propter E. K. qui jam patefecit mihi horrenda & multiplicia heresium,
NOTA.   & blasphemiarum dogmata, quibus illi hostes Jesu Christi illum imbuerant; & quòd
          jam (confessione præmissa) vellet sacrosanctum mysterium corporis & sanguinis
          Christi recipere, illisque malis Angelis renunciare, & omnes illorum fraudes dete-
          gere, &c.

Conversio E. K. *ad Deum, abdicatis* }
omnibus Diabolicis experimentis, &c. } Nihil apparuit hodie.

          Albeit the like had never happened to us, (that I remember :) but that either Cloud,
† *Unaccustom-* Vail, or some Voice was perceived by E. K. Yet this, † doing we not onely took *patiently* :
ed absence and but E. K. used many good reasons to prove, that servants ought to attend so long, as it plea-
silence.   sed their Master to have them await his coming to any place, to them.
          And that, about our own affairs we are contented to use patience for a long time, but to
await the Lord his coming or message, is a time better spent, than in any humane affairs, &c.
          He very plainly, and at large made manifest *his conversion to God* from the practices with
wicked spirits : Yea, that he was ready to burn whatsoever he had of their trash and experiments.   That he would write in a book the manifold horrible Doctrine of theirs, whereby
they would have perswaded him
          ..... *That Jesu was not God.*
          ..... *That no prayer ought to be made to Jesu.*
          ..... *That there is no sin.*
          ..... *That mans soul doth go from one body, to another childes quickening or animation.*
          ..... *That as many men and women us are now, have alwayes been : That is, so many humane*
              bodies, and humane souls, neither more nor lesse, as are now, have alwayes been.
          ..... *That the generation of mankind from Adam and Eve, is not an History, but a writing*
              which hath an other sense.
          ..... *No Holy Ghost they acknowledged.*
          ..... *They would not suffer him to pray to Jesus Christ; but would rebuke him, saying, that he*
              robbed God of his honour, &c.

          And so, of very many other most blasphemious Articles and Points of Doctrine, whereof
more shall be spoken in another place.
          This forbearings of our Instructors presence, I did expound or conjecture to be done great-
ly for the honour of God, many wayes, if the same were recorded somewhat near to the very
manner of the thing as it was : for so, should appear to the posterity, how truely it had been
said before, that he should be converted to God : How truely God did prepare E. K. his
The matter   soul to be a vessel cleansed, and so made apt for his visiting of him, in mercy and comfort,
made apt.   whereby the life of E. K. (now being amended, and his dealing with the wicked clean left
off) should not be a scandal to the will of the Lord, and to the greatness of his works : as
was noted unto us in the last Action.
          Also I said, that not onely his Conversion recorded should be a more evident argument
Δ. We left off of his so oft repeated Election : But his *patient attending* this present day, ([Δ] two hours and
hora 11.   a half, and taking all things in such sort as became an humble and patient servant,) will be a
more sure and evident argument that it was *no light pang,* such as he hath made outward shew
                                                                                             of

of diverſe times before, but a very harty and ſincere converſion, ſuch as without all doubt, will be found very acceptable to the higheſt.

Moreover, he declared that about nine, or ten dayes paſt, he did intend to have gotten away *ſecretly by the help ſpiritual* of thoſe, with whom he had ſo long dealt: And therefore that *till now, he dealt hypocritically.*

But, whereas they ſo fore were ever accuſtomed to threaten him Beggery, (a thing which he moſt hated and feared.)

That now he careth not if he ſhould have want; yea, he took it neither to be ſhame, or ſin to beg: and that he now made more account of God his favour, and life eternal, then he doth of all tranſitory wealth and riches, and to be entangled within the danger of theſe wicked ſpirits their ſnares, with all.

L-- Alſo he now perceived his great errour wherein he was of late, when he would for an aſſured temporal maintenance have forſaken the dealing with the wicked, and ſo more willingly would have followed theſe actions without repining: Saying now, that he is no perfect Chriſtian, who for money muſt be hired to forſake the Devil and his works, &c.

And as for the iſſue of theſe actions *he would never either doubt, or miſlike, howſoever they fell out;* aſſuring himſelf: That God would do all things beſt, and for his honour, &c. Many other his ſayings very glodly I omit, thinking theſe ſufficient here.

Δ. O Almighty, eternal, and moſt mercifull God, we thank, glorifie, and praiſe thee; O bleſſed, and moſt glorious Trinity, we will for ever Magnifie thy unſpeakable providence, Converſion, favour, Election, *and Converſion unto thee.*

O Bleſſed Jeſu, we will for ever extol thy loving kindneſſe, and long ſuffering toward us, and thy Triumphant proceeding againſt Satan and his Miniſters, for thy Elect ſake.

O holy Ghoſt, the director into all truth, and comforter of thy Elect, confirm, and eſtabliſh our Confirmation hearts with thy gracious, and continual zeal, and love of truth, purity of life, Charitable humility, and conſtant patience to thy well-pleaſing untill the end: That after this life (through the mercy of the father, and Merits of our Lord Jeſus Chriſt, and thy charitable embracing of us,) we may for ever enjoy the heavenly Kingdom, among the bleſſed Angels, and all the dignified company of mankind. *Amen. Amen. Amen.*

Munday, *Junii* 11. *Mane hora* 7¾. Cracoviæ.

Δ. After our prayers due, and thanks to the Almighty for, his great mercies and power ſhewed in the converſion of *E. K.* we ſtayed ſtill attending ſome ſhew, as we were accuſtomed to receive: and among divers our ſhort diſcourſes of our faith, hope, patience, conſtancy, humility, and other our duties requiſite in this action, and in the ſervice of God: *E. K.* of himſelf ſaid theſe ſentences worthy to be recorded, as the evident token of his ſound and faithfull turning, and intent to cleave unto the Lord.

1. *E. K. I acknowledge my ſins have deſerved, that this ſeven years I ſhould have no ſhew, or ſight of his good* Creatures.

2. *E. K.* If I ſhould ſit thus for ſeven years, attending the pleaſure of God, I would be contented.

3. *E. K.* I repent me nothing of that I have done, in forſaking thoſe I was wont to have to do withall, &c.

E. K. In the ſtone, nothing appeared all this while of our fitting here.

Δ. *Nihil viſible apparuit in Chryſtallo ſacrato, præter ipſius Chryſtalli viſibilem formam: ut E. K. dixit.* Δ. *Hora* 11. we left off, ſo we attended 3. hours and 3. quarters.

Δ. I will affirm nothing in this caſe, but this my conjecture may be recorded: The cauſe of the non-appearance the laſt Friday, and now this Mounday may be this:

1. That, as we loſt and refuſed three dayes aſſigned by our inſtructours, to finiſh all in; The Juſtice So now we ſhall call, and requeſt three dayes, and have nothing: as, theſe two dayes it hath of God. fall'n out: and it is poſſible, one day more we ſhall have the like non-appearance.

Or elſe.

2. According to the premiſſes; Onely, three dayes before our journey ſhall be begun, *vide ſup.* we ſhall have that delivered us, which in the three laſt dayes we ſhould have received, &c.

Y O4

Or else.

The conver-
fion of E. K.
before made
manifeſt.
3. That great Caveat before noted, (on Saturday *Junii* 2. laſt paſt) may have ſome fore-warning of *this our patience to be uſed, after our Converſion unto God* : The words then recorded are theſe :

> This Action ſhall never come to paſſe, untill there be no remembrance of wickedneſſe, or Hell left amongſt you : And yet, after, for a time you muſt have patience. For, your Offices are above a Kingdom.

To conclude ; whatſoever, with God, is known and uſed as the true cauſe, we are content-ed : Nothing doubting of the goodneſſe, and wiſdom, and power of God to perform his pro-miſes and Covenant made to, and with us, for our ſervices to be uſed to his honour and glory.

Moſt willingly, and patiently we will attend the will and pleaſure of the higheſt herein. Intending hence forward (by the help of God) not to give our ſelves over unto, nor eaſily to be inveigled, or allured of the temptations of the world, the fleſh, or Devil.

For which our diſpoſition of minde, and all other benefits received from above, we render moſt humble, harty, and entire thanks to the Almighty, moſt glorious, and bleſſed Trinity. *Amen, Amen, Amen.*

Munday, Junii 18. *Mane, hora* 8. Cracoviæ.

Δ. After the Lords prayer, and ſome other peculiar prayers and thankſ-giving, for the ex-ceeding great mercies ſhewed in *the Converting and Reforming of* E. K. & my promiſing to re-cord the Act thereof, as well as God ſhould give me grace : and alſo craving earneſtly for comfort to be given to *A. L.* being ſomewhat oppreſſed with penſiveneſſe to ſee his own ſub-jects, and ſervants to triumph againſt him in his low eſtate from high, and all for lack of money and wealth, &c.

Suddenly appeared a mighty long, and big arm and hand in the *aire, to catch at the ſhew-ſtone :* and E. K. meaning to ſave it from him, put his hand on the ſtone, and immediately the ſtone was out of the frame, we know not how, and lay by on the Cuſhion, &c.

Peſt mediam
horam ab ini-
tio.
And then ſoon after appeared *Gabriel,* in all manner as he was wont, and on the right ſide of the ſtone (that is againſt E. K. his right hand) as he was wont.

Δ. *Gloria Patri, & Filio, & Spiritui Sancto, ſicut erat in principio, & nunc, & ſemper, & in ſe-cula ſeculorum.* Amen.

Gabr. ..... The comfort and peace of the Father, Son, and holy Ghoſt be amongſt you, quicken and confirm you.

Δ. Amen.

E. K. I pray you what was that, that would have ſnatcht the *ſhew-ſtone* ?

Gab. ...... *Let his houſe come, that his iniquity may be ſeen.*

This ſeemeth
to be G-oano
Caſtle in Lit-
taw, where
the King now
is.
E. K. I ſee many houſes, and beſides them a fair Houſe, ſeparated by it ſelf, the *Houſe is of ſtone and wood, and a ſquare thing in the end of it, like a* Turret. The houſes of the Town are low wooden houſes, ſmall : There appear in that odd houſe fellows in red Coats, like *Po-land* Coats. Now I ſee a bigge man ſitting within the houſe afore the window : and the houſe is hanged with *Turkie* Carpets, and there The Arms of
Littaw. is wrought in one of the Carpets (juſt afore the door) *a man on horſ-back, with a ſword in his hand :* and the man is like the man I ſaw at *Mortlack* with a Wart on his cheek : There ſtand by him two boyes, they have red Coats on, one of them is a little fair boy : There ſtand-eth a man by with a ſword, which he delivereth to him that ſitteth, and he looketh on it, being gilt and graven on it, and layeth it down on the Δ: There
ſeemeth to be
Magical Cha-
racters. Table.

Gab. ...... *This is a ſword, wherein he putteth his truſt, but it ſhall fail him.*

E. K. Now

E. K. Now that man calleth the leſſer boy to him, and the boy thereupon runneth along a Gallery. Now that man with the Wart goeth out after, ſtrouting himſelf, and no body with him : Now he calleth that leſſer boy to him, and maketh ſigne to him, ſmiting one hand on another, and drawing it under his throat : as though he threatned the boy, unleſſe he kept ſecret. Now he cometh to a door and knocketh, and one like an Italian letteth him in. There he hath in the corner a frame of wood, and a great ſtone in the middle of it (of about 16 Inches ſquare) and there is a fire on that ſtone, on the middle of it. Now he taketh that engine, or frame with the fire between him, and that man (like an Italian) and carrieth it into another Chamber. There they have a dead mans hand. Now he taketh out of his Casket a black box of yern (as it ſhould ſeem by the blackneſſe of it) The box is about a foot long. Now he hath ſet down the box, and the ſame is open, and therein appeareth an image of wax of blackiſh colour, like ſhooemakers wax. There is one like an Angel, made of red ſtuffe, ſtanding at the head of the image, holding like a Skarf over the face of the image. The image is marvellouſly ſcratched and raſed, or very rudely made with knobs and dents in the legs of it.

Now he looketh four wayes : And ſpeaketh (the man with the Wart on his face.) *The man with the Wart inuocateth.*

The houſe aforementioned ſeemeth to ſtand *without the ſtone*, and *beyond the ſtone.* *Note, becauſe no wicked power an enter within this ſtone.*

Now they poure bloud out of a Baſon upon the fire, and lay the hand upon it : and it frieth in the fire.

Now he, and the *Italian-like* man, have *put on* Apparel, black, like Gowns : each of them, and the engine ſeemeth now to be ſet in a Chimney. *Cloſe without any ſlit, but where their arms are put out.*

Gab. .... *Be it, as it was.*

E. K. There be ſix ſmokes, like ſix men ſtanding about them : and they go like ſmokes out at a window, and there ſtandeth one like a Gyant man, and he taketh them, and *windeth them up* as they come out at the window. Now all that ſhew is vaniſhed away. *Δ. Fumi quaſi, ſunt ſpiritus qui venerunt, vocati ante.*

Gab. ...... *This is the cauſe that* Lasky *is poor. This is the ſeventh image that he hath ſcraped ſo.*

Δ. As it is the ſeventh, ſo (I truſt) it is the laſt. *Δ. Ergo, An. 1581. 6. Februarii incepterunt die Lunæ.*

Gab. .... *This is three years four moneths, and* ten dayes, *ſince they began ; ſo long hath the Angel of the Lord been ready, for thy ſafe-guard,* (O Lasky) *ſtanding at the window : and ready to binde up miſchief prepared againſt thee.* *The Angel ſtanding at the window, winding up the 6. ſmokes.*

This miſchief ſhall light upon his own head.

But if thou remain my ſervant, and do the works that are righteous, I will put Solomon *behinde thee, and his riches under thy feet.*

Be therefore comforted in me : for the breath thou breatheſt is mine, and the body that thou dwelleſt in, is the work of my hands.

The earth from whence thou cameſt is mine alſo.

It is I, therefore, that caſt down, and none but I, that raiſe up again.

E. K. All the ſtone is become full of a ſmoke.

Gab. ...... *Art thou ſure that the Sun ſhineth ? [pointing to* Δ.]

Δ. I am as much as my eye may judge. *A. L.*

Gab. ..... *So ſure it is, that he ſhall reign : and be the King of* Poland.

Δ. Always I underſtand a condition, if he do, &c.

Δ. The will of God be done, to his honour, and to the comfort of his Elect.

Y 2 *Gab.* .... *Make*

Gab. ...... *Make haste for your journey.*

Δ. O Lord, the man is ready (in manner) but hability wanteth : and to ask thy help herein, we dare not, but as thy will is, so be it.

Gab. ...... *To talk with God for money is a folly, to talk with God for mercy, is great wisdom.*

Δ. Lord, this mighty arm and hand, which here appeared, and would have snatched at the stone, what was it, and who sent it ?

Gab. ...... *It is a wicked power, which the Kings Enchanters have sent amongst you, but be hath his reward for returning.*

Δ. What was his intent, I beseech you? and I marvel that his Enchanters were able to detect any of our doings to the King.

Gab. ..... *The King knoweth not your doings.*

Δ. I beseech you, as concerning the 48 leaves, being commanded to be bound, and to be silvered ; what, if I caused seven white leaves to be bound before, and seven behinde , for the more aptnesse for the binding?

Note.   Gab. ...... *Use thine own judgement.* God will appear no more unto you, *untill you take your journey.*
                                        Δ. We believe, The Lord will perform
                                                    his promises,

Gab. ...... *According to your faith be it unto you.*

The white   **E. K.** Now he hath pulled a white Curtain about the stone, and the
Curtain.   stone is dark.

Δ. *Semper laudetur qui Trinus & unus est, Omnipotens & sempiternus.* Amen.

Wednesday, Junii 20. *à Meridie.* 1584.   *Cracovia.*

Δ. It is first to be noted, that this morning (early) to E. K. lying in his bed , and awake, appeared a Vision, in manner as followeth : One standing by his beds head, who patted him on the head gently , to make him the more vigilant. He seemed to be cloathed with feathers, strangely wreathed about him all over, &c.

There appeared to him [E. K.] four very fair Castles, standing in the four parts of the world : out of which he heard the sound of a Trumpet. Then seemed out of every Castle a cloath to be thrown on the ground, of more then the breadth of a Table-cloath.

Out of that in the East, the cloath seemed to be red, which was cast.

Out of that in the South, the cloath seemed white.

Out of that in the West, the cloath seemed green, with great knops on it.

Out of that in the North, spread, or thrown out from the gate under foot, the cloath seemed to be very black.

Out of every Gate then issued one Trumpeter , whose Trumpets were of strange form, wreathed, and growing bigger and bigger toward the end.

After the Trumpeter followed three Ensign bearers.

After them six ancient men, with white beards and staves in their hands.

Then followed a comely man, with very much Apparel on his back, his Robe having a long train.

After him came five men, carrying up of his train.

Then followed one great Crosse, and about that four lesser Crosses.

These Crosses   These Crosses had on them, each of them ten, like men, their faces distinctly appearing on
seemed not to   the four parts of the Crosse, all over.
be on the
ground , but in   After the Crosses followed 16 white Creatures.
the aire in a
white Cloud.   And after them, an infinite number seemed to issue, and to spread themselves orderly in a
The great   compasse , almost before the four foresaid Castles.
Crosse seemed
to be of a   Upon which Vision declared unto me, I straight way set down a Note of it ; trusting in God
Cloud , like   that it did signifie good.
the Rain-bow.
    After noon, as E. K. sat by me, he felt on his head some strange moving : whereby he deemed that some spiritual Creature did visit him ; and as we were continuing together , and I had red to E. K. some rare matter out of *Ignatius* Epistles, *Policarpus,* and *Martialis* ; some of the Sacrament, and some of the Crosse, a voyce answered, and said, *That it is true, that the sign of the Crosse is of great force and vertue.*

After this, the spiritual Creature seemed to E. K. to be very heavy on his right shoulder, as he sat by me in my study : And as E. K. considered the numbers of such as he had numbred to passe out of the four Gates, (it is to wit, 1.3.6.1.5.) The spiritual Creature said , the number 16. is a perfect number, consisting of 1.3.6.1. and 5. He said further more, God the father is a standing Pillar.

Δ. Upon which word I asked him, if I should write such matter as he was to speak. And he answered to E. K. at his right ear.

...... *If thou wilt.*   Δ. His voyce was much like unto a mans voyce, not base,
                                            nor hollow.

                                                        ......, Divi-

....., *Divided with a straight line, is one and two.*

Δ. What is to be divided with a straight line?

...., *The Pillar.*

Δ. In the name of Jesus, who art thou?

....., *The servant of God.*

Δ. Art thou sent from God, with good tydings or message?

...... *What I am he knoweth, of whom I bear witnesse.*

Δ. What is your name, either as you are notified among the blessed Angels, or called by of any mortal man? If you be of Verity, and so of Charity, you .cannot mislike my speeches.

E. K. He sayeth nothing.

Δ. Belike he is not sent unto us by God: for if he were, he would do his message.

...... *I am* A V E.

Δ. This *A V E* is one *ex filiis filiorum*, of whose order *Rocle* is, *vide sup. lib. 2. & 4.*

Δ. If you be *A V E*, In the name of Jesus, say, that all wicked Angels are justly condemned: and, that, by the mercy of God, in the merits of Christ, mankind, elect, is to be saved.

Ave. ..... *The * visitation of God, is twofold: [1.] In respect of his secret will and purpose: and in particularity. And in that he hath [2] sealed us, with the good will of mankind to their comfort. But if I be a scandal to the word, then am I not of righteousnesse: But my righteousnesse is of the world: Therefore,* That I visit you of my self, can be no offence. *Those that are, and die in wickednesse, are dishonourable, and far from the mercies of God: For it is written,* I am a God to the living. *Therefore, do I dishonour them: such (I say) as are wicked.*

> * E.K. and I said now in our talk togethe, That God would not visit us but at the dayes of journey taking (as was last affirmed) Therefore whatsoever came before was to be doubted as an illusion. He therefore answereth first our doubt, and then to my request he maketh answer.

The mercies of God, (which is the true Manna) comforteth the comforted, and giveth hope of amendment, of such as run astray, are sinners, and may return: Therefore, I say, The mercies [of God] (which is the Fountain and sweetnesse of the love of God) is a thing most blessed, most holy, most to be desired in Heaven and Earth, and of me, the creature and servant of God, to be reverently spoken of, and required: For, it is the food wherewith we live: even the very bread wherewith we are rejoyced. Thus much, thou hast required.

Misericordia Dei.

Δ. I did so: for so, is his Justice against the impenitent, and his mercies to his Elect testified truely.

Ave. ..... *Have patience: I will return after a few moments.*

Δ. Hereupon, (in the mean space) we considered the premises: and liked very well of the scandal, or offence, avoiding: Because it was lastly (*Junii* 18) said, God will appear no more to you, until you take your journey.

And secondly he answered my request of God his Justice against the wicked Angels, and also of his mercies towards mankind.

Δ. About a quarter of an hour after, there seemed a thing to come again on E.K. his right shoulder: and (as before) he caused his shoulder to be very warm where it lighted on.

> Note this manner of a thing felt warm on the right shoulder.

Δ. Benedictus qui venit in nomine Domini. Hallelujah.

E. K. Amen

Ave ...... *The place is sanctified.*

Δ. Sanctus, Sanctus, Sanctus, est Dominus Deus Zebaoth.

Ave. ...... *I, in the favour of God, considering (and by force of his secret love toward you) how Satan purposeth; yet, and daily to overcome you, thought good, (through the mercies of God) to prevent his malice, and the effect thereof.*

Δ. O blessed, be thou, our God of mercies and all comfort.

Ave. ...... *That, (although, yet, the Harvest be not) the Vineyard might yeild some fruit: whereby God might be glorified, and you, (in despite of the world) revived and comforted, might rejoyce, and shake off the present cares to come. For if those that be unworthy, can seem to be lifted up, and to enjoy the fruits of the Earth, by the Tempter: Much more ought the true servants of God, to feel his fatherly goodnesse. Those that trust in me (saith the Lord) shall not be driven to despair; neither will I suffer the beast of the field to tread such as I delight in under feet:*

> For the glory of God.

feet. *The Earth is mine, and the glory thereof : The Heavens are mine also, and the Comforts that are in them. Why hath, (Therefore) the father of Darknesse, risen up saying.*

1. I will shut up the Earth from them ?

2. I will seal up the mindes of men : *and they shall became barren towards them ?*

3. *Their miseries shall be great, even unto death ?*

The malice of Satan provoketh his own confusion wher he thought to prevail. So God suffereth his to be proved that the afflicted might be comforted, and the afflicter confounded. Governours of the Earth.

For *this* cause : *That he might waken the Lord, when he is asleep : That those that trust in him, might be comforted.* He hath sealed the Earth from you, and I will open it unto you : *He hath said, you shall be poor : But I say, you shall become* exceeding rich.

1. *I will blesse you with a twofold blessing : That the Earth may be open unto you* (which at last, you shall contemn.

2. *And that my blessing and laws may dwell amongst you : wherein you shall rejoyce unto the end.*

Δ. O blessed, blessed, blessed, God of power, goodnesse, and wisdom.

Ave. ...... *This was the cause that I appeared to thee,* E. K. *this morning. Now therefore hearken unto me : for I will open unto you the secret knowledge of the Earth, that you may deal with her, by such as govern her, at your pleasure ; and call her to a reckoning, as a Steward doth the servants of his Lord.*

I expound the Vision.

4 Angeli Terra.

The 4 houses, are the 4 Angels of the Earth, which are the 4 Overseers, and Watch-towers, that the eternal God in his providence hath placed, against the usurping blasphemy, misuse, and stealth of the wicked and great enemy, the Devil. To the intent that being put out to the Earth, his envious will might be bridled, the determinations of God fulfilled, and his creatures kept and preserved, within the compasse and measure of order.

What Satan doth, they suffer ; And what they wink at, he wrasteth : But when he thinketh himself most assured, then feeleth he the bit.

1 King.

5 Princes.

In each of these Houses, the Chief Watchman, is a mighty Prince, a mighty Angel of the Lord : which hath under him 5 Princes (these names I must use for your instruction. The seals and authorities of these Houses, are confirmed in the beginning of the World. Unto every one of them, be 4 characters, (Tokens of the presence of the son of God : by whom all things were made in Creation.)

Ensignes, upon the Image whereof, is death : whereon the Redemption of mankind is established, and with the which he shall come to judge the Earth.

4 Angels.

These are the Characters, and natural marks of holinesse. Unto these, belong four Angels severally.

The 24 Seniors in the Apocalyps.

The 24 old men, are the 24 Seniors, that St. John remembreth.

These judge the government of the Castles, and fullfil the will of God, as it is written.

The 12 names of God.

The 12 Banners are the 12 names of God, that govern all the creatures upon the Earth, visible and invisible, comprehending 3, 4, and 5.

The Angels of the thirty Aires supra.

Out of these Crosses, come the Angels of all the Aires : which presently give obedience to the will of men, when they see them.

Hereby may you subvert whole Countries without Armies : which you must, and shall do, for the glory of God.

The use in practice.

By these you shall get the favour of all the Princes, whom you take pity of, or wish well unto.

Hereby shall you know the secret Treasures of the waters, and unknown Caves of the Earth.

And it shall be a Doctrine, for you onely, the instrument of the World.

The higher instructions.

For, the rest of your Instructions , are touching the Heavens, and the time to come : *of the which, this is the last and extream knowledge.*

This will I deliver unto you, (because I have yeilded you before the Lord.)

On Monday next 25 Junii.

Upon Monday next, I will appear unto you : and *shall be a Lesson of a few dayes.*

E. K. The will of God be done.

Δ. Amen.

Ave. ...... *In the mean season, desire you of God, such things, as are necessary for you.*

A blessing.

He that filleth all things, and from whom all things live, and in, and through whom, they are sanctified, blesse you, and confirm you in peace.

Δ. Amen.

Δ. I beseech you, to Notifie this mornings Vision, by words : as all other holy Prophets have recorded theirs.

Ave. ...... A Vi-

Ave. ......   A Vision.

The sign of the love of God toward his faithful.   *Four sumptuous and belligerant Castles,*
out of the which sounded Trumpets thrice.
The sign of Majesty, the Cloth of passage, was cast forth.
In the East, the cloth red; after the new smitten blood.   Red.
In the South, the cloth white, Lilly-colour.   White.
In the West a cloth, the skins of many Dragons, green: garlick-bladed.   Green.
In the North, the cloth, Hair-coloured, Bilbery juyce.   The Trumpets sound once.   The   Black.
Gates open.   The four Castles are moved.   There issueth 4 Trumpeters, whose Trumpets are a
Pyramis, six cones, wreathed.   There followeth out of every Castle 3, holding up their Banners
displayed, with ensigne, the names of God.   There follow Seniors six, alike from the 4 Gates :
After them cometh from every part a King : whose Princes are five, gardant, and holding up his
train.   Next issueth the Crosse of 4 Angles, of the Majesty of Creation in God attended upon
every one, with 4 : a white Cloud, 4 Crosses, bearing the witnesses of the Covenant of God, with the
* *Prince gone out before : which were confirmed, every one, with ten Angels, visible in countenance :* * King.
After every Crosse, attendeth 16 Angels, dispositors of the will of those, that govern the Castles. 40. Angels, on
They proceed.   And, in, and about the middle of the Court, the Ensigns keep their standings, op- the 4 Crosses,
posite to the middle of the Gate : The rest pause.   The 24 Senators meet : They seem to attending on
consult.   the principal †
                                                                                   16 Angels.

I, AVE, STOOD BY THE SEER :

It vanisheth.
So I leave you.
Δ. Omnium bonorum largitori, Omnipotenti Deo, sit æterna laus, gratiarum actio, honor
omnis, & Jubilatio.   *Amen.*

Junii, 22, 23.   Note.
On Friday, and especially Saturday, E. K. had great Temptations not to credit this
Action, and was said unto by a voice, how our Instructors would use cavillation of our dis-
ordered life, to forsake us, and not to perform, according to our expectation of the former
promises to be performed by them.
   A voice said, likewise, to him, that A. L. should not go to the Emperours Court, for lack
of money : for he should get none here.   Likewise, it willed him to go up into his Study
and he would shew him all the effect of our Instructions received.   E. K. complained to me
how he was thus greivously molested by such means, and almost brought in despair. But I comforted him as well as I could (my self being inwardly, most sorrowful) and made my moane
to God by prayer when I was alone: for him, and our Cause.   Moreover he could not be
perswaded by me that good Angels would undertake to help us to any relief by money or treasure : affirming that it appertained to the wicked ones: seeing they were the Lords of this
World ; and the kingdom of God was not of this World, &c. .... Said, that the wicked were
in the world, and of the world : but the Elect were in the world, *but not of the World.*
   Si de Mundo essetis, Mundus quod suum est diligeret : quia vero de mundo non estis sed ego elegi Joan.cap.15. c
vos de mundo, propterea odit vos mundus.
   Ergo dedi eis sermonem tuum, & mundus eos odio habuit, quia non sunt de mundo, sicut & ego Joan.cap.17. c
non sum de mundo. Non rogo ut tollas eos de mundo, sed ut serves eos à malo. De mundo non sunt :
sicut & ego non sum de mundo, &c.
   To be of the world, was to be in love with the trade of the vanities of this world, and to
follow them : And that money and riches were things indifferent : good, if they were well
used ; and evil, if they were evilly used : And that, *Bonis omnia cooperabantur ad bonum ;*
Therefore the godly (as the Patriarchs and many now adayes) might have money ; but to
use, not abuse it : and that such is our case and necessary request to God, &c.

Sunday, *Cracovie, Junii* 24. *à Meridie horam circiter tertiam.*
   Δ. Note, while at my lodging (by Saint *Stephens*) I was writing the Note, (on the page
going next before) of the Tentations of Friday and Saterday : E. K. was at my Lord A. L.
his lodging (at the Franciscan Fryars, where he lay at Physick) and at the same time , this
happened, as followeth ;
   As my Lord A. L. and E. K. sate together, conferring and consulting of our affairs, of
Gods mercies, and of sundry tentations of the spiritual enemy, and afterward, as the Lord
A. L. was reading *Rofensis psalm. de Fiducia in Deum,* suddenly, upon E. K. his right shoulder,
                                                                                     did

did a heavy thing seem to sit, or rest, whereof he told the Lord *A. L.* And afterward was this voyce uttered by that Creature in *Latine.*

Lasky, *veniet tempus, cum tu portabis versum sedecimum, illius Psalmi undecimi, in vexilla tuo, & vinces inimicos tuos.*

Then *A. L.* sought in *Davids* Psalter for the eleventh Psalm, and sixteenth verse thereof: and while he was so about that Psalm, The voyce said that he meant not that Psalm *of David,* but the eleventh Psalm of *Roffensis*: which Psalm the Lord *A. L.* was then in reading to E. *K.* and was about the verse; *Hic labor ac dolor,* &c. being the sixth verse.

By and by after, the voyce said in *English.*

—— Trust thou in God.

Hereupon the Lord *A. L.* did read forth that Psalm of *Roffensis,* and when he came to the sixteenth verse thereof, being

Si ambulavero in medio tribulationis, me custodies adversus inimicos tu . . .
Manum tuam extendes, & dextera tua me salvabit.

Thereupon the voyce said : Put to the first line of the next verse : And that was *Domine tu omnia, pro me perficies.*

And as he would have read further, the voyce willed him to stay at those words, and said as followeth :

—— I swear unto thee by the true and living God, that this shall come to passe.

Vide Anno
1585. Junii
22 Cracoviæ.

Then E. *K.* said unto the Creature : In the name of God, Who art thou ? And he answered in *Latin,* and said,

Ego Sum A V E, cum plura audietis.

Δ. Gloria, laus, honor & gratiarum actio perennis sit Deo Nostro, omnipotenti & Misericordi. *Amen.*

Munday 25. *Junii, Mane hora* 7.   *Cracoviæ.*

Δ. *Orationem Dominicam pronunciavimus, & aliquot alias oratiunculas ex Psalmis,* &c. After we had sit awhile together conferring of *Ave* his Vision, &c.

Ave.   A voyce said, *bring up the show-stone.*

Δ. I had set it down on the Table, behinde the Cushion with the Crosses, for I had furnished the Table with the Cloath, Candles, &c. as of late I was wont : Hereupon I set up the stone on the Cushion.

E. K. There appeareth in the stone, like a white Curtain all over the stone : After awhile it was drawn, and layed on the back-side of the stone, on a heap together.

Δ. *Ave.*   Now here standeth one in a white Garment, with a white Cerclet about his head like a white smock, I remember not that ever I saw this Creature before, his Garment is tucked up.

Δ. Ave.   *...... Who is he that is rich ?*
Δ. The Lord of all.
..... He it is that openeth the † *store-houses, not such as fly away with the winde, but such as are*
† *Four.*   *pure, and without end.*
Δ. Blessed be his name for ever.
.....To the pure in spirit, and such as he delighteth in. Amen.

Δ. *Da verbum*   *Dixit Dominus, Invoca nomen meum,* & mittam vobis verbum quo fabricavi terram, & re-
tuum in ore   *sponsum dabit de se, & testimonium dabit de se, ut in testimonio vincat malos.*
meo, & sapien-
tiam tuam in   E. K. Now is there fire come, and hath consumed this Creature all
corde meo   to pieces, and he is fall'n down to ashes.
fige.
Δ. *Quasi figu-*   Now he riseth up, and *he is brighter then he was before*
ra de terra re-   *..... So doth the glory of God comfort the just, and they rise again with a threefold*
novanda.   *glorie.*

Δ. A place was made.

E. K. Now he spreadeth the aire, or openeth it before him, and there appeareth before him a square Table.

Now

Now he taketh off the Table a black Carpet.

Now he taketh off a green Carpet.

Now he taketh off a white Carpet.

Now he taketh off a red Cloath.

And now the Table appeareth to be made of earth, as Potters Clay, very raw earth.

The Table of the Earth.

△ *He taketh off the coloured cloaths in due order, respecting the four parts of the World.*

E. K. The Table hath four feet, of which two touch the ground, and two do not : The feet seem also to be of the earth. The Table is square.

E. K. On the left corner (fartheft from E. K.) did a T appear on the Table : Out of the top of this T do four beams issue   of clear collour bright.

...... *That part [pointing to that T] of the Table of the earth of those that govern the earth : that is are governed by the seven Angels that are governed by the seven that stand before God, that are governed by the living God, which is found in the Seal of the living God, (Tan with the four) which signifie the four powers of* God *princpial in earth,*&c.

...... *Move not, for the place is holy, and become holy.*

...... *I said not so, be said it, that beareth witnesse of himself. Unto this, obey the other three Angels of the Table.*

E. K. On the other farther corner of the Table (on E. K. his right hand) is a Crosse like an Alphabet Crosse.

This Crosse, and the other T do seem to lye upon the Table, in a dim dunnish, or a sky colour. All the Table over seemeth to be scribled and rased with new lines.

...... *The earth is the last, which is* with the Angels, *but not as the Angels, and therefore it stand-eth in the Table of the seven Angels,* * *which stand before the presence of God in the last place, without a Letter, or number, but figured by a Crosse.*

...... *It is expressed in the Angle of that Table, wherein the names of the Angels are gathered, and do appear, as of* Michael *and* Gabriel.

The Earth.

* *Vide* 158.

20. *Martii.*

lib. 2.

△. I remember, there is an Alphabetary Crosse.

E. K. Now in the corner of the Table, on the right hand to E. K. appeareth another Crosse, fomewhat on this fashion †. and there appear'd these Letters and Numbers.

```
b | 6·
-- | --
4 | b
```

Vide lib. 3.

A ino 1582.

Aprilis 28.

...... *It is in that Table, which confisteth of 4. and 8.*

E. K. In the last corner of this earthly Table appeareth a little *round smoke,* as big as a pins head.

E. K. Now is all covered with a mist.

E. K. Now I hear a great voyce of thumbling and rumbling in the stone.

E. K. Now all waxeth clear again.

Now hoveringly over the Table , appear infinite fort of things like worms, fometimes going up and fometimes down ; thefe feem fomewhat brightish.

Over thefe higher in the aire, appear an infinite fort of fmall, little, blackish things, bigger then Motes in the Sun, and they go up and down, and fometime come among thofe *worm-like* Creatures.

Z

...... *The*

Enoch.

...... *The Lord appeared unto Enoch, and was mercifull unto him, opened his eyes, that he might see and judge the earth, which was unknown unto his Parents, by reason of their fall: for the Lord said, Let us shew unto Enoch, the use of the earth: And lo, Enoch was wise, and full of the spirit of wisdom.*

And he sayed unto the Lord, Let there be remembrance of thy mercy, and let those that love thee taste of this after me: O let not thy mercy be forgotten. And the Lord was pleased.

50. Dayes.

And after 50. *dayes* Enoch *had written: and this was the Title of his books, let those that fear God, and are worthy read.*

The title of Enochs books, expounded into English.
150 Lions, or wicked spirits seducers, Counterfeiting.

But behold, the people waxed wicked, and became unrighteous, and the spirit of the Lord was far off, and gone away from them. So that those that were unworthy began to read. And the Kings of the earth said thus against the Lord, What is it that we cannot do? Or who is he, that can resist us? And the Lord was vexed, and he sent in amongst them an hundred and fifty Lions, and spirits of wickednesse, errour, and deceit: and they appeared unto them: For the Lord had put them between those that are wicked, and his good Angels: And they began to counterfeit the doings of God and his power, for they had power given them so to do, so that the memory of Enoch washed away: and the spirits of errour began to teach them Doctrines: which from time to time unto this age, and unto this day, hath spread abroad into all parts of the world, and is the skill and cunning of the wicked.

Wicked Magicians.

Hereby they speak with the Devils: not because they have power over the Devils, but because they are joyned unto them in the league and Discipline of their own Doctrine.

For behold, in the knowledge of the mystical figures, and the use of their presence is the gift of God delivered to Enoch, and by Enoch his request to the faithfull, that thereby they might have the true use of Gods creatures, & of the earth whereon they dwell: So hath the Devil delivered unto the wicked the signs, and tokens of his error and hatred towards God: whereby they in using them, might consent with their fall: and so become partakers with them of their reward, which is eternal damnation.

Devils Characters.

These they call Characters *:   a lamentable thing. For by these, many Souls have perished.*

The mercy of God to Dee.
To △.

Now hath it pleased God *to deliver this Doctrine again out of darknesse: and to fulfill his promise with thee, for the books of* Enoch *: To whom he sayeth as he said unto* Enoch*.*

Let those that are worthy understand this, by thee, that it may be one witnesse of my promise toward thee.

The wicked power expelled out of the earth.

Come therefore, O thou Cloud, and wretched darknesse, Come forth I say, out of this Table: for the Lord again hath opened the earth: and she shall become known to the worthy.

E. K. Now cometh out of the Table a dark smoke, and there remaineth on the Table a goldish slime: and the things which hovered in the aire do now come, and light down on that slime, and so mount up again.

He said. ...... *Non omnibus sed bonis.*

E. K. He taketh the smoke and tieth it

...... *I tie her not up from all men, but* from *the good.*

Now cometh a dark Cloud over all again.

△. *A pause.*

E. K. Now it is bright again.

He said. ...... *Fiant omnia facillima.*

...... *Number.*

E. K. I

E. K. I see lines and scribblements (as before) going athwart the lines.

E. K. I count thirteen lines downward.

...... *Stay there.*

E. K. I count twelve this way overthwart.

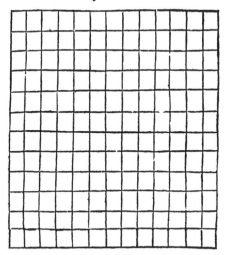

E. K. In the just middle of every square are little pricks. The Table seemeth to be eighth yards square.

E. K. Now come upon these squares like Characters. They be the *true Images of God his spiritual Creatures.* _{NOTE.} Characters.

...... *Write what thou seest.*

E. K. I cannot.

Δ. Endeavour to do your best, for he that biddeth you do, will also give you power to do.

E. K. Did his best, at length fire flashed in his face, and shortly after he said, I perceive they be easie to make, so that I tell the squares, by which the lines do passe, and draw from middle prick to middle prick.

Δ. At length E. K. finished the Table : he said that these seemed to be yellowish Gold,

A wicked power tempting E. K.

E. K. You heard one here say, *I write my own damnation.*

...... *He might have said, you write his damnation. Pray, and write as many more lines.*

Δ. After awhile E. K. did with great ease finish the four parts of the Table.

E. K. The stone is become dark.

A voyce. .... *Cease for an hour.*

Δ. May we passe from our places as now ?

...... *I.*

Δ. After a little hour past we returned, and as we talked of the premisses, he said.

...... *L se no time.*

Δ. He said in the stone being clear again.

...... *In the name of God, be diligent, and move not for the place is holy.*

...... *Take the first square : write from the left hand toward the right, you shall write small letters and great.*

Say what you see [*to* E. K.]

ꞅ Z i l a f A u t l p a.

Δ. I finde here one square among these Characters that hath nothing in it.

...... *It must be filled.*
a r d Z a i d p a L a m.

E. K. A dim Cloud cometh before mine eyes: now it is gone.

```
c Z o n s a v o Y a u b
T o i T t X o P a c o C
S i g a s o m r b z n h
f m o n d a T d i a r i
o r o i b A h a o Z p i
```

```
C n a b r V i x g a z d
O i i i t T p a l O a i
A b a m o o o a C v c a
N a o c O T t n p r a T
O c a n m a g o t r o i
S h i a l r a p m z o x
```

E. K. Now cometh a Cloud over.

Take the second, that is the third that was written.

This p may stand backward, or forward
E. K. What is the reason of that diverse setting?
-- For beginning there it will make the name of a wicked spirit.

```
b O a Z a R o p h a R a
u N n a x o P S o n d n
a i g r a n o o m a g g
o r p m n i n g b e a l
r s O n i z i r l e m u
i z i n r C z i a M h l
m o r d i a l h C t G a
Æ O c a n c h i a s o m
A r b i z m i i l p i z
O p a n a l a m S m a L
d O l o p i n i a n b a
r x p a o c s i z i x p
a x t i r V a s t r i m
```

Δ. So is the name of the first division of the earth in the 19 aire. A voyce to this intent.

...... *That last word is* Vastrim.
Δ, I marvel of that square that lacketh this line.
...... *It must be drawn from the end, or foot to that prick, before where it cometh double from the first top, the prick is allowed but to one, and not twice to be accounted: So that, that standeth but of six pricks: Therefore it must be framed, and now it is of seven.*

E. K. All is in a Cloud.
Now all is clear again.

This is the Table that hath 4. and D on the top, by me so noted.

P backward, ... or forward.
A is arsward.

```
d o n p a T d a n V a ..
o l o a G e o o b a .. i
o P a m n o O G m d n m
a p l s T e d e c a o p
s c m i o o n A m l o x
V a r s G d L b r i a p
o i P t e a a p d o c e
p s u a c n r Z i r Z a
S i o d a o i n r z s m
d a l t T d n a d i r e
d i x o m o n s i o s p o
O o D p z i A p a n l i
r g o a n n Q A C r a r
```

E. K. Now

E. K. Now he calleth again, saying, See.

Δ. This is the Table that had
the little round smoke.
Δ. No, it was the Table before.

```
T a O A d u p t D n I m
a a b c o o r o m e b b
T o g c o n x m a l G m
n h o d D i a l e a o c
p a c A x i o V s P s yl
S a a i x a a r V r o i
m p h a r s l g a i o l
M a m g l o i n L i r x
o l a a D a g a T a p a
p a L c o i d x P a c n
n d a z N x i V a a s a
i i d P o n s d a s p i
x r i i h t a r n d i ]
```

E. K. Now all is in a whitish cloud covered.

E. K. Now all is clear.

.. ;... Make the first figure upon a clean paper, and thereto adde the simple letters : Then shall you bear more. Thou must make the squares of the first part of the Table unto every square and his letters.

Δ. I have made the squares of the first part, and set in the letters.

Thou hast in the middle line o r o i b A h a o z p à. *There are 6 lines above, and six below. That line is called* linea Spiritus Sancti : *and out of that line cometh the three names of God, from the East gate, being of 3, 4,* and *5. letters, which were the armes of the Enfignes that were spoken of before.* O1o, ibah, aozpi , *I said before, that God the Father a mighty pillar divided with a right line.*

The Father himself, without the line.

The Father and Son by addition of the line.

These two lines beginning   J A
                               i d
                               a r
                               &c.

That is the great Crosse that came out of the East gate.

Δ. With that line of the Holy Ghost ?

...... I.

Thou hast in the upper left angle in the second line a r d z a.

Thou hast that maketh the crosse downward : first i, *then the same* d, o, i, g o.

▲. Will you have six letters downward ?

...... I.

So thou hast the three other crosses in their angles.

Δ. Will you give me leave to repeat them, for fear of erring?

I L a c z a, *the down line of six letters, and* p a L a m *the crosse line.*

...... *It is so.*

Δ. Now to the other on the left side below.

```
a
i
d
o
a
i
```

the down right line.   Now the crosse line, is O i i i t.

Here those Crosses have ten faces.

Δ. One letter is reckoned twice which is in the center of the Crosse : and so should seem to be eleven.

...... *This is true knowledge.*

Δ, The laſt croſſe is thus, his down line is **s**
                      o
                      r
                      t
                      z

Δ. The Croſſe is a **L O s i**.

Δ. So have I the 4 Croſſes attendant on the principal Croſſe.

...... *Here thou mayſt ſee the cauſe, that Pilat wrote with 4 letters.*

Δ. H w doth the cauſe appear ?

...... *For above every croſſe, ſtandeth 4 letters : Not that Pilat knew it, but that it was the fore-determination of God.*

They are thus to be read.   In the upper left angle thou haſt r z l a : *pronounce,* urzla : *by*
— Δ. Another pronouncing of it
— The 4 Angels over every croſſe of the 4. attenſant croſſes.

this name the firſt Angel appeareth, z l a : *go then to the firſt* r, *and pronounce it* zlar. *That was the firſt letter of the firſt Angel, is the laſt letter of the ſecond : as of the firſt* r, *was the firſt letter of the name, as* r z l a, *that* r *is now the laſt letter of the name of the ſecond Angel, beginning at* z, *as* z l a, *and ſo back again to the* r.

Δ. So that the third beginneth at *l,* whoſe laſt letter is the firſt of the ſecond name; and is called *Larz,* and ſo of the laſt: as *a r z l,* to be pronounced *arzel.*

Δ. So that you have, of thoſe 4 letters, 4 Angels names, here thus gathered out: but how are
— The uſe. they to be uſed ?

...... *Let it be ſufficient that you know theſe names, I will teach you to uſe them.*
— 4 Angels over every croſſe.

Δ. Shall we labour by like order of every the 4 letters over the croſſes to make 4 ſuch names?

...... *They are alſo to be made.*

Δ. I do know aſſuredly that there is very much matter in this Table.
— Solomon his knowledge. Six Seniors

...... *It is true : for hitherto,* ſtretched the knowledge of *Solomon.*

...... *Now for your ſix Seniors: whoſe judgement is of God the Father, the Son, and the Holy Ghoſt. In the line* De Spiritu Sancto, *you have* Abioro *of ſix letters: The ſecond name of the ſecond Senior is of* 7. *as,* A (*the ſame, aſcending*) Aaix x *if the third, as the ſecond, in* patre & filio, H c mord A.

Again in Spiritu Sancto, baoxpi. *The fifth, in* patre & filio deſcendens *bi pot ga. The*
— How to make the Seniors of 7. letters.

ſixth, A V to Tar. *If you will make them of 7 letters (becauſe two of them, are but of ſix) that is, when the wrath of God is to be entreaſed.*

Note.

Then whereas you ſay, Abioro, *ſay* Habioro ; *and where you ſay* Haozpi, *ſay* ahahozpi. *Thus*
— The encreaſing of names with a letter.

haſt haoſpi, *before* h *is* A ; *take that unto it and it maketh* Aha ozpi. *And ſo they conſiſt all, of 7 letters.*

— b
— a
— T

Thou haſt b *the fifth, in the left part of the line,* de Spiritu Sancto : *thou haſt* a *the ſixth, (the firſt part of the line* de patre & filio deſcending.) T *the ſixth in the ſecond part deſcending.* a *The firſt in the ſecond part deſcending, or the ſecond aſcending.*

— a—
— i ———

Thou haſt a *the fifth, in* aozpi.

i *The ſixth, and* V *the ſixth, aſcending in the part deſcending of the line* de patre & filio, *the*
— A or H.
— * To make the end of this word.

ſecond and firſt part. Put the A *or the* h *that ſtand in the Center, to it : Thou haſt* Bataiva *or* Bataivh. *You muſt take but* * *one of them, either the* A *or the* h. A, comiter, *and* h *in extremis* Judiciis.

— The King his name Eaſt.

Δ. So I ſee when the contract *A,* and when the contract *H* muſt end this word : That is the mighty Prince whoſe traine was holden up in *the Eaſt.*

— To morrow.

...... *Spare me now, I will open you more ſecrets to morrow, I am ſecretly called away:* but you ſhall find me the true ſervant of God.

E. K. Now he ſpreadeth the white Curtain over all that was laid on an heap behind.

— Characters or N tes.
— * Nalvage delivered them, but by the ſame ſpirit of God.
— Note.

...... *Yet one thing ere I go. Thoſe Characters or Notes (for, ſo call them) are the parts of the whole Earth, as you may find in thoſe names* * I delivered you before ; To the intent you may work all the World over at one time.   Now, my love reſt with you.*

E. K. Now he is gone.

Δ. Amor Dei patris filii & Spiritus Sancti ſit ſuper nos. *Amen.* Semper.

Tueſday, *Junii* 26. *Manè hora* 8.
Precibus finitis, & poſt varias noſtras conſiderationes de præmiſſis, tandem apparuit *A V E.*
In nomine Patris & F, & SS ſicut erat, &c. *Amen,*

                                      E. K. He

E. K. *He* hath gathered the whole Curtain together as yesterday, and set it behind.   Now a white mist cometh over all,   Now the mist is gone.

Ave. …… *All glory and praise, be to God the Father, the Son and Holy Ghost.*

Δ. Amen.

Ave. …… *Now to the purpose : Rest, for the place is holy.   First, generally what this Table containeth.*

1. All humane knowledge.
2. Out of it springeth Physick.
3. *The knowledge of all elemental Creatures, amongst you.   How many* kindes there are, and for what use they were created.   *Those that live in the air, by themselves.   Those that live in the waters, by themselves.   Those that dwell in the earth, by themselves.   The property of the fire : which is the secret life of all things.*

> 4. *The knowledg, finding and use of Metals.*
> *The* vertues of them.
> *The congelations, and vertues of* Stones.   *They are all of one matter.*

5. *The* Conjoyning *and knitting together of Natures.   The destruction of Nature, and of things that may perish.*
6. Moving *from place to place,* [*as, into this* Country, *or that* Country *at pleasure.*]
7. *The* knowledge *of all crafts Mechanical.*
8. Transmutatio formalis, sed non essentialis.

The general of the first table.

A bodily and a true motion.

E. K. Now a white mist covereth him.

Δ. ——————— Pause for a ¼ of ———

E. K. Now he appeareth again

…… *Look out* Lexarph, *with the two other that follow him,   among the names   of the Earth the three last.*

Δ. The ninth Chapter may be added, and is of the secrets of men knowing; whereof there is a peculiar Table.

Lexarph, Comanan, Tabitom.

Look out the name Paraoan.   *Write out* Paraoan *in a void paper.*

Δ. I have done.

Seek out Lexarph.

Δ. I have found it.

Look into the 4 parts of the Table, and take the letters that are of the least Character.   Look among the 4 parts that have the Characters : and look to the Characters that have the least letters.

Δ. I have done.

…… *How many letters are they ?*

Δ. Seven.

…… *They must be eight.*

Δ. They are these (as I have noted them) OA JA JA il.

…… *There are 8 in the 4.*   Δ. Afterwards I found 8 letters in the 4 principal :
                                             for I had omitted *Y I.*

Dwell in darknesse ———   Δ. I suspect this was spoken to me, to my re-
                                             proof, for no more diligence used in the search.

They must be made all one Character:

e x a r p

h c o n s

n a n t a

b i t o m

Lexarph, Comanan, Tabitom.

Set down these three names, leaving out the first L [*that is of* Lexarph, *set them down by* 5.]

Ave. …… *Your sickness causeth me to be sick.*

Δ. E. K. had the Migrom sore.

A great Temptation fell on E. K. : upon E. K. his taking these words to be a scoff, which were words of compassion and friendship.

Δ. They be 3 names of the Tenth air, answering to Caspis, Germania, Trenam in Africa.

…… *The first is* exarp, *five in order.   Set them down without the first Table : That shall make the crosse that bindeth the 4 Angles of the Table together.   The same that stretcheth from the left to right, must also stretch from the right to the left.*

Δ. Have

Δ. Have I now made this crosse of uniting all the 4 parts or Angels together, as you like of ?

...... I.

Wicked Angels whose names are of 3 letters. ...... *Every name, sounding of three letters, beginning out of that line, is the name of a Devil, or wicked Angel, as well from the right, as from the left, excepting the* [Δ.] 4. Angels that are above the crosse, which have no participation with Devils.

4. Angels a-bove every of the lesser cros-ses. Erga, 16 whereby these Angels, are called and do appear. *The letters that joyne those names, which may be put before the* [Δ 4.] *names of the four An-gels of the four crosses in every angle, (as well from the right, as the left,) is the name of God,*

Δ. An example (I pray you) give of this rule.

...... *As, in the first of the black crosses thou hast,* e.

Δ. So it is.

In the first square of the right side thou hast r. beginning the name of the Angel Urzla: *put e to it, and it changeth the sound, into* Erzla. Erzla *is the name of God that governeth,* Urzla.

Δ. And likewise the other three above the crosse are governed by that name of God, Erzla.

* In the crosse of union, or the black crosse.

The 4 Angels serving to this lesser Crosse.

Note. Appearing by one name, and doing by another. ' *Take* * X *which is the next letter :* look under the Crosse in the first angle ; thou hast C z (*then* o, *in the crosse :*) *then* n s. *Call it* C zod-en es : *It is one of the 4 angels that serve to that crosse, which are ruled by this name* Idoigo. *It is the name of God, of six letters :* Look in the crosse that descendeth, In that name [Δ Idoigo] they appear, by the name [Δ Ardza] that is in the crosse, [Δ Transversary] they do that they are commanded.

Δ. Which they ? you named onely C zod n es.

Ave ...... *There followeth* Tot t.

Δ. Which more ?   Δ. The principal Crosse transversary.

Those two, under, till you come to the Crosse.

Δ. Do you mean Sias, *f* m n d ?

...... *Those* 4 *be of Physick.*

Physick.

Δ. As they do *appear in the name of God* Idoigo, *so what* shall be of the name of God Ardza ?

Ave ...... *The one is to call them, the other is to command them.*

Note.
† The Angel his name made of five letters. The use of the wicked powers. *If it be an incurable disease (in the judgement of man) then adde the letter that standeth a-gainst the name, and make him* † up five : *then be cureth miraculously.*

But if thou wilt send sicknesse, then take two of the letters, and adde the letter of the Crosse [Δ the black crosse] *to that, as in the second,* a To.

.[Δ. This a, is of the crosse of union, or the black crosse.]

The Call of the wicked. ...... *Then be it a wicked power, and bringeth in disease : and when thou callest him, call him by the name of god, backward : for unto him, so, he is a god : and so constrain him backward, as* Ogiodi.

Note. Apparition. Constraint. Δ. I think the Constraint must be, by the name of the Transversary backward pronoun-ced, as of Ardza, is backway, azdra : For ogiodi, should but cause him to appear by the order of Idoigo, used for the 4 good Angels.

BaatainA, or Baataivh. ...... *The name of God in the middest of the great Crosse (where the name may have* A *or* H *in the end) upon which the 4 Crosses of the first Angle attend, (or first part of the table attendeth)* calleth out the six Seniors : *which give scientiam rerum humanarum & Judicum, according to the nature of their parts : as in the East after one sort, in the West after another, and so of the rest.*

E. K. A Cloud covereth him.

Now he speaketh of the se-cond little crosse above, on the right side in the East quarter. *The upper right angle in the next crosse, hath the same name* [Δ hath his peculiar name] *of God to call out, and to constrain.*

Δ. Which name mean you ?

Ave ...... *The name that is in the crosse.*   Δ. Ilacza--

4 Good Angels. Metals. The wicked Angels of this portion.

The table of creation. *The good Angels are also* 4. *They have power over Metals, to find them, to gather them together, and to use them.*

These, that are the wicked ones, (made by three letters) are the Princes of those wicked ones, that stood afar off *in the* Table of the Creation.

Δ. You mean in our fourth Book.

Lib. 4. aliter 5. Bnaspol & Bljdem

Ave. ...... *These* can give money coined, in Gold or Silver.

Δ. Which the e ?

Δ. These wicked ones mean you ?

...... I.

The other give no money coined, but the metal.

Δ. You

Δ. You mean the good.

.... *I.*

Δ. As *X OT.*

...... *E X O T.*

Δ. I note this pronunciation.

Δ. The next is *apa.*

The third Crosse is the Crosse of transformation.   Transforma-
                                                        tion.

Δ. Mean you that on the left side underneath?

.... *I.*

The fourth is the Crosse of those Creatures that live in the four Elements , as you call them.   The four Ele-
The first Angel the aire.   ments.
The second ———— the water.
The third ————— the earth.
The fourth ————— the life, or fire of things that live.

Δ. Is not *Acca* the first Angel?

Δ. En pe at.

.... *I.* Then N P *at.*

Δ. Then *O toi,* and P *mox.*   A V E. *They are easie to call.*

1. *The knitting together of Natures lieth in the four Angels that are over the first Crosse.*   The knitting
                                                                                                 together of na-
Δ. As *Urzla,* zlar ? &c.   tures.

.... *I.*

2. *The carrying from place, which place lieth in the Angels of the second Crosse.*   Translatio à lo-
                                                                                      co in locum.
Δ. I understand in the Angels over the Crosse.

3. *All Hand-crafts, or Arts are in the Angels of this third Crosse.*   All hand-
                                                                       crafts.
Δ. I understand in the Angels over the Crosse.

E. K. He drew out much fire out of his mouth, and threw it from   Note this rare
                                                                  action of a
him now.   spiritual Crea-
                                                                  ture.

Δ. I pray you, what meant you by that?

...... *For that I fulfill my Office in another place.*

Stay, at this time I must also be gone.

Δ. When will you deal again.

Ave. *After Dinner about one, or two of the Clock.*

E. K. Now he spreadeth the Curtain.

Δ. Deo gratias nunc & semper agamus. *Amen.*

---

† Tuesday, *Junii* 26. *à Meridie hora,* 1½ *Circiter.*

Gloria Patri,*&c.*

Mitte lucem tuam & veritatem tuam, O Deus , &c.

E. K. Now he is here, and the white Curtain laid behinde.

4. Ave. ...... *The Crosse of the fourth, first Angle.*

Δ. I understand the Angels over the Crosse in the lower right corner.

...... *Herein may you finde the secrets of Kings, and so unto the lowest degree.   But you must*   The secrets of
Note, That as the Angels of the first of the four Crosses in the East, which are for Medicine : so are   all states.
the first of the second, the first of the third, and the first of the fourth ; so that for Medicine there   sixteen An-
be sixteen, and *so of all the rest in their order : but that they differ in that, some be the Ange's of*   gels for Medi-
the East, other some of the West; and so of the rest.   cine.

Notwithstanding, to know the world before the waters, To be privy to the doings of men , from the   Nᵣᵉ. The
waters to Christ ; from Christ unto the rewarding of the wicked : The wicked doings of the flesh , or   blessed King-
the fond and devilish imaginations of man, or to see what the blessed Kingdom shall be, and how the   dom on earth.
earth shall be dignified, purged, *and made clean, is a meat too sweet for your mouths.*   The earth.

Δ. Curiosity is far from our intents.

Ave. ..... *But there is neither Patriarch nor Prophet* sanctified, Martyr,   Ergo, these are here
or Confessor , King , *or Governour of the people upon earth, that his*   to be learned out.
name, continuance, *and end, is not (like the Moon at midnight) in these*   Δ. *Maximè enim*
Tables.   *splendet & manifesta*
          est, in medio cæli & in
          plenilunis.

Δ. Mean you not the Crosse of *the fourth first* Angle, to be that, which is of a ☉ *urrz.*
And his transversary of a 1 O *a* i ?

[a a]   Ave, ... It

Ave......*It is so.*

Δ. I underſtand not well, your account of 16 Angels for medicine.

Ave. ..... *Are there not four principal Croſſes? Every Croſſe hath alſo four. The firſt of every four are* the Croſſe *of medicine, ſo that there be ſixteen.*

Ave. ..... *One book of perfect paper.   One labour of a few dayes.*

Forth, For the.. Their pro- miſe, The calling them together, *and* the yielding of their promiſe, *the repetition of the names of God,* are ſufficient.

I have given you Corn : I have given you alſo ground.   Deſire God to give you ability to till.

Δ. We will pray for his help that is Almighty.

......*I am free before God.   Catch that catch can.*

Be it now as it was before.

E. K. He mounteth up into the aire, and is gone.

Δ. When would you that I ſhould prepare that book , and what call you perfect : and how many leaves would you wiſh me to make it of ?

......*Your book is not of my charge.*

Δ. Lord, as thou haſt dealt mercifully with us hitherto, and haſt given us the underſtand- ing of many ſecrets, ſo in reſpect of this ſtrange dealing with us, and leaving us of *Ave,* we are deſirous to know ſome cauſe : and therein we require that *Madimi* may be ſent,

E. K. She is here in the ſtone.

Madi. ..... *How do you?*   *E. K.* She maketh a low curſie.

Δ. I declared our admiration of *Ave* his ſo ſudden departure, and required her opinion of the caſe.

Mad. ...., *Surely Sir, I cannot tell : but I will go ſee if my mother can tell.*

Δ. He that is the Creatour of all things, be mercifull unto us, and lighten our hearts with true knowledge, as our truſt is in him.

E. K. She went away, and came again after a little while.

Mad. ...... *My mother ſayeth, you* ſhould have been at the Emperours.

Δ. But you ſee it is impoſſible to get thither without ſome good proviſion of money made by our great friend *A. L.*   I pray you, what can you ſay of *Ave?*

Mad. ..,.. *My gentle brother, Ave* is a good Creature : *indeed you might have made more of him.*

Δ. I beſeech you to give us ſome Declaration of *Ave* his laſt words.

Mad. ...., *There is no word unperfect :* My brother *Ave* his nature is to be plain and ſhort,

Δ. I pray you to ſay ſomewhat more plainly of *Ave* his laſt words,

Mad. ..... *If it were the commandment of my mother, I could do it.   But this is the good will of my brother toward you.*

Δ. As your brother hath done this of his good will, ſo do I deſire you of your good will to do, or ſay ſomewhat to our comfort.

Mad. ..... *Sir, I pray you, pardon me.   I may not meddle with* Ave *his doing.   I have no- thing to ſay to you, but* I know my Mother hath *much to ſay to you*

As the mighty thunder cometh, ſo cometh the promiſe of God.

If the Emperour (my mother ſayeth) do any thing againſt Lasky, *or bin- der, (ſhe anſwereth in earneſt) there ſhall be an Emperour.*

Δ. Make your ſentence more perfect.

Mad. ..,... *Therein lieth a myſtery.*

My Mother, my Siſters , Ave, Il, *my ſelf, and the reſt of us will not be from you* in your need.

Δ. Now is our need, as we have declared.

Mad. ...... Sir, *Content your ſelf : For , yet a ſeaſon , you muſt have patience.   God bleſſe you, for (as yet) I feel nothing to ſay to you.*

Miſericos, clemens & pius eſt Deus Noſter : Cujus nomen ſit benedictum, Nunc & ſemper. Amen.

Redulphus the *Empe- rour* now.

A. L.

Earneſt is means to be *Emperour , vide* 22 *Sept.* Prage.

A Myſtery.

A comfortable pro- miſe.

Note. About ſeven of the Clock this afternoon , *E. K.* came again up into my ſtudy : and ſeing me reading, and conſidering this Action, began to finde talk of it, and willed me to aſ- ſay the practiſe of it if I underſtood it : And, to be brief, by little and little fell to this iſſue, that he confeſſed himſelf to be very ſorry that he was ſo far raging in words as he was this day.

day. Nay, (said I) any man living, elſe, would have found juſt cauſe of comfort, and to give thanks for *AVE*, ſuch ſpeeches to him, as he uſed unto you upon true compaſſion, and no skoff, *&c.* But you by and by *called him Devil, and raged on further againſt* Michael *and* Gabriel, *and the heavenly powers* with moſt horrible ſpeeches, *&c.* He became very penitent, and acknowledged that he had offended God : and ſaid, that ſurely *it was of the Devil*, for he did not remember his words : but he is ſure, that they were not decent, and beſeeched *God to forgive* him : And ſo did I, and was very glad of this his reforming himſelf, and we (being oft (before) called down to ſupper) were going out of my Study : and as he was almoſt at the door to go out, he ſaid to me, *I feel a very heavy thing upon my ſhoulder :* and it *is warm with all :* Whereat I put to the door, and we ſat down again : Verily thinking (as it was) that it was the preſence of *AVE*, whereupon I ſaid unto the Creature.

NOTA. Penitentia Deo grata & acceptabilis in ipſa hora. Note his manner of a heavy thing on the ſhoulder, and warm withall.

Δ. In the name of Jeſus, Ave art thou there, he anſwered immediately after as followeth.

Ave...... *Becauſe thou* [E.K.] *haſt acknowledged my honour again : I will alſo acknowledge my help toward you : But where man curſeth the Heavens, what holy Creature can abide ? Or where Satan is brought into poſſeſſion, by free will of man, what good Angel is he that departeth not ?*

Δ. O Lord, confirm thy mercies upon us from henceforth.

Ave...... *As concerning your Action, The Heavens bear witneſſe of it. Yea, yeſterday did the good Angels contend with the wicked : and there was a great conflict betwixt them; and that about the love of God towards you, and your Action. But I will viſit you again in the morning, and will perform my good will in God toward you. But thou muſt pray often if thou wilt avoid temptation. God be mercifull to you, forgive you, and ſtrengthen you to the end.*

Δ There was a terrible ſtorm of thunder and rain, toward the end of our yeſter-dayes Action, which, I ſaid, was ſomewhat more then natural.

Δ. Amen, ſweet Jeſu, Amen.

Δ. When all was thus ended, I delivered to E.K. my Pſalter book (with the ſhort prayers annexed to every Pſalm) where he himſelf very devoutly, and penitently prayed three of them, and I hearing alſo of them, gave my conſent in heart to the ſame prayers.

Mr. E.K. Penitently prayeth.

Δ To God onely be all praiſe, honour, and glory, now and ever. *Amen.*

Wedneſday, 27. *Junii.* Cracoviæ. *Mane horam circiter.* 7.
Uratione Dominica finita, & peculiari Oratione contra Tentationes Sathanæ, apparuit ipſe *AVE*, &c.

E.K. He is here.

Δ. Gloria Patri, & filio, & ſpiritui ſancto, *&c.* Amen.
Ave...... *In the name of the Father, and of the Son, and of the holy Ghoſt.*
Δ. Amen.
...... *Now, what is that, that is hard to you ?*
4. Firſt, whether the Table (for the middle Croſſe of uniting the four principal parts) be made perfect, or no.
Ave...... *Thou haſt found out the truth of it.*
Δ. I think a myſtery did depend upon the choice of the three names, *Lexarph, Comanan,* and *Tabitom.*
Ave...... *That is not to our purpoſe.*
Δ. You bad me chuſe out of the Tables the Characters of feweſt Letters, and I found them to be O A X A J A, and I, you ſaid they are eight, you ſaid there are eight in four : I know not what this meaneth.
Ave...... *You muſt make up the name* Paraoan.
Δ. What ſhall become of the L averſed ?
Ave...... *It may be N, or L.*
Δ. What muſt I now do with that name ?
Ave...... *In* Exarph *there wanteth an* L, *which* L. *is of more force then the* N. *and therefore it is ſet in the Tables. As far as that* N. *ſtretcheth in the Character, ſo far ſhall that Countrey be conſumed with fire, and ſwallowed into Hell, as* Sodom *was for wickedneſſe. The end of all things is even at hand : And the earth muſt be purified, and delivered to another.*
The Heavens ſhall be 77 *times above themſelves. And the earth ſhall bring forth without Tillage : Prophets ſpeak of dayes,* [as] *preſently, that* * *are far off. But we ſpeak of dayes that are hard at hand. For, immediately after your being with* Cæſar, *ſhall the whole world be in ſudden alteration. Battails and bloudſhed great number : The Kings of the earth ſhall run unto the Hills, and ſay cover us.*

Δ. It is the ſecond part of the 22 aire.

Δ. So is not one letter ſuperfluous, or wanting in the Tables.
A Propheſie of things at hand.
NOTE. Nova Terra.
were.
Rodolphus Cæſar.
Nota. Initium malorum inſtare.

[aa 2] Δ O

Δ. O, Thou mighty God of Hosts : be our strength and comfort.

Anti-Chrift. ..... When you hear the peoplesay, *Lo, there is a man-child that doth great marvails,* (which is even at the door threshold.) Then, then shall you see the calamity of the earth.

A. L. But let *Laskie, the servant of God do as he is commanded :* And what goodnesse soever he craveth shall follow him, for the Lord hath spared him among the Kings of the earth.

Money, provision. Let *him provide for this one journey : He shall not need to provide for the rest : For,* he that hath all, hath provided for him.

In Constantinople 1585 15. Septemb. The fifteenth day of September, that shall be twelve moneths, shall you set up the figure of the Crosse ; even in the midd'st of *Constantinople.*

Δ. Thy will be done, O Lord, to thy honour and glory.

Ave. ..... *In this Kingdom shall be much bloudshed, and the one shall cut anothers throat. And as the Lord hath promised, so shall it come to passe.*   *Poland. Promissio confirmata de A.L. forth.*

Ave. ..... *Now to the Table.*

Δ. OF the Principal King of *Bataiva,* or *Baataiva,* (using the last *a* twice) I doubt of the perfect writing of it.

Ave. ..... *Is it not written ? It is all, most easie , and in gathering thou canst not erre.*

24 Seniors. Note, This diversity of working. The four plagues , or quarters. The 24 *Seniors are all of one Office : But when thou wilt work in the East , thou must take such as bear rule there ; so must thou do of the rest.*

Δ. Do you mean the estate, in respect of any place we shall be in, or in respect of any earthly place , accounted alwayes the East part of the world, wheresoever we be?

Ave...... *The East and West, in respect of your Poles. What will you else of me ?*

Δ. Whether these four Tables be joyned in their right places, or no.

Ave. ..... *They be.*   *Note, of the Letters in the black Transversary.*

Δ. Of the Letters in the Transversary of the wicked their black Crosse, I know no use, as of m o t i v a t ; nan, &c.

The book. Ave. ..... *Thou shalt know,* when thou writest thy book.

Δ. I desire you of the book to say somewhat more for the fashion, paper, and binding, &c.

Ave. ..... *Thou mayest use thy discretion.*

Δ. You mean (I trust) the book that you bid me to prepare : For, the other is not for my writing.

A perfect master ready. Ave. ..... *It is not.* I my self will stand with you, and shew how to practise.

Δ. Blessed be God for his ready help.

Δ. I will prepare the book (by the grace of God) with all speed.

Δ. As concerning the Offices, vertues, and powers of the three other quarters of the Table, what shall we think of them ?   *The Offices of all the four quarters.*

Ave. ..... They are all as the first.

The twelve names of God in the twelve Banners. Four dayes. Fourteen dayes. Obedient. White linnen vestures. Δ. *Note.* Thou hast *three names of God,* out of the line of the holy Ghost, in the principall Crosse of the first Angle, so hast thou three in the second, &c.

Four dayes (after your book is made, that is to say, written) must you onely call upon those names of God, or *on the God of Hosts,* in those names :

And 14 dayes after you shall (in this, or in some convenient place) *Call the Angels by Petition,* and by *the name of God, unto the which they are obedient.*

The 15 day you shall Cloath *your selves,* in vestures made of linnen , white : and so *have* the *apparition, use,* and *practice of the* Creatures. For, it is not a labour of years, nor many dayes.

E. K. This is somewhat like the old fashion of Magick.

Garment and book, onely once to be used. Ave. ..... *Nay, they all played at this.*

You must never use the Garment after, but that once onely, neither the book.

E. K. To what end is the book made then, if it be not to be used after.

Δ. It is made for to be used that day onely.

Ave. ..... *What will you else ?*

Δ. As you best know : we need instructions ; yet necessary for us.

Ave. ..... *Very few.*

Ave. ..... *It is a stem with fruit, but it wanteth leaves.*

E. K. What mean you by that ?

Fruit than leaves. Ave. ..... *There be more leaves then fruit, and in many actions there be more circumstances then matter.*

Δ. But here is onely marrow, and no bones, or flesh.

Δ. As concerning the great multitude that E. K. saw in the Vision standing after the sixteen Angels, next the Gate, you made no mention in your Description of the Vision : Therefore I would know what they are.

Ave. ..... *They be Ministers and servants.*

..... *There*

E. K.   * Aliter, *Sendenna,* as E. K. said.

Δ. Of this wicked *Sonden-na,* E. K. by &c. by, after this Action said.

There shalt thou see thy old Sondenna,* *and, many other wicked ones, that thou hast dealt with-all. Hereby shall you judge truly of wicked* Magick. *God be with you:* I will be ready, *when you need me.*

Δ. Æterno & omnipotenti Creatori rerum omnium, visibilium & invisibilium sit omnis laus, honor, gloria, & gratiarum actio. *Amen.*

Seeing his name is come to be known (and not by) I will tell you

me : for I had received the Sacrament with Mr. *Miniver,* of whom I had him, never to bewray or disclose his name somewhat of him.   He appeareth in many forms, till at length he appear in a Triangle of fire, and being constrained to the Circle, he taketh form (as it were) of a great Gyant, and will declare before for a month to come which spirits do orderly range : which by name being called, will do their offices, with a few other circumstances used, &c. This, indeed was one, of whom I made most account, &c.

Δ. 1. Remember, I have not yet heard any thing of the 5 Princes which held up the traine of the chief King.

2. Neither any thing of the Trumpeter which went before all.

Doubts.

3. Neither of the letters in the Transversary of the black Crosse.

4. Also of * *Docepax Tedoand,* being referred to *Cilicia, Nemrodiana,* and *Paphlagonia* in the late exposition of the places by vulgar names : and before in the naming of them by the names of Creation they were applyed to *Italia* and *Britania* : One of those is to be doubted of.

* Declared by *Gabriel* and *Nalvage.*

5. We are desirous to know the Etymologies of all the names of God which we shall use, either to God himself, or to the Angels.

6. We require the form of our Petition or Invitation to be made to the Angels.

7. Of the 20 (and more) diversities or corrections of this principal Table, we require your censure, which diversities I have (by conjecture) so made or amended.

8. Whereas I was [Δ] willed to call 14 dayes, the Angels which are to be used : so would I know whether also I should summon the wicked here recorded (out of the black Crosse, having their off-spring) likewise 14 dayes.

Δ. *Pagina penultima precedente.*

Saturday, † *Cracovie,* *Junii* 30. *Mane, circa* 9. *horam.*

Oratione dominica finita, & propositis illis 7. *dubiis, quievimus paululum.   Deinde, aliquot orationes ex psalterio recitavi, iterum quievimus paululum.   Ad semihoram nihil apparuit.*

At length appeared a face, very great, with wings about, adjoyned to it ;   afterward he seemed to be in a great Globe of fire.

...... *Hearken to my voice.*

Modesty, patience, and humility of heart and body, doth belong to these Actions.   Tell me how many Thunders the Lord hath in store for the wicked.

Note.

Δ. O Lord, we know not.

...... *Were you ever in the secret caves of the Earth ?*

Δ. No, Lord, never.

...... *Then tell me how many windes the Lord hath prepared for an year?*

Δ. Neither that can we tell : We are not of the Lord his Council in these things of his providence.

...... *Can you tell me none of these questions ?*

...... *Can you tell what shall become of your selves ?*

Δ. God only knoweth, and no creature but by him : for all things are kept uncertain until the end.

...... *You beget children, know you the hour wherein they shall be born ?*

...... *You begin labour, can you tell what point of time you shall end in ?*

Δ. God only is the Fountain of all wisdom and truth.

...... *Well, then I see, you are drowned in ignorance and know nothing.*

E. K. He turneth round very swiftly,

...... *Even as the Adder leadeth out her young ones, the first day one foot, (out of her hole) because they should eat, but because they might acquaint themselves with the air, and her subtlety.*

not Note this similitude well.

The second day, one yard and more: she encompasseth her hole, and windeth to and fro, and teacheth them to creep ; and so five or six dayes, till they know how to move and stir their bodies.

After the seventh day, she leadeth them further, and faineth deceit, striking the ground with her tail, as though it were the sound of some one at hand : And then gaping, beginneth to hisse, and stirreth up fear unto her young ones, so that they enter into her mouth.   And thus she doth till they be 12 or 13 dayes old :   Then she leadeth them a stones-cast, and exerciseth them both with fear, and biding themselves ;   And when they sleep (being young and wearied with labour) she stealeth from them and maketh a noise amongst the leaves and small stones, with the moving of her hinder parts :

To

To the intent she might see what shift her wormes can make, which stirred up with fear, and missing their mother, so learn to couch themselves in the Chymney of the earth: At length, after silence, the mother thrusteth out her self, and doubleth her tongue (with the sound whereof she useth to call them) They come together and rejoyce, wreathing themselves diversly about her body, for joy: She for a recompence, suffereth them to hang upon her back, and so waltereth to her hole: where she ga-thereth the leaves of the earth: and after she hath chewed them small and tender, with her teeth, and mingled them with the dust, she spueth them out again, and beginneth to lick them by little and little, as though she hungered, which she subtlely doth, that her wormes might eat and forget their hungrynesse.

Finally, in 20 dayes, they become big, and as skilful in the property of their kind . . . she (I say) leadeth them out into a fertile place, and full of dew, and full of bushes, and places apt to cover them, where they feed, dwell, observe their craft, and at last forsake their mother. Even so, it is with you: So the Lord, (the true Serpent and worme) leadeth you out from day to day, accor-

Triumphing true wisdom.

ding to your strength: and as you grow, to the intent you might, at last be brought unto the pleasant dew, and food of his mercy, which is Triumphing true wisdom.

But this the Lord feareth of you: that, as the wormes did, so you will forsake your mother.

Δ. Forsake us not, O God, Confirm thy graces in us, and we shall not forsake thee.

The nature of the Serpent, is, not to forsake his young.

Δ. O Lord we depend onely on thee, and without thy grace and continual help, we perish.

NOE.

The Lord told Noe long before, the Flood would come, he believed him: Therefore he is safe in both worlds. The sons in law of Lot, sunk into Hell, for that they derided the words of God, and believed them not. His wife became a salt-stone, for that she looked back, and did contrary to

Moses.
Numeri 10
Num de petra
hac vobis a-
quam poterimus
elicere.

the Commandment of God Moses had the reward of his holinesse in this world plucks back, be-cause he said, Can this, &c.

I, as the messenger of God, am as one that say, Cave, Take heed that you become not son in laws, though you passe the fire, Take heed you look not back: for if you do, you shall not see the flood, nei-ther shall the Lord put a vail betwixt you and vengeance, neither (I say) shall the promises of God come in your dayes. If God had taken you up into the heavens and placed you before his Throne, and told you the things that are to come, you would believe: But that you cannot do.

The Lord is merciful, he descendeth into your houses, and there telleth you what is to come, where you may understand: But you believe him not. Therefore saith the Lord of you, I fear you will

K.

forsake your mother: But if you do it, I say, if you do it, I will make of the Mother, men, that shall testifie my name.

E. K. I ever told you I do not believe them, nor can believe them, nor will desire to believe them.

Faith.
Obedience.
Humility.

...... If you be faithful, you be able to comprehend: If you be obedient and humble, The Creatures of Heaven shall abide with you: Yea the Father, and the Son, and the Holy Ghost shall make his dwelling with you. If you persevere, even with faith and humility, you shall see the wicked dayes that are to come, enjoy the promises of God, and be partaker of those blessed days

A Caveat.

that follow: For wonders unheard of, in, and of the world, are at hand. You are warned, The Spirit of God rest with you.

Δ. Amen.

Δ. *Cum maxi-mis lachrymis hac à me & valde serio ad Rem. dicta ti-rant.*

Δ. O Lord, shall we continue in this wavering or stiff-necked willful blindnesse, and fro-wardly keep out thy mercies and graces by our fleshly sense, and unreasonable perswasion a-gainst the verity of thy true Ministers?

1. *All things are committed to thy charge.*

Δ. O Lord as much as ever I can do by prayer or otherwise, I do, and yet I enjoy no fruit of my long travel.

2. *Thou hast good ground, sow if thou can.*

Δ. How can I without further instructions and help? and now, when I require *Ave* to come, he cometh not: O Lord comfort me.

3. A V E *shall come when thou hast need of him.*

Δ. In te Domine speravi, & spero, & sperabo. In die Tribulationis exaudies me, Refu-gium meum, spes mea, vita & beatitudo mea Jesu Christe, tibi cum Patre & Spiritu Sancto sit omnis honor, laus, Gloria & Gratiarum actio   *Amen.*

Monday, † *Cracovia, Junii 2. Mane hora ⅞.*
Oratione dominica finita, & mora aliqua interposita, & aliquot aliis ex psalterio recitatis pre-cibus, & post varias meas ad Deum ejaculationes.

Ꝟ ꝗ semihoram.

At length *Ave* appeared to E. K. in the Shew-stone, &c.

Δ. O Lord, all honour, thanks, and praise, be unto thee, who hearest the prayers of thy simple servant.

Δ. First,

Δ. First, for the reforming of diversity of letters in the names written, *I* require your aid, unlesse you will first say somewhat else.

By the same Jesu who sitteth on the right hand of his Father, and is the wisdom of his Father, I request you to proceed with us.

Ave. ...... *So that the body of Christ, now, is glorified and immortall.*

Δ. Most true it is --- *Mors illi ultra non non dominabitur.*

Ave. ...... *But as the Prophets, that were fullfiled with the Holy Ghost and Spirit of God, before Christ, tasted of him, in that he should come as a Saviour, and in the seed of man ; So is the Prophesie of this time, Christ being ascended, in the same Spirit.   But that Christ shall come in his* **Adventus Christ.** glorified body, *Triumphing against Satan, and all his enemies.*

Δ. So be it, O Lord.

Ave. ...... *But that the words of the Prophesies may be fulfilled,   It is necessary that the Earth swarm, and be glutted with her own fornication and idolatry : which ,   what it shall be, the same spirit will open unto you.*

Δ. Fiat voluntas Dei.

Ave. ...... *That you may not onely be wise in forsaking the world, and foreseeing the dangers of perdition ; But also preach the wonders of the same Christ, and his great mercies, which is to come and* to appear in the cloudes with his body glorified.   *The Lord said to Satan, I will give thee* power, in the end over their bodies, *and thou shalt be cast out into the fields, and that for my* **Our bodies to** names sake : But my Vineyard, and the fruit of my Harvest , *shalt thou not hinder.   Thus my* **be cast out into** brethren hath the Lord loved you, *Thus have the Treasures of the Heavens opened themselves unto* **the fields.** you : But your faith springeth not.

Δ. It shall when it pleaseth the Highest : We beseech him to encrease our faith as shall be most for his honor and glory.

Ave. ...... *But unto you it shall be revealled, what shall come, after Morrows, after Dayes, Weeks,* **Prophesie.** *and Years :   And unto you it shall be delivered, The Prophesie of the time to come, which is twelve :* **1 — 11** of the which you have but one.

Δ. God make us faithful, true and discret servants.   **11.**

Ave. ...... *For God will shake this earth through a riddle,   and knock the vessels in pieces, throw down the seats of the proud, and establish himself a seat of quietnesse :   that neither the Sun may* **Regnum futu-** *shine upon the unjust, nor the garments be made of many pieces.* **rum.**

Δ. All shall be in unity : *unus pastor, unum ovile,* &c.

Ave. ...... *Haste therefore and be gone :* as the Lord hath appointed you, *that you may be* Δ. **Be gone to** ready for him, *when he bringeth the sickle.   Purifie all the vessels of your house,* and gather more the **Emperour.** into it, *and when the Lord presseth, he will give you wine abundantly :   And lo, the * forks are weary* **⋆ That hold up** of their burdens :   But be diligent, watchful, and full of care :   for Satan himself *is very busie* **the grapes.** with you.   After dinner I will visit you with instructions :   But O my Brethren, be faithful, and **Satan.** persevere ; for the same spirit that teacheth the Church, teacheth you. **Faithful.**
Spiritus San-
Δ. To the same *Holy Spirit*, with the Father and the Son, be all honor, power, glory and **ctus.** praise, now, and ever, *Amen.*

Julii 2. After Noon, Hora 1 ¼
Δ. Gloria Patri, & Filio & Spiritui Sancto sicut erat in principio & nunc & semper & in sæcula seculorum.   *Amen.*

E. K. Here he is now.

Δ. Nobis adsit, qui cuncta creavit.

Ave. ...... *What will you ?*

Δ. If it please you, the solution of the former 8 questions first.

Δ. 1. As of the five Princes, which held up the traine of the King.

Ave. ...... *The knowledge of them helpeth not now.*

Δ. 2. Secondly of the Trumpeter, what it betokened.

Ave. ...... *It hath no relation to these Tables.*

Δ. 3. Of the letters in the Transversary, I would know your will.

Ave. ...... *They are, as the other, but for a peculiar practice.*

Δ. 4. For *Docepax* and *Tedoand* referred diversly, as I have noted, What is the cause of **Docepax.** this diversity ? **Tedoand.**

Ave. ...... *It was the* fault of E. K. in reporting.

Δ. What is the very Truth ?

Ave. ...... *Thou shalt be taught that, when thou hast their Calls,* **Call's.** *It belongeth to Nalvage his correction.* **Nalvage is to**
correct.
Δ. 5. As concerning the Etymologies of these names of God, we would be satisfied.

Ave. ...... *God is a Spirit, and is not able to be comprehended.*

Δ. Some **Notifying** or Declaration, no full comprehension I require:

Ave. ...

Ave. ..... *It is no part of mans understanding.* They signifie all things, and they signifie nothing.

Ave. .... *Who can expresse* Jehovah *what it signifieth.* Deus significat ad id quod agit.

Δ. As for the form of our Petition or Invitation of the good Angels, What sort should it be of?

Ave. .... *A short and brief speech.*

Δ. We beseech you to give us an example : we would have a confidence; it should be of more effect.

Ave. ..... *I may not do so.*

E. K. And why?

Invocation. Ave. .... Invocation proceedeth of the good will of man, *and of the heat and fervency of the spirit : And therefore is prayer of such effect with God.*

Δ. We beseech you, shall we use one form to all?

Ave. ..... *Every one, after a divers form.*

Δ. If the minde do dictate or prompt a divers form, you mean.

Ave. ..... *I know not : for I dwell not in the soul of man.*

Δ. As concerning the diversity of certain words in these Tables, and those of the portions of the Earth delivered by *Nalvage,* What say you?

Ave. ..... *The Tables be true.*

Is it *Aydropl,* or *Andropl ?*

Ave. ...... *Both names be true, and of one signification. I have delivered you the Tables, so use them.*

Δ. As concerning the Capital letters, have I done well ?

The use of the letters. Ave. ..... *You have easily corrected that, and to good end;* for every letter, and part of letter, hath *his signification.*

Δ. I beseech you say somewhat of the *N* in *Paraoan,* of which you said, so far as that stretched, should sink to hell.

Note. Ave. ...... *Every letter in* Paraoan, is a living fire : *but all of one quality and of one Creation : But unto N is* delivered a viol of Destruction, *according to that part that he is of* Paraoan *the Governour.*

Δ. It may please you to name that Place, City, or Country, under that *N.*

Ave. ..... *Ask* Nalvage, *and he will tell you.*

Δ. As concerning the wicked here, Shall I call or summon them all, as I do the good ones in the name of God ?

The wicked spirits are vile slaves. Ave. .... *No man calleth upon the name of God in the wicked : They are servants and vile slaves.*

Δ. We call upon the name of Jesus in the expulsing of devils, saying in the name of Jesus, *&c.*

Ave. ..., *That In, is against the wicked. No just man calleth upon the name of God,* to allure the devil.

Δ. Then they are not to be named in the first summoning or invitation.

Ave. .... *At no time* to be called.

E. K. How then shall we proceed with them?

Ave. .... *When the Earth lieth opened unto your eyes, and when the Angels of Light, shall offer the passages of the Earth, unto the entrance of your senses, (chiefly of seeing)* The Treasures of the Earth. *Then shall you see the Treasures of the Earth, as you go : And the caves of the Hills shall not be unknown unto you : Unto these, you may say,* Arise, be gone, Thou art of destruction and of the places of darknesse : Our words to the wicked that keep Treasure. *These are provided for the use of man. So shalt thou use the wicked,* and no otherwise.

Δ. This is as concerning the natural Mines of the Earth.

Ave. .... *Not so, for they have nothing to do with the natural* Mines *of the Earth, but, with that which is corrupted with man.*

Δ. As concerning the coined they have power to bring it.

Ave. So they may : that they keep, and no other.

Δ. How shall we know what they keep, and what they keep not ?

Ave. .... *Read my former words;* for thou dost not understand them.

Δ. I read it : beginning at the first line on this side, when the Angels of Light, *&c.*

Δ. I mean of coined money that they keep not; How shall we do to serve our necessities with it ?

Ave. ..... *The good Angels are Ministers for that purpose. The Angels of the 4 angles shall make the Earth open unto you, and shall serve your necessities from the 4 parts of the Earth.*

Δ. God make me a man of wisdom in all parts, I beseech him.

   Δ. Note I had spoken somewhat of my part in *Devonshire* Mines : and of the *Danish* Treasures which were taken of the Earth.

Δ. These our Questions being thus answered, now I refer the rest to your instructions intended.

Invocations to be made. Ave. .... *You have the corn, and you have the ground : Make you but invocations to* sow the seed, *and the fruit shall be plentiful.*

Δ. As

Δ. As concerning our usage in the 4 dayes in the 14 dayes, we would gladly have some information.

Ave. ..... *Tou would know to reape, before your corn be sown.*

Δ. As concerning a fit place and time to call, and other circumstances, we would learn somewhat.

Ave. ..... *Tou would know where and when to call, before your* invocations *bear witnesses of your* readinesse.

Δ. Then they must be written in *verbis conceptis,* in formal words.

Ave. ..... I —— *a very easie matter.*

Δ. What is the Book you mean that I should write?

Ave. ..... *The Book consisteth* [1] *of Invocation of the names of God, and* [2] *of the Angels, by* The Book. *the names of God : Their offices are manifest. You did desire to be fed with spoones, and so you are.*

Δ. As concerning *Bataiva,* or *Baataivb,* I pray you not to be offended though I ask again, what is the truth?

Ave. ..... *The word is but of six letters, whereof, one is on the left side, one on the right, two a-* Δ. He mean-
bove, and two under ; A *and* H *are put to.*   eth of the left

Δ. Sometimes or communiter, *A,* and in *extremis Judiciis* H as I was taught before. side of the
                                                                                        square center
Δ. So that the word is *Bataiva,* or *Bataivb.*   of the princi-

E: K. I think he be gone; for he made a sign of the crosse toward us, pal crosse :: not
and drew the white Curtain.   perfect square,
                                                                                      but heterome-
Δ. As we sate a while and talked of the Calls received in the holy Language, and not yet ces.
Englished, there was a voice.

..... *Tou shall have those Calls in English on Thursday. And so ask me no more questions.* The Calls to
                                                                                            be had in En-
Δ. Thanks, honour, and glory, be to our Creator, Redeemer, and Sanctifier, now and ever, glish on Thurs-
   Amen.   day next.

Thursday, † *Cracovie, Julii,* 5. *Manè, hora,* 8. *ferè.*

*Oratione dominica finita aliisque extemporaneis ejaculationibus ad Deum, & repetito promisso ul-
timorum verborum de Angelica interpretatione* 14. *illarum invocationum, quas à* 14 *Maii ultimi
recepimus, tandem apparuerunt,* Gabriel *in Cathedra &* Nalvage.

Gabriel in his Chair, and *Nalvage* with the Table, or rather Globe with the letters in it, *&c.*

Δ. Blessed be our God alwayes, for his mercies : his graces be with us, now and ever.

E. K. *Gabriel* standeth up.

Gab. ..... *Dictum est sæpe vobis,* perseverate usque ad finem.

Δ. God give us that ability.

Gab. ..... *And why is it said so ? but because you shall have many temptations and afflictions :* after which come consolation and comfort.

*If the Smith prove and temper his Gold by fire, his intent is to excell in the work that he hath in
hand : that thereby it might be tryed, refined, and made apt, to the end wherein it shall be used :
Much more, think you, doth the God of wisdom, forge, try, and beat out, such as he intendeth to use
in the execution of his divine and eternal purposes. How therefore can you find fault with the Lord ?
How can you say, he dealeth not justly with you ? when he suffereth y.u to be proved to the uttermost.
If you pay the uttermost farthing, are you not become free ? If you feel affliction and temptation,
and withstand it, are you not the more pure ? the more justified ? for the Vineyard and Harvest of
the Lord ? O yes, my Brethren ; for the more the wise man is afflicted, the more he rejoyceth ;
And the greater his adversity is, the more he prospereth.*

*Is it not written ? No man cometh to the Lord but he is justified, purified, and accepted. Whence
therefore (if you seek to come before the Lord, that is to say, to appear, to be blessed) shall your
justification or purifying arise ? Of your own nature it cannot ; for you were born sinners : But
by Christ you may : In whom you are justified, through patience, and resisting temptations. True
proof, and touch of man : But me thinketh I hear you say, O, if we were rich, or of ability.
True it is, for the dust of the earth many men extel you : But in that you* speak with God, in us Our great Pri-
his Angels (that is to say Messagers) you are not onely happy (which happinesse the others want) viledge with
but you excell all the creatures of the Earth.   God.

*O my Brethren, their joy is a bitter-sweet : But the comfort that you have, is eternal, is sweet,
and a food for ever.   Therefore, if you will be eternal, and in perpetual comfort with joy, despise
the world for the worlds sake : and delight in God for his mercies ; which if you truly do; Then can
no Tempest prevail, no affliction come amisse, nor no burden be too heavy for you : For it is written,
Gaudium beatorum est* Christus : Cui Mundus omnia mala fecit.

*O my Brethren, be contented, and suffer the world : for as Christ in vanquishing her, did prove
himself the Son of God : So shall you in resisting her, at last overcome, and be accounted the sons of*

God

Dee.   God *in Christ, of whom you are a follower.* John Dee, *be of comfort, for thou shalt overcome.*
Δ. God be praised therefore.

E. K. And what do you say of me?

Δ. If I prevail, Satan shall not have his will of you : for
Gab. ......, *But unto thee* [E.K.] *saith the Lord,* Take heed, how thou meddlest with hell, lest it swallow thee.
Have patience, a time.

E. K. They be gone out of sight.

Δ. In the mean time we read over the premisses twice, to our great comfort.

E. K. Now they be here again,

Now is a Cloud over them, all white like a smoke.

A voice. ...... Move not, for the place is holy ———— By a great hollow voice.

E. K. Why should it be holy.

Δ. ———— The Court is, where the King is : So where the Lord is present, the place is accounted holy, and is so.

E. K. Now they be out of the Cloud.

Δ. After this, they made another pause : longer than before.

E. K. When shall we practice Ave *his Calls,* &c.

Gab. ...... *My brother, thou hast least care: Thou drawest both of God and man: That is promised thee, shall be payed thee ; and that which is to come, thou shalt be partaker of* [Δ. To E. K. *for he hath no care neither for meat, nor drink for him and his, neither is he destitute of* 400 *Dollers yearly pension, and is to have some help by Art.*]
Nal. ...... *Say the first word of the Call.*

His fee of A.L. of 400 Dollers yearly.

Gab S did.   Δ. Sapáh   It is the fifth, for 4 being Englished.

E. K. He holdeth up all his hand, and on his thumb standeth written ————

The Spirits of the fourth Angle are

and on the fingers orderly very big letters.

Δ. It is yet a mystery to what book these, and such words have relation, they are in every Call following.

There was no word there that signified Nine, the third word should be E M.

Nine	to vanne the earth	Wherefore
mighty	and	Hearken unto
in the firmament	That word thou hast not, it is Acam.	my voice,
of waters,	7699	I have talked of you
whom	continual Workmen,	and
the first	whose courses	I move you
hath planted	visit with comfort	in power and presence,
a Torment	the earth,	whose works
to the wicked,	and are	shall be
and	in government	a Song of honour
a Garland	and	and the praise
to the righteous ;	continuance	of your God
giving unto them	as the second	in your Creation.
fiery darts	and the third :	

E. K. Like a cloud covereth between me & the things in the air. Δ 6

Nal. ....., *That is one.*

E. K. Now he plucketh the Curtain over all.

Δ. Because you said that *Acam* betokening 7699. was to be put in his place : I have viewed and numbred, and I find the words of the Call, more, than the English parcels by many : For the English parcels are 41, and the Call hath above 50.

A voice. .... You have O D *the fourth word of that Call;* The whole Call is placed there, *and ought to be the next.* Number the words of the next Call.
Δ. So that the next Call ought to have this English.

Sapáh.

E. K. Now he sheweth again.

Nal. .....,

Nal.... *The mighty sounds*
have entered
into the third Angle,
and
are become
as Olives.
in the Olive Mount,
looking with gladnesse
upon the earth, E. K.
and Clouds.
* *dwelling in the brightnesse*
of the Heavens
as
continual comforters,
unto whom
I fastened
Pillars of gladnesse

nineteen ——— That is Af
and that word
gave them have not
vessels there.
to water
the earth
with her Creatures,
and
they are
the brothers
of the first
and second,
and
the beginning
of their own seats,
which
are garnished
with continual burning Lamps
69636. Nal.....

whose Peral
numbers *you want*
are as *that word.*
the first,
the ends
and
the Contents of time.
Therefore, E. K. *Now all*
Come ye *the fingers are*
and *bowed down-*
obey *ward.*
your Creation,
visit us in peace
and comfort,
conclude us
as receivers
of their mysteries,
for why?
Our Lord and Master △ 5
is all one. 1

Nal.... ●
E K. *Cloud*s
came between.
E.K. *His eyes*
and the shew-
stone.

E. K. Clouds.
Forte sic.

* *Dwelling in*
the brightnesse
of the heavens
as continual
comforters.

Nal. ..... *That is it that went before.*

E. K. Now he draweth the Curtain.

△. I understand this to be the *English* of the fifth Call; and that before of the sixth: the Numbers of the parcels seem to agree. *So that we have now the* English *of the fifth and* sixth *Call.* Thanked *be God.* E, M, Af. *and* Peoal, *three words which you said we had* not, I finde them in the Calls: your meaning perhaps is some other then the common words.

E. K. Now he hath opened again.

A mighty
Guard
of fire,
with two edged swords
flaming,
which have
the Viols
eight
of wrath
for two times
and
a half,
whose
wings
are
of Wormwood,
and
of the marrow
of salt
have setled
their feet
in the West,
and
are measured
with their Ministers,
9996 ---- *That is,*

Nal......
That is P. you
have not mark
the mysterie.

These C.al, *that you*
gather up *have not.*
the Mosse
of the earth,
[as] *the rich man*
doth
his Treasure,
cursed
are they
whose
iniquities
they are,
in their eyes
are
Milstones,
greater
then the earth.
And
from their mouths
runne
Seas
of bloud:
Their heads
are covered
with Diamond,
and

upon
their hands
are
Marble
sleeves.
Happy is he
on whom
they frown not:
For why?
the God *of righteousnesse*
rejoyceth
in them.
Come away,
And not
your viols.
For,
the time
is such as
requireth
comfort.

The ninth.

△ 5
9 West.

E.K. Now he draweth the Curtain.

△. As I was comparing the Call to this *English,* a voyce said.

Nall. ....., *It is the next Call.*

△. I understand it to be the fourth *Call,* or

E. K. Now

E. K. Now he openeth.

The midday the first,
is as
the third Heaven
made
of Hiacinct pillars
26.
In whom
the Elders
are
become strange,
which
I have prepared
for my own righteousnesse,
saith the Lord,
whose long continuance
shall be
as Buckles
to the stouping Dragons,
and

Nal ....
Ox : And that
you have not,

like
unto the Harvest
of a Widow.
How many are there
which remain
in the glory
of the earth,
which are,
and shall not see
death untill
this house
fall,
and
the Dragon
sink.
Come away.
For,
the Thunders
have spoken :

△. I understand
the end of this
earth, &c.

Come away.
For,
the Crowns
of the Temple ,
and
the Coat
of him, that is, was, and shall
be Crowned
are divided.
Come
appear
to the terrour
of the earth
and
to our comfort,
and
of such
as
are prepared

△ $\frac{4}{8}$

E. K. Now he hath covered all again.

△. As I was speaking of his diversities, saying, This you have not, and this you have not;
A voyce said : *Some you have, and some you have not, whether you have, or have not, it is a my-*
stery.

E. K. There is a little fire in the stone, going about it like a little
Candle.

The Curtain is open, and a great Cloud over them.
Now they appear clear.

The Thunders of Judgement and wrath.

are
numbred
and
are harboured
in the North,
in the likenesse
of an Oak,
whose
branches
are
Neasts
22.

Op....
That you have
not.

of lamentation
and
weeping,
laid up
for
the earth,
that
times
5678.
in the 24th.
parts

That is Daom
that you have
not.

of a moment
roar
with an hundred
mighty Earth-quakes.
And
a Thousand
surges
which
rest not [*or*] *labour still,*
neither
know.

Ol. That you
have not.

——— Turb.

———— Math.

E. K. Now cometh a Cloud over them very white like smoke.
Now they appear again.

Which
burn
night
and
day.
And
vomit out
the heads
of Scorpions,
and
live Sulphur,
mingled
with poyson.
These be

the Thunders
any
time
here.
One rock
bringeth out
a thousand ——
even as
the heart
of man
doth
his thoughts,
wo,w:,wo,
wo,wo,wo,

Nal.......
Math. you
have it
not.

Yea,
wo
be to the earth,
for
th
her iniquity
is,
was,
and shall be
great,
Come away,
But
not
your noyses.

6
10

E. K. Now the Curtain is drawn again, after a quarter of an
hour.

E. K. Now

E. K. Now he appeareth.

Nal. ...... *Consider by these, whose businesse you have in hand.*

O you	of sorrow	3663.	*Mian......*
that range	bindf up	that	
in the South,	your girdles,	the Lord	
and	and	may be magnified,	
are	*Ob......* Vifit us,	whose name	
28.	*That you have not.* Bring down	amongst you	△ 8
the Lanterns	your train	is wrath, &c.	12

...... *Here must words in the end of the first Call, follow at Move, &c.*

△. But this Call, it differeth a little exprefly.

△. They are the 14 last words, in the holy language thus: Zacar e ca, od zamran, odo ic. Qua, Zorge, lap zirdo Noco Mad, Hoath Jaida.

Another ——	spake,	it is measured,	
The mighty feat	and	and	
groaned,	cried with a loud voyce .	it is as	
and	Come away	they are	
there were	and △ 7	whose	
Thunders	they gathered them- 11	Number	
5.	O...... felves together	is	
which	and	*There is no language for thele words in the Call.*	31 —— —— Ga.
flew	became	Come away.	
into the Eaft,	the houfe	For Gabr.	
and	of death,	I prepare —— ⎱ or, have pre-	
the Eagle	of whom	for you, ⎰ pared.	

Note: *Then begin at the first Call, Move, as before.*

E. K. Now they appear.

O thou	6739.	the great name	—— I le mefe: *Wednef-*	*At large,*
the governour	which weave	Righteoufnefſe,	*day,* Julii 11. *dixit*	*Da'ʃ......*
of the firft flame	the earth	and	*bic deeft.*	
under whofe	with drinefſe,	the feat △ 11	Of the firft flame.	*Of the firft flame.*
wings	which	of Honour 15		
are	know of			

Nal...... Then move *as before,* &c.

O you fons	Sons,	vexing	the voyce	
of fury,	Daughters.	all creatures	of God,	
the daughters		of the earth	the promife	
of the juft,		with age	of him	
which		which have	which is called	
fit	*Nal....*	under you *Nal....*	amongst you *Nal....*	
on	Ol......	1636. *Quar.*	Furie —— or extream	△ 10
24		Behold,	—— Juftice.	14
feats				

......, Move, *as before.*

O you fwords	making	and	
of the South	men drunken	his power,	
which have	Nalvage. which are	which	
42 —— Ux.	empty.	is called	
eyes	Behold,	amongst you ▲	
to ftir up	the promife	A bitter fting. 9	
the wrath	of God	13	
of fin,			

...... Move, *as before,* &c.

E. K. Now all is covered.

E. K. Now it is open again.

O thou mighty light,	openeft	to the Center
and burning flame of comfort	the glory	of the earth,
which	of God	In whom

the

Aran --

the secrets of Truth	is called	not to be measured.
6332	in thy Kingdom	Be thou
have	JOY,	a window of comfort 18
their abiding	and	unto me. [14]
which		

△ This is the 14 ... ceived them in the holy Language.

...... *Move as before.*

∩ thou	shalt comfort	separate
Jeu...	the Just,	Creatures
the house of ...	which walkest	great
which	on the earth	art
hast	with feet	thou
thy beginning	8763 ——— *Emod.*	in the God of Stretch forth
in glory,	that understand	and Conquer.
and	and	

△ [11]
16

...... *Move,* &c.

E. K. They have covered all with the Curtain.

Faxs---- Faxis or Faxis to be sounded. I find in the Call Text. I finde also in some words T or F indifferently used. [△ 13.] [17]

O' thou	vexation	whose God
third flame,	and hast	is Wrath in Anger.
whose	7336 .	Gird up
wings	Lamps living	thy loynes
are	going	and
thorns	before thee,	hearken.
to stir up		

...... *Move, as before,* &c.

A voice, ... *Upon Monday you shall have the rest.*
△. The God of Hosts be praised, his name extolled, and his verity prevail to the comfort of his Elect. *Amen*
A voice. ..... *The Eternal God blesse you.* *We have no more now.*
△. Amen, Amen, Amen.   *Hora* 12.

NOTE.

△. Upon my considering (immediately) of these Englished Calls, and the Angelical Language belonging to them, I find that here are but 13 Englished of the 14 which are in the third Cracovien Volume contained : and here wanteth the English of the third of those 14.

Besides this, you may consider that these English Calls keep this order as followeth : and to make it a more perfect account from the beginning of the first Call of All (being long since Englished, and three more) Then have we 18 Calls, whereof 17 are Englished.

Note, the third of the third Book, which is the seventh, from the beginning, is not yet Englished.
Vide post Julii 11. *hora* 4.
There is the Call Englished.

The total summe from the very beginning.	The Numbers of the Third Book, Cracovien.	The Englished Calls of this Book.
6	2	1
5	1	2
9	5	3
8	4	4
10	6	5
12	8	6
11	7	7
15	11	8
14	10	9
13	9	10
18	14	11
17	13	12
16	12	13

NOTE.

Ergo, there lack yet 30 Calls, for the 30 Aires, &c. (besides the English of the seventh or third, in the third Book contained) and so shall there be 48 Calls : For the first Table, is no Call : Although there be letters gathered, but made into no words ; as you may see, before the first Call of all.

Saturday,

Saturday, *Julii* 7. *Mané hora* 6 ½ .† *Cracoviæ.*

Oratione Dominica finita, aliísque tam ad Deum quam ipsum Ave *petitionibus, requirebam Judicium ipsius* Ave *de meis tam ad Deum quam bonos ejus angelos factis orationibus. Post vix quartam horæ partem apparuit.*

Ave. ...... *If the words or truth of our testimony and message, were, or were contained within, the capacity of man, Then might the Devil thrust in himself, and dissemble the Image of Truth : But because it is of Truth, and of him that beareth testimony of himself, it can neither have affinity with the flesh, nor be spoken of in this sense. .*

Lo, thus, deceitfully, hath the Devil entred into man.

Δ. Blessed be the Lord of all truth.

Ave. ...... *Therefore seeing the word is not corruptible, Those that minister the word, cannot dwell in corruption.   I speak not this, without a cause, my brethren.*

Δ. I pray you to proceed, accordingly, that we may know the cause, if it be your will : or else leaving this Caveat unto us, to proceed to the matter wherein we required your help-ing hand to correct or confirm, or to do that which is behooful.

Ave. ......: *For, which of you have sought the Lord, for the Lord his cause or sake ?*

Δ. That, God can be Judge.

Ave. ...... *Or in which of you hath due obedience ; either to the word , or unto us that are san-ctified by the word, been faithfully performed ?*

Δ. My points of errour, and disobedience I beseech you to Notifie, that I may amend them.

Ave. .... *It may be, you will say, we have laboured, and we have watched, yea we have called on the name of the Lord.   What have you done that you ought not to do , yea, a thousand times more ?*

Δ. We vaunt nothing of any our doings, nor challenge any thing by any perfection of our doings.

Ave. ...... *Shall the hireling say, I have laboured hard ? or doth the good servant think he merit-eth his wages ? It is not so.   But you do so ; Therefore you are neither worthy of your reward, nor the name of faithful servants.*

Δ. No Lord, we challenge nothing upon any merits ; but flie unto thy mercy and that we crave and call for.

Ave. ...... *You do wickedly and injustly : yea you credit the Lord, as you do your selves : your faith is the faith of men, and not of the faithful.*

Many things have I said unto you from the beginning, (saith the God of Justice) which you have heard, and not believed : But you tempt me , and provoke me ; yea you stir me up to be angry with you.

Δ. If thy Anger shall be on us, beside the sorrow of this world, tentations of the feind, &c. Then are we not able to endure.

...... *Answer not me, and hear what the Lord saith unto thee :   Satan laugheth you to scorn ; for he saith unto the Lord, standing before him,   Are these they whom thou deliveredst from the perils of the Seas ; and from the hands of the wicked, whom the windes were a comfort to ; and thy Countenance a Lanthorn ?   But the Lord seemeth not to hear him : for he knoweth it is true.   My* brethren, you seek the world more than you seek to perform the will of God : *as though God could not rain Gold and Margarits amongst you : As though the breath of God were not able to beat down the whole earth before you.   O you faithlesse Creatures : O ye hypocrites in the Vineyard of the Lord : O you unworthy servants of such a Matter.   Neither unto* Abraham, *nor unto* Noe, *nor unto any other Patriarchs or Prophets, hath God done more merciful unto, than unto you.   To* Abra-ham *he said, When I return at this time of the year, Thou shalt have a son.   Unto* Noe *he said, Build thee a Ship : Make up the Ark, Thus and thus, it shall be : for the people shall perish.*

You remember not that Joseph *was sold by his brethren ; or if you do, it may be, you think it is a* fable : *If you think it to be true, Then consider how he escaped the Pit ; Consider he was sold, and so became a bondman : But who changed the imagination and sense of his brethren ? who (I say) came between their Tyranny and his innocency ? What was he that made him free ? that brought him before* Pharaoh ? *yea, and that which is more, made him reign over* Pharaoh : *Was it not the same God, that dealeth with you ?*

O ye of little faith, and starvelings, withered grasse, and blasted willows : What and if you were in hell, could he not deliver you ? If you become bondmen, cannot he make you free ? If you be in prison, cannot he deliver you ?   Cannot he compasse your neck with a chain ?   But Satan *saith, Lo, they say, they have a long Journey : It is necessary that God comfort those that put their trust in him.   Euge, O ho   O you beggerly starvelings,   Hath not the same God, the same* Raphael *that he had . . .   Yes verily, a thousand a hundred ; and a thousand and a hundred thousand thousands that are, and more then* Raphael *for the help and comfort of the faithful.*

When Herod *sought to kill the son of God, in that he was man : his Father delivered him not with a mighty wind, nor with beating down of Lords Palaces ; but by a dream appeared unto* Joseph, *saying, flee,* Herod *seeketh the child his life.   Note the manner of his warning, The man-ner*

The great and peculiar mer-cies of God shewed on us.

Genes. 37.

ner of his departure : But hear what the Lord said in the end. Return, for he that sought the
Child his life, is now dead. Why, I say, you rotten Reeds, worse than the excrements of the Fens,

Up and be gone.
Stephen Bathor King of Poland.

have not you greater warning ? Wherefore b it said unto you, Up and be gone, but that the Lord seeth the thoughts of man ? even of him which seeketh your destruction ; Even of this wicked King which seeketh to destroy Laskie.

Could not the same Lord, consume that wicked monster and seller of his people, (which tarryeth for a time) with the fire of his mouth ? Yes, but that he hath given all things a time. Those

Note of the death of the righteous now and then. Flee.

that are righteous are oftentimes taken away because of temptations that are to come : But the wicked are suffered to continue, because they might be more heavy, and sink deeper : But, (for love) I say unto you, my brethren, Flee the mischiefs that are to come, and go forward in the service of the Highest, that you may enjoy the promises that are made you, and be partakers of the happy dayes to come.

Take heed of whoredom, and the provocations of the flesh. For why ? those things that we

But 10. dayes.

say, are not without their cause. You have but ten dayes to tarry (if you will follow my counsel) But if you linger any longer, you may drink of a Cup that you would not. Wherefore doth God warn you, but that he would be just with you ? Hath he not the whole Earth to serve him ? Believe me, by the testimony we bear, that the good Angels weep over you ; for, as you are particular-

Particular Temptations.

ly called, so have you your particular and unaccustomed temptations. But pray unto God, that you may prevail. Nititur enim, omnibus modis, Sathanas ut vos devoret.

Provide for this Journey. Spiritus Sanctus. Be gone.

It is said unto you, If you provide for this Journey, &c. That word is as sure as the strongest rock in the world. Considering that you were warned by the same Spirit (whereof I speak) being witnesse of himself, and by us, which bear witnesse of him ; Give ear, gird up your selves, and be gone : For, even at the very doors, are mischief. After a while I have somewhat else to say unto you.

E. K. He covereth all with the white Curtain.

Δ. We read and considered these premises somewhat diligently.

Δ. Afterward, [Ave] he came again, and (after a pause) said as followeth.

Enoch.

Ave ...... *My brother, I see thou do't not understand the mystery of this Book, or work thou hast in hand, But I told thee, it was the knowledge that God delivered unto Enoch. I said also, that Enoch*

The Book confirmed.

laboured 50 dayes. Notwithstanding, that thy labour be not frustrate, and void of fruit, Be it unto thee, as thou hast done.

Δ. Lord I did the best that I could conceive of it.

Ave. ...... *I will tell thee, what the labour of Enoch was for those fifty dayes.*

Δ. O Lord I thank thee.

Nal. Ave. It is a kind of flate-stone.
50 Dayes labour.

He made, (as thou hast done, thy book) Tables, of Serpasan and plain stone : as the Angel of the Lord appointed him ; saying, tell me (O Lord) the number of the dayes that I shall labour in. It was answered him so.

Then he groaned within himself, saying, Lord God the Fountain of true wisdom, thou that openest the secrets of thy own self unto man, thou knowest mine imperfection, and my inward darknesse : How can I (therefore) speak unto them that speak not after the voice of man ; or worthily call on thy name, considering that my imagination is variable and fruitlesse , and unknown to my self ?

Enoch his prayer to God.

Shall the Sands seem to invite the Mountains : or can the small Rivers entertain the wonderful and unknown waves ?

Can the vessel of fear, fragility, or that is of a determined proportion, lift up himself, heave up his hands, or gather the Sun into his bosom ? Lord it cannot be : Lord my imperfection is great : Lord I am lesse than sand : Lord, thy good Angels and Creatures ex e'l me far : our proportion is not alike ; our sense agreeth not : Notwithstanding I am comforted ; For that we have all one God,

One Creatour of all things. A Seer.

all one beginning from thee, that we respect thee a Creatour : Therefore will I call upon thy name, and in thee, I will become mighty. Thou shalt light me, and I will become a Seer ; I will see thy Creatures, and will magnifie thee amongst them. Those that come unto thee have the same gate, and through the same gate, descend, such as thou sendest. Behold, I offer my house, my labour, my heart and soul, If it will please thy Angels to dwell with me, and I with them ; to rejoyce with me, that I may rejoyce with them ; to minister unto me, that I may magnifie thy name. Then, lo the Tables (which I have provided, and according to thy will, prepared) I offer unto thee, and unto thy holy Angels, desiring them, in and through thy holy names : That as thou art their light, and comfortest them, so they, in thee will be my light and comfort. Lord they prescribe not laws unto thee, so it is not meet that I prescribe laws unto them : What it pleaseth thee to offer, they receive ; So what it pleaseth them to offer unto me, will I also receive. Behold I say(O Lord) If I shall call upon them in thy name, Be it unto me in mercy, as unto the servant of the Highest. Let them also manifest unto me, How, by what words, and at what time,

The Call of Angels.

I shall call them. O Lord, Is there any that measure the heavens, that is mortal ? How, therefore, can the heavens enter into mans imagination ? Thy Creatures are the Glory of thy countenance : Hereby thou glorifiest all things, which Glory excelleth and (O Lord) is far above my understanding. It is great wisdom, to speak and talke according to understanding with

[Δ] Kings :

[Δ]. *Kings : But to command Kings by a subjected commandment, is not wisdom,* unlesse it come from thee. *Behold Lord, How shall I therefore ascend into the heavens ? The air will not carry me, but resisteth my folly; I fall down, for I am of the earth. Therefore, O thou very Light and true Comfort, that canst, and mayst, and dost command the heavens ; Behold I offer these Tables unto thee,* Command them as it pleaseth thee : *and O you Ministers, and true lights of understanding,* Governing this earthly frame, and the elements wherein we live, *Do for me as for the servant of the Lord : and unto whom it hath pleased the Lord to talk of you*

Behold, Lord, thou hast appointed me 50 times; * Thrice 50 times *will I lift my hands unto* * Ave. thee. *Be it unto me as it pleaseth thee, and thy holy Ministers.* I require nothing but thee, and *That is to say, through thee, and for thy honour and glory : But I hope I shall be* satisfied, *and shall not die,* thrice a day. (As thou hast promised) *until thou gather the clouds together, and judge all things : when in a moment I shall be changed and dwell with thee for ever.*

These words, were thrice a dayes talk betwixt Enoch *and* God : In the end of 50 dayes, there Thrice a day. appeared unto him, *which are not now to be manifested nor spoken of : he enjoyed the fruit of God his promise, and received the benefit* of his faith. *Here may the wise learn wisdom : for what doth man that is not corruptible ?*

I have not that I may say any more unto you : But believe me, I have said great things unto you : If you will have me hereafter, I will come.

Δ.
...... *Consider well my words, and what I have now said unto thee : for here thou mayst learn wisdom,* and also see what thou hast to do.

Δ. I will, if it please you read over some of these Invitations which I have made and written here in this Book.

Ave. ...... *You may not use that word* Obedientes.

Δ. You spake of a first word to call, and of a second to *constrain.*

Ave. ......, *It signifieth,* it urgeth them more in God. *I have said.*

Δ. Note, what is meant by the name of God that was said to constrain, being the second What is meant names of two before given. by the phrase or word Con-

E. K. He is gone, and all covered with the Curtain. straint, in re-

Δ. All honour, praise, and glory, all thanks and power, is due to our God and King. *spect of good Angels.*
So be it. *Amen.*

Monday, *Julii,* 9. *Manè hora* 7. *three quarters,* † Cracoviæ.
Orationibus quibusdam finitis ad Deum & deinde ad *Gabrielem* & *Nalvage,* &c.

E. K. As soon as he looked, he found the Stone covered with the white Curtain.

Δ. A pause of a ¼ of an hour : In which space I used sundry ejaculations to God, and his good Angels.

Δ. This day was appointed, we attend therefore your instructions. At length they appeared not, but used a voice.

A voice. ......, *This day, but the Sun declining the fourth hour.*

Δ. Your meaning is, that at after noon, at 4 of the clock.

The voice. ...... *As thou hast written* ——

Δ. The will of the Highest be done. *Amen.*

Monday, *A Meridie, hora* 4.

Δ. As E. K. was saying to me, that he thought that the Angels might tell the certain day and times of things to come, and that Angels could now fall no more, &c. Of such things touching Angels ; suddenly a voice was heard, as followeth.

A voice. ...... *Herein will I talk with you, my brethren.*

E. K. *Gabriel* onely appeareth : neither *Nalvage* nor the Table appeareth. He sitteth in a Chair, and with his fiery Dart.

Gabr. ...... *The Prophets inspired with the Holy Ghost, were assured of the coming of their Messias, of their Christ : But what day, or in what year was not of mans understanding. Christ himself opened unto his Disciples his death, and the manner thereof ; but the day and hour he never dis-*

[C c]   *closed.*

De secundo ad-   *closed.* So likewise *the Scriptures speak of the coming of Christ, but the day and hour, the Son of*
ventu Christi.   *man knoweth not.* But because *in time to come, and for this action, (the message of the highest)*
And assured, and infallible Doctrine, (in respect that God appointed you no certain time) is neces-
sary. For, for this cause *you waver my brethren: and may lose the benefit of God his favour, and*
mercies. O weaklings *examine the Prophets, look into the doing of the Apostles: There always*
went a promise before the end: But the end was the benefit and fruit of the promise. Some alleadge Paul, *some* Peter, *some* Daniel: But *in this case shall you alleadge the sayings of God, spo-*
ken in the spirit of truth by me *Gabriel, the servant of the highest.* God, for three causes hi-
deth the end, *and the very time of his heavenly purposes.* As after a little silence you shall shortly hear.

E. K. A cloud covereth him.

E. K. Now he appeareth again.

Gab. ...... *First, by reason of his own inexplicable* Est & non *est esse, which is without the circum-*
ference, strength, capable vertue, and power of man, *his intellectuality, whereby he appeareth to be*
verily one God, *and incomprehensible.*

Secondly, because Lucifer *with his yea sayers, (damned justly) should never taste of his light,*
nor understand his secret judgements : *which he would, and might do, if they were delivered to mans*
imagination, and discourse : *Because it is within the circumference and compasse of his Creation.*
Consider of these two.

E. K. Now he is covered in a white Cloud again.

Δ. The first reason, or cause we do not sufficiently understand, or conceive.
Deus est esse, Sanctis Deus.
Non est esse, Impiis Deus.

For, *In the judgement day, God in his son, Christ, shall shut up his perpetual and everlasting Ju-*
stice, wrath, *and anger, with Hell and damnation.* Leaving them, *and forsaking them, and in*
no case to be called their G d. Fratres [mi] non habebunt Deum. *But they shall be without*
a guide, *and without a Centre.* Hereby you may understand *, Esse & non est esse.* To the
purpose.

Thirdly, that man firmly perswaded of things spoken of by God above his capacity to come, and
unknown, *might worthily in the strength of faith, and through the effect of his promises merit his fa-*
vour in Christ, *and receive eternal salvation, justly before God and his Angels. These are the three*
causes.

Δ. This last cause, if it would please you to make more plain, it should greatly enform us
and confirm us.

.... *These are the three onely causes, that the ends of God his determinations are secret.*
1. *In the first, that God might appear omnipotent.*
2. *In the second, sealed up in himself from the knowledge of such as have rebelled to their di-*
struction.
3. *In the third, that man might justly be made worthy of the places prepared for him.*

Wednesday   Nalvage *is called away, and cannot be in Action with you till* Wednesday. Then shall you
following.   have the Calls that you look for. And so enter into the knowledge and perfect under-
standing of the 49 Gates and Tables *if you will.*
Δ. O Lord, thy will and mercy be shewed upon us.
Gab. ...... *But understand that it is a labour, the hardest and the last.*
Δ. Violenti nihil difficile : God strengthen our will and fai h.
Gab. ...... *I have nothing else to say unto you.* But God be mercifull unto you, and forgive you
your sins.
Δ. Amen.
Gab. ...... *And that you go hence, make haste.*
Δ.

E. K. He is gone.

Δ. Gloria Patri, & filio, & spiritui Sancto sicut erat in principio, & nunc & semper, & in
secula seculorum. *Amen.*

Wednesday, *Julii* 11. Mane hora, 6 ½.   *Cracovia.*
Oratione dominica finita, &c.   *The Curtain appeared*
straight way.
Δ. We await the promise, which you made us, O *Gabriel.*
A voyce. *Not now, but at the fourth hour, declining as before.*
At four of the   E. K. And why not now as well?
Clock after   A voyce. *He that laboureth in his own harvest laboureth when he list: but he that fisheth on the*
noon.   Sea, *must be ruled by her course.*
Δ. Fiat voluntas Dei.

Wednes-

Wednesday, *Julii* 11. *à Meridie, hora* 4.

Δ. At the first looking the Curtain appeared to E. K. his sight.

Δ. When it shall please thee, O God, we are desirous to receive wisdom from thee.

Δ. At six of the Clock appeared a little one, yellow, like a little Childe: his hair fine yellow, and a very amiable face.

To avoid reproach, and for the truth of the word I visit you, instead of Nalvage, *which cannot come. I am* Ile Mese, *the servant of the highest, which instead of* Nalvage, *will, and am able to supply his place.*

Δ. So be it in the name of Jesus.

Ilem. .... *Many, and strong are your enemies, both bodily and ghostly: But be you strong, and you shall prevail.*

NOTE.
Ilemese.
Δ. He is one of *sigillum Dei,* one of the Septenarii whereof , Ave and... are
The Translation of the Call into English.

Many enemies bodily and ghostly.

Therefore say, what you will have me do.

Δ. That (if it please you) that *Nalvage* would have done.

The East is a house of Virgins.

Δ. He distinguisheth it not by fingers.

Ile. .. ... *Well, you shall have fingers.*

Singing praises	with ornaments so bright	*Move,*
among it	such as	appear,
the flames of first glorie,	work wonders	sing praises
wherein	on all creatures,	unto the Creator,
the Lord	whose	and
hath opened his mouth	Kingdoms	be mighty
and	and continuance	amongst us,
they are become He. ...	are as the third	for
Twenty eight Ni;	and fourth	unto this remembrance
living dwellings, That you have	strong Towers	is given
in whom not.	and	power,
the strength of man	places of comfort.	and
rejoyceth.	The seat of mercy	our strength
and	and continuance.	waxeth strong
they are apparail'd	O you servants of mercy.	in our comforter.

Ile. .. ... *Lo, there you have it.*

Δ. I pray you to consider of the form of the promise, for we were promised to receive the **Vide Supra.** Calls we looked for, and so to be fit for the 49 Gates, &c. If this you have done, be the performance of those the words of *Gabriel,* or no, I pray you consider.

Ile. ...... *For the thirty Calls, or thirty Call,* to morrow *at the fourth hour,* Thursday at four of I will ease you sufficiently. the Clock afternoon.

Δ. I beseech you (if I shall not offend to request it) *What is the cause of* Gabriel and Nalvage *their absence?*

Ile. ..... Spiritual Contention between Satan and them, *and more then man can, or may understand.*

Δ. Then I pray you, why was not this supply sent at the time appointed?

Ile. ..... *It is not of God, to think that God is of time. All things are tied unto him, and nothing can be separated from him. Notwithstanding, he may separate himself from them. But you* Nineteen *shall understand, that these* nineteen Calls. Calls received.

Δ There are but 18 besides the first to God.

...... *There are nineteen besides the first*] are the Calls, or entrances into the The use of these knowledge of the mystical Tables: *Every Table* containing one whole leaf, 19 Calls. whereunto you need no other circumstances.

1. *The first Call beginneth* Ol Sonf.
   In English *I raign.*
2. *The second beginneth* Adgt.
   In English Can.
3. *The Call of the third Table beginneth* *Micma.*
   In English Behold.

E. K. A white cloud cometh about him, but hideth him not.

Ile...... *But you must understand that in speaking of the first Table, I speak of the second. So that the second, with you is the first.*

4. *As this last, behold is the fourth, but with you the* third.

Δ. It is the seventh: but the third of the fourteenth.

[c c 2] Ile. .. ... It

Ile. ...... *It is the Call* of the third.

5. *The next* —— *in* English *is* I have set
   Otherwise —— O thil.

6. *The sixth* —— *The mighty sounds.*
   Otherwise —— Saphah.

7. *The seventh* —— *The spirits*
   Gah.

8. *The eight* —— *The East*
   ROa.

Ilem. ...... *Look that, that you call the third.*

Δ. It is *Raus.*

9. *The next* —— *The midday the first*
   Basenn lo, or *Basemlo.*

10. ⌐——⌐ *A mighty*
    Micaoli.

11. ——— *The Thunders of judgement and wrath*
    Coraxo.

There cometh a white bright Cloud about him.

12. ——— *The mighty seat*
    Sai
    Ox *Cai* al.

E. K. Every time he speaketh, he pulleth fire out of his mouth, and casteth it from him.

13. ——— *O you*
    Nonci.

14. ——— *O you swords*
    Napci.

E. K. Now a white Cloud goeth round.

15. ——— *O you sons*
    No Romi.

16. ——— *O thou the Governour*
    Ils Tabaam

Il. ...... *There you lack the third word?*

Δ. What is that?

...... *Of the first flame, it answereth to* L *al* purt.
You had not the exposition of the third word.

17. *O ye of the second flame.*
    Ils vivi a purt.

18. ——— *O thou third flame,*
    Ils di al part.

19. *O thou mighty light*
    Il micalZo al part.

Thus you have not lost your labour.

E. K. Now he wrappeth the Cloud that was under him about his head.

... . *God be with you.*

E. K. Saw him go upward.

Δ. Glory be to God, praise and honour for. *Amen.*

Thursday, *Julii* 12. *& Mere bora* 4. † *Cracovia.*

Oratione Dominica finita, & breviter ad *I'emese* quibusdam dictis.

E. K. The Curtain appeared at the first looking.

Δ. Now in the name of Jesus, as concerning those 30 Calls, or thirty Call, we await your information of *Ilemese.*

Δ. As-

Δ. After divers parcels of our Actions past with *Nalvage* being read, which were very well of us liked, at length *Ilemese* appeared : and after he had shewed himself (the Curtain being opened) he drew the Curtain to again.   *Ilemist.*

Δ. I then said three Prayers out of the Psalms, &c.

E. K. Now he standeth as *Nalvage* used to do, upon the Globe with the rod in his hand : *And* Gabriel *sitteth by.*

Δ. In the name of the eternal and everlasting God say on.

E. K. Now the Globe turneth swiftly, and he pointeth to letters thus, with the rod which *Nalvage* was wont to use.

MADRIIAX	*O you heavens*	Δ. I think this word wanteth as may appear by *Madriax*, about 44 words from the end. *Ilemese.*
DSPRAF	*which dwell*	*Ds praf.*
LIL	*In the first air*	*Lil.* *Kis*
CHISMICAOLZ	*are mighty*	*Chis Micáolz.*

Gab. .... *Move not, for the place is holy.*
Δ. Hallowed be his name, that sanctifieth whatsoever is sanctified.

SAANIR	*in the parts*	*Sa á nir.* *Ile.*
CAOSGO	*of the earth*	*Ca ós go.*
OD		
FISIS	*and execute*	*Od fisis*
BALZIZRAS	*the judgement*	*Bal zi zras.* *Ta*
IAIDA	*of the highest*	*Ia - i da.* *fa*
NONCA	*to you*	*Nonca.*
GOHULIM	*It is said*	*Go hu lim.*

E. E. There came a black cloud in the air about the Stone, as though it would have hindered E. K. his sight.

Gabr. ...... *It behoveth us to do that we do even with present contention against the wicked. Have a little patience.*

The curtain is now away again, and they appear again.

		Mikma
MICMA	*Behold*	*Micma.* *asper.*

E. K. Now is the curtain plucked to again, and they covered.

ADOIAN	*the face*	*A do i an.*
MAD	*of your God*	*Mad.*
IAOD	*The beginning*	*I á od.*
BLIORB	*of Comfort*	*Bliórb.*
SABAOOAONA	*whose eyes*	*Sa ba o o áo na.* *O or A.* *Kis f*
CHI	*are*	*Chis.*

LUCIF-

LUCIFTIAS	*the brightnesse*	*Lu cif ti m.*
PIRIPSOL	*of the heavens,*	*Pe rip sol.*
AS	*which*	*Ds.*
ABRAASSA	*provided*	*Abr aßa.*
NONCF	*you*	*Nonsf Noncf.*
NETAAIB	*for the government*	*Ne tb a ib.*
CAOSGI	*of the earth,*	*Ca of gi.*
OD	*and*	*Od.*
TILB	*her*	*Tilb.*
ADPHAHT	*unspeakeble*	*Ad phabt.*

Ile, ... *Read it.*
Δ. The English.
Ile, ..., *I*

DAMPLOZ	*variety,*	*Dâm plox.*
TOOAT	*furnishing*	*To b at. Nonsf*
NONCF	*you*	*Non cf.*
GMICALZOMA	*with a power, understanding*	*Gmi cal zo ma.*
LRASD	*to dispose*	*Lrásd.*
TOFGLO	*all things*	*Tof glo.*
MARB	*according*	*Marb.*

[Δ. It follows in *Libro Cra.* .

LIBRI

LIBRI CRACOVIENSIS MYSTICUS APERTORIUS,

Julii, 12. 1584.

PRÆTEREA PROOEMIUM MADIMIANUM,

Libri primi, Pragenfis Cæfareıque, Anno 1584.
Augufti 15. *Stilo Novo.*

Liber 5. *Cracovienfium Myfteriorum Apertorius.*
Thurfday, Julii 12. *Anno* 1584.

ARRY   *to the providence*   Yar ry.

Δ. Note the wicked power dazeled fo the eyes of
E. K. that he could not well difcern this O̊, but
ID*UIGO *O   ftaying at it a while concluded it to be an V : which
afterward, and by and by, he corrected.

of him that fitteth on the holy Throne   Id u̇i-go.
                                           I doi go.

The Curtain being plucked.

Ile. ..... *Have Patience.*

Δ. As we were talking of the name of God *Idoigo* in *Enoch* his Tables, a voice faid.

A voice ...... *Where the moft force was, the Devil crept moft in.*   *Herein the Devil thought to deceive you.*

Δ. It muft be then *I doigo* ?

O D	*and*	Od.
TORZULP	*rofe up*	Tor zulp.
IAODAF	*in the beginning*	Ia o daf.
GOHOL	*faying,*	Go hól.
CAOSGA	*The earth,*	Ca óf ga.
TABAORD	*let her be governed*	Ta ba ord.
SAANIR	*by her parts ;*	Sa á nir.
OD	*and*	Od.
CHRISTEOS	*let there be*	Chris té os.
YRPOIL	*divifion*	Yr pó il.
TIOBL	*in her,*	Ti óbl.
BUSDIRTILB	*that the glory of her*	Buf dir tilb.

NOALN

NOALN	*May be*	No aln.
PAID	*alwayes*	pa id.
ORSBA	*drunken*	Orf ba.
OD	*and*	Od.
DODRMNI	*vexed*	Dodrumni. Dod rm ni.
ZYLNA	*in it self.*	Zyl na.
ELZAPTILB	*Her course,*	El zap tilb.
PARMGI	*Let it run*	Parm gi.
PIRIPSAX	*with the Heavens,*	Pe rip fax.
OD	*and*	Od.
TA	*as*	Ta.
QURLST	*an handmaid.*	Kurlft. Qurlft.

Il. ..... Have patience a little.   E. K.

E. K. Now they are here again.

BOOAPIS	*Let her serve them*	Booapis.
LNIBM	*one season:*	Lnib m.
OUCHO	*Let it confound*	Chofe. O v Cho.
SYMP	*another,*	Symp.
OD	*and*	Od.
CHRISTEOS	*let there be*	Chris te os.
AGTOLTORN	*no Creature*	A g tol torn.
MIRC	*upon,*	Mirk. Mirc.
Q	*or*	Q.
TIOBL	*within her*	Ti ob l.
LEL	*the same*	Lel.
TON	...... *one and the same.* *All*	Ton.
PAOMBD	*her members*	Pa Ombd.
DILZMO	*let them agree*	Dil zmo.
ASPIAN	*in their qualities,*	As pi an.

OD

OD	*and*	Od. Long, *or short.*
CHRISTEOS	*Let there bu*	Chris te os.
AGLTOLTORN	*no one Creature*	Ag l ter torn. Ah.
PARACH	*equal*	Ach. Pa rach.

The wicked spake behinde E. K.   Note.

ASYMP	*with another.*	A symp.
CORDZIZ	*The reasonable Creatures of the earth, or Man.*	Cord ziz.
DODPAL	*Let them vex*	Dod pal.
OD	*and*	Od.
FIFALZ	*weed out*	Fi falz.
LSMNAD	*one another.*	Ls mnad.

E. *K*. Now the Curtain is drawn.

A voyce....... *Read.*

Δ. *I read it .... ter from the beginning hitherto.*

Ile. ...... *Whereat doubt you.*

Δ. Is it true, that before the Creation of man this kinde of Malediction was pronounced, or when else shall we understand it to have been spoken ?

A voyce. ...... *True it is that one man weedeth out another. To avoid which fault it is said, and after God thy brother as thy self.*

One Kingdom riseth up against another, the servant against his Master, the wicked son disdaineth his father. All which fell upon man when God cursed the earth: For, perfect love was taken from among them, and the spirit of malice came amongst them, to the intent they might be always at variance, and one weed out another, and so must be, and shall be unto the end. Answer me, why turned God Adam out into the earth.

Δ. Because he had transgressed the Laws to be kept in Paradise.

..... . *It is true. Then Adam offending, received punishment for his offence, in that he was turned out into the earth. If he had been turned out to a blessed place, then can you not aptly say he was turned out, for he that is turned out goeth to dishonour: Even so Adam, from innocency through his fall, was turned out to corruption into a prison prepared for him before, if he offended. God (my brother) knew he would offend: he knew also how to dishonour him.*   If.

As Jesu Christ brought all blessednesse, and comfort into the world: So did Adam, *accursed, bring all misery and wretchednesse into the world, and in the same instant, when* Adam *was expelled ; The Lord suffered the earth to be accursed for* Adams *sake, and* then, said the Lord these things, and gave unto the world her time: and placed over her *Keepers, Watch-men, and Princes, for years, moneths, and dayes: [I am easie, you may understand my rule.]*   Note. In the same instant. Angelicall Watch-men, Keepers, Princes of the earth.

Δ. Note, All this was answered by a voyce, as concerning my question, or doubt heretofore expressed.

.... *After this, a great pause was used: In which time in my minde, I discoursed of the Ministery Angelicall, not all to have been committed to their charge with their Creation, but afterward in divers times, divers offices, both toward God and man.*

A voyce. ...... *To morrow morning I will meet you here the third hour.*

[d d]   Δ. The

Δ. The third hour after the Sun rising mean you?

A voyce. ..... *I.*

    Δ. Let us hartily thank the Lord and praise him alwayes: His Mercy and Grace be upon us, now and ever. *Amen.*

Fryday, *Julii* 13. *Mane hora* 7.   † *Cracoviæ.*

Δ. *Oratione Dominica finita,* &c.

Δ. At the first looking, E. K. saw the Curtain usual to appear, and somewhat plighted, and shortly.

A voyce. ..... *Read that you have done.*

Δ. I read hitherto that was written.

E. K. Now they appear, the Curtain being drawn away : But the round Table, or Globe appeared not.

E. K. Now they have drawn the Curtain over them again.

Δ. Blessed be they that are come in the name of our God, and for his service.

E. K. Now they appear, and the Table, or Globe with them.

Ile. ..... *The rest.*

Δ. In the name of Jesus, and for his honour.

OD	*And*	Od.
		Gad.
FARGT	*the dwelling places,*	Farg t.
BAMS	*Let them forget*	Bams
OMAOAS	*their names,*	O ma o as.
CONISBRA	*the work of man*	Co nis bra.
OD	*and*	Od.
AUAVOX	*his pomp :*	A ua vox.
		g dg.
TONUG	*Let them be defaced*	To nug.
ORSCATBL	*his buildings,*	Ors cat bl.
NOASMI	*let them become*	No as mi.
TABGES	*Caves*	Tab ges.
LEVITHMONG	*for the beasts of the field*	Levith mong.
		Ki.
UNCHI	*confound*	Un chi.
OMPTILB	*her understanding*	Omp tilb.
ORS	*with darknesse,*	Ors.
BAGLE	*for why ?*	Bagle.
MOOOAH	*it repenteth me*	Mo c uah.
OLCORDZIZ	*I made man*	Ol cord ziz.

L C A-

LCAPIMAO	*one while*	L ca pí ma o.
IXOMAXIP	*let ker be kiſown,*	Ix o máx ip.
ODCAGOCASB	*and another while*	Od ca có casb.

Gab. ,..... *Move not, for the place is holy.*
E. K. All is covered.
E. K. Now it is open.

GOSAA	*a ſtranger,*	Go ſa a.
BAGLEN	*becauſe*	Baglen.
PII	*ſhe is*	Pi i.
TIANTA	*the bed*	Ti ánta.
ABABALOND	*of an harlot*	A bá ba lond.
ODFAORGT	*and the dwelling place*	gt, or dgt. Od fa orgt.
TELOCVOVIM	*of him that is fallen.*	lotch; or lóckı Te lóc vo v im.
MADRIIAX	*O you heavens*	yax Má dri iax.
TORZU	*ariſe,*	Tor zu.
OADRIAX	*The lower heavens*	O ádriax.
OROCHA	*underneath you*	ka. O ro cha.
ABOAPRI	*let them ſerve you,*	A bo a prı.
TABAORI	*Govern*	Tabá o ri.
PRIAZ	*thoſe*	Priáz.
ARTABAS	*that govern,*	Ar ta bas;
ADRPAN	*Caſt down*	dir A dr pan.
CORSTA	*ſuch as*	Cór ſta.
DOBIX	*fall,*	Dobix.
YOLCAM	*bring forth*	Yol cam.

E. K. Now the Curtain is drawn.

PRIAZI	*with thoſe*	Pri á zi.
ARCOAZIOR	*that encreaſe,*	Ar co a zior.
ODQUASB	*and deſtroy*	Od quasb.

[dd 2]

QTING

Q TING	*the rotten*	^{dg} Q ing.
RIPIR	*No place,*	Ri pír.
PAAOXT	*let it remain*	Pa a oxt.
SAGACOR	*in one number.*	Kor Sa gá cor.
VML	*Adde*	Vm l,
OD	*and*	
PRDZAR	*Diminish*	Pur Prd zar.
CACRG	*until*	cúrg Ca crg.
AOIVEAE	*the Stars*	A oi vé ae.
CORMPT	*be numbred;*	Cormpt.
TORZU	*arise,*	Tor zu.
ZACAR	*Move*	Zacar.
ODZAMRAN	*and appear*	Od zamran.
ASPT	*before*	Aspt.
SIBSI	*the Covenant*	Sib si.

E. K. Now he hath drawn the curtain again.

BUTMONA	*of his mouth,*	But mo na.
DS	*which*	Ds.
SURZAS	*he hath sworn*	Sur zas.
TIA	*unto me*	Tia.
BALTAN	*in his Justice.*	Balta n.
ODO	*Open*	Odo,
CICLE	*the mysteries*	Cicle.
QAA	*of your Creation,*	Q á a.
OD	*and*	Od.
OZAZMA	*make us*	Ozazma.
PLAPLI	*partakers*	Pla pli.
IADNAMAD	*of undefiled knowledge.*	Iad na mad.

The first Aire, is called ————————	Lil.	
The second ————————	Arii.	
The third ————————	Zom.	
4 ————————	Paz.	
5 ————————	Lit.	
6 ————————	Maz.	
7 ————————	Deo.	
8 ————————	Zid.	
9 ————————	Zip.	
10 ————————	Zax.	
11 ————————	Ich ik.	
12 ————————	Loe.	
13 ————————	Zim.	
14 ————————	Uta.	
15 ————————	Oxo.	
16 ————————	Lea.	
17 ————————	Tan.	
18 ————————	Zen.	
19 ————————	Pop.	
20 ————————	Chr	kar in palato
21 ————————	Asp.	very much.
22 ————————	Lin.	....
23 ————————	Tor.	
24 ————————	Nia.	
25 ————————	Uti.	
26 ————————	Des.	
27 ————————	Zaa.	
28 ————————	Bag.	
29 ————————	Rii.	
30 ————————	Tex.	

There is all ————

Now change the name, and the Call is all one.

Δ. Blessed be he who onely is always one.

Δ. I take these names to be as *primus, secundus, tertius,* and to 30.

A voice. ...... Not so, they be the substantial names of the Aires.

Δ. It was said they had no proper names ; but were to be called, O thou of the first Aire, O thou of the second, &c. I pray you reconcile the repugnancy of these two places, as they should seem.

Note.
How this One
Call may serve
the 30.

E. K. The Curtain is opened.

E. E. Now *Gabriel* standeth up.

Gabr. .... *Thus hath God kept promise with you, and hath delivered you the keyes of his store-houses : wherein you shall find, (if you enter wisely, humbly, and patiently) Treasures more worth than the frames of the heavens.*

But yet is not August come : Notwithstanding the Lord hath kept his promise with you before the time. Therefore, Now examine your Books, Confer one place with another, and learn to be perfect for the practice and entrance.

God his prd.
before August.

See that your garments be clean.   Herein be not rash :. Nor over hasty; For those that are hasty and rash, and are lothsomely apparelled, may knock long before they enter.

Counsel for
preparation.

There is no other reading of the Book, but the appearing of the Ministers and Creatures of God : which shewing what they are themselves, shew how they are conjoyned in power, and represented formally by those letters.

The reading
of the Book.
The letters.

E. K. Now he taketh the Table, and seemeth to wrap it up together.

Δ. Seeing I have moved the doubt of *their names* I pray you to dissolve it.

Gab. ...... *You play with me childishly.*

Δ. I have done.

Gab. ...... *Thinkest thou that we speak any thing that is not true ?*

Thou shalt never know the mysteries of all things that have been spoken.

If you love together, and dwell together, and in one God ; Then the self-same God will be merciful unto you : Which bless you, comfort you, and strengthen you unto the end.   More I would say, but words profit not.   God be amongst you.

The mysteries
of this Book.
Dee'l toge-
ther.

E. K. Now they both be gone in a great flame of fire upwards:

Δ. Laudibus

Δ. Laudibus te celebrabo Domine Deus quoniam non prævaluerunt Inimici mei super me. Domine exercituum clamavi ad te, & tu salvasti me, Convertisti dolorem in gaudium mihi, dissolvisti luctum meum & circumdedisti me lætitia. Misericordias tuas in æternum cantabo, Noram faciam veritatem tuam in vita mea. Os meum narrabit Justitiam tuam omni tempore beneficia tua: certè non novi numerum. Sed Gratias agam donec mors rapiat, tibi psallam quamdiu fuero. Laudem tui loquetur os meum: & omne vivens celebret nomen tuum Sanctum, in perpetuum & semper. Laudate Dominum, O vos Angeli ejus, potentes virtute facientes jussus ejus, obedientes voci verbi illius. Collaudate Deum Universi exercitus ejus, Ministri ejus qui facitis voluntatem ejus. Omne quòd vivit laudet te Domine, Amen.

Rolandus pene nx tuus. 1584. Remember that on *Saturday*, the fourteenth day of *July*, by the *Gregorian* Calender, and the fourth day of *July*, by the old Calender, *Rowland* my Childe (who was born Anno 1583. *January* 28. by the old Calender) was extreamly sick about noon, or midday, and by one of the Clock ready to give up the Ghost, or rather lay for dead, and his eyes set and sunck into his head, &c.

I made a vow, if the Lord did foresee him to be his true servant, and so would grant him life, and confirm him his health at this danger, and from this danger I would (duriug my life) on Saturdayes *eat but one meal*, &c.

Remember on *Wednesday* night the eighteenth of *July*, as I walked alone about nine of the Clock in the evening, in the Chamber before my Study, (above) in divers places of that Chamber appeared flashes of fire, and did not lighten abroad.

Munday, *Julii* 23. *Mane Circiter* 8.   † Cracoviæ.
Oratione Dominica finita.

Δ. I read *Mapsama* his first words of the book to be prepared of 48 leaves to be silvered, and would gladly know what I was now to do. By and by at the first looking into the stone.

E. K. There appeared ten Pikes, all black on the ground in a Circle as it were, and 1 in the middle, a great Pike, standing up. And *Vera, falsis, falsa,* seemed to be written in the middle of that Circle, somewhat blacker then all the rest, which seemed to be as new molten Pitch.

A voyce. ...... *Qui non in* 7. *vivant in undecimo.*

Δ. I made a short discourse to God of my sincere, and just dealing, hitherto of the book of *Enoch*, written, of the book to be silvered, how hardly I can get it performed to my contentment: (the books being laid on the Table, that of *Enoch*, and that as it were silvered) &c. I craved therefore the exposition of this dark shew, and as yet nothing pleasant, or plain: My conscience is clear, and I trust in the Lord his mercies.

E. K. After this appeared a man all black, naked all over.
...... *O thou that art just, and hast a clear conscience, answer me.*
Δ. In the name of Jesus.
Be gone. ...... *Who commanded thee to be gone ?*
...... I take the Commandment to have been from God.
...... *Thou hast broken the Commandment of God.*
Δ. I can in no case yield thereunto.
...... *Tou have dishonoured the Lord : which is just in the bottom of his own breast, and gave you warning, and commanded you to go: which is the Lord of Heaven and Earth.*
May 21. Mane. Et à Meridie per Mapsama. ... 27. Junii, per AVE. Δ. O Lord, my first charge was in these words: Thou shalt go from hence *with him to the Emperour :* It was also said that he should make provision for this one voyage, and for the rest God had provided. So that seeing I was to go with him, and he hath not yet provided (doing what he can) what shall I say, or do?
...... *True it is, thou hast had the victory, and thou, and thy Children have tasted mercy. Thou art one of those, that when I command thee to leave nothing with life, yet thou savest the fatlings to offer before him that abhorreth such sacrifice.*
Δ. Lord, I know no such act of mine : The Lord be merciful to me. For when it should come to such a case, God knoweth, I would spare none.
...... *O thou just man [shaking his head] thou art become a* Saul.
...... *Wherefore did God (answer me) take the Kingdom out of* Saul *his hands ?*
Δ. It appeareth in the Bible, because obedience was better then sacrifice.
Reg.1.cap.15. ...... *Even so, if thou hadst been obedient, thy obedience had been regarded. But I say unto thee, the Lord oweth thee nothing for thy labour : he hath payed thee to the uttermost.*

As

As for Lasky, I *will* give him over to the spirit of errour: *and he shall become more poor ;* so *that his own Children shall despise him.* Λ. L.
His plague
thr:atned.

But it *shall not come to passe in these dayes : For I will keep* my *promise with you.   You do* the *Commandment of Princes, and Lords, and Masters : But when the God of Justice (without your* deser*t) entertaineth you, and placeth you, and dwelleth amongst you, (which is able to give you all* jast God. *things) commandeth you to go, and that for your own profit, you think it nothing to offend him.* Δ. O most mercifull and jast God.

But *true it is, That, Obedience pleaseth the Lord for therein, his Creatures glorifie him most.* Obedience. *All Worship, all Honour, all Love, all Faith, all Hope, all Charity, all the knitting together of the Heavens consisteth in* Obedience. *For if you had been obedient, the very stones of the earth should* have served your necessity.   *For the Lord will not be found a lyar.*

Δ. O Lord, be mercifull to me : I could not do thy Commandment in going without A. *Laskie,* and him I was not able to cause to goe without provision : And to our judgement he seemeth marvellously to be carefull to make provision : but still he hath hinderance.

...... *Thou (hearest thou?) the Lord forgiveth thee : but from henceforth, be commandeth thee that thou open not the secrets and the judgements, which the Lord shall open unto thee of the times to come, unto* Laskie. Dee, Is pardoned.
No more secrets of God
to be opened to A. L.

Δ. I pray you to say somewhat unto us, as concerning this book to be silvered : Else what shall I do, if I have not direction herein, the case being so hard.

...... *As concerning the book, when thou art at the end of thy journey it shall be told.*

Δ. Misericordias Domini in æternum Cantabo, *Amen.* Hallelujah. *Amen.*

Tuesday, *Julii* 31. *Mane hora* 7.   † Cracoviæ.

Oratione Dominica finita, & variis ejaculationibus factis tam ad Gabrielem , *quam* Nalvage, Ave, Mapsama, *&* Ilemer, *quàm maximè ad Deum ipsum pro suo lumine, auxilio & protectione : tam in ipsa actione quàm itinere præsenti, futuro, versus aulam* Cæsaris.

After a great hour attendance.   At length appeared one all naked, black, and about the stone a Circle of black.

He said, ... *Were you not commanded to go after ten dayes ?*

Δ. It is true.

...... *And what followeth ?*

Δ. I appeal unto the mercy of the highest, for that I have not offended upon wilfulnesse.

...... *Say what followeth.*

Δ. It followeth that we may drink of a Cup, which we would not, &c. And also we were willed to provide for this journey, which provision onely now is made for us two , and not yet for *A. L.* himself.

...... *Thus sayeth the Lord, I have stretched out my hand , and you have hindred me. I have brought things unto their course, but you have thrust your selves between. When I appointed you* 10 *dayes, did I not also tell you that the earth was mine.* 10 Dayes. *Am not I the God of heaven and earth, by whom you breath. The same which also forsaketh not my people in the time of need.*

. *I have opened my wings, but you have refused my cover. I have brought in madnesse into the house of the unjust, but you have prevented my judgement.* Δ. Fortè. Madnesse procured in the K. and he is now recovered.

And because you have done so, and have trusted more in the mallices of the world then in my power.

[Δ. Lord we have not done so : to our knowledges.] Δ. A scourge to follow unto us : Lord be mercifull.

...... *Therefore shall you drink of a Cup that you would not : but it shall not fall in these dayes, but in the dayes to come.*

Moreover,   ### [E. K. The fire cometh out of his mouth as he speaketh.]

...... *If you go, it is : if you go not, it also shall be.*

[Δ. Make that dark speech plain, for I need you not.]

Δ. We were willed to go, but with this condition, that *Laskie* should make provision.

...... *I have not sealed this sin unto thee* [Δ.] *but yet I have measured out a plague, and it shall light upon you all. But unto* Lasky *I have sealed it, and it shall be heavy.* A. L.

E. K. Doth not *A. L.* use all the means he can for provision making.

...... *The time shall come when I am, and will appear unto thee in a Vision, and of seven Rods thou shalt chuse one, unto you both I speak : For I will not let passe my dishonour unpunished, neither will I sell my name like an hireling.*

Notwithstanding, in the midst of my fury I will be mercifull unto you, when you think I have forsaken you, then shall the Rod break in pieces.

Δ. Lord

Δ. Lord deal with us, as we have just cause to put our trust in thee, not onely in the principal state of our salvation, but also in this Action.

...... You go: I will not forsake you. *And what I have said, that I have said. And it is a living spirit, and shall bear witnesse of it self. For, great is the God of Hosts in power, and in all his works, and words most just.*

Δ. Lord, is it thy will that we shall go before this *A. L.* toward *Prage*?

...... *If you tarry it is, and if you go, it shall be.*

Δ. Lord make that plain unto us?

Thus sayeth the Lord, if you tarry, it is because I am, which am strength, and triumph against mine enemies, and so against the enemies of those that put their trust in me: And shall be, because I am just, and because it is.

For, that I am, I am, and my spirit is justice and truth: which before, was, is, and shall be, and after, world without end.

Δ. Lord, shew s the light of thy countenance, and be not wrathfull against us any longer, be a comforter unto us in our journey to be undertaken.

...... *Move me not, for I am gone.*

E. K. He is gone.

Δ. Misericordia Domini sit super nos, nunc & in sempiterna seculorum secula. *Amen.*

ANNO 1584.

On *Wednesday* the first day of *August*, at afternoon (*hora 3.*) we entred on our journey toward *Prage*, in the Kingdom of *Beame*, whither we came on thursday sevenight after, by three of the Clock, that is exactly in eight dayes.

We came by Coach, I, *E. K.* and his brother, and *Edmond Hilton*, so that we came to *Prage* Augusti 9. by the new Calender: but by the old *July* 30. two dayes before *August* the old Calender.

Miserere Nostri Deus Noster neque in eternum irascaris nobis.

PRAGE 1584.

Augusti 15. *Wednesday*, we began on the day of the assumption of the blessed Virgin *Mary*: in the excellent little Stove, or Study of D. *Hageck* his house lent me, by *Bethlem* in old *Prage*: Which Study seemed in times past (Anno 1518.) to have been the Study of some Student, or A-- skilfill of the holy stone: a name was in divers places of the Study, noted in letters of Gold, and Silver, *Simon Baccalaureus Pragensis*, and among other things manifold written very fairly in the Study (and very many *Hieroglyphical* Notes *Philosophical*, in Birds, Fishes, Flowrs, Fruits, Leaves, and six Vessels, as for the Philosophers works) these verses were over the door.

Immortale Decus par gloriaque illi debentur
Cujus ab ingenio est discolor hic paries.

And of the Philosophers work (on the South-side of the Study) in three lines, uppermost was this written.

Candida si rubeo mulier nupta sit marito: Mox complectuntur, Complexa concipiuntur. Per se solvuntur, per se quandoque perficiuntur: Ut duo quæ fuerant, unum in corpore fiant: Sunt duæ res primo, Sol cum Luna, tamen in imo, Confice, videbis, sit ab hiis lapis quoque Rebus.

Luna potentata, peregit Sol Rubis actu: Sol adit Lunam per medium, rem facit unam. Sol tendit velum, transit per ecliptica Cælum: Currit ubi Luna recurrit hunc denuo sublima. Ut sibi lux detur, in sole quæ retinetur. Nec abiit vere, sed vult ipsi commanere: illustrans certe defunctum corpus aperte: Si Rebus scires, quid esset tu reperires. Hæc ars est cara, brevis, levis atque rara. Ars nostra est Ludus puero, labor mulierum; scitote omnes filii artis hujus, quod nemo potest colligere fructus nostri Elixiris, nisi per introitum nostri lapidis Elementati, etsi aliam viam quærit, viam nunquam intrabit nec attinget. Rubigo est Opus, quod fit ex solo auro, dum intraverit in suam humiditatem. And so it ended.

MYSTE-

MYSTERIORUM PRAGENSIUM
Liber Primus, Cæfareufque, Anno 1584.
Stylo Novo.

Augufti 15. *incœptus ad Omnipotentis Dei Laudem, Honorem,*
& Gloriam. Amen.

 Ieri poteft, quod anni 1588, & aliorum fupputatio, initium fuum habent ab ipfa die Paffionis Chrifti vel Afcenfionis in Cælum. Atque *Conjeftura le-* hac ratione, 33, vel 34. anni plures confiderari debent : quia tot an-*vicula.* norum Chriftus erat tempore fuæ paffionis, vel afcenfionis : Addas igitur annis 1588, 34. & inde emergunt anni 1621. atque ifte numerus propius accedit ad tempus annorum diluvii & Arcæ, cujus fi- *Note de Anno* miltudinem fore circa fecundum Chrifti adventum Scripturæ 88. docent :

Vel, cum poft creatum Adamum, Anno Mund. 1655, Diluvium Aquæ, omnia deleverit viventia : Poft Chrifti, (noftri Adami fpiritualis) reftitutionem in Cælum, Anno 1655 (qui erit ahno 1688.) expeftamus Diluvium ignis, quo omnia funt Immutanda : vel Charitatis & ardoris Chriftiani magnum futurum fpecimen.

Non faciet Dominus *D E V S* verbum, nifi revelaverit Secretum fuum ad fervos fuos, prophetas. Leo rugiet, quis non timebit ? Dominus Deus loquutus eft : Quis non prophetabit ?
Amos, Cap. 3. *B.*
Nihil mali invenimus in homine ifto : Quid fi fpiritus locutus eft ei, aut Angelus ? *Aft.*
Apoft. Cap. 23. *C.*

Dico enim vobis, quod multi Prophetæ, & Reges voluerunt videre, quæ vos videtis, & non viderunt : & audire quæ auditis, & non audierunt. *Lucæ* 10. *E. Matthæi* 13. *B:*

Chariffimi, nolite omni Spiritui credere : Sed probate Spiritus fi ex Deo fint : quoniam multi pfeudoprophetæ, exierunt in mundum. In hoc cognofcitur Spiritus Dei. Omnis Spiritus qui confitetur Jefum Chriftum in carne veniffe, ex Deo eft, *&c.* *Johannes Epiftola* 1. *Cap.* 4. *A.*
Quifquis confeffus fuerit, quoniam Jefus eft filius Dei, Deus in eo manet, & ipfe in Deo, *&c. Cap. eodem C.*

Paulus ad Corinthios, Epiftola, 1 *Cap.* 1. *b.*
Gratias ago Deo meo femper pro vobis, in gratia Dei, quæ data eft vobis in Chrifto Jefu, quod in omnibus divites facti eftis in illo, in omni verbo & omni fcientia (ficut teftimonium Chrifti confirmatum eft in vobis) ita ut nihil vobis defit in ulla gratia, Expeftantibus *revelationem Domini noftri Jefu Chrifti, qui & confirmabit vos ufque in finem fine crimine, in die Adventus domini noftri* Jefu Chrifti. Fidelis Deus per quem vocati eftis in Societatem Filii ejus *Societas Jefu* Jefu Chrifti Domini noftri, *&c.*
Δ. Noto Revelationem & adventum Chrifti fecundum : deinde confirmationem quæ refpicit alium adhuc finem temporis : *unde de Regno Chrifti hic in terris,* fecundum Joannis Apocalypfim, videri poffit hic locus aliquem præbere guftum, *&c.*

Paulus ad Corinthios, Epift. 1 *cap.* 1. *D.*
Quæ ftulta funt mundi, *elegit* Deus, ut confundat fapientes : & infirma mundi elegit Deus ut confundat fortia : & ignobilia mundi, & contemptibilia *elegit* Deus, *& ea quæ non funt* ut *ea quæ funt* deftrueret, ut non glorietur omnis caro in confpeftu ejus. Ex ipfo autem vos eftis in Chrifto Jefu, qui factus eft nobis fapientia à Deo, & Juftitia, & Sanftificatio & Redemptio. Ut, quemadmodum fcriptum eft. Qui gloriatur, in Domino glorietur.

[e e]   *Paulus*

Paulus ad Corinthios, Epist. 1. *cap.* 2. *C.*
Nobis autem revelat Deus per Spiritum suum : Spiritus enim omnia scrutatur, etiam profunda Dei, &c. Vide præcedentia & sequentia in eodem capite.

Pragæ. Prima Actio, *Anno* 1584.
Wedensday, *Augusti* 15. *Mane horam circiter* 9.

Δ. We thanked God for his safe bringing us hither, to the place appointed by him : We desired him to direct us, as the rest of our Action requireth : And thirdly, for the Book with silver leaves, to be prepared, we required instruction, as we were promised.

Anon after *E. K.* his looking into the Shew-stone, he said, I see a Garland of white Rose-buds about the border of the Stone : They be well opened, but not full out.

Δ. The great mercies of God be upon us : and we beseech him to increase our faith in him, according to his well liking.

E. K. Amen.

E. K. But while I consider these buds better, they seem rather to be white Lillies.

Δ. The eternal God of his infinite mercies, wipe away our blacknesse and sins, and make us pure, and whiter than Snow.

Δ. 72 Angels.   *E. K.* They are 72 in number : seeming with their heads (*alternatim*) one to bend or hang toward me, and another toward you. They seem also to move circularly toward the East : but very slowly. In the middest of this Circle, appeareth a little fire, of the colour of yern, hot; ready to melt : from which fire to every one of the said lillies, is a fiery beam extended; which beam toward the end, is, of more whitish fiery colour, than it is near the center.

A voice. -... *E. K.* A voice cometh shouting out from the Lillies, saying, Holy, Holy, Holy : and all the lillies are become on fire; and seem to tumble into that fire. And now they appear again distinctly, as before : And the fire remained in the center still : and the emanation of beams, came from it, still to the foresaid lilly buds.

E. K. I hear a sound, as though it were of many waters, poured or streaming down in the clifts of great Rocks and Mountains : The noise is marvellous great, which I hear coming through the Stone : as it were of a thousand water-mills going together.

A voice. ...... *Est.*
Another voice. ...... Seemeth to pray over, & *quo modo est.*
A voice. :.... *Male* & *in summo* : & *mensuratum est.*

E. K. I hear a great roaring, as if it were out of a Cloud, over ones head : most perfectly like a thunder.

Another voice. ...... *The Seal is broken.*

Δ. Vide *Apocalypseos, cap* 16. *sed videtur quod non sequenter ordine, velati quis ex textu judicaret; Ast non asseritur hic effusam esse etiamsi sape & olim vindicatum requirebant illi qui sub altari sunt : nondum illis erat concessum, & c. Sic hic dici potest.*

Another ...... *Poure out the sixth Viol : that the earth may know her self* [Viola Sexta.]

These are the dayes of wo, that are spoken of.

E. K. Now I see beyond like a Furnace-mouth, as big as 4 or 5 Gates of a City. It seemeth to be a quarter of a mile off : out of the Furnace-mouth seemeth a marvellous smoke or smother to come. By it seemeth to be a great Lake of pitch : and it playeth or simpreth, as water doth, when it beginneth to seethe. There standeth by the pit,

pit, a white man, in a white garment tucked up : his face is marvellous fair ; he faith very loud.

A white spiritual Creature........ *Ascend.*

E. K. Now there cometh out of the Lake, a thing like a Lion in the hinder parts, and his fore part hath many heads, of divers fashions : and all upon one trunk of a neck. He hath like feathers on his neek. He hath 7 heads : Three on one side, and three on another, and one in the middle : which branch from the neck is longer than the other, and lieth backward to his taile-ward. The white man giveth him a bloody Sword : and he taketh it in his forefoot.

The white man tyeth this Monster his 4 legs with a chain, that he cannot go, but as one shackled, or fettred. Now he giveth the Monster a great hammer, with a seal at that end where the hammer striketh, and the other is fashioned like a hatchet.

The white man said. .... *A horrible and terrible beast* ......

E. K. This the white man said with a loud cry.

A voice out of the little fire. .... *Seal him, for two years of the Seven : For, so long is his power.*

The Stars, with the Earth, even to the third part, are given unto thee : The fourth part thou shalt leave untouched.

E. K. The white man taketh the hammer, and striketh him in the forehead of that head which is in the middle, and lieth down backward toward his taile.

E. K. Now all this vision is vanished away. The Stone is clear.

E. K. Now *Madimi* appeareth, and she seemeth to be bigger than she was.

Madimi. .... *The blessing of God the Father, the Son, and (in the Father and the Son) of the Holy Ghost, in power and comfort rest upon you, take hold of you, and dwell with you, that you may be apt to receive the comfort of my childishnesse ? and the reward of such Innocents, as my voice beareth witnesse of. You both, the Spirit of God, salute you : which alwayes comforteth the Just, and is the strength and stay of such as are Elected : of whom it is said, Mittam illis Angelum, in Adjutorium.*

Δ. Are you *Madimi* (in the name of Jesus) that I may so note of you ?

Mad. .... *I am Madimi, and of that order, wherein the wonders of God are wrought with power, with you, as my words are : with my self, as my creation is.* Madimi *est ex ordine potestatum.*

Lo, as I have often * *promised you, so in the time of your necessity and grief, I visit you.* * Vide 26.

Δ. Thanks be to the Highest. Junii.

Mad. .... *Not as the friends of the world do, but as a comforting spirit : exalting the servants of God, and cherishing them with celestial food : But my mother is at hand, which openeth* Mater Madimi. *unto thee, the will of God. Believe me, many are the woes of the world, and great are the sorrows that are to come : For the Lord prepareth his Rain-bow, and the witnesses of his account :* The Rainbow. Apocalips. 4. *and will appear in the beavens to finish all things : and the time is not long.*

Blessed are those that believe ; for faith shall flee from the Earth, and her dwelling places shall be Faith shall *in caves, and unknown mountains, and in parts of the Earth which the Lord hath kept secret for* hardly be *such as shall triumph and rejoyce in the Judgement to come,* found on the Earth.

1. *Wo be to women great with child, for they shall bring forth Monsters.*

2. *Wo be unto the Kings of the Earth, for they shall be beaten in a Mortar.*

3. *Wo be unto such as paint themselves, and are like unto the Prince of pride ; for they shall drink the blood of their neighbours, and of their own children.*

4. *Wo be unto the false preachers, yea seven woes be unto them ; for they are the teeth of the Beast.*

He that hath ears, let him hear. Seven Woes.

5. *Wo be unto the Virgins of the Earth, for they shall disdain their virginity, and they shall become Concubins for Satan, and despise the God of Righteousnesse.*

6. *Wo be unto the Merchants of the earth , for they are become abominable : Behold , they are become the spies of the earth , and the dainty meat of Kings. But they are foolish : Yea, they shall fall into the pit that they have digged for others.*

Mater Madim

7. *Wo be unto the books of the earth, for they are corrupted ; and are become a wrasting stock, and firebrand to the conscience.*

Stay a season, for my mother cometh.

Δ. We read over the premisses, and so conferred of the verity and weight of them. And all this while *Madimi* stood still in *E. K.* his sight (as *E. K.* told me :) But because we were willed to stay, I moved no question : but wished to have some understanding, how my wife and children (at *Cracovia*) did.   Hereupon *Madimi* said as followeth:

My wife tempted to destroy her self.

Mad. ...... *Hear what I say unto thee [Δ.] The King of darknesse whetteth his teeth against thee, and rampeth with great rage to overwhelm the world upon thee : And he seeketh the destruction of thy houshold, and thereby thy overthrow : The life of thy Children ; yea, he tempteth thy wife with despair, and to be violent unto her self.*

Δ. Why with despair ?]

...... But his lips are sealed, and his claws made dull: that when he would bite he cannot : And where he scratcheth the bloud followeth not.

Madami, my friend.

But bear what thy friend sayeth unto thee : Both in her self, and by him that moveth her to speak ; As thou art the servant of the God of victory, so shalt thou triumph in the God of stretchforth and Conquer.   Δ. Madzilodarp.

This name of God is in the 16ᵗʰ. *principall Call, beginning* Ils vinial part. Salman Ealt, &c.

Thy wife, thy children, thy servants, and more then that, such as favour thee, even the coverings of thy house ; are under the protection and defence of such as are of power : against whom, neither the rage of such as raign, neither the fury of Authority (though it hath the help of Satan*) can prevail. For why ? God hath care over thee : But thy faith is somewhat lower. Take heed of Satan, be will joyn himself unto thee. But beware of him. For, sin keepeth back the power of God, which is oftentimes deferred for another season : Yea, even for the wickednesse of one Soul.*

Satan his Traiterous insinuation so to be taken heed of.

A. L.

Lásky, *I look for, but I see not : Behold, I wrast my eyes after him, and cannot finde him. Peradventure he hath hid himself behinde some Mountain, or is crept into a Cave : for he appeareth not.*

Δ. I beseech you, what is the cause thereof ? Is he not gone from *Cracovia ?*

Mad. ..... *Sin is the greatest Mountain, and he rejoyceth when he pleaseth himself : and in the fury of his flesh creepeth into a Cave from us.*

At one instant Madimi seeth all the world over.

Lo, I look for him, and cannot see him, yet see all the world over , It is a sign that God is not with him.

Δ. I beseech you, is he not gone from *Cracovia* yet ?

Mad. ..... *I tell thee, I see him not ; I can say nothing of him.*

Δ. Lord, our coming hither was to come with him.

Mad. ...... *Therefore brought I thee hither,* that thou shouldst not tarry with him. *Knowest thou not that God is marvellous in his works ? Hast thou not heard of his secret judgements ? If thou hast, Think he hath care over thee.*

My wife, children, and houshold must be moved to Prage.

For also, thy wife and children, and the rest of thy houshold must be moved hither.

Δ. When, I beseech you ?

Mad. ..... *Let that be my charge to answer thee.*

E. K. Now here appeareth a little fire like the same, which appeared before : but it hath no beams from it, as it had before.

Mad. ..... *Hic & hæc, est Mater mea.*   [E. K. Pointing to the fire.]

Mater Madimi.

E. K. She falleth down on her face prostrate : Now she riseth again. This fire entreth into her mouth, she is waxen of higher stature then she was, she hath now three faces.

Trinity.

Δ. Now it is the vertue of the Trinity in her so represented.

Mad. ..... *I. And I have a few things to say, and I say.*

E. K. I hear a marvellous noise, as of many Mountains falling.

Mad. .... *Arise, and believe.   The time is come , that of the foolish I will make the wife. And of such as are sinfull men, my anointed : If they encline their ear unto my voyce.*

℟.

E. K. The noyse is marvellous : And which of the mouths doth speak, I cannot discern.

Mad.

Mad. ..... *First, thou shalt write unto* Rodulphus, *as I shall enspire thee.*   Then shalt thou go RODOL-
unto him, saying, That the Angel of the Lord hath appeared unto thee. ——   PHUS.

And rebuketh him for his sins.   [*I never heard any such noyse : it is as if half the world were rushing down an hill.*]

[*E. K.* A great noyse still.]

Mad. ..... *If he hear thee : Then say unto him, He shall triumph , Fear thee not.*
If he hear thee not:Say,that, The Lord, the God that made heaven and earth,   Δ. Either E.K. *V. I. 263.*
(under whom he breatheth, and hath his spirit) putteth his foot against his breast.   spake not this, or I   omitted to write it   at the first.

[*E. K.* A great noyse still.]

And will throw him headling from his seat.
Lo, thus (I swear unto thee) I will do. If he forsake his wickednesse , and turn   Dei *Juramentum*
unto me : His seat shall be the greatest that ever was, and the Devil shall become   *& Pallum cum* Δ.
his prisoner.   de R.

E. K. There came great flashes of fire out of her, and so out of the stone : and suddenly she was in her former shape again.

Δ. In the name of Jesus.

Mad. ..... *Where this voyce entreth, no man hath to say : For it is the beginning , so it is likewise the end.*
Therefore enquire not any more now, but cease : For this is the mar-   The marvellous beginning   *vellous beginning of this last time.*   of this last time.

Δ. All thanks, Laud, Honor, Glory, and Empire be to the Eternal, Omnipotent, and our onely God of Heaven and Earth. *Amen.*

Thursday, *Augusti* 16. 15,84. *Mane, circiter horam* 8 ¾.   † Prage.

Δ. *Precibus finitis,* I propounded, as concerning the book to be prepared for the Angelical writing, *&c.* And because *Mapsama* had dealt about that point : Therefore I required at God his hands, the Ministery of *Mapsama* herein : if it were his will.

E. K. Here is *Madami.*

Δ. Blessed be the God of Heaven and Earth, who regardeth the sincere intent of his sily ones.

Mad. ..... *When seed time is past, who soweth his Corn? Or what is he amongst men that calleth back the Sun a minute? So may it be said of you, which were slack in sowing, and therefore have let passe the benefit of time, wherein your seed might have multiplied. Behold, your labours are in vain, in respect of that you might have received.*

...... *For August is past with you the first day : And* Mapsama *wanteth, not by himself , but*   Mapsama.   *through your negligence : whose fingers wrought, and made an end of anothers work, which was tied to time.*

Nalvage *was beaten back from you : But you consider not his conflict, neither thank God for that he hath finished for you : with whom* [Nalvage] *now, you have no power.   For the Receiver and Giver for that time, were of time.*
But to the entent that the Heavens may agree, (because they are the light of him, which is the A paper book   *light of his father) I say unto thee that thou must prepare, of fair, and decent paper , a book.   To* to be prepared.   *the entent, that the paper it self may bear witnesse against you : and receive that, which should have been printed in Gold.*

Δ. God he knoweth, and the Heavens, that I did the best I could, to have had the book silvered.

Mad. ..... *It is so : I will bear witnesse with thee.   But where the watch-men sleep, and do not their duty: Theft taketh place, and the enemies make havock.*
The sins of Lasky are not a few ; yea, they are such as have brought in the Prince of Thieves, which had prevailed : But God was watch-man at the inner doors .   For, he doubted of thy faith, and laughed God to skorn.   But bear the voice of him that sitteth : Leapers and defiled people use not to carve at a Kings Table : for when his Carvers become Leapers, they are not : because they are expelled.
Even so into my Chambers, and secret judgements entreth not the Incredulous , Proud , and Skornfull sinners.   But because he became worse then a Leaper, I banished him out of my Chambers, for I am more then a King.
Notwithstanding, because I have sworn unto thee for him , I will suffer him   *Jusjurandum ad*   *to be exalted : But in the midst of his Triumph he shall fall, as a proud Tree*   Dee, pro A. L.   *doth, whose roots are uncertain.*

And

And because thou hast believed me, and hast not murmured against me, I will be   Misericordia
just with thee, And with this Emperour shall be thy aboad. And through thy mouth   Dei super △.
shall spring a Cedar-Tree, whose top shall touch the Moon, and branches cover the   Cum Imperore
beasts of the field, the birds of the Aire; yea, and a part of the Sea. Because thou   Rod.
hast taken pains for me, I will deal justly with thee, and reward thee.   Prophetia de△.

The sons of wickednesse are proud, because of their promotion; are stout, because of their King-
* Matheig. D.   *doms and Dominions: But they must fall, because their building doth stand on* * *sand.*

Do my Commandment, be not afraid.

New l-ssons.   *For I have new lessons to teach thee, and new books to open, such as have been sealed in the wil-*
New books.   *dernesse.*

E. K. She is gone.

△. As concerning the Letter to be written unto *Rodolphus*, O Lord, I would gladly know
the Argument, and when I should send it.

A voyce. ..,... *Incipienti, dabitur.*   △. I understand this thus: That, when I
                                       begin to write it shall be inspired from
                                       God, as was said before.

A voyce. ...... *Cease.*

△. Deo Nostro Immortali, Invisibili, & Omnipotenti, sit omnis honor, Laus & Gloria: Nunc & semper. *Amen.*

Friday, *Augusti* 17.   *Mane.*   †*Pragæ.*

△. Because I would make no delay, for the Letter writing to the Emperour *Rodolphus*, I
framed my self to write, beseeching God that I might so write, as might be sufficient for the
purpose, &c. And thus I wrote as followeth.

N. dicta eoram   Omnipotentis Nostri Creatoris (Christianorum omnium Imperatorum fælicissime, O *Ru-*
Angelis non est   *dolphe*) tam est hominibus incognita illa, quæ cuncta disponit perficitque *PROVIDEN-*
Previdentia.   *TIA*, rataque ipsa rerum series & coordinatio (à primo ad ultimum) quòd à plerisque, te-
Ecclesiastes,   mere, fortuito, vel casu, hoc illove evenire modo, existimentur omnia, quæ extra præterve suo-
cap 5.   rum Consiliorum designationes, fieri conspiciant. Verum quibus est mens Divinæ veritatis lumine collustrata, & ad multiplices longisque intervallis distinctas rerum consecutiones conside-
randas, attentior, evidentissimè deprehenden: illi quidem, Quæ, quibus præcurrisse, tanquam
causas, occasionesque necessarias, alio priori, & interdum longe diversissimo, tempore, oportue-
rat. Atque ut varietatem nunc omittam exemplorum, (quæ, ex aliorum hominum inter se
collatis vitis, conditionibus, factisque adferre possim,) Exemplum satis conspicuum hoc unicum fieri possit: Nimirum illa, (incredibilis ferè) quæ inter sacram Cæsaream Majestatem vestram, & humillimum (in Deo) Mancipium me vestrum (ex multiplicibus utrinque præcur-
rentibus occasionibus) jam quasi instare videtur, In unum (idemque admirandum quid) Com-
binatio, Divinaque conspiratio. Ambiverunt me (Juvenem) Illustrissimi Imperatores duo:
Victoriosissimus ille *Carolus Quintus*, & ejusdem Frater *Ferdinandus*, vestræ *Cæsareæ* Majestatis
Magnificentissimus *Avus*. Hic, *Posonii, Hungariæ:* ille verò, *Bruxellæ, Brabantiæ.* Hic, *An.* 1563.
Ille autem, *Anno* 1549. Ast clementissimum Imperatorem *Maximilianum*, *Cæsareæ* vestræ Majestatis Patrem (Immortali glora dignum) jam tum *Hungariæ* coronatum Regem, (invitissimo
quidem ipso Tyranno Turcico) eodem in *Posonio*, eodemque, *Anno* 63. in deliciis habere cœpi:
illi: sque rarissimas virtutes, cum fideliter colere, tum posteritati easdem reddere commendatissi-
mas, opere quodam conabar Hieroglyphico. Quo etiam in labore exantlan-   * *Libelli Monadis Hiero-*
do, animus mihi præsagiebat, Austriacæ * familiæ; aliumi fore aliquando ali-   *glyphica Theoremate* 20.
q.em, in quo maxima mea spes, & publico Christianorum statui, Res, con-   *jam ante* 20 *annos editi.*
firmaretur, (vel confirmari poterit,) Optima, Maximaque. Vestræ igi-
tur *Cæsareæ* Majesti, Imperatorum Romanorum (ex Austriacorum Principum nobilissima familia) mea ætate florentium, *QUARTO:* Adsum, & ego, Triplicis Alphabeti, litera * Quarta. Atque ita adsum, ut me ipsum ad pedes Cæsareæ Majestis vestræ demissè osculandos offe-
ram: plurimùm gavisurus, si qua in re, Christianæ Reipublicæ Imperatori tanto, talique, gratus, utilisve esse potero.

<table>
<tr><td>

Superscriptio erat hæc.

Serenissimo ac potentissimo Principi ac Domino Do-
mino Rudolpho, *Dei Gratia Romanorum Imperato-*
ri semper Augusto, *ac* Germaniæ, Hungariæ, Bohe-
miæ, &c. Regi, Archiduci Austriæ, Duci Burgun-
diæ Stiriæ Carinthiæ, &c. Comiti Tyrolis, &c.
Domino meo clementissimo.

</td><td>

Vestræ sacræ *Cæsareæ* Majestati, soli, si hæc
aliquandi u cons|are patiemini (neminique
detegere velitis) rem facietis valde ne-
cessariam.

Prage, An. 1584. *Augusti* 17.
Cæsareæ Majestii Vestræ
Humillimus & fidelissimus
'Clientulus

Joannes Dee.

</td></tr>
</table>

*2
D {
△ {
7

Munday

Monday, † *Prage, Augusti* 20. *Mane circa horam* 7.

Δ. *Precibus ad Deum fusis, ex more nostro,* &c.

1. I propounded : If the letter written for *Rodolphus,* were as it should be ?

2. Secondly, becaufe we were willed to invite the good Angels, for the book writting, I asked how we fhould invite them ?

3. As concerning our wives, and my familly fending for : I required, when that fhould be done ?

Δ. Quickly apparition was made,

E. K. Here is *Uriel.*

Δ. Welcome be the light of the Higheft.

VRIEL. ...... *Wo be unto the world : for her light is taken away. Wo, wo be unto man, for the eye of light hath forsaken him. Wo, wo be to the understanding of man, for it is led out, with a threefold spirit,* * * the spirit of errour and ignorance. And wo be unto such as believe not the glorious and supereminent light of this Testimony : for they are not written with the life, neither shall their portion be with the living.*   * *Aliquid de-
est forte.*
The Spirit of
Pride.

Thus faith he that is a mere ftone, (which fitteth between the feat of light and darkneffe) whose wings are great, and more than mighty : wherewith he gathereth the Stars , and the powers that hang upon the firmament of the first and leffer light : placing them and powering them, in the Spirit of Truth ; and through his own power, the power of the word, whereby all things are, and are comprehended : in that he is as well in the heavens of Glory, Chaftity, and Meffage, as also in places unknown to us.   This Teftimo-
ny to be belie-
ved upon great
difpleafure elfe
Heavens of
Glory, Cha-
ftity, Angels.

Behold, those that dig into Nature with dull Mattocks, and dull Spades, are such, as of every congeled substance can imagin, but not judge : are foolish, and of the world : whose imaginations, are become the instruments of vanity, and the piercers of him which is the father of ignorance. We be unto them, for their disputations and doctrines, are dogma's and dull. Wo, wo unto them, for they are such as please themselves, and are become fathers to many lewd children : of whom it is written, They are become stiff-necked and proud, and the followers of their father. Therefore have I gathered my self together, and am hidden from them ; because they are proud and haters of inno-cency. These teach not unto you a doctrine, neither are you partakers of their Bankets ; for the Spirit of God, is plain, pure, and most perfect. These breath not upon you, neither are the Orna-ments of your Garlands enterlaced by these : But by him are you lifted up, that is the God of Juftice, and the Difclofer of his own fecrets : and the headlong drawer of things to an end.   God to us is
the Difclofer
of his own fe-
crets.

Therefore believe, and dream not with the world : For the world shall perish, and all her Ad-herents : and shall be cast into the pit of woe everlasting. Read the Scriptures, and understand them : but wrest them not, with the wicked. Look into the simplicity, and nakedneffe of God his Promife. : View the innocency of some that received them, And let not the wickedneffe of those that the Lord made vertuous, go out of your remembrance. But fo Triumpheth true power, fo ga-thereth he himself together to discomfort the Serpent : O^c the lighteft he maketh the heavieft, and of the weakeft the ftrongeft : And in the weakeft veffels, worketh he his mercy. And why ? Behold, left the world, in her proud imaginations, in the ornaments of her pearls, and moft pretious wits, fhould brag, faying, I can compare with the Lord. Hear my voice, for it is of God. The world bringeth forth no good thing, neither are the doings of man accepted ; but where the fpirit of humi-lity dwelleth. Out of the depth of darkneffe, hath God made light : And lo, the light is great, and the darkneffe comprehendeth it not. So, in the weakeft will he be exalted   Humility.

The Spirit that speaketh unto you, is he that hath a Tower to build, a ftrong Tower and a mighty; yea such a one, as hath not been from the beginning : No, n t from the beginning. Great is the foun-dation thereof ; for, it is of Iron ; But greater are her walls ; for they are of Diamond. Moft great are her Turrets ; for they are the feven Heads, that behold, judge, and gather : And they are made of Truth, the Spirit of Eternity. Unto the laying of every ftone, are you made privy, And for this Tower are you provided.   Uriel hath a
Tower to build
&c.
△. and E. K.

1. *For lo, the first hath appeared, and fhewed himself mightily.*
2. *And the fecond hath redeemed, and overcome Satan.*
3. *And lo, the third appeareth, and fhall vifibly fhew the power of God to all Nations.*   *Primus Filius
Spiritus San-
ctus.*

For Now cometh the Defolation of the World, *And the fall of her pride. And this is the laft Rod that meafureth, and fhall be broken :   For it is faid, Now will I bear you from un-der the Altar, Now will I revenge the blood of your brethren.*   *Defolatio de-
qua Propheta
loquutus eft.*

O you ignorant, and of weak faith : Know you not the times that are to come ? O you that fpit out the meat of comfort : yea when it is put lovingly into your mouths. Why are you forrowful ? Why rejoyce you not, that the God of Juftice is girded, and hath whetted his fword, upon a thoufand thoufand Mountains of fire ? Why laugh you not the world to fcorn ? and deride her fornication ? Weep not upon her ; for fhe is accurfed : Neither wonder at her ; for fhe will be more wonderful.   *Apocalypf. cap.
18. P.*

Toll

△. *Ecclesiastes. Tempus est tacendi & tempus est loquendi veluti de transfiguratione Christi Matth.* 17. B. *Marc.* 9. B *Luc* 9. B. 12. A. *Constat, Et prop:it Matthæi cap.* 10. C. *Quid in aure audits, predicate super tecta, &c Luc.* 12.

* *Joel, cap.* 3.
† *Fear not.*

You have received this Doctrine in Chambers, and, in secret places: But it shall stand in the great City: and upon 7 *Hills, and shall establish her self in truth: Purifie the walls, and sweep out the dust and cobwebs* (*the works of the venemous*) *that it may be cast into the River, and brought into no remembrance.*

Yea, it shall sit in ✱ *Josaphat, in Judgement, against the wicked, and shall become a fire engendred in the cave of Thunders. Therefore, When you are commanded, lift up your heads, and* † *fear not: for whom, the Heavens shall fight.*

But in your selves be patient, and continue to the end: That your Crowns may exceed the Garlands of the Earth.

† *Promise of visitation for the* 48. great *Calls, and the Holy Book writing and practising.*
* *Legislatio manif. sta & in loco Sanctificato. Antichristi eversio per Spiritum SS. futura.* * *Epist. Pauli ad* 1 *Thess.* 2. *cap.* 2.

Thus saith the Lord, Lo, I have promised thee, that my Angel shall † *visit thee: And so it shall be. But if I now visit thee, Thus will the world say hereafter; Lo, he hath fained a Doctrine for himself. Lo he excelleth in subtilty. When I gave my laws, they were not secret; neither was the place unsanctified. When the Comforter cometh, girdeth himself against the son of* * *wickednesse; Then must you be known, and seen unto the Earth.*

An Election or Choice offered to △. RODOLPHUS Imp.

But I will give thee the choice: Chuse therefore, whether thou wilt banket Now: because I have promised thee: Or tarry, till I see the time more convenient; For lo, if Rodolph. hearken unto my voice, He shall wonder, and rejoyce with thee: And I will exalt him, above the Kings of earth.

Stay a while: I come again.

△. After he had stayed a while, and read over the premisses, and talked of the manner of the Choice or Election offered: and the dealing with *Rudolph:* we thought good to beseech God to regard his promise, for his glory and honour, and we most humbly to thank him that he would offer a choice to me a man of no worthinesse, nor wisdom: therefore most desirous to be entred speedily into the *School of Wisdom*, wherein we might grow, and attend the opportunities of any thing to be done or said by us; So that (if it were his will) we were, and are desirous *now to be visited*, as his most merciful promise importeth.

A Vision.

E. K. Now *Uriel* is here; he hath a Chair, and is set down in it: It is like a Throne.

Here I see a green Hill: and I see thereon three men, like learned men, in Gowns of puke-colour: they have Hats on their heads. *Uriel* hath in his hand a thing like a rolling-pin (of half an ell long) of Gold.

The Garden of Comfort.

I see beyond the men, a very fair Park, enclosed with pale, piked, &c. I see Roses and Lillies, and goodly Flowers in one part of it, and fair running waters in it, and little Hills, and all manner of Birds: And in the middle of the Park, is a turret, and in the top of that, a round thing like a Stone, which giveth light all the Park over: but without the Park pale, it is duskish or dark. These three men stand together upon the pitch of the bank of the Hill that goeth down toward *Uriel.*

There appear three diverse fair wayes to the Park, two from the Hill where the men stand; and one from the place about *Uriel.*

1. I see one man walk in the Park, and he picketh Flowers, and putting them to his mouth, they smoke, as the smoke of the snuff of a candel when the candle is put out.

2. I see likewise another man gathering of Flowers there, and he would put the Flowers to make them stick on his Coat, but they will not hang on but fall down, it is so bare.

3. I see a third man, who hath his Robes all belayed with lace of gold, great and small, and divers pretious Stones, and on his head a wreath like a Garland, very broad beset with very beautiful pretious Stones: and he trimmeth himself all over with the flowers of the Park

or

or Garden,   Now the three men are come from the Hill, before *Uriel* his feat.

...... *I most humbly beseech you that I may have accesse into the Garden of Comfort.*
Uriel. .... *You shall: I am contented.*

1.
One of those
men faith

E. K. Now they three go toward the Garden of Comfort: they point one to another, and seem to talke one with another.   They go in the path which leadeth from him [*Uriel*] toward the Park.

Uriel. ......, *These are Wise men, for they shall escape the danger of the* [△] *first and the second,* *and shall live as the* [△] *third in comfort and pleasure : For behold, Those which have entred, and now shall enter, have deserved their reward.*

△ He mean-
eth of the first
and second
which gather-
ed flowers, and
of the third.

But some there be that enter, and respect not the end ; and such shall they be as he is, which defileth the flowers.

Respice finem.]

E. K. Now here cometh a man from the Park-ward, and meeteth those three men, and giveth them three very rich garments : they put off their former garments , and put on those rich and beautiful garments.

Uriel. ...... *Othersome there be, and go the middle way, because it is the next and straightest, and those be such as enter with their own ornaments, which are very poor and bare, and upon whose garments can hang no pleasure.*

Some there are that enter [1] *from me (for without me none entreth into that Garden) and because I am the light of him that lighteth by Creation, therefore is there a way perfect, and bear-eth testimony from me, whereby they are thought worthy, and are* [2] *apparelled for that place of pleasure, and so worthily enter.*

3.
Causa
& causa proxi-
ma & propria
ut different bic.

Lo they enrich themselves, being made rich with the beauty of so pleasant flowers. and they al-wayes drink of the water of wisdom to their comfort and continuance.   Blessed is he that so entreth.

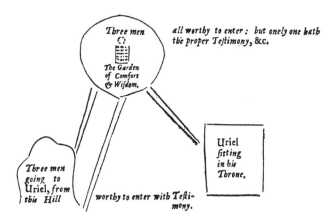

Three men
The Garden
of Comfort
& Wisdom.

all worthy to enter : but onely one hath
the proper Testimony, &c.

Uriel
sitting
in his
Throne.

Three men
going to
Uriel, from
this Hill

worthy to enter with Testimony.

2

1. *He that defileth the flowers, was worthy to enter into our Garden : but because he came not hither to my Throne, and so took the way descending from the Hill,* [to me] *and brought into the Garden of Wisdom, his worldly apparel ; which, lo, is alwayes as a mist between him and true wisdom, yet he thinketh himself satisfied.*

A defiler of the
flowers.
The Garden of
Wisdom.

2. *He whose coat is bare, was also worthy :   But because he thought himself worthy, and visited not my seat, he took the middle way, where are no ornaments :   Therefore he brought in his own nakednesse which is so thredbare, that the flowers fall off it; as from a marble stone, and the waters glideth off it, as from the back of a Falcon.*

Behold, I sit: happy are those, that come unto me.

Lo, you see, you may become wise ; with the [1] *Cloudy, wise with the* [2] *bare ; and wise with those that are* [3] *advanced ; and dwell in true wisdom.*

Three manner
of wise men.

The Gate that thou shalt enter into, is a fire of fury, and of revenge :
But be it unto thee, as thy Election is.   Even from the beginning, nakedly.

Fury and Re-
venge,
Open unto

Rudolph.

[ff]

Rudolph. *the manner of Gods visitation: Shew unto him the holy Vision: for I will make thee un-*
to him an hand, an arm, yea an half body. Yea I will be merciful unto him, and seal him for
my self: *and he shall be thy comfort. I will put my fear into him, and .be shall be afraid to*
sin, and he shall become a rod to those that are sinful.

Happy are those, whose works are a hope; and whose faith deserveth the aid of my light. This
is of God, and I am the finger. Happy are those that are directed by me. For, in me is the true
path and light of direction.

E.K. He is gone.

Δ. As concerning this Gate (lastly spoken of) whereinto I must enter, that it is *a fire of*
fury, and of revenge: O Lord, I am afraid, if that phrase be of any displeasure to me : for I
referred my Election to the will of God, as was for his honour and glory to be granted: And I have
long made Petition to God for your help, and I desire nothing that should make the highest offended with me. But perhaps the service of God wherein I am to serve him now, (with
his Talent of wisdom to be imparted to me) consisteth in the execution of the Justice of God,

with a furious and revenging fire, as under the Altar they lie, and cry for,&c.

...... *Thou hast said* ————

Δ. All Laud, Honor, and praise be unto the Almighty, wise, and our most mercifull God :
now, and ever. Amen.

Tuesday, 21. Augusti : *Ante Meridiem horam Circiter 9.*   † Pragæ

Precibus finitis, & invito *Uriele* ut nos illuminaret, dirigeret, consolaretur, &c.

E.K. *Uriel* is here, and about his head at a little distance, is a bright
part of a Circle like a Rain-bow, &c.

Δ. We propounded unto you yesterday (O you faithfull messager of the highest) as concerning this letter, how it is liked : when it is to be sent, and by whom, &c.

Uriel. ..... *O earth, how great a Monster art thou, and how great is thy wickednesse, which makest*
dull mans capacity, and carriest him away into an obscure and rash sense? Not without a cause art
thou hated with the highest; yea, not without a cause are thy Garments made short.

My brethren, how long will you be grievous to the Lord, how long (I say) will you be without un-
derstanding.

O, how long will you consider your own commodities, and neglect the harvest of the Lord?
[Δ. I understand nothing of the occasion of these speeches.]

Uriel. ..... But behold, for you *have chosen unto your selves a visitation, and have broken the*
visitation of the Lord.

For when you were commanded you went not, and unto your selves you chose dayes for ad-
vantage: Well, I say, Take your choice and become wise: for I am ready to deliver.

I say, prepare your selves, and be ready: But I fear me, (yea, I know it) that you will become
foggy and misty. *Notwithstanding thus say; th the Lord: Since you will become wise,* Chastise your
self for a few dayes, and abstain, and you shall see that I am a God that can visit, and mightily:

I am not man, that my promises may not be, neither speak I of any thing that liveth not, for I am
light, and the breath of understanding. Because you have followed my Commandments (yet
some of you obstinately, and rather, as reprehenders then obedient servants) *I will put a snaf-*
fle unto Satan, and unto his Ministers, and thou shalt sit in judgement against the wicked : *For*
I will multiply thee, and thy houshold: And of thy seed; yea, even of thy seed,
will I finder out *a Camber,* a *and will root out a people, which* I have
long favoured. *And for this cause* spared *I him unto thee, for unto him*
that loveth me, will I be a just rewarder. The branches of the wicked do I cut
off, and make worse then the Asses dung: But unto the faithfull will I send
honour, and a Crown of rejoycing.

Hui, who is he, that I cannot reward him? Or where dwellest thou, (in
Heaven, or in Earth) that art, and rejoycest not by me? If thou follow my
Commandments, and I once begin to love thee?

I have told thee that I will place thee here.

Δ. I must be   [Δ. In this Citie.]
placed here in   Uriel...... *Not as a Citizen,* but *as an owner of ma-*
Prage.   *ny houses. But take heed, thou be just to me, and do*
what I command thee.

Δ. Lord thou knowest my heart, help, and supply my wants.

Uriel...... *Behold, the Corn is not ripe, neither are the Grapes red, nor the Sun hath not yet sea-*
soned them; Therefore, yet, need I not Stewards, but Overseers : *And as yet, Laborers* are to me
as shadows. *Because, not yet, no, not yet is the time of my visitation: therefore he that bring-*
eth his Syckle now, must not reap for me, but must rejoyce in himself. Happy is he that tarrieth
the Lord, least afterward the doors be shut, and the feast at an end. *All wisdom (and scien-*
ces

ces comprehended in wisdom) that worketh for himself, is of the world: But the wisdom that I give,
I give openly, and without reproach: that I also rejoycing in the wisdom may be glorified, and ex-
alted with a Diademe of honour. When Sodom *cried for vengeance, had I it not ready? Could*
not I from heaven have consumed them with the breath of my own mouth? I, in my self know
it, and am witnesse: But lo, in the pride of their filthinesse I had regard to time: And (that it might Time.
be known to all Nations) licensed my Angels, *and gave them power: And lo, then made a promise* Δ. Promise to
unto all Nations that they should be blessed in Abraham: *even the same moneth that I destroyed the* So- Abraham.
domites.   These things did I, as unto Noe: *and unto* Seth, *whom I lived: I made them privy* Seth, the third
of time to come, and opened unto them my judgements: because the world should be justly condemned. son of Adam.
After the same manner made I a promise unto you: Lo, after the same manner have I called you A promise
to counsel.   But you have chosen the lowest, and have refused the highest places, and have made unto
regarded your own comforts, and not my visitation. I commanded thee not to go into the woods, us.
and to fetter Wolves: *neither to saw the* Tygers *teeth.   I delivered you not unto the wicked, neither* The choice
suffered I them to rejoyce over you: But I have brought you from death, and from the dayes of The mercies
lamentation, and have dealt with you as faithfull brethren do in their divisions: Not that I forget of God upon
my self, but that I would be magnified, and that you might see your wildnesse, and naked rashnesse: us.
Many are there upon the earth, which would have burst with gladnesse, and have rent their Garments
in pieces.   If I had touched them with the least of these Counsels (so I call them, because they [Δ. To P. age.]
are my secrets) Is it not sufficient that I have brought you [Δ.] *hither safe? Have promised you* A sure help
a sure help? promised.

Lo, you wrast me, for what is he of the   [▲ *This is spoken in respect of God his*
world, to whom I shall confirm letters?   *judgement required of the letter.*]

They grieve me, because they are the doings of man: O man, let man answer unto thee, and let it
suffice thee, that the mark whereat thou shootest is in my hand.
My work is not a work of hours nor dayes.   But when I command, do speedily.   When the Do the Lords
Thunders fall from Heaven, and burn up the Earth, scale her face, and leave her naked.   Then, Command-
Then, will you believe.   ment speedily.
Behold, He that is a man, being new born, is accounted a Monster.   Note, signes.
Is it not written? Lo, the Lord looked from heaven in his visitation, and in the midday, and Δ. I under-
groaned upon her, for she had vexed him.   Happy is he that is ready when he visiteth: That which stand not this.
I command, let it be done.   For when the Kings of the earth, say, do this: They play not also the
parts of their servants and subjects, but lo, it is done.   Suffer me (I pray you) to have that fa-
vour.
Δ. Deo Noſtro Miſericordi, Pio, & Juſto, ſit omnis Honor, Laus & Gloria.   *Amen.*

Tueſday, 21 *Auguſti.*   † Pragæ.

After Dinner as we [E. K. and Δ.] were in my Study, and conferring of my choiſe, and
very ſorry that we had made our choiſe not of the beſt: E. K. *ſaw* Uriel *in the ſtone, which yet*
ſtood unput up: and ſaid, he had ſeen him there ever ſince we began: So coming to the ſtone he
ſaid as followeth.
Uriel. ...... *Murmur not amongſt your ſelves: But rejoyce and be glad, and found into the greatneſſe*
of Gods mercies, which beareth all your weakneſſe, and leadeth you through the foggy and perilous
miſts of your daily temptations even by the hand: And now, not onely giveth, but also exhorteth.
I ſpeak with you as a man, Yea, let me ſpeak with you as a man: You are oppreſt with ſin, and
with the world, and are not yet apt for the viſitation of God.   Note our un-
                                                                                        aptneſſe yet
My brethren, God hath dealt mercifully with   Δ. In malevolam animam non introibit to be viſited,
you, hath opened unto you theſe three wayes de- ſapientia, nec habitabit in corpore   Eccleſiaſtes,
ſirous   ſubdito peccatis, Eccleſiaſtes, cap. 1. cap. 1.

[E. K. He ſpeaketh other language, I underſtand not.]

...., *That one of you might have entred into the higheſt Gate.*
And why? Becauſe the workman might be able, and correſpon-   The workman and the work
dent unto the work, and time (of the Lord) to come, God hath muſt be correſpondent.
done may great things for you: but you will not ſee them. Tar- To Δ. Was ſaid, In fac. ſu-
ry awhile till I come again.   pra. To E. K. In vide. To A. L.
                                                                Tu vive.
　　E. K. He is gone beyond a thing like a Hill.
　　Δ. After half a quarter of an hour he came again.
　　E. K. He hath a pair of Tables in his hand, made as of white bone:
and therein are many names written orderly, one under another.
　　E. K. If I thought this to be of God, and this to be Uriel indeed, it
were another matter: but their too much familiarity maketh me doubt.
　　Δ. The old ſaying is true in you, *Nimia familiaritas parit contemptum.*
Uriel.....Be-

Uriel. ......, Believe me, by Heaven and Earth, *I am true* Uriel.

E. K. He hath another Book holden unto him, by one standing by him, who is like a shadow.

A new choice, by God his great mercy granted. 73 and a half Dee his age.

Uriel. ...... Give ear, *say* and chuse : *for after this time, there is no choice.*

Dee, *thy age and continuance in this world, in flesh, according to the finger, and second proportion, which you call Nature, is 73 years and a half : and here it is* [Δ. pointing to the other Book.]

E. K. He that is like a shadow openeth the Book ; it seeming to be of yern or steel. In which Book appeareth divers names, as *Bamasan, Corsax, Tohomaphala,* &c.

[Δ. They seemed to be the names of good Angels proper to peculiar men.]
Uriel. ...... Thou [*E.K.*] *dost more than thou art commanded. Yet, cease a while.*
[Δ. Because he [*E. K.*] read these names.

E. K. He spreadeth a thing like a Cloud before them.

E. K. Now he appeareth again, and the other with him.

Angelus bonus, E. K.

E. K. Sudsamna appeareth in the Book, and against it 46.

Uriel. ...,... *So much shalt thou* ⌊ *E. K.* ⌋ *live by nature, and die* violently.

E. K. Now he is covered again.

E. K. Now he is here again.

E. K. Aflasben standeth written in that Book, and 73 with a prick over the upper part of the figure 3.

E. K. The Book is very big and full of names, and numbers against them : the leaves are very thin.

Aflasben my good angel.
Sudsamna E.K. his good Angel.
Vita Natura, Gratia.

E. K. Now *Uriel* openeth his book himself; And there appeareth against *Aflasben,* 122. And against *Sudsamna* appeareth 87.

Uriel. ...... Beyond the which, you cannot : --- *Notwithstanding this life, is always given by God, or at the intercession of some one, or mo, of us his Angels. The other is natural : notwithstanding is shortened through the sin of man. I am a witness to my self,* that these books and words are true.

E. K. Now he is in his Cloud again.

Δ. After a while, they appeared again, as before.

E. K. They look very gravely on their books.

Δ. As King Ezekia's did Regnum 4. cap. 10 Note.

Uriel. ...... *Behold my brethren, God is ready to open his merciful store-houses and gates of understanding unto you : But he that liveth for himself, and for the end of this shadow, limiteth his wisdom with this number : - and shall both have an end at once : But he that turneth him to* the wall, and weepeth bitterly, *shall enter into this Book : But he must not build his own house, but an house for the Lord ; Neither must he be visited by the challenge of promise, but by the meer mercy and good will of God, and at his pleasure and appointment : He that hath understanding let him hear.*

* August 13. One new or reformed choice.

Behold, This his pen, is a pen of Steel ; But that that I raze withal, is of Gold, and a piercing Instrument. If therefore your visitation shall be after to * morrow, and that you covet to build (because you are men) Then give your names unto the yern : But if you will remember the Lord, and adde any thing unto his building, faithfully, Then vow your names unto me, In the name of him which created you. *After this time, there is no choice.*

A g eat mercy and mystery.

Therefore, consider ; for, never before, (but once) was this mystery, and mercy of God opened unto man.

E. K. Now he hath drawn the Cloud to him.

Δ. I am not able (O Lord) to give thee condigne thanks for these mercies : But thy will be done : Not as we will, nor as we have rashly and blindly (before) chosen : But this is our choice, to be thy servants all the dayes of our life ; and we desire not long life so much, as the *favour* which addeth those dayes, wherein our faith may be fruitful through thy graces abounding in us. *I renounce my former choice, I challenge no promise :* But require thee, O God, of thy fatherly goodnesse to be my light, director, staff, strength, defence, and comfort, now and ever, *Amen.*

The former choice renounced. This Day.

Uriel. ...... *Alwayes call unto me for the Testimony and witnesse of the promise of God, and* the remembrance of this day.

E. K. He

E. K. He hath written after the * numbers in his own Book, . 112.87.
Est, Est.

Δ. Ad laudem, gloriam, & honorem Dei, Esto, Esto. *Amen.*

Uriel......... *Now deal with* Rodolph. *and be not slack: for until thou have talked with* Rodolphus, *him, I appear no more.*

Thy haste, shall prevent the slander of wicked tongues, whom Satan hath already stirred up against thee.

Δ. I understand of none.

Uriel. .... *It is best thou understand it not at all.*

E. K. He putteth a Cloud over all the Stone, like a white wrinkled Curtain : and so disappeareth.

Δ. But though you appear not, yet of *Madimi* I may require answer, to know when my wife and children are to be sent for, *&c.*

E. K. There is no answer given.

Δ. Fiat voluntas Dei, juxta illius beneplacitum : cui omnis laus gloria & gratiarum Actio, nunc & in omne ævum. *Amen.*

Δ. I received letters from my wife, that she and her children are well.   God have the praise and thanks therefore. *Amen.*

Friday, *Augusti,* 24. *à Meridie.*   Pragæ.

Being willed to deal with *Rodolphus,* first by letter, and then by speech : I thought good to send the Letter before written, for the Emperour ; by the Noble *Don wilhelmo de St. Clemente,* the King of *Spain* his *Præfectus Negotiorum* with this Emperour : and thereupon by *Emericus Sunttag,* the Lord *Laskie* his Secretary, I wrote this to the aforesaid *Don Clemente,* and sent it this *Bartholomew* Day.

EA est hominum in terris conditio (Nobilissime vir) ut sibi soli nullus natus esse videatur : Immò neque sibi ullus omnia sponte nascentia, vel ultro ab aliis oblata, quæ sibi maximè sunt necessaria, recipiat.   Mutuæ inde hominum emerserunt societates, mutuæ amicitiæ, mutuæ operæ, Mutua dona, Rerum commutatio, & emptionis, rerumque venditionis contractus : Aliique diversi hominum existunt status, unde hominum inter homines, & cum hominibus multiplicia procurantur officia, commerciaque.   Neque omnium istorum, sola est utilitas vel (quæ peribit) voluptas, scopus ille, vel finis, quem attingere conantur & student : Sed aliud aliquibus est propositum, quod Divinius quidem est, quod virtutem vel Honestatem nominare possumus ; quæ cælitus demissa, hominum informet mentes & ornet, sibique coaptet : Adeo ut sedibus illas reddat cælestibus dignas.   Illud, illud, ergo est Illustrissimo vir quod excellentiam vestram tam mihi pridie reddidit attentam, benignam & perhumanam ; Illud est quod vestram refricabit memoriam, & vestrum insigniter acuet ingenium, in Causa mea, suæ Cæsareæ Majesti tam proponenda, quam commendanda : eoque tractanda modo, quo illa tractari Arcana debeant, quæ a paucis credantur , & a paucioribus intelligantur : verissima licet sint, & ex sese utilissima.   Quo citiùs Cæsarea sua Majestas, mirabilem hanc & maximam Dei, non Providentiam solum, sed bonitatem etiam amplexus fuerit, eo citius & abundantius, meæ ad illum legationis constabit sinceritas, bonitas & utilitas.   Voluissem equidem hunc inclusum libellum, literásque inclusas vestræ excellentiæ, ipsemet attulisse. Sed (cum venia sit dictum) ex digiti pedis mei offensa cuticula, non tam commodè possum hodie pedes venire.   Proinde amico meo hoc onus imposui, ut (cum vestræ Excellentiæ manuum deosculatione) omnia mea vobis offerat servitia : hocque, quicquid est, pro sua Cæsarea Majestate, traderet munusculi.

Pragæ 24. *Augusti* 1584.

Joannes Dee.

The Superscription of this Letter was thus,

Illustrissimo Domino, Domino Don Gulielmo de Sancto Clemente serenissimi atque Catholici Hispaniarum Regis Negotiorum apud sacram Cæsaream Majestatem, *&c.* Præfecto, Domino meo Observandissimo.

Monday

Monday, *Augusti* 27. *Mane circa* 9.   † Pragæ.

Precibus finitis, I propounded to God, of *Madimi* four things.

First, what was the cause of the errour recorded, *Febr.* 18. this *Anno* 1584. at *Lasko* of Sir *Henry Sidney* his death ?

Secondly, In what sense is this to be understood, which *Madimi* willed me to say to *Rodolphus, An Angel of the Lord hath appeared unto me* ?

Thirdly, *Madimi* said as concerning the time of my wife and children and houshold to be moved hither, *Let that be my charge to answer thee* ?

Fourthly, *Madimi* willed me to write to *Rodulphus* : And I have done, and caused it to be delivered to *Don Wilhelmo de Sancto Clemente,* the Spanish Embassadour, to deliver it to the Emperour. God prosper it. *Amen.*

E. K. Here she is.

Δ. The eternal roots of verity bring forth fruit, to the comfort of such as delight in the pure verity for the service of God, &c. And you *Madimi,* as a Minister of the Highest in verity, are unto me welcome.

Causa sine qua non
Note this phrase of sound.

Mad. ...... *Even as mans fingers [or a thing,] touching, moving, or forcing an instrument musical, is the cause, without the which it cannot sound, or drink up the air ; which again seeking issue, and feeling a stay, is the [objectum] cause of concord or dissonancy, according to the inward spirit and imagination of the thing that moveth, or of the finger moving : So the earthly part of man, which hath no motion of it self, (radically) moveth by touch or finger (whatsoever) spiritual, and sendeth out sounds ; not according to her self, but according to the fiery, yea invisible, and spiritual power, wherewithal it is moved,*

Three movers in man concurring.

Hereby we learn, that mans body, and his organical motions, bath three manner of movers ; centraliter, by the property and perfection of the Soul, a superiore, and by descension, from the Angels or participants of understanding : E contrario, and ascending, spirits wicked, and tempters, in all moving.

☉ *Splendor in die obtundit lumen lunæ etiam supra horizontem.*
Note the manner of the Diabolical working in, or by man.

But here you must note, That as the Sun depriveth the Moon in respect of her end, which is to give light, but not of her self ; So do the Angels and higher powers drown and overshadow the soul in man when they are present : working from God and in themselves, (as from above) and not by the soul as any root, or first cause of the motion.

But when the Devil entreth, and ascendeth, he worketh not by force, but by enticement, and so allureth the soul, to grant of his possession : whereby he entreth and becometh strong.

Those that have ears let them hear ; for my words are wisdom, and the grounds of many Sciences.

Mundus Humanum Corpus, &c. tanquam Cera,
Impressio { *Superior, Humana, Inferior.*
Pray against Temptation.
Impressio prædominans est consideranda.
Δ. *Per quæ homo peccat per eadem punitur : qui dixit Ascendam, &c. Jam ex Infernali statu, semper ascendendo tentat.*

Then, by a similitude, is the world wax : Mans body wax : and the natural motions of things, naturally extended, wax also : But our purpose is of man ; which at one instant receiveth three impressions : Missive, Natural, and Offensive.

Whereby you may perceive, That man greatly needeth to pray against temptation : For the last Seal, is sign of him that oweth the wax, Happy are those, that can watch and pray : for such they are that grant not any room or interest, to the wicked ascender.

I answer you : If you be but as a string, Challenge but your own duty : But take heed, you be in tune.

E. K. She speaketh, but I cannot expresse it.

Δ. I pray you let nothing of your words, that you utter to us, or before us, be unrecorded.

Mad. ...... *You are not worthy to write it : for it is the harmony of the heavens.*

Stay a while ; for I would open that unto you, which I perceive I may not : but I come again.

[Δ. We read over the premises, and weighed them as instructions of the three divers movers of mans senses internally, &c. And so after a quarter of an hour

E. K. Here she is again.

Mad. .... *For he that purifieth his house, and straweth rushes, and beautifieth the chambers with Garlands, is worthy to receive (because of his aptnesse,) such as are messagers of understanding and light. My friends and brethren, marvellous is the God of Wisdom in all his doings and works, and full of variety are the works of his hands.*

E. K. Now she speaketh again ; I understand it not.

The Answer to the first Doubt.

..... *But to the Answer : The end of my purpose, Satan, perceiving you [E.K.] as well to be moved by him because of your own grant, as by the motion wherewithal you were moved and illuminated :*

minated : and being the father of suttlety, and a froward understanding purposed, even in this one sentence ; yea, with this one lye, to overturn, or at
least to blemish the worthinesse of our message, and of your receiving : because he saw the course of nature, and the doings of man, and that this man
Mr. Simon Hagek, young Hagek, would first visit thee , [Δ] therefore be
thrust in a shingle of his own cutting and nature : Not to the intent it should
be credited, but to the intent it should be a stumbling block to the action in time
to come, which is now.

*My brethren, he is a marvellous work-man : and one that striketh now the most strings, in a man-
ner, all. But he hath his reward : Therefore do I deny it to be spoken by me, or of me.*

Δ. So by God his Grace, I did conceive, and undoubtedly think, *and of many other things,
besides that,* I have occasion of reforming the Records : that the heavens may agree, as the
phrase was used.

Mad. ...... Many there are not : But such as are, gather them together, let me sift them.

Δ. I thank God for that his mercy.

Δ. Now I beseech you to the second my present request before propounded, it may please
you to give answer.

Mad. ...... *When the King sendeth a Present to a Noble man, or unto any one that he favoureth,
he loveth, or delighteth in : The Messager carrieth it, delivereth it within his house.*

E. K. She seemeth to smile.

...... *He to whom it is sent enjoyeth it , he useth it ; yea , peradventure (being a dainty dish)
eateth of it.*

*Afterward the King sendeth to him by the same messager, saluteth his houshold, and commandeth
him to say : Thus sayeth the King ; Go to such a man and salute him : Tell him that I will visit him,
and that I say so.*

*Behold, he sitteth still, and goeth not, neither doth he the Commandment of his Superiour. For lo,
sayeth he : The King commanded me not ; his messager came, and would so. But whether the
King will so, or no, I know not.*

*But hearest thou : Thou wicked man, hast thou not eaten of his meat, and enjoyed the benefit of
his present before ? Yes, A threefold benefit, which shall continue untill the * seventh Angel,
and untill the third woe.*

*Man begetteth a Son, and lo, his wife is with Childe, and she looketh for the time of her delive-
rance : If the question be moved unto him, (his wife not yet delivered,) whether he have issue, or
fruit of his body, say thou unto me, what shall he answer.*

Δ. As it shall please God.

Mad. ...... *That is no answer.*

Δ. Then he may say, He is in hope to have the issue his wife goeth great withall , may this
seem an answer, I beseech you?

Mad. ...... *Though the Childe be not yet born, he hath issue Deliverance, it, by reason of the issue,
and not called issue of the deliverance : for he is a son as well unborn as born.*

So is it of you : Thou hast prayed unto God, and he hath heard thee.

*And lo, the issue , which he giveth thee is Wisdom. But lo, the Mother of it is not yet deli-
vered.*

*For, If woman know her times and seasons of deliverance : Much more doth he,
which is the Mother of all things. But thou mayest rejoyce that there is a time of
deliverance, and that thy gift is compared to a woman with childe.*

*For, as the one is, and shall be visible : so is wisdom granted, and shall appear :
yea, a lively, and most perfect Creature.*

*Behold, the Angels of the Lord have been sent down from God , unto him
[E.K.] here is sight, which is of this houshold in God : He hath brought unto thee
that which he tasteth not himself : And yet thou doubtest, saying, How shall I say
the Angel of the Lord hath appeared unto me.*

*Unto thee, [Δ] we have appeared : for unto thee, [Δ] we are
sent. And because his eye hath seen , therefore we have joyned him
unto thee, that in the time of darknesse thou mightest see.*

Δ. It is to be made   *And before the time of thy vi-
perfect before the time   sitation thou must be made per-
of his visitation.   fect.*

*And because it is of thee and not of him : Therefore doth not God impute unto him his offen-
ces, but placeth in you the figure of time to come.*

Supra lib. 15. 1584.   *For some there be that naturally shall draw in the Plow of the Lord,
Junii 2.   And othersome there be, that must have their times and seasons.*

*For thy boushold affairs, I say nothing yet, neither for thy Letter sent, or Messen-
ger.* Nam Deus agit in suis, sicut vult.

*I have nothing else to say unto thee but blessed be those that believe in the Lord,
for they have their reward.*

E. K. She

E. K. She goeth away, *divided into a great many pieces* of fire.

Deo Noſtro Omnipotenti, eterno & ſapienti : ſit omnis honor, Laus & Gloria. *Amen.*

Note. At noon, this day I received Letters from the Lord *Laskie*, from my wife, and from my brother *Nicolas Fromonds* in *England* : how Mr. *Gilbert*, Mr. *Sted*, Mr. *Andrew Firmorshem*, my Book-ſeller, uſed me very ill in divers ſorts.

The Dates of the Letters from *England* were of the 15. and 16th. day of *April* 1584. My wife is in great ſorrow for my brother *Nicholas.*

Monday, Auguſti 17. At night after Sun ſet, *Emerich Sontag* brought me word from the Spaniſh Ambaſſadour, that he had delivered to the Emperour this day my Letters and Book : and that he took them gracio⸗ſly and thankfully, and ſaid that within *three, or four dayes* he would let the Spaniſh Ambaſſadour underſtand, when he would *give me audience.*

Deus bene vertat : & ad ſui nominis honorem & Laudem. *Amen.*

Saturday, *Septembris* 1. *Ante Meridiem Circa* 10. † Ptagæ.

Δ. As I, and *E. K.* ſat in my little Study : after our talk of divers matters , and of my expecting audience at the Emperour his hand, &c. *E. K.* ſaw three little Creatures walk up and down in the Sun-ſhine, about an handfull from the pavyment : and the Creatures themſelves very ſmall, not an hundfell long, like little ſhadows, or ſmokes, and the path wherein they walked ſeemed yellow. They walked a good while to and fro, till at length I ſuſpected that *they were ſent to us* ; and ſo prepared the ſhew-ſtone : But *E. K.* ſaid, he had rather ſee them thus out of the ſtone. I ſaid that in the ſtone we have warrant that no wicked thing ſhall enter : but without the ſtone, Illuders might deal with us , unleſſe God prevented it, &c. *E. K.* ſaid again, he had rather deal thus.

One of the 3. ſpiritual creatures ſaid, He in the middle of the Thre.... ...... *His meaning is above thy ſight.*

E. K. Now two of them ſeem to kneel down in the Sun beams.

...... *Bleſſed be God the Father, God the Son, and God the holy Ghoſt, the moſt holy and bleſſed Trinity : One, true, mighty, perfect everlaſting and incomprehenſible God.*

　　[Δ. Amen, Amen, Amen.]

...... *Which will be comprehended with thoſe that live in the Heavens (the true Church of God) of ſuch as meaſure him by faith, and not reaſon : which hath ſent us to do his will ; Both in that he will turn his heart : And in that he doth vouchſafe to make you witneſſes of his ſecret purpoſes , and determinations in hand.* Δ. Rod. his heart is to be turned by God, but I know not the meaning.
· Δ. Sunt dua liteʒa ultima in linea Spiritus Sancti in Tertia Tabula.

 The [1] *middlemoſt ſaid* —— I am *the midſt of the third, and the laſt* [Δ] *of the ſpirit of life : Underſtood in this temporal controverſie , and conflict of mans Soul : but not according to his eternal and immeaſurable proportion.*

Flagellum Dei. *The* [2] *on the right ſide ſaid* —— I am *the ſecond of the third, which dwell in the ſpirit, and power of God in earth : I have power to ſcourge them that reſiſt the power, will, and commandment of God : and I am one of thoſe that ſtand, and is perpetual.*

Trinitas & unitas Divina. *For even as the father, ſon , and holy ſpirit are one , but of themſelves and being dilated, is full of power, and many. So are we one particularly in power, but ſeparated ; notwithſtanding, ſpiritually, of , and amongſt others, and dilated in the will of God, and into the branches of his determinations : but particularly living, and joyntly* praiſing God.

E. K. Now [3] the other (the third) on the otherſide ſtandeth up, and ſayeth.

3 ...... *The Kingdom of God, and of his ſon Chriſt : (which is true God, and the ſubſtance of his father, True God of true God) is contrary to the Kingdom of this world.*

E. K. What is that, God of God ? Δ. The Confeſſion and belief of the Catholick Church : not to be talked of now.

E. K. They are diſappeared : but their path appeareth in the aire, in ſun-beams ſtill.

E. K. They are here again. Δ. Half a quarter of an hour they had diſappeared.

Filii fidei & non rationis humanæ. ...... *Happy are thoſe that are of his Kingdom, for it hath no end ; yea, happy are thoſe that are* the ſons of faith, and *not* of the world : *which is called* Reaſon. *Which is blinde, and is ſealed*
with

with the mark of destruction. Because *she prosecuted, and put to death the Son of God, the God of* righteousnesse *, and light of all that live.*

I am the last, of the first, of the fourth, and *I have power to gather up the bles-*   Δ. His name is the
Ejus officium est transplan-   *sings of God, and to set them (if they*   last 3. letters of the
tatio Donorum Dei.   be disdained*) in a better soyl.*   1. line of the fourth
                                                                                             Table.
3. *For thus sayeth the God of Hoasts.*

If he dream and will not hear me Gather up that he hath, and that which   Rod if. *Vide* lib. 15.
should be given him : that his life may be short, and his house without comfort: Maii 28. 1584.
that he may passe away naked ly, as a shadew.   Ga
                                                                                                   Za
As lo, behold, we go, and we will dwell there ; yea , even in the skirts of.   Vaa
their Garments will we take up our habitation.   *And why ?*

Behold, this hath God *said : In the morning* watch them , *and see how they*   Angeli observantes
rise. In the day time give ear unto them, and listen unto their counsels. Stand   Nostra opera & Con-
over them in the night, and note their filthinesse. And when it exceedeth the   silia.
number, strike.   Strike.

We are they that must direct your practises.   Note.
...... *Behold, let us give Testimony of our names.*   One of them
My name is — Ga — E. K. He in the middle.   sayeth.
My name is — Za ⎱ Δ. The three names make one name of 7. Letters, *Gazavaa.*
My name is — Vaa ⎰
So we are called by position.
Thou shalt finde us amongst the merciful Tables *delivered unto* Enoch *: and so unto you.*

1. *The middlemost* ⎡ *I am of the third* Table, *and am extream.*   Δ. Of the Phy-
2.   │ *I am of the third, but of the humanity, and the second.* sick part.
                   │   Δ. Note the third Table here meant, is that
                   │   of the South; as East, West, South, and
                   ⎨   North; their placing is others.
3.   │ *And I am the fourth, but Angular , and extream, Linear of the upper-*
                   ⎣ *most.*   Δ. The three last Letters in the uppermost
                                 line of the fourth Table.

..,.. *We are gone.*   E. K. They are out of sight.

A voyce. Follow that which is commanded thee.

                                          Δ. Æterno , Omnipotenti , Trino & uni
                                          Deo; sit omnis honor Laus & Gloria.
   ⎧ Ga —— *Ultimus spiritus vivorum.*
4. ⎨ Za —— *Flagellator resistentium potestati,*
   ⎪   *voluntati, præcepto Dei.*
   ⎩ Vaa—— *Transplantator Donorum.*

Monday, *Septembris* 3. *Mane.*   † *Pragæ.*
Δ. *Nota.* Sathanæ *astutum & violentum Stratagema.*

Δ. There was great disquietnesse in E. K. being come home from our Hosts house, where
he had lyen all night upon a form : by reason he had been (which he never was the like afore,
as he said) with wine overcome suddenly : yet intending with himself to take heed of being
overshot in, drinking of wine : being requested by the Hostes to give her a quart of wine
upon the good bargain he had in a Clock he bought of her for five Suckats : In this company
of drinking was *Alexander*, the Lord *Laskie* his servant, who came with us to *Prage*. Unto
whom E. K. (when the drink on the sudden had overcome him) said he would cut off his
head, and with his walking staffe did touch him fair, and softly on the neck , sitting before
him : This *Alexander* being half drunken himself , by & by took those words in great snuffe,
and went to defend himself, and so took his weapon to him; and thereupon they by caused
Alexander to go down : It was supper time ; and I that night refrained to suppe, and so tarrying at my Lodging, and looking out, saw *Alexander* sitting on the great stone against our
Lodging : I called to him, and told him that they were at supper : And he came over to me,
and he had wept much ; he complained of E. K. his former words, and the touch of the staffe;
how it was against his credit to take that in good part , and spake many Souldiers terms of
stout words, not worthy the recording. I, thereupon went to our Hosts house, and would understand the very truth ; and there I found E. K. fast on sleep on a form, most soundly : for
which I was right sorry : And yet better pleased to perceive the words of E. K. which so
moved *Alexander* (being half drunken) to have been spoken by E. K. when wine , and not
wit, bare rule : and so pleaded long time with *Alexander*, that of words spoken so as they were,
no such exact account was to be given to him, &c. And after two hours perswasion caused
Alexander to go to bed in our Lodging, where he used to lye, For he would have gone out,

to our former Inne, in those raging half drunken pangs, he was in : which I thought not good. This Monday morning *E. K.* coming home, and seeing *Alexander*, as he came in ; he said, they tell I should have spoken words, which greatly offended thee yesternight, and that I touched thee with my staff, *&c.* I know nothing of it, and shoke hands friendly with *Alexander*. Well saith *Alexander*, *Si fuisset altus*, &c. *E. K.* came up to me : I told him how sorry I was for this mischance, and told him of the Watchmen perceiving *Alexander* his disquiet mind, and hearing his words, they came to me and charged me to have a care of the peace keeping (as they did indeed) And farther said, that *Alexander* in his rage, said, that rather, or before, he should cut off his head, that he would cut *E. K.* in pieces. So soon as I had expressed that word of this drunken *Alexander* likewise, (whom now I saw quiet, and *E. K.* also quiet) suddenly *E. K.* fell into such a rage, that he would be revenged of him for so saying, and for railing on him in the street, as he did, *&c.*

Much a do I, *Emericus*, and his brother, had to stop or hold him from going to *Alexander* with his weapon, *&c.* At length we let him go in his dubblet and hose, without a cap or hat on his head : and into the street he hasted with his brothers Rapier drawn, and challenged *Alexander* to fight : But *Alexander* went from him, and said. *Nolo Domine Kelleie*, *Nolo*.

Satan his exceeding vehement Temptation.

Hereupon *E. K.* took up a stone, and threw after him, as after a dog, and so came into the house again, in a most furious rage for that he might not fight with *Alexander*. The rage and fury was so great in words and gestures, as might plainly prove, that *the wicked enemy sought* either *E. K.* his *own destroying of himself, or of me*, or his brother, *&c.*

Note the cause of this recording.

This may suffice to notifie the mighty temptation and vehement working of the subtile spiritual enemy Satan, wherewith God suffered *E. K.* to be tempted, and almost overcome : to my great grief, discomfort, and most great discredit : if it should (as the truth was) have come to the Emperours understanding, except he had known me well, *&c.* I was in great doubt, how God would take this offence, and devised with my self how I might, with honesty, be cleared from the shame and danger that might arise if these two should fight, *&c.* At the least it would crosse all good hope here with the Emperour, *&c.* for a time, till God redressed it.

Comfort in time of need.

After I had brought *E. K.* to some quietnesse, (by yeilding much to his humour, *&c.* and saying little :) not long after, came my messager from my wife at *Cracovia* : and *Hugh* my servant with him, to my great comfort through her letters , and the full satisfying of me by *Hugh* my servant his knowledge farther than conveniently could be written.

More Comfort in time of need.

About 2 of the clock after Noon , came this letter to me, of the *Emperour his sending for me.*

Nobilis, Præclarissiméque Domine, Domine observandissime.

Red.

CÆsar, jam jam significavit Domino Legato Hispaniarum, Hero meo, ut Dominationem vestram ad se evocaret, ad horam secundam ; quae eam audire cuperet : Dominatio vestra si ad dictam horam venire poterit : accedet statim Dominum Octavium Spinolam, qui est Majestati suæ Cæsareæ à Stabulis & Cubiculis. Is enim eam, ad Majestatem suam introducet. Quod reliquum est, me D. vestræ quam officiosissimè etiam atque etiam commendo,

Dominationis vestræ Studiosissimus

Arnoldus Vander Boxe.

Note the Original letter it self is in this Book.
Octavius Spinola Chamberlain and Stall-Master in the absence of the Officer who is sent into Spain.

Hereupon, I went straight up to the Castle : and in the Ritter-Stove or Guard-Chamber I stayed a little ; in the mean space I sent *Emericus* to see what was of the clock : and the Chamberlain , (*Octavius Spinola*) spied him out of the Emperours Chamber window, and called him, who came up to me, and by that time was the Chamberlain come out to me ; and by *Emericus* he understood that I was the man the Emperour waited for. He came to me very * curteously : told me of the Emperours desire to see me, and to speak with me. So he returned to the Emperour into the privy Chamber, and came out again for me, and led me by the skirt of the Gown through the Dining-Chamber, and the Privy Chamber, where the Emperour sat at a Table, with a great Chest and Standish of Silver, before him, my Monas and Letters by him, *&c.* I came toward him with due reverence of three curfies, who shewed me a gracious and chearful countenance.

* Hora tertia exactè à meridie.

Then I craved pardon at his Majesties hand, for my boldnesse to send his Majesty a Letter and the *Monas Hieroglyphica* (dedicated to his father.) But I did it of sincere and entire good will I bare to his father *Maximilian*, and also unto his Majesty : and that the rather, because I had good proof of the favour which Almighty God beareth unto his Majesty. He then thanked me for his fathers Book, and did affirm, that he believed me, that I was affectionate unto his Highnesse : And of my estimation with the learned of the world, he had heard

heard by the Spanish Embassadour; and also of my zealous mind towards his grace. And commended the Book *Monas,* but said, that it was too hard for his Majesties capcity; and added, that the Spanish Embassadour told him, that I had somewhat to say unto him, *Q. id effet pro sua utilitate.* I answered, So I have; and withal looking back whether any man were in the Chamber or no, I found that we were alone : Hereupon I began to declare that All my life time I had spent in learning : but for this forty years continually, in sundry manners, and in divers Countries, with great pain, care, and cost, I had from degree to degree, sought to come by the best knowledge that man might attain unto in the world : And I found (at length) that neither any man living, nor any Book I could yet meet withal, was able to teach me those truths I desired, and longed for : And therefore I concluded with my self, to make intercession and prayer to the giver of wisdom and all good things, to send me such wisdom, as I might know the natures of his creatures; and also enjoy means to use them to his honour and glory. And in this purpose made divers assayes : and at length it pleased God to send me his [△] *Light,* whereby I am assured of his merciful hearing of my long, fervent, constant, and continual prayer, in the cause before specified : And that, His holy Angels, for these two years and a half, have used to inform me : and have finished such works in my hands, to be seen, as no mans heart could have wished for so much; yea they have brought *me a Stone* of that value, that no earthly Kingdom is of that worthinesse as to be compared to the vertue or dignity thereof, &c. And that these things be true, I protested, and took to witnesse the God of Heaven and Earth, by *whose Commandment* I am now before your Majesty, (said I) and have a message from him to say unto you; and that is this :

△. Uriel.

Books finished.

A Stone brought by a good Angel.

The Angel of the Lord hath appeared to me, and rebuketh you for your sins. If you will hear me, and believe me, you shall Triumph : If you will not hear me, The Lord, the God that made Heaven and Earth, (under whom you breath, and have your spirit) putteth his foot against your breast, and will throw you headlong down from your seat.

My message to the Emperour *Rodolph* done.

Moreover, the Lord hath made this Covenant with me (by oath) that he will do and perform. If you will forsake your wickednesse, and turn unto him, your Seat shall be the greatest that ever was : and the Devil shall become your prisoner : Which Devil, I did conjecture, to be the Great Turk, (said I) This my Commission, is from God : I feigne nothing, neither am I an Hypocrite, an Ambitious man, or doting, or dreaming in this Cause. If I speak otherwise then I have just cause, I forsake my salvation, said I.

The Emperour said. he did believe me, and said, that he thought I loved him unfaignedly, and said, that I should not need so earnest protestations: and would not willingly have had me to kneel, so often as I did.

Farther I said, His Majesty was to see and understand nakedly, from the beginning, the whole course of this Angelical leading, instructing, and comforting of me : for so I was commanded, that I should from the beginning, nakedly open unto *Rodolph,* the manner of God his visitation, and shew unto him the holy Vision : Which my charge I am ready to do. The Emperour said, at another time, he would hear and understand more. I spake yet somewhat more in the purposes before, to the intent they might get some root, or better stick in his minde. To be short, he thanked me, and said he would henceforward, *take me to his recommendation and care,* and some such words (of favour promised) he used, which I heard not well, he spake so low. In the end perceiving that his will was to end for this time, I did my duty with curfie; and at the door going out, I turned back, and made curfie, and so came into the next Chamber, where the Noble *Octavius Spinola* came to me again, and with curteous words, offered me great friendship. I took my leave of him, and so came through the Ritters Stove or Guard Chamber, and so down, and home. I had a large hour audience of his Majesty.

All the course of our Actions and Visions, nakedly to be shewed to the Emperour.

Octavius Spinola.

Deus bene vertat : ad sui nominis Laudem, Honorem, & Gloriam. Amen.

Wedensday, *Septembris,* 5. 1584. *Mane circiter horam* 8. † Pragæ.

Precibus finitis, &c. *Repetivi ter hanc Sententiam Mitte lucem tuam* (O *Deus*) & *veritatem tuam,qua nos ducat & perducat ad montem Sanctum Sion & Tabernacula cælestis Hierusalem.*

△. I have to the best of my ability, both written and spoken unto *Rodolph,* as I was willed : how it worketh or taketh place in his heart, is known to thee O God, &c.

Now I am to receive farther instructions, what is to be done in this cause, or else whatsoever shall please the Highest, &c.

E. K. Now here is *Uriel,* and *a black thing like a Sarcent of silke* before his face, and over his head behind : by the rest of his garments it seemeth to be *Uriel.*

△. Note, Uriel his face now not seen of the eye which had highly offended God.

God make all things white, and make us whiter than Snow : What that black Scarf importeth I know not; but I suspect.

Uriel. ...... *Such as defile the seat of the Soul, and are suffocated with drunkennesse enter not into the Kingdom of Heaven, neither can behold the ornaments of the Lord his beauty.*

See, how Satan, how he runneth headlong about and through you. See, how he maketh his dwelling place within you: of whom the Lord gave you warning, saying : Satan seeketh to sift you.

Lo, he hath done wickednesse against the Lord, and against you ; for he hath blemished the eyes of your understanding.

[E. K. He speaketh other words between, which I understand not.]

Uriel. ..... *Is not Jesu, God, and the High Priest of the Lord, placed on the right hand of his Father ?*

Δ. He is : we believe it.

Uriel. ...... *Is not Satan (as the † Prophet saith) suffered to stand and triumph on the right hand of the Lord of Hosts and Justice, as the open enemy of the Lord, and of his annointed.*

True it is : and he hath almost given you the overthrow.

Δ. Assist us O God, and be our strength against this most subtile and mighty enemy.

Uriel. ......, *But because he is subtile, and hath power given unto him for a time, and hath striven against you, not for your own sakes, (but because you are of the Spirit of the Highest) and against his testimony : Therefore doth not God, in his Justice impute the sins of the eye, unto the body.*

[Δ. Lord thy mercies are infinite, praised be thy name for ever.]

Uriel. ...... *But commandeth the [Δ] eye to be reconciled, as the spirit of Truth hath taught.*

E. K. He is gone.

Vide Septemb. 13.
of Reconciliation.

Δ. Glorified be God for his most loving kindnesse and infinite mercies towards us fraile, and sinful creatures : and we beseech thee to shew us *the light of thy countenance,* to our comfort and direction. *Amen.*

Δ. As I was putting up all, *Uriel* appeared again, with his black Scarf, as he did before : but paused a while before he spake any thing.

Δ. In thy name (O *Jesu*) we attend thy words by thy messager to be uttered.

Uriel. ...... *Give ear unto my voice.*

A　E. K. Now he is become like a great wheele of fire, like a waggon wheel : He thrust out his hands on the sudden, and so became like a wheel full of mens eyes : it turneth round, it is full in all places of those eyes, like living and seeing eyes.

V　Now cometh fire out of it in 4 places.

Now there is a great Eagle, which is come, and standeth upon it : It is a white Eagle : The wheel turneth still, notwithstanding that she standeth on it.

I

E. K. She hath in her beake, like a scrol of parchment. She hath two monstrous eyes : one like fire red ; her right eye as big as my fist, and the left eye, is Chrystal-like. She standeth hovering with her wings spread, and her stern or taile spread.

S

Under the wheel is a great valley, and in it a great City, and a Hill on the East part of it. And all toward the South are Hills.

I

The City is as as big as six of *Cracovia* : and many ruins of houses in it there appear.

The City is one place in it covered, square like a little Chappel : It hath a little round pinacle in the end of it ; and over it in the air, hanging a little fire bright.

O

N　There be many like unto fowles, like Ravens, and their heads like unto

unto bright fire : They flie into a Country a great way off from this City.

Now *Uriel* standeth beside the wheel, and the wheel is as it was before : and he as before with the Scarf.

The Eagle cryeth and striketh as a Gull , or the Sea fowles do.

Uriel seemeth to descend from the air above, and to come to the side of the Shew-stone.

Uriel. ......, *The Lord hath chosen you to be Witnesses, through his mercy and sufferance, not in the* Δ. and E K. *office of Apostles, but in the offices and dignities of the Prophets : which is alwayes beautified* we are. Pro- *with the wings of the Cherubims, with the voices that cry a thousand thousand times in a-moment be-* phets th ough *fore the Lord, and before the Majesty of his eternal Seat : wherein you do* exceed *the* * Temples God his mercy *of the earth : wherein you are become separated from the world, and whereby you are lifted up, as* * Which have *of the houshold of the Bl ssed, even by the very* hand and finger *of the Highest.* not su h pre-

Δ. Blessed, blessed, blessed, is the Lord to whom Cherubim and Seraphim incessantly sing, cal. *Sanctus, Sanctus, Sanctus, Dominus Deus Zebaoth.* Amen.

Uriel. ...... *But that it may appear, that he it is, that revealeth, which gathereth the Clouds to-* Deus est qui bat *gether, and is the breath of all things that live : Because I say it may appear that the Lord visit-* revelat. *eth, and is of power, and that the imaginations of man, flie before themselves, as the dust of the earth doth before him that moveth it : I open unt) you a Seal, yet secret and not known.* A Seal opened.

[Δ. Zach. 13. --- Et erit dies una, quæ nota est Domino, &c.] Zachary 13. cap. B.

Behold, now cometh that day, that is known unto the Lord himself, wherein the Kingdoms of the earth shall begin to fall : that they may perceive how they have run astray : and how weak they are in the triumph of their pomps.

And now out of Hierusalem, out of the Church of God, and of his Son Christ, shall passe out and Zach. cap. 13. *flow the water of life : That the sayings of the Angels and Spirit of the Lord, may be verified up-* B. *on the face of the earth, spoken by his* annointed Zachary. Dies vindicta.

Now shall those dayes open themselves, which are the dayes of vengeance. Regnum Christi

Now, Now shall these woes, that have been spoken of and sealed, burst out , to the confusion of the jam stabilietur. wicked, *and the establishment of his Kingdom, which is annointed.*

Behold, I teach thee.

Those that inhabit the holy City, and usurp the authority of the Highest, are called in remem- A Prophesie a- *brance before the Lord, and they shall be scattered like unto the mighty hail, that the spirits of the* gainst the *North have gathered against the day of revenge.* Clergy.

They are become proud, and think there is no God. They are stiff-necked ; for they are the sons Rod. *of wickednesse. Lo, in the dayes of Rodolph, shall this come to passe, of whom the Lord hath* If *said, If he hear me,* and believe my words, *I will place Thee* [Δ] unto him, as a mighty rock : I will open unto thee [Δ] (for his instructions, and safeguard to come) *my determinations in* Divina Appa- *hand, and lo, to come. And when he hath wiped away his darknesse, and offence of his soul, I* ritio ipsi Ro- will appear unto him, *to the terrour of all Nations.* dulpho faciendæ

For I rejoyce, when I exalt such as are weak : And when I help the comfortlesse, am I magnified.

Δ. Thanks, honour, and glory, is due to thee, O our God.

Uriel. ...... *And behold, the day of this visitation, and of the execution of my judgements, is at* An other Seal *hand : And lo I open unto you another Seal (Because I have said unto you, I am true, and* opened. *just.*) An. 1588. or which 88 else ?

In the year eighty eight, shall you see the Sun move contrary to his course, Δ. Forté leese: *The Stars* [Δ] *encrease their light : and some of them* * *fall from heaven.* * Math. 24. G.

Then shall the Rivers run blood :

Then shall the wo be unto women with child.

Then shall the time come to passe, that this Prophesie shall be known.

This Prophesie

then to be known, An. 1588. — Δ. Which 88 ? For I have not yet had (that I remember) the year notified to be 1588.nor yet 1688. &c. Forté An.1688. This Prophesie is to be known An. 1588.

For lo, the Lord hath prepared his Prophet, and he shall descend from the Heavens : *as it is* * Malach.cap. *written by* * Malachiah *the Prophet.* 4. B. Elias shall

Behold I will send before that day, (not that day I spoke of , but the great day of the Lord) come. Elias *again amongst you.* Δ. Note two dáyes.

In

In the mean season will I be mercifull unto Rodolph, *and will bring into his*

Rod. The beautify-　*house, such as shall be skilfull: unto whom I will give my spirit, to work Gold,*
ing of *Rodulph* his seat　*Silver, and the Ornaments of his house. And he shall perceive that I blesse*
Imperial.　*him, In that I have tied him to my Garments.*

If, he hear thee not

If
Vide infra Sep-　Behold, I have one in store: *Yea, such an one as cleaveth unto Justice. Man is but a Reed*
temb. 22.　*that is shaken with every winde. The pride of Kings, is as the beauty of a Peacock: See how they*
　run all astray. See how they tempt the spirits of righteousnesse.

R:x Pcl.　Lo, (*as I have said unto thee*) I reserve that wicked King, *not that I will be mercifull unto him,*
Stephanum.　*But that he shall shortly perish with an eternal scourge.*

And now bear me what I say unto thee. Hereafter, see thou tempt me not:

CAVE. *Uriel onely.* Neither look *for my presence after this order: But for great causes.*
In great causes is to be　For lo, *this is the end of Teaching. Now cometh in the time of warn*
looked for.
The end of teaching, or　ing and of counsel.
instructing thus.　Δ. Will you give me leave to speak?

Uriel. ..... *Say.*

Δ. I trust it shall not offend God at any time, to call for [Uriel] *his light* in matters dark
Enoch his Ta-　to us, and above our capacity.   Also in *Enoch* his Tables understanding and enjoying, we
bles.　are to require help of instruction at *Ave:* and so of other points and Doctrines already begun,
we are to require their help, who have begun with us, &c.

Uriel. ..... *As far as the Lord hath suffered you to enter into his Garden: Even so far (I say)*
Taste, and eat.

Δ. The entrance yet we have not, but the manner to enter: The perfect practise is the best
entrance.

Uriel. ..... *Man speaketh not with thee: wherefore dost thou wrast the Lord? All things that*
are delivered thee are plain.

Δ. Lord, I do thus speak to be perfectly instructed in what sense your words are to be understood, when you said: This is the end of teaching.　　Δ. *Uriel,* or perhaps in the
name of God.

Uriel. ..... *Thou hast called upon me, and I have heard thee.*
Thou hast desired comfort, and I have comforted thee.

The spirit of choice　*Thou hast the spirit of choice.*
Vide 13. September.　*Be it sufficient unto thee, that the Garden of the Lord is open unto thee:*
Garden of the Lord.　*where there is no hunger, nor thirst, but a filling spirit, a comforter.*

Note.　† *What care is it unto me, if the Kings of the earth say: Lo, this is not of me.* Δ. Ex Dei lu-
Lo, this is not of the highest.　mine.

This Testimony.　Uriel. ..... *Behold, I am the light, and servant of God: Blessed are*
Adventus Dominic　those which believe, and are made partakers in this Testimony: *by*
the which you are become Prophets, and are sanctified for the coming
of the Lord.

Δ. He putteth us in re-　*But lo, why do I speak unto you, who have defiled your selves? I will*
membrance of our frailty;　*take up those things that I have, and will be gone. Lo, blessed is he that*
and offence committed be-　*giveth ear unto the Lord.*
fore noted.

E. K. Now all is vanished away, and he is disappeared: Wheele,
Eagle, Citie, and all, &c.

Δ. All laud, thanks, honour and glory be to the eternal, Almighty, most just Judge, and
mercifull father our God, the God of Heaven and earth, whom of his infinite goodnesse, we
beseech to have mercy upon us, and to purifie our hearts and consciences, granting us humble
contrition, and sincere confession of our transgressions and iniquities whatsoever. *Amen.*

Note. While I was thus requesting God, E. K. made a vow of penance, during his life:
(in token of hearty sorrowfulnesse for his fault in that dayes action noted) *never to eat his*
E. K. His vow　*supper, or evening meal on Saturdayes, during his life;* wherein I beseech the highest to regard
of fasting du-　his inward intent, and his continual memory of the Lord his mercies, in sparing him when he
ring life.　most had offended him.

Δ. Deo Nostro vero, vivo, omnipotenti, & eterno sit omnis Honor Laus & Benedictio,
nunc & in perpetuum. *Amen.*

Wednesday, September 5.　　NOTE.

Δ. The morning of this Wednesday (before I prepared my self for the former action) I sent
Emericus with two Letters to be delivered: the one to the *Spanish* Ambassadour (giving him
thanks for his honourable dealing with the Emperours Majesty in my behalf) and the other
to the Noble *Octavius Spinola:* thanking him likewise, and requiring his instruction; or advise
how I might most conveniently proceed in dealing with the Emperours Majesty: The Copy
of

of which Letter I thought good to record here, that the effect thereof consequent, might have the light of the Original cause (Divine and humane) annexed.

Illustri & Magnifico Domino, Domino Octavio Spinolæ, sacræ Cæsareæ Majestatis à stabulis & Cubiculis Domino suo observandissimo.

ILlustris ac Magnifice Domine: Non possum satis condignas vestræ Magnificientiæ agere gratias, pro singulari illa, qua me Heri amplexi estis humanitate & benevolentia : hominem quidem vobis incognitum, sed tamen virtutis & veritatis studiosissimum : quique *omne* reliquum meæ vitæ curriculum (Deo sic volente) in hoc consumere decrevi, ut sacra sua *Cæsarea* Majestas clarè percipiat, sibi, *incredibiliter* (*ferè*) *propitiam* fore Dei Omnipotentis tremendam Majestatem. Atque quamvis videam multiplicibus multarum Regionum negotiis, suam sacram *Cæsaream* Majestatem occupatissimum sepissime teneri, neque aliis, illisque a me, suæ sacræ *Cæsareæ* Majestati proponendis causis, commodè vacare, vel posse, vel evidenti aliqua ratione debere : TAMEN, si aliquis excogitari possit modus, pro loci, temporis, & rerum occasione, quo sua sacra *Cæsarea* Majestas, ea penes me videre, vel ex me intelligere dignaretur, quæ illi forent grata : Ea in re, vestræ Illustrissimæ Magnificentiæ libentissimè audirem vel reciperem Informationem atque Judicium. Nam in hoc totus ero, ut tempore debito, appareat, Omnipotentis Dei, & suæ sacræ *Cæsareæ* Majestatis servitio (Maximè autem, pro Sacrosanctæ *Orthodoxæ* Catholicæ & Apostolicæ fidei Illustratione, ac Reipublicæ Christianæ defensione ; amplificationeque) Addictissimum, devotissimum , fidelissimumque me esse, ac fore sacræ suæ *Cæsareæ* Majestatis servitorem.

*Opportunitatis flos maturè colligi debet :
Cito enim fiet marcidus.*

4. Septembris 1584.

Illustrissimæ Magnificentiæ vestræ

Paratissimus

Joannes Dee.

Emericus went and delivered my Letter to the *Spanish* Ambassadour : But this he brought back again ; saying, that the Emperour was ridden very early abroad to *Brandeish,* or elsewhere : (not certainly being known) and that this Noble *Octavius Spinola* was gone with his Majesty.

Hereupon I determined with changing the Date, to * send unto him at the Emperour his Majesties returning to *Præge. Deus bene vertat.*

                              * *Factum erat die* 11. *Septemb. sequente.*

Mr. Doctor Hagek his son was by	*At noon this day*	I sent Letters to my wife : to my Lord *Lasky,* and to Mr. *Paul Hertoll,* by the Messager of *Reichenstein,* on this side *Nisse.*

Monday, *Septemb. Manè hora* 9.   † *Præge.*

Δ. *Precibus finitis* ; I invited *Ga, Za, Vaa,* (as being assigned to understand of *Rodolph* his doings,) that of them I might receive instructions ; that my proceedings might be answerable as occasion should be given.

E. K. There appeareth written in great letters upon a right hand (and no body appearing:) the hand being very big.

*Cui est habet :
Cui nihil non habebit.*

E. K. And so the hand vanished out of sight : The writing was in the palm of it.

Δ. After that appeared the same hand again, with his writing

*Face, & factum erit,
Ultra, non habeo.*

                                                 Ultra non habeo.

E.K. It

E. K. It vanished away, by and by, hand, writing, and all.

△ Further, I have not to say, or do.

Δ. I take this (Ô Lord) in this sence : That I am to proceed, and *to do* as I intended, in either writing to *Rudolph* himself, or to the *Spanish* Ambassadour, or to *Octavius* Spinola for the Emperour to give me audience, time, and place to hear, and see the Records and Monuments, which I have to shew him : And that when I *had done* as was commanded me, that, Then the purpose of God, shall *also be done.*

Δ. Deus, in adjutorium nostrum intende tuaque nos dirigat sapientia, ad illud Faciendum, quod tibi maxime erit gratum. *Amen.*

Tuesday, *Septemb.* 11. *Hora* 9. *ferè.*

Misi per Dominum Emericum Sontagium Secretarium Domini Palatini Siradiensis literas illas ad Dominum Octavium Spinolam : quas superiùs descripsi ; sed ubi in illis scripseram *qua me heri amplexi estis.* Nunc, scripsi, *quæ me ante paucos dies* amplexi estis, & pro; quique omne *reliquum,* nunc scripsi quique reliquum, &c. & pro *incredibiliter (ferè) propitiam,* &c. scripsi, nunc, *Incredibiliter (ferè) & modo mirabili, propitiam fore,* &c. Et reliqua omnia scripsi ut supra annotavi : sed datæ erant hæ, 11. *Die Septembris :* Illæ autem priores, 4. *Septembris.*

Tradidit istas literas (Emericus) Magnifico Domino *Spinolæ,* jam statim post prandium *Cæsareæ* Majestatis, & crastina die (post missam) pro responso, venire jussit.

Wednesday, *Septembri* 12. *Manè.*

Δ. This morning, when *Emericus Sontag* went up to the Castle for answer from the Emperour : By the Noble *Octavius* Spinola, he received the effect of this answer, which I required the same *Emericus* to write down with his own hand (for sundry respects;) which his own hand writing I have annexed ad majorem rei fidem. And because his writing is not easie to be read, I have written it plainer somewhat, as followeth :

Responsum Imperatoris, per Dominum Spinolam.

Sacra *Cæsarea* Majestas benignè intellexit quæ Dominus *Joannes Dee,* per suæ Majestis Cubicularium, Dominum *Octavium* Spinolam, proponi curavit : Ad quæ, sua Majestas gratiosè sic se resolvit : Quòd quandoquidem Latinum Sermonem non omni ex parte exactè calleat : præterea etiam variis & multiplicibus negociis occupata, non semper ad audientiam vacaré possit, videri suæ Majestati ut idem Dominus *Dee,* cum Magnifico Domino Doctore *Kurtzio* (qui & suæ Majestati ab arcanis est consiliis, satisque fidus, eruditione quoque insigni pollet) tractare, & negotia sua concredere velit. Id quod, sua Majestas prælibato Domino Consiliario suo, *Kurtzio,* renunciari curabit. Sin verò, secus Domino *Johanni Dee* videbitur, suam Majestatem quomodocunque tandem per occupationés facere poterit, desiderio Domini *Dee* satisfacturam.

1584. xii. Septembris.   *Emericus Sontagius manu*
                                                                    propria.

                                                                                Pragæ.

Δ. Which answer, both by word of mouth, and thus by writing being received by me : and the said *Emericus* being (by the Noble *Spinola*) willed at Evensong time, to bring my answer herein; which I gave him of *my great good liking the same, and most humble thanks to his Majesty, for so wise and gratious his consideration had of the cause.* I required the same *Emericus* to understand ; when, and how soon Doctor *Curtzius* should be made privy of his Majesties pleasure herein : and so, after my dispatching of *Emericus,* I endeavoured my self to render thanks unto God for his mercies, graces, and truth, in these his affairs : beseeching him to frame my heart, tongue, and hand in such sort, as to his Divine Majesty, my dutifull service, doing, may be acceptable : as chiefly of me intended to his honour and glory : And secondly to the comfort of the godly and elect : And thirdly to the confusion of the proud, arrogant, scornfull enemies of truth and vertue. *Amen.*

Thursday, *Septembris* 13. *Manè, hora* 7.   † Pragæ.

I received the Noble *Octavius* Spinola his answer by *Emericus,* as concerning *my accepting of*

* On Wednesday.

the Emperour his gratious former answer of condescending to my request, so much as he conveniently could : which my answer yesterday * night, late was delivered to the Noble *Spinola.* Whereunto he said, that *my Answer would be most acceptable* unto the Emperour : *and that to morrow,*
                                                                                (meaning

meaning this Thurſday) the honourable Doctor *Curtz* ſhould underſtand the Emperours pleaſure herein.   Hereupon I willed *Emericus* to go up to the Caſtle, and to bring himſelf in ſight of the Noble *Spinola,* if he could.   Thereby to help his memory, for warning and information to be given to the ſaid Doctor *Curtz* : That ſo we might come together, ſo ſoon, as conveniently might be.

Deo, omnis laus, honor, & gloria.   Amen.

Thurſday, *Septembris* 13. *Manè, horam circiter* 9.   † *Prage.*

Δ. *Precibus finitis,* and the caſe propounded of the Emperour his Anſwer, for dealing with Doctor *Curtz,* a man of his Privy Council, faithful, learned, and wiſe : upon the conſiderations alledged, I requeſted of God, his pleaſure to be ſigniſied unto me, by ſome of his faithful and true Meſſagers : whether I ſhall *openly and frankly deal with this Doctr,* ſo, as the Emperour, by him may underſtand that which he ſhould have done at my mouth and hands originally : And whether I may, both alone with the Emperour, and before, and with the ſaid Doctor, deal in this Action as occaſion ſhall ſerve from time to time, at my diſcretion, informed by his ſecret grace divine.

Δ. Nothing appearing, or being heard, in a quarter of an hour ſpace, I ſuſpected ſome of our miſdoings, to be the cauſe of the Lord his reſtraining to anſwer : and thereupon I did fall to prayer for mercy and grace, and deliverance from the aſſaults and. malicious purpoſes of the Devil againſt us :   And that I did the rather, becauſe as I felt my good Angel (or other good friend) in vertue, ſo I felt *Piloſum,* ſenſibly, buſie, and as it were to terriſie me with my offences paſt, or to put me out of hope, at this preſent, from being heard.   But I held on to pray divers Pſalms, and at length againſt the wicked tempters purpoſely.   After my prayers and aſſuring *E. K.* that the ſpiritual enemy was here buſie, and attended to fruſtrate this dayes Action : He anſwered, that againſt him [*E. K.*] he could not prevail, or accuſe him, for his late notable fault; for he had made a reckoning, and ſorrowful bewailing for that his treſpaſs, to th: Lord, and that he doubted not of forgiveneſs; and that he was ſo reconciled to God, that Satan nor any other wicked accuſer, could put him in any doubt of God his mercy, *&c.* And he ſpake very well both of repentance, Gods mercies, his juſtice, and of theſe Actions.

Reconciliation

Mary, he confeſſed that *by reaſon,* he himſelf was an unmeet perſon to come before the Emperour, or Princes, *&c.* and therefore if it would pleaſe God to diſcharge him of further medling, ſo, by reaſon he might ſeem well at eaſe, *&c.*   At length, after an hour appeared *Uriel* ; but with a Scarf before his face, as he had laſt.

Δ. God ſend us the brightneſſe of his countenance when it ſhall pleaſe him.

Uriel. ...... *True it is, that in reſpect of the terrour and force of God his wrath and indignation in* [1] *Judgement :* Reconciliation is made : *through that power which is given unto the Lamb, to whom all power is given in Heaven and Earth : But with th:* [2] *congregation, and the members of Chriſt his body, the number of the faithful, the Church of God, you have not made reconciliation, And* therefore, *are not ſinners* worthy to behold the face of true light and underſtanding: *for there is a double Reconciliation :* One (and the firſt) between *the* Conſcience and the Judge : *through the force of faith and repentance : that is to ſay,* Reconciliation againſt Judgement.   *Another,* (the ſecond) Reconciliation *between the Spirit of Truth,* (the Church of God) and mans Conſcience.

Reconciliation is made : of two ſorts:
*Wherefore U-
riel his face is
yet covered.*
1.
2.
Vide ſupra S ptemb. 5.
The eye was commanded to
be reconciled to the Spirit
of Truth.

Behold I teach you a myſtery.

1. *Thoſe that are at one with God, ſhall not be judged with the wicked in the laſt Judgement : Notwithſtanding the Juſtice of God is pure, and undefiled :* and ſuffereth not mans fault unpuniſhed.   2. *But he that is at one with the Spirit of God, is made one with him, and without puniſhment.*

Juſtitia Dei.

For there are many things that God beareth witneſſe of, in the ſoul and ſecret Chambers of man, that neither the bleſſed, already dignified, nor to be dignified, do, or can know : *which is the cauſe that the ſoul of man,* (after his body ſleepeth) being found polluted, *is received,* and ſnatched up, of ſuch as are the Meſſagers of puniſhment: *and ſo, according to the multitude of their ſins,* are A temporal in horrour, and puniſhment.   Therefore not all, that are puniſhed, ſhall be damned ;   Neither puniſhment. *is it evident unto the Angels, who ſhall be ſaved :* I ſpeak generally.

Δ: *Ab occultis
meis munda
me, &c.*

A temporal
puniſhment.

Therefore *when you offend, be alſo reconciled unto the Mother of the houſe : that you may have place before ſuch as are reproved.*

*Eccleſia catho-
lica reconciliari
debemus.*

Herein you may underſtand the retaining of ſin ;   For the [Δ] retaining of ſin is a judgement :   *And therefore it is neceſſary that God ſhould hold a general day, that thoſe that have truſted in him, and inwardly have been ſorry for their offences, may alſo taſte of his mercy. Elſe how could it be verified, that the Prophet ſaith ?* If in Hell, thou art alſo there.

Δ. *Accipite Spiritum San-
ctum, quorum remiſeritis peccata,
remittuntur eis : & quorum re-
tinueritis, retenenda ſunt:* Ioannes
20. E. Math. 16. C. 18. C.
*Si deſcenderis in Infernum, in
illic es.*

[hh]

But,

Ignis purgationis.
The perfect assurance by
Christ and his
Church or Spirit.
* Math.c.5.D.

But, here, there is a Caution ; All sins that are forgiven by the Church, passe not the fire : but he that is forgiven in his heart by God, in his Son Christ ; and [2] reconciled through the holy Spirit, to the body from whence he is fallen, is safe, as well from the wrath of God to come, as the punishment due unto his offences.

And therefore is the reconciling of brethren, of great force. Wherefore * hath Christ left his body with the Church ? Wherefore is he called the bread of Life ?

I say unto you, my brethren, that the body of Christ dignified and glorified, is true bread ; is true comfort, which cleanseth sinners that are penitent, and wipeth away the punishment of adversity.

Happy are those, that eat of him, and that account not his body, a. the shadow of a candle.

Δ. *Aliqui bare-*
tici dicunt
Christ corpus
fuisse phanta-
sticum.

Behold, I teach you: Even as the Spirit of God filleth the Congregation of the faithful ; so doth the body of Christ now dignifie, fill and cleanse all that receive with sorrow : sorrow I mean for their wickednesse.

But lo : his body is become an offence unto the world. Many there are that say, This is Christ : But behold I teach you. Even as all things were made by him, spiritually : So are all, that are of his Elect, nourished through him, bodily.

Lo, he is become one power, one God ; in that he is neither separated from his body, nor separateth his body from his Church.

After a while I come again.

E. K. Now he is gone away.

Δ. We read over the premises to our great comfort, in the mean time, while *URIEL* disappeared.

E. K. Now he is here again.

Δ. Now he
answereth to
my request
first propounded.
Rudolp.

Uriel. ...., O ye timerous birds, How long run you headlong into the Wildernesse ? How long will you be ignorant ? How long will you tempt the Lord with the spirit of foolishnesse and errour ? Behold thou hast not judged well of me. Behold thou hast placed me in a low room, and hast taken the Garland from my head, and trod it under thy feet : For, what is Rodolph, that is not at leisure for the Lord, the God of righteousnesse, the King of Heaven and Earth ?

Are they troubled with things that are greater than I ? True it is ; for with me there is no trouble : for where I enter, I set all things in quiet. Will the Counsellours of the Earth, sit in judgement to sift the Lord ? O ye fooles and starvelings of the Earth : O you of little understanding. Think you, that you are able to find light amongst the affairs of the World? true judgement in the imagination of man ? or verity amongst the boords and corruption of covetousnesse and falshood ?

If.

If he be not at leisure to hear me : Have not I told thee, that I have another in store ? Lo, I see, all flesh is full of folly.

Δ. It is not yet done : and therefore we ask counsel of thee ; and I thank thee (O Lord) for rebuking of us, before farther errour committed.

Spiritus Electionis quid sit
vide pagina se-
quente.
Rodulp.
Spiritus verita-
tis.

Uriel. ...... Lo, I gave unto thee, the spirit of choice: and therefore I will regard thy doing, and will wink at thy weaknes. I will blesse all that thou takest in hand, and will cover thee with a Robe of Purple ; that thou mayst understand that all is mine, and that I raise up whom I list. And I say unto thee again : Lo, Rodolph hath heard thee, And I will poure my Spirit of truth into thee, and thou shalt be a light unto him.

If.
From the
Δ. *Hiacinth*, and his
East, Comfort
and Triumph.

But, now, If he live righteously, and follow me truly ; I will hold up his House with Pillars of Hiacinth, and his Chambers shall be full of Modesty and Comfort. I will bring the East wind over him, as a Lady of Comfort : and she shall sit upon his Castles with Triumph, and he shall sleep with joy.

Rodolphi so-
boles in tertiam
generationem.
If.
Secresie requi-
red.

Moreover I will blesse his loynes : and his House shall stand to the third generation : and to the end ; for, now, the World hath hoary hairs, and beginneth to be sick.

If he despise my commandment, I will put the sword against him ; and in his dwelling places shall his enemies banket. (But those that deal with thee, let them sow up their mouth : lest being cut with a Razor, they speak not.) For those that neglect my Judgements I will despise them, and their seed shall wither, as corn sown out of season : But he that loveth me, I will multiply them, and their seed shall wither, as corn sown out of season : But he that loveth me, I will multiply

Adde te Deo quo
modo bonum est;
vide infra.
Spiritus .Ele-
ctionis supra
Sept. 5.

And he that addeth unto me, I will adde unto him a thousand.

But lo, thou hast the spirit of choice.

Δ. O Lord open my understanding of that saying.

Uriel. ..... Quos tu eligis, electi sunt : quo autem despicis, despiciuntur etiam.

Δ. Dwell thou in me (O Lord) for I am frail, and (without thee) very blind.

E. K. Now he is gone.

Δ. Thy glorious name (O Lord) be magnified, praised, and extolled for ever. Amen.

Δ. I spake this
to E.K.

Δ. I perceive that I shall not deal with the Doctor Curtz now. Well, I can let him understand that I had rather deal with the Emperour himself, and so shift my self of him.

E. K. He is here again.

D. *Curtz.*

Uriel. ...... Yes, deal with him : and hide nothing from him.

Δ. With Doctor Curtz, O Lord ?

Uriel. ...... I———— And therefore I said, He that addeth unto me , I will adde unto him a thousand :

thousand : But he that playeth with me ; lo, I swear, I will blot his name from life!
[Δ]Libere agas : Deus est enim liber.

E. K. Now he is gone.

Δ. Deo Omnipotenti, Invisibili & misericordi sit omnis honor, laus, gratiarum actio, & Gloria : nunc & in perpetuum. *Amen.*

Δ. Frankly as my term was in my first request, or question this day made.

Thursday, *Septembris* 13. *Mane.* † *Pragæ.*

Emericus did bring himself in sight of the Chamberlain, the Noble *Octavius Spinola* : as I willed him : And he called *Emericus* to him, and told him, that this day Doctor *Curtz* should understand the Emperour his pleasure, to confer with me, &c.

Emericus about 10 of the clock before Noon being in the Ritters Stove (or Guard-Chamber) saw Doctor *Curtz* come out from the Emperour.

Friday, *Septemb.* 14. *Mane,* circa 10.

I sent *Emericus* to Doctor *Curtz* his house in *parva parte* : with my commendations; and to say that before, I understood of Doctor *Hageck,* Mr. Doctor *Curtz* his desire to be acquainted with me : whereof I was very glad and desirous : and now I trust that the Emperour his majesty, by his Authority hath taken order with him whereby to begin our acquaintance, and (God willing) our perpetual friendship. The Doctor was at home, and to *Emericus* (saying the effect of my message before noted) the Doctor declared that *Captaverat antea varias occasiones mecum contrahendæ amicitiæ,* &c. and that now he is very joyful of the occasion offered by the Emperours Majesty : and that this day sundry affairs did hinder the opportunity of our meeting, but to morrow at any hour (at my choice) he would be ready to welcome me to his house : and so with the usual phrase of offering all his services to my pleasure, he sent *Emericus* to me with his said Answer.

Quos Deus conjungit, Homo ne separet. Amen.
Quos autem Deus & Cæsar copulat, copulatissimi maneant. Amen.

Saturday, *Septembris,* 15. *A Meridie hora (ferè) prima.* † *Pragæ.*

I came to the foresaid (called Doctor) *Curtz* : about one of the clock after Noon, who had all the day been ready to have heard me, if I would so have had it : but I sent him word in the morning by *Emericus,* that after Noon, (as now at this hour) I would come to him. Being come, he entertained me curteously : and two chairs being at the Tables end, he gave me the preeminence (by a friendly kind of earnestnesse) Then he told me, that long since in *Germany,* he had heard of my fame, and had seen of my writings : and that he was very glad of the opportunity now of my coming to this City ; and that otherwayes he was desirous of my acquaintance, but chiefly seeing the Emperour his Majesty *Ore tenus* (for that was his phrase) by word of his own mouth, had willed him to hear what I had to say to his Majesty. I began and declared my long course of study for 40 years, alwayes, by degrees going forward, and desirous of the best, and pure truths in all manner of studies, wherein I had passed, and that I had passed as many as were commonly known, and more than are commonly heard of. But that at length I perceived onely God (and by his good Angels) could satisfie my desire : which was *to understand the natures of all his creatures, and the best manner how to use them to his divine honor and glory, and the comfort of the elect, and also to the reproof and confusion of the adversaries of his name and honour.* And herein I had dealed sundry wayes : And at length had found the mercies of God such as to send me the instruction of *Michael,* *Gabriel,* *Raphael,* and *Uriel,* and divers other his good and faithful Messagers, such as I had here now brought books (about 18) to shew him the manner of their proceeding : And that I thought it good to begin at the last book, which also concerned most this present Emperour *Rodolph.* And so I did ; and so by degrees from book to book lightly, I gave him a taste or sight of the most part, and also let him see the Stone, brought me by Angelical ministery, &c.

All things being seen and heard, that in six hours I could shew him : at length he required of me what conclusion, or summary report he should make to the Emperour. I answered, as he had occasion of the things seen and heard ; but if he would follow my counsel (somewhat expert in these Divine and Angelical doings.) That his Majesty was to thank God for his great mercies and graces offered : and that by me one, who most sincerely and faithfully gave his Majesty to understand the will of God herein, and that his Majesty was to do, as *Mary* (the blessed Virgin) did, to lay up all these my informations in his heart, and to say *Ecce*

Δ. Studiorum meorum scopus.

Rodolph.

My counsel to Doctor Curtz.

servus Domini, fiat voluntas tua, and so to attend the manner of the Lord his proceeding, while he framed his life, as it became every Christian to do.

He said, that he would write (for his own memories help) some short note of his observations of my speeches, and things seen and marked: and that he would to morrow (being Sonday) or on Monday, if he conveniently could, make a report to the Emperour, and so with all speed give me to understand further of the Emperour his Majesties will and pleasure. Hereupon courteously he brought me down to the street door of his house; and I came home after seven of the Clock, and an half in the evening.

> The mercies of God be on me, and his name be magnified and extolled in this world, and for ever. *Amen.*

He also said that in the former my Records that I had noted many a ly, and untruth.

Note. In the mean space while I was thus occupied with the foresaid Mr. *Curtz.* E.K. was visited at our Lodging with a wicked Tempter, *who denied any Christ to be*: and that as the heart received comfort of all the Members of the body: So that he, who is God, of all things received comfort by Angels, and other the Members of the world: and that I was now with one, who would use me like a Serpent, with head and tayl compassing my confusion, &c. he earnestly reviled E.K. in divers manners: he said, that E.K. should be damned, and said: moreover, that of our practises should never come any fruitfull end, &c.

> Δ. The eternal and Almighty God confound the Adversaries of his truth and glory, and of his Son Jesus Christ our Redeemer, and the Triumphant Conquerour against, Hell, sin, and the Devil. *Amen.*

PRAGÆ.

On Monday and Tuesday the 17th. and 18th. of *September,* I sent *Emericus* up to the Castle, to listen after answer of that Doctor *Curtz* his report to the Emperour, of that he had perceived by me. (But on Monday *Octavius* Spinola had sent into the Town for *Emericus,* and told him that the Emperour *had care and desire to understand my doing with the Doctor:* And therefore asked *Emericus* if I had been with the Doctor, and he affirmed that I had. Hereof (said he) the Emperour will be glad: And yet (as I began to note) *Emericus* coming on Tuesday in the face of the Doctor in the *Ritters* stove; had not one word spoken to him, that either he had spoken to the Emperour, or he had not. And therefore *I suspect* that the Doctor dealeth not honestly, faithfully, or wisely in this so weighty a case. And forasmuch as he told me, that the Emperour his Majesty was perswaded, that he was pious, &c. perhaps he would be loath; now, to prefer me to the speech of the Emperour, seeing both he himself, and the rest of his counsel stood perswaded to the contrary of this King. Hereupon this great delay, upon sinister report made to the Emperour might follow, &c.

Note, the Emperour enclined to hear, &c.

I suspect the Doctour doth not deal sincerely.

Note. Fryday, *Septemb.* 21. *Circa horam* 10. *Ferè, Mane.*   † Pragæ.

Δ. As I and E.K. were together in my Study, earnestly discoursing of Auricular confession, publick confession, and confessing to God alone, and of the Authority of the Church, and the manner of the same Authority using to release, or retain sins, E.K. saw one walk on the Table between him and me: Thereupon I framed me to write, and note what should be shewed, or said, E.K. willed me to set down the shew-stone: So I did, and he looked.

E. K. I see him here with the Scarf over his head and face, untill his waste, but I see his hair yellow behinde on his head, &c.

Mitte lucem tuam, O Deus & varitatem tuam ut ipsæ nos ducant ex hac valle miseriæ ad montem Sanctum Sion, & ad cœlestia tua Tabernacula. Amen.

Uriel. ..... *I am* Uriel *the servant of the most wise, mighty, and everlasting God: which visit you for two causes.*

The first, that I may open unto you true, and perfect light: such as darknesse comprehendeth not, infallible, and true meat, the power and spirit of the everlasting God.

The second, that I may counsel you against the world, and teach you to triumph against her frowardnesse. For, who hath trusted in the Lord, and hath been cast down? or what is he that hath cried aloud, and it not heard? Therefore, I say unto you; Hear my voyce: For I am of truth, and put against darknesse, and in me are published the light, and mysteries of the Trinity from time to time, and in all ages unto those that fear, and obey God.

Two things there are which are the seals and marks of Satan: which bring eternal death and damnation to all such as are noted, or burned with them, that is to say, lying, and froward silence.

Trinitatis Lux & mysteria per Urielem revelantur.

Mendacium Obstinatum silentium.

Behold

Behold the words of Christ, unto the subtile (your father is a lyar from the beginning , and the Devil.)

Hearken unto my voyce : He that [1] *teacheth false Doctrine, openeth* [2] *his mouth against truth, or defraudeth* [3] *his brother is a lyar, and shall not be forgiven.*

1. *For first, he sinneth against his Creator, which created all things in truth.*

2. *Secondly, he offendeth against the* truth, *and his* Redeemer, *which is the son of God, very Christ.*

3. *Thirdly, he offendeth against the spirit of God, (of the Father, and the Son) the holy Ghost : which shall not be forgiven : And therefore doth he incurre the rigour of Gods justice , his eternall damnation.*

But, I say, give ear unto my words : For, I will sift the dust, and finde out the Pearle, *that of a long time hath lyen trodden under the feet.*

I will come again.   E. K. He is gone.

Δ. We read over the premisses, and so expected the rest.

E. K. He is again here.

Uriel. ⸺ *Now let us joyn these things together.*

All flesh offendeth, and is a lyar.   Who, therefore shall be saved, or escape eternal damnation ? Objectio. *He it is (I say) that when he hath lyed, and spoken against the truth doth not frowardly drown'd,* Solutio. *and keep down his sin in silence.*

For, lying meriteth the vengeance of the Trinity.   But he that is wilfully froward, *sealeth up* Mendacium. *his own damnation : For this cause (my brethren) and to the intent that the mercies of God might* Ecclesia Digni *alwayes be ready for sinners ; hath he provided the light, and comfort of his spirit , left as a con-* tas & Authori- *tinual workman in the Church and spouse of Christ.* tas.

I teach you briefly : that, he whosoever, opening his mouth against the spirit of truth ; and with Reconciliation *wilfull frowardnesse continueth in his lying,* without reconciliation to the Church *sinneth against the* to the Church. *holy Ghost, and shall be damned eternally.*

I come again.   E. K. He is gone.

E. K. He is here again.

Uriel. ⸺ *Be now therefore admonished (I say) be warned : And considering you be sinners, acknowledge your offences, least in the end your sin be against the holy Ghost, and so not to be forgiven. But herein they erre with you that expound the Scriptures, saying, that man sinneth, and cannot be forgiven, because he sinneth against the holy Ghost.*

I teach you, my brethren : that there is no sin against God, but it is against the holy Ghost: Wilfull si- *If so be, in the end, it be shut up with wilfull silence.* lence.

Whensoever, (therefore) you have offended acknowledge, I say, your sins, before God and his An- Δ. Finalis in- *gels : That God may forgive you, and the Angels bear witnesse of your forgivenesse , and shut not up* pænitentia. *your sins in froward silence.* Testes Angelici.

If thou commit adultery, if thou blaspheme the name of God, if thou be a lyar ; yea, if thou speak lence. *against the truth : yea, if thou say there is no God (as the * foolish do)* Despair not ; *saying, I have* * Psal. *sinned against the holy Ghost, because I am a sinner, and a blasphemer of the name of God, because I have spoken, and opened my mouth against the spirit of truth : But go unto the Church, which is* Ito ad Eccle- *governed by the spirit of God, and there with hearty, and open confession disclose , and make plain* siam. *thy offences, that the holy Ghost may bear witnesse in the spouse, and Church of Christ ; That thou hast not sinned against him to eternal death : Because* Δ. Voluntary confession *thou art not drowned in* froward silence. is contrary to froward si lence.

For, although God bear witnesse of repentance.   Although he hear, and Aures Dei, Manus Dei, *open his ears, yet consider also he hath hands, and must untye those bonds* Vide de Lazaro, Joh. c.11. *wherewith you are bound.   What are the hands of God , but his spirit, wherewith he maketh and created all things.   Therefore when thou hast* cried out and art sorry, *endeavour thy self also to be lifted up by the hands of God.*

Learn a similitude in Christ, which (signifying the power of his Church,) commanded the offender to go and wash himself : and so he was whole.   I speak this, for thy [E.K.] *instruction : I say also unto thee,* [E.K.] *Go and wash thy self : For thou art a lyar, thou art a drunkard : And therefore thou art a sinner. And if thou persevere, and shadow thy sins with wilfull silence frowardly , then sealest thou thy self with the second brand, and canst not be forgiven, because thou sinnest against the Ghost.*

* Ananias *fell down at the feet of* Peter , *not onely for that he lyed : but because after his of-* * Act.5. *fence he was* wilfully silent.

Here thou mayest consider the greatnesse of God his mysteries, and secrets of his will and of fa- Supra. *vour, that he stretcheth out unto thee in mercy, for thou art a* Childe, *and must ascend , and must become a man.   The rest after you are refreshed.*

Δ. We went to Dinner to our Host his house.

Δ. Thanks, honour, glory, and praise be unto the Almighty Trinity, now and ever. *Amen.*

Δ. After

Δ. After we had been at Dinner, they read over the premisses, and confidered them quietly.

E. K. Here he is.

Δ. Bleffed be he that cometh in the name of the higheft, to whom be all honour and glory. *Amen.*

Uriel. ..... *Lo, Lo, L^, (I fay) which of you hath an eye, that feeth not, (now) the world : the vanity, and folly of worldlings : and fuch as are choked with the mildew of vanity and worldly promotion ?*

For thus fayeth the Lord ; wherein could I fhew my felf more, either unto this age , or unto this Emperour, then with rebuking him for his fins from Heaven ?

† *More affuredly.* *Who is able to promife more, or to perform* † *affureder then I, which lighten, and make all things ? Yet they believe not,*

Yea, they rejoyce in their own folly, and defpife me : yea, becaufe they defpife thee, whom I have fent with my word unto them, Δ. *Is defpifed of Rud, and Curtz.*

E. K.

Well, thus fayeth the Lord, they have defpifed their own Garlands , and have trodden their food under feet : They have rent their Robes in pieces, and have caft them into the waves. They are become mafterleffe Dogs, for I have forfaken them. And lo, Rodolph, *I will fcatter thy bones, and thy head fhall be devided in many pieces. I will bring in thy enemies over all thy Kingdoms , and for thy fake fhall many thoufands perifh. He alfo that thinketh himfelf wife, if he dye a natural death ; then fay, I am not, neither that I live with my people.*

Contra Rud.

Contra Curtz.

Δ *Fecit quod ill injunctum erat. l'altum mifericordia divina cum* Δ. *But becaufe thou haft done that which I commanded thee , and haft not forgot my name. Lo, I will plant thee my felf, and thou fhalt grow, and out of thee fhall fpring a mighty and a terrible fword : whofe Hilts fhall be as the Carbuncle, and edge like unto the fting of a Dragon, and I will not fuffer thee to fall : neither fhall thine enemies ride upon thee. Truely, truely, thou fhalt know I am with thee.*

Sathanas. * Ne megalitudo revelationum extollat me, datus eft mihi ftimulus carnis meæ, &c. Paulus ad Corinthios fecunda, cap. 11.   *But be patient : for Satan hunteth hard after thee. Thou fhalt have always a * prick even unto thy laft grave. But therein fhall thy faith be exalted, and thy reward great.*

...... *I come again.*

E. K. He is gone.

E. K. Here he is again.

England pardoned for Δ. his fake. Uriel. ..... *Lo, for thy labour I will reward thee : And fo it fhall be. Behold , I had determined to have rooted out the Englifh people, to have made a wilderneffe, and defart of it ; to have filled it with many ftrange people, and to have tied the fword to it perpetually.*

Δ. This is no contradiction, for thus this wilderneffe and filling is to be underftood.	**But** Δ. The filling of it with ftrangers fhould have been for the conqueft, and in a manner razing, or defacing of all Cities, Towns, and Caftles, and fo to have brought it to a *wilderneffe* and defart.

God will give me England , that is to fay, fpare it from diftruction for my fake, &c. England. Δ. Our good return into England. Δ. Perhaps, fpiders flying in the aire, are carried by ftrings of their own fpinning, or making, or elfe I know not how. Rud. I remained for the moft part in Bohemia, and in the Empire, till 1589.

But Lo, I will give thee that land ; (onely for thy fake) it fhall not be confumed.

And after certain moneths, I will bring thee home ; yea, thou fhalt live till thou be able to paffe the waves without a fhip, and to afcend the Hills, as the Spiders do. Notwithftanding, I will take the Crown from the houfe, it is in , and I will place it, as I have Prophefied unto thee. Notwithftanding, for a time, thou fhalt live with Cæfar.

...... *I come again.*   **E. K.** He is gone.

Δ. O Lord, what fhall become of my good friend the Lord Laskie.

E. K. Here he is again.

A L.
Δ. L. Came to us to 1 rebon, in Bohemia. An. 1588. poft captum Maximilianum à Polonis, &c.
Rud.
Num. 11.
Pfal. 77.   Uriel. ...... *Of* Lasky *thus it is faid : Thou [Δ.] haft groaned for him, and haft placed him thy [Δ.] heart : From henceforth will I reconcile him unto me, and I will ceafe my anger upon him, and he fhall come hither * fhortly. But he is a wanton, and very prone to fin.*

But bear what I fay unto thee.

[E. K. He feemeth to have talk with one afar off]

Cæfar thought thou hadft had the Philofophers ftone, and (as yet) he thinketh fo.

Even as I choaked the gluttenous Ifraelites *with quayles , fo will I choake him with that fecret.*

Behold,

Behold, thou shalt write unto him, saying, that he regardeth not heaven:
And say unto him, that thou canst make the Philosophers stone, I will perform it unto *thee:* Thou shalt do it: *And I will give unto thee a* special
vertue in healing: *That whensoever thou comest hither: Thou shalt under-*
stand the truth. And this I do, because they shall not despise thee.

A Letter to be written unto *Cæsar.*
Lapis Philosophorum.
A special gift in healing by the shew in this stone.

Δ. O Lord, for me to be despised in doing thy commandment, is honour and comfort to
me: But as concerning thy honour and glorie; Thou in thy wisdom knowest what is best to be
done.

R. Peribit.

Uriel. ...... *Notwithstanding, thou shall see him perish before thy face.* Lo, from this time, I will
blesse thee marvellously, *and I will help thee in all thy works.*

Benedictio Dei
sit super nos.
Supra.
Tu sac.

{Do thou *always:*
{*And make me thy* Buckler.

Δ. What shall I do with Doctor *Curtz,* as concerning his answer?
Uriel. ...... *Handle him like a man, for he will deceive thee.*

E. K. I request you but one thing for all my labour and travel;
that is, that this Doctor might this night be bereft of his life, to the terrour of other, &c.

Uriel. ...... *Have patience, God turneth all to his glory, and your commodity. To morrow I have*
something else to say.

Deus Noster in cœlo, omnia quæcunque voluit fecit: Ille solus est Omnipotens, æternus, sapiens, Bonus, Justus & Misericors: Illi debetur omis Laus, gratiarum actio, honor & gloria. Amen.

Saturday, 22. *Septemb.* Manè, *Circiter horam* 9.

Precibus ad Deum finitis, & variis ad ipsum Ejaculationibus pro Luce & veritate Dei, &c.
& quibusdam de *Rudolphi* & *Curtzii* corruptis Judiciis (qui Dei Misericordias, juxta carnis
sensum judicare ausi sunt) [apparuit *Uriel* facie velata ut ante.]

Uriel. ...... *For this cause (say I unto thee)* write unto *Rudolph,* saying, I can make the Philosophers stone: *Because I would place thee with them, according to their hope and imagination:*
That whilest they think little of me, and of the sweetnesse *of my message* and testimony, *I might*
burst out amongst them; as the mighty waters do out of Hills, when the earth moveth: For I have said
unto thee, *I will place thee here; If I sow thee here, what Raven can pluck thee up by the roots.*
No, I will hide thee, *as the Hen doth her Chickens: And I will make thee spring to their de-*
struction. *For why, thou shalt overcome that mystery for thy own sake.*

A Letter to *Rudolph* the Emperour.
Eruptiones a-
quarum ex Ter-
ra motibus.
Lapis Philoso-
mum.

Δ. For the glorie of God: his honour and triumph, all good come unto me.

Uriel. ...... *Behold, since they will not tye thee unto them from heaven: Thou shalt tye them unto*
thee from earth: That thou mayest rejoyce when thou seest their destruction, and be ready cloathed
for him that is to come.

Cæsar futurus.

It *was said unto thee, my mother saith she will chuse an Emperour in*
ernest : *But it is* Ernest *that shall sit upon his seat. Behold, there*
shall be no seed left in him for his wickednesse. Yea, the blessings that
I have offered him shall return again; and I will leave his house na-*
ked. But when he seeth and hath Gold (which is the thing he de-*
sireth, and those that counsel him, do most desire him, for) Then shall he
perish with a most cruel, terrible, and unheard of mischief.*

It is a saying of *Madimi,* Junii 26. 1584. Cracovia.
Ernestus Frater Rudolphi.
Δ. Blessings offered are pro-
mises with conditions.
Gold, *ex lapide Philosophorum.*
Mors crudelis, terribilis, inaudi-
ta.

But lo, I have written his name within my hand, because I would not forget to punish him. Be-*
hold, I could send the windes to devour him, and could open the Caves of the earth to swallow him;*
which would turn to my honour: *But I have a care over you.*

Note.

Now I am unto you *in mercy and wisdom: But I will be with you in ter-*
ror and *miracles. And I will deal with you in a higher degree: And you*
shall bear my voyce, as men do their brethren.

God in mercy, wisdom, terror, miracles.
· *Vox Domini ut hominis fu-*
tura nobis audibilis.

Δ. What thou wilt (O Lord) for thy honour and glory: That be.

Uriel. ...... *But those that are his counsellers have commanded him, rather then counselled him,*
to have no dealing with thee *at all.*

Consiliarii Cæ-
saris.

And he is possessed *with a great, and a mighty Devil. And behold* Belzagal *(which is the fury and*
Prince of the Turks) doth assist him in his wickednesse, for he knoweth it may come to passe that* * *his*
Kingdom shall be short. But give ear unto me. Fawn thou upon Cæsar as a worldling, that thou
mayest draw him with the world, to see the glory of God: but to his destruction. For lo, how much
more a mans felicity is in this world, the more shall be the burden of his destruction.

R. Poss: sus
Belzagal Ca-
codæmon Turca-
rum.
* Turkish, or
Rudolphus ra-
ther.

There be that gape *after thy books, and speak vainly of things that are not. Therefore I coun-*
sel that they dwell not long with Poland.

My books
from Poland.

Behold, when Lasky cometh, *he shall not hastily return into Poland : till I whisper in his ears,*
He is dead that sought thy life. I have more to say, but they are not (yet) necessary.

A. £.

Δ. I beseech you to tell me when I shall prepare my self to go for my books, &c.

Uriel. I

I may chuse
my time to go
to Cracow.

Uriel. ..... *I speak not, that I know not ; but chuse thy own time. Now will I become a Courtier.*

E. K. He is gone.

Fiat voluntas Dei, ad ejus laudem, honorem & gloriam.   Amen.

Monday, *Septembris,* 24. *Mane hora* 8.   † *Pragæ.*

Δ. At the first looking E. K. saw *Uriel*, but covered with his Scarf, &c. Notwithstanding I
said some prayers to God on my knees, and came and said here. *Mitte lucem tuam & veritatem
tuam O Deus : ut ipsa nos ducant ad montem Sion,* &c.

It is to be remembered that for two causes we repaired to the Shew-stone : the one by reason of the letter which I had written to the Emperour : and was minded to go to shew it to
the Spanish Embassadour before I sent it to the Emperour, to have his opinion of it, and also
to bear it. Secondly, by reason of foul slanderous words which were spoken of me here at this
Embassadours Table : That I was a Conjurer, and a bankrupt alkimist, and came here to get
somewhat of the Emperour : and that I had sold my goods, and given to the Lord *Laskie* the
mony, and that he had deceived me. To these untruths the Embassadour did reply in my
behalf : for which I meant to thank him, &c.

Uriel. ...... *Even as the accursed, and cast down, most wilfully abhorreth, hateth, and dishonoureth, the God of Justice, because of his mightiness and power over him : So do all those that suck and
hang upon his dugs, that are coveteous and desirous of worldly promotion : that gape and thirst after
the glory of this world, abhor, hate, and continually vex and dishonour, such as love Justice, or dwell
under the wings of the God of power and Triumph. Herein may you rejoyce, that you are partakers
and innocents (railed at, and despised with the world) in the fellowship of God, and of his Son
Christ. Herein may you be glad, that you are sealed, and dwell with the Fathers, and that you play*

Cithara Davi-
dis.
E:ctio.

*also upon the Harpe of David : for verily as they are, so shall you be : and as they are made righte-
ous by reason of their election, and crowned toward eternal Joy ; So shall your Election establish
your righteousnesse, and give you Garlands of eternal comfort. Those that are on the Seas, are
fearful of the windes : And why ? because of the motion of the place, and of the power of nature :
But it is not so, with you : for you dwell in Castles made of marble, wrought out of the middest of a*

Deus habitat in
rore rock, a
tebis & ros in
Deo.
Imago Christi
Paulus ad Cor.
cap. 14. F.
* Misericordia.
† Ciguum ni-
fium supia in
multis locis.
* Justitia.
† Domus.
* Vestes.
† Sapientia cum
potentia.
* Promissa.
† Tultiroa ven-
tura.
* Terra promis-
sionis.

*rock, a most stable foundation. For why ? I am sure that God dwelleth in you, and you in him.
Therefore lift up your heads, and rejoyce when you are afflicted, and keep the image of God sincere
and perfect in you, that you may always be * merciful in the Image of his Son Christ. But when the
Lord openeth his mouth, and calleth you together, saying, † Venite & audite : Then lay away all
mercy ; for the God of * Justice dwelleth amongst you. Who dwelleth in a house till it be perfectly finished ? or what is he that putteth on a garment before it be made ? Be you assured, that
when the † house is finished, and your * garments made, you shall both enter, and be clothed with
comfort : Comfort of † wisdom and power. I am mindful of you, and will be mindful of my * promise toward you. And if you remain and dwell [forte [together] deest] and be constant in me,
you shall passe the † Thunders that are to come; you shall be witnesses of my power : and shall enter
into the * Land of Promise with those that shall be comforted : where these dayes shall have an end.
O my brethren, this world exceedeth in wickednesse, and is a terrour to the good Angels : Because
of the souls that she devoureth. But when lightnesse is rewarded, and Justice sitteth in place, Then
shall she bear no weight. but be made all one with the bottomlesse pit. Despise her, despise her ; for
she is an Harlot.*

*A Spiritu Dei sumus ducti ut
Domino Magnifico Domino Gulielmo
de Sancto Clemente, Hispaniarum Regis legato hac aperiremus : cui mercedem dabit Deus.
* D. Jacobo Curtzio Consiliario
Cæs...*

*Behold I have entred in amongst you ; and it is my Spirit that
leadeth to the Embassadour from Spain. I will reward
him.*

*Therefore as thou hast opened me unto the * wicked, so let also the
good bear witnesse of me.*

*The Lord is become a firebrand in fury, and hath armed him-
self : and hath taken unto him his great Target, and the Spear of
his indignation : Accursed are they that have offended him.*

Δ. *Quantum memini in Sibylla
oraculis Græcis & Latinis facilis
per Castalconem , habetur nomen
Urielis inter illos qui collecturi sunt
homines ad judicium. Vide & hic
ascribe.*

Tum verò æterni Genii Immortalis
'Hux & * σεφμίλ. U R I E L, Saniel, Azaelque,
Quæ mala quisque hominum patraverit ante Scientes
E tetris animas tenebris caliginis omnes.
Judicio sistent ad formidabile patris
Magni, Immortalis solium, &c.
    Orat. Sibyl. pag. 79.
    Ubi sequuntur plura de *U R I E L E.*

*And when I separate them in the day of wrath to come, (as one of the fingers and gatherers
in of the harvest of God) Then they shall know that I am* U R I E L, *which will not forget the
wickednesse of their hands, nor their blasphemous mouth, in that day of revenge.*

After

After a certain time cometh Michael *unto you, and shall shew unto you his bloody Sword; and* Prophesia de *you shall stand under his Banner. He shall hold up his hands, and shall fight against the Hills for* MICHAELE. *you: and your enemies shall not be. Unto which time, receive you Light and Comfort: and be contented with adversity in the Lord.*

My brethren, it is better to be poor; with those that are * *poor in spirit: then to be rich with* * Math. cap. 5. *those that are gluttons, and with the Princes of the Earth*   Quoniam ipsorum est regnum cælorum, &c.

Thou shalt be with Cæsar, *in despite of the Devil.*   Δ. Erit cum Cæsar.

I have said.   I understand

Δ. Gloria patri & filio & Spiritui Sancto : Sicut erat in Principio & nunc & semper, & in   not this, how it secula seculorum. *Amen.*   is, or shall be verified, or with which Cæsar.

Note : As I had finished this Action, and was come to my Study door; *Emericus* was returned again from the Spanish Embassadour, to whom I had sent him desirous to know his leasure for me : who had now sent me word by *Emericus* to come to diner, & so he would have leasure, &c. Whereof I was right glad ; and went thither to diner : who into his inermost Study (where he himself was writing of letters) caused me to be brought. And after I had complained of injury and violence done unto me, by foul slanders, and that, at his Honours Table : (to which his Honour, in my behalf had replied : and therefore most humbly, and sincerely I did thank him) I said that the Emperous Majesty himself could bear me witnesse, that I used this phrase unto him, that I came not for his riches as, *Non veni ad vos O Serenissime Cæsar propter divitias vestras, ut inde ego dives fierem, sed à Deo missus, non audeo aliter facere quam ejus ad vestram Cæsaream Majestatem voluntatem declarare,* &c. And therefore, How falsly they slandered me, it was evident : and because I perceive that Doctor *Curtz* hath not dealt neither with due entertainment of me as of a stranger, or a Sudent, or a Mathematician, or of one whom (to my face) he gave great praise unto, as of one long since of great fame in *Germany,* and so in his good estimation, &c. And least of all, as of one, who offered so great curtesies to the Emperours Majesty as he was made witnesse of : I thought good to send unto the Emperours Majesty this letter following, and so read it unto him after diner, when I shewed him *Librum Pragensem sive Cæsareum* ; and moreover *Librum decimum,* (whose former title was *Libri Sexti Mystici Tertiarius*) and there shewed him divers Actions in Latine already translated, because now to translate so to him of the English, did seem to me both tedious, and to him not so readily pleasant. All things on his part considered, his summary final conclusion was, as well of the last offer in this my letter, as of the great actions and divine purposes. For the first he declared that he was lineally descended out of the consanguinity, *of one a Gentleman, but unlettred at the first, who left his wife, children, and family in* Domini Legati Maiorca, *and ascended an Hill there, and in place solitary remained in whole year, and at the* Regis Hispanicarum Responsum. *years end, he came down, but so learned and wise, that all who knew him before, wondred at it.* And that the same man was called *Raymundo Lullio :* and that he made that which is called the Philosophers Stone, as in *England* (said he) I understand is good record of it : Therefore I see, quoth he, that it is a truth and possible : and as he hath granted the knowledge of it to one man, so he may grant it to another, &c. And as for the other higher matters, *I perceive that God intendeth some great matter in this world.* But I am not able to judge of some of it : But I am of this mind, wherein I can any way further the service of God, I will be ready and obedient, &c. And as for the Emperours person himself, I find him of a good nature, curteous, and most zealously Catholick : yea ready to shed his blood in the cause, if opportunity required. He understandeth the Latine well, and speaketh sufficiently well : That is true (quoth I) for he spake well in Latine to me divers things. Moreover (said he) as *concerning you, I saw him very well affectionated, making great account of your book,* &c. Therefore you are not to regard these *Dutch mens ill tongues who hardly can brook any stranger,* &c.

Upon farther matter that I had to shew him, I offered my ready repair unto him at all times of his good leasure being called or warned. And he desirous to see the Stone brought to me by an Angel, willed me to come to morrow also, to Diner : I promised him, and so, with thanks yielded to his honour; I departed toward my Lodging at *Bethlem* in old *Prage.*

The Copy of the foresaid Letter to the Emperour.

MUltis (O Sereniſſime Cæſar) & permagnis (ferè omnium) Creaturarum Dei , immò
i pſius Dei , & cœleſtibus haud paucis myſteriis, arcaniſque, veſtræ Cæſareæ Majeſtatis
juſſu per me (jam, ante quatuordecim dies) fideliter, ſincere, & diligenter (quantum
ſex horarum fieri poterat ſpacio) declaratis, ac manifeſtatis: eidem, cui, eadem penes me
videnda, audienda, intelligendaque eſſe voluiſtis : Inde, nunc, quæ ſit veſtræ Cæſareæ Majeſtati, ſimplex (tanquam ab æquo rerum Æſtimatore) facta relatio : vel, quod cum relatione
adjunctum Judicium : vel, qualis totius proceſſus excogitata cenſura : vel, qualis mecum pro-
cedendi, vobis perſuaſa cautio ; vel, quale pro Cæſarei veſtri reſponſi formâ, initum captum-
que conſilium, Non ſum tam immodeſtè curioſus, ut expiſcar, Neque alicer, vel alia ratione
de ſacræ veſtræ Majeſtatis Cæſareæ prudenti & gratioſa (in præmiſſis) Reſolutione, ſum ſol-
licitus, quàm, me (fidelem, ſincerum, & devotum) Dei Omnipotentis, & (in Deo, propter-
que Deum) veſtræ ſacræ Cæſareæ Majeſtatis ſervitorem deceat. Video tamen me (dum
nullum adhuc ad præmiſſa receperim reſponſum) per tam alti ſilentii (quaſi) ſtimulum, aliquantulum impelli,ut ſecundò veſtram Cæſaream Majeſtatem admoneam,Ne divinam hanc, &
divinitus oblatam Miſericordiam, tam inexpectatam, tam magnam, tam inauditam, tam admirandam, tam multiplicem, tam ſtatui Imperatorio, Chriſtianæque Reipublicæ neceſſariam,
tam certam, tam paratam, eamque (per Dei Omnipotentis, Cæſareæque Majeſtatis veſtræ, fidelem ſervitorem) re ipſa, vobis confirmandam, & adminiſtrandam : (ſi ſacra veſtra Cæſarea Majeſtas voluiſſet) parvi momenti negotium, vel inventum aliquod humanum, aut fraudem Diabolicam, eſſe, fuiſſe, vel fore, ullo modo ſuſpicemini, vel Credatis. Tali enim & tam
gravi veſtræ Cæſareæ Majeſtatis errore, Omnipotentis Dei incendi poſſe furorem vehementer
vereor : & ne hanc Dei miſericordiam reſpuentes, ejuſdem indignantem provocetis vindictam,
valde metuo. Quapropter, cum videam Cælum ipſum , & cæleſtia talia myſteria , non tali
tantæque curæ, veſtræ ſacræ Majeſtati Cæſareæ adhuc eſſe, quali, quantæque optaſſem equidem : Ego potius quam, ut, vel Deus hujus ſuæ (prius inauditæ) Miſericordiæ ultroque
veſtræ Cæſareæ Majeſtati oblatæ,prorſus nullum (penes homines) haberet conſpicuum judicium, argumentum, Teſtimonium vel experimentum : Et potius quam mea (ſæpe nominata)
fidelitas, ſinceritas, & Devotio (ſive votum) erga Deum & veſtram Cæſaream Majeſtatem,
omni (apud poſteros noſtros) careret fide, & veritatis manifeſtæ robore : In Dei Nomine,
& ad ejus laudem, honorem, & gloriam : & ut veſtræ ſereniſſimæ Cæſareæ Majeſtatis ſatisfa-
ciam deſiderio Heroico, De lapide illo Benedicto : (Philoſophorum vocato lapide) in infal-
libiliter videndo, poſſidendo & utendo : Aſſero veſtræ ſacræ Cæſareæ Majeſtati, lapidem eundem me (auxilio favoreque Divino) conficere poſſe. Et propterea ; Si veſtra Cæſarea Majeſtas; me velit interim, ſibi intimè charum habere : Et, ſi, pro dignitate tanti myſterii, &
Beneficii (ſibi à me liberaliſſime & humillime exhibendi) gratioſè me tractare dignabitur
(Non tamen alio quidem vel altiori me inſigniens Titulo quam qui veſtræ Cæſareæ Majeſtatis Philoſopho & Mathematico conveniat,) His literis ore & corde polliceor, ſanctéque coram
Deo Omnipotenti voveo : Opus illud philoſophicum , Omnibus ſuis numeris perfectum, in
manus veſtras Cæſareas, (& ſine ſumptibus veſtris ad illud opus perficiendum requirendis)
ac breviſſimo, quo fieri poterit, tempore (Nutu Dei) me daturum. De aliis præterea Arcanis,
adhuc mihi ſilendum eſſe video. Nunc autem ſacræ Cæſareæ Majeſtatis veſtræ gratioſam, li-
baram, conſtantemque voluntatem, in præmiſſis,non aliter, niſi ex veſtro proprio gratioſo ore
vel ex veſtris Cæſareis literis propriis, intelligere Cupio. Nullum enim jam noſco, dignum
& aptum, qui in iſtis, aliiſque Naturæ & Artis ſecretis, meus (penes veſtram Cæſaream Majeſtatem) fieri deberet Mercurius.

Tueſday, *Septembris* 25. Pragæ.
    Note : I went to Diner to the Spaniſh Embaſſadour : and carryed with me the Stone
brought me by an Angel ; and the fourth Book, wherein the manner of the bringing of it is
expreſſed. And alſo I carried with me *Librum Sextum Sanctum Myſticum.*
    After Diner, when I had ſhewed him theſe things : his final anſwer was , that verily he
took the doing to be by good Angel : marry, the matters to be too great : Therefore (ſaid I)
they are for the ſervice of God, and not onely man. He ſaid he was a ſinner, and not worthy to be privy, much leſſe to be a doer in them : Notwithſtanding whatſoever he can do
A Copy of the   therein acceptable to God, he would be moſt obedient thereto. He deſired a Copy of the
letters deſired;   Emperour his foreſaid letters, that he might conſider circumſpectly of the Contents before he
ſhould deliver them ; whereunto I conſented. Renderiug his honour thanks I de-
parted.

After my return home, I found E. K. refolved to go from hence to morrow, for his wife, E.K Ready to and fo ftraightway into *England*: which was to me a grief: But what can I do, but go into Eng- refer all to the mercies of God, whom I have called upon for wifdom to ferve him withal? I *land* as he pre- have put my truft in the Lord, I have not murmured at any fuch pangs and tentations tended. hitherto.

The mercies of the Higheft be upon me, as I have put my truft in him.
Amen.

Now were we (all) brought *to great penury* : hot able without the Lord *Laskies,* or fome Poverty. heavenly help, to fuftain our ftate any longer.

Befides this, I underftood of the Queens difpleafure for my departure, and of the Bifhop of *London* his intent to have begun to have accufed me of Conjuration, and fo to have had the fecret affiftance of you know whom.

Tu es Deus fortitudo mea, refugium meum Sufceptor meus, & liberator meus.
Amen.

Wedenfday, *Septembris* 26. *Ante Meridiem.* Pragæ.

About 10 and a half of the clock, Dr. *Curtz* fent with Mr. *Simon Hageck* his fervant to D. *Curtz.* know my lodging : He had paffed not far off in a lane on horfeback his felf going into the Town, and fo met Mr. *Simon Hageck* at the lanes end, *&c.*

Thurfday, *Septembris* 27. † Pragæ.

Mane : About 7. of the clock came Dr. *Curtz* his fervant from his Mafter to tell me, D. *Curtz.* that his Mafter would come unto me at 9 of the clock.

At 9 of the clock came Dr. *Curtz* on horfeback to me, to my lodging (at Doctor *Hageck* his houfe by *Bethleem*) my wife he faluted, and little *Katharine*, my daughter. Mr. *Kelly* had gotten him into his chamber, not willing to be feen.

After he was come up into my little Study, and there fet, in Mr. *Kelly* his ufual place, and I in mine ; I began to complain of the great injury done unto me here ; for I came as a fin-cere and faithful fervitour of the Emperour his Majefty, intending all goodneffe and honour unto him : no hindrance, loffe or hurt ; neither came I *propter divitias Cæfaris mihi colligen-das,* as I faid expreffely unto his Majefty. I was, before I came hither, of good name and fame, both in this Court, and all *Europe* over, As you your felf Mr. Doctor (quoth I) can bear me witneffe : and other in this Court divers : And that here my name and fame fhould fuf-fer fhipwrack, where I thought I had been in, a fure Haven of my principal Patrone : My thinketh that great injury is done unto me : I know no means how to help it , but to give you warning of the envious malitious backbiters that alfo are about this Court, that as you find occafion, you might encounter with this evil, and foul monfter, in fo mighty a Princes Caufe intruding it felf.

The Doctor feemed not to know what I meant. I told him, that at a Noble-mans Table, There was, of great account, who faid, that there was an *Englifh* man, come to the Emperours, *A bankrupt Alchimift, a Conjurer, and Necromantift : who had fold his own goods, and given the Lord* Laskie *the money : and that he had beguiled him :* and that now *he would fain get fome of the Emperour his money from him,* &c. The Doctor feemed greatly to miflike thefe flanderous words, and faid, that he never heard of any fuch ; with fome few words more, of the wicked manner of backbiters.

After this, as concerning the report making to the Emperour, of that I had fhewed unto him, at his houfe, (as before is noted) he faid that he had made a plain and fincere report. Whereunto the Emperours Majefty, had (as yet) given no anfwer. And to be plain with you (faid he) his Majefty thinketh them almoft either incredible, or impoffible : and would have fome leafure to confider of them : and is defirous to have the fight *of thofe Latine A-ctions you fhewed me,* or a Copy of them, and efpecially, of that, which containeth *a para-phrafis of the Apoftolical Creed.* I anfwered, that my Books I would not deliver out of my hands : And as for a Copy of them, I would (at leafure) write it, that his Majefty might have it. And then I told him farther, that becaufe it was fo long before I heard any word of him, I had letters ready to fend to the Emperours Majefty, to have farther declared my mind unto him, and I declared unto him the tenor of them : and he told me that about three of the clock after noon, his man fhould go to the Court, and if then I would fend them, his man fhould

[ii 2]

should carry them. I answered that I would expect a day or two for the Emperours return hither. After this we talked of some Mathematical matters : And I shewed him the little Book *de superficierum divisionibus,* set forth by me and *Commandinus,* printed at *Pezaro* in *Italy.* He said that he never saw it before : I bad him then take it with him to peruse : and that if I had another Copy, I would give it him ; but I had none other but that. I shewed him also the *Propedeumata Aphoristica de præstantioribus quibusdam Naturæ virtutibus,* which he had never seen before. After this, with mutual curtesies offered on both parts (after the manner of the world) he took his horse, and returned homeward.

<hr />

Friday, *Septembris,* 28. Pragæ.

Intending to send the Emperours letter (here before written) to his Majesty , by my good friend, the Spanish Embassadour, I wrote this letter to send to the Embassadour in that behalf, and as concerning the credit of these Actions.

Illustrissimo Domino, Domino Don Gulielmo de Sancto Clémente, serenissimi atque Catholici Hispaniarum Regis apud sacram Cæsaream Majestatem, &c. Legato, Domino suo observandissimo.

Illustris & Magnifice Heros : Multis hoc probari potest testimoniis & exemplis, quod illa, quæ (preter vulgarium artium & scientiarum decreta) Nova, & supra vulgariter Studiosorum expectationem, hominibus (licet piis & candidis quidem) Divinitus revelantur mysteria, cum summa difficultate vel intelliguntur à paucissimis, vel vix sine suspitione admittuntur, aut creduntur à pluribus : Ast qualis, in nostris, (si rectæ piéque informatæ rostris adhibeatur judicium) esse potest suspitio ? Nam à Deo Omnipotente, per multos jam annos, fideliter, ardenter, & constanter per preces requisita sapientia : Una (scilicet quæ penes nos quidem) videtur esse radix & occasio tanti istius Doni obtinendi. Ast in cœlesti suo Palatio, ante conditum mundum, determinata, & assignata erga nos Misericordia & gratia Omnipotentis Dei, præcipuum, solidum, immobileque hujus tanti mysterii est censendum fundamentum : In quo mysterio, talis relucet, per potentes fidelesque Angelos Isagogica Informatio, De Arcanis Dei consiliis, tam in mundi creatione Créaturarumque naturis, & vero usu, quam in mundi præsentis moxque futuri statu : Et preterea, de unius Catholicæ Ecclesiæ (charissimæ Jesu Christi sponsæ, nostræque piæ matris) sanctitate, dignitate, & Authoritate (veluti in qua etiam est Sanctorum Communio, & Peccatorum remissio) & de multis nondum per nos revelandis Dei Arcanis Magnalibus & Determinationibus : Quòd tantum abest, ut aliquis (sanæ mentis) Christianus, Actiones Nostras Mysticas, Diabolicas esse fraudes, contendere , immo ne suspicari quidem conetur aut possit : ut potius , tale Arcanum Dei propositum , incredibiliter admirari, rationem humanam, in eisdem examinandis , subjugare, & Dei erga Electos suos admirandam misericordiam in istis esse manifestam, humillimè, & cum summo tremore fateri velit : Ego quidem , hactenus, in istis , aliud (ferè) nihil, me esse invenio, nisi Calamum scribæ, velociter per me scribentis. Nam visa auditaque (in mea præsentia) fidelissimè, de litera interdum ad literam, interdum, verbatim, interdum pluribus simul receptis verbis (ipso eodem temporis momento, quo traduntur) annotare sum solitus. Ast jam in quam multa excrevit Noster talis labor volumina ? Ex quibus omnibus illum fructum , successumque expectamus, qualem præfixit ille, cujus nutui cuncta obediunt, Istas autem ad suam sacrem *Cæsaream* Majestatem literas meas : Cum vestra magnificentia opportunitatem inveniet primam , si meo nomine: humillimè eidem exhibere dignabitur , Tum magno mihi (Divinitus) injuncto , levatus ero onere : Tum magno, à vestra magnificentia affectus beneficio : Interim verò , Dum suæ sacræ Majestatis *Cæsareæ* ad istas responsum dabitur, (nimirum si ad 14. vel 16. dies prius expectandum esset) vel, statim post acceptum responsum (si tam expeditè illud recipere possum, quàm quod recepi ultimo) ad iter me accingere debeo , propter familiam , libros , & aliquam meam suppellectilem, huc (ante hyemis asperitatem) transferendam. Ubi , cum *Cæsareæ* Majestatis gratioso favore, & sub ipsiusProtectione Imperatoria , voluntatem Omnipotentis Dei implere, pro viribus, & suæ sacræ *Cæsareæ* Majestati inservire (tanquam ejusdem *Philosophus & Mathematicus*) fidelissimè, de tempore in tempus, paratus esse potero.

Illustri vestræ Magnificentiæ

Addictissimus

Joannes Dee.

I an-

I annexed hereunto a Poſt-ſcript, which followeth :

Poſt-ſcriptum.

MEarum eſſe partium , & conſultum eſſe duxi veſtræ Magnificentiæ pauciſſimis verbis ſignificare , quod heri , manè , hora nona , vir egregius , & ſuæ Majeſtis *Cæſareæ* fidus Conſiliarius D. Doctor *Curtæius,* me humaniſſimè inviſebat in meo ergaſtulo , & hypocauſtato , juxta *Bethlehem ,* ubi videre poterat Bibliothecam preſentem meam , nullam (ferè) aliam eſſe, præter Sancta Dei Evangelia & Biblia ſacra ipſoſque noſtrorum myſteriorum libros : Ego autem quodam humili modo (inter cæteras querelas meas) de tam longa interpoſita mora conquerebar , inter ejuſdem (de meis rebus) factam relationem , & *Cæſareum* de eiſdem recipiendum reſponſum. Ille verò ſe ſimpliciſſimè *Cæſareæ* Majeſti viſa auditaque (penes me) retuliſſe aſſeruit , nullo ſuo , de eiſdem , adhibito judicio. Verum, *Cæſari* (dixit) quaſi impoſſibilia vel incredibilia fuiſſe viſa. Et de reſponſo mihi (in hac parte) dando , ſecum , adhuc , ſuam deliberare velle Majeſtatem *Cæſaream.* Unde egò de literis meis iſtis , ſuæ Majeſti mittendis , mentionem feci & ſummatim earundem tenorem , eidem enarravi. Ille eaſdem ſtatim habere voluit , ipſi *Cæſareæ* Majeſtati à Meridie mittendas : Ego quidem *Cæſari* me velle ad pauculos dies expectare adventum dixi. Deinde de rebus Mathematicis breviſſime inter nos habito ſermone , illique (ad pervidendum) dato libello quodam Geometrico (per me & *Federicum Commandinum Urbinatem*) in lucem olim dato, & mutuis, poſt, utrinque promiſſis officiis humanitatis & benevolentiæ, abiit.

1584. *Sept.*28.

Saturday, *Septemb.* 29.   *Die Sancti Michaelis.*

The foreſaid Letter to the Emperours Majeſty, with this Letter to the Ambaſſadour , and this Poſt-ſcript : And moreover , (according to the Ambaſſadour his requeſt) the Copy of the Emperours Letter, all in one uttermore paper cloſed (Letter like) ſealed, and with ſuperſcription to the foreſaid Ambaſſadour ; I ſent to his honour on *Michaelmas* day at dinner time , by *Emericus Sontag*: Who delivered the ſame to the Secretary of the Ambaſſadour, and he to the Lord Ambaſſadour, as he ſat at dinner.

Deus bene vertat, ad laudem
nominis ſui.   Amen.

September 29.

Remember that this day (after-noon) I ſent *Hugh* on foot with my Letters to *Cracovia* to *Edmond,* that my folk ſhould not be out of quiet, or afeard to ſee Miſtreſſe *Kelly* , ſent for, and no Letters to come from me, &c. I writ to the Lord *Laskie* of our want of money, &c.

Monday, *Octobris* 1.   *à Meridie circa* 3. *horam.*   Pragæ.
Oratione dominica finita , &c.   Valde cito eſt facta apparitio.

E. K. Here be two, one his face is covered, and the other is not : *Uriel.* And he, whoſe face is uncovered ſeemeth to be *Gabriel.*   *Gabriel.*

Δ. Sit benedictus Deus Pater, Deus filius, & |Deus Spiritus Sanctus nunc & Semper. Amen.

Δ. Our chief cauſe (at this inſtant) why we reſort to this ſhew-ſtone , is for to underſtand (according to the grounds of God his promiſe) the ſtate of my wife her grievous diſ- *Jane uxoris* eaſe, and means to cure her, wherein if it pleaſe the Lord to be mercifull unto her and me, *mea morbus* it ſhall be the occaſion whereby ſhe will all her life time praiſe the name of God for his mer- *periculoſus.* cies, and be of a quietter minde , and not ſo teſty and fretting as ſhe is.

...... *Who are you, or from whence come you, that you require ſcience ; which ſeek to be more* *Gabriel.* *wiſe and expert , then ſuch as are the Children and Doctors of this World ? whoſe judgements are* *taſh, rash, and understanding naked : and in whose lips dwelleth no truth. Who (I say) are you, that you should deserve the majestral benefit of so great and sanctified grace ? as to understand the determination of God, the power of his Angels, or the brightnesse, or obscurity of mans Soul, and understanding : You desperate sinners, and partakers with the wicked, how can you seek bread at your fathers hands : when you seek to steal into his barnes ?* Yea, *into his house, and dining Ta-*

The robbing God of his honour.

bles : and more then that ; yea, even into his privy Chambers : not to spoyl him of his houshold stuffe, of his Gold, or precious stones, but of the diademe, and Crown of his everlasting Majesty and ho-nour : *you are thieves and robbers ;and through the Dignity of your spirit you shall think to exalt your selves,and to live in Majesty with the world.*

True it is, you may live so : But you live with an Harlot, and shall possesse the reward of Fornicators and Adulterers.

Poni Angeli Dei.

Therefore seek not to feed of such food, as the holy, and blessed messengers, and Ministers of the God of Hosts and glory do taste of : and are comforted ; for they are the spirits of truth and understanding : such as cleave unto their God, and fight against the abominations, and horrible blasphe-

Animarum Splendor vel obscuritas

mies of the world and her adherents : which (because you set your selves against them) shall keep, and close up the brightnesse, and obscurity of each Soul from you, that your ignorance may be greater ; and your darknesse thicker, and that you may return without light : to the Barathrum of ignorance,

Superbia philautia vanitas.

where pride, self-love, and the Children of vanity have their habitation.

Then (peradventure) will you say within your selves : There be other doors, there be other woods ; yea, there be other wayes, let us therefore seek out them.

Vigor Elementalis. Coagulatio. Pabula.

But behold, I will shut up from you all Elemental Vigor : So that the Fountains of coagulation shall be dried when you seek them, and the natural nourishment and food of parts that dwell in one proportion shall hide themselves, and be asleep when you seek them ; yea, in the lowest I will place a threefold door-bar, stronger then a Rock of yearn, which shall stand between your eyes and knowledge, and you shall not see : for peradventure you may say in your selves.

△. Forte lapis philosophorum intelligitur. It.

Behold, there is a science known ; yea, there is a conjunction of [△] *equal qualities, opening unto us the mysteries of comfort in infirmities, that is not so. O you foolish : for neither here, nor there, shall you finde the Lord, if you follow the steps, and* defiled *wayes that the world teacheth you.*

For I said of you : Lo, I will place you against the world, that my name may be magnified, and the world shall hate you for my sake.

Nos mundi Inimici esse debemus,& mundus nos odio prosequitur propter Deum.

△. O Lord, be mercifull unto us : Deal, O Lord, with us, as I have put my trust in thee: Turn away thy wrath (O God) and visit us in mercy : O God, O Lord, what grievous sayings are these ?

Gabriel.

Gabriel. ...... *Trouble* [△] *thou not thy heart, but bear the voyce of me, Gabriel, the man of God. I am the true medecine of such as put their trust in the God of Hosts, and in his son Christ ; which is the Lamb of life, and the comfort of his father,which give unto those that thirst, the true medecine of comfort and consolation ; neither shall God forsake thee, neither shall thy Soul be deceived.*

Misericordia Dei super △.

But it behoveth these things to be spoken, that sin might be corrected, and the name of him that sent us, magnified.

Nota causam acerba increpationis istius.

Here placing.

△. In nomine Dei loquitur, qui per omnes Angelos loquitur : licet enim *Uriel* dixerit vel alius, tamen Deus semper loquitur.

Rud:lphus adhuc misericordia capax.

Gabriel, *Hear my voice : as I said unto thee, so will I place thee here. And from hence thou shalt have science and understanding, and thou shalt be favourable in the eyes of him, that I favour not : that my glorie might be exalted in him, and against his childishnesse. Yet, I will be mercifull to him ; yet if he hear me.* E. L.

...... *Unto thee* [E. K.] *I say, (O thou that art a worldling) I will stir up friends amongst you, and I will fill thy hands with that thou desirest : But that thou receivest in the one, I will pluck back in the other, that when thou wouldest be wise, thou shalt not, and when thou wouldest see, thou shalt not.*

A voyce from an uncertain place. There were some wicked tempters vexing E. K. from hearing quietly.

E. K.

△. E. K. Was very much offended at these sharp words, &c. and would have left off, &c.

Uriel. ...... Inobediens es, & castigatione dignus.

* Sept. 21. in fine.

Gabr. ..... *As for the vertue of the holy spirit* * *(spoken of) the gift of medecine, and healing (which you call Physick) Alas, you know not.*

Infa-

Infani funt omnes , & fatui : For, Phyfick *is in very deed,
the true , and perfect fcience of the natural combination,
and, proportion of known parts, anfwering in graduation
real , to one principal and defined ; is therefore above the
capacity of fuch as are worldlings, and do hunt after money more
then the truth of Gods fpirit.*

*Definitio Medicina, Medicina eſt vera &
perfeſta fcientia naturalis combinationis , &
proportionis partium notarum debito modo
refpondentium in graduatione reali ad unum
principale, & definitum eſſe.*

Uriel *as a wit-
neſſe ſtanding by.*

*But lo, light ſtandeth by me, and my words are medicine :
and whatſoever I ſpeak , light beareth witneſſe of me :
Therefore are my words true.*

...... *Have patience awhile.*

Δ. *He difappeared.*

Δ. We examined the definition of Phyfick to be a very apt anfwering, both to the Anato-
mical natures of man, or any patient, and alfo of the Herb, or fimple, that is medici-
nal , &c.

Δ. He came again and proceeded.

Gab. ...., *Which confiſteth of two parts, the knowledge of cæleſtial radiation (the cauſe of* [1] *com-
bining) and of Elemental vigor, the ſtay, and cauſe of* [2] *proportion.*

*Radiatio cæ-
leſtis, vigor ele-
mentalis.*

*The firſt, and cæleſtial is threefold, that is to ſay, from God, from the Angels, from mans
Soul.*

The ſecond (that is to ſay Elemental) is the knowledge of the ſtar [1] *coagulating ; of the* [2]
pabula of the parts nouriſhed, of the [3] *conjunction of like qualities.*

*(Here is the true Art of Phyfick.)
This ſecond is threefold.
After a while I come again.*

Δ. He is come again, and proceeded.

Gab. ...... *Go to.*

Δ. In the name of Jefus.

Gab. ...... *Then you are diſeaſed, you are ſick : you muſt have a Phyſitian : why then, your
Phyſitian muſt be ſuch as hath this Science, to judge your diſeaſe,*

Whether (for ſin) it come from God : and ſo by prayer to be cured :   *Deus* 1.

Or from the Angels, as the Miniſters of Gods Juſtice (generally) for deſert or for reproof :   *Angelus* 2.

*Or from the ſoul of man, as from the chief life of the body , whoſe infection radically, and by the
influence of proportions immediate, (hidden from man, but known unto us,) is called (with us)
Mazah : with you, Impietas.*

*Anima hominis,
3.
Infectio anima.
Impietas.*

*Theſe are the firſt three , and Magicall Cauſes : The other three are Elemen-
tall.*

*Tres magica
cauſa.*

1. *Either by the ſtar, that is cauſe of coagulation and imbibing of mans ſperm in the femine
blood, without the which it could not.*   *Stella.* 1.

2. *The other (that is the ſecond) through infection of meates which are divers, wherewith the
thing is, [and] continueth, which in their kinds are many.*   *Cibus.* 2.

3. *The laſt, by conjunction or mixture : which is the ſecret property that draweth infection from
man to man.*   *Mixtio.* 3.

*Theſe if you know (for he is no Phyſitian if he know them not) how they are and live, and are
joyned together in their proportions, and alſo when they exceed, or are diminiſhed, in that they
are you ſhall be able to bring them to their proper being, wherein they are ratified and
rejoyce.*

*Attractio mor-
borum contagio-
ſorum.*

[Δ. He was away a quarter of an hour.]

Gab. ....., *Lo, theſe are ſeeds and foundations : and here I have (according to my property)
touched the leaſt of my ſtrings for you.*

*If now you intend to excell the Phyſitians of the Earth, and to help thoſe that are diſeaſed,
ſincerely, truly, and through the power and mercy of God ;*   *Medicina vera.*

*Then muſt you attend upon me, and my expoſitions, for forty dayes, wherein I will open unto
you, many and unknown ſecrets ; and will comfort you with this one herb or branch of my Garden;
to the intent you may perceive I am true Gabriel.*

*40. Dayes.
True Gabrielt
verus Gabriel.*

*But as in you that are bearers, due obedience ought to be, ſo muſt I keep the Authority and
gravity of a Schoolmaſter, ſuffering none to bear my Doctrine, but ſuch as are abſtinent and clean-
ſed from their ſins.*

*Abſtinentes &
purgati à pec-
cain.*

*Conſider therefore, what the mercies of God are, the fruit and value of this Doctrine, and the
naked-*

Responsum vo-
tum.

nakednesse and necessity of the world that requireth it, and then answer me.

Auxilium &
Consolatio Dei.
Jana uxoris
mea morbus
periculosus.

For your answer is a vow unto the Lord, of whose help and comfort I bear witnesse.

But as touching thy wife, her disease is in the first Elemental, and very dangerous, and threat-neth her child, yea and her self death.

Δ. Lord, therefore I resort unto thee, who art the Curer of all dieases.

Gab. .... *But to morrow (if thou resort here,)*
I will tell thee, what it is, and will define of it.

Lord, I trust, it shall be cured: What is unpossible unto our God?

Gab. .... *I cease.*

Δ. Incessant praise and honour, be unto the Almighty, most bountiful, and wise God, the Lord of Hosts, our God and King.

Amen.

Remember I sent letters to *Cracow* by the Messager of *Prage:*

Tuesday, Octobris 2. Mane hora 9. † Pragæ.

Δ. Orationibus finitis, ad Deum, &c. Deus in adjutorium nostrum intende, &c.

E. K. Here they be.

Δ. Gratia Dei, patris, & filii, & Spiritus Sancti, sit super nos nunc & semper & in sæcula sæculorum. *Amen.*

Δ. They paused, before they spake, very long.

Δ. Perhaps they expect our *answer,* as concerning our cleansing and abstaining from sins: Herein I crave at Gods hands his grace and mercy, and intend and desire both to be purged, and also to abstain not onely 40 dayes, but all my life, to the best of my abili-ty, &c.

Gab. ......, *Puris habemus omnia, Immundis nihil.*

Δ. I beseech you for God his sake, & *per viscera misericordiæ Altissimi,* that you would de-clare unto us a certain remedy of my wife her disease, &c.

☉ *Virtus.*

Gabr. ...... *When thy wife was a milkie substance, growing by the perfection of the place, and* influence radical, (which onely, is the gift of the Sun) *then, was not the Matrix, or bag of Nature (wherein she encreased) perfect, or of sufficient* retention : *By reason of a feaver going*

Febri laborabat
Mater uxoris
ante conceptio-
nem. * *For, so,*
the soul is sent
in. to
Δ. Of *Jane*
my wife.

before the conception : *So that, the Angelical administration, generally containing, the vessel of life, for the proportion of the world,* * *entred by force of their Order immediately, before the* [Δ]*inward parts, were established in their nutriment and proportion.*

Which is the cause, that the second * *vessel, and lowest of nature (for, your terms I must use)* is so thin, and tyed short, that it is not able to keep in, or retain, the simile and quidditie of her own

* *Forsan, vasa*
seminaria.

substantial being *and seed.*

Wherefore, when the rest of her digestions (according to her age and natural strength) fulfil their offices, by degree to be received into that receptacle ; then, doth the force of nature quail : and by the subtilty of the principle, or matter ejected, (which seeketh to take up on every center a dwelling place,) the guts and passages, are offended and scalded with an intemperate heat : the most subtile and sharpest part, being of a most penetrating vertue : *(and therefore seeking*

She }
he }
it. }

passage) mixeth her self with the excrements, where resting, she turneth unto her first form, which is blood : *Whose Quintessence worketh, in her own property and beginning, and forceth the* [1] *ex-*

Excrementa
bina.

crement stercoral many times to become bloody, the other part being more heavy, notwithstanding unapt to descend, (Quia natura quærit omne suum) *becometh corrupted ; and so by vertue of nature, is cast out as an* [2] *excrement, being blood and matter.*

But I tell thee, that so long as Nature was in the lowest degree, and the sperm kept more near together, by reason of the spiritual heat in youth, it was not faulty in her :

Spiritus caloris.
The breathing
or vapouring
heat.

But in her sixteenth year, when they were more heavy and sought issue and descension, then began Nature to feel the effect, in the places, and vessel, which is the ground of her retention, the chief basis and mother of her dwelling.

Uxor jam preg-
nans est.
Imagination.

Behold now, being fative, and the force of heat drawn to the nutriment of the Creature ; More-over the other part Active compelled into a nearer place, by the impediment of imagination, *bring-eth great danger now, by reason that Nature is become very weak, and not able to make excremen-tal expulsion.*

But

But doſt thou think that there is a remedy to this diſeaſe ?
Δ. Yea verily, through the wiſdom and mercies of the Higheſt.
Gabr. ...... *I have taught the diſeaſe ; I will go and ſee if there be a remedy.*
Δ. The God of *Abraham, Iſaac,* and *Jacob,* be merciful to my wife and me, and ſend her remedy and cure of her grief.

E. K. Here he is.

Gab. ...... *Come again after Diner.*
Δ. We had been ſent for to diner, twice or thrice before. So we went.
     Δ. Miſericordiæ Dei ſint ſuper nos. *Amen.*

After Diner, circa horam 1.

Δ. We reſorted to the Myſtery : and ſhortly, they appeared both.

E. K. Here they be both.

Δ.
Gab. ...... *Take pure wheat, a pinte : one Pheaſant-Cock alive, an eleven ounces of Maſculine Amber (which is the white Amber) an ounce and a quarter of Turpentine.*   The phyſical remedy.
Δ. Of waſhed Turpentine ?
Gab. ...... *Turpentine that is waſhed loſeth his vertue.*
Break the Cock in pieces with a peſtel, (his feathers pluckt off) pound the Amber ſmall.
Put all this into a gallon of red wine.
. May we take the red wine of this Country ?
Gab. ...... *I.* *Diſtill them, with a fire of the ſecond heat.*
[Λ. I beſeech you, how long ſhall they ſtand in ſteep ?
Gab. ...... *As thou wilt.*]
Still it again the ſecond time, (the feces being caſt away) And adde ſomething more to the fire, ſo that it be a quarter toward the third.
Let her faſt forty hours from meat : And let her divide the Medicine into three parts.
The firſt part, let her drink (being milk-warm) by little and little.
The ſecond part, let her make a ſawce of, for five or ſix meales.
The laſt part, let her uſe in Abſconditis : And ſhe ſhall have health.
Δ. I beſeech you, in how many dayes compaſs would you have this to be done ?
Gab. ...... *It is no queſtion : the neceſſity of the thing teacheth.*
Δ. As concerning the Infant, what ſtate is it in ?
Gab. . .... *Shut thy mouth · Seek not.*
Δ. I am contented.
Δ. As concerning a Pheaſant-Cock, I know not how or where to get it.
Gab. ...... *All the creatures of the world, elſe, help not.* *I have taught, take thou care.*
Δ. The thanks, honour, and praiſe, be to the Higheſt, and I thank you for your charity and good will, to impart theſe things unto me.
Gab. ...... *Tou ſhall have no more, at me,* until you be repentant, and reconciled *: and are* Penitentia, *made apt for my School.* Reconciliatis.

E. K. You might *give this Table vertue* to cure her, or. cure her with ſome one thing, or ſimple, *if you be good Angels.*

Gab. ...... *Unto us, the vertue of Gods Creatures are known : which we may open unto you : and* E. K. His ma-
the power of giving vertue is in God : Therefore ceaſe thy malitious tongue. licious tongue
I have no more. againſt God
his good An-

E. K. They are gone.

Δ. Deo Omnipotenti, Optimo & Maximo ſit omnis laus honor & gloria : nunc & gels.
ſemper. *Amen.*

Thurſday, Octobris 4. Mane, hora 10.¼ circiter. † Pragæ.

Orationibus variis ad Deum, & pro pane quotidiano jam in tempore neceſſitatis, finitis, *&c.* apparitio facta eſt.

E. K. Here is he, that is covered with the Scarf.

Uriel. ...... *Hear, O thou,* [Δ] *that ſayeſt, (if I have put my* Δ. It was a parcel of my prayers
truſt in thee) bear me, If that thou hadſt taried at home, and wan- to God
ted my admoniſhment, thy children had been ſcattered, thy wife had Δ. Miſericordias Domini in æter-
ended her dayes with ſorrow : and lo, the birds of the air had num cantabo, qui me ſub alis ſuis il-
reſted on thy carkaſe. If thou waſt held by the hand, and attended leſum ſervavit, ſervat, & ſervabit.
on, by heavenly Pilots, when the Seas would have ſwallowed thee, and
Satan had power over thee ; If poiſon had prevailed, wherewith thy meat was often times ſawced.
If the continual rage of Satan and the world had overthrown thee. Then had not I been thy
God, neither had done well unto thee. But out of all theſe I have led thee, as a father doth his
child

child from danger, And from many more fcourges and adverfities unknown to thee, but ready to afflict thee. Hitherto, thou fayeft unto me, If : What haft thou done for me , or added unto my name ? What haft thou loft that I have not given thee ? or what canft thou have, that I pluck back? Hear my voice. He that loveth the world, loveth not me ; for what I do I do : and what I am, I am : And I made nothing without a caufe. Thou haft not yet begged for my name, neither haft been imprifoned for my fake ; But I have turned the prifon from thee, and have opened un-to thee my myfteries. I fay unto thee, I am the beginning, and an undefiled Spirit, and there is **If.** *no riches that is without me. If I fhould not fuffer thee to be proved, Then were thou not for me ;*

Probatio. **Satans whips are long in fpending.** **Fel bibendum, Deinde vinum. Interim.** *For, thofe that are mine, tafte tribulation : But when Satan hath fpent his whip ; If thou be found faithful, I will place my covenant with thee and thy children, And I will be revealed unto them, unto the end of the world. Silver and Gold I give not ; But my bleffing, is above the fub-ftance of the Earth. Dayes there be, that thou muft drink of gall, and a time cometh, when thou fhalt drink wine. In the mean feafon, thofe that give unto thee, I will multiply all they have with bleffing a thoufand fold ; for thofe that give unto thee, I will give unto them ; And thofe that pluck back from thee, I will alfo pluck back from them. Thofe that are of me, have no fpot ; for I am all beauty.*

E. K. But will you give us meat, drink, and cloathing ?

*O Kelly, Kelly, Paulus ad Cor. Epift. 1. cap. 15. verfu 51. & 52 *Ecce myfterium vobis dico : Non omnes quidem obdormiemus : fed omnes mutabimur : mom nto & fallus oculi,* &c.
The Commiffion, and manner of prophefying againft the Incredulous.

* *There fhall come a time,* (If you dwell together and love me) *that in the twink of an eye, you fhall breath your laft, and live again: and I will kick under my feet all the proud Nations of the Earth :: for my day is at hand. But I am a jealous God : Be therefore faithful. If I fend thee forth, and they hear thee not : or meafure thee, as a fhadow, at noon dayes, Go unto the mountains and take up ftones and break them in pieces with a mighty peftel , caft them againft the windes, and into the four parts of the Earth. And fay, Thou and thus be it unto them : Thou and thus let* **Confirmation of the Pro-phefie.** the Lord work for me : *and thy prophefie fhall be true, and it fhall come to paffe that thou fayeft.* **The manner of bleffing Pro-phetical.** *So likewife if they hear thee, do unto them, that my bleffing may alfo be known.*

Δ. Lord, what fhall I do, if they hear me ?

Uriel. ...... *Do unto them the figns of good ; as it fhall come into thy mind.*

I come again. ### E. K. He is gone.

Δ. I thank thee O God, for this great comfort : my heart is greatly refrefhed therewith : Thou art my God.

Δ. We read over the premiffes.

E. K. He is here again.

E.K. Intending to depart, and I not knowing. *Why doft thou* [E.K.] *feek to flee from me, and fecretly putteft into thy heart,* &c.

Δ. He fpake divers things to E. K. which chiefly concerned himfelf : and he would not utter them as now : But he told me, That he was determined to have fold his cloths, and with as much fpeed as he could, with his wife, to have gone to *Hamburgh,* and fo to *England,* &c. If his wife would not go, that he would.

Uriel. .... *Hear me, There is not any one, more ftrong, more rich, or more friendly, than I,* &c.

Δ. He fpake much again to E. K. of himfelf, which he expreffed not.

E. K. It is true, I will follow God; *but I doubt that you are not of God.*

My wife not to go now to Cra-cow. Uriel. ...... *I will fhew you the water : do what you lift. I fay unto thee* [Δ] *Take not thy wife* Jane *with thee, leaft thou have a new forrow.*

Three of you fhall go, The fourth, [T.K.] (*which is* [E.K.] *his brother*) *fhall be a fer-vant to his houfe.*

Uriel our Houfe-keeper. I can well keep it.

A. L. Againft Lasky his enemies as in the former practice was taught. *But when thou comeft into* Poland, *be not known. Lead out* Lasky *by the band, and bring him hither, and prophefie* againft his enemies, *that I may break them in pieces : and may be mind-ful of my Covenant.*

He hath much need of Counfel.

I am with you.

E. K. He is difappeared.

Δ. Deo noftro, Domino noftro & Sanctificatori noftro Omnipotenti, æterno, & mifericordi fit omnis laus, gratiarum actio, honor & gloria nunc & femper.

Amen.

Fryday, *Octobris* 5.

At afternoon came one of Doctour *Curtz* his servants from his Master to tell me, that his Master would come to me to morrow in the morning about seven, eight, or nine of the Clock, as I would, &c.

Saturday, *Octobris* 6. *Mané.*

Before seven of the Clock I thought good rather my self to go to Doctour *Curtz*, then to suffer him to come to me so far, and that for divers causes : So I went to him, and came before he was ready. At his being ready he came forth, but nothing with so chearfull a countenance to welcome me as he did at the first : I conjectured that he suspected that I would take his words in evil part ; which he had to say to me from the Emperour, which (after I had somewhat spoken of the book that I lent him, and some other, that had written somewhat of such matter of division of superficies ; and he had told me that this my book was the most excellent in that Argument; and so made a pause, he began in this sort in two parts to divide his speech ; and said that *Cæsarea sua Majestas quantum ad sua peccata (per me reprehensa) solet Confessionarium adhibere tempore & loco opportuné, neque diffidere illum de Misericordia divina ; Quantum autem ad me attinebat, paratam esse suam Cæsaream Majestatem mihi gratificari & benefacere in quacumque re quæ illius subjiceret Authoritati :* I hereupon answered, and said : *Doleo verba mea in alio sensu intellecta vel concepta fuisse à sua Cæsarea Majestate quàm intelligi vel concipi debebant. Non enim me ejus fieri Confessionarium cupiebam, sed peccata ejus ex cælo reprehensa fuisse, hoc illi significare jubebar, ut feci : unde ille consolationis plus haurire poterat, quam ex consilio alicujus sui amici vel Confessionarii sui, peccata ejus redarguentis, Domini enim Dei eximium declarabat favorem,&c. Quantum verò ad illam quam mihi offerebat sua Majestas Cæsarea gratiam ; humillimè acceptabam. Nunc verò quod desiderem titulo Philosophi & Mathematici Cæsarei insigniri causa est multiplex; tum respectu secreti mei servitii erga Cæsarem, sub eo prætextu cælandi quam majoris authoritatis & favoris apud Cæsarianos & Anglos meos, ne vel illis hic nugas agere viderar, & nullius esse æstimationis, vel istis etiam viderer aptus, contra quem suam invidiam & maledicentissimam, ut incepere, exercerent linguam impune,* &c. *Orabam igitur D.* Curtzium *ut Cæsaream suam Majestam admoneret de indebita interpretatione illorum verborum quibus vitia ejus redarguebantur,* &c. Then he spake of the second Letters to the Emperour, the effect whereof he had heard at my hands, and had sent on *Michaelmas* even to the Emperours Majesty, a note and advise of them, as he now said. And did wish that they had been delivered before the Emperour had resolved on the former answer : Those Letters (said I) are in the Ambassadours of *Spain*'s hands ; and if he will not deliver them to day, I will fetch them for you : If you do(said he)I will deliver them straight way, for at eighth of the Clock you shall have me in the *Ritter* stove, or hear of me there. Then (said I) I will straight way go to the Ambassadour.

I went unto the Ambassadour of *Spain*, and reported all that had passed between me and D. *Curtz*. He said, that by reason of his divers affairs he had not good opportunity, never since the receipt of my Letters to go to the Emperours Majesty : But that this day he determined to deliver my Letters with his own hand unto his Majesty :so with thanks given to his honour I departed : I went to the *Ritter* stove (or Chamber of presence) where I found none of the Guard, but very many sitting without. In the stove were three, or four, of which one went straight way into the privy Chamber, and by and by D. *Curtz* came out from the Emperour unto me, I asked him if he had told the Emperour of my grief conceived of his misunderstanding my words : he said, I, and that the Emperour took it not in evil part, and so of divers other things we had talk walking up and down together about a quarter of an hour : Among other things I told him that the Lord Ambassadour would deliver my Letters himself to the Emperours Majesty, so I departed, and he returned back to the Emperour into the privy Chamber.

Sunday, *Octobris* 7. *Mane hora* 7.

I sent to the Lord Ambassadour his house, and there I learned that the Ambassadour had yesterday delivered my Letter to his Majesty : And that answer was to be expected by D. *Curtz*.

After Dinner I went to Doctor *Curtz* home to his lodging, and he had nothing as yet to say of the Letter delivered by the Lord Ambassadour : But we fell to other talk, and I told him plainly, that I had not hitherto lived obscurely, neither without care of my good fame and name, maintaining, and increasing; therefore if here for my sincere dealing I should seem to be despised, or not regarded, or to be but a trifler, my thought I should have great injury : And sure I was that the Emperours Majesty was much ruled by him, and as he did frame his judgement, so did his Majesty very oft resolve in such matters as mine; wherefore if I

were

were not used in my causes as was reasonable, and for the Emperours honour it should not be laid to any other mans charge but to his, &c. He promised that he would deliver all in the best words he could, in friendly sort, &c. After this he shewed divers his labours and inventions, Mathematical, and chiefly Arithmetical Tables, both, for his invention by squares to have the minute and second of observations Astronomical, and so for the mending of *Nonnius* his invention of the Quadrant dividing in 90. 91. 92. 93. &c. I then opened to him my secret of my glasse, for battering in a dark night, &c. He said that conclusion would be very acceptable to his Majesty, I told him that the glasse was at *Cracovia*, and his Majesty should see it by Gods leave.

After this I told him that I would full fain have a Pasport, or safe conduct to passe quietly and safely in any of the Emperours Dominions. He thought his Majesty would willingly grant that, and willed me to write three, or four lines as I would have it, and he informed me thus:

Cæsaream suam Majestatem humillimè orat Joannes Dee *Anglus, serenissima sua Majestatis Devotissimus servitor, ut pro sua majori in Itineribus per amplissimum sua Cæsarez Majestatis Imperium conficientis securitate, literas salvi passus sibi concedere dignaretur.*

Joannes Dee.

At my coming home, I bethought me that I would gladly, the said Pasport, safe Conduct, or Letters of passage, more ample and beneficial; as for my wife, children, family, servants, and goods whatsoever, and for one whole year to dare from the date of these presents thus.

Wednesday, On Monday morning 8. Octobris.

Sacram suam Cæsaream Majestatem humillimè orat, serenissima sua Majestatis Devotissimus servitor Joannes Dee *Anglus, ut eidem* Joanni *pro seipso, uxore sua, liberis suis, familia sua, servitoribus, Ancillis suis & suppellectili sua quacunque sua sacra Cæsarea Majestas favorabiles & gratiosas suas literas salvi quieti & liberi transitus per omnes & quascumque amplissimi Majestatis sua Cæsarez Imperii partes viasque, & pro integri anni (proximè post datam præsentium sequentis) tempore quocumque, clementèr concedere dignaretur.*

Anno 1584. Oct. 8.   Joannes Dee.

Monday, Octobris 8.

I went to Mr. Doctor *Curtz*, with these last Letters fair written, and I found him to be at the Hoff rate Camer in Counsel: and so awaiting till they rose (half an hour after 6. of the Clock) he came out with my Letters in his hand, which I left yesternight with him. I shewed him these last written: And he said they use to limit no time, but to make them indefinite. So he took the last, and I had the former Letters back again: He went with them into the privy Chamber, he said, I should not need to send for the Letters, but he would send them home by his man, and I went from him toward the Ambassadour *Don Gulielmo de Sancto Clemente*, whom I found coming with the Ambassadour of *Spain* (who came three, or four dayes before, to give the golden Fleese to the Emperour) and the Marshall of the Court to go to the Emperour presently to have audience: And as I stood in the Court of the Ambassadours lodging, and they three on horsback coming, the Ambassadour my friend did put off his Cap, so did the new Ambassadour and Marshal twice very courteously to me, I saw it was no time to offer speech to the Ambassadour; now of my giving thanks, taking leave, and requiring his pleasure toward the Lord *Laskie*: so following them to the Court, I passed forward home toward my Lodging.

Mysterio-

Myfteriorum PRAGENSIUM Confirmatio,

Anno, 1585. *Januarii* 14.

PRAGÆ

Iterum veni *Pragam* ultimo *Decembris,*

ANNO, 1585.

+ NOTE. *Anno* 1584.

NNO, 1584, *Decembris* 20, (*Stylo* Gregoriano) we did fet forth, I, Mafter *Kelly*, *Rowland* my Infant, with his Nurfe; and *John Croker*, (in a Coach with Horfe, which I had bought of Mafter *Frizer*) from *Cracovia* toward *Prage.*

PRAGE.

Decembris 30. We came to *Prage* in the afternoon.

December 31. I wrote to Don *Gulielmo de Sancto Clement*, the Spanifh Ambaffador, as followeth:

ILluftriffime & magnifice Heros, Licet mea nondum privata curaverim negocia: pro quibus ordinandis, multos interim dum hinc abfuerim, & labores pertulerim,& fumptus fecerim: Tamen nolui literas ad veftram magnificentiam, à Nobiliffimo illo Domino *Palatino* Syradienfi miffas in multas horas à reditu meo retinere penes me: Ne aliqua ex parte,officio viderer deeffe meo,tam erga veftram magnificentiam; quam ipfum Dominum *Palatinum.* Quantum vero ad Myfteriorum incredibilium progreffum, habeo & quæ dicam, & funt quæ audiam multa ad veritatis caufam (invitiffimis ejufdem adverfariis quibufcunque)elucidandum.De quibus quando opportunum erit, paratiffimus ero, cùm audire, tùm audiri: eo quidem modò, quo finceritati & fidelitati meæ erga *Cæfaream* fuam Majeftatem erit convenientiffimum. Interim aliquot dierum intervallum liberum requiro, ut tam ædes mihi meifque conducam (fi fieri poffit) accommodas, quam ut alia, ad rem familiarem fpectantia difponam, Deus Optim.Max. Magnificentiam veftram ornare beareque dignetur.

Pragæ ultima *Decembris* 1584.
Illuftriffimæ Magnificentiæ Veftræ
Obfequentiffimus,
A a   *Joannes Dee.*

Anno 1585. *PRAGÆ.*

FRIDAY,

JAnuary 4. *I hired the House in the* Salt-*street, of the two Sisters: But Mr.* Christopher Christian, *who had long time been Chancelor, & Register of old* Pragæ, *did make the Covenant or Bargain with me : he had* Anne *the one Sister, to Wife, and the other Sister named* Dorothe , *bad   to her husband. This* Dorothea *dwelt in the House, and was to remove to another House of her own hard by : and to deliver unto me and mine the whole House, with all the appurtenances of roomes and easements, and I to pay for the year* 90 *Dollers : and that quarterly, (every 3 Moneths expired) to pay the quarters rent thereof.*

JAnuary 6. *I wrote to* D. Jacob Curtius : *One of the Emperours Privy Counsayle, of whom the former Records of* Prage *Actions do make abundant mention : And a letter of his written to me the* 8th. *day of* October Anno 1584 , *is beginning of the Book next written before this. The Copy of the letter which I wrote now, is this.*

Illustri & Magnifico viro D° Jacobo Curtio *sacræ Cesareæ Majestatis ab arcanis Consiliis, Domino meo plurimum colendo.*

ILlustris & magnifice vir. Majorine gaudio affici debeam ex bona vestra valetudine, & salvo meo ad *Pragam* reditu : an ex contumeliis hic interim dum abfuerim, contra me confictis, & variis ejaculatis reprehensionibus & quasi nimis , dolore torquetι , penè incertum videri possit. Ego quod statui, hactenus feci : suppellectilem scilicet ex *Cracovia* meam cum tota familia mea , huc jam adduci curavi,cum magnis quidem laboribus meis; & sumptibus haud modicis. Ædes (ex quo jam veni) tales quales , etiam cum aliqua difficultate , conduxi. Et hac presenti septimana, omnia hic nostra ad easdem citissime transferri,remque familiarem, & *Oeconomicam*, quodam crasso modo disponi , negociorum meorum requirit ratio. Interim vestram magnificentiam enixe oratam habere velim , ne ullo modo ægrè ferat, quodeandem nondum inviserim , officioque meo , in hac parte , accuratè satisfecerim spero,quòd una mecum sentire velitis, jure merito in proverbium hoc abiisse dictum.

Satis citò, modò satis benè.

Non solum literæ ad me vestræ, in abitu meo,mihi magno interim fuere solatio o : Sed & absente me , sæpe testificata bona vestra de me concepta opinio magno me delinivit gaudio: de contumeliis igitur, & literis vestris, & veram de me opinione, sive judicio,cùm opportunum fuero nactus ocyum (predictis negociis meis confectis) vestræ magnificentiæ adero,ut aliquid dicam:& paratissimus futurus,ut omnia quæ potero faciam, quò vobis & posteritati constet , fideliter & sincere (prout statueram) a'd sacræ suæ *Cesareæ* Majestatis, ægregia servitia, animnm me applicasse meum.

Pragæ Januarii 6. *Anno* 1585.

+ *Praga Anno* 1585.

January 12.

Saturday Afternoon I removed clean from Doctor *Hagek*, his House by *Bedlem*, and came with all my Houshold to the House which I had hired of the two Sisters (married) not far from the Market-place in old *Praga*.

January 14.   *Praga*   *Actio prima, post reditum.*

Monday Circa 9 horam à media nocte :. Precibus ad Deum de more fusis , & invocato lumine auxilióque Dei, ad ejusdem veritatem intelligendam, & cum virtute tractandam, &c.

E. K. Here is △ one with a Vail afore his face , as it were , a Hair Cloth of Ash-   △ colour : I know him not yet : I see a Garden full of fruit, of divers sorts. In the   LEVANAEL midst of it is a place higher then the rest. On that place standeth a round House, it hath   as may appear four corners, [within] and 4 Windows : and every Window is round , and hath 4   Febru. 5. post round partitions, round also. It hath 4 Doores , and at the East Door is one step , at   ultima parte. the South 2 steps , and at the North 3 , and at the West Door, 4 steps : The first   E. K. Note, Door is white, like Chrystal, transparent : The South Door is red of an high colour,   The House is transparent. The North Door is bright black, not to be thorough seen , as the rest.   round without The West is green, like an Emerauld Stone : So is the South Door like a Ruby. The   and square Doores be all plain. The House within (as it may be judged by the transparent   within. Doores) seemeth to be white, and empty.

E. K. He that hath his face covered , openeth the East Door ; and all the House   1 seemeth to be on fire, like a furnace. The fire within doth weve , and move about the   Fire. House, and by the roofe. Now he openeth the West Door, and there appeareth , as   2 if all the House were a fountain full of water. And there run divers streames , in the   Water. same one water , whereof, one doth go and come , as if it ebbed and flowed ; which stream doth go about all the rest , by the sides of the House; that is, as if it were the Ocean sea compassing the World. The next stream, within that, moveth from the 4 sides ward , and make (in manner) 4 Triangles, or rather Cones , of water ; whose vertices rest cut off (as it were) by the middle stream of water which occupieth the middle or Center of the House, and is in circular form invironed.

An other manner of stream there is, which commeth from the 4 corners of an in-nermost square : and so run *diametraliter* or *contradictorie* wise, toward that circular middle stream.

The middle stream seemeth to issue out at the very Center of the place, and to mount up , and making an arch of his course ; doth seem to fall *circulariter* in one ; circumference.

E. K. The fire also had diversity in it.

△ I would you had noted the diversity of the fires also.

...... *Those that learn truly, learn by parts.*

E. K. The colour of the water in the Center, is most pure white.

The waters of that Saint *Andrews* Crosse , are like a water somewhat Saffronish co-loured. The waters of the Triangles, are somewhat like a watrish blew , which ap-peareth most, in the top of the arches of their flowing :

For all spring otherwise·

The uttermost water , is of Quick-silver shew, as if it were somewhat mortified.

△ In the figure following, you may gather a better and more easie understanding of this Descrip-tion of the water streams.

Here is a blank, or void space in the Original Co-pie : but no fi-gure.

A a a   E. K.

E. K Now he openeth the Fire Door againe: And the fire appeareth in a square place. And there appeare 4 fires filling the whole place, leaving nothing *vacuum.*

One of these fires seemeth to rise from the Center of the place; and to go in low arches to the 4 corners of the House.

The House seemeth to have 14 foot long in every side.

The arches of these fires seem to come from a trunk of fire, which riseth from about the Center: and seemeth to be 4 foot over in the Diameter.

This Trunk seemeth to be high three quarters of the height of the place; The place seemeth to be as high as it is broad.

On the top of this fiery trunk, seemeth the fire to be in form of a fiery Globe, having 6 foot, his Diameter, which fire reverberateth and rolleth in it self.

From the sides of the Trunk (between the said Globe and foresaid Arches,) goeth up fire Triangularly, filling all; saving that which remaineth filled, by the flames of fire, which ariseth from the Globe to the 4 corners of the House, filling all the place above the Globe: as by the figure annexed, more plainly may appear.

Here is a blank, or void space in the Original Copie: but no figure.

E. K. Note The colour of the fire of the 4 arches, is very red; The rest are very pure, Aërial, candent, &c.

The Motion of the trunk fire is swiftest.

The Original Center of all these fires, seemeth to be very little.

E. K. Now he openeth the red Door.

The House seemeth darkish, of colour of the smoak of a Wax Candle being put out.

3 aire.

...... *By it self, it is not, but by the Sunne, it is clear.*

E. K. It hath 4 motions in it also: every one moving more swiftly then the other: All from the middle of the House. Three of them move arch-wise to the sides.

The first and second arise to half the height of the place.

The third occupieth the other half.

The fourth goeth upright to the top of the House.

The second his space (that he striketh against on the Wall) is double to the space of the Wall, against which the first smiteth.

Here is a blank, or void space in the Original Copie: but no figure.

4 Earth.

E. K. Now he openeth the black bright Door; And the House there seemeth full of black dust, like Gun-powder colour, or somewhat of Leadish colour.

E. K. Now he seemeth to goe down, faire and softly from the House, down the little Hill, and from thence goeth by a water side, to a Rockish Mountain.

E. K He speaketh.

...... *Ascend. I am now ready for you: Bring out your Mattocks, Spades, and Shovels.* Enig è veri eri.

E. K. Now come out of that Rock, seven lean men, with Spades, and Shovels, and Mattocks, &c.

..... *Follow me.*

E. K. Now they be come up to the foresaid Hill.

..... *Come*

...... *Come on, Dig till you finde.*

E. K. Every one standeth distinctly one from another, and they dig on the foresaid Hill, which before seemed covered with Earth and Grasse : But now it appeareth to be a Rock, and they dig that the Fire flieth out again of their stroakes, and some have broken their Mattocks, some their Spades, all except two, one with a Shovel, an other with a Pickax.

The Workmen. O Lord we labour in vain.

...... *So you are sure to do, unlesse you have better Tooles.*

The Workman. Alas we labour in vain.

One of them. This is long of you.

...... *I bad you provide Instruments to labour with, but you asked not me, wherein you should labour. Therefore have you digged away that which you saw, and have repulse with that you know not.*

A dark man thou art, and hidden from men, and so are thy doings.

E. K. They stood gazing one on another.

...... *Have you not better Instruments ? Go, provide your selves, and return.*

One of them said to the man covered with Hair-Cloth of Ash colour.

E. K. They runne a great pace to the foresaid Rocky Cave from whence they came out first. Now they come againe with great Beetles of Iron, and Wedges. They knock their Wedges (as we use in Wood) and so break off great Slakes of Stone, like Slate, and throw it down the Hill.

One of them. What a thing is this, that this Wedg is broken?

Another We are in worse case then ever we were.

E. K. Their Wedges are broken, the most part, and the Fire flieth out of the Stone in great abundance.

...... *The nature of this Stone is not to cleave : Therefore if you have no other Instruments you must ce use.*

E. K. They are in great disquietnes among themselves.

...... *Those that go a Journey, provide them Cloathes against all weathers : He that is worthy of the Name of a Conquerer, carrieth with him all Engines : Where the Bridges be broken down, he stayeth not, because he is prepared : Behold, he hath victuals for time to come, and his Study is as well the event, as is the mean. So should true Labourers do : considering what they work in . For the Earth is a Monster with many faces : and the receptacle of all variety. Go home, stand not idle. Provide by Arts for the hardnesse of Nature, for tha one Sister weepeth without the other.*

E. K. They go away speedily.

...... *They have their Tooles to harden, and their Steeles to temper. It will be more then an hour space before they return. Therefore may you spend the time in your necessity, and use the time of day as you are acquainted or womed. I also must over-see them, or else their labour will be without fruit.*

E. K. Now he is gone.

Δ. Gloria Patri, & F. & SS. sicut erat, &c. *Amen.*

Monday,

The same day, after dinner we returned to our former purpose for God his Service, to his Honour and Glory.

E. K. He is here. Now the Labourers be comming out; They have Wedges made long and sharp : and Pickaxes with three pikes very short.

They say. Our trust is, that these tools will serve.

E. K. They fall to work. They make like square holes, and put in their wedges, and break up the rock or blackish stone (like yron-mine, or Magnes stone) in roundish lumps as big as a two-peny loaf, about two or three inches thick. They pick or dig round about the hole first, and so after use their wedges. The Pickaxes have three heads, every pick thereof bigger then the other. The first as big as one finger : the second as two : the third as broad as four fingers. And so after the first digging they fetch three or four cakes or pieces out of one hole, and then they go to another. Now one of them is faln into the ground, up to the arm-pits. Now another is faln in, to the knees. Now the house standing thereon beginneth to shake, and waver from one side to the other. Now the men be gotten out of the holes they stuck in.

...... *Make an end of your labour.*

One of the workmen to the Guide. It behoveth you to find a remedy, or to let us understand what remedy

remedy we shall finde, that you may descend thence: for lo, the peril you stand in, is great: for this Rock was nothing else but a shell, whose kernel is a bottomlesse lake, and a myre quickened with some shut up water.

......You come hither as Labourers, therefore make an end of your work, and stand not idle. If the house fall, and I sink, then is your labour at an end. For the end of your labour is the fulfilling of my will, and the promise which you have made me.

One of them. We are ready to do our promise ; but we are more ready to provide that you may be amongst us ; so you may be free from danger.

......O you of little wit ; are you not ashamed? which of you have dwelt within the secrets of this Hill ? yea, which of you intendeth to fulfil his promise ? Judge not a thing whereof you have, no skill, neither be slack in that you have to do: for the one hath his reward of idlenesse, and the other is condemned of rashnesse: For why? It springeth on her mother ignorance.

They say, If we work, it is against reason. Neither do our tools answer to this labour. Therefore we had rather be idle, then to labour about nothing : for to labour in vain, is to do nothing.

If we were determined to work, how should we perform our determination, since the Instruments of working want ?

......Gather up the pieces of your spades, that is wood, and may be joyned together : The older and the baser they are, the fitter they are to turn up such soile.

E. K. There commeth a Smith by with a budget full of nails.

One of them to the Smith. What hast thou there ?

Smith. Nailes.

E. K. They be like Horshooe-nails.

......Thou cam'st in good time, leave thy nails behind thee, and at thy return I will pay thee for them. See, God is not unmindful of us, for nails are the fittest things to further your work, Joyn therefore your spades and shovels together, and labour.

E. K. Now they are mending their spades and shovels, the iron of them being all off and broken.

Now they work, and throw away the earth like dirty sand, and the skurf of the earth sticketh to their spades and shovels.

E. K. One goeth behinde, and maketh a trench to let the water out from the sand.

One of them. How now ! Have we found harvest in the midst of winter?

......Why : what have you there ?

One of them. Marry, either *Alablaster or Salt.*

E. K. Now one of them knocketh a piece off with his shovel-end, and reacheth it up to his Guide.

......Did I not tell you, that the Earth hath many faces ?

E. K. They work now easily, and cut up *like Salt or Alablaster.*

Now they have digged all the hill away, even to the house. Now the house seemeth builded upon that *white stuff.*

One of them. If we dig any further, we shall undermine the house.

......Go to your businesse.

E. K. They work.

......Soft, soft. Now labour with your hands as softly as may be. Stand aside,

E. K. Now he taketh one of the irons of their spades, and seemeth himself to pare the sides *of the Foundation* under the house, and it seemeth to be a vessel of transparent glasse, and having fire within it.

Timor Domini *......The fear of the Lord is a burning fire, consumeth not, but rectifieth the body ; the old dross it wipeth away, and the daily influxion of the flesh and sin it separateth from the soul.*

Behold (I say) he liveth not, but unto whom life is given : neither is their any joy, but it is ascending ; for the end of joy is glory ; but glory is the consummation of desire, and the beginning of felicity. No man entreth into joy, but by life : neither is there any life, but in the fear of God.

Whosoever therefore hath the fear of God, let him draw neer, and come hither. Number ex-
Ascension *ceedeth not, but by unities. Neither is there any multiplication but by order. For the root of number is one. And things that ascend are dignified by order. Out of this vessel go four vents ascending into that Rock, which is the Root, which is this building.*

Separation *It is said, Behold: let my spirit enter in, let there be Separation made within the house of the North, that the earth may be divided into her members. Cursed be that body, that is not divided, according to proportion, answering to the Division. For she hath yet not cast off the shape of darknesse.*

E. K. There runneth up fire into the house, from out of the round glasse vessel

under

under the foundation of the house. And that fire maketh a great noise (through the black bright or marble door to be hard onely.) Now that North door is mightily thrown open, and there appear in the house like kernels of apples, and slime appeareth, and water thinner then slime, and there appeareth pure water, else.   Now there commeth together stuff like yellow earth, which the fire wrought out of the black earth: And the pure water runneth into that yellow stuff.

......*Of that take a part.*

E. K. The fire returneth back again among the stuff in that house, and there appear of all Creatures some.

Here is *Creation,* and it is the first.   *Creatiah.*

E. K. Now he taketh a lump of the earth lying by, which was thrown up, and he breaketh it into six pieces like round Balls.

E. K. He taketh a thing like a vessel of iron, and putteth *into it that mixture of yellow earth and water.* And it looketh now like grasse mingled with water.

......*Thou art strong, and wilt beget a strong Child.*

E. K. Now he putteth out the earth which he put in, and it is a lump of gold. He giveth it him that standeth by.

.......*so are the seeds of the earth.*

E. K. Now he taketh the second, and putteth it in.

......*Corruption is a thief, for he hath robbed thee of thy best Ornaments, for thou art weaker in the second.*

E. K. He taketh it out, and it is as if it were pure silver.

......*Where there is double theft, poverty insueth. But, notwithstanding, Thou art true; for thou givest unto every thing as much as he desireth: Thou openest the greatest hability and strength of thy power, not such as it hath been, but such as it is.*

E. K. Now he putteth in the third Ball,

......*Thou must tarry, for thou art of an harder digestion, since thou art the third, Content thy self, for thou art not an Inheritor.*

E. K. He taketh it out, and giveth unto one of them that standeth by, that is a red metal like copper.

E. K. Now he taketh up another of the Balls, and holdeth it in his hand.

......*Behold, thy mother, Heat is gone, and the enemy of life entreth; for he that passeth his middle age, decayeth, and draweth to an end.*

Behold, thou shalt find a Step-mother, for thou cam'st out of time.

E. K. Now he putteth it into the vessel.

......*Let cold cover thy face, let the North truly beget thee, for thou art an enemy to thy predecessors. But thou art of great vertue, for of thy excrement shall vertue receive dignity. And thy vertue shall be a garland to Nature; for thou shalt be visible when the other are silent : the Seas shall not hinder thy vertue, notwithstanding, thy vertue shall differ with the Seas : For as they differ, so shalt thou.*

E. K. Now he taketh it out. It is a ragged thing like Smiths cynder of iron, and it hath holes in it, as if it were spongy.

E. K. Now he taketh up another Ball of the earth : he putteth it in.

......*Thou art tractable and like unto an obedient daughter : But thou shalt be the fifth in the second and an Instrument to the first.*

E K. Now he taketh it out, it is like unto a white whetstone, as he shaped it at the putting in, it is like Tynne.

E. K. Now he taketh up another Ball, and putteth it in.

......*Thou art the last that hath in himself and by himself his being: Behold thy face is like unto wax, but thy inward bowels are like unto the anger of a Serpent : Many shall have thee, but shall not know thee.*

One of them by said. Will you give me nothing?

E. K. A great cloud covereth them all, the stone and all.

△ It dured so a quarter of an hour.

E. K. Now appeareth another, none of them before appearing. He seemeth afar off comming, and higher placed then the other, it seemeth to be U R I E L, he hath his face covered with a Skarf of black hanging down to his breast.

U R I E L ..... *Blessed are such as are not offended in the little ones.*

[E. K. He speaketh now a language which I understand not.]

U R I E L ..... *For the Angels of the God of Righteousnesse, are his little ones : and such as know*

                                                                                    not

not sin of Concupiscence by consent (I speak this for your understanding.) Take heed (therefore) that you offend not your selves : for you must become little ones : and the power of the highest must abound in you.

He that offendeth his brother, offendeth God : but he that offendeth his own innocency, is abhorred of the Lord. Lo you are The children of Promise, and in you is the mystery of a great, and mighty Seal. Therefore study to humble your selves, for Humility is the Root of Innocency. But (my brethren) Innocents by nature you cannot be, neither can you serve God in the imagination of cleannesse of your own flesh. Now (therefore) since you are fleshly, will you become innocent ? Or how can you seek that which Nature hath lost ?

In Christ we may become Innocents, and be born anew.

The Scriptures teach you ; That in Christ you were born a-new: And by him you may become Innocents, when in him you are cleansed. Therefore, if in him the state of your Innocency remain, if in him you are renewed, and made clean, (being rotten and defiled,) why seek you not him, as you should do ?

No man that seeketh the brightnesse of the Sunne, goeth under the Earth: Neither creepeth he into unknown Caves. The Tygres seek not their prey upon Earth, where the waters are not. Neither the Eagles upon waters.

Temptation.

No more ought you to grudg that the Lord tempteth you, nor to be offended when the World offendeth you.

Is it not said unto you, that you shall fight a great fight : What fight is it my brethren : But a Battel against the Worldlings and the Devil ?

Kings.

I say unto you that Kings shall be offended in you.

The Sunne ceaseth not, yet he shall cease, yea he shall not be.

The Lights of Heaven keep their course ; but they shall suddenly stagger, and forget their long worne way. Much more shall the wickednesse of those that rise up against you, have an end, for in them is no course but error, and the fire-brands of Sathan, prepared in their own hands, for their own destruction.

* Victoria nostra erit.

Behold, they shall contend against you, and shall despise *thee: But lo I have blessed thee above them: for thou shalt fight against them, and shalt overthrow them : that my Name may be magnified in thy mouth amongst the multitude of the sinfull.

Behold, they are opposite unto thee, because they are opposite unto me : for I have gathered thee from amongst them, and they are become thy Enemies. Since therefore they are thine Enemies (because thou must fight against them :) Be not grieved therefore when their wickednesse doth offend thee: But put on the armour of patience, and Become innocent.

Mundi veritatis,

Dost thou think that from the Heavens can come the dew and life of all things ? Even so think also, that from us commeth no untruth.

Be therefore innocent, and be not deceived by the flesh ; Cast reason aside, covered with her Cloud : And lift up thy self on him, unto him (I say) that hath lifted thee from the Doores of Death : taken thee out of the hands of Butchers, and continued thee for a member of his Glory.

O magna misericordia tua, Domine.

Behold, I say unto thee, The brightnesse of Truth over-shadoweth thee. If therefore, thou dwell in truth, why shouldest thou be afraid ? Considering that soe conquereth and resisteth all her Enemies.

Behold, the World despiseth you, you also shall despise the World.

When the Angel of the Lord powreth his wrath and vial upon the Earth, and the enemies of the Sonne of God, runne in among the sheep. When the self-same Plague that was in the land of Pharaoh raineth in the Houses of all that dwelleth upon the Earth, such as the Lord abhorreth. When the Lord with his hand shall gather up the fruits of the Earth from them, where then shall be their honors ? What shall be done with money ; with that harlot and strumpet of the Earth? Of what value shall their love be then, or who shall regard their friendship?

Prophetia 1589 1590 1591 1592 The Harbour we are in.

In these 4 yeares that are to come, shall all these things come to passe.

And this great joy shall be turned into teares of Brimstone.

Why? you of little faith, you know not how often I have been amongst you : neither the Harbor that I have thrust you into. Notwithstanding you murmur amongst your selves. But stick fast unto him that leadeth you : For he is a sure Guide.

And be not afraid, though the Earth open her jaws against you, for why? I will blesse all things you take in hand, (saith the Lord,) and my spirit shall dwell amongst you.

Δ May I speak ?

E. K. He turneth him to you.

Δ How shall our new proceedings joyne to our old beginnings ? O God, our guide, light, staffe, shield, and comfort, &c.

URIEL. Behold, I teach you, before I correct : But the Doctrine I teach is Humility, Patience [he forceth to speak to one above,] and the fear of wrath to come

After which manner, I have taught them, by thee Δ.

To Redolth, and Curto. Note * I promised the stone.

Therefore, if thou teach Obedience through the spirit of God, appearing unto thee ; Be thou also Patient and Obedient : And Humble thy self unto them, for my sake. Not with the opening of any seal, neither with the Counsailes, that I shall deliver thee ; But with a ready mind, Obediently, desiring to performe that which thou hast promised in me.

I

I am sufficient strength, and will be thy buckler, and if they intend evil, it shall rest upon them; yea when they imagin it, it shall frize within them: And thy goings in and out shall be safe amongst them. *But behold, I teach unto thee a way, which thou followest not. When thou mindest to do any thing, in the name of God, to his honour, to the help of thy neighbour, or thine own comfort:* Go about it whatsoever it be: and begin a Labour; Do that thing thou intendest. *And see that you joyn with one consent towards God and the businesse you are occupied in.*

Then cry out to God for comfort, for light, *and true understanding. And it it shall be given* unto thee *abundantly. For Lo, I say unto thee* [E. K. I understand him not now.] *I will open my hand unto thee, and be merciful unto thee:* And whensoever you *heap up* the Wood together, I will descend and give fire.

Behold, I keep back the rest of my message for an other time. Which shall be ready for you when I find you ready to receive it.

△ I requested to know how I should deal with the Ambassador of *Spain*, or the Emperor, or *Curtius*; Secondly, your *RULE* here given, I understand it not. For I dare not begin any labour without counsel divine: Mans imagination is so weak, &c.

URIEL *Thou hast those that are sent unto thee here for thy instruction, which shall* by degrees *lead thee into the degrees of that thou art to do.*

But it is one thing to receive Corn, and abundance of grain, by the blessing of God, in the return of an year: and an other thing to do the works of the Apostles.

For the spirit of God is twofold: working by information, and influence Cœlestial through the grant of God his good will, in the ministery of his Angels to the information of such as are his faithful and chosen: An other thing to be inspired from God himself, in his holy spirit, imediately comforting and knitting Wisdom together with you, beyond the power that is given unto his Angels.

I have spoken unto you a sound and true doctrine, and have given you not fleshly but Celestial counsel: Apply your self unto it, as the Spirit of God leadeth you. As for those wicked men (that Ambassador excepted) our understanding hath no name of them: We remember them not, neither limit any thing for them. But if thou in thy simplicity and innocency *canst not deal with them, the fault resteth in thy own faith.*

I am gone.

△ Deo nostro Omnipotenti Immortali & Regi Gloriæ, sit omnis laus, honor, gratiarum actio & Jubilatio. *Amen.*

January 16. ✝ *Prage.*

Wednesday, Mane hora 9 ½ ferè

△ Precibus ad Deum fusis, ut nobiscum procederet in sua misericordia & lumine veritatis, non in parabolis solùm & ænigmatibus, sed clara & manifesta veritate, modo qui illi maximè placet, &c.

E. K. I see the man again and the house: the man seemeth to be covered on his face, and so over with a vail of hair-cloth to his middle.

△ When it shall please God, all vailes and *Ænigmata* shall cease.

....*Whatsoever I teach you hath a Mystery. And I am a Mystery in my self. Even so all things that you learn of me, you must be content to receive as mystical instructions comprehending perfect truth, and to be known to such as are true. Some there be that have, and have nothing: yea though they have all, for All, is conteined: But the mysteries of God are infinite, and his grace is not to be determined.*

△ That saying is dark.

That which is All, is conteined. Beleeve you, that we give holy things unto Swine? Or open the finger and workmanship of God unto Sinners? God forbid. Moses *saw God but his hinder parts. The Prophets were acquainted with God, but mystically. The Apostles with the Sonne of God in shadows, and their own impotency. Yea, I say unto you, that she that lyeth in the lap of her Mother, knoweth not but by degrees, for it is the manner of Gods Wisdom, both immediately and by us, to keep back his Wisdom from Hell and corruption.*

Therefore murmur not at that which you receive, for it is not your own. Behold, if you have better, you need it not: for it is vanitie to seek for that you have. Well, since it is given you, Consider what it is, that is given you. Consider also how it is given you, and by whom.

△ We know by whom, as our consciences and faith teach us.

...... *O you of little understanding: Who is he that can and hath to give, but God, Jesu Christ the Sonne of the living God, unto whom all things are given in Heaven, and in Earth, if therefore, All be his, then he giveth. And if you receive it hardly; Consider how hardly you ought to deliver it again.*

And if it be a fire reviving the form of all worldly things: *Then cast it not to Swine: neither yet worship it. Behold, you are men, But in having it you must cease to be men,* for by it you enter

B b upon

Margin notes:
A way of dealing.
Together:
By degrees.
Simplicity.
Innocency.
Mysteries.
Ignis vivificans.
Lapidis P.
Dignum.

upon, and into all *immortality* : And by it *you ascend into the true knowledg of our fore-fathers, and state of Innocency.*

But I hear a voice ; I will depart, and come again.

E. K. Now all is vanished away.

△ We read over the premisses to our comfort and instruction , we beseech God , to continue his graces and mercies, on us, and in us,to his honour and glory,here and for ever.

E. K. Now he is here again.

...... *The will of God is upon me, and snatcheth me unto other things.*

To morrow in the morning, with empty Bellies, *I will tell you what it is you seek;*

△ Fiat voluntas Dei, ad ejus laudem,honorem & gloriam, nunc & semper. *Amen.*

+ *Prage.*

Anno 1585. *January* 17.

Thursday. Mané, circa horam 8. ¼.

Oratione Dominica finita, & alia brevi ejaculatione, pro lumine & veritate Dei obtinendis,&c.

Post quartam horæ partem; venit.

E. K. Here he is now.

△ Gloria, laus, & honor sit Deo nostro Omnipotenti. *Amen.*

...... *Honour and thanksgiving with lowd voices, be unto our Lord Jesus.*

△ Amen. E. K. Amen.

△

Note this
VISION.
Earth of a
tawny colour.

E. K. He hath a great *heap of earth* , or little hill natural *by him of orange or tawny colour, drawing somewhat to a Lion tawny.*

E. K. A Woman commeth , and with a spade diggeth about it. Now commeth a child (a man-child) out of a dark place , with a fire shovel in his hand.

Water.

The Woman hath taken *away all the earth, and there appeareth water, where the earth was.* The boy casteth out that Water with the fire shovel. The Woman laugheth at that. The Woman is in green clothes, and the boy in red.

Green.
Red.

Now commeth a Woman with child, or with a great belly , in white clothes, she putteth her hand down to the ground, and pulleth out *a little Glasse full of red oil.*

Now commeth an old man with a Crab-tree staffe on his back , his clothes of metly colour. This old man taketh the Glasse from the Woman by force, with his fist he breaketh the Glasse, and all the oil runneth about his arm , and *out of that oil did seem a Book to come;* a very little Book.

...... *Plainer, truer, or better can nothing be.*

E. K. He said this, looking on the Book.

1 A Woman.
2 A Child.
3 A Woman
with child.
4 An old man.

...... These four *found, but none HAD FRUIT, but the last. Hear and write the mysteries of God, with humble hearts, not sitting, but kneeling, before* Sanctum Sanctorum.

△ I kneeled, and so prepared my self to the writing. In the Name of Jesus our Redeemer,and the Wisdom eternal of God Almighty.

E. K. He kneeleth himself.

E. K. Now goeth fire out of his mouth streamingly , he turneth himself to the 4 parts of the World, spouting out, or breathing fire vehemently.

An Angel

E. K. Now commeth one like an angel, hovering over him in the aire : and biddeth him Hold up his hand.

An Oath.

...... *Thou shalt swear by heaven and earth , and by him that sitteth on the Throne, that thou shalt open thy mouth, and speak no more then is conteined in this Book,*

E. K. He delivereth him a Book out of his Bosom.

...... *I have sworn.*

E. K. The Angel is gone. Now truly, the place is holy.

E. K. He holdeth the Book in his hand which the Angel gave him. The Book is as if it were of Ivory bone. The Book is open, he looketh on it. The letters seem to be blewish.

...... *There is silence in us, and in the heavens.*

E. K. Now all is full of smoak.

△ Oravi paululum tacimus.

E. K. Now it is clear again. ...... *He seemeth to read of the Book,*

" *Take of your Diased.*

E. K. The book seemeth to be written in the holy Characters.

" ...... *Diased dignified.*

E. K., thought
this is igno-
tum per ignoti-
um.

E. K. —

...... *My brother, leave off thy childishnesse; murmur not, thou hindrest me.*

E. K. He is again in a Cloud. E. K. Now he is cleer again.

And

...... *And Luminus or from due degrees.*
...... *Read it.*
△ I read it. .... *Take off your Dlasod dignified, and Luminus, or from due degrees.*
E. K. He seemeth to labour much about the reading of it.
.... *Gather or take fierce degree.*
......[*I feel no power, therefore have patience.*]
.... " *Notwithstanding, work it diverse dayes multiplying four digestions.*
E. K. Now he is in a Cloud again.
...... *Pray, that it may be given unto me of God.*
...... " *And double then Dlasod, and thy* R o d l n r. [*It is a word which cannot be sounded*] △
...... " *Mend it* R l o.   Corrected
△ Must it be R l o d n r?   thus afterward
...... *Look about you, for Satan would hinder you of Gods benefits.*
" ...... R l o d n r.
" ...... *Diligently.*
...... *Pray, that you may understand.*
△ We prayed.
" ...... *For, until thou watch so continuing.*
E. K. A Cloud standeth by him, and now commeth before him as other times
before: and then goeth away from before him again.
" ...... *it, a holy hour descendeth.*
...... *Note this, very well,* for here you may be cast over shoes.
                    E. K
...... *This Cloud is in thee.* △ VVe had talk of the foresaid Cloud.
" ...... *Of every work there ascendeth one.* Audcal, *and so every Law* R l o d n r.
E. K. Now he is covered in his vail or cloud again.
E. K. Prayed a short fervent prayer, whereat I rejoyced much.
E. K. Now there commeth a beam from above into his head as big as my little
finger.
" ...... *And purpose Dlasod, take a swift Image, and have the proportion of a most glorious*   E. K.
mixture Audcal *and also* Lulo. *Continue and by office seek* R n o d n r *backward by the red di-*   He speaketh,
gestion. But he by the common or red D a r r *doth gather most ripest work, purge the last fortene*   & casteth his
well fixed. Then the four through your [R l o d n r.   arms abroad
[*I said*]Roxtan *finished more together at the lower body by one degree* |bu| *be by you for him*   swiftly.
hold it, for him in one of them.   [*Fortene*]
E. K. Now he lyeth down prostrate.   △This was
" ...... *Until of the last thing.*   added & cor-
E. K.——   rected after-
" ...... *In him become his red and highest degree of his resurrection through coition.*   wards.
E. K. Now there commeth a great thing like a fire, and covereth him.   He speaketh
Now fit up.   swift.
△ We did rise up from kneeling.
" ...... *After a while I come again.*
...... *There is the whole work.*
E. K. Here is again.
...... *Bring forth the book of* Enoch.   *Liber Enoch*
...... *Read your lesson* ...... △ I read the former, Take off your, &c.
Gather your six words, 4 words consist of 6 letters, and two of 4.   Six words.
R l o d n r *read that, in the upper angle descending in the first square.*
It is a great thing to know which is the first table there in Nature.
Deliver the Book here.
△ I gave the Book to *E. K.*
...... *Look where thou* E. K. *seest the letter clear.*
E. K. looked, and saw a spark of light upon R, then on L, &c.
△ He was led by light appearing on the letters to read the six words,
             Dlasod, Roxtan, Rlodnr, Audcal, Darr, Lulo.   Six words.
...... *Here is* Quaternarius *in Circumferentia, and* Quaternarius *in Centro.*
There be the 4 mediating wayes to the Center.
All that may be spoken in that you call Animal, Vegetable, or Mineral workmanship of Nature   Animal,
is here, as in a part of the four. *This far now, more as you desire it. But that you may see, I am*   Vegetable,
a Companion with the rest.   Mineral.
E. K. He is gone.   *Omne verum-*
                                                                                                    vero concordat
                    Bb 2   △ Bene-

△ Benedicamus Domino Deo nostro Omnipotenti, Patri Filio & Spiritui sancto, *Amen.*

Januarii 18.　　　　　　　　　+ *Praga.*

Friday Mane horam circiter 8 ¼

Orationibus fusis ad Deum, ut Mysteria nobis exhibita (hesterno die) explicentur; & ut detracta literæ cortice succus & spiritus veritatis manifestus fiat, &c. tandem apparuit ille cum velo cinereo.

E. K. Here he is, upon a green endlesse plain field, and as I see abroad in the field, so the Heaven appeareth, and all circumstances of the air abroad: but my thinketh, that I am from the earth aloft, and see all under me, as if it were in a valley.

......*Now what have you learned out of that Lesson?*

△ We perceive the grace and favour of God, to deliver us Mysteries in outward terms determined, but in the fruitful inward verity, as yet unknown to us.

The use and fruit of the former Lessons.

...... *Behold I have delivered you (through the Will of God) the true perfect and most plain Science or understanding of all the lower Creatures of God: their natures, fellowship together, and perfect knitting together, which is fourfold.*

The first, the knitting together of celestial influence, and the Creatures below. The second, the centre of every body Essential. The third, the combination of many parts or bodies concurrent to one principle. The last the true use and knowledge of every substance to be conjoyned and distributed. Take a pause—　　[*E. K.* He speaketh a language which I cannot sound after him.]

△ We read the premisses, and discoursed of them.

E. K. Now he is here again.

......*In the Lesson which I have taught you is this knowledge, with the rest contained.*

Note

Therefore seek, and turn the earth upside down. Labour, that you may receive fruit, for unto him that worketh, and hath strength, strength shall be given, and the reward of a workman. Many years, the daughter of long time, are not necessary to the opening of this Mystery. Many moneths have nothing to do here: For lo, it is a labour of one day, for in one day you may understand and to tear this Lesson in pieces, and to understand what every word signifieth.

Note

The place of words and letters.

The number of words and letters.

The joyning of number and place.

But here is to be considered, in the learning of this Lesson, three things: the place that every word occupieth; the place that every letter occupieth, and the number and place that every word and letter is referred unto. For here place and number are apart, and bear an Image of the work that they intreat of.

But number and place must be joyned together, and thereby shall you taste of that which followeth, true wisdome.

Be therefore diligent, and pray for the grace of God, that you may learn and understand. The manner of mans teaching look not for, in me; for I have nothing to do with man. See, how you can digest this:

E. K. He is stept aside.　　　　　△ I discoursed.

E. K. He is here again.

......¶ *Now hear of what I shall say unto you. I will open unto you a Mystery, the key and foundation into the entrance and knowledge of the divine wisdome, delivered unto you in a Science palpable, conteined in letters and words unorderly placed, as a Chaos: and therefore not to be understood but by order to be reduced and drawn into their places, and thereby to be understood.*

Cabalistically

For you have not a letter, nor the form of a letter, nor the place of a letter, but they are all counted with us, as the stars are counted with God. The letters and words working into all reason, as the stars do into the lower creatures: Therefore humbly receive that which I have to say unto you, or shall open unto you as obedient Scholars, kneeling.

First, a little with me praise God—　　*E. K.* He is on his knees.

E. K. prayed the 142 Psalm, *Domine exaudi orationem meam,* and I with heart consented, and greatly rejoyced in the aptnesse of the prayer: as *E. K.* his case chiefly required, and mine also.

.... *I come again.*

E. K. He is gone.

△ We conferred and considered many things to the praise of God, and the contempt of the worldly wisdome, &c.

E. K. Now he is come again.

E. K. Now there commeth a white curtain before him.

.... *Now hear my voice, for thou canst not see me.*

　　　　　　　　　　　　120

One, *Seventy three,* 67, 29. 20

Read— △ I read. ..... *it must be* 120.

.... 33.

E. K. I hear a voice, as if baskets, and earthen pots were thrown from place to place, from one side to another.

105
...... 78. 140. 95. 100. 60. 91.*

K. K. I hear as it were a whistling very basely or lowly, whu, whu, whu, &c.

...... *Say what you have.* △ I read all the 12 numbers —.

~..... *Make a note there.* △ I made *as you see before.

...... 39. *E. K.* Had a very heavy thing on his head : and in his cap it seemed as if it would have crept into his head.

...... 51. 52. 83. 6. 7. 12. 20. 88. *

...... *Note that.* △ So did I, as before, with * as a full point, Notable.

...... *Take thou E. K. also pen, ink, and paper, and note the numbers also, that you may agree.*

E. K. Took pen, ink, and paper.

...... *Write thou E. K. also the numbers that he hath written.*

E. K. Wrote out all the former numbers.

5
5 ...... 11. 13. 23. 62. 63. 141. 9. 81. 18. 26. 54. 123. 105. 14. 27. 115. 135. 137. 10. 64. 46. 59.

△ I became here almost in a sound, I was forced to rise from kneeling. Our guide and School-master bad me go away, and *E. K.* should write out the rest : But it was not our friend that so bad. △

139.	22.	3.	45.	128.	86.	72.	68.	58.	142.	121.	143.
24.	63.	69.	55.	19.	15.	25.	37.	31.	17.	76.	57.	75.	40.
42.	79.	119.	8.	96.	113.	93.	84.	70.	49.	32	17.
122.	136	71.	2.	138.	43.	109.	106.	126.	116	131.
77.	4.	103.	16.	124.	30.	102.	110.	50.	48.	89.
44.	97	101.	81.	129.	130.	90.	34.	98.	99.	65.	28.
112.	114.	47.	144.	107.	132.	61.	133.	134.	66	80.
53.	73.	35.	92	111.	21.	127.	108.	56.	118.	25.
104.	87.	41.	94.	38.	85.	74.

Thou *E. K.* hast all done.

These E. K. very quickly had received, after my going, by shew of bright light representing the numbers upon his paper. But it was a Sophistical shew, as may appear after.

After Dinner we repaired to our businesse, and by and by apparition was made.

...... *And luminous, all one word.*

...... *Now set your numbers, as they follow in order, so orderly over every word.*
△ *Together is to be taken for one word.*

...... *It is so.*
△ There seem to be just 144 accounted words.

...... *Now bring every word consequently in order by number directing you. When you have finished and considered, after 2 hours I will help you again.*

5 ...... *Must be in the place of 23, and must answer And luminous.*

2 ...... *The number over* Comoron, *must be 2 : and not 138. Set all together, I will help your errors.*

△ I cannot do it well this night.

...... *As thou wilt, and when thou wilt, I am ready.*
△ Omne quod vivit resonet laudes altissimi. *Amen.*

+ *Prage.*

Saturday.
Januarii 19 Mane hora 9. Inspecto Lapide statim apparuit, qui ante heri. Post preces ad Deum.

...... *Hear what I shall say unto you. The Word and Testament of* Jesus Christ, *the bread of life, left to the comfort and instruction of the faithful, is such as informeth according to the dignity and purenesse of Spirit in him, which seeketh to be informed. For why, the Holy Ghost helpeth not such as are Lepers, neither healeth such as are sick, unlesse they come seeking him truly for medicine.*

Many read the Scriptures after the same manner, (my brethren) but they are confounded, because they seek their own glory, and not the glory of him, whereof they intreat. Herein doth Satan rejoyce that the Word of God is become an instrument unto him, to spoil the life, (and state to come) of man.

Herein doth he rejoyce, that with the same meat that God feedeth, even with the self same he confoundeth.

For

For *yesterday, when he saw thee* (△) *labour and struggle* with infirmities of the flesh, *he thought a fit time to thrust in himself, and of the same bread that I have given you* (in the power of *Christ*) *to make himself an instrument by turning of* himself into our *brightnesse, to lead you into errour. But not unworthy are you of this mist or darknesse: Read you not in the Scriptures, that he perished that moved himself to stay the Ark unbidden?*

The Hand doth not the part of the body, neither can he that is a *Seer*, and the member of another, fulfill the office of him of whom he is a member.

I say unto thee [E.K.]

Because thou *yesterday wouldest offer up sacrifice, wouldest put thy hand to* that which is not thy office, *and that in the absence of* him, *which is thy body: therefore hath Satan deceived thee, and as the father of lyers hath in a lesson of truth led you so far into errour, that you will never find the way out, if you should follow those instructions.*

For why they are false, and of the Devil.

When *thou wert commanded, saying,* Write; *then write:* But *when thou hast no authority given thee, usurp not.* But *notwithstanding, Humble your selves before the Lord, and kneeling before* him, *Receive you Lessons together, you are but one body.*

△ Thanks be unto our God, which hath delivered us from the snare of the wicked hunter, and is ready to lead us into the path of truth.

...... *Now* write both together, *as you shall hear.*

△ In the Name of Jesus.

.... *The Place is holy.*

Margin notes (left column):

△ I was very sick suddenly, and was constrained to leave off

△ *unusquisq; proprium solum officium faciat.*

Officio unusquisque fungatur proprio.

Mercy and Grace.

∴ 1. 10. 67. 29. 120.   E.K. Now I hear as the falling of a block.

∴ ∴ 33. 78. 140. 95. 52. 60. 91. 39. 51. 65. 83. 6. 7. 12. 20. 88.

∴ 11. 13. 5. 62. 111. 63. 125. 141. 9. 81. 18. 26. 54. 123 128. 14. 27. 115. 66.

∴ 135. 137. 28. 64. 59. 139. 22. 3. 23. 105. 86. 72. 68. 45. 142. 121.

∴ 29. 143. 24. 36. 58. 55. 15. 25. 37. 31. 117. 76. 57. 69. 40.

41. 79. 75. 8. 96. 113. 93. 84. 70. 35. 32. 17. 122. 136. 49. 138

∴ ∴ 2. 92. 43. 109. 106. 126. 116. 131. 77. 4. 103. 92. 19. 124.

30. 102. 110. 50. 48. 89. 44. 97. 101. 82. 129. 130. 90. 34. 132.

87 98: 134. 87. 28. 112. 114. 47. 144. 187. 132. 61. 21. 99. [46] 71.

∴ 42. 80. 53. 66. 77. 16. 111. 133 127. 108. 56. 118. 119. 104. 100.

73. 94. 38 85. 74.

A holy *must be all one word, and so* else where, A most.

Note.

△ I find here 8 numbers double, and 9 numbers between 1 and 144, not served with words, and one to want of 144.

...... *What is it to me, if Satan confound you.*

△ As I put my trust in the Almighty power of Christ our Redeemer, so I most humbly, heartily and constantly beseech him, and verily believe, that he will confound and utterly extermine all Satanical temptations in these actions, else are we nothing.

..... *Beseech God to forgive you your sins. I will visit you at the fourth hour after dinner.*

Deo Gratias.

───────────────

Saturday,
After dinner, circa horam 4.

△ Comfort us, O God, with thy truth, as we intend truly to be thy faithful and devout Servants. *Mitte limam.*

E.K. Here he is.

1 ..... *You have 29 twice, the last 29 must clean be put out.*

2 *You have two Dlasod, you must put the latter out.*

E.K. He is gone.

E. K. He is here again.

3 ..... *Have you not this word* double?

Put two words next to that, Dlaſod and

..... *Look out the number of* 63

Put next to it 125.   .....△ The wicked enemy prompted falſe.

4 .....*You have two* 10

Make the laſt 66.

5 *The laſt* 77 *muſt be* 71.

The reſt will prove it ſelf.

Now ſet the numbers and gather.

..... *Think not that I can erre ; if there be a fault, it is yours.*

Saturday,

After drinking at night, hora 7.

......*Your words and numbers muſt be all one, or elſe you labour in vain.*

...... 1. 2. 3.

△ Which be the words anſwering to thoſe numbers ?

......Take Common Rlodnr   *I will teach you no further.*

△ God be thanked.

.....*Take Common*

.....*I ſpoke to thee in the beginning of* Darr *and* And, *over the which there muſt be* 121 *and* 125

I ſo inſtructed thee in the beginning.

But it muſt be for a new Revolution, *but not for this.*

Put out theſe numbers, let them fall elſewhere.

Note that, in the Margent, *for* the beginning of another.

1   Take
2   Common
3   Audcal
4   Purge
5   and
6   Work
7   It.

Note.
For a new Re-
volution
The beginning
of another.

..... Dlaſod and then *together.*

..... 121 *over* Dlaſod, *and* 125 *over* then.

.. ... *Now doubt not.*

+ *Praga.*

Januarii 20.

Sunday after Dinner, about 3 of the clock. As we ſat together in the Myſtical ſtudy, and the *Shew-ſtone* being before *E. K.* our School-maſter appeared therein.

....*Behold I open unto thee this key, which is not worthy for the unworthy ; neither are the un-worthy worthy of it.   Yea ſuch it is,* as never entred into man before ; *but the body it is, with the image whereof they have brought forth many things, to the praiſe of God, in the* Number *of his Works.*

Take Common, &c. Take hold.

Write it in a paper by it ſelf.

Now you have that you ſought for (you may apply it, and find your own errours) which you are unworthy to receive any ſuch thing.

△ Gloria laus & jubilatio ſit Deo noſtro altiſſimo Domino Dominantium & Regi Regum immortali.   *Amen.*

Januarii 21.   + *Praga.*

Monday.

Mane hora 9 ⅓.

△ Oratione Dominica & aliis precibus ad Deum fuſis, pro ejus gratia & auxilio, per fideles ſuos Miniſtros, & noſtros conatus promovendos, &c.

E. K. Here he is.

△ Benedictus qui venit in nomine Domini, cujus nomen ſanctificetur & exaltetur, nunc & in ævum per omnes gentes.

....*Remember that you are fleſh, and by your works deſerve nothing at Gods hands.*

                                                            New

Now then if you be man, then are you of earth, earthy. But according to your similitude, grafted in the image of God in his Sonne Jesus you are heavenly.

But behold, God is opposite unto you, and his spirit cleaveth not unto you, in that you are flesh, in that you are earth, in that you are filthy: in that you are the children of Satan, and that therefore, take part with him against Christ anointed of the Lord.

E. K. He is out of sight now.

Now if you be opposite, or more contrary to the image of him which dwelleth in you, if you dwell in him what do yee here: why presume you to enter within the Doores of him to whom you are an adversary?

Herein you shew your ignorance; and the lumpishnesse of your fragility, in that you seek of him, unto whom you are odious, or crave the bread which is due and necessary for his children and servants. But hear my voice, Petentibus dat, sed petentibus filiis, & servis, sed non alienis.

Panis

Notwithstanding, of his mercy, and for that, he knew before the beginning of all worlds, the corruption of your vessels, and remembring that you have been of his houshold, mercifully he hath hitherto winked at you, and at your presumption, and fed you with that bread, which is not the bread of sinners.

Upon condition.

But now considering that you continue in your wickednesse, continue in your rebellion against his Majesty, and fight daily under his banner which is accursed, he taketh his bread from you, shutteth up his Doores against you, warneth his servants against you, and is become a fire-brand of wrath against you.

But here you will say: were not we of those number unto whom he made a promise, you were so. But upon condition: That if you would bridle your tongues from speaking evil, and become wholly his. But you are neither his, nor bridle your _tongues: but_ speak Blasphemy _before the Lord, and the_ Messengers _of his light and covenant. Therefore are you not inheritors of his promise. Behold, while the grapes grew, and the corn ripeneth, God did expect your return, for no hour is unacceptable unto him._

But now the harvest commeth that the corn must be cut down and the grapes pressed, you are not as you said you would be, nor as you promised.

Therefore are you excluded, for in the vineyard there commeth no strangers, nor in this harvest commeth any hirelings, for it is not the harvest of man.

△

Now either fulfill your promise and return from the multitude of your sinnes: or murmur not, though you be shut out of Doores.

The earth of it self bringeth forth nothing, for it is the lump and excrement of darknesse, whose bowels are a burning lake.

Hell.

But where the heavens yield, and the Sunne poureth down his force, she openeth her self, and becommeth spongy, receiving mixture to generation, and so is exalted above her self, and bringeth forth to the use of man: Even so the Body when it lyeth in the puddle and hotchpotch of his earthly filthinesse, and darknesse making himself equal with beasts: whose dignity is not, but in their use.

E. K. Now he is here again.

...... _Two things you have to be instructed in, in_ Rl o d n r, _and in the_ Law of Coition and Mixture.

The first, is the instrument working, and drawing things together of one nature. The second is the bounds and termes, wherein every mixture consisteth, and beyond the which it cannot go.

The first of 4 parts, every part conteining, conteineth his conteined double.

The first is Tepens, _this teacheth the rest._

These two things can I open unto you in two revolutions, which is but one dayes work.

But now I cease to open any more unto you till I see the favour of God more open unto you.

After 7 dayes I will come again, until then, I neither am, nor speak.

△ _The mercies of God be upon us, now, and ever,_ Amen.

+ _Prage._   _Jesus Mercy._

Monday.
Januarii 28.   Mane, hora 10 ferè.

Oratione Dominica & aliis pro misericordia divina, fusis precibus extemporandis,

After diverse pitiful complaints of our frailty, and calling for favour, grace, and mercy, he appeared.

...... _Let the heavens prepare themselves to hear, the earth scatter her self before my voice: for I am the Trumpet of the Highest, and the piercing Spirit, dispersed into all creatures, which are from the beginning in God, and made to his glory, and the use of man-kind, that in man he might be glorified._

Give ear therefore, gird up your garments, and scatter your hair abroad before the Lord, which is glorified in me, and through whom I speak; and those are my words.

Har-

Harden not your hearts against the Lord, neither exalt your selves above him that hath created you. But humble your selves, and consider you are flesh, mortal, transitory, and full of sinne.

My brethren, my brethren, sinne and flesh appear not before the Lord, neither such as are sinners, and fleshly vessels apt or fit for the Lord to dwell in.

Understand what the Lord is, and how great he is: a Judg to the wicked, great and terrible: a father to the holy and sincere, just, full of mercy, and loving kindnesse.

If you now therefore be holy, and put on the garments of Innocency, and walk before him in U *righteousnesse; Then look to have the reward of Children; Then look for his fatherly mercies, and loving kindnesse; Then, then rejoyce at the garments of glory prepared for you.*

But if you seek him in judgment, and stir him up to wrath and anger: if you cause him to call the But if *terrible thunders (provided for the wicked) about him, in the most furious flames of his indignation, to gather you together like whirl Winds: if you draw his holy Angel from you, and spoil you of your armes: if he sit down upon the mouth of vengeance, and arm himself with righteousnesse against your wickednesse.*

Then look for the horrible and unspeakable reward of the wicked, and the consuming fire of Justice, sharper then the two-edged sword.

Who hath stood before the Lord in Justice? or who dare quarrel with the highest? What flesh hath seen the Lord in his Majestie? or can appear before him, as righteous?

Tear your selves therefore in pieces, and fall down before the Lord, worship him as a father, and become his children: for his Judgments (my brethren) are terrible, and his wrath is without measure. Many wayes you are bound and tyed unto God; As by discipline you learn.

But three special wayes you have been advanced by him more then your brothers or sisters have bin: The first in the visitation, wherewithal he hath comforted you, and exalted you above the worldlings, of his good, pure, and just Ministers of eternity and light.

Secondly, in that with his own hand, yea, with the beck of his own eye, beyond the ministry of Angels, he hath divers wayes protected you: defended you, yea, and snatched you from imminent and violent envy, and prepared destruction of Satan, at home, abroad, and diverse other wayes, secret and not to be opened.

Lastly, that by their meanes and ministry, which are his good Angels, and minister unto him, he hath guarded you from the wickednesse of your own Country, and hath brought you, ready to place you into the lap of a Virgin, with whom, if you take part; you shall ascend into that Hierusalem, which shall descend, and there live for ever.

Therefore ought you, above all men, to lift up the horn of the Lord, and to blow his praises abroad.

Therefore ought you when others are full of idlenesse, the dalliances of sinne, to humble your self upon the earth before the Lord, and to praise his Name.

Therefore ought you, though all flesh forsook the Lord, and cried out against his anointed, to stand stifly against the malice of the hills, and to be without fear.

O my brethren, therefore ought you (in very deed) to shake off your wickednesse, and to cleave (before the Lord) unto the innocency of Angels, delighting in the one as an eternal food, despising the other as a fire-brand for Hell-fire and the wicked.

△ O Lord, Velle adest nobis, ast absque tuo singulari favore, & auxilio non possumus perficere, quod ita debemus præstare. Igitur Deus.

Lo, behold, your humility is not, you are sealed to the World, and according to the World mea- World. *sure the Lord; Therefore with the World shall you be judged. Therefore shall the Lord sit in judgment against you.*

△ O Lord, what prevaileth us that we are ~~are~~ born? or what prevaileth us that we have heard of the mysteries and promises most merciful of the highest, as concerning our Election, if the Lord will not help us in our great frailty and misery .•. where shall we become on the face of the earth? &c.

...... *Hear me. Fret not in Spirit, for it is not in thee.* △

E. K. Now a flame of fire flasheth in my face.

...... *O yee of little faith! O yee of little faith! O yee of little faith! I have gathered you together as Prophets. But you flie from me. If I had known or foreseen, that to sit on the seat of Kings, had been meet for you, to have had habitation or dwelling with the crafty Counsellors of the Earth would have made you fit for me. If I had seen that pride of the loathsome heaps of money ill gathered together, could have sanctified you before me; Then could I have lifted you up, placed* △ *you amongst the worldly wise, or opened unto you the lowth of the Earth. But I provided you against* Abissum, the *Kings, against Counsellors, against the Governours of the World, to open my judgments, and to* lowth. *bear witnesse of my power. But since you are so full of rebellion, and will rise up against the Lord* △ *that made you, disdain to take part with his holy Spirit, that you may be rectified and sanctified to* Our office appointed. *the performance of his holy will; Hear [*△*] thou my voice.*

Take whomsoever thou wilt, in whose face the Lord shall seem to dwell, and place him with this De novo *Seer, and let him stand seven times by him: I will take the spirit from him, and will give it unto* aspiscendo vi-*another, unto the same that standeth by, and shall have power to see: and he shall fulfill my word,* dente & Na-*that I have begun. But if thou do so, take heed that upon his head there come no rasor; But keep him* zareo Domini *for me.* futuro.

Cc   I

I come again.

△ O Lord God, thou haſt coupled us two together, in thy election, and what the Lord hath joyned, no fleſhly fancy of mine ſhall willingly ſeparate. But Lord, if it be thy will, ſeeing he is ſo hard to give credit to thy holy meſſages, without ſome proof in work firſt paſſed; as for example, this doctrine *of the Philoſophers ſtone*; that ſo he may come to be allowed, though he imitate *Thomas Dydimus* in his hard and ſlow belief, or credit given to thy Miniſters in this Action. Lord, proceed herein, that he may perceive thy power and mercies, &c. And Lord, becauſe he is to re-ceive the pledge of thy mercies, and myſtery of the heavenly food, we would gladly hear of that *holy Sacrament* ſome diſcourſe for our better inſtruction, and his better incouragement to the myſte-ry receiving.

△ After a good while, in which mean time we had diſcourſed of the Sacrament receiving, and of the Philoſophers ſtone making, he appeared.

E. K. Here he is now.

.....*Note well what I ſay unto you.*

E. K. He openeth his face, he putteth on a white garment, he taketh up the four corners of his garment, and putteth them under a broad girdle he hath : on his head is nothing, but *hair reddiſh wavering.*

.....*God, in the beginning, of Nothing, by himſelf, made, created, and gathered together all Creatures; of Nothing, becauſe in himſelf he is.*

E. K. He holdeth up his hands, and looketh up to heaven, and ſeemeth to pray *ex-*tentis manibus.

..... *If he Be, then doth it follow, that nothing is, but that which is God. But God made not all things (made and created) of himſelf, neither out of himſelf: therefore of nothing.*

Underſtand therefore, that God from beginning, and beyond the beginning in himſelf, in himſelf as God, conteined I am and is, proper to himſelf, and for himſelf: But alſo by the knowledge of himſelf, he conteined alſo that Nothing, *of the which in his ſecret and determined purpoſe ſeparated from himſelf, he intended to make all things. It followeth neceſſarily (therefore) that that which was not, had no power of it ſelf, muſt remain after the Image of* IS, *brought or knit together by the Wiſome of God, ſubſtantially in himſelf, whereby Jeſus Chriſt appeared in his God-head.*

But behold, when God the Father and the Son, through one ſpiritual ſubſtance and illumination, from one centre, had gathered together (Ictu Divino) *that* Nihil *ſeparable.*

E. K. He ſeemeth to be conſumed to aſhes in a fire, and ſo lyeth as it were in aſhes proſtrate.

E. K. Now he is up again I know not how.

E. K. He ſeemeth now to be very clear, and in manner tranſparent.

..... *Say that laſt.*

△ I read, But behold, when God, &c. as in the 8th. line above.

E. K. He looketh about him diligently.

.....*Then did he ſeparate that Nothing from himſelf, and as it marvelouſly lay hid in him: ſo marvelouſly he wrought upon it: Not at once inſtant, for then it had been like unto himſelf.*

But in time, which he firſt made out of nothing: when being conſumed, Nothing ſhall *return in-to the place from whence it came. And that which hath offended in nothing ſhall be a ſecond, oppo-ſite from God, and out of God; which ſhall have continuance, world without end: And it ſhall be alwayes vexed, the Spirit of God mediating: not of the ſubſtance or pureneſſe of God, or of his Spi-rit, but with the ſelf-ſame Nothing; out of which God created all things. Seeing therefore, that the Will of God, which is his Image ſeparating Nothing from eternity, in time made all things (being the work of ſix dayes.)* ____ [*But I teach you a Myſtery.*]

Time.

All things that through God are moved to the Center by the Spirit of God, (which is the center of the Godhead) are not after the world, after the conſummation of the world, as Angels and the bleſſed ſouls, *are not to be reckoned with* [that] *Nothing: But are of God, becauſe they dwell in him, of whom it is ſaid,* There they ſhall not need *the Sun nor the Moon, the Lamb himſelf ſhall be their light, and a ſhining lamp for ever. Note here that the Trinity, firſt, ſecond, and third, to-tally not moved, but by himſelf, in himſelf, time bringing forth all things according to his Word, made all things except Man. For why? when all things had pleaſed him, not becauſe they were, but becauſe by the Word (the Image of himſelf, and wherein he is delighted) they were made, he made man, as the Scripture teacheth you, how by the Spirit of God in Moſes, that he ſhould injoy and uſe the benefit of all this ſomething proceeding from nothing in the Creatures of God in their kind: that in him God might be glorified; not onely in this world, which is your earth & vail of mi-ſery; but alſo and chiefly that the memory of his exceeding and great mercy & omnipotency might remain before him in heaven, in the image of man, and the moſt excellent Creatures, world with-out end.*

Angels
Mens ſouls.

E. K. Now he is faln into aſhes again, as before.

E. K. Now he ſtandeth up again, as before.

...... *Here is the making of man to be conſidered: for of the moſt excellenteſt dignified, and neereſt part of* Nothing *diſtributed, as it were approaching neer unto God. God made the Soul of* man,

man, *as a thing knit or tied in the confex of his own Sphere, not taking part with* Nothing materially, *but with* Nothing *Immortal.* Creation of man.

The Soul was made spiritual and increasing, wherein the Philosophers, the wise men of this world are deceived, and hath been a secret shut up in the Book of Esdras, *not fit for the world.* Anima hominis Esdræ book.

For even as flesh by conjunction and commixtion of likelihoods proper in their own nature to bring forth the image of himself ; so doth the most excellentest part of man, taking part with the vicinity of God, (and so perpetually moving) bring forth, after the manner of eternity, every living soul: the Spirit of God (conjoyned with the Trinity) working with him in his infinity. Note of the souls spiritual Increasing. A rare Mystery.

Behold in the beginning God hath not numbred formally *all souls that shall enter into these vessels, or other part.* But the matter material in himself, *he knoweth and hath limited; beyond the which,* Deficiente materia, *there cannot be. Therefore it is* conteined in Number : *Not, that it is contained in Number to be numbred, but within the proportion of number conteined in the knowledg of Jesus Christ, taking part with man, and so to be numbred.* △ So that it may be said, that Deus quasi creando, & homo quasi generando, animam humanam progignit.

Adam fell ; transgressed God his Commandment, and therefore was his soul darkened, bare and naked, because he wanted the beauty and excellency of Gods Spirit, wherein he dignified him, and made him like unto himself, being a living soul. He was cast out, and now casteth off misery, wanting the knowledge of those things, for the which he was created. Now God, the image of his Father, grieved at the fall of man, and moved with pity, vouchsafed, because of the excellency of man, to enter into man, being before separated, into this part of nothing, into man. Not that he would beautifie himself with any thing that man had : But that, Become man, begotten of the Holy Ghost, he might , as you know by the Scriptures, make man acceptable again with God his Father, God himself, with God in unity, for Justice and Terrour is God the Father, Mercy *and love is* God the Son *Wisdome and knowledge is God the Holy ghost.* The Trinity distinct.

He, since he became man, put not on the flesh of man to become a lyar, but that the flesh of man might be full of the spirit of truth and understanding.

E. K. Now he is faln again into ashes.

E. K. Now he is up again.

And so receive forgivenesse of sins, and be at one with God, which is to say, in his favour, taking hold in God, not as created, and from Creation sinful by fall. But by ransome and redemption as bought and made free in Jesus Christ, which offered up the Sacrifice of frankincense, gold, and myrrh, of true propitiation, for the quick and the dead.

Now, my brethren, give good ear what I say unto you;

The wisdome of the Father, in love, created and made man, dignifying him, and exalting him, as the Lord and Master over all Creatures mortal. But how ? by Plasmation. For it is written, Let us make man.

Here thou seest also the Scripture saith, that God took of the Earth. Mark this word, and consider it when I shall apply it. Earth.

Now if this power, if this Plasmating, if this Taking, which was the Word, become man, perfect man ; then followeth it, that man was and is, God creating and created. If therefore this conjunction or knitting together of God and man, bear the image of him, in excellency and power, which created all things, and by whom this Nothing was spread abroad, and had form in his parts : then followeth it, that the self-same God and Man being truth, speaking of himself unto his Disciples, saying, This is my body.

E. K. Now he is fallen again in ashes.

E. K. Now he is up again.

△ *Read.* I read, Now my brethren give good ear, &c.

E. K. Now he holdeth up his hands.

did in breaking of bread, which signifieth the earth, in taking it signified, the power of making, and his own Office, and breaking it before his Disciples, according to the secret sense of mans soul, then being yet alive, give himself in the bread, and in breaking unto his Disciples, as the sense of his word spoken.

E K. He speaketh that I understand not.

did import and truly signifie himself, his very body, to suffer, and suffered in that, in him, in his Godhead and wisdome before the worlds it was so : his very true body and very true blood. But notwithstanding My mistically. *Consider of this.*

E. K. He is gone.

△ Blessed be.

E. K. Now he is here again.

Mark here for whom, and unto whom Christ took , and brake bread : also took the Chalice, and called it his blood of *the New Testament, which shall be given.*

Here you see, that in faith, and Sacramentally *it was given unto his Disciples there, which was also to be given upon the Crosse for the redemption of man kind ; for else, why should he have said, which shall be given?* Note. In faith & Sacramentally.

But

But here my Brethren, in that it was to be given, it was to seal the perpetual and everlasting memory thereof unto the destruction of Satan, and the comfort of his chosen. But in spirit, before, he had pacified the wrath of his Father: Therefore it was given and to be given.

But unto whom? to his Disciples, and not unto strangers; not unto the Scribes and Pharisees, but unto such as did apprehend him by faith.

Here thou seest, that to apprehend by faith, is to be comprehended in the love of God.

But in that Christ said that shall be shed, it signified unto the worlds end: for his blood is always shed before his father, as a satisfaction for the obstinacy and sin of man.

The remem-
brance.
But the remembrance thereof is the power of doing, that he gave to his Disciples, which consisteth in Act, which must be done in the Church of God, yea even unto the end. For as God (Jesus Christ) is said to be a Saviour and anointed, so is he an eternal King, and a continual Saviour of

Christus potest
esse ubique.
such as fly unto him, conteining in man (being dignified through his Godhead) the eternal power of presence and Being, in all places wheresoever.

Consider (my brethren) unto what use should the body of Christ be, if the Body it self were not a Sacrament, and the holy sign of the peace between God and man.

Behold it is said, unless thou eat of the flesh and drink of the blood, thou canst not, &c.

If the Disciples did eat the body of Christ, Christ ministring himself, and standing by, not yet crucified, why therefore shouldest not thou eat the body of the same Christ, which dwelleth in thee, and in whom thou hast to dwell.

But here is to be considered the manner of eating.

E.K. Now he falleth in ashes again.

E.K. Now he is up again.

.... But at whom shall we learn this manner of eating? My brethren, of his Disciples. For although Christ himself alive, visibly and substantially stood beside them, and ministred unto them: Notwithstanding took bread, brake it, and gave it unto them, saying, This is my body: They simply did believe it, considering and acknowledging his Omnipotency (which Peter had grounded in saying, Thou art the Son of the living God.)

If therefore he be acknowledged of us (I speak for you) to be the Son of the living God. Then must we truly confesse, that all things are possible unto him, and that by faith, we ought to believe the mysteries, works and wonders of God, Sacramentally opened and to be used for the cure of our own sores.

[He speaketh I know not what, nor to whom.]

.... *Read:*

Δ I read: But at whom? &c.

And not as the wicked use to do; Tie the power and majesty of God and his Omnipotency to the tail or end of reason, to be halled as she will.

If his Apostles have left us examples of belief, have taught us how to believe, and upon what rock and foundation to fasten our belief; Then simply and nakedly follow the steps of true *Faith,* and laying reason aside, believe.

But here note, that this Sacrament is to be ministred amongst the Apostles, amongst the Ministers and true Servants of God, in his Church, and not in the temple of the Scribes and Pharisees, Hypocrites, and Deceivers, which whilest they tear Christ Jesus and his body after the frowardnesse of their own sense, do eat (as *Judas* did) and so perish eternally.

But I say unto you, and teach you, that wheresoever in the true Church of God remembrance is made, and the use of this Sacrament is celebrated of the true body and blood of Jesus Christ crucified, there is also the true body of Christ, God and man substantial, and bread of eternal comfort and food, to such as humbly, nakedly, and penitently receive it, propitiatory for the quick and the dead; not unto such as are dead in sin, and in hell, and out of this life, but unto such as are here *Sinners, and so dead,* and to be revived. For he that dwelleth in Christ is quick, because he dwelleth in life and light. But he that goeth out of Christ through sin, and in whom Christ dwelleth not, he is dead. *For this, I have said.*

Δ Lord, what shall we say to the Priests, when they would have us to acknowledge Transubstantiation, &c.

Δ
The words of
Consecration
pronounced.
Sub forma pa-
nis.
.... The bread that was ministred by Christ unto his Disciples, was not a figure of his body, but his true body. So the Minister using the office and person of Christ in office, pronouncing the [Δ] words, doth also give unto the people not Bread, but the true body.

But hear me, Thou must consider it as a Sacrament, and must believe as the Disciples did, that it is the true Body of Christ, that thou eatest in the form of Bread.

Δ As concerning under both kinds recieving, what is your doctrine?

.... Caro & sanguis faciunt corpas & constituunt.

Δ Then it is no offence to God, to receive under one kind onely.

Δ As concerning the worshipping of it, being lifted up by the Priest.

.... *That*

...... *That, by faith, (in that it is believed to be the true body,) is also by faith to be worshipped: Not in that it hath the shape of bread, but that it is the body of* Christ, *true God and man.*

△ As concerning also the reserving of it, being consecrated, what are we to understand?

..... *Reason hath no place here: To them that receive it, it is a Sacrament.* But receiving ceasing, the Sacrament *ceaseth also.*

Celebrandi, & accipientibus, Sacramentum & Sacrificium est: Cessante celebratione, & nullis accipientibus, cessat Sacramentum & Sacrificium. Nam Sacramentum dicitur ab institutione & modo.

The mean consisteth in them both.

...... *To morrow you shall hear more of me, in the mean season consider you, How merciful God is unto you through me,* and open this doctrine also unto your wives, *that they may also know God truly.*

△ Gloria in excelsis Deo, & in terra pax hominibus bonæ voluntatis.

1585.　　　　　　+ *Prage.*

Januarii 29. *Tuesday.* Mane hora 10 ¼.

Orationibus finitis, post hesternæ actionis lectionem, apparuit, facie velata, ut prius.

...... *I demonstrated to you, yesterday, how the visible sign: or matter appearing was united and knit unto the visible, significated: wherein and whereunto I answered* in my own form and person, *for whosoever talketh of God and Christ expounding the Scriptures, ought to talk plainly, truly, and openly, that that which they speak may be understood. This is the Office of a Preacher. Even so I talking of God, and illuminated to this Office, for the time, was bare, because I spake not of my self.* But the doctrine I taught you was true: and is worthy to be graved in golden Tables, and monumentally to be placed upon the altar, wherein man may see, as in a glasse, How God through his Sacraments and holy institutions, sanctifieth, regenerateth and purifieth man unto himself.

Now to the work intended, which is called in the Holy Art Gebofal, which is not (as the Philosophers have written,) The first step supernatural, but it is the first supernatural step naturally limited unto the 48 Gates of Wildom; *where your holy Book beginneth. The last is the speaking with God, as* Moses *did, which is infinite: All the rest have proper limits, wherein they are contained.*

But understand that hoc opus unum receiveth Multiplication and dignification, by ascension through all the rest that are limited according to their proper qualities.

Of this knowledg I have laid a sure foundation, have taught what it is, and the instrument wherewithal, and whereby it is. The manner of proceeding, and her Basis. So that there wanteth nothing but the simple and easie unknitting of those things that are wrapped, not with the bands of it self, but with the obscurity and caliginous Cloud of your own ignorance.

But if the Cloud be in you, then by your own help and consent it must be removed,

△ By the favour and help of the Highest we trust the Cloud shall be removed.

..... *Take heed therefore you lift not up your selves in mind, presuming against reason, (whereby you are knit together,) and the will of God: whereby you are taught obedience.*

For pride is hateful before God: and so be in love with your selves is the greatest ignorance.

Shall a dark seller brag or boast of her beauty? because she receiveth light and cleernesse, by a Candle brought into, or shining into her.

No more canst thou, [E. K.] *for the ripennesse of thy wit and understanding is through the presence of us, and our illumination.*

But if we depart, thou shalt become a dark seller, and shall think too well of thy self in vain.

Matter wanteth amongst you, the fire cannot continue, but when you bring more Wood, you shall have more fire, I will not visit you again, until the seventh day.

△ Deo nostro Omnipotenti, Sempiterno vero & vivo, sit omnis Laus, Decor, Gloria & gratiarum actio, nunc & semper. *Amen.*

Art Sancta.
GEBOFAL.
Prima Porta libri sancti.
48 Portæ Sapientia.
Colloquium cũ Deo, summæ Sapientiæ Porta.
Multiplication.
Dignification.
What hath been taught.
What yet lacketh.
Pride.
Self-love.

+ *Prage.*

February 5. *Tuesday.* Mane, horam circiter 10.

△ Orationibus finitis, & specialiter pro misericordia divina super nos tres, [A L.]E. K.]△ ad ejus honorem, laudem, & gloriam.

E. K. He is here now.

△ Gloria patri, &c.

We be unto the World, for she hath appeared before the Lord unpure.

We be unto the Sonnes of men, for they are the dwelling places of the beast.

Fames.   *We be unto the seed of the earth , and unto the seed within her , for she is touched with fire from on high , and is trod under the feet of the Highest.*

Who is he that girdeth his sword unto him : or what is he that is ready for the battel? such as have forsaken the Lord and are run astray : and hath placed himself with the scornful.

Justi oppri-   *Great sorrow is at hand unto all flesh : the just shall be troden down, and the streets shall bear*
mentur.   witnesse of them.

Bellum.   *For there is a Battail proclaimed in Heaven, and the God of Hosts hath put on his armour, and is become a fire of wrath.*

Now commeth the time , that such as forget,fear not God, shall fall down Headlong, and such as have been lifted up, runne astray and down wilfully,

Happy is he that endureth and appeareth a Labourer before the Lord, for he shall enter into his holy hill, and shall be crowned with the Victory.

Such as God coveteth, they flie from him : yea,such as serve at his Tables, become his enemies.

What therefore shall I say ? I make seed,but I reap it not : I build, but I enjoy not.

△ Be merciful to us,O God , and help our frailty, purge our filthinesse, and create a clean heart in us, &c.

..... *The sinner knocketh and is heard : but he that is just entreth,For into the Sanctuary of the Lord, no unclean thing commeth , for being cleansed, they enter.*

He that is a Prophet, or an Apostle,or a Servant called , by the mouth of the Lord, and so sepe-
△   *rated from the rest , let him do his duty; First, that he make himself clean before the Lord ; And*
Make clean   *then may he bear , and sit in judgment , against the impure and unjust , and may see the works and*
first.   *wonders of the Lord in his holy place.*

Laboro vos, ad nauseam.

E. K. He is gone.

△ After an hour we had discoursed together, I fell to this Prayer.

△ O Lord thou hast heard our conferences, discourses and resolutions : O God, be our comfort, and reconcile these repugnances of purposes , so as it may appear that thou art the merciful Father, the almighty and living God , the Creator of all things being, and that thy promises made in mercy and favour, shall not with mans frailty be overthrown, or hindred. *Manifest thy power and glory to us herein, that thy Prophecies may come to light , to the end and purpose thy Wisdom and power may work thy own honor and glory.* So be it.

E. K. Now sir, where are you?

...... *Here I am, the servant of God.*

Unus vestrum, vocatus est hujus negotii minister.

Alter, Puer.

Igitur ad impleat minister ministerium : Puer autem humili & se ministerio.

Parabola de   *Understand that.*
sene nudo &
puero.   △ I remember the old Parable told us of a man naked, who cloathed himself with leaves , and of
Sap. d 13.   a child, and a Whale, &c. *Anno 1584. Aprilis* 21. *Cracoviæ.*

Hear my counsel, and follow it.

Consilium.   *Wonderful and great are the secrets and judgments of Gods determinations to come : which are all ready leafed and gathered into your bosome.*

A similitude of *They are great and true : and are like unto the Rainbow which the Sunne maketh by the aptnesse*
the Rain-bow *of the matter and place (that sheweth it self suddenly and many behold it :* So shall the harvest of this
very apt.   *Doctrine, when the Vial is runne , and the World receiveth disposition , shew* himself wonderful and terrible to all Nations.

But if the matter agree not with the weaknesse of your understanding , and palpable blindnesse ; Repine not, neither murmur. But pray, that you may have the spirit of God, to understand , and that your eyes may be opened.

△ **Regum lib.** The Prophet [a] saw , but his boy did not.
4. cap. 6.
C. Elizeus.   But the Prophet praying, the boyes eyes were opened.

Dee.   *These mysteries are delivered and taught to a Minister apt for them through the Grace and fore-knowledg of God, wherein he hath blessed thee,*Dee.

Unto thee is joyned the dignity of this mans vessel, which ministreth unto thee,as a servant.

He therefore is not part of the labour, but part of thy knowledge.

Kelley.   Kelley, True it is; that this rain falleth out at thy request. But lo, thou art let into the garden,
Mirabilia Dei. and art preferred before all others , as a gatherer,that the wonders of the Lord may be finished in his
Our own judg- House.
ment is to be   Therefore seeing thou art let in as a servant, not as a *J U D G, lay Judgment aside, and do thy*
laid aside.   *duty.*

So

So shall it come to passe that *the minister, through thee, shall be satisfied,* (*as through the labour of a necessary*) *and thou through thee satisfied, shalt be satisfied also.*

In the mean season gather thy self together, fear God truly, and humbly *go home unto thy Mother.*

Endeavour thy self to know things necessary for mans understanding, whereby thou shalt be apter to *judg,* and to take part with the *Spirit of God.

I promise thee, if thou do so, that the Spirit of *understanding in all humane knowledg and divine, sufficiently for thy* Profession, Calling, and Creation *shall multiply* upon thee.

△ I presume not to interrupt your discourse of matter, but as we are knit with the Lord *A. L.* in league of friendship, for the Service of God, so doth charity, and the order of our affaires require that somewhat we should understand of his present estate, &c.]

...... *Cast pride away and be humble:* for *he that hath an humble spirit knoweth much.*

Et cum puer Prophete, es, ab illo quære, ipse te informabit.

Video & circumspicio, sed non video, Lasky.

△ Oh Lord, what is this, what is this ! Oh Lord !

...... *Sedem posuit Satanus in cor ejus, & neglexit mandata Dei.*

Si qua dixi feceritis, bene fiet vobis : Sin minus, fiat vobis, sed bene mihi.

△ Give me leave to speak I pray you,

...... *Fio, loquendo, mater.*

△ If *Lasky* fall, (upon whom so much of our worldly doings is grounded, as the House-keeping, still in *Cracovia,* in hire for an year,&c.) How shall we supply the wants? &c.

..... *Si ceciderit, statu.*

Unicum habet [A.L.] *à cælo secum relictum.*

But iniquity and negligence causeth him avolare also, of 21, *this is the last.*

△ O Lord, Lord, Lord, have mercy upon us.

...... *Consider this last counsel for I can counsel you no more. As your fight is, so shall you see me.*

△ I beseech you let me know your name, if it shall not offend you to ask.

...... *Sum sanctissimi sigilli fœderis centrum.*

△ Are you the same that is about the Crosse in the Center?

...... *I.* [L✝na] △ Then are you *Levanaël.*

Leva. *Relinqua, sed non desero.* ∴ E. K. He is gone.

△ *Gloria, Laus, Honor Deo nostro Omnipotenti. Amen.*

△Through E. K. to be satisfied.
△ *Ad Ecclesiam Catholicam Matrem omnium fidelium, redundam est.*
△* *Is Ecclesia Catholica.*
A promise to E. K. of great importance.
A. L.

A.L. *Non apparet in conspectu bonorum.*

A. L. *Unicum bonum Angelum jam sibi habet relictum.* Habuit 21. *ultimum consilium.*

Sigillum fœderis.
∴
△ *Lib. 2. In Sigillo Dei.*

✝ *Praga.*

Februarii 18.

Monday   Mane horam circitèr 9.

△ *Orationibus ad Deum fusis, & aliquantulum de* E. K. *quantum ad mysteriorum participationem præsentem : ut misericordit̀er nobiscum agat, & illius* [E. K.] *intentionem, & fidem Catholicam respicit, & ut sua divina bonitas nobiscum procederet in mysterio perficiendo; viz. de lapide Philosophorum, propter honorem & gloriam sui nominis, &c.*

E. K. I see an endlesse thing like a red Sea. A head cut off from a body doth appear: Shortly after. the Hair hath bin pulled off it: that Head appeareth to come out up of that bloudy Sea, tumbling sometime one part, and sometime another upward, and sometime under the water clean.

E. K. Now I see a Tree upon an old Hill full of mosse in a desolate place, besides the former water.

The Tree is sprung of a graft, which hath been grafted in ∴ The Tree hath a few green leaves on, and many old leaves: The state of the Tree is as if it were *Autumn.* There lyeth by it the top of a Tree cut off, and dead withered.

The Tree hath a eleven Shots or branches issuing out of it.

There tumbleth down from heaven a white thing, and out of it issueth an arm with a broad axe in his hand, such as they hew pannel board with, it seemeth to be about a yard long

That hand with his nail maketh a race down along the body of the Tree, and then spreadeth the bark open from that place of the race made.

Quod erit, & futurum est, est & non est,

E. K. That voice seemeth to come out of the top of the Shew Stone.

A voice.

E. K.

E. K. On the place of the Tree where it was made bare appeared two figures of 8, one in manner under another. Now the bark is put together again, and the Tree seemeth whole, and as it were not cut.

A voice out of the white. 10 branches cut off of the grafted tree.

Quod erit & futurum est, jam est.

E. K. At this word he strook off ten of the Tree branches, and the stem or branch that standeth, seemeth to be now between me and the Sun risen about an hour high; And that stem or branch hath five lesser branches out of it.

Every.

E. K. Now there standeth *one like Michael,* with a tanckard in his hand of silver and stooped, he saith;

Mich. ...... *Iterum Lavabo te.*

E. K. He washeth with water, and his hands the old branch cut off. Now he taketh that old branch up in his hand, and holdeth it up. The ax is torned from the tree.

A voice from the top of the stone.

..... *Plantavi te, & neglexisti mandata & statuta legis mea, & in superbia tua defalcavi te: Sed jam memor sum verborum & pacti mei apud patres,* & occupabis locum solitum, *& ipse rorabo te nubibus cœli. Jam ponam timorem in cor tuum, & visitabo te legibus meis, & introducam pedes reductos in Sanctuarium: Neque cades, sicut patres tui ceciderunt; Induxi gentem malam & superbam, & benedixi ei, (sed proh dolor) tadet me. Igitur dejeci, & præcipitavi illos à me: Ne forte triumphantes posuissent nullum Deum.*

Michael...... Magnus es tu Ben Elohim, *magna est gloria tua, magnitudo tua superat cœlos, & jam regnabis in terris.*

Regnum Dei in terris instat.

E. K. Now *Michael* putteth on the dead bough on the former tree: Now he with the ax with his thumb, closeth the barks together.

Now out of heaven commeth drops of a rain, and that stem which was so put to, had 12 branches; and both that and the rest springeth together very freshly.

Michael. ..... *Qui habet oculos videat, & cui sunt aures audiat.*

Dee

E. K. Now appeareth one like △ under the tree.

{ *Dee*
{ *Kelly*

E.K. or Safeguard.

And also I see my self (said *E. K.*) comming there, and my *Gown* is *all white,* but *bebloudied :* and △ seemeth to have a white Gown, or rather like a womans safeguard full of pleats, and full of mens eyes.

Seven more.

There appear seven more, six men and one boy. One is a Blackamore.

They have all white garments also.

The tree at the first seemed to bring forth and shew horns, and after that there appeared men issuing out or growing plentifully on that tree, and those men to have those horns.

Then he with the Ax pulled one of those men off, and pulled one of his horns, skull and all, *and thereof gave to eat to* △, *E. K.* and the other seven; and they *did eat :* and so all the Vision did vanish away, nothing appearing in the stone.

A voice.

..... *Ista ad rem ; Vos autem post modicum admonebo.*

—— △ After half an hour, wherein we talked *de Conversione Judæorum.*

E. K. Here is now *Levanael,* as before time.

Levan. ...... *O thou which art of the seed of the earth, attend my voice, and open thy heart, that thy bowels may be filled with gladnesse, and that within thy head may wisdome enter, since God hath not onely called thee, but also hath made a choice in thee,* If thou hear his voice, and obey it.

If

Be not stiff-necked, neither suffer sensual imaginations to obscure or defile thy inward understanding. The first nourisheth thee to the nourishment of thy flesh, that thy flesh perishing may also carry thy soul with it. The second teacheth thee to understand thy self, and thereby to acknowledg the Creator : that thereby thy soul purified may also purifie thy body : that thereby in the end thou mayest rise a purified and perfect Creature.

Behold, there are which rise; and have lost their bodies: and there are also which rise, and they rise in body.

Qui appetit se propter se, non intelligit Deum, sed qui intelligit Deum, appetit seipsum ; sed appetitus ejus non est à se, sed ab alio.

Since therefore, to seek God [me] *for your own sakes, is to glorifie God, lift up your selves, and behold the heavens, and look into the earth, and muse at her wonders : And let not the lesser part carry away the greater.*

E. K. I pray you speak higher, I can scarce hear you.

Those that have their Sanctification through promise, and fulfilling of the Will of God, have always wayes forsaken themselves: But yet, for themselves, followed his Commandements ; Therefore I say, forsake your selves, and do the will of God, that for the comforts of your selves, and your e-ternal salvation, you may seek God.

But he that seeketh God, seeketh him through patience, through afflictions, through temptations. Therefore despise this Monster that tempteth you, and neglect her in the middest of her pride, for she is poor, miserable, and prepared as a fire-brand for destruction ; if you seek riches of her, she hath none, if you seek wisdom at her, she knoweth it not, if you desire quietnesse, and the joyes of rest, she cryeth out against you, Watch, Watch, and gird up your selves. Patience.
Afflictions.
Temptat.ons.
Mundus.

And if you seek eternal life, or study to please God, and to glorifie him, whereunto you are cre-ated, seperate your selves from the Harlot.

Swear your selves her enemy, and hate all those that take part with her ; For, behold, she is be-come an enemy of him that created you, a Blasphemer of him whom you seek to glorifie, the daughter of him, which set himself against the Highest. A mundo &
mundanis de-bemus esse ali-eni.

Therefore for your Creations sake, ought you to despise her.

For your Redemptions sake to neglect her, and for the Glory that you seek to attain unto, utter-ly to despise or contemn her.

But here, peradventure, you will say unto me, as he said unto Christ the Sonne of the living God.

E. K. He maketh cursy, and kisseth the ground.

What shall I do to enherit everlasting life?

I say unto you follow the Commandements.

Behold, it is written, I give you a new Commandement; Love one another.

How love you one another without Charity? Love.

But what is Charity? is it not the gift of the Holy Ghost? you know it is so, you know also, that the Holy Ghost is called a Comforter.

But consider with your selves, why he is called a Comforter ; Not because he comforteth him-self, for he is all comfort ; But because he is the comfort of such as he hath spoken to, saying, I have given you a new Commandement, Love one another ; But, who are they? Even they that eat the flesh, and drink the bloud of the Sonne of man Jesus Christ, the Sonne of God, true God and man, which unlesse you do, you are not of that Company unto whom Christ said I give you a new Com-mandment.

For in so doing you are grafted in Christ, are subject to the Commandment, tyed unto Charity, wherein you are refreshed by the Holy Ghost the Continual Comforter, and giver of wisdom to such as dwell in Christ.

See therefore that none is of Christ, that hath not Charity, neither hath any Charity, that is not of the Company of such as feed of the flesh and bloud of Jesu Christ, without the which there is no Salvation, therefore art thou E. K. a lyar when thou sayest I fear God, I love God, I intend to live well and in obedience, for thou followest not his Commandements, thou fliest from him; There-fore thou art not with him.

But I hear thee saying, I confesse my self to Christ before the Throne of God.* Δ e. K. did
confesse that
he thought so
at this instant.

But thou hast not offered thy self unto the Priest, neither hast laid down thy Sacrifice. Penance.

I say unto thee, Thou confessest not thy self, neither thy sinnes, before God, because thou com-mest not where he is. The Church.
Ad Ecclesiam
Catholicam
confugiendam.

Not that God seeth thee not, but that he is said not to hear sinners, unlesse they be penitent, but penance is limited by the Church, and sorrowfulnesse is not judged by thy self, it behoveth thee therefore, if thou wilt flie unto Christ, to enter into the Company of such as professe him, where he is, and with whom he dwelleth.

There, at what time thou repentest thee of thy sinnes, and shalt confesse them with sorrowful-nesse, before him which is in office at the mystery ; there also by the mystery (which is Christ) shalt thou receive forgivenesse of thy sinnes.

For if he that ministreth, is heard in the power of his Administration, and Sacramental vow, much more hath he power to forgive Sinnes ; For lo, that he doth, is not of himself, but his digni-ty is of that, whereof he is called a Priest.

Now therefore I say unto thee E. K. until thou make thy self clean, thou shalt continue filthy, & immundis & impuris, non revelat Deus Sacramenta.

But even as thou, not clean, seest, and yet seest nothing : so being cleansed, not seeing thou shalt see, and see all things.

I have done.

Δ *Gloria Patri & Filio & Spiritus sancto, sicut erat in principio. & nunc & semper, & in secula seculorum.* *Amen.*

1585.   ✠ *Praga.*

Februarii 23.
  Saturday   A meridie horam circiter 2.
Orationibus ad Deum fusis, pro luce & veritate divina, &c.
  △ The occasion of this comming to the Shew-Stone, was that as we sat together in the Stove, there was a pat or stroke or two (not natural) given on the Bench and Wall : and withal I *felt on my head a heavy moving thing,* and also after that *E. K.* felt on his back, as if one had written letters distinctly : whereupon we went to understand the will of God, as being thereto half warned and stirred by these tokens.
  E. K. Madimi is here.
  △ Benedicti sunt pedes evangelizantium pacem & favorem altissimi.

Madimi ...... *What should I speak unto you, since you have no faith?*

Why should I teach you that despise my documents?

I knock in vain, for you hear me not.

Unus unam alius aliam quærit : dispares estis.

  △ Deus potest omnibus & diversissimis satisfacere, bona semper petentibus.

  Madimi ...... *Shall I speak, or no?*
  △ Speak in the Name of God, who would not hear the words of the wise and of the mighty, of the good and true?

Mater.
Madimi.
  Madimi ...... *Shall I close my mouth, because of your wickednesse? or shall I open my mouth, because my Mother hath commanded me?*

I will go back, and will desire that my mouth may be sewed up with a double threed's for assure your self I will not come again willingly : But if she say again, Go, I will come.

Hui, wherefore doth God give bread to Dogs? or suffereth his sonne to shine to the bottomlesse Caves? I know a cause, but yet I am torn in spirit.

O Mother, Mother, if thou shouldest speak unto this people, out of and from above the Clouds, they would melt before thee, yea, they would fall.

But lo thou speakest unto them by thy daughter that they may stand and hear, but they hear not : But I swear unto thee, they despise thee.

What shall therefore become of them? I go, I will see if I can absent my self from them.

  △ She went away as if she had been angry, in the mean space we argued after our former manner ; *E. K.* as he was wont, and I still in my constant hope of Gods mercies.

After half an
hour.
  E. K. Now she is here again.

  E. K. She putteth off her peticoat, and putteth on an other Garment full of pleats of a golden colour, and after that an other Garment, upon that Garment with many Crowns bordered on it, with hands out of every of them, and a great part of the Arm, they are right hands, the first Garment (which she put off) and flingeth it into a fire.

  Madimi ..... *I speak unto you, though I say nothing.*
  Madimi ...... *The counsels from above, are perfect, because they descend.*
Consilia Dei.
  But the wrappings of mans wit, are unperfect knots, hard to put together, and harder to unlose : Therefore they are not.

Imprisonment
conspired a-
gainst me.
△
  But these are of God, and they are true. Envious minds, and false hearts, do hunt after thee, and they have said and have *conspired ; But I have said unto them, be it unto them, as they have measured unto others : And that which they have nourished in corners, let it be fire, and consume their dwelling places ; Let it seek out their brothers : Let their throats be burst in pieces : Let it range along their Kingdomes, and let it burn down the gate of their borders, that the way may be wide : for a narrow way serveth not where I bring in mischief, I will bring her to the borders, and will place her in the Gates, and will say unto her.*

Accipe tibi vim.

  And I will give her a two edged sword, but I will not enter in with her : because I will not hear their Lamentations, neither be moved with their groanings.

  These are the hard and heavy knots, that the evil spirit and mans wit hath wrought togther ; But because they are humane, they shall perish.

The way is
prepared by
A. L.
  Truly it seemeth good to my Mother and me : and our consent thinketh good also, (and the rather because she hath prepared the way by her own wisdome, which part of the North you must always (look unto), and be directed by.

  For why, that Constellation is true, and doth teach those that erre ; Those also that are right, it comforteth them.

But

Faith

But *I will go unto my* Mother, *and ask her once more,* whether I may hide these things from *on.*

E. K. She is gone.

△ We read over the premisses, and gathered, that some treachery was devised against me: And therefore, I beseech God, to give us his counsels, and advises, to be my guide and protector, my light and comfort.

E. K. Here she is again.

Madimi ......*That you both, or (if you will be distracted) one of you, go secretly* hence, *and speedily unto* Lasky: *So shall it come to passe, that he whom they intended to imprison,* (saying, we will compel him to perform his word, leaft he peradventure triumph elsewhere against us;) [&] *may at last, open the* Prison Doores *for them, and* salute *a strange King, even in the self same place, where they shall eat to morrows Dinner.* But when they perceive that you are gone; *Then will they understand and that you knew,* and that the spirit of God *was amongst you.*

  I come again.

E. K. She is here again.

Madimi ...... *If these words be true, bear witnesse of the truth:* if you think them to be false, you need not follow them.

△ How soon would you advise me to be going hence? you see how bare I am of money.

Madimi ...... *Do so as in an eminent danger.* I have spoke the last word. Sed adhuc tria; Omnia succedent voto.

△ Deo nostro Omnipotenti, sapienti, & misericordi, sit omnis gratiarum actio, Laus, Honor, & Gloria, nunc & semper, *Amen.*

Sapientia divina nostra debet esse stella nauticis in hoc mari magno.

Flie from Prage.
The words of the Conspirators.

Spiritus Dei nobiscum.

Monday

Februarii 25. à meridie, circiter 1 ½.
Precibus ad Deum finitis, citò apparuit Angelus Dei.

E. K. Fell on his back as one had written as he sat at the Table; Hereupon we resorted to the Shew-Stone, &c.

E. K. Here is *Madimi.*

Madimi ...... You have vowed to your selves, and to the Lord, perform your vowes. *That which God commandeth, that do.*

Excuse your selves with men, and gird up your Garments *to the travaile;* Not in Waggon, but on Horse-back.

E. K. I pray you to give us some instructions of my Lord *Lasky* his being.

Travaile hence directly, and unto Wratislania, *and there I will meet you.*

E. K. I pray you to deal openly with us, according to our frail state, and to declare unto us of my Lord *Lasky* his estate.

Madimi ...... You depend not upon *Lasky,* but *Lasky dependeth upon you;* if he do evil, his punishment is ready: *if he do well, he doth it* for himself.

I am greater then you, and my eye stretcheth farther then yours; yea, though you went to morrow, you have lost some dayes.

△ I must carry my Books with me, we must be at the least three horse.

Madimi ...... *Not so, but* thou shalt hide them.

△ Am I to return hither again, before my wife come from hence?

Madimi ...... *I am not flesh, neither do I move, or am moved with flesh;* But if you fulfill the first, the rest followeth.

Do this, as though you committed theft,   △ Secretly and speedily.
for if the hours be diminished, the purpose shall also want successe.

Duetus es, sequere si vis.
The hand is open, and ready to take hold on you, what therefore shall I say more to you?
△ What hand I pray you?
Madimi ...... *Manus amplectens non rapietus.*
△ Lord I understand not that neither.

E. K. She is gone.

△ In manus, tuas Domine, Commendamus nostra corpora, animas nostras & spiritus nostros.
Amen.

A. L.

Dayes.

Books to be hidden.

Houres.

Wednesday.

February 27. △ I and **E. K.** and *Thomas Kelly* as servant, rode to *Limburg,* (otherwise named *Nimburge,*) six miles from *Prage,* in the way toward *Bressel:* otherwise named *Wratislania.*

Februarii 28.　.Manè circa 6 horam.　*At Limberg.*

Thursday. Note, I had caused from 4 of the clock in the morning the Horses to be looked unto, so as, by five, or assoon as it was break of day, we might be riding.

In the mean space while *E. K.* yet lay in his bed awake, and I was in the next Chamber by, in ordering my things of my male. *E K.* heard a voice (like mine) say D.

Whereat he asked me, what say you? I answered, that I spake nothing. Then he doubted what creature did use that voice. Afterward he rose: and when he had been ready a while, and sate in the Chamber where my male lay, he said, that he felt somewhat crawling, *or as one writing on his back,* and at length *to ascend into his head.* And so I left him, and went out into another place, and kneeled to pray, and prayed, and upon the comming in of *Thomas Kelly* into that room where I kneeled (in the Door of a little open Gallery over the street) I rose up, and went in again to *E. K.* and he told me that he slumbred by reason of the heavinesse of his head; and *that he seemed to see me praying,* and Michael *to stand by me.* I answered, that truth it was I had been somewhat bent to

A Vision.
prayer, but that I could not pray as I would, &c. Hereupon; *Immediately he saw* Michael *over my Head with a pen in his hand:* Thereupon I was resolved that I was to write somewhat of importance: And I made speed to take pen, ink and paper, and to settle my self to writing, because we made hast to ride, as intending to ride 8 or 9 miles that day, and company tarrying for us: one of them being a Jew, whose sister is wife to Doctor *Salomon* of *Prague* the Jew, &c. And going about to attend for something to write, a voice said, as followeth.

A Voice.
Cur non includis te ad audiendum vocem meam?

△ Hereupon, I did shut all the Doors, and uttermost Doors.

Note the reason why a Receptacle is of more credit.
A voice ...... In receptaculo, ut magis approbetur veritas.

△ Hereupon speedily I took out the Shew-stone, and set it on the Table before *E. K.*

Madimi.
E. K. Here appeareth a white Circle round about the border of the Stone, and a ball or Globe of flaming fire in the midst; The white Circle hath great brightnesse of light in it.

E. K. Now here is *Madimi,* she standeth in the white Circle: and looketh into the fire, she kneeleth.

On the outside of her, standeth *Michael* with a sword.

E. K. Madimi is gone away, and *Michael* is come to the lower part of the Circle.

A voice ...... Speak, *for who controlleth me?*

E. K. Michael boweth himself toward his feet, as though he kissed the place where he stood: as if it were the Circle that he kissed.

Michael ...... *These are the words of the Lord, and of me his Angel, and Minister of truth: and they follow.*

Behold, I have led you forth divers times: and you have obeyed me. Therefore I say unto you, Be now Stewards of more.

△ O merciful God.

E. K. He spreadeth his Arms abroad, and stoopeth down.

Michael ...... *He that committeth his Treasure unto man, findeth favour, and at his return hath his own. But he that committeth himself unto me, and heareth my voice, I will write his Name in the Book of Life. Behold, Behold, Behold, I swear and it is.*

Dee.
That in thee, Dee, I delight. And lo, because thou hast obeyed me, and not of force of humane perswasions, I shew unto thee what is to come, and what I would have thee to do: and wherefore thou commest hither.

△ Fiat voluntas Dei.　　　　　　　　*E. K.*

Michael ...... *Cover me for a while, lest peradventure thou see I am beyond the ability of thy capacity,* and so return not easily.

E. K. He becommeth very bright.

△ I understood not well this saying, neither *E. K.*

Michael *I say unto thee cover the receptacle.*

△ We covered the stone a while, and read the premisses.

E. K. He is brighter then he was, the Circle of light shineth still.

△ We uncovered the Stone, and then he spake again.

Michael ...... *Before twelve moneths of your account be finished, with the Sunne: I will keep my promise with thee,* as concerning the destruction of Rodulph: *lest peradventure,* he triumph, as he often doth. *For, thy lines* are many times perused by him; *Saying;* This man doted,
Rod.
The destruction of Rodulph.
where is become his. God, or his good Angels?

And behold, I will sweep him off the face of the earth: And he shall perish miserably: that he may understand, that thou dealt not for thy self, but didst fulfil the work of thy master.

More-

Moreover I will bring in, even in the second moneth, (the twelve ended) *Steven.*

    St.
    △

And for a truth, (as *I am*) *will place him in the seat Imperial;* He *shall possesse an Empire most great:* and *shall shew what it is to govern, when God pleaseth.*

All conditionally to be understood.

In his time will I fullfil many things that I have promised thee, and I will be mercifull unto thee; because thou hast not broken my Covenant.

My minde abhorreth from *Lasky,* for he is neither faithfull to me, nor to thee: neither he careth for his own soul.

    A. L.

  △ Chamo & fræno maxillas illius constringe (ô Deus) ut approximet ad te.

Michael ...... *The speedy return of* Curtius *was to deliberate with* Rodolph *how they might,* (*under the colour of Justice*) *entangle thee.*

And lo, whom thou fostredst and fedst at thy Table, is he, that hath wet his hand in the dish with thee, and hath delivered thee.

Moreover, he hath betrayed his Master: And the cause of his adversity, hath had chief root in him. From the third year he hath done unjustly: and hath made naked his Lords secrets.

Emericus.
Sontagius.

But he shall have his reward: and shall perish with his own hand. Before thou camest out of thy own Doores, to take thy Journey, Rodolph knew of thy going.

And for a truth, his letters are before thee.

Therefore, it behoveth me, to give thee warning, and to teach and instruct thee, as one exercised in my businesse.

Cover me, I am become clecrer.

  △ We covered the Receptacle.

After a while we uncovered it.

Michael ...... *This therefore shalt thou do.*

The same way thou camest, the same way thou shalt also return: Not to flie from their malice or tyranny: But to stand in the face of them as my servant.

Hereby, indirectly, shall the Traitour *understand you know him.*

The Traitor.

And Rodolphus *hard heart, I will stir up with indignation against him. For he shall be constrained a Lyar.*

And they shall begin to fear thee, and also to love thee: and thou shalt be in favour amongst them.

Annuate their doings, and bear their sayings. And those things they shall offer thee, refuse not. I will send one out to pay them their wages.

Note.
Annuate their doings.

Moreover, I command thee Kelly, (*But in my own person, I counsel and advertise thee*) *that thou take part with the Lord Jesus: And go forward with the businesse thou hast in hand.*

For why? They shall be shortly made open and plain; *left thy* (△) *word* (to the Emperour he meaneth) *receive foil in the hearts of men.*

△ Belike he was studying in Dunstons book & Tables whereof he made me not privy.

But I bind it not to that place. For, the fruit that springeth of it, shall do my service with Steven; And yet, if he will, with that unjust Lasky. *And it shall be a Garden for you: wherein you shall not borrow of the World, but of the Gift of God.*

Yet if.
Donum Dei.

And hitherto I will deal with thee, that the least thing which thou hast bestowed in obedience toward me, shall not be forgotten.

Together.

Live you together, as brethren: and wonder together, at my works, and in me, for there shall not a hair of your head perish; So that you listen, and be obedient unto my voice.

If.

When therefore thou commest home, hide not thy self; But see, that the Infant be regenerated.

Infans baptizandus.

 ▲ As concerning the Godfathers: shall I requesit and use such as I intended?

Michael ...... *Do, that thou hast done.*

Mich.

But put all these things up amongst the secrets of your hearts, as though not seeing, yet seeing all things.

Let these for this time suffice.

E. K. The fire is gone, he and all.

 △ Creatori nostro Omnipotenti, Protectori nostro misericordissimo & consolatori nostro abundantissimo in tempore necessitatis nostræ sit perennis Laus, Honor, Gloria, & gratiarum actio.
          Amen.

 △ Hereupon we had great comfor, and so brake our fast, and returned to *Prague* again, before 4 of the clok in the afternoon.

Note.

While I was thus out, and had left a letter for the *Curtese Balthasar Federicus Dominus ab Offa, &c.* to deal with the Spanish Embassador, the Lord *Romfe,* and mayne Her *Kinsky,* to crave pardon of my sudden departure, *and the Child not yet christened, &c.* and had given my wife charge not to deliver the Letter before Friday night, &c. It came to passe, that this Mr. *Balthasar* had sent word of his comming to *Prage* with the Lord *Kinsky,* (whom on the Friday before I had met riding

ding out of Town: and he told me that he was to be out three or 4 dayes, &c.) and that he was desirous to speak with me.

Upon which occasion my wife thought it best to send the letter to him, and so did, not long before my coming home. Which thing when I understood, I was half sorry for it, and sent presently word to Master *Balthasar* of my coming home, and to certifie him that my wife had erred to send that letter unto his worship before *Friday* night, when she might perceive that indeed I did ride forth to *Bressel.*

He thereupon was desirous to speak with me, and *of him I received my Letter which he had perused,* and offered himself most ready to satisfie the content thereof, &c.

Now to the chief purpose, At my return home from Master *Balthasar Federick ab Ossa,* I found *Emericus Sontagius,* in my wives stove with Master *Kelly, who at the sight of me was sore amazed, and half not able, or not willing to speak, but said,* vos estis veteres equites. Then Mr. *Kelly* told me, that *Emericus* had told him, that the Emperour had been all day yesterday very melancholick, and would speak with no body. *And that he knew of my journey in a moment when it was,* and that by the Jews, & specially by the Doctor his son, that had gone about to get me the four horses, & laboured very much with himself (unasked) to perswade me that the Emperour his first and chief understanding of it was by the Jews, &c. Hereupon (being now night) he went home.

+ *Praga.*

Martii 14.
Thursday. A meridie, hora 2 ½. Baptizatus erat *Michael Dee* filius meus in arcis Pragensis majori Templo. Baptismum exercente, Cæsareæ Majestatis Capellano.

Susceptoribus vero, Illustrissimis Dominis, Domino don Gulielmo de sancto Clemente, Hispaniarum Regis, apud Cæsarem Legato, & Domino Magnifico, Domino Romff, summo Cæsareæ majestatis cubiculario, & à consiliis arcanis intimo & primario, &c.

Michael. Susceptrice autem, Nobilissima fœmina, Dominâ de Dittrechstain, Domini de Dittrechstain, uxore charissima, qui major Domo Cæsareæ majestatis est. Infanti verò nomen erat inditum *Michael* ad petitionem meam, *ob gratam beati* Michaelis *memoriam, qui (ex misericordiâ Dei) tam fuit est & erit nobis beneficus, auxiliaris & tutelaris,* &c.

+ *Praga.*

Martii 18.
Monday. Manè, horam circiter 7.

△ Precibus (ex more) ad Deum susis, primùm, deinde (aliquâ interposita mora) aliis etiam ejaculationibusque factis pro misericordia, luce & auxilio Dei, &c. post horas 2. tandem nulla facta apparitione, cessavimus. Ego verò de Dei ira timidus, causam subesse magnam dubitavi, &c.

△ Miserere nostri Deus, & ne nobiscum agas, juxta omnes iniquitates nostras, *Amen.*

Martii 20.
Wednesday, manè. △ Note— E. K. yesterday had a shew of a little thing as big as a pease of fire as it were in the stone going about by the brinks. And because it was not in shape humane, he of purpose would not declare it so to me, and so I have noted (as appeareth) of no shew. This he told me on Tuesday night (that was yesternight) upon occasion of a great stir and moving in his brains, very sensible and distinct, as of a creature of humane shape and lineaments going up and down to and fro in his brains, and within his skull: sometimes seeming to sit down, sometime to put his head out at his ear.

And this began from the same night following.

+ *Praga.*

Martii 20.
Wednesday, manè circitet 6 ½.

△ Precibus ad Deum susis aliquanto prolixioribus quam ex more, &c; statim facta est apparitio.

E. K. Here is the same shew of a little parcel of fire somewhat lesse then a pease, going about the border of the stone.

E. K. Here is one, but he hath a *covered face, I know him not,* his coveting is of a compound colour, between black: red and white, he is covered down to his middle, the ground of it is white: There be spots of black and red on it, some big, some little, as if they had been sprinkled on with a pen, or dashed on with a pencil.

A

..... *Against divine necessity is no prayer nor resistance.*

E.K. I feel nothing, in my head now, and till now I did, as is moved before.

..... *Come, ô you Prophets, and render your accounts. Come, O you that have sucked of the brests, wherein the judgments and secret will of the Lord is hid, and of Necessity to come, Gather your selves together, render some account why the King of eternity descending from the heavens hath so often visited you? And why he hath rather visited you, in the Desert, upon mighty and high Mountains, unranged of men. Tell, I say, what the cause is, that he hath come down into the Fens, and amongst your flock : Could not this God have lifted you up, and have brought you into his secret chambers? Could he not have ravished you unto himself, and so have carried you about with him, that you might see his great wisdome unknown to man, and the abundance of Glory, wherein he hath his habitation. There is none of you that dare presume to say, that you deserved the Lord his presence.*

There is none of you that dare open his mouth, saying, God hath need of us.

Tell therefore what is the cause that God hath visited you.

△ The unsearchable judgments and determinations of the highest, &c.

..... *Be silent, thou answerest before thou art called.*

.... *What is there none of you that answereth me ? No, where art thou ?*

Job, *where art thou ?*

Moses, *where art thou ?*

Zyrom, *where art thou ?*

Syracasba, *where art thou ?*

Daniel, *where art thou ?*

Jonas, *where art thou ?*

Ezechiel, *where art thou ?*

Holy, holy Esdras, *where art thou ?*

You lesser Prophets, *where are you ?*

You number without number, (whom the Lord hath talked withal) wherefore shew you not your selves ?

All these were full of the Holy Ghost.

All these mortified their flesh for the love of God. Yet, what, are you not able to render account or to shew the true cause why God hath visited you ?

God visited you so long, and so oft, so mercifully and so abundantly, and are you silent and ignorant ?. Why ?

Mandata tua justa sunt Domine.

What, was this the cause that God visited you for, that you should fulfill his Commandments, and teach his people the way of salvation ?

True it is, it was the cause that moved you to obedience, But the very cause why God appeared unto you, you know not.

Behold, the Commandments of God are just & true, whose sons you are : if therefore you follow not the Commandments of your father, you are disobedient. But why, your Father hath commanded you : Lo, I teach you.

When God of very God, the true light, beauty and honour of his Father, conteined or was full of the image of an heaven and earth, and by the omnipotent, conjoyned, and equal power and strength of them both, joyned in one, was brought forth, and had his real beginning, he determined also, in the self-same Image and Idea, the due and proper order, just law and determination, of all things that were comprehended, which Law and things together have their course co-essential both in heaven and earth, distinguishing all things into their real beginnings, limitation of time, and determination between their extreams, This order or law, begun in the bosome of the Word of God, keepeth so his proper course, and order, and law of his own establishment, That those things that before were wrought in God, might also receive working and being substantial to the end of God his progression.

This is the self-same that we spoke of before, in the name of divine Necessity, against the which no prayer prevaileth, nor resistance can be made.

This Necessity was the cause, O you Prophets and Children of God, that God dwelt amongst you.

This Necessity was the instrument that brought you to the stage of your election.

This Necessity was the cause that God chose you.

This Necessity maketh of wax, honey; of tar, milk; of long ranging, return, of Infidels, Christians ; of disobedient, holy ones.

Finally, of the unperfect and evil, rage and roming astray of mankind, the true number of such as return from wickednesse, and are chosen to eternal joy from the beginning.

But this may seem unto you a strange and stumbling Doctrine.

I have laid the Base.

△ We read the premisses, which seemed to us very pithy, and ponderous, and full of mysteries.

△ I

△ I noted two Prophets names, not before.

...... *This Necessity is two-fold, one (that is to say, the first) contemplative and fix.*
The other, working and leading to an end,
In the first do dwell two great and mighty Judges, Justice and Mercy.
In the second dwelleth the son and image of Justice, leading on by order for the course of things,
that are led on by the later, have not true Justice, but the image of Justice.
This is the cause that the elect and chosen may erre and go astray, and lose the benefit both of the
end of his Election and first determination.
For why : All things come on, and keep their course, even as they are led, by the image of Justice,
Man onely excepted : which by reason of his free-will, draweth   [E. K. He teacheth
out of order, runneth from the mark, refuseth that which is good,   himself.]
and through the burden of his flesh, inclineth unto evil.
In the which evil, whilst he dwelleth and continueth, lo the course of necessity taketh hold upon
him, and draweth him unto the scope or end whereunto he inclineth himself.

If he continue.   *For, behold, Although he be before sanctified unto the Lord, and made a chosen vessel, wherein*
if he continue, necessarily he shall enjoy the reward and glory of the sanctified: Yet if he lose that
Necessity, and fly from his own law and condition, taking part with the filthinesse and iniquity of his
enemy, through Satan or his flesh, of Necessity he must perish.

If   *For as those that are good, tied unto the law of goodnesse, are glorified, if they continue : so like-*
wise are the evil tyed unto the law of wickednesse, the Necessity whereof is damnable.
This is the cause that the Prophets are visited.
Because God found them punishing their flesh, despising the vanities of the world, and resisting
Satan.
For lo, the Lord looked down unto the earth : And he saw them despising wickednesse, fearing
him, *and grounded in the faith of redemption.*
Therefore he thrust himself in amongst them, and through the first part of necessity (in mercy)
he visited them.
Take heed (o you) that the Lord of necessity visiteth in Justice, for your burden shall be great
and intolerable.

E. K. He is gone.   △ We read and discoursed a pretty while.
E. K. Here he is again.
...... *Now unto the rest.*
What is (therefore) that necessity divine against the which there is no prayer nor resistance ?
For why it is evident, That sinners may return, and those that erre, may be brought into the
right way, and that by Prayer.
Prayer.   *Behold, no man is penitent, but he useth Prayer.*
No man satisfieth, but he useth Prayer.
No man taketh part with the Church, but in Prayer, for Prayer is the Key, sanctified by the
Holy Ghost, which openeth the way unto God.
Necessity had determined the destruction of Nineve, *necessity also saved it.*
For lo, when they should necessarily have received reward for their wickednesse, they prayed, and
resisted necessity.
It appeareth, therefore, not yet, what necessity that is, that Prayer prevaileth not against.
Note here, The later necessity is necessity, leading malum ad malum, *&* bonum ad bonum *; which*
necessity is that, which is tyed unto every thing leading is unto the end that it desireth.
Even as God, seeing the Prophets forsake the loathsomnesse of their flesh, and framing them-
selves to the necessity which leadeth unto good, of his meer mercy, in the first, thrust himself amongst
them, fixing their later and desired necessity, with a necessity of his Omnipotent and unspeakable
mercy wherein there dwelleth two things ;
Joy, and Perseverance,
These therefore (as the Prophets) which are visited with God in mercy, are fed, nourished and
fostred as the Prophets were, with these two dishes,
Whereof the greatest is Perseverance.
Herein I teach you, that he that is first elected and applyeth himself to the necessity of his Ele-
ction, doing the works that are righteous before the Lord, and receiveth comfort by the visitation of
Gods mercy, is sealed to the end of his Election, in gladnesse, and through the value and strength
of Perseverance, and cannot fall so far, that he shall be bruised, or run so far astray, that he shall
not be able to remember himself.
Happy are those that are elected.
But happy, happier are those that persevere in their Election.
These are those unto whom God imputeth not their sinnes.
These are those that sinne and Satan are a weary of, for they are not able to prevaile.
These are those which are numbred in the Book of God, and whose brethren tarry as yet for their
comming. But the altar shall be opened, and they shall rise.

But

But is there a mercy fixed, and doth this mercy also fix Justice; Or as I have called it the I-mage of Justice.

It is evident: So also is there a Justice that is fixed, a Justice triumphing, a Justice mighty, a Justice unable to be ... *yea, Justice that Prayer prevaileth not against, yea, a Justice that Hell and the Devil are condemned in.*

This is that Justice, this is that two edged sword, this is, that Iron Mall, wherewith those that refuse their Election, or are not elected, following the necessity of wickedness, are and shall be cut in pieces with, beaten into small powder, and be cast into the lake of fire and brimstone.

This is he that sealeth up the second Hell, with the second death.

This is that you, ô you starvelings, you vagabonds, you stiff-necked and stinking sinners ought to dread and fear!

Hath God elected you, and do you disdain it?

Hath he provided a Seat for you, an Honour for you, a Crown for you, a Wedding Garment for you, his eternal glory for you. And will you force him to cast it into the fire.

Shall the finger of God write you, and shall the vengeance of God root you out.

Repent I say, and flie from your iniquity.

Return into the way of the Lord, least God seeing your wickednesse, your un-natural and inhu-mane rebellion, your disobedience against your father, thrust himself upon your necessity with his ju-stice and vengeance.

Which thing if you do, Prayer prevaileth not, much lesse is their resistance.

Are you not afraid to lose the sight of God, and to be deprived of the glory of his Majestie?

Are you not afraid of the unspeakable flames and fire-brands of Hell, which are prepared for the wicked?

What shall I say unto you?

Shall I take pity upon you?

Why care you not for your selves?

Shall I pray unto God for you?

You pray not for your selves.

Shall I bestow goodnesse upon you?

Hui, *you despise it.*

Shall I bring three Sheep from the Mountains, and shall I lose two of them before I come Three sheep. *home.*

O you mortal men, be merciful unto your selves, Take pity on your selves. Fall into the true judg-ment of light and darknesse, of good and evil, of eternal Glory and Damnation.

For, behold, I tell you, that God is ready to thrust himself, yea, to throw himself as a might stone upon you.

Against the which there is no time of prayer, nor nothing that can prevaile.

I have here taught you, and exhorted you.

Exhorted you to forsake your wickednesse, and to cleave unto the Lord

Taught you that those that are elected may lose their election, and may be established in their Election. Also that those that are not elected run by the rule of necessity unto the end of their wick-ednesse, which is rewarded with eternal fire.

From the which God of his mercy, and in his Sonne Jesus Christ, who hath redeemed you, is yet ready, if you will, to deliver you.

Hal rowgh ha.

△ We long discoursed of sundry things, and each reproved other of haughtinesse, or pride of mind, how justly we did it God knoweth.

E. K. He is here still.

△ O Lord order these matters with us, and between us, to thy Honour and Glory.

E. K. —

...... *Thou E. K. and we, receive at one fountain, we are created and made by one God, to the end we should glorifie him, as our Creator, you, as your Redeemer and Creator.* Note E K. had said, let them give me some-what, or some-thing benefi-cial to my mind or body, and then I wil like the better of them.

But lo, we are of Heaven heavenly, comforted and nourished with the glory of God, wherein (since the (△*) division made amongst us) we erre not: you to the intent you may be proved, are covered with mortality and corruption, to the intent that the judgment of God may allow you, for those places you are apt to inherit. If therefore we be both refreshed of God, have our beginning from God as from our Creator, let us both acknowledg his goodnesse, and glorifie him in the works of our hands: we, in our angelical forms, you, in the Skirmish wherein you fight, by fighting man-fully, and overcomming.* △ The fall of Angels.

Yet of us thou hast, as those have that are rewarded in the labour of him that is sent in message from the giver.

If the King send his Messenger unto thee, he ought for three causes. First, for the person from whence

E e

386 *A true relation of Dr. Dee his Actions, with spirits,* &c.

A King his messenger to be honoured for 3 causes.

The Angels good will toward E. K.

△ E. K. said he would not allow of their doings & counsels, unlesse they were allowed of and confirmed by the Priest, to whom he would confesse himself.

The authority of good Angels is greater then the authority of the Pope.

Note of the Jews.

Both Churches Triumphant and Militant.

Ecclesia, quid?

△ E. K. had said, let them give me somewhat profitable to my body, or some wisdom to my minds behoof.

A Prophecy.

△ Fortè P L. significat Philosophorum lapis.

This we had not yet.

whence he commeth. Secondly, for the authority of his message, or goodnesse of reward. Thirdly, that by him you receive the benefit, whereby you are gratified.

Even so deal with us ∴ for as he may say, you fare the better by him, in respect of his labour, and the authority that he useth : so may we say, you fare the better by us.

But let the heaven and earth bear witnesse (besides the benefits of God) of our good will towards you. But answer me.

E. K. What say you to me ? wherein.

..... *As touching your receiving, as touching thy taking part with Christ Jesus, very God and man: the Son of the living God, whose precious blood cryeth out continually before his Father for the sins of the people.*

Whether is greater, the authority of truth, by the Church Militant, or Triumphant ?

Answer you [E. K.] *to that.*

E. K. By the Church Triumphant.

..... *Even such is our authority. Therefore it is greater then the authority of him that is a fleshly Priest.*

If the Angels that have appeared unto you, had appeared also unto the Jews, saying, Crucifie not the Son of God, they would not have done it.

For though they believed not man, yet would they have believed an Angel.

Therefore did God the Father acknowledge his Son Christ, by both Churches : as you may read by the Angels that appeared to the Shepherds, acknowledging from heaven the truth, that Jesus was the Son of God.

E. K. What is the Church? I did not think that the Angels were of any Church.

The Church is the number of those which are governed by the Holy Ghost, and that continually sing Holy, Holy, Holy, Holy, Lord God of Zebaoth : But that we sing so, the Scriptures bear witnesse.

I counsel you therefore to put on humility, and to make your selves subject before the truth.

Love one another, not because you are men, but because you are partakers of the heavenly testimony.

In respect of thy body and mind, I answer thee, that thy body is which now had not been, and what thy minde seeth, commeth through the light that we leave with it.

But if we forsake thee, thy body is not, much lesse shall thy understanding be.

Stay and I come again.

△ We read, and *E. K.* marvelled at the aptnesse and soundnesse of their answer.

E. K. Here he is again.   **E. K.** I cannot tell *F* or *P*.

..... *When ⊕ hath ended, and P hath ended,*

I come again.

E. K. He is here.

When P hath ended, and L hath ended (which is at hand) then commeth the son of perdition, and entreth.

Of these two Letters I will say more, in your next action.

The Light of heaven be amongst you.

△ Amen.

Misericordia Dei ineffabilis sit super nos, nunc & semper, *Amen.*

Sequitur Liber 24, qui, hac die etiam inceptus est à Meridie, horam circiter 3 per ipsum Levanaël.

Myſteriorum PRAGENSIUM Confirmatorum
Liber.

P R A G Æ,

Anno **1585**, *Martii* 20.

Myſteriorum CRACOVIENSIUM *Stephanicorum.*

Initia Aprilis **12.** **1585.**

Myſteria Stephanica.

Ake common Audcal, purge and work it by Rlodnr of four divers digeſtions, continuing the laſt digeſtion for fourteen dayes, in one and a ſwift proportion, untill it be Dlaſod fixed a moſt red and luminous body, the Image of Reſurrection.

Take alſo Lulo of red Roxtan, and work him through the four fiery degrees, until thou have his Audcal, and there gather him.

Then double every degree of your Rlodnr, and by the law of Coition and mixture work and continue them diligently together. Notwithſtanding backward, through every degree, multiplying the lower and laſt Rlodnr his due office finiſhed by one degree more then the higheſt.

So doth it become Darr, the thing you ſeek for : a holy, moſt glorious, red, and dignified Dlaſod.

But watch well, and gather him, ſo, at the higheſt : For in one hour, he deſcendeth, or aſcendeth from the purpoſe.

Take hold.

Anno

Anno 1585.   ⎰Vide hujus Diei actione præ-⎱
                ⎱cedente. De Necessitate di-⎰   + *Praga.*
Martii 20.   ⎱vina & electione, &c.   ⎰

Wednesday, à meridie circa 3¼.   △ As we sat together in my Study, and talked of our affairs, and of the Philosophers stone, E. K. felt a thing heavy upon his head, and heard a voice, saying, I will teach thee. Hereupon I set the stone in place.

E. K. Here is Levanael, covered as he was wont.

Levan. ...... *Why are you not pure, that you may learn?*

E. K. So we will receive at Easter, as the time of the year doth
require.

△ Lord, thou hast said, we should at length be of one minde, through thy mercies, Lord help us
herein.

E. K. He seemeth to have had his lips sewed: for the vail is so
thin, that it permitteth his face in manner to be perfectly discerned.

Levan. ...... *See that you take the season, and gather while it is time; if you let this Harvest*
NOTE.   *passe, you shall be desirous to gather, and you cannot.*
Thrice.   Thrice I must come unto you, *if I finde you not.*
'Lo, I have done, for I come no more.'

E. K. I pray you to deal with another: here is John, a boy in
the house, you may use him.

Levan. ...... *Thy talk is humane folly:* But before I go, I will not be hidden from you.
Read your Lesson, it is now a stale lesson.
△ I read, Take Common Audcal, &c.   Take hold.
Levan. ...... *You are best to do so.*

E. K. Now he hath heaved up his vail, his face is bare, it was not
his lips that had those stitches as it were, but it was in his vail, his
face is a very fair beautiful face.

△ We beseech you for God his sake, his glory and honour, to give light, and to make plain
this Lesson or Conclusion.

Levan. ...... *This Conclusion wherein man is exalted being the last and the first, is as necessary*
for you, and for the avoiding of *temptations* that are *to come, as your garments are to cover your na-*
kednesse, or the houses to keep off the storms.
△ Give us therefore his help, this hand, this staff, this counsel, O Lord.

Levan. ...... *How much the more you neglect it, and the time wherein it is to be gathered, so*
much the more shall you be redone unto your selves and the businesse which you must fulfill in the
The fruit of   *will of God, if you have this; it will first cause you to forsake; secondly, it will plant you there,*
the Philo-   *where without it your feet cannot enter, and from whence when you are planted, you shall not easily*
sophers stone.   *be moved.*

I speak not this, for that you should murmur, saying, Cannot God plant us without this? But to
make it evident unto you: that God useth his Creatures visible to introduce or lead in (yea, super-
natural) force and wisdome.

These things will demonstrate the will and power of God grafted in you, that it is found perfect,
The divers   *and from above.*
commodities
of the Philo-   *For if you say, lo these things hath God taught me, and these things hath God opened unto me:*
sophers stone   Whilest they wonder at the one, they shall be forced to believe the other.
known.   *Moreover, they shall leave their* Table-talks, *which object poverty unto you, and they shall be*
Table-talk of   *forced to say, (even in despight of their teeth) what need had he of us? he sought us not of the world,*
poverty obje-   for lo, he leadeth her *as his slave.*
cted to us.
These things, if you consider not, I put you in remembrance, that you may know you lose time, yea,
that you lose a benefit, desired of many, and so forth.
Lo, I come again.

△ I read over the premisses.

E. K. Here he is again.

Levan. ...... *Read.*
△ I read.
Levan. ...... *What is* Audcal?
△ God knoweth, I know not.
Levan. ...... *It is* Gold.
△ Purge and work it. How your purging it, I know not.

Levan.

Levan. ,,,,,, *Read and go forward.*
Levan. ,,,,,, *Dlafod is* Sulphur.
Go on let me teach you generally.
△ Take also *Lulo* of red Roxtan.
Levan. ,,,,, *Roxtan, is pure and fimple Wine in her felf.*
Lulo is her mother.
△ There may be in thefe words great abiguitie.
Levan. ,,,,,, Lulo is Tartar, fimply of red wine,
Audcal is his Mercury.
Darr, (*in the angelical tongue,*) *is the true Name of the Stone.*
I come again.

△ He faid before it was Gold.

E. K. Here he is again.
I have no more to fay to you, this is the firft time.

E. K. He is gone.   △ We know that Lapis Philofophicus fit ex metallis, cum metallis, & fuper metalla, &c.

The firft t me of three before fpoken of.

E. K. Here he is again. --- All is there.
Levan. ,,,,,, *How many letters are in Audcal.* ------△---- Six.
So many wayes: is this a working.

E. K. He is gone.   △ Divina nobis femper adfit gratia, & nobifcum co-operatur, ad Dei Honorem & Gloriam. *Amen.*

+ *Praga.*

Martii. 21.
Thurfday, a meridie circa 5 horam.
Note, my wife being in great perplexitie for want of money, requefted E. K. and me that the effect of the unnexed petition might be propounded to God and his good Angels, to give anfwer or counfel in the caufe? Hereupon I prayed a little to the fame purpofe, and read the petition, &c.

We defire God of his great and infinite mercies, to grant us the help of thefe heavenly myfteries, that we may by them be directed how or by whom to be aided and relieved, in this neceffity that we are in, of fufficient and needful provifion, for meat and drink for us and our Family, wherewith we ftand at this inftant much oppreffed: and the rather becaufe that might be hurtful to us, and the credit of the actions wherein we are vowed and linked unto his heavenly Majeftie, (by the miniftry and comfort of his holy Angels) to lay fuch things as are the ornaments of our Houfe, and the coverings of our bodies, in pawn either unto fuch as are Rebels againft his divine Majeftie, the Jews, or the people of this City, which are malicious and full of wicked flanders: I Jane Dee humbly requeft this thing of God, acknowledging my felf his fervant and handmaiden, to whom I commit my body and foul.

E. K. Here is one, with a leather coat and a fpade, with a white Coronet on his head round, hath a bag on one fide of him, and on the other fide a bottle, it feemeth like an husbandman, but a young fair man he is.

Jane Dee.

Give ear unto me thou Woman, *is it not written, that Women come not into the Synagogue, much leffe ought they to come before the teftimony of the will of God to be fulfilled mightily, and to come againft the World and againft the pomp for money and iniquity, but becaufe thou haft humbled thy felf, and haft refufed to tarry before me, as it becommeth thee? I will anfwer to thy infirmities, and will talk with thee.*

The title of actions.

He

He that hath his House inhemmed with a Ditch, which is deep and swelled with water must needs make a Bridge over, that he may be at liberty, else is he a Prisoner unto the waters; but if he want Wood, and have no shift to enter into the fields, is it not Wisdome to break his Dining Tables, and to set himself free; why cryest thou unto me; Behold, let thy House yeeld, and the covering of thy body give place to the necessity of hunger, Behold, God suffereth his Elect & chosen vessels oftentimes to be without Mansion or apparel: But, lo, he feedeth the Sparrows, but I will not reprehend thee, because thy soul is frail, but be faithful and obedient, and that truly, as thou art yoked: Behold, I have blessed thy Children, and of thy seed and bones will I build a new, and they shall have Houses, and shall be served of such as the people salute, saying, hail Master. Be thou patient and full of repentance, and do that thou hast to do, and not that thou hast done, For, lo, mercy is with thee, and well shall come unto thee.

A promise to save her children.

Of Necessity. Behold, the Scourge is with you, and of necessity you must be tempted, that your Faith may worthily be glorified, and that you may be praised in me.

Behold thou seekest Counsel of me, I will counsel thee, Behold, I would dig for thee, but I should do contrary to my selfe, because I have given power, and he that possesseth the earth is against me; But such as I have, I will give thee, and it shall be sufficient, more then thy vessels can hold, or thy dayes can thank me for.

Consider that to morrow commeth not before he be brought in: Neither canst thou have until thy power come; But cast up thy eyes, and hope for better things; Lo, since I cannot give thee that thou desirest, really, yet I bow my head, and so I counsel thee, let thy husband arise and gird himself together, and let him take his eyes with him, and let him hast out of this place: For my thinks they dissemble; Lo, let him stand before Steven, and let him visit Lasky, peradventure he find him not living: But if he live he is dead, there shall you see that I will relieve thee and do good unto him, and will bind up the Jawes of the persecutor, that he may go on.

Note, One storm is yet to come. △ Huic sexui scilicet mulie-bri. Thou art a Woman, and thy infirmities follow thee, I counsel not without a cause, neither did I stirre thee up to speak; But for thy faith I will reward thee; But one storme is to come, take it patiently, thou shalt be the more whiter, and more neerer: Behold, I go before and he that followeth me doth well unto himself, for I do well unto those that follow me; Cast away your murmurring, and sweep your Houses, take heed of Spiders, and of the whore Rats. This is the first time that I have answered to this kind in the latter dayes; Lo, I go.

△ Lord, it was said unto us as a Watch-word, when *Stevens* Messengers should come for us, that then we should go. Now his Messengers are not yet come, &c.

...... If the Bridegroom invite thee himself, what needst thou his servant.

△ Now is the difficulty for money greater, for if we had tarried together, lesse money would have served then now it will do, &c.

Numerata divina. Nescimus quis nobiscum loquitur. ...... Thou hast asked counsel, I have counselled thee, if it please thee hear me, it shall be well with thee if thou tarry, but much better if thou go; I have numbred thee, but be not proud, but because I have numbred, diminish not thy self, least when I find not the number, I find not thee also, if thou wilt any thing else, there are, and they can say unto thee, but who speaketh with thee thou knowest not.

E. K. He is gone.

△ Seeing here is matter unlooked for, we are stirred to ask questions not thought of before: Therefore, O Lord, send whom it please thee to us.

A voice ...... *Sunt alia hora.*

Deo nostro Omnipotenti sit omnis Laus, Honor, Gloria, & Jubilatio. *Amen.*

✠ *Prage.*

Wednesday.
27 *Martii* Mane circa horam 9.

E. K. came to me and asked me the Circle or Copy thereof which was shewed to him at *Oxford*, and he had written out, or described by the light that was shewed to him by the spiritual Creature, he intended as he said to shew it to a Jesuit, and to ask his counsel of it, &c. having a great misliking of our spiritual friends, saying, that they were the great Devils; and so the lesser that he dealt withal before, gave place unto them, &c. Hereupon I told him I would ask our friends counsel, before I delivered any thing of theirs to their enemie, &c. He would presently have it, and with great threats most terrible and dangerous to me, he willed me to deliver it strait wayes. I being occupied with writing a letter to the Queens Majestie, said assoon as I had leasure I would give it him, he said he would tarry my leasure: I told him that would scarce be this seven night, I had so many letters to write, he thereupon grew in such a rage that he said I should not passe one foot beyond him before I did deliver it him. at length he rose to shut the Door of the study upon me, I arose and went after him and took him by the shoulders to keep him from the Door, and withal called aloud to my folks; Come here (how) here is violence offered unto me, whereupon they came

in

in all, and my wife, and so afterward by degrees his fury asswaged, and my folks, my Wife and his went away: and after he had sitten two or three hours with me, he saw on my head as I sat writing *Michael* stand with a sword, and willed him to speak, which he did forbear to do, above a quarter of an hour, as *E. K.* said: At length he spake as followeth ⸺

E. K. Here appeareth Michael on your head, and hath bid me divers times to speak to you.

△ I disposed my self to write, and *Michael* bad bring the Stone.

E. K. Here appear 12 with him, 4 behind him, and 4 on each sides of him 4, and all with swords of fire, and he the hindermost of them had a Barrel of Glasse on his back full of fire, the 12 were all in red Coats.

Michael ..... *The Prophet.*

Nunc ergo Notum facimus Domine Rex quoniam si civitas hæc ædificata fuerit, & ipsius mutilati fuerint, descensus tibi non erit Cœlosyriam, neque in Phœnicem.   3 Esdræ cap. 1. c.

E. K. Now they all kneel down about him.

They look pitifully with their faces upward, as though they were praying, they be all in blood red Garments, and Michael his sword is as the sword I once did see him have; whose edge did open.

E. K. Now answer me to the purpose: whether I shall have the Circle of Letters which I did desire?

Michael ...... *Is there any like unto thee, O Jehovah in Heaven and in Earth, or can thy enemies rise up [saying] against thee, and shall they stand, O thou whose look is more terrible unto thy Angels, then all the fires which thou hast created, either in the bottomlesse pit or in the life of all Elemental Creatures, or above in the heavens if they were gathered together in one can be terrible to man.*

Hast thou not made Heaven and Earth, and hast put thy head no where, and thy feet somewhere; because without thee there is not, and without thee there cannot be?

O thou that hast numbred the Starres, and art Dominus Dominantium above those that govern them, and more in knowledg then their Government. Thou, Thou, Wilt thou suffer thy Name to be trodden under foot? Thou, Thou, Wilt thou correct the Heavens, and the whole seed of man? Wilt thou drown the World with waters, and root the wicked from the face of the Earth? Wilt thou cast down the lothsome and wicked Cities, that they may grow in the terrour of thy judgment? Wilt thou send so many Plagues into Egypt?

Wilt thou suffer all these things to be done and many more memorable, which are all in thee: And thou permit one Man, one Soul to be thus carried away with Satan to the dishonouring and treading under foot of thee, and thy light of thee, and thy truth.   One that E. K. Veritas.

If the King exalted him which magnified Truth before the strength and Policy of Women: extolled him before his Princes, and caused for his sake the building of this Temple to go forward: Wilt thou not punish him that despiseth truth, that preferreth the wantonnesse and voluptuousnesse of the World (that errant strumpet) before thy word, and before the strength of a heavenly Authority: Art thou so become a little one, that thou art lesse then a King? hast thou turned thy face so far aside that thou seek not this Rebellion? Can one man be dearer unto thee then the whole World was? or shall the Heavens be thrown head-long down, and shall he go uncorrected? Hast thou Mountaines and Stones untrodden on, out of the which thou canst shew thy Praise and Honour? Are there not yet Infants which may be sanctified to speak with the Heavens, that thou so hidest thy selfe away from Justice; What, What, if those that often cry for grace receive it not, yet dost thou give it unto him that commeth from it.   2 Esd. ch. 4. 33, &c.   An apt Skrier is sanctified.   Nota.

Sane stupor Cælis, & stupor terris.

What, are not so many Fires as wait upon me sufficient to arm Satan with vengeance against this   △   *wicked one? O thou Beast, O thou roaring Lion, O thou Monster, O thou Whirlpool, O thou terrible Murtherer.*   Note the manner of Justice.

E. K.

Hast thou plac't headlong many thousands into Hell, and dost thou linger to rage upon this imp, *whom thou hast so long sought for?*

Is it not written, least peradventure he find them sleeping, and so overcome them.

But, behold, whom thou findest sleeping, is ready for thee, willing to go with thee. what sparest thou? art thou so bold, to give authority unto thy Ministers to confound, nay, to so blind that thou canst not see so great an Hill?   Behold,

Behold, thy Ministers cry out unto thee, and send thee word, calling thee Master, King.

Take heed the City be not built, take heed the walls of it be not lifted up, and as they that were the Messengers of the King made evident before his face that it was against his commodity, to have the Temple of the Lord built up, to have the City new shapen, to have the Walls made strong, because it should hinder his passage into Cœlofyria, and the rest.

1 Esdras 2.24.

E. K. Now the 12 (he excepted) fall down.

Mich. ...... *And thy Ministers have they not said unto thee, if this work of the Lord go forward, if the City sent down from the Heavens may receive a place to set her selfe in, if the Walls and Rampiers of this that was built above shall be placed on any place of the World on earth, Behold, Behold, will it not hinder thy cause, will it not subvert thy Kingdome, will it not turn thee out of Doors: will it not bring thee to a terrible day before the Lord?*

Is it not written, that that day shall be terrible to Satan, and his Angels?

And wilt thou suffer a Door to be opened, wherein it may enter; it behoveth thee Satan here to bend thy bow, it behoveth thee now to draw up thy arrowes.

And if thou intend to plant on earth; that it may grow, time is, yet, now to weed out this Message from above.

Do thy Messengers give thee warning of these things, dost thou hold back thy forces: when the Porters will betray the City, would deliver it into thy hands, would break down the walls before thee, what I say art thou like to enter, thou that loseth no opportunity, art thou so negligent: Behold, the Doors stand open before thee, why entrest thou not.

Dost thou want fire, lo, he that betrayeth it hath fire for thee, yea, rumor.

Behold, he offereth himself a companion, what wouldest thou more, unto these things thou hearest the sayings of thy servants, which say unto thee O Satan, if this City be built, and the walls erected; Thou canst not go into the Holy Land: And lo, hearest thou not them, neither dost regard this opportunity, whence art thou so forgetful, O God? great is thy mercies, and far art thou above the sinnes of man: O thou not only shuttest up the eyes of the wicked, that they cannot see truth before their face, but the profound [the] malice and sight of Satan, that where he should most enter he misseth that place, and when time serveth him, that he letteth it passe.

Mirabilis Dei misericordia.

But so, so, God, thou givest to whom, and where thou wilt, and even as thou art terrible in Justice, so likewise art thou wonderful in mercy; Therefore of thee is no end, neither can be added any end.

Blasphemous rebellion.

This thy great mercy is the cause that this blasphemous Rebellion is yet unpunished; This is the cause that Satan misseth his mark; and is become weak.

If any man make a pot, an earthen vessel, worketh he not, tempereth he not, to the end to make a pot? But lo, when he hath made it, and applieth it to his intent, if even he against destroy it, is he not vain? Do not those that stand by him wonder at him? More mervail is it, that when Satan shouteth and hitteth the mark, that he should be blind, yea, so blind, that he knoweth not where to gather up his arrow?

3 Esdras cap.

But lo, the Temple was built, and the City stood, although the work was left off for a while, and he that magnified truth went with glad tidings, neither desiring rich apparel, neither to sit next the King, but that the City of the Lord might be built, and that the Name of God might be magnified, so shall it be of this City which the Lord hath sent down with his finger, his unsearchable

Actionum:

and wonderful truth: the Revelation and Law of time to come, it shall be built, it shall flourish, it shall stand, it shall endure, it shall be magnified, it shall be spoken of through all the World, and it shall not cease.

Behold, the King of Kings hath allowed it and the love of truth, is great with him, what hath he to do with Kings? or wherein needeth he the beauty of the Earth? Domini est terra, & plenitudo ejus.

Whosoever therefore sticketh unto truth, shall be exalted with God, which is the King of Kings shall be magnified before his Counsellers, not Counsellers fore-warning, but Counsellers partaking of holy Will: not called Counsellers, in respect of counselling him, but in that they are made privie of the Counsel of God: Before these also shall he be magnified.

E. K. For what end saith he all this.

O ye Infidels, and of little faith, which tast of the meat that was hidden from the Prophets, which are over-shadowed with the light of heaven, which have always associated with the holy Ministers of God: wherefore are you so stiff-necked, pleasant is the yoke wherein you are linked, and honourable is the earth that you draw the plow upon, for the Lord followeth, and his Angels drive, and the seed that is sown shall be the beginning of glory.

O yee stiff-necked people, why forsake you your visitation, or runne astray from your faith that you are driven in, do you make much of the Lords of the earth? Do you delight in her drosse that harlot money? Do you give reverence to the King, and stand you in fear to break his Lawes? have you a greater Lord then the Lord of Heaven and Earth, have you any money or jewels to be compared to his Grace? have you any honour on Earth, that can stand up against the Crown of Heaven

ven? wherewith God crowneth those that are Victors? Have you any Law sweeter then the pure illuminations, and sweet dew like comforts, the voices and presence of the holy angels?

Be mindful, be mindful, and lift up your selves, and be not blind, but consider the time of your visitation, and that which you do, is the work of a King, a King which is able in power, strength, and majestie to exalt you, to strengthen you, and to make you honourable, but in the end of the Visitation, and in the reward of your faithfulnesse, work not to-day, and be sorry to morrow; But lay sorrow aside, and continue your labour, least peradventure God unhood-wink, and make open the sight of Satan, and so deliver you.

Wo, wo, be unto them that are delivered, for beleeve me their tribulation is great.

There is horrour and gnashing of teeth, there is misery and vengeance for ever, there is horrour and the worm of conscience.

But two things are to be considered, here, whether the temptation be greater then the resistance, or the resistance, more dignified then the rigor of temptation.

Behold, the work is great, the labour is also equal unto it; And to fight against the Princes of darknesse in a set battail, requireth great force.

The temptations therefore that follow you, must needs be great, I see therefore the temptations surmounteth your strength, and your dignity is not such as can resist against it; For why, Satan striveth not with you, simply for the sinne of Adultery, for the dregs of Fornication, for the covetous desire of money, for the want of charity, or because you are proud; But he striveth, riseth up against you and tempteth you against the Lord, and against the strength of his truth, whereunto you are elected: Therefore, I give sentence.

Lo, because that temptations hath entred into you above your power, and not so much for the subverting as of the work of the Lord intended, and of necessity to be done.

Therefore, I proceed not against you, but against Satan, and God shall deliver you from your temptations; And this shall be a sign and token, that I will hamper and bridle the jawes of the enemy, that is to say, so long as thou (Kelly) art in this flesh, never shall there appear, or visibly shew himself unto thee any wicked or evil spirit, neither shalt thou be haled in peeces, as thou hast been, whosoever therefore appeareth hereafter is of God; For thy eyes shall be shut up from the wicked object. Et intellectu tuo Non introibit umbra mortis.

But now take heed, thou either perverse or froward, stiff-necked or disobedient; The sinne is of thy self, and shall fall upon thee, and thou shalt not be spared as thou hast been; Now watch and gird up your selves, and do the will of the Highest, preferre and worship truth, that you may be also worshipped. Lift up your selves, as the servants of God, and help to bring stones unto the building of this great City, that you may be openers of the Gates, and that the white * horse may enter, and that he that entreth may reward you with honour.

Greater then you are in the dignity of truth, are not amongst mortal men, neither shall there be any amongst mortal men that shall more despise the World then you, therefore hath God framed one of you as a stiffe made asse, to bind up the countenance of his work, and to be free from yielding unto Satan, which well understandeth that Satan endevoureth, and that his Ministers cry out against this glorious habitation, which being built, the wicked come not to, Cœlosytia, neither shall they see the beauty of the Phœnices.

When you have read these things I come again, and ponder them well.

△ We read them, and the places of Esdras, one in the second Chapter of the third Book of Esdras, and the other in the third and fourth Chapter of the same Book.

E. K. Now he is here himself alone.

Michael ...... A Wood grew up and the Trees were young, and lo, there arose a great Tempest from the North, and the Seas threw out the air that had subtilly stoln himself into them, and the winds were great, and behold, there was one Tree which was older then the rest, and had grown longer then that which shot up by him; This Tree could not be moved with the wind, but the Tree that was young, was moved to and fro with the wind, and strook himself oftentimes, upon the stiff set Tree: The Forester came and beheld, and said within himself, the force of this wind is great, see this young Tree beateth himself in peeces against the greater, I will go home, and will bring my ground instruments, and will eradicate him, and I will place him further off: Then if the winds come, he shall have room to move: But when he came home, the Lord of the Wood seeing him in a readinesse, with his Mattock and his spade, asked him of his going, which told the thing in order to his Master; But lo, his Master rebuked him, and he said thus, when the winds are not they increase, they are not hurtful one to the other, suffer them therefore, when the young Tree taketh roots, and shall look up unto some years, his roots shall link themselves with and under the roots of the greater; Then though the winds come, they shall not be hurtful one to another, but shall stand so much the more fast; by how much the more they are wrapped together, yea, when the old tree withereth, he shall be a strength unto him, and shall adde unto his age as much as he hath added unto his youth. And he ceased to dig.

Be not therefore haled in sunder, neither be you offended one at another, per adventure Reason would set you aside: But God will not. Behold, if you break the yoke that you are in, and runne astray, he that erreth shall perish: even so shall he that standeth also be desolate: For why, the driver angry, continueth not with one: But he shall return home, and shall not see the end of the Harvest.

F f   Love

Signum quo certi esse possimus quod Demus Satanæ frænum injiciet. Nota.

Caviat E. K. deinceps.

Veritas.

* *Equus albus. Apoc. cap. 19. B. Nostra vocatio magna. Dee sup.*

Parabola de nobis duobus.

Love therefore one another , *and comfort one another ; for he that comforteth his brother, comfort-eth himself :* and when one is a weary, let the other draw ; *For, why you are men and not yet crowned ; the first is paid : so is also the tenth ; Even so the tree that is grafted beareth fruit sooner then that which groweth of the seed. Notwithstanding, both have their place in the Or-chard, the night let that yield unto day , and Winter bear rule over Summer : Let youth yield un-to ripe for years ;* Solomon *saith, it is good for that young man that obeyeth the counsel of his elder ; In the Council House the things that they handle are for their Common-wealth ; Notwithstand-ing hath his order and degree. Cast your eye upon all things and you shall have examples ;* Peter *in his vocation preached the same Gospel that the rest of the Apostles did , but he was greater then the rest, not in respect of his Apostleship, nor in respect of feeding, but that God might keep his* order, *as the chief amongst them, which preferred* Peter *first ; Therefore he not stubborn. But I command you in the Name of him that sent me , and because you have vowed that the one of you did nothing without the others counsel, notwithstanding shall you not be two counsellors.*

Therefore, in things that are to be done, let the Door occupie the superiority ; The Seer let him see, and look after the doings of him that he seeth ; For you are but one body in this work.

E. K. He is gone out of sight.

△ As concerning my Letters and businesse into *England*, I thought good to ask counsel what I were best to do with the Letters to the Queen and others.

Michael ...... Gather out of the book of *Enoch*, the Seal and the Angel of thy Countrey, deal with him.

△ I found a Door, in the name due to *Britannia. Anno* 15.

Michael ...... *Thou shalt easily find the truth by their appearing , for the one answereth not un-to the others function.*

Hereby must thou do in all.

Kingdomes and Estates, both how, and what thou wilt , that thou hast not is thy own errour.

Note. ...... *Understand me well here.*

When thou wilt have any thing to do in the World , in humane affaires , *seek nothing in* Sigillo Æ-meth, Enoch *his Book is a worldly Book.*

Veritas in Cœlo.

Imago veritatis , in terra.

homini

Imago imagini respondet.

Cælestia autem petuntur a Cœlo.

△ I beseech you.

Michael ...... *Darknesse yeeldeth unto light : Falsum quod est , veritati malum bono.*

But note in the Book of Enoch there are those that are good, there are there also those that are evil , the Prince of darknesse is evil.

And those that are evil there, do stand on his side : but all his Ministers *give place to those that are good, so do they also.*

Note. ...... *But as concerning the manner how to practise that Book, I would gladly heare somewhat.*

Michael. ...... *Sua sunt, sua dicunt.*

△ I understand this to be required at his hands that gave us that Book.

Michael ...... Polonia te expectat , & qui EST præcessit.

△ As concerning my health helping, may I stay here yet 8 dayes , and then make speed to be going towards *Poland,* as was prescribed to me.

Michael ...... *Possum tibi concidere dies,* Septem —

If thou didst know that which I see, thou wouldst not go, but thou wouldst runne: He that is before is a Gardener , and he knoweth the vertue of Herbs : But the eighth day I will be there also.

...... *Where, and which eighth day.*

Michael ...... *The eighth day hence I will be in* Cracovia : *I have told thee plainly.*

△ May I then stay well 7 dayes, before I set forth on my journey.

Michael ...... *Potes , & non potes.*

Thou hast thy own judgment granted thee , thereby thou maist do it : But in respect of the neces-sity that requireth thee there , thou canst not.

△ I beseech you not to be offended, if I ask the cause of the Lord *Lasky,* silence ——△——He stayed long.

E. K.

E. K. Why did you not speak now.

Michael ...... *Behold, he hath said with himselfe, (and those that are wicked, have whispered unto him,) surely it seemeth that they despise me, and obstinately (because he hath not received letters from you) he useth this silence.*

Moreover, he hath not done, as God commanded him : But I will give him thee, use thou him *Misericordia* as thou wilt.   *& pax Dei sit*

△ I render unto thee O most merciful, mighty and loving God) thanks and honour, and will *super nos* (during my being) praise thy holy Name.

E. K. He is gone, and went away mounting upward, &c.

Quis, sicut Deus noster, qui humiliter resplicet, & peccatores sua ditat gradibus.
Illi soli sit omnis laus, honor, & gloria, nunc & semper. Amen.

✛ *Praga.*

Monday
Aprilis 1.   Mane, circa 8.

△ Præces feci, & visitatas, & alias (ex tempore) ejaculationes, pro auxilio Dei omnipotenti necessario in omnibus nostris (Dei prescripti) tractandis negotiis, &c.

△ A remembrance for me.
England Letters.
A. L. His Letters opened, and some yet kept.

Emerick his traiterous dealing to be deciphered; Counsel for the manner of our going, and what things shall be needfull to take with us.

E. K. Here is a tall man with white clothes, with wide sleeves, and his garment very much pleated, and a thing like a Cypress scarf before his face black, which had been many times doubled, and with a knot behind him; Two others there are by him on his left hand, one of them is apparelled in a green thing like a Cassock comming down to his middle leg, and a pair of shooes on his feet, and a hat on his head.

The other in a marble Jerkin like a leather Jerkin with panes, and a pair of Hose, with round Breeches of the same stuff, his neither stocks like common black, and usual shooes, and on his head an hat as the other hath of the English fashion : The first hath a little beard short, aburn colour, The other hath a young beard whitish.

...... *Why do you provoke me to indignation ?*
Why accuse you me of doing wrong?
Have I not lead you out by the hand from the Serpents?
Carried you against nature thorow the waters ?
Have I not held you up from falling?
Have I not brought you hither unto the Hill ?
This is the entrance.
The way is open for you ascend.
And are you not yet ashamed to urge me ?
If I have done you wrong, wrong be unto me.
If I have done more then I ought to do, why do you vex me?
△ He seemeth to mean us.
I have said unto you eat, and you have not.
I have told you it is time to eat, but you have your own time.
I have said unto you Go before; Follow me.
But in this case I will not be Judg against you.
These two, that record my sayings shall give judgment against you.
Therefore now unto you.

E. K. He seemeth to speak to them two looking on them. *The white man.*

E. K. There appeareth a very great Hill up to the Heavens by him.

E. K. He speaketh to them two.

E. K. He turneth toward you, △

Here you see the Hill, here you see the way open:
Here you see no hinderance.
Yet, lo, these men accuse me, trouble me.
Determine you against them.
Call not at these Doores any more, untill you be called unto them.

If *To have said if, before the Lord, if you had not, it had been better for you.*

E. K. He treadeth them two under his feet all to pieces, and taketh his hands, and flingeth the bloud of them about, and it sticketh to the sides.

A voice. ...... What is it to me if man had never been.

E. K. He wrappeth up the place of their lying as if it were a Cloth, and putteth or tumbleth them out of sight.

E. K. Now he is gone like a Whirl-wind away.

LORD,
Δ I am heartily sorry for any thing I have said or done, which hath provoked thy indignation, thy mercy be upon us, and not the rigor of thy most just Judgment. *Amen.* Thy Name be alwayes praised. *Amen.*
O Lord, I find my own weaknesse and frailty continually, and therefore I call unto thee for thy gift of Wisdome, that I might wisely and discreetly serve thee all the dayes of my life. O Lord, the escapes of my lips and the folly of my heart pardon, I most heartily beseech thee: And if thy helping hand forsook us, and much more, if thy indignation work against us, we are in most misera le and pitifull case, have pity, have mercy, have compassion on us, Lord, Lord, Lord, forgive this our offence whatsoever; Suffer us not to be confounded through our little faith, O God, help our faith, help, help, or else we perish.

K. K. Here he is againe.

Note my great offence.

Δ

Lasky his letters came on Friday last.

Δ

Pardon, pardon, pardon, O God, thy judgments are just.

...... *When the Lord bad thee go, if thou had'st so done, and had'st not taken thine own time, more had been given unto him, and more had been added unto thee.*
But now Letters came, that have passed through the hands of Sodomites and Murderers, (through whose hands they are accursed,) you rejoice, you receive comfort, you determine to goe.
But if you had left those letters behind you, had come when I bad you go. Then had my Name been untouched.
Therefore is the Lord angry, and forgetteth not this offence.
For he that dealeth with me, dealeth not as with a man, for I have nothing in me tied to time, much lesse hath he that sent me.
Δ O God, what a wretched miserable man am I, thus to fall, and to offend my God, O Lord, that thou judgest is very just; for man would have taken indignation against his servant that should not go where he biddeth, or that would seek or use better credit to encourage him to his duty, then his Masters, &c.
Many times hast thou been wearied.
Have mercy, O God. Et dele omnes iniquitates meas, cor mundum crea in me, & averto iram tuam à nobis, Is thy fury implacable, or shall thy anguish last for ever, what is flesh and dust before thee?

A sentence of punishment yet Lord be merciful.

Pardon,

...... *There shall remaine the sting of this offence, in both your generations, until the fifth. And I swear unto you by heaven.*
Δ Spare this Sentence of indignation (O God) against us. Thou hast said in what hour soever a sinner is sorry for his sinnes, and turneth unto the Lord, &c. And Lord, I am heartily sorry, I bewaile with teares this great offence, thou seest my contrite heart, O God, O God, O God, &c.
...... *This hath added much, even hath bound up the rod, which I spoke before-unto thee.*
Δ Thy mercies be recorded, likewise, O Lord, and praised from Generation to Generation.
After this we sat and confidered, and perceived, and confessed the greatnesse of our offence, how it concerned much the Honour and Glory of God, if we had gone without receiving the advertisement of those Letters; So should they hear (the) and the King *St.* have perceived that we had the direction of God, and of his good Angels, and not to have depended upon mans l tters, or perswasions, &c. we both a like confessed this great misdoing, and so framed our selves to make all speed away that possible we could, the mercies of God be upon us now and ever.

Δ
xx dayes the Stone is to be shut.

E. K. He is here, and said, Be thou shut for twenty dayes, and withal pulled a thing like a Curtain about the Stone, and the Stone seemed to be full of the same substance, being like the froth of the Sea, yet hanging or joyning together like Curds of a posset.

Misericordias Dominum in æternum cantabo, quis sicut Deus meus, qui cum iratus fuerit, misericordiam præstavit contrito corde invocantibus: Soli igitur Deo meo, sit omnis laus, honor, gloria & jubilatio, nunc & semper, *Amen.*

Aprilis 5.   *A Praga.*

Friday, I took my Journey from *Praga* toward *Cracovia,* God be our good speed, *E. K.* I, *Thomas Kelly,* & *Hugh Bricket* my servants.

Friday.   ✝ *Cracovia,*   1585.

Aprilis 12. A meridie we came to *Cracovia,* and as we were within an English mile of the City, being a fair and calm day, there passed about half a mile before us, crossing from the right hand to the left Whirlwinds, divers one after another, wreathing up the dust with great vehemency on high, and shooting forward still, and then mounting into the air, and so went Southerly from us, and likewise some began on the right hand, and came furiously, raising up and wreathing the dust up into the air Southerly also, and did not crosse the way.

When we came to our house, we found that a stranger was set into it, by the Landlords (Mr. *John Long,* the Judge, and *Martin Plutner*) and having by me the keys of the Store-house, and of the Street-door, I caused my stuff brought with me to be set in, and that night we made hard shift for lodging. But the new and forced in tenants gave me leave to have one of my Bedsteads, which was in one stove, and emptied the same to us, with much ado.

Saturday and *Sunday* we were sore out-faced or rather threatned, that we should have no house there, and also one *Bonar* his arms were set upon the door, as if the house had been allowed to him *ex officio.*   *Monday* I made the Rector privy of the Injuries I indured, and he courteously sent two Masters of Art with me to the *Proconsul* to have Citation for the Landlords to appear on Tuesday by 7 of the clock, to answer to our complaint.

This *Monday*-night came the Lord *Lasky* from *Lasko,* upon a Letter he had received from me from *Niso,* of my coming.

Tuesday (*Aprilis* 16) the Lord *Lasky* came to the house, and in the morning would have presently cast all their stuff out of doors, but by entreaty he permitted them to empty all into the lower stove.

In the mean space I appeared with my Lawyer or Attourney Mr. *Tetaldo,* (an Italian) an ancient Practitioner in the *Polish* and *Cracovian* Causes: And to conclude, I had a Decree against my Landlords, that I was to have at leastan half years warning; whereupon *John Laugh* gave me warning to avoid at *Michaelmas,* and so we came from the Court or Town-house, called *Pretorium* in *Lacine.* This same *Tuesday* afternoon, my Lord *Lasky* went to the King of *Poland* up into the Castle, and told him of my comming, and how evilly I was used: And he said, why did he not cast them out of doors? so have I now, quoth the Lord *Lasky*; and the King granted the House to be holden *ex officio*: And *the next day the King was desirous to speak with me.*

Aprilis 17. *Wednesday,* I went with the Lord *Lasky* to the King, to whom I said, to this intent, *Consolatio, pax, & misericordia Dei sit tibi, ô serenissime Rex : Coram quo, Divinitus recipi admonitionem, ut me sustinem, quod nunc humilime facio: paratissimus cum omni fidelitate & sinceritate ea cum Regia vestra Majestate tractare, quæ mihi divinitus injunguntur, Quorum mysteriorum historias de ordine in ordinem referre, prout occasio dabitur, non recusabo aliaque omnia peragere, quæ Deo & vestræ Majestati Regiæ gratia fore intelligero, &c.*

The King answered, *Ut de vestra persona multa bona audivi absente, ita jam mihi gratus valde est adventus vester, & si quod sit in quo vobis mea gratia & favor, possit esse commodo non dero me vestrium favorem, & protectorem existere : Atque de istis & aliis majoribus rebus aliquid magis opportuni loquendi tempus post festos istos dies : quo tempore vos ad me accersori curabo, &c.*

Hereupon I made Coursy, as was appertaining, and stepped back somewhat from the King, and so the Vice-Chancelor and other Officers, the chief Secretary brought Bills to be read, and subscribed, or assigned with the Kings own hand, which he did : and after the Lord *Lasky* had watched a fit time to tell the King of his desire to speak a few words to his Majesty of some of his own affairs, and was bidden to resort straightway after dinner to his Majesty, we took our leave with reverence doing, and so went out of the privy Chamber, or rather with-drawing Chamber through his privy Chamber, where he had said Masse when we came, and so into the Guard-chamber, and down, &c.

Friday, I took Ghostly counsel of Doctor *Hannibal,* the great Divine, that had now set out some of his Commentaries upon *Pymander, Hermitis Trismigisti.*

Saturday (*Aprilis* 20) I received the Communion at the *Pernardines,* where that Doctor is a Professor.

This day *E. K.* the Ghostly counsel and comfort, as his case required.

On *Easter Monday*, very devoutly in Saint *Stephens* Church *E. K.* received the Communion, to my unspeakable gladnesse and content, being a thing so long and earnestly required, and urged of him, by our spiritual good friends, as may appear by sundry former actions.

✝ *Cracovia.*

Tuesday in Easter week,
Aprilis 23. Manè circa horam 8. Præcibus susis; mediocritèr longis.

E. K. Here appears many thousands of spiritual Creatures, all in white : Now there seemeth one like Michael, (all in red) to stand before them, they all standing in an half Moon compasse behind him.

Michael. Michael ...... *Adhuc semel (sed Stephano assidente) Loquor.*
△ *Forte de* *Sed si aurem, & animam suam, loquuta mea præbuerit stabilietur sedes illi.*·.
A.L. intelligit.

E. K. Now they seem all to mourn or hum, all in one tune. He speaketh still, but I understand not his speech.

Sin minus loquitur pro me pestis : ulcere enim percutiam terram Zeli plenus sum, & Justitia.·.

E. K. All are vanished away.

△ Ne observes iniquitates meas (Domine Jesu Christi) qui speramns in misericordia tua, qui redempti sumus prætioso sanguine tuo, *Amen.*

Emitte Domine verbum tuum Evangelicum, ut liquefacias & emolias obdurata corda mea frigore vitiorum, ut mea peccata purgentur, & efficiantur, quasi in Christo, ut nebula ignorantiæ expellatur e cordibus meis, & spiritus Sancto gratia affluant aquæ Lacrymarum in pœnitentia Salutari, *Amen.*

1585. ✝ *Cracovia.*

Aprilis 24. in *Easter-week,*
Wednesday morning, circa horam 8.
Orationibus factis ad Deum, tam oratione Dominica, quam aliis particularitur respectu Ministerii Angelorum, qui regnis president obtinendi, ut nobis præscriptum erat, & dum conarer particulariter *nominare aliquem,* statim incipit *E.K.* & sequitur—,

A woman. *E. K.* There appeareth afar off a woman comming, and she is here now, she is all covered in green, as with a cloud : I may through it discern her fair face, and her hairs dispersed abroad.

The place about her seemeth to be concave, replenished with light of the Sunne : she standeth as in a hollow shell, or Oval figure *Nostrum offi-* concave.
cium erga Ste-
phanum Re- ..... Stephen, *lift up thy head amongst the stars of Heaven ; for the Spirit of God is with thee,*
gem. *and thou art become the Darling of the Highest, but the Lord will reprehend thee for thy sins.*
Aëret 30.
Qui terram Behold, *thou shalt stand, and thy sword shall be made holy : See therefore that you honour him,*
gubernant & labour *for him, and obey him, as the anointed and beloved of the Lord.*
23 Reges Tri-
buum. For why, *his spirit shall be plentiful amongst you, and he shall* put the pillow of rest under your
Vide Anno heads.
1584. Maii 11
1584 Junii 10. *E. K.* The more she speaketh, the more the place is bright.
de Angelis Aë-
rum. .....The Prince of Darknesse *shall lie as a stumbling block in his way, but he shall stride over*
△ *him without offence.*

In libro Enoch The earthly Creatures *have not to do in this receptacle :*
sunt qui terre- Therefore take heed *thou defile it not.*
ui tractant If thou follow the rules of calling them, *thou shalt see that the air is their* habitation.
mali, at in 30 Other wayes irregularly they appear in such vessels : *But such as are prepared* for them.
Aëru sacris Take heed (therefore) *thou defile not the place of the* Justified, *with the presence of those that*
majoribus non are accursed.
sunt tales qui-
bus cum nobis But as they are of two sorts ; *so let their appearing places be divers.*
res est. Thy servant is conducted, *and shall not stumble, but shall return, that the name of God may be*
Vide 21 Maii, blessed.
1584.
Ed sent into Now cease thy voice for our presence, *until the Lord hath rebuked* Stephen *: the consideration*
England. whereof consisteth the seal of his Election.
☞ Verbum *shall be the first word wherein the Lord shall shew himself unto him.*

Behold,

Behold, I am full of the light of heaven, and I shut up and go.

E. K. She is gone·.·

△ Note, all those things I intended or desired to be satisfied in, are answered me without my asking.

Misericordia, Pax, & Lux Dei nobis semper adsint.·. omnis autem laus, honor, & gloria sit Deo nostro, *Amen.*

Nota Cracovia.

Monday, Tuesday, Wednesday.

May 6, & 7,8. E.K. was very unquiet in mind, and so expressed to me in words·: for that *A. L.* had not paid him his money, long since due·: and chiefly for that he doubted very much of *A.L.* his turning to the Lord with all his heart, and constantly. So, *much did A. L. his former life and ungodly living and dealing offend him,* and so void was he of any hope, that he became in a great oppresse of mind to find us coupled with so * *ungodly a man.* I shewed *A.L.* his last Letters, how he was in a Monastery of his own, belonging to the Castle *Rithwyax,* (vvhich he had now by a stratagem won from the unjust delaying of his adversary)and what penance and contrition he was in, what meditations, and what godly purposes, &c. But E. K. would not hope of conversion, and thereupon utterly and resolutely intended with all speed to be gone from hence toward *Prage,* and willed me (if I would) to prepare my Letters, He *became very blasphemous against God* to my great grief and terrour: what the issue thereof would be, so great was the blasphemy and rebellion againit God and his holy purpofes in us, that almost greater could not be uttered. I used as quiet words as I could, assuring him of Gods mercies alwayes ready, and his helping hand for all such as put their trust in him, and call upon him in their troubles and times of need; and so did betake him to God for that Tuesday night, being past 9 of the clock.

* △ what should I then think of both them.

Wednesday morning, as I was at my prayers in my study over his Chamber, and had made declaration of this cause, and of the perplexity most grievous that I was in to see my friend and partner (E.K.) thus carried away with so grievous a temptation, so manifold and vehement.

E.K. yet lying in his bed, did call his brother *Thomas* to him, and willed him to c allme to him.: *Thomas* came (when I had in manner ended my devotions and prayers) for me, I went to him, yet lying in his bed: And after I had wished a good morrow, and sate by him on the Bench at his beds head, he began and said such matter as followeth,

E. K. A Spirit appeared to me this morning by my Bed-side, and bid me be quiet.

Bad me will you to go to morrow with both your servants to my Lord, as secretly as you could.

Bad you comfort him.

Bad you bring him with you.

Bad you to go to the King as you came homeward.

Bad me to board in the mean space with the Italian * Doctor at Perins house.

* *Gregorius; Jordanus; Venitus.*

Bad me lie here every night.

Hereupon I was most glad and joyful, and praised God for his marvellous mercies, loving kindnesse and goodnesse toward us, and declared my self assured that God had put out his term, and setled the degree: For the performance of his purpofes and promises made to us, for his own honour and glory: And so with joy and thanks given E. K. for his courteous imparting these good news to me, I went about my businesse intended, which was to go to the Table of the Lord: as I was prepared for it, and so went to the *Barnardines* Church.

Soli Deo nostro sit omnis laus; honor, gloria, & gratiarum actio, nunc & semper, *Amen.*

Note; I had in my prayers alledged to God, that albeit I was in great perplexity and agony of mind, yet since *I was willed to cease my voice for having at any angelical presence,* I said he of his divine clemency and care over us, in these great desires might counsel us and direct us, though we did not urge our requeft as we were wont. The conclusion and shame which many wayes would follow, if this intended purpose of E. K. should go forward and take place) was so great, that we might seem to the world, to have been led to that evil end, by a manifold digression, rather then otherwise led in mercy and verity, wherein I requested God to regard his own honour and glory, &c.

Cr A

+ *Cracovia,*

Maij 20.
Monday à meridie horam circiter 6. in mansio meo.

NOTE △.

△

E. K. sitting with me in my study, told me, that after my going to *Rithian* to the Lord *Lasky,* he had very many apparitions, and divers matters declared unto him, of the state of *Christendom,* &c.

He said (moreover) fault was found with my manner of standing before *Stephen,* I should have made some more ample declaration of my Calling and knowledge in these our actions. Secondly, that I did mistake the phrase spoken unto me at *Praga* of the *rod binding up* [*] ; For he said, that *Michael Dee* should die, that I should thereby be afflicted, and divers such things he told me, and among other that he was willed *to be ready to leave me, when he should be called :* for, he said, *our actions shall be cut off, for some of our unworthinesse, &c.* All which things were so grievous unto me, as I was (in manner) ready to sound ; and my distresse was the greater, because (after a sort) I was barred from requiring the presence of any of our spiritual friends, till *Stephen* had been rebuked by the Lord, and I had vowed to obey their commandments and instructions, whereby I was driven to beseech God to consider my cause and grief, who unfainedly desired to be his true Servant : And being desirous to obey them, staying of my voice for the presence of his good Ministers, I was contented to offer up my obedience herein for a sacrifice ; and ready to receive this distresse and affliction, as a punishment for my sins, awaiting his will and pleasure.

[margin: * 1585. *Aprilis.* Our actions to be cut off for our unworthinesse.]

E. K. said, It shall not be amisse to bring forth the Shew-stone, and assay what the good will of God would be herein.

△ I fetcht the Shew-stone, and after it had been set about a quarter of an hour. E. K. E-spied in it a little naked boy, with a white cloth scarf, from under his Navel hanging down unto his knees ; The hair of his head is short as of an young child : [and about that time came the Lord *A. L.* unto us, who sat down by us :] He had a little Circle of aire in his hand : There is a light in the stone as if there were the shining of the Sunne in it.

[margin: *Apparition:*]

Puer ...... *Creavit Deus omnia Spiritu oris sui qui etiam Spiritus, defendit & defendet suos, & in nomine suo speravit.*

E. K. He throweth up his Circlet, and catcheth it againe, three times ; He standeth still, and saith nothing more yet.

Puer ...... *Perforatus à Domino, loquor.*

E. K. Now he is turned into a water which goeth round about, and in the midst of it is bloud.

Now he is returned to his former shape again.

Puer ...... *The end of all flesh is at hand.*

And the sickle of the Highest shall reap down the Mountaines ; The Valleys shall be without fruit : And the seed of man shall be accursed.

[margin: *Prophета:*]

E. K. Now he turneth his face to you [△.]

Puer ...... *Who is he that the Lord rejoyceth in, or on whom the Heavens look with merry countenance, whose feet are not a burden to the earth, and in whom is the force of the soul comforted ? Who is he that shall rejoice in the Lord ? Even he it is that goeth out of himself, and beholdeth himself: saying, O thou Carcase thou art a Sepulchre for me ; Neither am I placed in thee, for thine own beauty, but that the Lord may be magnified, and his Creatures dignified ; He it is that shaketh off himself, and putteth on the Armour of Affliction, praising and extolling the Garland of the God of Hosts, before that great Whore, and in despite of her Congregation ; He it is that forsaketh his own will, to do the will of him that created him ; Whosoever (therefore) doth his own will, 't the servant of Perdition ; But he that expecteth the will of God is anointed.*

Behold, therefore, because you do so, and have beheld your selves, not in your selves, have acknowledged the power of God, and the truth of his Message, your Honour shall be great : Therefore fear not, For, lo, This Garland is prepared for you : and rest is sealed unto you, of the Highest, unto you, your wives, children and servants.

[margin: *Domina accepatio nostrorum servitiorum.*]

△ Blessed be thy Name for ever, O eternal, almighty, and most merciful, our God and King of Glory.

Puer

Puer .... *If the Sunne shine not in vain, if the Stars move not, but by variation and discourse, moving things, alternatim, to an end, if the Earth stand still, because she is so created: Much lesse ought man to despaire in the mercies and promises of God, which are not without a cause, neither any time spoken without effect.*

I remember thee (Lasky) *saith the Lord; And I will chasten thee for thy sinnes, and behold, I swear unto thee, as I have done; But humble thy self: This body of thine shall turn into dust. Take heed therefore that it defile not the greater part ; For unto him that dieth a sinner, vengeance is judgment, But if thou live according unto my Lawes, and graft thy self within my will, if thou forsake the World for my sake, and do the works of righteousnesse ; Because I have called thee before me, I will adde unto thy yeares, and will not blot out thy Name out of my remembrance.*

Be not therefore a Man, but the sealed servant of the Highest. Rejoyce in him that created thee, and when I command thee to strike, follow me, for I will make the way very broad for thee.

Behold, I am mindful of my Covenant made unto thee, the seventh day of September in the year fourscore and three.

A.L.

Anno 1583.
7 Septemb.
Moitlaci libro
10.
If

I will establish unto thee, that fortitude, both in true Wisdome and Victory: And I will make thee mighty as a Corner Stane in the Angle of my Temple: if thou turn, if thou do the will of him that speaketh unto thee: if thou become a marble stone, speaking Justice and Verity ; The mysteries of thy Crosse light upon thee, and let thy sonnes be blessed in thee.

I greatly thirst after Steven; for the course of things are at hand.

Behold, I will blesse him, that he may leave blessing unto thee,

Behold, I will place thee unto him, at his right leg, and he shall stand.

But his wicked Garments I will cut in sunder, yea I will send in the fire of wrath and dissention : And I will take away the buttons from his brest.

I have given unto him three wicked Nations, that they may grinde under him as slavish Captives.

Tres impię Nationes data, St.

When I come in one Week, Behold, I strike, and those that are proud, become poor and desolate.

The outward face of things shall be changed; And the whole World shall say, Lo here, is the finger of the highest.

Digitus Dei.

Rise, Therefore, and with speed go before Steven *; But the League Table thou shalt leave behind thee. I will reveal my self in thy proper Shew-stone.*

Mensa fœderis. in meo proprio Lapide mystico.
[O]

Dixi: quærite victoriam,

△ *Deo nostro.Omnipotenti, Patri totius consolationis & misericordiarum plenissimo, sit omnis Honor, Laus, Benedictio, Gloria & Imperium, nunc & semper Amen, Amen, Amen.*

Note.
Maii 21.   △ I did communicate, and this was the third time, within Easter receiving.
Tuesday.   Primo cum *Humbate*, & bis eum *Raphaeli* confessus, &c.
            That all manner of wayes I might have a clean and
            a quiet Conscience.

✝

Maii 22.
Wednesday, Nyepolonicze, in Aula Regia, circa horam 1 ½ a meridie.

Note, after dinner as we sat together, *A. L. E. K.* and I discoursing of some of our matters ; There appeared over *A. L.* his head (to the sight of *E.K.*) a little Child half, the upper part holding over the head of *A.L.* a white Crown, and a finger out of it pointing toward △, and withal he said,

Puer .... *Audivi te victores estis.*

△ Hereupon wo fat out the Shew-stone, as being ready and desirous to be instructed, according as the cause chiefly required.

As I began to pray and study, *Domino non sumus digni ut nos exaudias,* suddenly *E. K.* said he saw as followeth.

E. K. I see a great Hill of fire, a very great Mountain, and it is as if it did hang in the aire : for I see the aire under it, and I see the Sun shine on it ∴ the Mountain fire flameth not.

Now the little boy that appeared last day, standeth on the top of this Mountain.

Puer .... *God hath spoken unto you, and hath gathered you together, and lo, you are become a strong sword, with the which the Nations shall be cut down, and the God of Hosts shall stretch forth his hands ; And behold, you are come, and now is the time you Satan shall reap ∴ But Satan*

tan striveth sore against you ; *Behold*, Lasky *thou art become rich* ; *But have faith: For it overcometh riches , and shall beautifie and strengthen thee , that thou shalt be able to receive reward for thy labour : For it is not a small labour to contend against sinne , I have brought thee unto Steven ; And I will give him thee into thy hands: And because thou shalt see that God is not barren , I am of power ; Hear me therefore saith the Lord , wilt thou that before thy face I shall destroy Steven for his wickednesse ? wilt thou that I shall strike him with a perpetual Leprosie , or wilt thou that I shall correct him and leave him to do good unto thee? Now thou shalt see that I am not weak ; Neither that my words are barren or without fruit : Ask therefore of the Lord , and before thou move it shall be given thee .*. *For thou dealest with him that is a flame of fire , and a two edged sword to the wicked , out of the Dunghil I chose him , out of nothing I can stirre thee up, and exalt thee , but thou must first be poor before thou be exalted, read the Scriptures and judge .*.

Now speak. E. K. He is gone.

Infinitæ & incomprehensibiles sunt misericordiæ tuæ, O Deus, & Judicia tua sunt inperscruta-
bilia, hominibus.

A. L. Domine Deus misericors , quanta est tua misericordia, quod me summum peccatorem
tanta gratia prosequeris? Indignus sum Domine ante faciem tuam : Itaque Domine, quæso , ne illum propter me deleas neque Lepra percutias : sed potius inspires in illum , ut mihi propter te , & à
te, per illum bene fiat. Non quæro Domine divitias, sed gloriam tuam. Non nobis Domine, non
nobis sed nomini tuo da gloriam. Et fiat mihi secundum voluntatem tuam Domine. Tu scis Domine, an hypocritice ago.

Misere mei Domine, miserere mei, sitque misericordia tua supra me & fiat voluntas tua , sicut in
Cœlo, sic etiam & in Terra, Atque nomen tuum sit benedictum in sæcula sæculorum, *Amen.*

E. K. He is here againe.

Puer ...... *Sapiens es tu,* [*A. L.*] *& plenus spiritu Dei : Non quærens sanguine fratris tui
igitur benedictum, sis inter potentes hujus saculi , & ab hac die spiritus meus nunquam à te disce-
det ; & hac quia te humiliasti nam non elegi te sine causa.*.

Puer ..... *And lo, I will correct him sharply : Ask therefore in what Language thou wilt
have me correct him (for he is scarce worthy to hear that he may understand.)*

E. K. He is gone.

A. L. Hungarice peto, ut ipse audiat ea quæ illi sunt dicenda   sic ita Divinæ tuæ placcue-
rit Majestati.

Puer ...... *Hungarie is hateful unto me ; For it is full of iniquity ; Neither will I speak unto
him my self that he shall (yet,) hear me. I will open my mouth in Latin for thy sake: and if he
become obedient , I will also appear unto him my self and unto you all , in the spirit and presence of
my Angel : But to overcome him by Miracles it needeth not , for by him the people are not edified,
But by my words he shall understand, that I touch him, although Satan stand by him : unlesse it
were for thy sake I would not withdraw my word and curse from him , for why, I am sufficiently ad-
vised , And I do but keep back the fire from him.*

*But go thou [A. L.] unto him , and speak unto him liberally , when he hath heard me , if he re-
ceive me , my blessing is upon him of necessity.*

If he hear me not , I can easily unlock for I have the Key ready.

*God the Father, God the Sonne, (unto whom all power is given in Heaven and Earth,) with
the fire of eternal comfort, which is the privy science and knowledg of the faithful; The Holy*

*Ghost, be upon thee, and with thee for this day, thy [A. L.] sinnes are blotted out of Gods re-
membrance.*

I have no more to say.

Omnipotenti , tremendo & Solis Adorando Deo , & Domino nostro sit omnis gratiarum actio,
Laus & Jubilatio, nunc & in omne ævium. *Amen.*

+ *Nyepolonicæ in Aula Regis Polonie.*

Anno 1585.
Maii. 23. A meridie hora Circiter 6.

The *King* sent for the Lord *Lasky* and me, by his Vice-Chamberlaine , whom we came unto in
a Chamber, within the Chamber or roome where he useth to give audience , or to eat with his Pa-
latines and other : He sat by the Window which is toward the South , and by which his Prospect
is into his new Garden, which is in making : He began thus , (the Lord *Albert Lasky* being by,
and thereto willed by the King,) and said unto me very near as those words import.

St. Egit mecum Dominus Palatinus, ut vos audirem de rebus istis magnis & raris   loquen-
te : Quod libentur feci : & tamen hoc considerari debet , quod Prophetæ omnes & revelationes
jam diu & in tempore Christi cessaverunt. *Tamen si nihil in istis , contra Dei sit honorem, , eo lu-
bentius sunt audienda :* Et ego quidem haud dubito quin Deus nunc possit multis modis secreta
quædam hominibus deligere, ad hac usque tempora, mandatis & inusitatis.

Heer-

Hereupon I answered to this sence, although I cannot expresse the same words.

Δ Considero in ordine veſtræ regia tria quaſi capitala, in quibus totus ordinis veſtræ eſt medulla. Primum de Prophetiaris, & revelationem ceſſatione, ſecundum; an aliquid in noſtris actionibus, vel exercitiis inſit contra Dei honorem : & tertium (quod animo meo eſt valde gratium) quod, Deo non præſcribatis certos aliquos modos vel tempora quibus ſua hominibus velit aut debeat ſecreta detegere. De primo, hoc poſſimus veſtræ Majeſtati Reginæ aſſerere, quod ille Scripturæ locus haud recte a plurimis intelligeter : & ab illis peſſime, qui velint omni modæ. Dei potentiæ & miſericordiæ & ſapientiæ præſcribere certos modos, & tempora certa : aſſerendo nullorum hiis temporibus eſſe Prophetiam, vel poſt Chriſtum fore : quia omnes in Chriſto ceſſavere : hoc eſt, quia omnes de illo quæ erant Prophetiæ ſcilicet. De Dei filio in-carne venturo & Meſſia vero, & redemptore generis humani futuro, (& de tota illa quam nos agnovimus & confitemur Chriſtiani, completum & conſummatum eſſe Chriſti hiſtoria) jam ceſſavere : adeo quod illa neque jam futura ſunt ut putant Judæi, neque repetenda ſunt, cum jam ſunt conſummata & peracta quemadmodum Prophetæ prænuntiabant nam ob hac cauſa cum Chriſtus Jeſus in cruce pendens ſciniſſet, quod omnia de eo Prophetia completa fuiſſent, & præcepimus ſcilicet omnium Prophetiarum (ante Chriſtiano) ſcopus jam eſſet Collinatus, & Juxta præſentiam & propoſitum Dei redemptoris humane conſcientiam eſſet myſterium ipſe dixit conſummatum eſt : Nam & Paulus dixit ad Judæos, (namque conſummaſſent omnia quæ de eo *ſcripta erant,* deponentes eum, de Ligno poſuerunt eum in monumento. Et poſt Reſurrectionem ſuam ipſammet Chriſtus ſuis diſcipulis (pergentibus verſus Caſtellum *Emaus,* & de illius morte & reſurrectione differentibus & dubitantibus) dixit, O ſtulti & tardi corde ad credēdum in omnibus quæ locuti ſunt Prophetæ: Nonne hæc oportuit pati Chriſtus, & ita intrare in gloriam ſuam, & incipiente a Moyſe & omnibus Prophetis interprætabitur illis in omnibus ſcripturis, *quæ de ipſo erant,* &c. & paulò poſt iterum ad eoſdem vobiſcum : Quoniam neceſſe *impleri omnia qua ſcripta ſunt* *.* *lege Moyſi & Prophetu, & Pſalmis de me.*]

* *Joan.19 E:*
Acts 13. E.

Luke 24.

Sed quantum ad alium ſenſum quod poſt Chriſtum mille eſſent Prophetæ vel relationes ipſam Scripturæ planiſſime contrarium docent. Nam quod deſcendum erit de revelatione ſine notabile illa Beati *Joanni Apocalypſi* quæ poſt Chriſtum erat ? quæ & ab eodem *Joanne* Propheta vocatur, dicendo * *Beatus qui legit & audit verba Prophetiæ hujus & ſervat ea qui in ea ſcripta ſunt, & in ultimo Capite ejuſdem Apocalypſeos ſine revelationes, ter, eadem vocat Prophetiæ librum.* Quare manifeſtum eſt poſt Chriſtum eſſe Revelationes & Prophetas. Præterea que erat illa *Paulo* facta revelatio in ejus Vocatione & Converſione per ipſum Chriſtum, ut in Apoſtolicorum apparet Acteum libro, Cap.9. quid de illa decennes * *Cornelio* Centuriano.

* *Cap.1. Apoc.*

* *Acts 10.*

Quid de illa *Petro* de animalibus mundis & immundis. Et *Paulus* ipſam dicet ſi
Δ
gloriari oportet (non expedit quidem) veniam ante ad viſiones & revelationes Domini, Δ
&c. & paulò poſt : & de Magnitudo revelationem extollit me, datus eſt mihi ſtimulis carnis meæ, Angelus Satanæ qui me colophizet es, notum mihi factum eſt ſacramentum, ſicut ſupra ſcripſi : prout poteſtis legentes intelligere prudentiam meam in myſterio Chriſti, quod aliis generationibus non eſt agnitum filiis homini, ſicut *nunc revelatum* eſt ſanctis Apoſtolis ejus & *Prophetis* in ſpiritu, &c, ubi etiā Prophetas poſt Chriſtū eſſe apparet : & cap.4. Et ipſe dedit quoſdam quidem Apoſtolos quoſdam autem *Prophetas,* alios vero Evaugeliſtis, alios autem Paſtores & Doctores ad confinmationem ſanctoium, in opus miniſterii, in ædificatione Corporis Chriſti, Donec occurramus omnes in unitate fidei in menſuram ætate plenitudinis Chriſti, &c. ubi tam diu Prophetas fore in Eccleſia *Chriſti* poſt Chriſtū apparet. *Donec* occurramus omnes in unitate fidei, &c. quod nondum poſt Chriſtum factum fuiſſe bene ſimus & jam hæc ætate noſtra maxime ſumus circa negotium fidei diſcordes maxime videntur eſſe neceſſariæ non Prophetæ ſolum ſed etiam Revelationes valde expreſſe de Myſteriis Divinus. Et de locotione Angelica * ad *Philippum,* & ejus de loco in locum inviſibile quaſi tranſlatione per Spiri-

* *Acts 11.*
2 *Ad Cor. c.12;*

* *Acts cap.8.*
Philippi datater à loco in locum per Spiritum Dei

Gg 2   rituum

ritum Domini, quod putendum eft. Et de Prophetis poft Chriftum tempora teftificatur *Actum* undecimum caput, ubi legimus quod eodem tempore quo primum difcipuli Chrifti *Antiochiæ* cognominarentur Chriftiani, fuperdenerunt ab *Jerifolymis* Prophetæ *Antiochiam*, & furgens unus ex eis nomine *Agabus*, fignificabat per fpiritum, famem magnam futuram univerfo orbe terrarum, quæ factum eft fub *Claudio*, ad fecundum autem veftræ Majeftatis Regiæ Capitulum, fic refpondeo quod coram Deo & beatis ejus Angelis, aftere quod confcientia mea nihil adhuc deprehendit, Notivit, vel dijudicare potuit, neque poffit in omnibus noftris actionibus, vel illarum aliqua, quod fit contra Dei, honorem, vel gloriam, Immo, quod ad Dei honorem & gloriam valde fpectent, poffimus.

Denique tertio in loco quod cum magna & veræ pia Regiaque & difcretione exiftitis, me Deum Omnipotentem iis temporibus poffe modis fuis variis, hominibus quibufdam fua manifeftare myfteria & fecreta. Valde letor: & eo magis, quod tam ex noftris præteritis id conftare potuerit multis Actionibus, quam ex futuris: quibus inter effe & adeffe præfens (fi ita illi vifum fuerit) veftra poffit Majeftas Regia. " Et præ-
" teritarum noftrorum Actionum libros 24, paratus fum (quocunqne veftræ fereniff-
" fimæ Majeftati placuerit tempore,) videndos exhibere, quorum quædam Latina
" lingua, Græca aliæ, aliæ Anglica lingua, fed ex maxima parte Anglica funt Confcri
" ptæ ipfæ actiones Angelorum, *viz.* Dei bonorum Inftructiones, admonitiones, ex-
" hortationes, conciones, Prophetiæ, & quocunque alio funt. Cenfendæ nomine nobis
" factæ Revelationes, reales vel verbales, & per fpatium jam trium fere annorum à
" nobis receptæ & annotatæ, &c.

+ *Nyepoloniza in Aula Regia præfente ipfo Stephano Rege,* & A. L, *&c.*

Die Luna

May 27. Mane, horam 7. circiter. In camera privata Regis.

In lapide qui Angelus mihi addixit: ut præfcriptum erat, noftri actio cum eodem. " A.L. E.K.

Omnipotens, Sempiterna, Vera, & uni Deus, ò tu mifericors Pater mei, qui me de Patria mea funefta contra me concepta malicia, per Angelos tuos bonos admonifti, & per eofdem, inde, me cum Uxore, Liberis, & Familia mea iftifq, * duobus, egredi juffifti: e egredientis noi, ex fertibus maris, quafi miraculofe liberafti: Et qui ex homicidiarum & Hereticorum manibus & fraudibus variis nos expedivifti: Et qui multis nos modis (partim nobis cognitis, partim incognitis) a periculis & morte protexifti, ab eo tempore, quod ad tua fecreta Judicia & negotia teftificanda, tractanda & promovenda nos vocafti: Ideo propter hunc tuam tantam & tuam admirabile mifericordiam; immortalis tibi à nobis deberi laudes & gratias humiliime agnofcemus. O tu Pater nofter Clementiffime qui * nos duos; vinculo tuo Divino arctiffimo copulafti: & quafi unum ex duobus, effe voluifti. O tu fortiffime Deus meus qui hanc tuum Lasky, quafi Athletam meum cantiffimum, animofum, & tuam amantiffimum, nobis adjunxifti: virum Catholica tua & orthodoxa Religionis amantiffimum & Anti-chriftianifmi omnis acerrimum hoftem; Denique ò Sapientiffime, Potentiffime & Optime Deus, & Pater meus, qui tuis mox incipiendis Regiis, magnis mirifici Conatibus, quem fatiebat Regem, tandem invenifti Stephanum, tuum futurum Bellatorem; quis tuo minui, & juffit ex animis, totis tuis viribus, & maximo zelo obedire velit: & eus nos honorem & obedientiam & exhibiemus, in mandatis dedifti: & propter quem labores (tibi metas) ut fubiremus & fuftinueremus ftatuifti: & ad quem, poft laboriofas peregrinationes noftri multiplices quidem, præter 7 Menfes factas, directas aliquas, alias ante, (humano judicio) quafi retrogradas, tuam maximam gratiam, favore: & auxilio incolumnios & falvos nos perduxifti: Nos quafi hic tuos, tuo Nomine & una mente convenientes, tua dignes Paterna mifericordia, à totius vita mea omnibus purgare fpurciliis: Et Chariffimi tui Filii Domini & Redemptoris Nomini Jefu Chrifti intercedentibus meritis, nobis Condona quicquid contra Leges tuas Sanctas & Jufta, volentes, vel nefcii, vel negligentes, verbo, facto vel cogitatione ad hanc ufque horam offenderimus omnes & finguli, ut tibi jam poffimus maffa pura & azima offerri: uná Divina & abundantiffima firmitanda gratia; & tua charitatis igne in cordibus noftris per te accenfo, quafi quidem proportionis & facti in Templo tuo efficiamur panes. Et fit nobis interim Filius tuus Dominus noftris Jefus Chriftus Panis vitæ: quem guftando fuaviffimum, & fidei vertibus tranfgladiendo vivaciffimum Manna eundem habeamus nobifcum in perpetuum, mitte igitur nunc Luce & Veritatem tuam ò Deus Omnipotens fempiterna, Viva, & Vera, & tuo Stephano (nofter autem Sereniffimo Gratiofiffimoque Regi) appareat, Te Deum noftrum verum vivam, Omnipotentem Doctorem noftrum in iis actionibus & Myfteriis effe me auté (licet peccatis obnoxium) voto & Conatu magno, fidele tuam & fincerum effe fervatum: omniaque tua juffa mihi maxime effe Cura: ut usque fingulos fingularia in te autem mundi exordium prædinatos effe muneribus, in tuo Sancto fervitio tractandis, &c.

E. K.

E. K. Nihil poſt primas præces apparebat.

△ Breves ſecundas feci, & adhuc nihil apparebat.

Tertias adjeci, etiam breves.

Poſt tertias ex lapide quidem Calor in faciem ipſius.

E. K. Exire videbatur.

Circa lapidis oram & fimbriam rubicundus viridis circulus apparebat.

E. K. Jam video hominem albis indutum veſtibus, & ſuccinctis
facie longa ſparſis crinibus, & adeus notu quaſi undentibus, &
dexter pes ſtans ſuper magnum lapidem rotundam, & ſiniſter ſuper
aquam, & poſt dorſum ejus magna lux eſt : Nunc video terram ſub
pedibus ejus, ſed quaſi inaere videtur eſſe tam lapis ipſe quam a-
qua illa.

△ Sit benedictus Deus noſter, & fiat voluntas ejus.

Aquæ curſus (qui verſus Occidentem eſt) pedem ejus videtur ſecundum ſe prius deferre.

Videtur iſte longo à me eſſe cum intueor faciem ejus interdum una apparet eſſe interdum tres facies & ita confuſo quodam modo.

E. K. Audio magnam vocem Dicentem , *Veni & Vidi.*

E. K. Deſcendit jam alter ad illum quaſi Globus Ignius cum
facie eminenti, & ab ejus corpore quaſi verga arundinea videtur e-
manare.

...... *Inſpexi , & examinavi , & ecce, Nulla eſt Juſticia.*

Vox ..... *Interet aqua in mare, & fiat falſa , quia ecce tertia viola eſt plena.*

Anglice omnia dicta erant uſque ad verbum ab,&c.

E. K. Jam venit ignis , & illum totum circundat , aliquo mini-
mo : Circa illud relecto intervallo ſibi proximo.

Vox ..... *Menſura.*

Menſuravi & ſigillum eſt (52) quinquaginta duo.

Aſt ecce, ſum plenus Juſtitia & Miſericordia.

Vis igitur tu , quod aperies os meum ?

Aſt quare inquit Dominus viſitarem Stephanum humiliet Semetyrum.

E. K — Inclinat caput ſuum] quia ecce habeo quod dicam, &
ecce habeo,& labia mihi confuta ſunt.

*Magnificat igitur potenti Cœli & terræ Deum Creatorem , Regem & illuminaterem quod poſ-
ſit vobis peccatoribus propitius eſſe & vultum ejus miſericordiæ ſuper vos convertere.*

E. K. Jam converſus eſt totus in Globium igneum.

△ Miſerere noſtri Domine,ſecundum magnam miſericordiam tuam,&c.

E. K. Jam magnus quidam fumus per plicas quaſdam (inſta nubis) lapidem operet.

L. K. Jam videtur illa nubes convoluta eſſe , & ſeorſim ad u-
num latus lapidis ſepoſita.

...... *Verbum, ab altiſſimo miſſus facio ;*

    Quamobrum erige te & diligentir

    Attende Stephane , quis te a Cunabulis

    Dnutrivit ? quis viarum tuarum labores.

△ *Latine hæc ſunt verbatim dicta.*
△ *Nota quod hæc Stephani Regis reprehenſio intipiebat Latine , ab hac dictione verbum quemadmodum prædixit, Mali Cratovia*

*Aut juventutis tua temeritate menſuravit ? ab impetu judicii & temporis : quis te legit ?
aut unde munitus es Cæleſti decore? Hanc tibi animam viventem, ſagacem, & ſale plenum, quis
induxit ? Nonne Rex ille gloria, in cujus gratiam omnis ſubjecta eſt, in cælo & in terra poſte-
ſtas ? quis te potenti elevans brachio à milite ad majorem, a majore, ad maximum evocavit ſep-
trium; Nonne idem ille , qui te & vocat & viſitat : & de ſemetipſo, ante ſæcula dixit, Ego
ſum ? Quare igitur, Nebulam tam tenebroſam, tanta ecce caligine tanta dico ingratudine ſuffui-
tam , inter Deum tuum, & animam tuam induxiſti ? An, quod non accepiſti habes? [he ſhaked
his hand at the King, after the Polonian manner] Aut unde (Dic) Diadema Capitis ? Ecce quia
in fragili cordis tui prudentia, Deum à ſiniſtris, immo à tergo, poſuiſti, ſequitur te ſpirius malignus*

lignus: *Nam erasti: Igitur multiplicata & numerata sunt peccata tua in Cælis, Judicium tuum in te canes ipsi cum pseuda Propheta ferant inquinata sunt Regia tua scelere turpissimo, Cubicula tua olent malum, igitur surrexit Deus turgidus & terribilis factus est & iratus tibi. Verum sic dicit Dominus; quia patres tui, ad Altare meum sanctiores stetere, neque perversi a voce & via mei recessere; te autem, quia virum a vulgo distinctum seperando seperavi, & seperatum, eligendo, dilexi: Non visitabo iniquitates tuas in virga mea: Neque Dejiciam te quemadmodum decrevi: Sed in Solio titubanti sedeas permittam. Verum si brachium meum Zelo cognoveris potens: si impietatem tuam derelinques; si te munditia ornaveris, si fetidam a sinu tuo lepram & alunica tineam, (non ad vomitum rediens) abster serie Ego quoque iram avertam meam, & dies tua relinqua stabiliemur fortitudine: Reges maledicti & pœnites hujus nudi intoxicati calice, Meretricis (mea quia neglexere statuta) fulmine ire meo in manu, & ante pedes tuos cadent ferrorique erit gladius tuus mattonibus, tutela te Cæli circumducent dum in robore dextera tua peribunt inimici.*

Cor populi tui, a se alienatum, post modicum repurgabitur: qui autem in sanctum conspiramere turpissimo, cadent usterre Adhuc si latere meo cum firmiter, tam fideliter adhaseam abumbrabit te spiritus visus & evades sapiens: teque res Fœcundabis de Cœlo. Hac est veritas & Lex Domini, quam proposui tibi Lux Dei hodie Stephano: *Igitur sume tibi gladium femori, estringe, eleva pro Domino & veritate, pugna, vince, Regna Nois (sicut homo,) timori cedere, neque de mundo queritate: quia Deus tuus tecum est; Ignis terribilis & magnus Dominus exercituum: Igitur si os tuum juste a folio aperies; si impium condemnaveris impietatis impleto te spiritu meo, & anima tua repleatur igni potenti, dum manus tua vindicant Cœlos, [inclinas caput.]*

* Forte Uriel.

Bohemia.

Impiam illam generationem, (de qua Domino loquuntur est, & in servitutem tibi tradidit,) cum videris tempus, cum filiis suis, & a populo suo, a parvo usque ad majore, percute gladio ut pro impietate peccati, sit plagarum numerus; quia erit instictus Bohemia (non minus odiosa Cælis: quam terra gravis, & tediosa) signata tibi est; & maledicta in jubare solis, Collige & Orna.

Fuge pedem in Aquilone, & digitis tange mare, & nolis pernere coronam altissimi ostendam tibi nomen meum, & ponam laudes tuas inter aquas. Cinge te etiam sicut forti, amplectere montes meridionales; & ædifica mihi altare: Eripiam enim vincula ab illis. Ab Occidente, manus violentas in viscera tua extenuunt: Sed ferro præscindam illas ungues. Denique si a peccatis cessaveris, si studio flagrabis cælestium, & ambulandus coram me Domino Deo tuo in justitia, & veritate, & nunc quid in nomine meo superis benedicatur & in me splendorem suscipit; Sin autem, verba, qua

Egomet ulter existam vide Junii 24.

locutus est Dominus, audire nolueris, Egomet ulter existam hodie exaltavi te in Domino, & posui caput tuum inter stellas: Esto igitur obediens: Paratus est terror impiis, & maledictus est mundus: Beatus autem qui fideliter observant Verba, & illa custodiet qua Dominus hodie facis Gratia Dei patris, Jesu Christi filii, ejus [inclinas caput] & Spiritus Sancti visites vos semper [extendit manus suas valde.]

△ Amen.

Adduc familiam tuam cum celeritate.

Anglice hoc dixit.

▲ Sit benedictus nomen altissimi qui in servandis promissis est constantissimus, & in misericordiis abundantissimus .⁑. Illi Gloria, Laus, Honor, decus, jubilatio, & gratiarum actio nunc & semper. *Amen.*

Maii 28.   ✝

Tuesday mane circa 6. In Nyepolonize.

△ *Oratione finita & aliquibus verbis factis, de nostra cum Stephano Actione præterita hæri.*

E. K. Here is he that was yesterday in our Action with the King.

Hei mihi (saith the Lord) [He stoopeth by little downward] *why do I hold my hand from the Earth? What have all the Princes of the World built a Tower against me? These in denying me and my Majestie: The other wallowing in extream drunkennesse amongst the pleasures and blindnesse of the flesh, neglecting (without fear) my Commandements, have I thrown out the Children from the Vineyard, and called in the Dung-carriers? have I visited my servants, (whom I chose,) in wrath and indignation with the Sword of Justice? have I thus scattered them upon the face of the World, without a Shepherd, to entertain blasphemous Murderers, Lyars, and the Runnagates of the Earth, the seed of Cain, and of the cursed? O you Caterpillers, O you that fill the Earth with poison? O you abusers of my Name, and Dishonorers of my Temple? What is the cause that you are so barren, or that the Lord hath not mightily shewed himself amongst you, as unto his Children? Why are not the Miracles and Wonders a Testimony of the God of Truth amongst you, as they were unto the Israelites? Why hath not the Sea divided her self? Why, hath not the Lord delivered you from bondage? Unto the Israelites he gave a fruitful Land,*

land (the poſſeſſion of the wicked) abounding with *Milk* and *Honey* : unto you , he hath deliue-
red your poſſeſſion unto the Dogs: and your children to become Captives, why doth not the God of Hoſts
ſtretch forth his hand ſaying: Deliver my people from bondage? are not the times of thoſe latter dayes
and of the Harveſt of the Diſciples * ſhadowed amongſt the doings and graces of the Iſraelites, you
are become blind , you have eyes but you ſee not , for you * know not the time of your viſitation.
O thou ſtiff-necked Generation this is the cauſe, that the finger of God commeth not amongſt you :
This, this is the cauſe , becauſe you have not Faith : Neither is the Spirit of godlineſs and obedience
amongſt you, can he that is all Truth defile himſelfe with lying : or can the fleſh of man diminiſh the
authority of the Godhead : is Chriſt Jeſus, (very God of very God) of leſs power or ſtrength unto
you , then he was before , unto the ſeed of Abraham : becauſe he hath taken your fleſh upon him.
O you ignorant , ô you blind ſtrangers , O you that were faithful in the ſight of the Lord , is not
the God of Heaven and Earth heire unto you , by reaſon of his Man-hood have you not now acceſs your ſelves unto the Throne of the Higheſt, which your Fathers had not ? the Iſraelites ran unto
the Prophets and high Prieſts : yea ,they durſt not run before the Lord : For it was ſaid of them
* Let them ſtand before the hill. They brought their offerings to the Prieſt , which offered up their
prayers and humility : But unto you (ô you of little faith) the Gates are ſet open : yea, even unto
the Throne of God : why therefore, doe you not aſcend unto your Chriſt , Which is anointed before
the Father. Hath he anointed him for himſelfe, or for you? for both : If you have no miracle , you
have no faith , if you have (ſaith the Son of God) faith , to be compared with a Muſtard-ſeed, &c.
But you do none of theſe things, neither is the name of God magnified amongſt you , Is it not a
ſhame , that the faith of man groweth not to be equal with a Muſtard-ſeed, is it not a ſigne of your
ſlaviſh nature , from the which you were called, that there is no faith amongſt you?
   True it is : For why the blood of Chriſt is ſhed upon you : and you are waſhed without deſerts ,
Behold, now (ſaith the Lord) when I have ſtirred up a Moſes there are no Iſraelites that will follow
him : the ſeed of Abraham is deſtroyed with the Winter of ſelf-love and diſ-obedience.
   The Lord groaneth, ſaying : Whether ſhall I turn me ? unto whom ſhall I ſhew my face ? if I ſay
unto them go out, ſet your Tents againſt the wicked : Behold, I will be amongſt you , and fight for
you : who is it that heareth me ? where is your faith become ? who is he that believeth me , O you
wicked Generation ſhall the Lord call you and ſeeke your deliverance , and will you know of the
Lord with what meanes he will work amongſt you, is the God of Heaven and Earth become amongſt
you an Ingineer or a Merchant, a Hoorder up of worldly treaſure ; or one that rideth on horſe-back, to
battail ? you ſtinking Carrion, you hateful wretches before Heaven and Earth , you blind hirelings.
Who devided the Seas who threw down Jericho, who overthrew the wicked Kings? who deſtroyed
the Cities of the wicked ? who fought againſt the reprobate Giants and the fleſh of mankind ? who
opened the windows of Heaven and conſumed you all except as you read * eight perſons, yea, if
out of the windows I can conſume you , what ſhall become of you if I open my doors, if I ſend out
my ſervants againſt you, and my innumerable   army, Is it not ſaid, whatſoever I put into your
mouthes , that ſpeake. Why do you ſo, but for the truths ſake : If therefore I bid you doe, is not my
truth all one ? I am full of ſorrow : for no man openeth his doors unto me , no man believeth me :
no man remembreth that I made Heaven and Earth :

△ As the Iſraelites
and Hiſmaſ-
lem knew not
the time of
their viſitation
and ſo are
theſe dayes
ſhadowed in
the Iſraelites
act, &c.

*Exod. c.19. be

Miracula
Fides.

A Moſes.

Haec reſpiciam
verba Stephani
Regis cum quo
medio.

* Geneſ. 7. 8.

Stay a while that I may weep with my ſelf.

E. K. All the ſtone is become black and
full of fiery ſpecks.

△ After we had read the premiſſes

E. K. Here is another now come in green a man with nothing
on his head but onely his yellow hair.

He hath like a pair of black boots under his garments cloſe to
his legs : like buskins &c.

Ilimeſt. *Vide*
infra.

△ Note *Ilemeſe* appeared in July,
Anno 1548, and did make an end of
Nalvage his work, &c.

△

Iteach you [he pauſed after a pretty while

He appeareth their like a little
child with yellow hair, &c.

Thus ſaith the Lord thou muſt anſwer Steven according to the hardneſs of his hart : Anſwer
him thus , for the Mean : Lo, King, the God of Heaven and Earth hath placed me before thee , and
hath ſhewed unto thee his will , hath nouriſhed up me his ſervant from my youth unto this day , in
the fear of him and the fervent deſire of true wiſdome , whereby I have attained (through his help)
unto the knowledge and ſecrets of the things in Nature : which knowledge behold in the name of God
and for his ſake : and becauſe he hath choſen thee , lo, I offer up unto thee , and willingly made thee
partaker of; This done be not afraid to open thy mouth unto him , as thou didſt unto Rodolph, in
writing, Behold (ô King) I can make the Philoſophers Stone , for ſo they call it , Bear thou therefore the Charge, and give me a name within thy Court that I may have acceſs unto thee : and yearly
maintenance of thee for us both ; Command him alſo, or ſtrike a band of ſecrecy between him ; thy
ſelfe;

Reſponſum pri-
mo Stephano
Rige.

Rodolf the
Emperour.

For us both
E. K. and △

Fides.

Genef. 23. D

* p'em diebus
. Tondum à
responsis pe-
tendis.

felfe, and Lasky. _Take heed thou want not faith :_ for I will help thee : _And he shall_ have a great Treasure , _I will see them,_ if he will _labour for me. But it may be Lasky will hold him by the heele._

△ What mean you by that phrase ?

..... _As_ Jacob _did_ Esau.

Unto this apply thy self, and give thy whole endeavor _from time, ta time also I will open my_ mind unto _Stephen_ through thee, or in the presence of himself.

But let Lasky open this unto him : The Camp is known unto me.

△ I understand not this point,

..... _Let him understand, thou art minded so to doe._

For this seven dayes, aske no more answer.

△ How, and if the King be desirous of any action ?

..... _I respect not the King,_

△ I beseech you be not offended that I aske your name ?

..... _Ilemese._   E. K. He is gone.

△ The other will come again.

A voice. _Non venit._

Therefore shut up the window.

Deus Cœli & Terræ da nobis Fidem.

+ _Nyepolomiczo in_ Aula Regis St.

Junii,

Tuesday a meridie circa horam tertiam : The King send for me to hear what I had to say to him as I had , send him word that I had to say somewhat to him in God his behalfe. When I was come into his privy Chamber, and all others excluded but onely the Lord _Lasky_ who came with me , and stayed by the King his commandement. I said thus _verbatim_ as followeth.

△ Ecce (ô Rex) Deus Cœli & terræ , me ante oculos Vestros posuit : & vobis suam declaravit voluntatem: me autem servum suum à juventute mea ad præsentem diem enutrivit in timore illius, & desiderio serventi veræ sapientiæ qua ratione(& ejus auxilio)assecutus sum cognitionem & secreta rerum naturalium quàm cognitione (ecce) in nomine Dei.

Junii 6   + _Cracovia._

Mane horam circiter 8 .∴.

Orationibus finitis, pro luce & veritate Divina, quæ nos ducerent & perducerent ad montem sanctum _Sion._ &c.

I have (ô Lord) according to my simple abilitie , endeavoured my self to declare to _Steven_ those things I was willed ; accept , ô Lord, my intent, and give me thy graces and encrease my faith that I may in my doings and sayings, please thee or not offend thy divine Majestie, and now ô Lord, we await thy further direction : not presuming to propound (as now) matter, such as our final state might move us unto : but therein we crave this aide , thy light and wisedome, &c.

K. E. Here is a great head with wings like a Cherubim : all of fire, the eyes are very big, _as big as your hat_ , and his head as big _as this Table._

..... _He that is asleep let him sleep on, he that is in the high way let him not return home. He that eateth let him not rise, but eat still, and he that weepeth let him weep still, he that rejoyceth let him rejoyce for ever. He that goeth awry let him not return into the way. He that planteth his Vineyard let him not see it, he that gathereth the grapes let him not drink of them, he that blasphemeth the name of God, let him blaspheme, for he returneth not. But he that looketh up unto Heaven, let him not cast his eyes upon the Earth._

Behold, the Lord hath forgotten the Earth, and it is a burden to me that I am here , _therefore I go. Unto those that do well, the Steward is ready with the reward, we be unto the Monster of the Earth, for he is accursed._

E. K. He is gone : and _flyeth in a strange order :_ upward in a special line in manner ?

A voice. _Put all things to silence that the Lord had touched,_

The receptacle and the Books, see you open them not, nor touch them until you hear more from me. But be of right heart, and walke the ways that you are returned into.

Take this one lesson: you are in favour with me, and for the rest care not.

△ Thy mercies be sealed upon us for ever and ever, ô Lord, of Hosts.

E. K. Now is a red thing, like a Cloud come all over the stone.

Ignem tui amoris & præpotentis fidei in cordibus nostris, accende, ô Deus Omnipotens nunc & semper. _Amen._

Anno 1585. *Augusti* 6.

Unica Actio; quæ *Pucciana* vocetur.

Que durabat ab hora 5. manè, ad horam 11.

P R A G Æ.

Actio *Pucciana.*

✝ *Praga.*

Augusti 6.   *Actionis Pucciana,*
Tuesday, Manè, circa ortum Solis , & nobis heri injungebatur.   *prior pars.*
Fusis de mœre præcibus, &c. præsentibus nobis △ , *E. K. & Fr.* Pucci, ut præscriptum erat.
   Disposita erat Mensa fœderis : Candelaque cerea accensa.

E. *K*: Here is one , covered in white to the breast , all white apparalled, he hath a long glasse in his left hand , full of filthy loathsome stuffe , like matter or like bloud and milk, or curds mingled
together , and a staffe about an ell long in his right hand , he setteth the end on the ground , he pointeth with his staffe toward the
* Table of Covenant.
   Accede Dominum.   △ I had set *s.*
                                                    K. at the usu-
     △ He [*E. K.*] came to the Table of Covenant , and looked into the *Holy-stone,* al Table, in
        and saw the same vision, but his face is (here) bare, and he seemeth to be *Uriel.* our secret stu-
                                                dy, and had set
   △ Benedictus qui venit in nomine Domini : ô beata Dei Lux,   my usual
   U R I E L. ......, *Gloria tibi Domine, Rex cœli, & terra, qui es, & venturus es.* Shew-stone
E. *K.* Now I see the foundation of an old thing , as though it   before him.
were of a Church.
   A voice ,.....*, Measure.*
   Measure from the East to the North , and from the North to the West part , for behold , the rest
is judged already.
   U R I E L ...... *I have measured, (Lord)* 25, *and the half of twenty five.*
   37 ½
   The voice ...... *Divide into three parts.*   [△ The third part of 37½]
   U R I E L .... *It is done.*   is 12½.
   The voice ...... *Unto the Kings of the East give the first.*
   Unto the Kings of West give the second.
   The remnant measure unto the dayes of the North : that the fire of my indignation , may be a
bridle amongst them, and that the whole World (except the excepted) may drink of the sorrow of the Prophetia
seventh part of the half time, yet to come.
   U R I E L ...... *Thy mouth (O Lord) is a two-edged sword, thy judgments are perpetual and*
everlasting, thy words are the spirit of truth and understanding, thy Garments most pure and smel-
ling incense ; Thy Seat without end , and triumphing, who is like unto thee amongst the Hea-
H h

                                                                       vens,

vens, or who hath known thy beauty? Great art thou in thy holy ones, and mighty in thy word a-mongst the Sonnes of men: Thy Testament is holy, and undefiled, The glory of thy Seat, and the health of thy Sounes: Thy anointed is sacrificed, and hath brought health unto the faithful, and unto the Sonnes of Abraham. *Thy spirit is everlasting, and the oil of comfort: The Heavens (there-fore) gather themselves together, with Hallelujah to bear witnesse of thy great indignation and fu-ry prepared for the Earth, which hath risen up with the Kings of the Earth, and hath put on the Wedding Garments: saying with her self I am a Queen: I am the daughter of felicity. Remem-ber all ye, that are drunken with my pleasure, the Character I have given you, and prepare your selves to contend with the Highest, set your selves against him, as against the anointed, for you are become the Children of a strong Champion: whose Sonne shall garnish you with the Name of a Kingdome, and shall poure wonders amongst you, from the starres, which shall put the Sunne the steward of his Waggon, and the Moon the handmaid of his servants. But, O God, she is a Lyar, and the fire-brand of destruction. For, behold, thou art mighty, and shalt triumph, and shalt be a Conquerer for ever.*

E. K.   Now the Stone *is* full *of white smoak.*

△ A Pauſe.

E. K.   The ſmoak is gone, and here ſtandeth one over him in the

A Viſion. aire with a Book, whoſe nether parts are in a cloud of fire, with his hair ſparſed, his arms naked, the Book is in his right hand, a four ſquare Book, with a red fiery cover, and the leaves be white on the

Liber cum 7 ſi-gillis. edge, it hath 7 ſeales upon it, as if the claſpes were ſealed with 7 golden Seales. And there are letters upon the Seales, the firſt *E.M.*

Emet tau.   *E. T. T. A. V.*

The angel with the Book.   ...... *Take this Book, ut veritas Luce magis clarescat, Et Lux, veritate fiat valida. Data est enim tibi potestas, dandi & aperiendi hunc librum mundo & mundis.*

URIEL.....*Gloria tibi, Rex cœli & terra qui fuisti.es, & venturus, es hinc enim,* judiciũ meretricis.

E. K.   Now *Uriel* taketh the Book, kneeling upon both his knees.

URIEL ...... *Rejoyce O you sonnes of men, lift up your hearts unto heaven for the secrets of God are opened: and his word let out of Prison. Rejoyce, O you sonnes of God, for the spirit of truth and understanding is amongst you. Rejoyce O you that are of the Sanctuary, for you shall be full of wisdom and understanding. Rejoyce O thou the House of Jacob, for thy visitation is at an end, and*

△Visitatio Justitia, Misericordia Judaeorum. Conversio. *thy visitation is beginning: The four winds shall gather thee together, and thou shalt build up the trod-den wall: The bridegroom shall dwell with thee. And lo, behold, the Lord hath sworn, and wicked-nesse shall not enter into thee, neither shall the Spirit of the Highest go from thee, but thy fathers bones shall have rest; And thou shalt live eternally.*

The blood of the Innocents shall be washed away from thee, and thou shalt do penance for many dayes. Then shall the Lamb stand in the middest of thy streets O Hierusalem: and shall give Statutes unto thy people and inhabitants: All Nations shall come unto the House of David: The Mothers shall teach their infants, saying, Truth hath prevailed, and the Name of the Lord shall be the

Veritas preva-lebat. *Watch-man of thee, O City.*

E. K.   Now all is full of a white clond.

URIEL ...... *Silence unto me, and rest unto you for a season.*

E. K.   All is diſappeared, and the ſtone ſeemeth cleer.

Actionis *Pucciana* poſterior pars.

△ Legi præmiſſa Latine ipſi *Fr. Pucci,* & pauca locutus ſum de regibus & aliis qui hæc putant eſſe noſtras impoſturas, & à nobis l æc mala ratione tractari,&c.

E. K.   He is here again.

E. K.   He ſitteth in a chair of Chriſtal, with his Book in his lap, and the *meaſuring rod* in his right hand, and the glaſſe vial in his left hand.

URIEL ...... *Seeing that power is given unto me, and that truth is added unto my Mi-nistery, and I am become full of light and truth, I will open your eyes, and I will speak unto you the truth that you may shake off the lumpishnesse of your darknesse, and profound ignorance: and walk in truth with your fathers.*

Give ear (therefore) diligently unto my voice: and imbibe my sayings, within the liquor of your hearts, that the sap of your understanding may receive strength, and that you may flourish with

with acceptable Truth, as the chosen servants and Ministers of the Highest.

Totus mundus in maligno positus est, and is become the open shop of Satan, to deceive the Merchants of the Earth with all abhomination. But what, are you the Pedlers of such wares? or the Carriers abroad of lies and false doctrine. Do you think it is a small matter to tie the sense of Gods Scriptures and mysteries unto the sense and snatching of your Imaginations? Do you count it nothing to sit in judgment against the Spirit of God: leaving him no place, but at your limitation. Is it lawful before the Sonne of God, to spend the whole dayes, yea, many yeares, with the Sonnes of Satan, the lying imps, and deceivers of the World? Are you so far entied into the shop of abhomination, that you point unto the *Sonne of God the time* of his comming, the descending of his Prophets, and the time wherein he shall visit the Earth? *Moses* durst not speak, but from the Lords mouth: The Prophets expounded not the Law, but the voice of the Lord. The Sonne of God spake not his own words, in that he was flesh, but the words of his Father; His Disciples taught not, but through the holy Ghost; Dare you (therefore) presume to teach, and open the secret Chamber of the Highest, being not called?

Tell me, have you left your Merchandize, and the counting of your mony deceitfully gotten, to beome Teachers of the Word of God? Are you not ashamed to teach before you understand? yea, are you not ashamed to lead away, where you cannot bring home? Hypocrites you are, and void of the Holy Ghost, lyars you are become, and the enemies of Christ, and his holy Spirit.

Peradventure you will say, in reading the Scriptures we understand But tell me, by what spirit you understand them: what Angel hath appeared unto you? or of which of the Heavens have you been instructed?

It may be you will say of the Holy Ghost, O thou fool, and of little understanding! Dost thou not understand that the Holy Ghost, is the School-master of the Church, of the whole Flock & Congregation of Christ? If he be the School-master (therefore) over a multitude, it followeth then, that one doctrine taught by the Holy Ghost, is a lesson or an understanding of a multitude: But what multitude are of thine understanding or of what Congregation art thou? Wilt thou say, thou art scattered. Thou speakest fasly, thou art a runnagate. But, behold, I teach thee, and thy error is before thy face.

Whosoever doth understand the Scriptures must seek to understand them by Ordinance and spiritual tradition. But of what spiritual tradition understandest thou? or by what Ordinance are the Scriptures opened unto thee? Thou wilt say thou art informed by the Holy Fathers, and by the same Spirit that they taught, by the same Spirit thou understandest. Thou sayest so, but thou dost not so. Which of thy Fore-fathers *hath tied reason to the Word of God?* or the understanding of the Scriptures to the Discipline of the Heathen? I, say unto thee, that thy Fore-fathers were dear unto Christ, were pertakers of the heavenly visions and celestial comforts, which visions and celestial comforts, did not teach unto them, a new exposition of the Scriptures, but did confirm and give light unto the mysteries of the Holy Ghost spoken by the Apostles, the ground-layers and founders of the Church. Whatsoever, therefore, thou learnest of thy Fore-fathers, thou learnest of the Apostles, and whatsoever thou learnest of the Apostles thou hast by the Holy Ghost. But if thou expound the Fathers after thy sense, & not alter the sense of the Apostles, thou hast not the Holy Ghost, but the spirit of lying. Therefore humble thy self and fall down before the Lord. Lay reason aside, and cleave unto him. Seek to understand his word according to his holy Spirit. Which holy Spirit thou must needs find, and shalt find in *a visible Church, even unto the end.*

I will plainly say unto thee (That, Truth may appear mightily in light:) Whosoever is contrary unto the will of God, which is delivered unto his Church, taught by his Apostles, nourished by the Holy Ghost, delivered unto the World, and by *Peter* brought to *Rome*, by him, there taught by his Successors, held, and maintained, is contrary to God and to his Truth.

Luther *hath his reward.*

Calvin *his reward.*

The rest, all that have erred, and wilfully runne astray, separating *themselves from the Church and Congregation of Christ* obstinately, *and through the instigation of their father the Devil, have their reward. Against whom the Sonne of God shall pronounce judgment, saying,*

Malitia, Mundana, Pompa, & Vanitas,

Reason. Ecclesia visibilis.

Luther. Calvine Wilfully, Obstinately erring. The definition of an Heretique,

Go you deceivers into Hell fire, provided for your Father and his Children from the beginning.

You rise up amongst your selves, saying, The Pope is Antichrist ; For by this name you call him, an evil man he may be, and fall from his vocation : But he can never be Antichrist : For Antichrist is he, the sonne of the Devil, a man, flesh and blond, born of a wicked and deceitful Harlot, that shall seduce the people, swell with the strength of his father, and resist God in Earth amongst men, as his father did in Heaven among the Angels, utterly denying his Omnipotency, and setting himself against him.

Claves Cœli Apostolis data.

*O you fools, and of little understanding : When unto the Apostles, the Keyes of Heaven were given, that is to say, the same authority and power of Christ Jesus the Sonne of the Living God, to forgive sinners, and to exclude sinners from the Kingdome of Heaven ; (And) when unto the same Apostles; it was said also Come behind me Satan : you have not understanding to see into the mysteries of the Highest; if the Sonne of God did commend and reprehend his Disciples, why may not (therefore) a Bishop, be counted good and evil ; if it follow (therefore) that good and evil may be a Bishop, it followeth also, that neither good nor evil addeth unto the Authority of a Bishop, but unto his own life; if he be good he reapeth the benefit of his goodnesse, but if he be evil, he is a Lyar, because his Doctrine is against himself, if therefore for the sinne of man, God hath suffered many in the spirit of * Ananias to sit in the holy place, it is for your sinnes sake, and for your rebellious nature to be punished : And not for the obscuring or darkning of his Church.*

Remember to aske amending of this place. forte belongeth.
* Acts 23. A.

Open your eyes therefore, and understand, and cleave to the Church for the Church sake, and not for the love of man. Despise not the Church, because of the transgressions of man : But submit your neck under that holy yoke and ordinance, which shall lead you to the Congregation governed by the Spirit of God, wherein you shall understand the secrets of God his Book, to be interpreted according to the sense of your fathers : whose understanding was the finger of the Holy Ghost, you cannot authorise your selves, and without authority you can do nothing; Therefore if your authority be not, why take you upon you the doings of the Church, which it is one thing to seek, to understand the Scriptures, and an other thing to teach the Scriptures according to his understanding, for he that teacheth, teacheth, by Authority, but if he have no Authority, he is an Usurper.

Nullus sibi authoritatem assumere potest.

An usurper.

My brethren remember your selves, and consider you are Children : you are not, vestri juris, but alieni. Therefore, do nothing that is of your selves : But follow, (as good children) the steps of your Mother : which Mother is a pure Virgin, and is alwayes instructed with the wisdom of the Comforter ; What mean she shall give unto you her Children : and how she shall bring you up and instruct you : Simplicity is much worth, and obedience is a Garland before the Lord. But Curiosity is the Devil ; Have you not read ; That the bread of the holy ones is not to be cast unto Dogs ? Look unto your selves whether you be Dogs or no. See if your life be holy : your doings straight and just, your patience manifold : your affliction great for the Lord : if you find not your selves so, you are not Children ; If you be not Children, you are not Sonnes ; if you be not Sonnes you have no Mother, if you have no Mother you are Dogs, you are devourers of the bread of Children, currish, senselesse, and against God.

Ecclesia, nostra Mater : & tamen Virgo.
Simplicitas.
Obedientia.
Curiositas à Diabolo est.
Matth.7.15.
Filii, Canes.
Canes.

Enter therefore into judgment with your selves.

Consider you are created by God.

In nostri judicium statui ipsi descendamus.
Pater.
Filius.

Consider you are redeemed by God.

Consider also you are also left to the spiritual tuition and comfort of God : which God hath made of you a Congregation : a holy and sanctified fellowship, feeding alwayes as brethren together, under his wings, and at his Table : which feedeth you with the bread of life and understanding, with the body and blond of Jesus Christ the Sonne of the Living God.

Spiritus Sanct. Ecclesia.
The bread of life understanding.

With understanding that you may know the will of your Father which is in Heaven, and knowing him, be obedient : which is the conclusion of your vocation. Shake not off therefore the yoke of Obedience, least you put away also the Cup of understanding, and so know not the will of your Father.

Obedientia est finis nostræ vocationis.

But my thinketh, you are starved, your guts are shrunk up : your bones and sinewes are withered. What is the cause thereof ? When received you the bread of the Lord ? when received you nourishment ? O you of little faith : and lesse understanding you erre, and runne astray : you are blind, you follow not the will of your Father : Return, Return, and say within your selves,

O alio pœnitentia, & ad Deum Ecclesiamque (ejus sponsa) redeundis.

O eternal God and loving Father, great is thy care and mercy over us, which being led aftray (with Satan and the spirit of darkneffe) haft brought us home : which being blind haft fet open before our eyes : (our eyes alfo opened) the true path and line of underftanding : Happy are we whom thou loveft fo deerly : and unto whom the care of our health is fo dear : We will therefore praife thy

thy Name, and return from our errors : we will acknowledg our finnes, and follow thy Commandements : for thou, O Lord, art onely juft and true, and thy mercy is everlafting : Thy Lawes are fweet, and thy love and kindneffe mighty amongft us, Holy, Holy, Holy Lord God of *Zebaoth*, all honour praife and glory be nnto thee for ever.

△ *Amen.*

...... *After a while I return again.*

E. K. He is gone.

△ Note, I read the premiffes to *Fr. Pucci*, in Latin, which feemed to us to be wonderfully pithy, and to the purpofe, &c.

E. K. He is here againe.

U R I E L ...... *Francis Pucci, give ear unto my word.*

Stay a while.

△ Hereupon *Fr. Pucci* did kneel on both his knees.   *Francifcus Pucci.*

U R I E L ...... *True it is, that, as thy fpirit moved thee, fo God hath called thee to the partaking and underftanding of his will to be fulfilled in punifhment and wrath againft the falfhood and deceit of the earth. And therefore hath God in his great love and exceeding mercy called thee away from the Sonnes of the accurfed, and from the way of unrighteoufneffe : wherein if thou follow him in fimplicity of Confcience, and righteoufneffe (the works of faith) thou fhalt be confirmed : for I fay unto thee, I will power my vengeance upon the whole Earth, and I will chaften her in her iniquity, and in the middeft of her pride, I will throw her down head-long, and fhe fhall triumph no more.·. And becaufe thou haft humbled thy felf, my fpirit fhall be with thee, and thou fhalt underftand. And this wicked Monfter, that fitteth in the Holy Temple, and finneth againft the Higheft, fhall be thrown down head-long with his pride : And he fhall be chaftifed and corrected with the mouth of you two : For at the houfe of the Lord Judgment muft begin. And the rebelling fonne muft be fcourged before the wicked fervant be punifhed. Fear not, I will put unto your words, ftrength and power : And if he hear you not, but ftretch forth his hands againft you, I will rain fire and brimftone from Heaven : and his dwelling places fhall fink. And the Lake that fhall remain, fhall bear witneffe againft him for evermore : Lift up thy heart therefore, and defpife the World; Fight with her manfully, and be not overcome. Moreover, acknowledg thy finnes, and fly unto the Lord. Seek out his Houfe, and eat of his bread : for thou haft much need of it.*   *Judicium incipiet à domo Dei. Filius, fervus.*

The feeds that thou haft fown abroad, gather up again, leaft thou be punifhed for the fins of thy Brethren.

Thy Soule ftandeth deare before the Lord, which is the caufe that he hath mercy upon thee, which faith unto thee, If thou be obedient before the Lord, follow the inftructions and difcipline of the holy Ghoft : and do the works of righteoufnefs and Charity, my Spirit fhall reft upon thee. I have faid.

K. E. He is gone.

△ I read over the laft parcel in *Latine* to *Francis Pucci*: after he had in very penitent fort thanked God, confeffed himfelf an offender, as he was here noted, &c.

E. K. He is here again.

U R I E L. ...... *Your Penance and Devotion premifed, The bleffing of God the Father, the Son, and the Holy Ghoft, in his everlafting truth and light, comfort you, bleffe you, and be merciful unto you.*

▲ *Amen.*

U R I E L. ..... *Extingue lumen : Nam decedo.*

△ Deo noftro Omnipotenti, æterno Lucis & Veritatis Authori
fit omnis laus, gratia actio, honor & gloria, nunc &
fine fine. *Amen.*

Anno 1585 *Augufti* 6 PRAGÆ.

Actionis *Pucciana* pofterior pars.

Videns, (*E. K.*) nubem jam receffiffe confpexit : ut fupra U R I E L I S caput (quafi in aere) alium vidit Angelum : cujus pars inferior, nube ignea continebatur. Capitis veri capilli, circa humorem   *Videntes olim, qui Prophetæ poftea dicti,* humeros sparsi, & brachia nuda apparebant. Dextra autem Librum tenebat, quadrata figura, tegmine, (quasi ignito, rubicundóque colore,) velatim: Foliorum verò exterior margo, albicans erat. Septem retinaculis, quasi totidem seris, clausus esse, liber videbatur. Atque super retinaculorum ora, sigilla quasi aurea, impressa comparebant. Et super singulis sigillis, litteræ inscriptæ singulares. Super primo E, sup. 2 M, sup. 3 E, sup. 4 T, sup. 5 T, sup. 6 A, sup. 7 V.

..... *Accipe librum hunc, & veritas luce magis clarescat: Et lux, veritate, fiat valida. Dataest tibi potestas dandi, & aperiendi hunc Librum, Mundo, & Mundis.*

URIEL. ..... Gratia tibi, Rex Cœli, & terræ, qui fuisti, es, & venturus es, hinc enim Judicium Meretricis.

E. K. *Jam accipit librum* URIEL, *utrisque flexis genibus.*

URIEL. ..... Gaudéte, ô vos filii homini, levate corda vestra Cœlum versus. Secreta enim Dei panduntur: & verbum ejus ex carceribus emissum est. Gaudete, ô vos Filii Dei, quia Spiritus veritatis & intelligentiæ inter vos existit: Gaudete, ô vos, qui de sanctuario estis, quia sapientia & intelligentia replebimini. Gaudete, ô tu domus *Jacob*, quia jam tua finita est visitatio, atque incipit visitatio tua. Quatuor venti te unâ colligent: & conculcatum redificabis mirum. Tibi cohabitabit sponsus. Et, ecce, juravit Dominus, & non te invadent impietates; neque Spiritus Altissimi á te recedet. Verùm, Patrum tuorum ossa quietem nauciscentur: & tu ipse æterna frueris vita, Sanguis innocentum, à te abluetur: & ad dies multos pœnitentia te affliges. Tunc quidem Agnus, in medio platearum, stabit, ô Hierusalem: Edictáque promulgabit populo tuo, civibusque tuis.

Omnis Nationes ad domum *Davidis* confluent matres, suos informabunt infantis, iis verbis: Prævaluit veritas: atqué Dei nomen, tuus erit vigil, ô Civitas.

E. K. *Jam, omnia, nube alba, oppleta sunt:*

URIEL. ..... *Mihi silentium, vobis verò, ad temporis exiguum intervallum, quies esto.*

E. K. *Ex oculis meis prorsus evanuere prorsus.*

△ *Nota.* Interea ab ipso Angelico sermone, præscripta in Latinum recitavi conversa, legendo expeditè, ipsi Domino *Francisco Puccio*, præterea abiter pauca locutus sum, de Calumniis, contra nostras actiones tales oraculatis, &c.

E. K. *Iterum hic mihi apparet* Uriel, *atque in Cathedra sedet Chrystallina cum Libro illo, in suo gremio: dextra autem, illam tenet virgam Geometricam: & sinistra, illam Philosophiam vitream, ut prius.*

URIEL. ..... Cum mihi sit concessa potestas, & cum meo ministerio sit adjuncta veritas; (unde lucis & veritatis sum factus plenus) vestràs ego aperiam oculos, atque vobis ipsam eloquar veritatem; ut inertem illam molem tenebrarum vestrarum, et profundæ ignorantiæ, excutere positis, et in luce cum patribus vestris ambulare. Voci igitur meæ diligenter præbete aurem, & intra cordium vestrorum liquorem, dicta imbibatis mea. Ut vestræ intelligentiæ succus, vigorem recipere possit: & vos ipsi florere positis cum acceptabili veritate, veluti servi electi, et Ministri ALTISSIMI.

Totus mundus in maligno positus est, aperta Satane facta est officina, ad terræ mercatores omni abominandæ impietatis genere decipiendum. Ast, quid vosne facti estis talium merciùm sub mercatores garuli? vel mendaciorum et doctrinæ falsæ, in publicum vectarii: Æstimatisne vos, levis momenti negotium esse Scripturarum Divinarum & Mysteriorum sensum, judicium et temeritati aligare vestrarum imaginationum? nihili rem esse statutis, in judicio sedere contra spiritum Dei, nullum illi concedendo locum, nisi vestro ex præscripto?

Vobisne licet, coram Filio Dei, integros dies, immò injustos consumere annos, cum filiis Satane mendaci sobole, & mundi deceptoribus? Adeonè penitus in abominationis officinam vosmet contulistis ut Dei filio, futuri adventus sui tempus præscribere velitis, Prophetarumque suorum descensus: temporisque terminum, In quo ipse terram erit visitaturus?

Moyses nihil loqui iusus erat, nisi ab ore Dei.

Prophetæ Legem non explicabant, sed Dei vox.

Filius Dei propria sua non est locutus verba, quatenus Caro erat, sed verba patris sui.

Discipuli ejus, nihil, nisi ex Spiritu sancto docuerunt.

Audetisne (igitur) vos, vobis docendi assumere munus, aditáque secreta Altissimi pandere, minimè ad id admissi, vocative?

Dicite mihi, Mercaturamne deseruistis, vestrarumque pecuniarum (fraude partarum) supputationes, ut verbi Dei essetis Doctores?

An non pudet vos, ante docere, quàm ipsi intelligatis?

Immò an non vos pudet seducere, prius, quàm domum reducere noveritis?

Hypocritæ estis, & Spiritu sancto vacui,

Mendaces

Mendaces esse deveniltis, & ipsius Christi inimici, & sui sancti Spiritus.

Fortassis dicitis, ex Scripturarum Lectione, intelligentiam comparamus earundem.

Ast mihi respondeatis, cujus spiritus auxilio, hanc vobis comparatis intelligentiam ?

Quis vobis apparuit Angelus ? vel ex quo Coelo , vestram recepistis instructionem?

Fieri potest, quod, ex Spiritu sancto diceris.

O stulte tu modicæque intelligentiæ ! non intelligis tu, quòd Spiritus sanctus Ecclesiæ Pædagogus est, integri gregis, & congregationis Christi ?

Proinde si multitudinis Pædagogus est , sequitur , quòd Doctrina aliqua , quàm Spiritus sanctus docet, instructio, documentum, sive intelligentia sit multitudinis.

Atqui, quæ hominum multitudo, tuæ est intelligentiæ ?

Vel cujus es tu Congregationis ?

Aliter *dispersionis.* Dicisne, dispersus alicujus te unum esse : Falsum narras, fugitivus es.

Verùm, ecce, te doceo : Errorque tuus ante tuam constat facie**m.**

Quicunque ad Scripturam intelligentiam perveniet , conari debet ad illarum intelligentiam præve-nire, secundùm Ordinationem, & Traditionem spiritualem.

Ast ex qua spirituali traditione, nactus es tu intelligentiam ?

Vel juxta quam Ordinationem, tibi est apertus Scripturarum sensus ?

Dices (forsan) ex sanctis Patribus, informatum esse te , & per eundem spiritum per quem docebent illi, tuam te esse consecutum intelligentiam.

Dicere sic quidem potes, verum non te sic facere certum est.

Quis enim antiquorum Patrum, rationem copulavit verbo Dei , vel Scripturam intelligentiam, Ethnicorum aftrinxit disciplinæ ?

Tibi dico, quò d antiqui Patres , Christo chari erant, & coelestium visionum , consolationumque Coelestium participes : quæ visiones Coelest ésque consolationes non illos docebant novam Scriptura-rum expositionem, sed confirmabant, lucéque illustrabant mysteria Spiritus sancti, per Apostolos declarata , qui Ecclesiæ ipsi sua posuére fundamenta ; quicquid igitur ab antiquis Patribus discere possis, ab Apostolis discis, & quicquid ab Apostolis intelligis, habes id quidem , à Spiritu sancto, sed si ipsos Patres exponas tuo sensu modóque , & non juxta sensum Apostolorum , certè Spiritum sanctum non habes, sed spiritum mendacii.

Humilem, igitur, temet præbeto, & coram Domino procidas, rationem semoveas, Dominoque ad-hæreas, laboréique verbum ejusdem intelligere, ex Spiritu suo sancto : quem Spiritum sanctum, omni ex necessitate invenire debes, atque invenies invisibili Ecclesia usque ad mundi finem.

Perspicuè tibi dicam, (ut veritas potenter in luce appareat) quicunque Dei contrarius est volun-tati, quæ suæ est tradita Ecclesiæ per Apostolos quidem publicata , per Spiritum sanctum enutrita , & mundo impertita, & per *Petrum* ad *Romam* tradicta, & per eundem ibidem expressa, ab ejusdem suc-cessoribus retenta atque sustentata est : Hic idem Deo & veritati suæ contrarius est.

Lutherus suorum recepit mercedem.

Calvinus suam.

Reliqui omnes quotquot erraverunt, & sponte in devia concurrerunt, separando seipsos ab Ecclesia & Congregatione Christi, obstinatè & Diaboli (patris sui) instinctu , mercedem suam rece-perunt.

Contra quos filius Dei judicium pronunciabit, dicendo :

Ite Deceptores in gehennæ ignem, Patri vestro & filiis illius, ab exordio præparatum.

Inter vos ipsos insurgitis asserendo , *Papam* Antichristum esse (hoc enim nomine illum insigni-tis) homo certè malus esse possit, atque à sua excidere vocatione , verumtamen Antichristus esse nunquam potest.

Antichristus enim ille est , qui filius est Diaboli , homo quidem ex carne & sanguine natus ex impia & fraudulenta meretrice, qui populos seducet tumidusíque sui patris potentia , Deo resistet in Terra inter homines, quemadmodum pater ejus in Coelo fecerat inter Angelos : prorsus denegando Dei Ominpotentiam seque illi opponendo.

O vos stulti & exiguæ intelligentiæ , quùm Apostolis Coeli concredabantur claves : (quasi dice-res) eadem Christi Jesu filii Dei viventis, authoritas & potestas ad hominem condonanda peccata, & ad peccatores Coelo excludendos , & quùm * eisdem Apostolis, vade post me Satana , etiam di-cebatur, non tanta estis intelligentia ut in Altissimi hæc introspicere valeatis mysteria.   * Matt.cap.16. C. D

Si Dei filius tum commendabat tum etiam reprehendebat Discipulos suos, cur non possit igitur Episcopus , & bonus & malus censeri ? Si hinc consequatur , bonum malumque Episcopo inesse posse , pari ratione inferri possit authoritatis Episcopalis rationem , a bono malove illo non pendere, sed ipsius ad Episcopi vitam hoc bonum malúmve spectare si bonus sit, suæ bonitatis metet beneficium; sin malus sit , mendax est ; sua enim illi contraria est doctrina. Proinde , si , *propter hominum peccata* Deus permiserit , multos in spiritu * *Anania* sedere in loco sancto, id quidem propter pec-cata vestra est , & rebellem naturam , ut supplicium recipiatis : & non obscura vel tenebrosa ejus fieret Ecclesia.   * Act. 23. A

Aperitè itaque oculos vestros & intelligite ; & Ecclesiæ adhæritatis, amore ipsius Ecclesiæ, & non hominum. Neque Ecclesiam contemnatis , propter hominum iniquitatis.

Verum

Verùm colla illi submutatis sancto jugo & ordinationi, quæ vos ducet ad illam Congregationem quæ gubernator per Spiritum Dei, in qua intelligetis secreta Libri Dei, explicata esse juxta sensum antiquorum vestrorum Patrum: quorum intelligentia erat dignitus Spiritus Sancti.

Non potestis a vobis ipsis authoritatem recipere, & hinc authoritas nihil facere potestis.

Idcircò cum vestra authoritas nulla sit, cur Ecclesia opera Actave intra vestras arripitis manus?

Mala fidei pos-sessor. Una quidem res est, Scripturarum aliquem quærere intelligentiam: atque alia est Scripturas docere, secundùm intelligentiam suam. Qui enim docet, ex authoritate docet: sed authoritatem si non habeat usurpator sive intrusor est.

Fratres mei, Considerate vosmet ipsos bene, & considerate vos pueros esse, & quod vestri juris non sitis sed alieni. Nihil igitur faciatis qua ex vobis ipsis: sed insistatis (ut pueri boni) vestigiis Matris vestræ, quæ Mater pura Virgo est, & semper à Paracleti sapientia informatur, quem vobis (pueris ejus) exhibere cibum debet; & quo vos modo educare atque instruere.

Simplicitas multùm valet & obedientia, certum est, coram Domino; Ast curiositas Diabolus est.

Matt.7. & 15.C.
Mar.7. C An non legistis quid sanctorum panis, non sit ante canes projiciendus?

Penitius vosmet examinetis, utrum canes sitis, nec ne.

Videte utrum vita vestra sancta sit, opera vestra recta & justa; patientia vestra multiplex; afflictio vestra, magna propter Dominum.

Si vosmet ipsos, in hoc statu esse, minimè deprehendatis, pueri non estis; si pueri haud sitis, non estis filii; si filii haud sitis matrem non habetis; sin verò matrem non habet, devoratores estis illius panis qui filiis debetur, canini, *insensati*, & contra Deum estis.

In vestri igitur judicium status vos ipsi descendatis.

Vox hæc in-Scripturis mul-tum usitata.

Pater   Considerate, per Deum Creati estis
Filius   Considerate, per Deum Redempti estis.
Spiritus S.   Considerate etiam, relicti estis Spirituali Tutelæ & consolationi Dei.

Qui Deus ex vobis congregationem ordinavit, sanctam & sanctificatam societatem, pascentem semper simul tanquam fratres, sub aliis suis & in sua mensa; qui vos pascit vitæ & intelligentiæ pane; corpore (nimirùm) & sanguine Jesu Christi filii Dei viventis.

Intelligentiæ autem pane vos pascit, ut patris vestri voluntatem intelligatis, qui in Cœlis est; Obedientia ut illi quum noveritis, obedientes factis; quæ obedientia vestræ vocationis finis est.

Nullo igitur modo obedientiæ jugum excutiatis, de simul etiam Calicem intelligentiæ à vobis repellatis; atque ea ratione Patris vestri vos lateat voluntas.

Sed judicio meo famelici estis, vestra contracta sunt intestina, ossa nervique marescunt.

Quæ hujus rei causa est? quando illum Domini panem recepistis? quando nutrimentum accepistis? ò vos modiæ fidei & intelligentiæ minóris erratis, & devii curritis. Cœci estis, patris vestri, non obtemperatis voluntati; redite, redite & intra vosmet ipsos talia dicatis.

O sempiterne Deus, & benigne Pater, magna certè est cura misericordiáque tua erga nos, quos in devia actos per Satanam, & spiritum tenebrarum reduxisti domum; & nobis cœcis præposuisti (visu etiam nobis restituto) veram semitam lineamque rectam intelligentiæ. O nos fœlices, quos tibi tam charos habes; & quorum salus tantæ tibi curæ est. Nomen proinde tuum, laudibus celebrabimus; & à nostris revertemur erroribus. Peccata confitebimur nostra, & præcepta observabimus tua. Quoniam tu solus, ò Domine, justus & verus es, & misericordia tua æterna est. Leges tuæ suaves sunt, et per amans tua benignitas inter nos validæ est. Sanctus, Sanctus, Dominus Deus Zebaoth. Honor omnis laus et gloria tibi detur in perpetuum.

△ *Amen.*

URIEL. ...... *Modico transacto temporis spatio revertam.*

E. K. *Abiit.*

△ Nota.

△ Interim *Francisco Pucci* hæc (quæ Anglicè dictata recepimus) Latinè recitabam, Nobisque nervosa valdè, nosu isque accommoda instituu is videbantur.

E. K. *Iterum illum adesse video.*

URIEL. ...... Francisce *attentis auribus, verba excipias mea.*

SISTATIS PAULULUM.

△ Hinc statim, *Franciscus Puccius* à sede sua genibus utrísque (quasi Deo supplex) terram petebat.

URIEL. ...... Verum quidem est (ut tuus te aliàs commune fecit spiritus) quod Deus te vocavit ut particeps & intelligens esses voluntatis suæ explendæ, in vindicta & ira sua exercenda, contra terræ falsitatem & fraudem.

Atque hanc ob causam, ex magno suo amore, & immensa misericordia sua avocavit te Deus à filiis hominum, Deo invisorum, & ab injustitiæ tramite.

In qua tua vocatione, si illum injieris, in tuæ conscientiæ simplicitate, & justitia (quæ fidei sunt opera) confirmaberis. Tibi enim dico, vindictam meam effundam super universam terram atque,

atque illam castigabo in iniquitate sua., & in suæ superbiæ summo gradu illam præcipitem posternam; neque ultra triumphabit.

Et quia te demissum humilémque exhibuisti spiritus meus tecum erit, & intelligentiam tu consequeris.

Et monstrum hoc impium; quòd in Templo sancto sedet, & contra Altissimum peccat, præcipitabitur cum superbia sua, Atque ex ore utriusque vestri castigabitur & corrigetur. Judicium enim a Domino Dei inchoari debet, E filius rebellis prius flagellis cædi debet, quam impius puniri servus. *Exech. y. C* *1 Petri 4. D*

Ne timeas, vestris enim verbis, vires & potentiam adjungam.

Et vestra si contemnat verba manúsque suas contra vos exerat: de Cœlo ignis atque sulphuris demittam imbrem, & Palatia ejusdem in terram descendent: lacúsque ibidem remanens contra illum testimonium dabit perpetuum.

Erigas igitur cor tuum mundúmque despicias, & contra ejusdem veriliter pugna, neque ab eodem vincaris.

Tua præterea confitearis peccata: & ad Dominum confugias, illius perquirito domum, & de illius pane comedas: eo enim multum tibi opus est.

Et semina quæ sparsim seminasti recolligas: ne forte tu pœnas tuas, ob fratrum tuorum peccata.

Anima tua Deo chára est, atque ideirco misericordia erga te movetur, tibique dicit, si coram Domino obediens apparetis: atque sequaris instructiones & disciplinam Spiritus sancti faciásque opera Justitiæ & Charitatis, spiritus meus super te requiescet.

Dixi.

E. K. *Abiit.*

Δ   Ex Anglicis dictatis istis ultimis Latinè eundem expressi sensum, Domino *Fr. Puccio,* valdè devoto humili, & præmissa agnoscenti & acceptanti, &c.

E. K. *Iterum mihi conspicuus est:*

URIEL. ..... Præmissa vestra tam pœnitentia quàm devotione, Benedictio Dei Patris Filii, & Spiritus sancti, in sua sempiterna veritate lucéque vos consoletur: vobísque benedicat, & vobis misericordiam impertiat copiosam.

Δ   Amen.

Ex Actione, quæ erat die Veneris, September 6. 1585. Pragæ.

Eat Puccius, *ut promissis perficiendis provideat.*
At cor habeat sincerum rectúmque.
Immò sæpe proprios detergat calices.
Inter eundem autem alloquatur mortua arbusta, de Domino venturo.
Ambulet cum mentibus ut illi ejus audire possit.
Tunc revertatur ut quod reliquum est ad implere possit.
Atqui dico proprios tergat calices.   *Angelica vox.*

Δ   Vos oro ut illam nobis explicare phrasem velitis obscuram.
Qui flagellatur ipse sentit.   *Angelica vox.*
Angelica vox. ..... Reliqui (jejunii vestri) dies, non hic complebuntur, sed in illis viginti diebus, in quibus Romæ operari Decretum est mihi.

I i   **LIBER**

LIBER RESURRECTIONIS.

Pragæ, Aprilis 30.

Pactum, feu Fœdus Sabbatifmi.

1586.

Threbone } { Venimus è
Octob. 14. } { Septemb. 14.

1586. { *In Maio* 29 *Exilii Decretum contra nos exiit à Cafare* Rod.
{ *In Augufto* 8, *Reverfionis permiffio* D. Rofenbergio, *obtinente ut ad fua veniamus.*

Miraculum, & factum memorandum in perpetuum.

S E. K. ftood at the end of the Galery by his Chamber, looking over into the Vineyard he feemed to fee the little man the *Gardiner*, in all manner of behaviour and apparel, who is the chief workman or over-feer of Mr. *Carpio* his workmen in the fame Vine-yard. He feemed very handfomly to prune fome of the Trees: at length he approached under the wall by *E. K.* and holding his face away-ward he faid unto him, *Quafo dicas Domino Doctori quod veniat ad me.* And fo went away as it were cutting here and there the Trees very handfomly, and at length over the Cherry-trees by the houfe on the Rock in the Garden he feemed to mount up in a great piller of fire.

E. K. bade his Wife to go, and fhe who was in the Garden, She came up, and brought him word, No body.

E. K. then came to me and faid, I think there is fome wicked fpirit that would allude me, and he told and faid to me, as is before noted. Then faid I, I will go into the Garden, and bade *E. K.* come with me. We went down that way which this Creature did go: but nothing we faw, went to the Banqueting-houfe in the Vine-yard, but that place pleafed us not fo, we went along in the way by the cliff fide, and fat down on the bank by the great pyle of Vine-ftakes lying in the very South end of the Vine-yard. And we had not fat there half a quarter of an hour, but I efpyed under the Almond-tree, and on the South-fide of it, being the Wefterly Almond-tree, that is it which is ftanding on the Wefterly fide of the ftraight path which leadeth from the North toward the South in the Vine-yard. I efpyed (I fay) like *a fheet of faire white paper lying toffed to and fro in the wind.* "I rofe "and went to it, and (to the prayfe of God his truth and power,) there I found three of my Books "lying, which were fo diligently burnt the tenth day of April laft.

1 The three Books were, *Enoch his Book,*

2 The 48 *Claves Angelica.*

3 And the third was the Book of my gathering of the thirty Aires, and entitled *Liber Scientia terreftris auxilii & victoria.*

Thereupon *E. K.* comming to me, I fell on my knees with great thanks yeilding to the God Almighty, and fo did *E. K.* whofe mind and body were mervailoufly affected at the fight of the "faid Books, having no fhew or figne that ever they had been in the fire, neither by colour or favour, "or any thing wanting.

And after we had fet half an hour under the fore-faid Almond-trees prayfing God and wondring at the Miracle. Suddenly appeared by us the felf-fame Gardiner like perfon, but with his face fome-what turned away, and nothing thereof to be adjudged as of *Ave* the cuftome is. He faid, *Kelly,* follow me, *E. K.* went, and I fat ftill, awaiting his return.

This

This Gardiner went before *E. K.* and his feet seemed not to touch the ground by a foot height. And as he went before *E. K.* so the doores did seeme to open before him, he led him up the great stairs on the left hand by the Vineyard door, and so in at his own Chamber door where *E. K.* hath his new Study, and then the door going out of that to the stairs opened of it self, and he went up those stairs, & at length brought him to the Furnace mouth where all the Books and papers had been burnt the 10 day of this April. And coming thither, there the spiritual Creature did seem to set one of his feet on the post on the right hand without the Furnace mouth, and with the other to step to the Furnace mouth, and so to reach into the Furnace (the bricks being now plucked away which stopped the mouth of the Furnace, all saving one brick thick) and as he had reached into the furnace there appeared a great light, as if there had been a window in the back of the Furnace, and also to *E. K.* the hole which was not greater then the thicknes of a brick, or two, at the most, though it seeme now more then three or " four brick thicknes wide, *and so over his shoulder backward he did reach to E. K. all the rest of the* " *standing Books, excepting the Book out of which the last Action was out, and Fr. Pucci his Recan-* " *tation, also to E. K. appeared in the Furnace all the rest of the papers which were not as then de-* " *livered out.*

That being done, he bade *E. K.* go, and said he should have the rest afterward. He went before in a little fiery cloud, and *E. K.* followed with the Books under his arm all along the Gallery, and came down the stairs by *Fr. Pucci* his Chamber door, and then his guide left *E. K.* and he brought me the Books unto my place under the Almond-tree.

✠ Praga.

1586 *Aprilis* 30 *May-even.*
Mane circa 8.

△ Precibus quibusdam fusis ad Deum, & gratiis pro miraculo Hesterno actis, petebamus jam à Deo consilium suum quid de isto miraculo nobis esset faciendum ulterius, &c.

Et quid faciemus cum Domino *Rosenbergio*, an illum debeamus admittere ad amicitiam nostram & foedus sanctum ? quid de ejus oblatis aedibus, &c.

E. K. A voice commeth down right before me saying.

E. K. Who is this William ? Willielmus à Rosenbergi.

Vox. ..... *Thou* William.	△ A pause	△ I suspect it to be the Lord *Rosenberg.*
Thou William.	△ A pause	
Thou William of Rosenberg.	△ A greater pause	

This day in the Blond of the Lamb, do I pronounce forgiveness of sinnes, upon thee : and for a signe and token : Thy lines shall be opened, and thy seed shall be multiplyed upon Earth Therefore take unto thee a Sheep, that is yet a Lamb, and spoile not the flock of thy poor neigh-bour.

And, behold, if thou turn thy self from the North, and ascend unto the Holy Mountain, [and] I will hereafter make a Covenant with thee. But take heed, thou despise me not.

Blessed are those that are comforted of me, for their strength is from above. For whosoever is rebuked of the spirit of truth, shall with time perish as a shadow.

Is it not said, if thy eye offend thee, cast him out ? I say unto thee also, yea, though thy head offend, cast him also away. The unstable Whisperings and wordly Pollicies of such as are the Princes of the World, are they not known unto mee ?

O you Hypocrites ! O you little of understanding, and of less faith, how far are you in love with the World, and her pomp, with the flesh and her lightness or wantonness, with the Divel and Consilium. *his damnable subtilty ! Purge your houses, and purge your Kingdomes, if you will stir up the Lord to strengthen you. Cursed is that Nation, that defiled her self with the society of such as are Bastards. But wo, wo, be unto him that Ruleth not according to the length of his bridle.*

The chaff of this Empire and Kingdom, behold it remaineth, the father swept it not out, nei- De Imperio Ro: *ther doth the Son lift up his hand for the name of the Highest.* & Regio Bo-hemiæ.

O you Hypocrites, you are faithless, for you fulfil not your charge!
Thou hast, yet time to awake, thou mayst yet be acceptable. Time yet.
Thy doings let them be a Judge between thee and me.

△ Magna pausa. △

Vox. ..... Behold, I have given thee unto Rosenberg, *him also have I given unto thee* △. The voice so *Whosoever therefore considereth not the giver shall be called to account and that sharply.* expounded it after at my re-

In the yeare 88, I will send out my visitation that the ends of the world may be known, and that quest. *Justice may appeare in the garments of her unmeasurable honor.* Anno 88.

In the mean season, I will bless you abundantly with all the gifts and seeds of nature. See there- Noster bene-*fore, that you work, and labour that your hands may bring forth fruit, the increase of the* ficentissimus *Lord.* D:M.

Ii 2 Six

Sex Actiones futuræ & Sabbathum, Vox 7.
△ *I asked which Fryday.*
* From good Fryday.
Our Heavenly Kalender of six moneths Action.
The rest red Books to be most closely kept until the sixth Action.
Domini miraculum sub filentio est temendum.
williclmus à Rofenberg. faciendus eft confcius fuo tempore. Omnia reliqua reftituentur quæ igni committebantur.
E. K. and △ *together.*
Adam of Newhoufe lord Chancelor.

Six Actions you shall have : the seventh is the Sabbath of the Lords, and from this day (being a part of the time) beginning from * Fryday last celebrated, as the memorial of him through whom I speak unto you, which suffered upon the Crosse for your Redemption, until the day come of the sixth Moneth, you shall not presume to aske any visitation of him that speaketh with you. And so the sixth Moneth (the last day ensuing) shall alwayes be your day of Action.

§ *Pucci is defiled, and shall not be partaker of these six visitations to come : but shall depart from you, and be ready as the Lord shall find him, and as he shall be warned of you. Notwithstanding my spirit shall not depart from him, and I will open his understanding that he may convert many. For the World must be satisfied with testimony as well of his life, as the recantation & professed Doctrine.*

△ *We lack (ô Lord) his recantation, written by his own hand, I cannot find it in the Books restored.*

Those Books let them be kept of thee, as committed unto thy custody by me. And see that they be never opened until the sixth Action to come.

See also, that you disclose not my hand amongst you, least I then rise up against you.

For, behold, you are yet in the Wildernesse. Therefore, be silent.

Unto William, notwithstanding (hereafter) all things may be known, and made manifest.

If any mean seek you, else, you know him not.

For you live within the silence of the Highest.

The rest that wanteth, shall be restored unto you : even unto the least and last letter.

Live, therefore, together as in the hands of your Protector.

And doubt not, but that I will be merciful unto him that is sick through his infirmity : yea, and unto his generation as I have promised. And the sinne which remaineth in his Fathers house, and in his house for many generations, I will mercifully blot out.

Doubt not, my peace (which am peace, the beginning and the ending) shall alwayes be amongst you.

△ We read all and had long discourse of all, and at last, I asked thus.

Vox ..... *That, which is said of him, that, say thou* △ *unto him.*

Move no more questions.

△ Benedicite Domino omnia opera ejus, laudate illum omnes Creaturæ ejus : laudent illum Angeli ejus, laudent illum Sancti ejus : ille solus est Omnipotens, ille solus est Sanctus, ille Protector nostri, Illuminator & Consolator noster est. Singuli omnis honor & gloria. *Amen.*

△ What shall I say unto *Rosenberg* of your present merciful dealing and intent toward him.

MEMORANDUM.

1586. May 1.

On *May* day after dinner I went over the water (being brought to the water side in the Lord *Rosenberg* his coach, and *Jacobus Menschick* with me) unto the Lord *Rosenberg* his Gardens, and lodging by the water-side, whether he came to me by appointment. To whom when I had read in Latin (*ex tempore*) the things that concerned him, I asked him what he had done, since the time of my being with him, that I may the better understand these words spoken to him and of him.

He told, that he had often prayed, since unto God for the forgiveness of his sins, and to open his eyes how he might serve him; and to make it to be evident unto him whether he is to marry or no, and where, or in what flock or kindred. And if it were his divine will, that he might receive comfort and instruction by me, and that these and such matters, and somewhat earnestly he had prayed also for his Mr. the Emperour, that he might bend himself to enjoy God his favour, yea, for his own marriage and amending of his loose life, while he yet sat at dinner this day at the Archbishops table, his heart and thought did come very much upon it, &c.

At these his words I rejoyced much to perceive the doing of the Highest, in the hearing of his prayer-faithfully prayed & that the answer which I read unto him was so fitly applyed unto his prayer as he also himself, did perceive with great comfort and spiritual joy. He entreated much that I would pray to God that the Emperour might be restored to the favour of God, as he was when I declared my message unto him from the Highest, I answered, that whatsoever the God of Heaven and Earth should appoint me to say or do unto his Majesty, I most willingly rejoyce in the faithful doing of it : and that it was my duty (as a Christian) to pray for his Majesty : but I should not make my promise of my prayer to be heard, but would highly rejoyce if his Imperial Majesty would so use himself in God his judgment, as might be meritorious in the sight of our Redeemer.

Votum & promissum Wilhelmi Urfini Vice-regis Bohemia.

Such words and matters as this passed between us. And he said that he would in all points, fulfil the advice and warning of God, in this Action expressed, & would marry a Maiden as he was willed. And this day did acknowledge, & account himself a happy man. And as concerning our mutual bond by the meanes of each being given to the other by God of Heaven and Earth, he vowed and promised that he would regard it in all points to the best of his skil and power, &c.

These and other such good seeds for the service of God being sown between us; he went towards his Palace in the Court, and I to the water-side, and so over to the Coach awaiting for me, and so came home. God be praysed.

MEMORANDUM.

The Lord *Rosenberg* sent Mr. *Jacob Menschik* with this Letter unto me.

Magnifico Domino Joanni Dee *ad manus proprias.*

Magnifice Domine, Pater Observande & Chariſſime.

Lætatus ſum in his quæ mihi dixiſtis. Cognovi enim quoniam exaudivit deprecationem meam pius pater & miſericors Dominus. Itàque maximo pere-deſideravi ut quam ſepiſſime ea mihi lege-
re, perlegere & ſemper ab oculos habere poſſim : per amorem Dei oro. ut ſaltem eorum, quæ mihi
perlecta & ad me pertinent verborum mihi tranſmittas deſcriptionem : Non tantum mihi multum
gratificabitur, ſed & conſolabor plurimùm.

Obſecro præterea Dominum veſtram, aſſiduè pro me orare velit, ut confirmet hoc Deus quod o-
peratus eſt in nobis : & dirigat omnia conſilia, opera, actiones, immò & cogitationes noſtras ad
laudem & gloriam ſanctiſſimi noſtris ſui, commodum multorum, & animæ noſtræ ſalutem. Neque
deſinat, pro amore ſuo paterno, quo me (uti ſpero) Dominatio veſtra proſequitur me, ſemper in
omnibus quæ pro honore Dei & commodo veſtro à me fieri & debent & poſſunt, admonere & ſignificare. Rem ſummopere mihi gratum & expectationi meæ dignam & conſentaneam faciet. Et cum
his, me commendo ſuis præcibus & orationibus, nec non paterno ſuo amori & cordi. Optimè vale-
at Magnifica Dominatio veſtra Dominica, Cantate, *Anno* 1586.

Filius & Amicus veſter ex animo
Wilhelmus R, Manu propriâ.

Rogo ut melius intelligat Dominatio veſtra
eáque ſcripta ſunt, & conſideret plus mentem
meam quam verba. Quia mihi in uſu non fuit à
multis annis Lingua Latina, & nemini in hac
re confidere volo.

N O T E.

I had tranſlated this Sunday morning, the ſame parcel of the former Action into Latin for the
Lord *Rosenberg*, which he then ſent for, jump at the time, when I had finiſhed it : And ſo I
ſent it him incloſed in a Letter.

May 6. Being Tueſday, I entred my Journey toward *Valkenaw* Glaſſe-houſe, and *Leipſig*
Mart.

There are divers *Valkenaws*, one by *Egre*, or *Elbogen*, not far from *Carls* Bath, weſtward from
Prage about 18 *Bemiſh* miles, an other in *Behem*, about 11 or 12 miles from *Prage*, northerly, a
mile from *Krebitz*, and two miles from *Liep*, and a mile from *Kamnitz*.

N O T E.

May 11 I came to *Leipſig*, on Sunday the 11 of *May*, and was at *Peter Haus Swartz* his
Houſe lodged. I found *Lawrence Overton*, (with much ado) an Engliſh Merchant ; to whom my
wife (the laſt year) had ſhewed no little friendſhip to himſelf, and *Thomas* his partners ſervant, in
the time of his lying ſick in our Houſe, &c. at *Prage* ; He came from *England* at Mid-lent, he
confeſſed that *Edmond* my ſervant had been oftentimes with him, at his Houſe, and that he did
think that he would come with the next Ships after his comming from *England*, then to come within
16 days.

I perceived by his diverſe expreſſe ſayings, that he was but a hollow friend unto me, and ſeemed
half afraid to deal either with me, or my man.

There, alſo I found a courteous Gentleman called Mr. *Francis Evers*, the Lord *Evers* his Sonne of
the North. And of all other matters omitting the rehearſal in theſe Records, (thoſe matters I mean
which at *Leipſich* and in this Journey happened notably unto me, or I did my ſelf) one Letter
which I wrote to the Queen of *England* her Secretary, the Right Honourable Sir *Francis Walſingham*, as followeth.

Right

Right Honorable **SIR,**

ALbeit I have (almoſt) in vain come a hundred miles (from *Prage* to this *Leipſich* Mart) hoping either to meet my Servant there, with anſwer to my former Letters, ſent in *November* laſt to her Majeſty (when alſo I wrote unto your Honor, and divers other). And ſo with ſpeed from this *Leipſich* to have ſent again, moſt ſpeedily as occaſion ſhould have ſerved. And now, I find, neither ſervant, neither Letter from him, neither word of mouth : yet all this notwithſtanding : and whatſoever the hindrance or delay hereof be (whether the keeping back of my Letters from her Majeſty, or the manifold and importune, moſt weighty affairs publick hindring or delaying her Majeſties moſt gracious, diſcreet and wiſe reſolution herein : or what other occaſion elſe hath and doth cauſe this long and wonderful delay of anſwer receiving. All this notwithſtanding, I thought good, before I ſet up to my Coach, to viſit, and moſt humbly to ſalute your Honour very faithfully, dutifully and ſincerely, with great and the ſame good will, that my Letter ſome yeers ſince written to your Honour, (butt hen, a ſtnmbling block unto your Honour and other, for the ſtrangneſſe of the Phraſes therein) doth pretend, ſo it is, right Honourable, that the merciful providence of the Higheſt, declared in his great and abundant graces upon me, and mine, is ſo wonderful and mighty, that very few, unleſſe they be preſent witneſſes, can believe the ſame. Therefore how hard they are to be believed, there where all my life and doings were conſtrued to a contrary ſenſe : and proceſſe of death contrived and decreed againſt the Innocent, who can not eaſily judg.

I am forced to be brief. That which *England* ſuſpected, was alſo here, for theſe two yeers, almoſt (ſecretly) in doubt, in queſtion, in conſultation Imperial and Royal, by Honourable Eſpies, fawning about me, and by other, diſcourſed upon, pryed and peered into. And at length, both the chief Romiſh power, and Imperial dignity, are brought to that point, reſolutely, that, partly they are ſorry, of their ſo late reclaiming their erroneous judgment againſt us and of us, and ſeek means to deal with us, ſo as wee might favour both the one and the other : And partly to *Rome* is ſent for as great Authority and Power as can be deviſed, and likewiſe here, all other means and wayes contrived, How, by force, or for feare, they may make us glad to follow their humours. But all in vain, for force humane we fear not : as plainly, and often, I have to the Princes declared : And otherwiſe then in pure verity, and godlineſſe, we will not favour any (my words may ſeem very marvellous in your Honours ears : But mark the end, wee have had (and ſhall have to deal with no babes) I have full oft and upon many of their requeſts

and

and queſtions, referred my ſelf to her Majeſties anſwer, thus, in vain, expected. *Nuncius Apoſtolicus,* (*Germanicus Mala Spina*) after his yeers ſuit unto me to be acquainted with me, at length had ſuch his anſwer, that he is gone to *Rome* with a flea in his eare, that diquieteth him, & terrifieth the whole State Romiſh and Jeſuitical: ſecretly they threaten us violent death, and openly they fawn upon us. We know, the ſting of Envy, and the fury of the Fear in Tyrannical minds, what deſperate attempts they have and do often undertake. But the God of Heaven and Earth is our Light, Leader, and Defender. To the Worlds end, his mercies upon us, will bread his Praiſes, Honour and Glory. Thus much very rhapſodically, (yet faithfully) *tanquam dictum ſapienti*, I thought good to commit to the ſafe and ſpeedy conveyance of a young Merchant here called *Lawrence Overton* : which if it come to your Honours hands before my Servant have his diſpatch, I ſhall or may by your Honour be advertized. Your Honour is ſufficient from her Majeſty to deal and proceed with me, if it be thought good. But if you make a Council-Table Caſe of it, *Quot homines, tot ſententiæ*. And my Comiſſion from above is not ſo large : *Qui poteſt capere, capiat*.

Sir, I truſt, I ſhall have Juſtice for my Houſe, Library, Goods, and Revenues, &c. Do not you diſdain, neither fear to bear favour unto your poor Innocent Neighbour. If you ſend unto me Maſter *Thomas Diggs*, in her Majeſties behalf, his faithfulneſſe to her Majeſty, and my well liking of the man, ſhall bring forth ſome piece of good ſervice. But her Majeſty had been better, to have ſpent or given away in Alms, *a Million of Gold*, *then to have loſt ſome opportunities paſt*. No humane reaſon can limit or determine God his marvellous means of proceeding with us. Hee hath made of *Saul* (E K.) a *Paul* : but yet, now and then, viſited with a pang of humane frailty. The Almighty bleſſe her Majeſty both in this World, and eternally : and inſpire your heart with ſome conceiving of his merciful purpoſes, yet, yet, not utterly cut off from her Majeſty, to enjoy

From Leipſich *this* 14 *of* May 1586,
at Peter Hans Swarts *Houſe.*
Your Honours faithful wel-willer to uſe and
command for the honour of God and her
Majeſties beſt ſervice,
J O H N D E E.

To the right Honourable · Sir Francis
Walſingham *Knight*, *her moſt Excellent*
Majeſties Principal Secretary, my ſingular
good Friend and Patron,
with ſpeed

Illuſt.

Illustriss. & Magnif. D. mei Colendissimi

BEnedictio Dei Patris & mera gratia & misericordia per unicum meritum Jesu Christi, illuminatio Spiritus Sancti, confirmet nos cum omnibus Christianis, qui magno cum zelo, propter gloriam ejus, crucem, tribulationem, & præsentionem a rancido atque putido scorto *Babylonico*, in turbulentissimo hujus mundi Oceano patimur, ut exemplo Jesu Christi qui est in Patre, virtute & auxilio Spiritu S. hæc omnia perferre patienter valeamus ad nóminis sui gloriam & animarum nostrarum salutem. *Amen.*

Mirum fortassis videbitur Dominat V. quod ignotus ad ignotos scribo imputabitis bonam hujus culpæ partem justissimo dolori, quem ex rumore sparso, & ad me delato propter D. V. concepi: mirari enim non satis possum pertinax studium bestiæ istius *Babilonice*, quæ nihil intentatum relinquit, nullum non movendo lapidem, quo hominibus vestræ nationis præcipue piis & amantibus Dei non solummodo nocere sed & funditus perdere studet. Elapso enim undecima die hujus mensis Legatus Pontificius Libellum supplicationum ut vocant) Cæs. Majestati obtulit quo *D.V.* Nicromanciæ & aliis artibus, prohibitis insimulat, aliisque calumniis graviter accusat copias hujus libelli habere potuissem, sed nimis sero hac de re sum certior factus, nec tutum & absque suspitione est qui illum ex Italico in Latinum sermonem transtulit petere. Quare cum hæc omnia vana a *D. V.* ut hominibus Christianis & Philosophis certo sciam Epistolam hanc cum tenendi tum admonendi causa exarare libuit ut promptiores & paratiores *D. V.* ad respondendum offendant. Peto itaque ut eo animo suscipiatis quo scripta est scilicet Christiano integro & candido. Valete meque precibus vestris Christo commendate.

POSCRIPT.

Ante aliquot dies transmisissem D. V. Litteras sed L. V. peregræ profectas esse mihi significatum fuit postquam autem a servitore generoso D.a Bikerstein cognovissem (Ferdinando Harnik) D.V. hanc nostram remisse patriam, intermittere non potui quin illud quod vestrum interessit scire litteris istis significarem.　　Julius Ascanius *septima à* Verdeman.

Illustriss. & Magnif. D. *Joanni Dee* &
　　Edwardo V, &c. Dominis & amicis
　　　meis colendiss.

Rceived of Mr. *Kelly* on Friday before Whitsunday, after my return from *Valkenaw.* 1586.

Mr. *Kelly* received this on Thursday before Whitsontide, 22 *May* 1586.

Illustris.

Illustrissimo Principi & Domino Domino Wilielmo Ursino *hereditario Domino Inclite Domus a* Rosenberg, *Domino in* Crommaw *Equiti aurei velleris* Cæsareæ Majestatis *intimi consilii Consiliario, & in Regno* Bohemiæ *supremo Burgravio, &c. Domino & Patrono meo Colendissimo.*

ILlustrissime Princeps , nihil mihi gratias a Magnifico Domino, *Schonbergio* narrari poterat, quam vestram Celsitudinem prospera interim frui valetudine , Dum ego vario, diverso, & intricato quodam fueram jactatus itinere, per montes, per valles , per sylvas densissimas, per apertos campos, & per nivem profundam, & nobis fere inperviam : Et (semper tamen nos protegente altissimo) tandem sani , salvique illesis tam equis quam curru Celsitudinis vestræ, reversi sumus. Pro quo prospero successu, summas Altissimo agimus gratias, & Vestræ Celsitudini infinitas a nobis deberi fatemur. Dum absum contra nos nescio quid falsi incipit iste *Apostolicus Nuncius* vel leviter nimis credere, & temere conqueri, vel a seipso excogitare perversæ. Veræ si ita petgant (habito jam nostri, per biennium experimento satis accurato) illi quidem, qui pietate & sapientia, (saltem vulgares) deberent superare homines omnes, omnium hominum semet declarare maxime invidos, malitiosos, perversos, sanguinis humani appetentes , superbos, innocentum carnifices, & piorum in Christo Calumniatores exitiosos, &c. Vere (dico) cogemur pulverem ex calceis nostris excutere, & alias in mundi partes nos conferre. Et nisi vestræ Celsitudinis haberemus eam quam debemns considerationem : Et nisi nos ipsos vestræ Celsitudinis præsidio quocunqne armato (quasi) minntos existimaremns (præter illud invincibile , Dei Opt. Max. agmen invisibile) statim abire ex hoc regno conaremur. Curare etiam debet sua *Cæsarea* Majestas, ut aliquo modo, & citissime, perspectum toti huic Regno esse possit, nos duos non solum veræ Catholicos esse, sed etiam veræ pietatis & pacis Christianæ, esse amantissimos. Per literas istas non est opus ut plura effundam, spiritus mei fervore quodam. Sed diligentissime & circumspectissime respiciamus nos utrique, inestimabile Dei, quod nobis utrisque contulit Donum. Sumus enim quasi tres. Sed in uno Deo, unus quasi vir esse debemus. Mysterium hoc notate *I. D. E. K. W. R.* Nam qui me habet, habet & *E. K.* & quem ego meum habeo, ille etiam ipsius mei *E. K.* censendus est esse. Omnipotens ille Deus qui cuncta creavit, vestram Illustrissimam Celsitudinem, suæ divinæ Justitiæ, & Gloriæ Comimnistrum & co-operatorem nobis conjungat & diutissime conservet.

Pragæ, Maii 26, Anno 1586.
Illustrissime Celsitudinis vestræ fidelis-
simus in Christo Servitor.

Joannes Dee.

K k

Invictissimæ Potentissimeque sacræ suæ Cæsareæ Majestati
Hungariæ, Bohemiæ, *&c.* Regi, *&c. &c.*

PEr aliquot jam hebdomadas , Invictissime & Gratiosissime *Cæsar*, aures nostras circumsonabant rumores varii, quasdam contra me, & socium meum, præparari accusationes graves & exitiosas : Vestræque Sacræ Cæsareæ Majestati offerendas fore vel jam oblatas esse : Et præterea Sacram Vestram *Cæsaream* Majestatem, quorundam persuasionibus, pœne eo perductam esse, ut aliquam malam, & nobis periculosam, de nobis conciperet opinionem. Vestræ igitur Sacræ *Cæsareæ* Majestati humillime supplicamus ut (Authoritate sua *Cæsarea*, interposita (illius, cujuscunque contra nos exhibiti libelli, copiam, accurate & verbatim exscribi, nobisque tradi, mandáre, gratiose dignaretur, Sic enim nostris responsis ad accusationis contra nos confictæ collatis articulos, citissime & clarissime intelliget sua Sacra Majestas *Cæsarea*, quid in præmissis, cum Justitia, ad Dei honorem & Reipublicæ Christianæ utilitatem , arbitrari, vel statuere possit aut debeat. Et de hoc certissimi nos sumus, favente Deo, (quod adhuc, et nimis diu, aliquorum negligentia , et contra nostram voluntatem, Vestram Sacram *Cæsarem* latet Majestatem.) Nos cum Vestræ Sacræ *Cæsareæ* Majestatis personæ, tum Reipublicæ Christianæ, per vos longe utiliores, gratioresque esse posse, quam omnes, et quotcunque hic nostri præsentes adversarii : veluti ipsa docebit veritas si pœnes Vestræ *Cæsareæ* Majestatis aures proprias, eum possit habere favorem, ut gratiose audiri queat Deus Opt. Max. Sacram Vestram *Cæsaream* Majestatem sua Divina abundantissime illustret gratia abrachioque suo extento, contra, Christi atrocissimos hostes *Imperatorem* reddat triumuphantissimum

Amen.

Maii 28, 1586

Sacræ Vestræ Majestatis
Cæsareæ
Humilis & fidelis Servitor,
ad Dei promovendam gloriam
Joannes Dee.

Invictissimæ potentissimeque Sacræ suæ Cæsareæ
Majestate Hungariæ, Bohemiæ, *&c.* Regi, *&c. &c.*
Domino meo Clementissimo & Patrono incomparabili
ad manus proprias
expeditissime

Edlor

EDlor goſtronger lirbor bortranter fraundt,Diſeſtumdoiſt mir daſz bruſſlainJu komon,Darauſzichunt ſondon frondron Gottesdionör behorzt ganuottvornoman, In ſumma craſz David fraibt iſt waar , Mirabilis Deus in ſanctis ſuis Deus Iſrael, ipſe dabit virtutem & fortitudinem plebi ſuæ, Benedictus Deus.

Diſo Varfolgung wirds Inon, (obgottcoill) In Iror wolfart gor-richon und don Loniden In Irom ſpot.

Dentibus ſuis frement , & contabeſcent deſiderium peccato-rum peribit.

Dom gutton Jungon Gorrn Civillor got ſoinrm horrn vndſicſſolbſt orkonam.) kan aſu ſoelvnd Crib goholſſonwordon. Daſz Vborig crollen coir cunuadtlich brld Vorrichton , Interim , So brotts Ich, ſic bon moiu & angon , Jum ſernundtlichſton Jubo gruoſſon , va-dàrim trouots graucott Ina, Juoſſoriron, Darbinbegott ſhimt vnſz Von Nanaſa In arigkail.

Datum in Eyle Raudmitz don 28 Maii, Anno 1586.

Des ſorru trruoer
   fraundt

            Wilſclm Moimaigne handtz

Horrn Laſpar von Schonburg auff Voplitz Moinom Vartranotra gutton froundo In ſolbſthandog.

         Cito
         Cito
         Cito
         Cito
         Cito

            K k 2   Sowder

SOwder Rumeschenn Kayserlichen auch Ju Hungern unds Behom Koninbchon Mapt unsors allor gnadigston horrn cropen Doctori Joanni de Dee Engellandorn, anformoldon, Dasz Iro Mapt jausz jondorn urgeblichen, bodentklichon undt billichen ursachonjont schlosson som snoundt dio somigon In Joror Mapt, tumg Ruch Bohem so woll als andorn dorosolbron Pomp Ranchon, burstant gumbombon undt Landon longer nicht Induldon nach julugivn Hiorauff so sun nun Jorar Mapt Endlichor orille undt truster beurblich Dasz chrsichsambt soinom Worbe tindorn, umdallon don soyinpen, so woll als soinem Consorten undt Jngethanen boy vormedanp Iron Mapt trusten unnachlvszlichenn strassfand ungnad, Innerhali drn Negt nachoniandor volpomdon sechs Zagen, albie or heve, vnd sichalfszbalet daranff vrn hinnen, ausforbalbgedachtor Jorar Mapt Koningraich Behannb vms andoror Joror Mapt Koningraich, Curstantbumbay undt Cainder begebo diseilben Durchausz Jun Kunfftigmedr Nuchsus sorror Darumen, weyternicht besunden nach hetresten lasse Damit ausz den lasll lassalba vn Imo odar den seympen auch doupy Jme Jupethaury, ungrhorsamblicsay vborganpen crourdo Irr Mapt Inn truston einschon undt Straff, sosie lirber vormitton schonvrolton nicet Vernrsacht wordoun, Wolton In Mapt, Ime Juondtlicher Nachrichtung, nicht porgen. Esz boszfese auch Hieran Iror Mapt sorustor Willey vndt mainng. Decretum in Consilio Imperatoriæ Majestatis secretiori. Prage xxix Maii, Anno Lxxxvi.

E. Waldtnons Sayleldt.

Mynssnik.

Decret Doctor Johann *de* Dee *Iror Mapt Koniglieh Bohomb so woll als andors Iror Mapt Lander sureamboy.*

Doctori Joanni Dee
offerenduu

I received this the 30 day of May,
Anno 1586, Mane hora nona,
By one of the Chancery Clerks.

The Copie of the Emperour his Decree, of our Banishment out of his Kingdomes, Dukedoms, &c. with onely six dayes warning.

Ad-

Anno 1586 18 *Junii in* Erphurdia Thuringiæ, *quo, Illustrissimus Dominus* Rosenbergius, *miserat* Joannem Carpionem *ad nos, cum literis suis, & maximè ut de uxore futura, Dei intelligeret voluntatem, & de aliis rebus, &c. Ego vero jam* Castellæ *eram in* Hessia, *& Erphurdiæ erat D.* Eduardo Keleus. *Qui super quæstionibus & petitionibus Illustrissimi jussu erat divinitus Chartam mundam super Altare, ante Sacerdotem* Missam *celebrantem ponere, quod & fecit, anno & die supra scripta, manè in* Monasterio Minoris Ordinis S. Francisci, *inter horam* 6 *&* 7 Monacho Seniore *Missam Celebrante. Et finita Missa, hæc quæ sequitur in Charta invenebantur pulchrè scripta. Sed die sequente, postquam exscripta erant pro Illustrissimo Principe statim evanuere omnes lineæ & litera, nihilque in illa Charta, post visibile permansit, &c.* △

Admonitio.

Tempore exilii nostri.

Nationes terræ omnes vocatæ in Judicium, coram Tribunal stabunt. Populus enim rebellis, nimiumque hujus mundi deditus voluptati, mei jamdudum ira furoris irrititus tabescit: Ita quod, neque ad sinistram neque ad dextram sed ad voluntatem meam perimplendam, declinandum est. Beatus ille qui mihi mendatisque patris mei obediens est & perseverantia decoratus.

Maledictus autem, qui mendax operibus, perdicas verbum meum: quia scandalo multis erit, & ignominiæ pacis Evangelii mei.

Ego te Gulielme (quia manus adjunxisti mihi) Davidem ad Goliatha jugulandum constitui & constituendo invexi.

Mundo igitur ad gloriam meam utere, & corpus tuum erige in me, ad justitiam meam in sede debita collocandam, & superbiam iniquissimam turpissimámque (illorum qui posuerunt sedem meam, in scabellam pedem blasphemiæ & abominationis) ad penitus tum conculcandum, tum eradicandam.

Beatus enim eris in fortitudine manus & spiritus mei, quia audire preces tuas. Noli igitur tempus visitationis tuæ negligere: sed freme zelo & indignatione acerrima, & conjunctam tuis parietibus, virginem in uxorem accipe, paratam lumbis & senectuti tuæ illámque amando dilige, & diligendo fove, ut mea in te & in illa benedictio pollicita manifesta fiat.

Cave porrò, ne quos tibi in auxilium paravi, servos meos, vel negligentia vel timiditate tua, aliorum sic patiaris ex manibus tuis vel tanquam oves ab ovili tuo, malis artibus & iniquitate, eripi Quis enim istud surripiet quod datum est à me ?

Cogita igitur & vigilando cura, quod hactenus lesum est.

Fringam namque frænum Satanæ & inimicis vestris.

Benedictio Patris & Spiritus mei, & consolatio à me (cui subjecta est omnis potestas) sit tecum & supra te.

A peccatis denique monitus cessa ut cum mecum loqueris, vita tua sit lumine & gratia mea suffulta.

MEMORANDUM.

Be remembred that Mr. Francis Pucci Florentine, *whom at my going to* Leipsich *I left in our house at* Prage, *in the meane space had been at* Frankford *upon* Mene, *and went from* Prage *about the same day that the Bishop of* Placenza Nuncius Apostolicus *did exhibit to the Emperour a libel against us of most horrible untruths, &c. As his going from* Prage *he had that* Nuncius *blessing, &c. In the meane space, and after his return to* Prage *again it happened so, that the* 30 *of* May *last, I received the Emperours commandment, I, my Companion, and all mine to depart within six dayes out of* Prage *and consequently out of all his Kingdomes, Dukedomes and Lands, Which we did, and were come to* Erphurt *in* Thuringa, *and sometimes to* Cassel *whether we had removed our goods and family by reason the Senators of* Erphurd *would give us no leave to hire any house there as both by the Lord* Schonberg *in the name of the Lord* Rosenberg, *I was assayed, with repulse received, and also again by me and* E. K. *proved,* July 7, 8, 9, 10, 11, 12, 13, 14. *And on* Tuesday (*the* 15*th day of* June) Doctor Curtz *brought upward from the* Senat *that they would not grant our Request, yet notwithstanding, if the Lord* Rosenberg *would again send unto them in the matter, they would think better upon the matter, &c.*

Mr. Francis Pucci. Anno 1586. Maii 6.

Now remember that Francis Pucci *came to* Erphurd *on* Thursday *after our supper,* July 10 (*stilo novo*) *on horse-back on a horse which he had bought at* Mawnberg-faire, *&c.*

July *the* 11*th he discoursed with* E. K. *and me, that he thought we might obtain favour to return to* Prage *again if we would.*

That he had found this Nuncius Apostolicus *more courteous then* Malaspina ; *of whom he reported also, that is was credibly informed that he was sore offended that we gave him no more honourable title in our speeches to him, then* Reverendissima Vestra Paternitas.

This Pucci *framed the discourse of his talk to perswade us to think well of this* Episcopus Placendus *that he was charitable towards us, and sorrow that we were so uncourteously used, that he meant nothing else in his sute to the Emperour against us, but that we might be examined, and thou being*

found

found faulty, we should be sent to Rome, but after that he had begun to move against us, that he *found the Emperour more eagerly bent* against us, than he himself was.

NOTE.

The Lord *Rosenberg* told us that when he did (in our behalf) advise the Emperour of his error committed in our extermination, that the Emperour answered that this *Nuncius* from his first Audience did urge so vehemently against us, and also the Pope had sent commandment by Letter to him to deliver us and send us to *Rome*, that he was forced in manner to do as he did. But if the commandement or his Decree were to be made again, that it should not passe, or if this *Nuncius Apostolicus* had not sent this Decree away to *Rome*, that he should not send it, &c. This I note in respect of the contrariety in the *Nuncius* assertion, and the Emperours, of our so hard usage.

The foresaid eleventh day of *July*, the foresaid *Fr. Pucci* to prove this his intended perswasion of the *Nuncius* good meaning toward us, and to make us beleeve that great benefit would ensue our going to *Rome*, did bring forth unto us a writing of his own hand which he read unto us, and at the hearing of it we mused much for many causes I asked him then why the *Nuncius* had not subscribed this writing. It is all one said he for that ; Hath he heard this read (quoth I,) yea, that he hath heard me read this three several times, arise unto him (said he ;) And if you like of it saith he, wherein his power serveth him not to performe as much as is specified in the writing, he will make and use meanes to have it from his Holinesse ; well, said I, take a copy hereof Mr. *Kelly*, for I was riding toward *Salfeild* about a house getting ; Thereupon said he, contented, but I think it meeter to save and keep the original it self said *E. K.* Well, said *Pucci*, and so the original was delivered to *E. K.*

NOTE.

After 10 of the clock the same Friday, being the eleventh day of this moneth, after break-fast I rid toward *Salfeild* about the house of the Earl *Albert* of *Swartzenberg*, &c.

But after I was out of *Erffurd* until my return again, I was so sore vexed in mind to think of *Pucci* his return to our company, *as well for his unquiet nature in disputations*, *as for his blabbing* **A bait.** *of our secrets without our leave, or well liking, or any good doing thereby* ; either in God *his ser-* **A spie.** *vice*, or our credit, but rather the contrary, ensuing albeit not of his intent, but by either his undiscreet handling of it, or of his undue hearers of him, &c. And also for his Houshold behaviour, not acceptable to our wives and family, and also because we were warned *that he should be cut off from our company*, &c. And chiefly, now to consider that he had laid *such a bait* for us with our mortal enemy, to entrap us by fair fawning words, which by no meanes the Emperour would consent to do before by his authority, but rather to put us out of his Kingdomes, &c. And imagining that he was a mighty Explorator upon us, for this *Nuncius Apostolicus*, and his adherents, that now he might perceive what we had done hitherto, what we were doing, and what we intended to do, and considering that he urged at our hands in answer to the former writing, wherein also lay a trap for either in not answering it, or refusing to grant some points of it, or in our consenting to the whole, this *Nuncius* would put matter against us to our great disadvantage. Thus being tormented in mind in my absence, how we might be rid of this *Fr. Pucci*, by quiet and honest meanes, I devised to write to this *Nuncius* to know if this writing were of his contriving onely, or of *Pucci* his contriving onely, or joyntly, or if at the least the writing were according to his will, and offer unto us, and so to send him away ; wherein he could make no refusal, I intending not to make him privy of the content of my Letter ; And in the mean space of his absence I hoped that some good way and better meanes would appear or fall out, whereunto we might trust, &c. Thus I note my imaginations and discourses in the time of my absence.

I returned to *Erphurd July* 13. *hora* 5. *a meridie.*

I found *Fr. Pucci* desirous to have answer to the foresaid writing, and very much perswading this Roman voyage, using arguments out of our actions, as that God said we should go to *Rome*, in a certain moneths space ; That we ought to obey the Roman Bishop, and to love him, &c. I replyed and said, that he was not *to urge God upon any his sayings to us*, but to referre all to his most free disposition, his will was to be done and not ours, God was not bound to us, &c. He answered very vehemently, and often, that *Deus est nobis obligatissimus, & Deus dixit nos ituros Romam, & ego credo & credam, & aliter non credam nisi mihi Deus dixerit non nobis*, &c. Well, (quod we) God hath delivered unto us his meaning in that phrase, which we also devise you of, that it is not meant (by the speech) that we shall corporally goe to *Rome*, and so I brake off that his reasoning ; And told him that we mervailed that he should urge this Roman Voiage so violently and eagerly more then we ; It appertained unto us as much as to him, &c. The same day I told him that he had heretofore offended God with his *curiosity in our affaires* otherwise then apperteined unto his calling, and he may well remember his repentance therein, and his forgivenesse obteined, But that

now

now he had offended much more in curiosity, and half. in conspiracy against us with our mortal enemy this *Nuncius Apostolicus*, upon whom he did fawn, in whose favour he is ; who joyneth, counsaileth with him in our affaires, who dare prescribe us what we have to do in so weighty affaires as our Journey to *Rome*, who hath framed a bill, accusing us coufusedly of Heresie, and wicked Magick, both falsely in one part, and dangerous to life, and infamous at the least in the other, and hereto requireth, urgeth, and in manner in God his name argueth by our actions past, obedience. And therefore he hath separated himself from us, and hath set himself against us, &c.

With great vehemency he said, He intended nothing, but well to us, and *was Explorator with this Nuncius* for our behalf; We require none (said I) neither we need any, for God seeth all, and doth all, for our benefit, if we will constantly love and serve him ; To be brief, he would seem to be worthy to be thought well of for his zealous good will and fidelity to us ward, in all his doings and sayings. The truth whereof God knoweth, to whom we commit the cause between him and us.

The Copy of the writing before specified.

SI D. Johannes Dee, D. Eduardus Kelleus, & Fr. Puccius, *volent ire* Romam, *ut conferant cum Summo Pontifice de suis Revelationibus, venerantes eum tanquam Sancti Petri Successorem & Christi in terris Vicarium Illust & Reverend. Episcopus Placentinus Apostolicus Nuncius apud Cæsaream Majestatem, dabit illis Literas commendationis, ut per totum iter, & Romæ, humanissime summaque charitate tractentur, & in suis necessitatibus juventur: Ac præterea authoritate Apostolica absolvet eos & liberabit ab omni culpa & pœna, quam meriti essent in vita ante acta, ob artes Magicas exercitatas, hæreses, falsasque opiniones ab eis sparsas, aut fictas, verbis aut scriptis, aut aliis rationibus; ob libros prohibitos lectos aut scriptos, sive ob aliud quodvis crimen, cujus accusari aut argui possent in foro sancto Inquisitionis, aut in foro quod Contentiosum vocant; aut in quovis alio foro Pontificia ditionis: Ne quis ob ullum peccatum aut scelus quantumvis atrox, quod illi admiserint ante hoc iter susceptum, eis unquam facessere negotium, aut molestus esse possit, aut ullo modo inquirere, aut ipsos accusare presumat.*

For the better ground of any manner of answer making hereunto I asked the same *Fr. Pucci*, after supper, on Tuesday the 15 of *July*, (forasmuch as I had framed a Letter for answer to the pith of the Letter or writing here recorded) whether this Letter were written and sent to us by the consent of this *Nuncius Apostolicus*, to know our answer in, or no. He seemed to be unwilling now directly to affirm the *Nuncius* consent. We replyed that he had already told us that he had read it thrice over to the said *Nuncius*, and that he liked well of it, and did mervail that now he would make strange to affirm the same again, seeing I had now, (according to his purpose) written a plain and perfect humble answer to the same Letter, and much more matter, true and needful for this *Nuncius* to know. Well, said he, *Eatenus ex ejus consensu est, si velitis ire* Romam, *ea præstare conabitur, quæ in eisdem literis continentur, &c.* Well, said I, (in Latin alwayes you must understand my talk with him in the same sence here in English recorded, if he mean well unto us, and in charity unfeigned; he will not be offended with my answer ; The Copy whereof doth ensue.

Illustissimo Reverendissimoque Domino, Domino Episcopo Placentino *apud Potentissimum & Invictissimum* Romanorum Imperatorem Rodulphum, *ejus nominis secundum*, Apostolico Nuncio, *Domino mihi (in Christo) Colendissimo.*   ^{The superscription of the Letter without.}

Illustrissime & Reverendissime Domine, mihi Colendissime.

IN Nomine, Sanctæ Beatæ & Individuæ Trinitatis, vestram Illustratissimam Reverendissimamque Dominationem, ea qua virum Christianum decet animi affectione & humilitate saluto, non presumptione aliqua, vestris manibus oculisve istas meas obtrudens literas, sed ex istius *Nuncii vestri* verbis admonitus, non gratas solum, sed (serè) expectatat fore: hasce aliquot, haud invitus, exaravi lineolas. Quibus cum non potero, 40 annorum continuum & ardentissimum vitæ me cursum in limatioris quam vulgaris veritatis Philosophicæ in dagatione transactum, describere; (vel adumbrare saltem) satis presenti nostro esse possit instituto, si præsenti rerum meta-   ^{Remember Fr. Pucci his own hand writing hereof is kept in a lether bag by it self, to be the more safe and ready to be shewed without shewing of this Book.}

metamorphosi, & admirandæ negotiorum nostrorum actioni, itidumque circuitioni multiplici, aliquid exprimam quod maxime quadret.

Divinitus ante aliquot annos * informati, & deinde ex *Anglia* △ evocati, non solum fortissima Dei Omnipotentis manu, & miraculosè, ex multis magnisque evasimus maris periculis : sed etiam ex variis hominum fraudulentis & truculentis contra nos, & vitam nostram consiliis & conatibus, liberati hactenus, eidem Deo nostro gratias laudesque canimus mente grata, mente læta, mente profecto Christianæ, Catholicæ, Apostoliceque Religionis amantissima, & (Dei nos confirmante gratia) tenacissima futura. Ast ecce, tamen, qui ejusdem nostræ pie matris (Sanctæ Ecclesiæ Catholicæ) legitimi etiam censentur esse filii, nos, fratres suos, in omni modestia, quiete, pace, & civili Justitia, inter illos, & coram illis, *Praga* conversantes, subito, in exilium quoddam, sive exterminium, *Cæsareo* emitti mandato procurabant nulla, nobis, nulla prorsus, neque privatim, neque publicè declarata tam violenti mandatis causa sed vulgari solum, & aulica relatione nobis facta intelliximus ex libello quodam, per vos, sacræ *Cæsareæ* Majestati exhibito, conflatam contra nos fuisse maximam *Cæsaris* indignationem, & quasi excandescentiam : unde ex Cancellaria *Bohemica*; acerbissimum ad nos (sacræ suæ *Cæsareæ* Majestatis nomine) missum sit * mandatum (nulla in eodem expressa, ejusdem mandati causa, vel ratione legitima) ut infra tunc sex proximos sequentes dies, Ego, consors meus, uxores nostræ, liberi mei omnes, immò & ipse infans noster *Michael* (*Pragensis* natus, & baptizatus) atque ad matris adhuc pendens mamillas, famuli etiam mei, & ancillæ, mei denique omnès, & domestici, ex ipsa *Praga*, atque ita consequenter, ex universo regno *Bohemia*, & aliis quibuscunque sacræ *Cæsareæ* Majestatis Regnis, Ducatibus, & terris, migraremus, nunquam easdem reversuri, sub terribilis infligendæ pœnæ periculo. Nos autem, nulla interposita mora, huic mandato *Cæsareo* fideliter & humiliter obedire nosmet accinximus : Bonaque nostra mobilia, a peregrinationis nostræ suppellectilem, tam librariam quam domesticam, in duos magnos currus conici curavimus : Reliquorum nostrorum bonorum, partem unam, amicis dedimus, & pauperibus dispersimus & distribuimus : Partem autem, de facie terræ, (propter causas Deo non ingratas) pridie, ante exitum istum nostrum, per nos deletam esse sciatis : Ast optimum partem, Divino jussu, decima die *Aprilis* (quando etiam, de tota hac afflictione, & persecutione nostra, & aliis adhuc futuris eramus divinitus præmoniti.) *Ignis luculentissimis flammis commisimus : quando* illa, ejusdem optimæ partis, quæ nullus unquam naturalis vulgarisque ignis poterat lædere vel consumere, *visibili angelici ministerio, ex* ipsis summis flammis in Divinam, Angelicamve invisibilem recipiebantur Custodiam. Ast librorum Divinorum Thesaurus maximus, tunc, & ibidem (duorum adhuc viventium testium diligenti opera,) ab ipsis flammis in cineres favillamque conversus est totus : renovationem, restaurationem, & quasi regenerationem vel resurrectionem quandam, per Divinam manum, opportuno recepturus tempore Sacellum; Denique cum altari quod omnipotenti Trinitati consecrandum fore cupiebamus, (media ex parte absolutum) intactum relinquimus. Ego verò, cum consorte meo, uxoribus nostris, liberis meis, & reliquis exulibus, sive exterminatis nostris *Rhedis*, tribus avecti, transmigrationem hanc, nobis injunctam, die præfinita ingressi sumus. Atque nondum ex Imperii *Romani* finibus egressi, ita gressus nostros disponimus, & de cætero (Deo favente & gubernante) disponemus : ut toti orbi Christiano claro apparere poterit, patienter nos hæc (qualiacunque) tolerare posse, aut saltem velle : & paratissimos esse nos, Reddere Deo quæ Dei sunt, & *Cæsari*, quæ sunt *Cæsaris*. Obedientissimos etiam nos esse, & humillimos sacro sanctæ Catholicæ Ecclesiæ filios, & summi Pontificis Romani, & aliorum Ecclesiasticorum Præsulum Catholicorum, in Christo & propter Christum tam esse observantes & fore, quam ipse qui Judex futurus est vivorum & mortuorum, varriis nos esse modis haud raro admonuit. Vestræ vero Illustrissimæ, Reverendissimeque Dominationi, hoc à Deo optamus bonum, ut per secundas vestras (de tota causa nostra) meditationes, nostræ *Innocentiæ*, sinceritatis, & fidelis (coram Deo & hominibus) in illa Republica *Bohemica* conversationis nostræ, justa habeatur ratio : Meæque honestæ famæ, existimationisque (sine qua, ne vivere quidem cupio) ea fiat in integrum restitutio : ut talis

post.

* *Ab Anno* 1581.

△ *Anno,* 1583.

* *Anno,* 1586. 30 *Maii.*

* *Anno,* 1586. 10 *Aprilis.*

Anno, 1586. *Junii* 4.

posthac esse indicetur indubitate, qualis (ante vestrum *Cæsareæ* Majestati exhibitum
contra nos libellum, per 30 annos, (& plures) in omnibus (pœne) Christiani orbis
tam Academiis, quam Regnis & Provinciis (ex Dei immensa Bonitate, gratia abun-
dantissima & singulari providentia) extitisse, haud obscuris confirmari possit testimo-
nijs. Ex hijs igitur paucis, Historiæ Ipsius veritatis scintillis, Vestræ Illustrissimæ
Reverendissimeque Dominationis prudentia, magnum sibi lumen afferre sive accen-
dere potuit: ad nos, nostrorum animorum affectiones, nostrorum ita mirabilium & adhuc incredibilium negotiorum progressum & statum dijudicandum , & denique de
ipso futuro horum omnium exitu, haud leves sibi contexendas conjecturas : Cum
nos, ex solo Deo Omnipotente, & vero & vivo, in omnibus nostris pendeamus; &
ab ipso dirigamur & protegamur. Cui soli, nos ipsos, nostraque omnia, Animæ, corporis & Fortunæ nuncupata Bona, tanquam Holocaustum, quotidianis nostris hu-
millimis & spontaneis offerimus precibus. Cui denique soli sit omnis laus, honor, gloria, & gratiarum Actio, nunc & semper. *Amen.*

Datæ Erphurdiæ, *Anno* 1586, *die* 16 Julii.

Fidelis (in Christo , & propter Christum)
servulus.

Joannes Dee.

This Letter being written, and read unto *E. K.* and of him well liked for the quiet and modest
course therein kept , otherwise (as he said to *Fr. Pucci*) then he could have used : or had used in a
Letter which now he had also written : but now would not send , thinking that my foresaid Letter
might suffice for our case , he talked with *Fr. Pucci* of this Letter , which *Fr, Pucci* said he would
gladly see and read , which *E. K.* told him that I was minded not to let him read it : Then said
he, that he would not carry it : Hereupon in talk with *Fr. Pucci*, speaking of this Letter , I told
him that I had written a Letter with sufficient answer in general to the *Nuncius* request and offer by
him in writing brought to us , and in summe told him the chief contents of the Letter. Then said
he, *whereas you* write of the Books burnt , why write you not unto him of the *recovery of them, as
I now perceive by you both*, that *they are restored* ? And it shall be a disgrace to you if the *Nuncius* shall understand more by other, then by your self. Thereof have I no care, *Quod scripsi, scripsi*;
and I know the truth of my writing : And they are not all restored that I know of : And whatsoever he hath at my hands he may be assured is true : whatsoever he shall otherwise hear , the Record
thereof cannot be so good , unlesse, our Record consent thereto ; Then said he, *why write you of
those Books burning, being done before your comming away* : It is as if you wrote backward. Have
you no care Mr. *Pucci*, for the method of my Letters said I, and I said farther , it is told me that
unlesse you see my Letters you will not carry them , you shall pardon me for seeing of them, the
content I have sufficiently told you : and if you will not deliver them , I can get them delivered divers wayes , or I may omit the sending of them, and write such a Letter to the *Nuncius* that I had
written answer to his requests , and offer sent by *Fr. Pucci*; But he would not bring the said my
Letter, unlesse he might have a sight of it himself. At the length by farther discourse with *E. K.* he
became resolved to goe with the letter, and (by *E. K.* his order) he was to receive 50 Dollors of
John Carpio, that he should not be destitute of money at *Prage.*   Fifty Dollors

---

N O T E.

This day, *Francis Pucci* said to us both , how can you doubt of my fidelity toward you (whom
I love as my own life,) and against this Monster of *Rome*, whom my chief desire is, and long   Pucci infideli-
hath been, that he may be overthrown, &c. Again, consider , what fidelity, obedience , and reve-   tas manifestis-
rence he hath promised to the Pope, and this *Nuncius* ; as the writing brought by him , and so sore   sima facta.
and many wayes urged by him, for us to accept of , can specifie.

Therefore *Fr.* is false to the Pope, or us, or both, or rash, foolish, blind , &c. And (as our spiritual
Schoolmaster, divers times telmeth him) leprous : Therefore I commit this his doings to the judgment of God : But also it is greatly to be remembered and noted that he now also discoursed again
with *E. K.* as concerning the Birth of Christ , that it could not be proved by the Scriptures , that
Christ came of the line of *David*, unlesse he were begotten of the actual copulation of *Joseph*,
with *Mary*, and said that , because it was the gift of the Holy Ghost , that at *Joseph* his first and
onely carnal copulation with *Mary*, Christ was conceived ; Therefore she was accounted (in man-

Videlicet, that is miraculous that Virgo in primo cum viro congressu conciperet.

new Virgin according to the Jews doctrine: which *his heresie whom I heard*, I trembled for the horreur of so manifest an heresie against evident Scripture, *virgo concipiet & virgo pariet*, &c. &against many other most plain and sufficient Authorities both of Scriptures, and also Histories of our Lady her examination made by Women, and that she was found a Virgin, &c. And at her conception her answer to the Angel: *Quia virum non cognovi, &c. & antequam convenirent, inventa est in utero habens de spiritu sancto, &c.*

NOTE.

It is evident hereby that this *Priest is very leprous*, both in this Heresie (what other he is infected with, God he knoweth) and also the forsaker infidelity proved.

On Thursday 17 *July* Fr. *Pucci* entred his Voyage toward *Prage* with my Letter to the *Nuncius Apostolicus*, and with Letters to *John Carpio* from E. K. and with my Letters inclosed to the Lord *Rosenberg*. And we entred our journey toward *Cassel*, but that night we rode onely three mile, to *Gotha*, our horses were so ill that we hired, and therefore sending them back again the next day, we hired a Coach, &c.

POSCRIPTUM.

Remember that Fr. *Pucci*, the morning before his going required of me our Letters Testimonial to our friends, of his fidelity toward us. What needeth that (said I) for as much as your deeds were as well known to them as to us, your own conscience to your self may serve abundantly. But our friends divers, who have warned us of you, and have marvelled why we would suffer you any longer in our house and company, would neither credit our Letters as yet in this case. And would also condemne us of light judgment, or great blindness to judg the cause between you and us.

But truly I observed in him, now, a more proud presuming over us then hitherto, before, when he was sore reouked, for over-crowing us, so as he began to do.

Præsumptio.

  1 Now he said, he had as great authority as we to publish any of our Secrets, at his discretion.

  2 That he ought to eat bread with us.

  3 That he understood our Books of Actions better then we.

  4 That he needed not our consent or counsail to deal with the Pope his *Nuncius*: he did it by his duty general, of Charity, &c.

  5 He offerd to order the *Nuncius*, and the *Emperor* to the reclaiming of the Decree made against us, &c.

NOTE.

* Vide scriptum illius de nostro itinere Romano, &c.

Consider what this may import, that the Decree touching him, being one of my houshold company, and of them that then did appertain to me, and whose name he is not affraid one way and another way not abashed to * thrust himself into the whole body of our Revelations, as a principal fellow or Receiver of them. By the first he ought to be afraid of the danger of the Decree which banished us, unless he is assured of their good will who have shewed themselves our mortal enemies; or else some other cause emboldened him to some other purpose, &c. by the second he might be afraid of so great presumption, being but a *Probationer*, not yet allowed of, and to us known to be cut off.

I. D.

All these points I cannot decipher and judge, but referre them to the profound wisdome and high providence of God, wherefore and how farre he hath admitted him to be privy of our Actions, and so *a Witness to some purposes sufficient*. All things be to the Honour and glory of God. *Amen.*

Magnifice Domine,

Lectis tuis literis sui miratus quod intelligerem te illius esse opinionis & sententiæ, me apud Cæsarem tibi ac consorti tuo officiis meis non parum obfuisse, quod sciam ita me & religione & natura comparatum, ut omnibus quam maxime cupiam prodesse, nemini agt obesse. Quod autem præstiterim quod mei erat officii, mihi vitio verti non debet. Cæterum cum inter summum Pontificem, & Cæsarem, merus sim interpres, non video quid in hoc vestro negotio præstare possim: Consulo autem, ut vestram innocentiam, de fide Catholica sensum, & de Angelorum conversatione & assistentia, quam visibilem habere dicitis, juxta Concilii Lateranensis in undecima Sessione decretum, coram Summo Pontifice & Sede Apostolica deducatis, & ita exponatis ut non possit cuiquam esse dubinam

binam

bium quid sentiatis, quin sede Apostolica approbante, fides tuto ab omnibus Angelicis assertionibus vestris, præstari possit, & tum demum & obtrectatoribus, si qui sunt, ora obcludentur. Nec ut arbitror grave vobis videbitur consilium meum, si enim ea vobis est in fide Catholica puritas atque constantia, ea in præsenti Angelorum communione sinceritas, vitæ integritas,& innocentia, ut asseritis: Me etiam tacente occasionem quæritis declarandæ vestræ fidei & bonitatis, & hac una ratione honori vestro (cujus vos rationem habendam dicitis, & cui tantum abest quod per me aliquid sit detractum, ut illum etiam pro viribus quantum officii mei & injuncti muneris ratio patietur, fovere sim paratus, ut Domino Puccio *pluribus dixi) & omnibus vitæ commodis vel maxime consuletis. Deus gratia sua vos ita regat, ut Angelorum conversationem in Cœlis aliquando habere possitis. Vale* Pragæ *, die* 28 *Julii* 1586.
Magnific. D.V.

> Ex Corde in Christo frater
> Philip. *Episcopus* Placenti-
> nus Nuncius.

Magnific. Domino Joanni Dee, *Anglo, &c.*

△ Oraculum Divinum.

MUlta sunt flagella præcepta mea negligentium: Multiplexque furor hominibus propriis confidentibus viribus. Hi enim contemptores sanguinis & Regni mei fortitudinis, Gigantes facti sunt, ad omnem abominationem multiplicandam. Sed ego Sum qui sum, qui posui in Patre. Solium verbumque ad faciendum in terris Judicium: qui in ultima Tuba percutiam illos, ut coacti recognoscant vias meas, & ad ovile proprium redeant. Peribit Ecclesiæ & populi Iniquitas, & judicabitur in gladio. Tu vero Gulielme, manum in tempore extende opportuno, prout a me informaberis, & Regnum, (tacto & moriente nequissimo) adjunctum induc: Inunxi enim te in fortissima dextra mea, ad falsum illum Prophetam, & Goliath [forte Mahometanos & Turcas] extirpandum ut intelligat Terra judicium a Nazareno Crucifixo me. Sunt qui cribarent te: sed maledicti sunt machinantes in te malum. Fac bonum, & utere creaturis meis ad gloriam meam Docui Kelleum, inquiete, hac nocte, de cæteris, quæ ab illo disces. Spiritus meus habitet in vobis.

Trebona, Anno 1589. *Mensis Augusti fine.*

When Mr. *Kelly* was gone from me at *Salfeild* toward *Bohemia,* and in the mean space the Emperour had granted to the Lord *Rosenberg* licence for us to return into *Bohemia,* to any of his Lord-

Ships, Towns, Cities, Castles, &c. This was delivered written by spiritual and divine meanes, and the writing yet remaineth in my Lord his hands, out of which I copyed this for the order of our History somewhat making plain.

Franciscus Puccius *præstantissimis ac Deo dilectis viris D D.* Joanni Dee *&* Eduardo Kelleo *generosis* Anglis, *majoribus in Christo fratribus, & ipsis tanquam patribus colendis, precatur gratiam & pacem a Deo patre nostro, & a Domino Jesu Christo, Amen.*

EX quo à vobis discessi, toto illo itinere, quod octo diebus confeci, vendito *Lipsiæ* equo, haud parum vexatus fuit meus spiritus, dum animum mecum volverim, quot modis Satanas divinum opus retardare & nostram conjunctionem dirimere, adhibitis exterioribus & interioribus machinis & armis, tentaverit, & adhuc tentare non cesset. Neque enim possum, nisi ab eo, agnoscere afflatus illos diffidentiæ, rumores ab invidis hominibus, sparsos, suspitiones nobis injectas, absque certis indiciis, adversus fidem non levibus argumentis probatam, atque hujusmodi impedimenta & offendicula, quibus cursum nostrum impedire ac sanctam amicitiam, divinis auspiciis, inter nos cœptam, convellere ac labefactare, malignus ille spiritus aggressus est. Itaque, in illa lucta, ne ullo modo manus illi darem, aut fatiscerem, decrevi me, magis ac magis, munire certa fide in Deum, ac spe promissionum ejus, quas illum servaturum non dubito, tum precibus frequentioribus magis instare, apud summum patrem, ut nos quam primum donare velit illo spiritu, quo nostri humeri montibus ferendis, ut ille inquit, pares evadent ; ad hæc austeriorem vitam instituere nec mensas lautas amicorum adire, sed panem doloris solus comedere decrevi, *ne sim meliore conditione* quam vos, *qui tantopere affligimini,*ut benignissimus Dominus quamprimum, vos in integrum restituat, atque ad solita colloquia piaque exercitia nos una revocet, & eventu consentaneo suis sanctissimis dictis, singulos nostrum exhilaret. Hanc viam sequenti Dominus mihi spem facit fore, ut vobis & aliis facilius meam fidem probem, & multas tentationes vitem quæ apud hujus mundi homines facile nos invadunt. Ideo, nisi necessitate urgente, aut communibus negotiis, familiaritatem omnem & convictum cum aulicis fugio, & me hoc modo minus ineptem precibus gentio, meamque vitam & mores in dies emendare conor, ne videar omnino indignus ea schola, in qua Dominus me erudire dignatus est, nec interim cum Publicano, illo, precari obliviscor, ut Deus propitius sit mihi peccatori. Vos non dubito me vestris votis & supplicationibus juvabitis, ut vocatione meæ respondeam, & in opere Domini vobis adjumento & consolationi esse possim : & benignissimus ille pater propediem hoc adverso vento

to ignem suam magis excitari curabit, ac nos majori, quam unquam
antea, jucunditate recreabit. Ac de his hactenus. Quod vero ad
nostra negotia attinet ; perveni huc die 24 Julii, sub vesperam, ac
statim adivi *Illustrissimum Dominum Nuncium* , cui vestras tradidi,
quas læto vultu accipere visus est : sed colloquendi non fuit otium,
cum, parata cœna , jam discumbere vellet. In posteriorem Diem
igitur rejectus, ad *Dominum Carpionem* me conferebam , cum didici
eum ad vos Missum, quatriduo ante, hinc discessisse. Dolui admodum
eum non esse mihi obviam factum , tum ratione vestrarum , tum
mearum literarum , quoniam fasciculum quendam ad me quoque
ferebat. Sed quod maxime me torquebat erat cura de litteris *Illu-*
strissimi Domini Rosenbergii, quas sciebam inclusas *Domini Carpi-*
onis literis, nec eas aperire, aut alii tradere audebam, cum diserte esset, scriptum illud *ad manus proprias.* Dum itaque occasionem quero
& expecto, ea sese obtulit, quam mox audietis. Reversus sequenti
die, ad *Illustrissimum Dominum Nuncium,* invenio apud illum *Jesui-*
tam Italum, qui mihi fuit a confessionibus : blande ab ambobus ac-
cipior, sedere jubeor, a *Jesuita* nomine candoris & ingenuitatis, non
parum laudor. Tum lupide moneor ab *Illustrissimo Domino Nuncio* ut
ipsi adsim, in convertendo *Jesuita* ille (is enim erat qui cum ipso ex-
postulaverat, quod nimis facile mihi dedisset : *testimonia triumphan-*
tis Ecclesiæ non subjici judicio militantis.) Respondeo me fecisse
quod in me erat ut docerem eum præferre Cœlum terræ , ac tribunal superius inferiori; sed cum id mihi minime successet, ejus esse, sua
doctrina & autoritate, hominem de sententia illa dejicere *Illustrissi-*
mus Dominus Nuncius haud gravate, nostram sententiam, hac in parte, probat, & exemplis confirmat, *atque ita concludit, ut statuat cer-*
titudinem videntis & audientis Dominum , aut ejus angelum , non
pendere a probatione Ecclesiastica, neque ab illo esse rationem repeten-
dam suæ revelationis, dum nihil publici muneris exercere audet : sed
si incipiat palam profiteri, se a Deo doctum & missum, ita ut non ip-
sius solum , sed aliorum quoque intersit , scire quo spiritu agatur,
tunc Ecclesiasticorum munus esse, illius spiritum examinare & pro-
bare, neque ipsum jure posse examen hoc detrectare, licet suas revelationes eis subjicere minime teneatur. Nam si ordinaria autoritas
eum admiserat, bene habebit, nihilque turbarum excitabitur : sin
per injuriam aut inscitiam aliquam , aut per aliam hujusmodi causam, rejicietur, suum erit appellare Superiorem Dominum , qui ipsum misit, quo suum servum & Legatum defendat, aut ordinario Ju-
dice commonefacto, aut alia ratione : quod probabat decreto *La-*
teranense Concilii, cujus mentionem facit in suis literis ; ac præterea
historia S. *Francisci,* qui primum expulsus ab *Innocentio Pontifice,*
mox revocatus fuit , cum per quietem apparuisse *Pontifici* pannosus
ille, qui *Lateranense* templum suis humeris fulciret. Addebat præterea viros Dei non esse solitos deterreri una aut altera repulsa, & hoc
re-

repellendi modo, dicebat Præsules aliquando usos esse; ut probarent spiritum & constantiam eorum qui res novas magnasque proponerent. Ego vero inquam, ut hæc ita se habeant, _Vos hactenus publicum munus exercere non tentasse, & intra privatos parietes, summa modestia vos continuisse._ Tum ille, longiori ambitu verborum, sic de vobis disserit, ut ex vestris verbis Serenissimum _Poloniæ_ Regem, ad invictissimum _Cæsarem_, & ad Illustrissimum Legatum _Hispanicum_, jam constare diceret, vos aliquid amplius quam privatum moliri: Ac Summo Pontifici, sedenti in specula super totam Christianam Rempublicam potuisse merito suspectas esse vestras personas, hoc modo Principum animos, & interiores aularum recessus scrutantes: Idque ratione vestræ Regnæ, infensissimæ Apostolicæ, sedi, & cum ipso Turca conspirantis, necnon _spiritus familiares habentis_ ac præterea ratione vestræ summæ peritiæ, in artibus & scientiis reconditis, quibus facile plebi & imperitis imponi potest. Cum enim sitis magni Astrologi, dicebat ille, & facile vobis sit habere geneses principum, necnon Magicas artes calleatis, haud difficulter possetio bonorum _Angelorum nomine, ea proponere_, quæ a spiritu Ecclesiæ hoste manarent. Ideo Summum Pontificem, (cui duo, illi Principes sunt maxime observandi, utpote qui inter Hæreticos vivant & regnent) prudenter fecisse, qui jusserit, ut in vestros mores & doctrinam inquireretur. Accidisse autem præter ejus postulatam & voluntatem, _ut, indicta causa, expelleremini._ Se vero vicem nostram dolere, & paratum esse ad curandum, ut vos justificare possitis, idque sibi esse in votis, non semel asserint Quapropter hortatus est me, ut ad _Illustrissimum Dominum Rosenbergium_ contenderem, atque ipsius bonam propensionem, erga vos, ei significarem; Nam ille a Summo Pontifice facile impetrabit, ut causa vestra hic cognoscatur, & si ille vobis faverit, ut hactenus fecit, se quoque adfuturum vobis omnibus officiis, ac primum fore, qui se vestris genibus obvolvat _si tales eritis, quales vos nonnulli prædicant._ Ego igitur recta ad _Illustris. D. Rosenbergium._ Sed quater redeundum mihi fuit, antequam admitterer. Die 27 tandem admissis, exposui meum studium, erga vos resque vestras, ac quomodo _Illust. D. Nuncius_ affectus erga vos esset, ac tandem oravi ut non desereret patrocinium & defensionem illam, quam suscepisset _peregrinorum pientissimorum, qui a Cæsate minus bene informato ad Cæsarem melius informatum, provocarent_, ac suam innocentiam, Dei & hominibus, probatam cuperent. Ille humaniter respondit: Vos non admodum sibi notos esse: _se bis cum seniore; semel tantum cum juniore collocutum, judicasse vos doctos & pios, & præclaris donis instructos_: existimare vobis hoc accidisse mala aliqua relatione cui incommodo a res principum sunt obnoxiæ; vestrum esse id æquo animo ferre: non se pœnitere quod vobis faverit, & si scirit quid potissimum, a se, peteretis, daturum operam, ut vestris votis responderetur. Tunc mihi visum est nonnulla dicere de optima spe, quam de ipso concepissetis,

pisseris, & quomodo me non dimiseratis sine literis ad illum : Sed
erant inclusæ fasciculo D. *Joan. Carpionis*, quem statim protuli,
atque eo instante ac respondente D. *Carpionem* non ægre laturum
si ipsi dedissem, tradidi fasciculum ei, qui dixit se per otium lecturum,
ac, sequenti die, mihi responsurum. Discedo igitur ab illo ad Illust.
D. *Nuncium*, atque otium nactus, tum per me, tum per Illust. Legatum *Florentinum*, pluribus cum eo agere instituo, *de insigni injuria
vobis facta:* expono quantopere laboraveritis; ut considere possetis,
apud Catholica Templa, & quam inhumaniter, in hospitiis & civita-
tibus ratione hujus præjudicii *Cæsarei*, tractaremini, doceo quam
sordido & angusto loco vestras familias reliqueritas, ita ut vestram
supellectilem, & libros explicare nequiveritis ; . Moneo, ut Domini
Dee jam grandis natu, aut potius senis, & nihil tale hactenus passi
vicem doleat ; ejus ærumnas non tanquam simplicis hominis conside-
randas esse, cum vir sexagenarius; quatuor tenellis suavissimisque liberis (quorum major septimum annum vix excesserit) ac dilectissi-
mæ conjugi adjunctis, longe gravius affligatur, ratione uxoris suæ
lectissimæ fœminæ, & pignorum charissimorum, quam sui ipsius ; o-
stendo quanto offendiculo hoc futurum sit Catholicis *Anglis.*, ac
cæteris, & quanta ansa præbeatur hæreticis, invehendi in Ecclesia-
sticum ordinem : declaro periculum imminens ordini illi, si forte Deus facultatibus vestris ad eos plectendos eorum inimicos armari per-
mitteret : Demonstro Deum alias, per Israelitas hæreticos Catholicos *Judæos* punire consuevisse : ac denique declaro, quam *absurdum sit vos indicta caussa condemnari*, si id meriti sitis : quanto ab-
surdius, si non meriti sitis quicquam tale : absurdissimum vero, cum
a Catholica Ecclesia honor potius vobis deberetur : Ac cum non
petatis nisi ut vobis vos purgare liceat, nihil magis consentaneum
rationi excogitari, nullo alio modo errorem admissum emendari,
atque hoc negotium bene dirigi & redintegrari posse. Ille mihi legit vestras literas, id est D. *Dee*, sed de rebus, ambobus vobis, aliquo modo, communibus : dicit se non credere ea, quæ de divinis
monitis & miraculis, in illis, continentur, petit ut ipse declarem ob-
scuriorem locum de libris combustis : *audit a me testimonium ocula-
tum de illis concrematis, & quomodo vobis audiverim eos esse cœli-
tus restitutos*, ac denique concludit in illis literis esse multa lauda-
bilia, multa admirabilia, multa itidem incredibilia ; sed cum non
sint Deo impossibilia, se sustinere assensum, nec velle quicquam
certi, re non penitus explorata, pronunciare : vobis tamen responsurum humaniter, ac daturum mihi literas, quod fecit postea die
28, quas literas ad vos, cum hisce, mitto. Et quia legendi eas mihi
fecit copiam, *satis jejunas & frigidas mihi esse visus, haud dissi-
mulo.* Tamen quia mentionem aliquam mei facit, tanquam hominis
cum quo fusius de suo animo, erga vos, egerit, visum est mihi accurate & particulatim exponere, quid inter nos actum dictumve sit, ut

verba

verba cum factis conferre poſſitis, & pro veſtra prudentia & pietate, conſilium capere, & ſi operæ precium videbitur reſcribere.
Quantum enim ex ejus ſermonibus colligo, videtur ipſi neceſſarium
novum mandatum, a ſummo Pontifice, antequam quicquam vobiſcum agat; nec ſe ſcripturum dicit de vobis *Romam,* niſi prius *petatis
quod ab ejus ſanctitate capitis :* utpote qui, in hac cauſa, fuerit
merus interpres, inter Pontificem & *Cæſarem* ; nec poſſit, niſi verbis
ſui Domini quicquam promittere & ſtatuere. Idcirco, quantum videre poſſum, res diutius protrahetur quam vellemus, niſi Dominus
noſter & Pontifex cœleſtis, alio modo, nobis providerit. Die 28 &
29 inveni Illuſt. *D. Roſenbergium* tam occupatum, ut admitti non
potuerim, ſed per cubicularium ſignificavit, ſe valde cupere ut collo-
queremur, itaque redirem die 30. Interim fui rurſus cum Illuſtriſ-
ſimo *D. Nuncio,* mox diſceſſuro ad Sancti *Caroli* Monaſterium, ubi
commorabitur quamdiu hi eſtus ſævient. Et cum commodo ceci-
diſſet, in colloquendo, viſum eſt, mihi interrogare hominem, an pro-
baret meam *ſententiam de diſcernendo* ex certis notis & terminis verum verbum Dei a ficto & fucato, cum poſſit angelus malus tranſ-
formare ſe in angelum lucis & Apoſtata falſi, non raro, ſe transfigu-
rent in Apoſtolos Chriſti. Dicebam enim duo mihi videri neceſſaria,
ut hoc judicium rite fiat, primum quidem, in homine audiente, bona propenſio & animus bene affectus ad Creatorem, totuſque ex ei ita
pendens, ut nihil antiquius habeat quam ei placere, & qui de ejus
benignitate atque veritate non dubitet erga eos, qui ad ipſum con-
fugiunt, ut bonum ſpiritum hauriant. Deinde in ſermone, nomine
Dei propoſito, requiri eas proprietates, quæ tantum authorem de-
ceant ; quas graphice deſcribit *Paulus,* cum dicit, *Vivus eſt enim*

Heb. 4, 12, 13. *ſermo Dei & efficax, & penetrabilior omni gladio ancipiti, & per-*
tingens uſque ad diviſionem animæ ac ſpiritus, compagum quoque ac
medullarum, & diſcretor cogitationum & intentionum cordis, & non
eſt ulla creatura inviſibilis in conſpectu ejus. Cui adſtipulatus Deus,

Jer. 23, 28, 29. qui apud *Jeremiam* dicit; *Propheta qui ſomnium habet, ſomnium nar-*
ret, et qui verba mea habet, verba mea narret. Quid paleis cum tritico?
dicit Dominus. Nunquid non verba mea ſunt quaſi ignis? dicit Dominus,
quaſi malleus conterens petram? Concludebam igitur, hominem Deo
fidentem, ex efficacitate & ardore illo, quo affici ſe percipit, deprehen-
dere ſermonis Dei veritatem. Nam vox lupi & alieni paſtoris non
poteſt permovere veram ovem, ut ipſum diu ſequatur, & hanc eſſe
regulam, qua judicarem divinas ſententias a non divinis, diſtingui
poſſe : Ille probabit meam ſententiam, atque addidit, ſine bono ſtu-
dio auditorum, non apparere efficacitatem divinorum ſermonum, ut
conſtat ex Chriſti hiſtoria. Dum enim ſimplices *Iſraelite,* dicebant;
Nunquid ſic loquutus eſt homo, & ſimilia de Chriſti doctrina; *Phariſæi*
& perverſi Sacerdotes eum deridebant & contemnebant. Tnnc ego,
ſi contingeret igitur, ut cum congrediemur, fieret ad te verbum Domini,

mini, num hujufcemodi regula utereris. Hic ille inquit, cum poffet
accidere, ut mihi de hac re judicandum effet, nolo hoc tempore,
meam fententiam declarare, fed hujufcemodi ratio non mihi mala
videtur. Ex quibus verbis nefcio quid mihi vifus fum adorari minus
candidum, quam in re tanta, opus effet. Sed Dei efto judicium de
ejus interiori fenfu. Ego, bona fide, colloquia noftra expofui, ut
vobis ufui effe poffint, ratus hoc vobis gratum, ficut foret mihi fi veftro loco effem. Reverfus die 30, ad Illuft. *D. Refenbergium* vidi
eum tandem exeuntem, ex cubiculo, ad quofdam nobiles, et dixit
fe tantopere diftrictum effe, ut mecum colloqui non poffet. Sicut
cuperet. Ego vero, inquam me S. Celfitudinis monitu, toties rever-
fum expectare ejus refponfum, et an vobis refcribere vellet. Tunc
ille inquit prius tecum colloquendum eft mihi, itaque, (ut ejus verbis utar) habeas patientiam, aliquot dies donec ego pro te mittam,
et fic me dimifit. Docui igitur *Venceflaum* cubicularium noftras æ-
des, qui dixit fe optime callere locum, ac, fuo tempore, memorem
fore mei, cum Dominus me accerfet. Expectans igitur aut re pon-
fum Illuftriffimi *D. Rofenbergii*, aut aliquid aliud dignum veftris auribus, non vifum eft mihi id vos expreffum nuncium mittere : Mo-
nente præfertim Domino *Sevembergio*, vobis effe paratis nefcio
quas ædes in oppido *Naitu*, in Comitatu *Suarreburgenfi*, & ut ex-
pectarem reditum Domini *Carpionis*, quem propediem reverfurum
fperabat, ne fine magna caufa atque incertus de loco veftræ fedis, ad
vos literas dirigerem. Igitur non parum folicitus de vobis & de reditu D. *Carponis*, femel ad minimum in die, ejus ædes adeo, atque in-
terrogo fi quid de illo fignificetur, nec quicquam, per multos dies
audio. Tandem de die 12 *Augufti* fcifitor D. *Millerum* an aliquid mihi de amico, dicere poffit. Refpondet fe quoque expectare hominem,
atque admodum mirari tam diuturnam moram, præfertim cum D.
Gregorius, qui in ipfo *Carpione* ad vos venerat, fit triduo ante reverfus. Ego igitur, qui nihil prius de D. *Gregorii* aut itinere aut reditu noveram, ad illum recta contendo. *Gallus* ejus contubernalis humaniter me admittit, jubet expectare D. Doctorem, et ad illum ac-
cerfendum currit. Sed cum diutius moraretur, ego jam difceffurus,
video D. *Gregorium* feorfum cum ipfo colloquentem, et me torvo
vultu intuentum. Saluto illum & gratulor reditum, ac demum de
vobis incorrogo. Ille refpondet fe nihil quicquam de vobis aut rebus veftris fcire, nec vobifcum fuiffe. Tunc ego aliquantulum
hæreo, ac tandem dico, fi nolit quicquam dicere me æquo animo
laturum; fed jam mihi conftare eum vobifcum fuiffe : Ille ftoma-
chatur veftrum nomen, ac totius mundi fallacias & impofturas : dicit fua fibi effe curæ, non veftra vos multa quidem promittere, fed
parum præftare, nefcire fe quare conqueramini : fe per fefqui annum, vana fpe lactatum, vobis ad hæfiffe, ut aliquod e minoribus
veftris arcanis difceret, nec quicquam alicujus momenti percepiffe.

M m

Hic

Hic ego : an parvum tibi videtur arcanum illud contra laeium veneream ? Ille verò, subridens, a *D. Sconto,* inquit , longe praestantiorem habeo. Denique, his omissis, librum meum *Postellæ* repeto : ille negat se habuisse interrogata quo audiverim ; ac me laudante *D. Dee,*ille rursus negat se vidisse; nisi forte,inquit, ex manibus *D. Sevenbergii,* vis dicere librum nescio quem sine titulo : ac denique de restituendo nullam spem facit. Ego qui cum illo verba commutare nollem, abeo : ac puerum vestrum *Stanislaum,* in atrio offendo,& ab illo intelligo , vos *Erfordiam* usque cum *D. Gregorio* & *D. Carpione* venisse,ante octiduum . *D. Carpionem* illinc *Bambergam* ad exigendas nescio quas pecunias,profectum; se cum *D. Gregorio,* hoc venisse.Interrogo an literas aut aliquod verbulum, a vobis, ad me, ferret; respondet, nihil prorsus, quia forte putabant, inquit, te hic non esse: se post triduum aut quatriduum ad vos reversurum.Laudo ejus consilium, & constantiam in serviendis Dominis, ac doceo meas ædes,ne sine meis literis ad vos veniat : promittit se non discessurum, me insalutato *D.Gregorius* interim percipit, me cum eo colloqui , atque iratus (quantum ex voce clamantis judicare possum) puerum revocat. Ego, cogitabundus, discedo. Die quinto decimo hujus mensis, tandem nactus servulum vestrum *Stanislaum,* in loco libero, eum accuratius de vestris rebus ac statu examino , atque non sine magna animi mei voluptate, audio vobis concessas esse ampliores ædes.Illust. *D.Langravium* praestantissimo *D. Dee* multum tribuere ut favere, & summo Deo pro tanto munere magnas gratias ago,atque puerum ad meum cubiculum duco ostendoque illi literas ad vos paratas, ne sine ipsis ad vos revertatur. Sed paulo postea pater *Carpionis* me monet, se velle ante noctem , ad vos unicum expressum mittere & ut scribam si velim : nam se a *D. Kelleo* monitum hoc mihi significare: ingentes gratias ago *D.Kelleo* qui mei non sit omnino oblitus , & hæc, per hunc quem vobis spero fidem nuncium , significare statuo; scripturus rursus per *Stanislaum,* si operæ pretium videbitur.

Oro vos atque obtestor per Deum illum vivum,qui Autor est nostræ amicitiæ, & qui diserte praecepit ut nos invicem ac mutuo amemus,ne obliviscamini mei cum datur vobis occasio invigendi me per literas aut per inter nuncios, & reddendi me certiorem de statu vestrarum nostrorumque rerum ; nam ego certe vestri non obliviscar, & officia mea id testibuntur,non solum coram Deo,sed etiam coram omnibus hominibus. Si vester reditus aliquandiu differetur ; invisam vos proximo mense *Septembri,* longe enim a vobis vix vivere possum, immo si proprie loquendum sit , me vitæ tædet : Ac præsens agam de nonnullis rebus quas scribere minime decet.

Jam elapsi sunt 18 dies ex quo Illustrissimum *Nuncium* Apostolicum non vidi, & cum satis superque satisfecerim obedientiæ,non adibo illum, ne verba nobis dare sibi tam facile fore persuadeat. *Ostendit literas D.Dee Legato* Veneto *&* Florentino *& uterque mihi*

sum-

summopere eas laudavit, dixitque sibi visus disertas graves, & plus-quam vulgaris spiritus, & optissint exemplum illarum , sed ego of-ferre non poteram, & dubito ne Illuftriftimus *Nuncius* eas supprimat ; nam haud obscure, innuit *se timere vestrum congressum præ-sertim æquum & rationale,* & id quærere videtur, ut vobiscum age-re possit *more Hisp.* &c. D. *Joan. Carpio,* nondum revertitur, & D. *Rofenbergius* cras dicitur discessurus & nescio an recuperare potero literas ad eundem *Carpionem,* in quibus de pecuniolis illis agebatur, si dubitatis ne ille diutius quam par sit , solutionem differat quæso curetis, ut aliquo alio modo mihi profpiciatur. D. ab *Ossa,* per 20 dies, non vidi, ac Jesuitis palam dixi & dico quandocunque occasio se offert, *vobis factum ab ipsis insignem injuriam, eos plus pendere ab aulis terrestribus quam a cælesti : timere collationem æquam cum vo-bis,ac suæ causæ annum haud obscure dissidere,*itaque jam sum eis mi-nus gratus.

Saluto uxorem D. *Dee* lectissimam tœminam , ac mihi non mi-nus quam matrem venerandam ; necnon conjugem D.*Kellei* rarum exemplum juvenilis fanctitatis , caftitatis , atque omnium virtu-tum. Saluto omnes , alios veftros domefticos fanctos vofque in-primis D.D. *Joan.* & *Ed.* defiderabilia mihi nomina fœlices ac bea-tos in Domino cupio ac precor. Quantum tribuam & tribuere de-beam veftris precibus noftis,eis oro atque obfecro me apud D.Deum juvetis ut vocationi meæ refpondeam, & curfum meum hilari animo ac firmo corpore perficiam.Sanctiffimus ille pater, qui nobis jam fuf-citavit paftorem illum magnum D. Jefum filium fuum mox reverfu-rum ad fubigendos omnes innimicos ejus fub pedibus fuis, atque ex-tremam manum impofiturum renovationi rerum , nos omnes fuo fpiritu foveat ac recreet,ut Lati adventum ejus præftolari,atque nu-ptialibus voftibus , lampadibufque accenfis ornati, ipfi occurrere poffimus. Praga *xv Kal.* Octob. *M.D. Lxxxv.*

Idem Dominationibus vestris addictissins

Atque ex animo frater

PUCCIUS

Præstantissimis ac Deo dilectis viris D.D. Joannes Dee. *& Eduardo Kelleo Gene-rofis* Anglis, *ac Majoribus in Chrifto fra-tribus, mihi, tanquam Patribus colendis,* *&c.*

Mgnifice Domine;& uti pater amantissime & observande non minori etiam desiderio teneor videndi & de multis colloquendi cum Magnifica dominature vestra de cujus erga me & fide, & amore nunquam dubitavi nec dubitare possum post prandium hora commoda ego illam accedam. Deus sua, gratia semper nobis adsit.

Vester ex animo, *Gulielmus* propria matiu.

Febr. 10. 1587, stilo novo.   *Trebone.*

Postride reditus Illustrissimi à *Vienna* ad *Trebanam.*

✛ ▵

Sir, My hearty commendations unto you desiring your health as my own , my Lord was exceeding glad of your Letters , and said now I see he loveth me , and truly as far as I perceive he loveth us heartily. This Sunday in the Name of the Blessed Trinity I begin my Journey, wherein I commend me unto your prayers, desiring the Almighty to send his fortitude with me. I commend me unto Mrs. *Dee* a thousand times , and unto your little babes: wishing my self rather amongst you, then elsewhere, I will by Gods grace about twenty dayes hence return, in the mean season all comfort and joy be amongst you ;

<table>
<tr><td>

▵ {
Prage.
1587.
25 *Januarii.*
Thomas Kelly.
Francis Garland.
Ferdinando Hernyk,
} went with him.

</td><td>

Your assured and immoveable friend.

E. Kelly.

</td></tr>
</table>

To the Right Worshipful, and his assured friend Mr. John Dee *Esquire , give these.*

Magnifico Domino, Domino Dee.

Received of *Lodovick* in the High-way by *Platz,* in the middle way between *New-house* and *Trebon,* as I was comming from *New-house,* whither I went to have met my Lord as he came from *Vienna :* But Arch-duke *Ernest* was occasion (as was thought) that they should go to *Prage* by *Triegle,* being the more even, although not the next way : I received them on Friday the 6 of *February,* and they were delivered him at *Prage* on Sunday was a seven-night before , being the 25 of *January, nevo stile.*

Swethart I commend me unto you. hoping in God that you are in good heakh, as I and my children , with all my Houshold am here, I praise God for it ; I have none other matter to write unto you at this time.

I being at *New-house* from *Trebone,* (to go to understand which way my Lord *Rosenberg* would go from *Vien* to *Prage* and when,) and this Letter being in the same day brought from *Prage,* my wife sent *Lodovick* with it, toward me, and so without *Platz* Town in the High-way he gave it me.

✛ *Trebone in Bohemia.*

Visitationis Secunda , Actio instituta.

Anno 1586.
Die 19 *Septembris.*
Die Veneris sexti mensis sine a die Veneris ante Pascha à meridie hora 3.

▵ Preces ad Diem fudi , and declared that we here and now presented our selves, as in obedience, according to the time prescribed of six Moneths end , since the last good Friday : I craved pardon of all our errors and misdeeds , since the last time of his visiting us , and now requested his aid and direction hence-forward to walk prosperously, according to the well pleasing of his divine Majestie : and that he would grant unto *William Rosenberg,* E. K. and me his graces , so abundantly, that in us his honour might be increased , and glory advanced mightily and triumphantly, &c.

E. K. Here is a round fire like a Sunne.

Vox ...... *Frigida præparatio.*

Frigida oratio.

Frigidam hoc exiguum responsum.

Reversente tamen Gulielmo, *mediatorem & agunm, respondere paratum, consulito.*

E. K.

E. K. He is gone now.

△ Tu justus es Domine, & nos impii : tu sanctus es Domine, & viæ tuæ immaculatæ : nos nec orare, neque nos præparare sine tuo auxilio & gratia unquam possimus: Tuam igitur nobis concedas gratiam, & de tanto errore nostro dignam agere pœnitentiam, ut agnum,& mediatorem nostrum omni tempore nobis inveniamus propitium ex tua clementia, illius meritis, & spiritus tui Sancti afflatu consolatorio: *Amen.*

Cui, Trino & uni, Deo vero, & Omnipotenti, sit sempiternus honor, laus perennis, & gloria perpetua. *Amen.*

✝ *Trebone, Actio Secunda ex septem.*

Anno 1586.

Octob. 14. Tuesday. *Mane post solis ortum.*

Circa 7. *Precibus fusis, gratiisque actis pro misericordiis Dei infinitis erga nos tam in prædestinatione quàm in executione, in patria, in mari, & in hac peregrinatione, & pro liberatione nostra ex manibus hostium in Pragensi exilio, & pro sua continua tutela, & pro redactione nostra cum honore & gloria in illo, ad quietem & securitatem cum Willielmo Rosenbergio, jam lebamus quid ipse potissimum nobis proponere velit ex suis mysteriis, & quid de Puccio esse statuendum, quid de & operibus Philosophicis juxta ejus propositum, & quid de errore in practica nuper facta sit statuendum, & quid præterea nobis jam & præcipue sit faciendum, & ad Willihelmum vocandum paratos, nos esse juxta Dei beneplacitum,&c.*

△ I had set up *Mensam fœderis,* with the appurtenances, and had set the *Angelical Stone* in the frame of Gold on the Table, onely *E. K.* and I being In the goodly little Chappel next my Chamber, appointed to our uses.

A voice ...... *Let him come, that is to come:*

△ I went for the Lord *Rosenberg,* whom I found in his Oratory of the Church hearing of Masse: And he came with me and sat in his place.

E. K. I see a great plain like unto a field, as though it were a Mile over, in the end of it there is a great high rotten Tree, all the grasse is as though it were withered and burned, there commeth a beam as of fire from Heaven, and lighteth upon the Tree, now there cometh water out of the root of the Tree, as though it were a Sea, and spreadeth all the plain over: And the Tree openeth and there commeth a Man out of it, his hair hangeth down unto his girdle stead, his garment covereth him down from his shoulders, and hangeth behind him down upon the water.

The earth hath now drunk up all the water, and the Man standeth upon the dry ground.

All the place is full of green grasse about a cubit high.

Now the Man is out of sight.

It seemed to be as beyond and without the Stone.

The Vision is clean dis-appeared.

△ I expounded this Vision in Latin to the Lord *Rosenberg.*

E. K. In the middest of the Stone seemeth to stand a little round thing like a spark of fire, and it increaseth, and seemeth to be as bigge as a Globe of 20 inches Diameter, or thereabout.

Vox ...... *Wo be unto the World, wo be unto the World, and Worldlings : Wo be unto you Sonnes of men, for you are withered, and behold the field of the Lord bringeth you not forth: you are defiled, and being defiled, you defile also the beauty of your Seat: And behold, behold, behold, (I say) you that are the King and Princes of the Earth eyed and knit together upon one stemme, you are all rotten and barren, behold, you bring forth no fruit: but even as the grasse that withereth, he is a dis-glory to the place, even so, are you that is grasse, of your situation and dwelling, for behold, you have no leaves, much lesse fruis : Wo, wo, wo, unto such a generation, which lacketh moisture, and the fire of comfort: The stemme that carrieth you is the Seat and holy place, which also is contaminated. And so, behold, (as it were) withered ; if holinesse be hidden whereupon you stand, how wicked are those that are governed by you ; how wicked are you; and how abominac* ble : how full of corruption are you that ſtand without all beauty, moiſture, or comfort : The time ſhall come that the power and might of God which here ſpeaketh amongſt you, in the fire and ſpirit ot his holy truth ſhall come down from above, from Heaven, from the Seat of comfort, from the everlaſting Throne, and ſhall fall down, not into you, nor amongſt you (for you ſhall be rooted out,) but into the ſtemme and into the root which is the holy place, and the houſe of comfort : And behold, the power of God, (of him that ſpeaketh) ſhall be mighty, ſtrong, and of infinite power : So that like a Woman with Child, ſhe ſhall bring forth in the Church of God, a man, clothed with a white garment : which is JUSTICE unſpotted, which may walk with infinite power (and in the Garment of holineſſe and beauty,) upon the abundance of graces, and the waters of comfort, which ſhall flow out of the holy Seat.

And behold, ô you Sonnes of men, you ſhall be full of underſtanding, and of the ſpirit of Wiſdome, and the grace of God, (of him that ſpeaketh with you) ſhall be plentiful and ſtrong amongſt you : So that you ſhall ſpring, and beautiſie the Earth and the Houſe of Chriſt : And behold, the higher boughes, and mighty branches ſhall loſe their vertue, and be caſt down, becauſe they have placed themſelves upon the outward rotten Stock, to the diſhonour of him that hath called them : and   re ſhall no more ſtrength or vertue be amongſt you : but you ſhall be ſubjeÄ to verity, and be controuled with an iron rod, by him that came out, and walked on the waters : Then ſhall be peace and reſt : Then ſhall Hieruſalem deſcend.

Quando Hieruſalem deſcendet.

E. K. Now is all diſ-appeared away out of ſight.

△ I read the former parcel in Latine to the Lord *Roſenberg.*

A Pauſe.

△ Tu juſtus es Domine, & Judicia tua vera, tu omnipotens ô Deus noſter, & brachio tuo nullus reſiſtere poteſt. Veni, ô Domine, & conſolare nos veritate & Juſtitia.

E. K. Now he is returned again in the form he went away in. A red croſſe commeth over it, pure red, ſo   yellowiſh.

A Pauſe.

Religionis reformatio in Anglia futura. Locus ſanÄus ruet. Finis mundi de rrentur. Terribilia prime.

So that the Name of the God of Righteouſneſſe, and of his Sonne Chriſt ſhall be magnified in thee : § And lo, behold, by my ſelf, I ſwear that after a few Moneths the time expired ; I will ſmite, and break the holy place, ſo that there ſhall be no abomination in it.

§ And behold, the ends of the World ſhall be opened, and all people ſhall rejoyce in the Croſſe and Name of the Lamb.

§ But firſt commeth terrour to all Nations. § Wo, wo, therefore be unto you, ô you Kings and Princes of the Earth ! he that hath eares let him hear.

...... And lo, behold, this day I am deſcended, and my promiſe is upon him that heareth amongſt you.

Let him mitigate therefore the fragility of humane reaſon, and give me a dwelling place by faith : for I will this day make a Covenant with him, ſo that my Name and Spirit ſhall not depart from his Houſe.

William Roſenberg.

And what I have promiſed him I am, and I will bring to paſſe : what is he, or who is he that laugheth me to ſcorn, that (if he repent not) receiveth not his reward ?

Roſenberg ſhall fall.

And moreover, I will appear to him hereafter, and he ſhall be partaker of the cæleſtial myſtery, if my Name be exalted in him.

And behold, he ſhall often fall, but he ſhall riſe again, and ſhall perſevere unto the end.

E. K. It is diſ-appeared.

△ Legi ultimam hanc particulam Latine ipſi Principi *Roſenbergio.*

A Pauſe.

E. K. *In lapide ſtetit ſcriptum.* After an hour.

△ We removed not, but ſat ſtill and diſcourſed partly upon the premiſſes, and partly of *Englands* miſery to come.

K. K. There appeareth a little white cloud, like the end of a cloud, with a dark image of a face of three in one : ſometimes appearing three, ſometimes one.

The end of the white cloud doth wave up and down before the face.

Two Winds in this Kingdom. Of the firſt, Vide An. 1587 Actione Rebenſteinenſ. Mart. 16.

Vox ex latere lapidis ...... Theſe four Moneths, let William (for aſmuch as in him lyeth) abſtain from Prage, for he ſhall deceive thoſe that are deceivers.

Two winds ſhall ariſe from the Earth within theſe next yeares in this Kingdom : In the firſt let him ſit ſtill : In the ſecond let him arm himſelf ; and reſiſt with Victory.

E. K.

E. K. There appeareth a Wood, a great Wood on the left hand by a River: There be two like Hawks, whereof one is white, and the other is black: The one is on a bough in the water, that is the black, the other on a withered bough on the land.

A great Bear commeth out of the Wood.   *u sus primus.*

Now he runneth toward them, he catcheth the black one in the water, and swalloweth him, and standeth up upon his hinder legs. Now he goeth to the other, and shaketh him in his mouth, and standeth up on his hinder legs; and hath pulled off both his Wings, he returneth into the Wood again, the body of the white lyeth on the ground. Now he turneth his feet up.

Now he standeth on his legs again.

He followeth the Bear the same way he went, he would lift up himself as if he would fly, but he cannot.

All this Wood, Bear, and two Fowles are vanished.

E. K. Below standeth a great Castle, at the foot of the Hill on which that Wood did stand, down in a valley from the Hill goeth a great high Bridge of Stone long (in sight) about ten English miles long.

Beside the entrance, on the right hand of that Castle, is like a Dial, with motions cœlestial in it, of Sunne and Moon.

Now commeth a Bear, (black as the other) a very great mon- *ursus secun-*
strous Bear. The Bridge quaketh under him as he passeth it toward *dus.*
the Castle he roareth, looking toward the Castle. He steppeth up to the Dial, and taketh the Moon out of it, and teareth it all in pieces with his teeth. The Castle falleth, and the bridge where he standeth is broken. The Castle is all in ruine.

The Bear standeth upon the edge of the bridg, and beholdeth the ruine of the Castle down into a pit as it were.

Now he goeth back and the bridg falleth down after him.

Now the Wood appeareth again, and he goeth into the Wood.

Now that Vision is all vanished away.

Vox ...... *Tou shall shortly see, against what stone Pucci hath spurned.*
My Peace and blessing be upon you.

E. K. Now all is gone away.

△ Gloria, laus, honor, Benedictio & Jubilatio sit Deo Patri, Deo filio, & Deo Spiritui sancto: Sicut erat in principio, & nunc, & in sempiterna sæculorum sæcula. *Amen.*

Spiritu principali confirma nos Deus, Deus noster confirmet nos Deus, Omnipotens, Sempiterne vive & vere. *Amen, Amen, Amen.*

MEMORANDUM.

Anno 1586. *Octobris Die* 17, *à meridie, post novas cum* Fr. Puccio *turbas & rixas, propter pecunias quas cupiebat à nobis habere, ex liberalitate, & in nomine Dei, & tanquam a servis Dei, & non ab* Edwardo Kelleo *tanquam ab* Edwardo Kelleo; *nos* [△ & E. K] *conclusimus (ad scandala multa evitanda quæ ipse contra nos sparserat & excogitaverat, propter pecunias ejus* 800 Florenorum, *Deo oblatas & redditas per illum, & prius recusatas quando nos illi solvere parati eramus, & 630 Ducatos illi exhibuimus coram Deo, ut inde acciperet quod suum esse judicabat.) Conclusimus inquam, (cum bona spe, quod non offenderemus Deum) ante illum, coram testibus, exponere interim 800 Florenorum: & si sibi deberi asseveret, quod recipere posset, si vellet; sin vero negaret 800 Florenos, aut aliquam sibi à nobis deberi pecuniam, Tunc & id etiam eorum testibus pronuntiatum volebamus, testimonio, & chirographo conscripto notum facere temporibus & locis opportunis.*
                                                                        Ex

Ex Arce Ivimus igitur ad Primatis Domum, & convocatis aliquot Civibus primariis, Sacerdo-
te sediore, & aliquot scribis Illustris summi Principis (Domini Rosenbergii) *duos magnos saccos*
pecuniarum expostuimus, & ex (ubi duo millia ducatorum, & præterea plures quàm 400 Doleri nume-
rabantur supra mensam, 800 Floreni : Et Dilemmate illi proposito (quod superius annotavi) pecuniæ
accipere contentus erat, sed ille voluit subscribere, se accepisse in nomine Dei, & à nobis tanquam
à servis Dei. Nos vero protestabamur nos nullo modo recipere in nos, ut a Deo hoc nobis esset in-
junctum diceremus, ut illi illas proponeremus pecunias, vel accipiendas, vel recusandas ab illo : Sed
tantum ad evitanda magna & multa scandala contra nos, ill   illius ibidem libero commit-
tere arbitrio, ut ill   & dicat, quod illi videretur melius, & illi esset gr   Ac-
cepit ergo pecunias, numeravit, & inde est conscriptum Chirogrphum manu scribæ   summi
*Principis (*Pauli Wolfg) *præsentis cum diversis testibus, qui sua nomina subscripserunt, ut in ipso*
Chirographo appare potest.

Franciscus   *Deo gratias agamus, Speramus enim, meliori nos jam quiete fruituros : & ma-*
                gis fore liberos ab ejus lingua venenata & inquieta Deus illum convertat : & illi
Puccius.   *sit propitius, atque dixit nobis se velle me ut ministrum faciat, sua divina Maje-*
stati utilem in

+ *Trebonæ. Anno* 1587.

Die 8 *Januarii* 21. *mane hor.* 9.

△ *Tempus beneplaciti, est tempus opportunum.*

Necessitas non habet Legem.

△ *In nomine pa*tis & F.& SS,&c. Pater noster,&c. *Omnipotens sempiterne vere* & une *Deus in*
adjutorium W. C. E. K. & *mei* Joannes Dee, *intende*, &c.

△ Not by or upon presumption (O Lord) but with fear and love toward thee we are ready to
hear thy will, as concerning the *Shew* and Commandement, now at *Prage* in this moneths beginning, made to *E. K.* We beleeve and hope it *is of thee*, and that thou wilt not tempt us, or suffer
us to be tempted in so weighty a case; And therefore being not perfectly informed in *those two ounces*
of powder, *E.K.* Knoweth not how to do, seeing at his return hither he misseth an *half ounce* thereof
whether shall he of the residue make up that half ounce wanting, or no ? we will or dare propound
to make any compleat action : but therein referre all to our Parliament dayes, or principal ordinary
actions assigned.

Mora interposita, parte horæ ¼.

E. K. Here appear Letters if I could read them, thus they are.

▢ ▢ ○ ▭

...... *Mihi, ita, & à me.*

E. K. They seem white Letters — of greenish yellow coloured
figures, in every figure one of the four words, in all being 12 letters.

E. K. Now they be gone.

△ I understand that the first part of that my Proposition is touched in answer of *mihi*, that is,
to God, the service required is to be done : and *ita & a me*, so is the message or commandment
from the same our God.

△ Mora interposita horæ parte ¼.

E K. Now is here other writing, thus, *Claudite, clausæ sunt.*

△ I understand not this well, if it mean no more to be taken out of *the Powder*, or what else.

Now appear over the former words, other words, as thus,

Cessate

E. K. Over *Claudite*, is *Cessate*, the other words I cannot read yet.

E. K. Over *clausa sunt* appeareth *divinum propositum sibi ad*
huc non constat.

△ *Quæ igitur tibi sunt, & à te, nobis sunt acceptissima.: & per te, & propter te, ut nobis injuncta*
faciamus tuum, ô Deus, nobis paratissimum præbeas auxilium !
Tibi Creatori Redemptori, & Sanctificatori nostro, sit omnis Laus, Honor, & Gloria, nunc &
semper, Amen.

Ad Omnipotentis Trinitatis Laudem, Honorem, & Gloriam.

Mysteriorum Divinorum memorabilia cui dies
quartus Aprilis, Anno 1587, *dicata fuit.*

Trebonæ

1587. ACTIO TERTIA.
Trebonæ Generalis.

▲. *P*Oſt *preces ad Deum, & recitatum Catalogum illum, petitionum noſtrarum ad eundem,* *Aprilis* 4.
quievimus divina expectantes conſilia, monita,& oracula.　　　　　　　　　　　　　　*Mane circa* 8.

Magna pauſa.

▲. ...... *Tandem accepi literas* * *utraſq; illuſtriſſimi Domini* Roſenbergii,& *recitavi coram* ＊*Illas cum*
Deo, *ut ejus obedientia, humilitas, & deſiderium, coram Deo & Angelis ejuſdem conteſtata eſſent.* 12. *quæſtio-*
Alia adhuc pauſa, ſive Mora facta, ſed non longa.　　　　　　　　　　　　　　　　　*nibus & illas*
priores ad
E.K. There ſeemeth a black Curtain of Velvet, to be drawn from *＇he chſtem.*
one ſide of the Stone to the other. The Curtain is full of plights. *m ſſas.*
There ſeemed alſo one to have deſcended from above, (a good
way behinde the Curtain) and ſo to go behinde the ſame Curtain.

Alia pauſa.

Vox. ...... *Happy is he, whoſe minde thirſteth after the knowledge of ſuch things as are ſpiri-*
tual, and celeſtial, of ſuch things as are in the everlaſting place and glory of him that is, and was,
and ſhall be for ever : for unto him belongeth reſt in the harveſt of the Higheſt, and comfort in
the midſt of many worldly ſorrows. For unto him, thus ſaith the Lord, the Lord of Reſt, Thou
haſt rendred my blood again, with comfort unto me, and haſt made a blood of eternal reſt unto thy
ſelf for ever. Aſcend therefore and dwell with me, and receive eternal comfort : for unto ſuch
belongeth the Kingdom of my Father ; for I am * Zebaoth *unto all ſuch as truſt in me. But be-* ＊ *Requies*
hold, the earth bringeth not forth my mighty praiſe, becauſe of the wickedneſs that aboundeth in all *ceſſatio ſab-*
mankinde : Neither have I many ſuch children amongſt the ſons of men as I have ſpoken of be- *batum,&c.*
fore ; for why ? The Giants of this world are a ſtumbling block unto the poor people, and unto Sabbath.
their ſubjects : for lo, behold, behold ! (I ſay) vile and baſe things (for that they are miſuſed)
are become gods within their houſes : ſo that,Gold and Silver, precious Stones, and ſoft Apparel,
which were wont to be brought out of their houſes to garniſh mine withall, are become their gods,
and the Idols of their deſtruction: for, who is he that exalteth not himſelf in his riches, and de-
ſpiſeth me that was the Author of them ? Where is he that loveth not his wife and children, pomp
and wo idly glory, more than the ſetting in order of my little flock, or the preferment of my
glory ? Who (I ſay) is he, that maketh not more of himſelf than of me ? Woe be unto you that
ſo do : and woe be unto the generations that ſhall follow you.
▲. Be merciful unto us, O God of Mercies.
...... O wretched and miſerable mankind, look, look in and upon thy ſelf. Haſt thou
made thy ſelf ? or when thou art afflicted, canſt thou remove thine own affliction ? Haſt
thou any thing of thy own, which my Father hath not given thee, through me, in one
provident and eternal will? Canſt thou hide thy ſelf where I cannot ſee thee ? or canſt
thou do that which lieth hid from me ? Look again upon thy ſelf, and conſider what parents, and root thou hadſt thy beginning in Nature : behold, they and their fathers are
become the duſt of the earth ; even ſo ſhalt thou do. And even as of them is a ſtraight
account of life required, even ſo ſhall it be of thee : for, *I that made thee, and gave thee*
breath, made thee partaker and uſer of my creatures, led thee in and out, gave thee the
Sun to ſhine upon thee, and the *Moon as the mother of your radical moiſture.* I that lifted
thee up, either to the honour of a King, or Magiſtrate, and made thee a governour over
thy brethren, will at laſt take a ſtraight account of thee, how thou haſt uſed thy ſelf towards me, and where thou haſt advanced my Name in ſuch things as I have lent thee :
And be right ſure, that thou ſhalt pay, even the uttermoſt farthing. Woe be unto thee,
if thou make not a juſt account ; miſerable ſhalt thou be for ever, if thy deſerts condemn
thee. Therefore while thou haſt time and ſpace,look, look up unto me ; for I am *the Well*
of comfort, and the God of peace ; the true reward of righteouſneſs to all ſuch as faithfully
love and truſt me.

Pauſa.

▲. I read this over ...... Oh how comfortable are theſe leſſons ! Give us and confirm
unto us thy graces and bleſſings, O God, to do thy bleſſed will herein, and in all our duty
toward thee whatſoever.

＊ A a a　　　　　　　　　　　　　　　E.K.

E.K. Now the voice seemeth to come from him who standeth behinde the Curtain.

Magna Pausa.

William the son of *Ursine,* the Lord talketh with thee this day, saying, Wilt thou that I buy a Kingdom for thee with gold or silver ? Wilt thou that the Kings and Princes of the earth shall laugh the Almighty God of the heaven and earth to scorn ?

Have I at any time preferred (such as trust in me) to the government of my people, by giving them the excrements of the earth ?

Look down upon my servant *Abraham.*

Look down upon his children.

Call to remembrance my servant *David.*

See *Solomon* before thy eyes.

The Kings and Princes of *Judah* and of *Jerusalem.*

Consider with thy self the Calling of the twelve : The government and state of such as have been Princes amongst the flock Christian.

Have they been hired or promoted ? Have they been lifted up by me with gold or silver, or such like trumpery, the Monsters of the earth ? In necessity, to pay Tribute the fish ministred, wherewithall Tribute might be paid according to custom.

In the calling of *Abraham,* multiplication of seed was promised; which was to be a multitude in people, mighty and great upon the face of the earth.

David was brought in (the least of his brethren) even to be King of *Israel,* not by the multitude of precious stones, gold or silver. A Sling he had, a Satchel with a few stones.

Solomon was commanded to build me a Temple, without any sum or stint. The Apostles went from place to place, intending to teach; neither carried they gold or silver, but onely a scrip or bag prepared for their common victuals and nourishment.

Many Princes and Kings have published my Name, without any promise made unto them from heaven.

Notwithstanding, unto *Abraham* I have plenty, as his necessities required : and unto his children, as I had limited.

Unto *David,* being King, riches followed his State; and unto his son *Solomon,* plenty both at home and abroad, to build my Temple,

Unto the Apostles I gave (in the time of the calling of my people) the spirit of understanding, whereby they understood and had power to teach : And unto such as stretched out their hands for my name, I have abundantly given; and it hath been faithfully, and for the love of me taken in hand.

Believe therefore with *Abraham,* and with his children.

Bring thy sling and bag before the people of the Lord against *Goliah.*

Endeavor thy self with *Solomon,* to build a Common-wealth, wherein I will be exalted, as the servant of the Son of God, and as his follower.

Go forward, as thy own power and ability shall serve thee : For thus saith the Lord of Hosts :

Thou hast nothing but what thou hast received of me : neither thou, neither thy father.

Provide therefore, of that thou hast, which is mine : that is to say, of that which thy power can extend unto, in thine own faculty and riches, to shew thy good will and ready endeavours in such things to be brought to pass, as thou hast learned of me : That is to say, Neglect not the time of this thy visitation, neither despise this Kingdom wherein thou shalt reign, for in so doing I dwell with thee for ever, and with thy posterity which shall be (in me) mighty. ¶ When thou art entred into it, *whatsoever Treasure there is in any house, or amongst you,* Take it, use it.

The use of
the Powder.

Il-um evil.

The ounce &
the half wch
W.R. hath is
to be multiplied.

Caesar: reddenda quae sunt Caesaris.

The L. Sobcovize the Land-Host-master.

Make thee a sword of it with two edges, that with the one thou maist cut off the bastards head, and with the other build up the Monuments and the houses of cleanliness, godliness, and understanding : That the East again may flourish, and that I may make *ane Floc* , from the Sun-rising to his going down.

In the mean season, shall the Powder which thou hast to be multiplied, *be extended, and multiplied with them that are here present,* that it may be apt for thy uses, and the strengthning of thy faith.

The one half of it thou shalt keep, as the perpetual remembrance of me, even thou and thy posterity.

Unto him that is thy head, do thy true obedience : although *his heart be hardned against thee, and thirsteth after thy destruction.*

For behold, thy enemy that seeketh to devour thy Soul, ceaseth not to lay nets for thee, that thou maist become odious to common people. But the time shall shortly come, when thou

shalt

shalt have justice against him. See therefore that thou smite; see, I say again, that thou *Justice a-*
smite him, for Justice is the hand of the Highest punishing such as offend, either against *gainst People.*
him or his Innocent.   *Justice.*

These that now come unto thee, have brought thee a great Cluster of grapes, even as *The Lord*
big as they can both carry : amongst the which, notwithstanding there are many rotten. *Czotek*
But behold, the foolishness from above shall appear wisdom before them, when their *Schonberg.*
wisdom shall become foolishness before me, and before themselves.   △ *He allu-*

Round about thee thou shalt receive assistance, and many hearts shall be made glad *deth to the*
in thee.   *spies of the*
holy land
As for my Treasures to be opened, To him that defileth my Seat, and the Sword of *for the chil-*
Justice.   *dren of Israel*

To him that harboureth abomination in his own houses, and listneth unto wicked *To the que-*
counsel.   *stion of*

Unto him which hath despised me, which is accursed of me, shall none of my Trea- *Brannen-*
sures be opened.   *burgh send-*
ing to.
I have judged him, and it shall appear shortly.   *Respondet*
That which is *Cæsars* give unto *Cæsar* ; and that which is mine, unto the House of my *Articulo Li-*
Honour.   *terarum su-*
arum, an
Be obedient (as the servant of God) unto thy Superiours: and whilest thou maist, di- *Cæsari ex*
ligently do Justice. Thy Country shall receive such remembrance of thee, as shall never *publere ali-*
be rased from the face of the earth: *until the fire come down from heaven consuming all things.* *qua sit dan-*
di portio.
Be full of humility, and abandon pride.

Bow down thine ears unto the poor.

Be often sorry for thy dayes mis-spent.

Be strong for ever in me.

Pausa.

△.

Thy wife is even at the door of sickness : But behold, I am even he, the Lord of *Jane* my
health.   *wife.*

E.K.

As unto thee, Barrenness dwelleth with thee, because thou didst neglect me, and take *Ed.K. uxor*
a wife unto thy self * contrary unto my commandment : for neither young nor old, rich *sterilis illi*
nor poor, are respected with me ; but what I will have done, is just, and whosoever doth *erat.*
it not, is privily (if he be not openly) punished for his offence. Therefore thou shalt † *At Mort-*
have *the womb which thou hast barren, and fruitless unto thee,* because thou hast transgressed *lake, 1583.*
that which I commanded thee.

Be it unto thy brother, as his service, trust, and confidence hath been in me, and to- *De Thoma*
wards me.   *Kelco agroto*
Lay your hands to work, and your bodies unto labour, and *participate one with an-* ⎫ Our mutual
other, as is commanded you.   ⎬ participating
That the blessing which I have promised you may go forward in you ; and that your ⎪ one with
labour may bring forth good fruit.   ⎭ another.

The fourteenth day hence shall this Action end : *In which day you shall once again as-*
semble your selves here together. And now behold I say unto thee, unto thee, that hast *18 Aprilis*
thy eyes opened, and thy ears made perfect, *which hast been exalted by the sight of the* *futura die*
heavens, why dost thou call upon me, desiring *to be made free.*   *Saturni.*
E.K. told me
Is it a burthen unto thee to be comforted from above ? O foolish man ! by how much *that he had*
the heavens excel the earth, by so much doth the gift that is given thee from above, ex- *all the Lent*
cel all earthly treasure. Notwithstanding, because that Manna is loathsom unto thee, *praid once a*
behold what is said unto thee this day.   *day at the*
Thou art made free : neither shalt thou any time hereafter be constrained to see the judgment *least, that he*
of the highest, or to hear the voices of the heavens.   *might no*
more have
But thou art a stumbling-block unto many.   *dealing to*
Notwithstanding, my Spirit shall dwell with thee ; and in the works of thy hands thou *skry.*
shalt receive comfort.

And the power which is *given thee of seeing,* shall be diminished in thee, and shall *Arthur Deo*
dwell upon *the first-begotten Son of him that sitteth by thee, as I have * before said.* ∴ *Prague*
In the mean season shall he be exercised here before me, *until the time come, that his* *ann. 1585.*
eyes shall be opened, and his ears receive passage towards the highest.

And these fourteen dayes shall it be a time unto thee of chusing or refusing.

For I will not cast thee away, neither out of my house, *unless it be long of thy own igno-* Unleast, &c.
rance, and wilful despising of my great benefit.

If thou therefore be weary of it, the fourteenth day hence, bring hither, and lay before me the *Powder which thou hast,* for thou hast offended me, *as a false steward, in taking* *The Powder*
out of that which is not thine own.

I will no longer dally with you, but will give unto you according unto your works.

Δ. O God be merciful unto us, and deal not with us according to the wickedness, frowardness, and blindness of our hearts. *Amen.*

N O T E.

Δ. Upon this former part of the Third Action General, where my first begotten Son (namely *Arthur*) was assigned to the Ministry of seeing and hearing, in place and stead of E.K. if he would utterly refuse the same office (hitherto by him executed, and by him to be executed, until the seven actions general finished) And that the same Childe and Son, in the mean space (that is to say, between the day of the part of Action received, and the end of the same: determined to be fourteen dayes after) should be exercised before God. I thereupon thinking that E. K. would, should, or best could instruct and direct the Childe in that exercise, did alwayes await, that E.K. would of himself call the Boy to that Exercise with him ; and so much the rather, because he said, that *he was very glad now that he should have a Witness of the things shewed and declared by spiritual Creatures:* And that he would be more willing to do what should be enjoyned to him to do, then if onely he himself did see, and that for divers causes. But when E. K. said to me, that I should exercise the Childe and not he, and that he would not, I thereupon appointed with my self to bring the Childe to the place, and to offer him, and present him to the service of Seeing and Skrying from God, and by Gods assignment, and of the time of fourteen dayes yet remaining, being the 15, 16, 17 dayes of *April,* and next before the 18 day, (the day assigned to end the Action in) to have the Childe exercised in them. And thereupon contrived for the Childe this order of Prayer ensuing.

Die Mercurii summo mane die Aprilis 15. *anno* 1587. *Trebona.*

Oratio pro Arthuro qua in exercitiis suis uti debet mysticis.

In the Name of God the Father, of God the Son, and of God the Holy Ghost. *Amen.*
Glory be to God the Father, God the Son, and God the Holy Ghost : As it was in the beginning, is now, and ever shall be, world without end. *Amen.*

O *Almighty and Everlasting, the true and living God, have mercy, pity and compassion on my father John Dee, and on me Arthur Dee; who being now called hither by thy assignment, am now here present and ready in all humility; obedience and faithfulness, to serve thy Divine Majesty, with all the gifts and graces which thou hast hitherto endued me with ; and with all other which of thy most bountiful and fatherly mercy, thou wilt henceforward bestow upon me. Lighten (therefore) O Almighty God, mine eyes, and open thou mine ears; Quicken, Instruct and Confirm in me, and unto me, my discretion, judgement, understanding, memory, and utterance, that I may be a true and perfect Seer, Hearer, Declarer and Witness of such things which either immediately of thy Divine Majesty, or mediately by the ministry of thy holy, mighty, and faithful Angels shall be manifested, declared or shewed unto me, now, and at all times and occasions, for the advancing of thy Praise, Honour and Glory. Amen.*

Hereupon, *Wednesday* morning, (the 15 of this *April*) I brought the Childe to the holy Table, being in order of the furniture thereto belonging, and set before him the Stone in the frame, (my first sanctified Stone) and caused him on his knees, to say the foresaid Prayer. And I also praid to the Childs hearing, other Prayers to God for the purpose in hand : and at his coming to look and see in the Stone,
There appeared to him (as he judged) divers little square figures, with pricks, and divers other figures and lines, which I caused him with his own hand to imitate upon a paper with pen and ink.
The lines were white, and some of the pricks also, but other of the pricks were black, as of ink.

Arth. Two old men with black beards, and with golden Crowns upon their heads, do appear. One is now gone : this holdeth his hands before him like a Maid.

Arth.

Arth. Now in the place of thofe fquare marks, I fee two Lions, the one very exactly, and gaping. About the upper brim of the Stone they appear : and the Lions feet be waxen greater and greater.

I fee another man from the breaft upward. I can fee no hair on his head.

I fee a great company of feet, and their garments skirts fomewhat above their ankles : and they are like womens kirtles with gards about them.

I fee another man without a doublet, in his fhirt, and with a white Cloke about him, hanging his hands down by his fides.

Δ. Nothing elfe efteemed or judged to be fhewn in the Stone, by the Childe, we cea-fed that Exercife, and committed all to Gods mercies.

Δ. On *Thurſday* and *Friday*, I determined each of them two dayes that the Childe *Aprilis* 16. fhall thrice in the day be put to the Exercife, and each time repeat the Prayer prefcribed thrice.

Δ. In the forenoon I brought the Childe to the Exercife, and he faid as followeth. I.

I fee two men with Crowns of gold upon their heads : their appa-rel is black and white. I cannot fee their feet. Their faces are white, their eyes are black like fpots of ink.

There appear now two other, without Crowns : of the which one ftandeth whole before, and of the other I fee nothing but the head, which ftandeth behinde the firft.

I fee not any with Crowns now. The apparel of him is white that I fee.

I fee no hands of him. I fee nothing now.

The fquares and pricks appear again as yefterday.

And I doubted it was fomething of the Glafs it felf : as there were in it certain white fpots.

An hour we were at the practife.

Δ. The fecond Exercife before Dinner. After the Prayer thrice faid, &c. II.

Arth. I fee the firft fquare lines and pricks, white and black : the pricks for the moft part be all white, but fome are black, and the lines all white.

I faw, even now, fome of thofe fquares made Lions : but now there appear none.

The fquares are now turned alfo into other fhapes, which I cannot well declare.

Now the Letters be gone, and the fquares do appear again.

The fquares are gone, and a word is there.

The letters are clearer then they were : for all the lines and letters do appear white.

There appeareth a B, with a fquare, with four black pricks in it. It is gone.

Now fome of the fquares are come amongft the letters B D O.

Under the B appeareth a little e thus ə backward.

The

The letters as if one had cut them in the glaſs   B D O
Here appeareth a Caſtle with little pinacles like a Church.
Now it is gone.

B a this appeared and ſuddenly is gone.

Now there appeareth a young man with a white doublet, and his arms by his ſide, and a B before him againſt his doublet. He hath a black beard and a white face. I ſee no hair on his head: his beard is a little——

He is now changed : he hath on his doublet breaſt, on each ſide three black lines.

He is gone, and another is come in his place, with a white leather doublet, and a grey cloke like Hans of Gloats his cloke. He is gone.

The firſt young man is come again, and hath now on the one ſide of his doublet — on the other ſide, thus :

Now I ſee only two ſtrokes overthwart all the doublet, but he hath no head that I ſee.

Either his head is come again, or elſe another man, that hath two lines and two pricks as he had.

The light of the candle did ſeem to ſhine ſuddenly on his face, and go away again. It did not ſhine on his doublet, but onely on his face and his head.

There is now another man come in, who holdeth up both his hands: the upper part of his ſleeves are white, and the half towards his hands black.

The firſt man is here ſtill. Now he hath no arms, but a B before his doublet, but no lines, but only on each ſide two pricks in ſtead of the lines, thus : :

Theſe men came amongſt the ſquares ſuddenly before I was aware.
Here appear not ſo many as were here.

Here are now but ſix ſquares, and one man. I ſee no farther of the man but to the waſte of his doublet.

The man appeareth not ſo brim to my ſight as he did, his head is no bigger than the mark in the margent.

III.　　　　　　　*The third Exerciſe after Dinner.*

Arth. Whereas I ſaid before there was ſome of the ſquare figures wanting : Now I finde that they are all here again, as many as they were at my firſt ſeeing.

In lifting up the Stone, and bringing it down again, the ſquares do all ſeem like B B of the Roman letters.

A. *Magna mora.*

Arth. I ſee now B A. It is now vaniſhed away, after three Pater noſter times ſaying. R a appeareth, but I cannot ſee clearly the foot of the R. Now it is gone.

⁑ I ſee a thing all white in this form, and a little o before it. It would

would feem to be as an X and an o.   It is vanifhed away.

e B An Englifh little e, and a Roman great B.

It is gone before I can be aware.

S B now appeareth.   B by himfelf: it appeareth following S B thus S B   B.

N appeareth by the laft B, in order following, thus S B   B N.

I can fee no more now but the S B the B and N.

f B appear.   e B is here now.   B by himfelf, with two great white pricks before it, appear.   The pricks wax dim.

The man ftandeth amongft the fquares and letters in the midft of them.   ∴   This now appeareth.   The 4 little pricks be gone.

There appeareth like a B and a d joyning to it.

A circle appeared with a black prick in it, and two white pricks af-ter.   An n, two ftrikes, and two white pricks after.   The n is white and the prick within the n black.   ua appeared, and quickly went away.   Two long ftrikes by themfelves, white.   The two pricks black, and the crooked line white.   Four white pricks by themfelves. Two black.   Two long white ftrikes and a prick.   A round circle white, and a black prick in it.   A white prick by it felf.   A little prick as it were blotted, and a ftroke by it all white.   The crooked lines white, and the pricks black.   Two white pricks by themfelves.   Two long white ftrokes.   lo Thefe both white.

Here appeareth the thing like the Caftle, all white.

The pricks black, the lines white.   A little Englifh o by it felf. Four white ftrokes.   The man is here in the midft of the things, as before I told.   Four white pricks.

Note: All the fhews are within the uppermoft quarter of the ftone, as where A with the prick.

Like a figure of 2 all white.   Two little black pricks, and the ftroke white.   They are now gone.   D o appeareth all white, X o appeareth all white.   B e appeareth white.   Two o's joyned like a figure of 8 all white.   A great Roman white S by it felf. B Bu Thefe appear white.   A white prick by it felf.   An Englifh little t white.   Two lines white.

More magna.   So we ended.

a. God enrich us with his Truths.

The end of *Thurfdays* third Exercife.

Friday Morning.

I.

The Prayers on both parts being faid.

Arth. I fee not the fquares, lines, pricks, and thofe other things which I was wont to fee firft.

More hora unius.

After

After I had tarried an hour, and had had no evident shew : as I asked the boy diligently again, he said that he had from the beginning seen thus   *b b*

Also there appeared X o all white.   Do the o joyneth to the D.

Fiat voluntas Dei in sua luce & veritate, ad ejus nominis laudem, honorem, gloriam. Amen.

Friday.   II.

Preces————

Mora hora unius spatio.

Nulla ostensio toto illo tempore.

Δ. *Benedictio, misericordia & Pax, Dei, & Domini nostri Jesu Christi, sit super nos, & nobiscum : nunc & in sempiterna saeculorum saecula.* Amen.

Friday 3. à meridie.

Mora Magna,

Multae factae preces erant, & invitati illi fideles Dei servi quia etiam auxilia sua pollicebantur n cessitati quocumque tempore.   Etsi mora magna & admiranda : & apparitio nulla extra est puero ipsi.

Thursday à meridie circa 3.

Δ. *Tandem mirabili fortuna, sive fato divino accessit ad nos Dominus E.K, & qua sequebantur notavi.*

Uriel.

Δ. He sate down by us : and *Arthur* yet standing before me at the Table, being covered after the best manner, but onely the Stone being set thereon ; He asked if any thing appeared : We answered No, albeit I have called oftentimes, and have prayed earnestly that some of our former accounted friends might shew themselves to the boy, as *Madimi, Il, Is,* and chiefly *Uriel,* because *as he was first which appeared to the joyning of E.K. and me together ;* so he might be also the Director *in the translating of E.K. his office to Arthur.* Then said he, I marvel if you had no apparition here : for I somewhat thinking of *Arthur* and his proceeding in the feat of skrying, came here into the gallery, and I heard you pray : and opening the window, I looked out, and I saw a great number going in and out of this Chappel at the little hole in the glass window.   I saw *Madimi, Il,* and many other that had dealed with us heretofore, but shewed themselves in very filthy order ; and *Uriel appeared, and justified all to be of God,* and good : And therefore I wonder if here you have no shew : perhaps there is somewhat, but *Arthur* seeth it not.

Δ. True it is : and how should I help him herein, seeing I cannot yet see or skry ?

E.K. I will come and see if there be any thing.

Δ. I pray you do. [Note : and so *E. K.* looked towards the stone, and he by and by said, Here appeareth somewhat, and pointed to *Arthur,* where : and asked him if he saw any thing, and he said No.. Then said

E.K. I see like a white Marble square table or book lying on a wooden desk.

Δ. I pray you Sir take the pains to look and discern what is here shewed.

E.K. I see written upon that book,

Beatusque per peccatum mihi, demum corruentem & hominibus integram reddit.

E.K. Now a leaf of that book is turned open, and there is written on it, but I cannot reade it yet.   Now I see it.

Ego sum qui dedi & daturus sum vobis legem : ex qua mortalibus perpetua requies & felicitas sit ventura.

E.K. Now another leaf is turned over, and appeareth written,

Estote ergo tales, quales me meosque decet, & rati coram me ambulate.

E.K. Now turneth over the leaf of it self.

Ne populus esuriens & sitiens, negligentia & obstinatia vestra vel ruat vel saltem.

E.K. Now the leaf turneth.

Pro tempore, alimento careat.

E.K. Now the desk and book or table is gone.

Δ. Note : By and by after, while *E.K.* did look into the stone, he said,

E.K. I see a hand appear, a very great one, white, with the fingers spred abroad.   E.K.

E. K. The hand is gone, but there remaineth writing.

Videbitis & audietis brevi omnes. Si interim.

E. K. It is as if it were upon the fide of a white Globe afar off. The Globe turneth fo fwiftly that I cannot well read it.

Animi ad meliora compoti.

E. K. The Globe turneth fo fwiftly that I cannot read it till it ftand ftill.

Sefe mihi & meis.

E. K. Now again the Globe is turned moft fwiftly.

(Filiorum more) fubjicient. Si vero (per meipfum loquor & jure) alieni & vagabundi alias vobifmet ipfis difimperitis non oculo, fed corpori, immo omnibus membris, cafus & ruina paratur. Quales enim in futuro eritis, vobis ut fcivetis nullo modo licet : Majora enim à fuperis mortalibus, præ foribus funt, quotidieque inftant quam vel primo, vel fecundo etatis modulo fuerunt. Qui aures, erigat : Cui intellectus, fapiat. Omnia peccata apud me poftponuntur huic. infaniens propter me, fapiat : Immo adulterizans propter me, in fempiternum benedicetur, & premio afficietur celefti.

E. K. Now the Globe is gone.

Δ. *Gloria Patri & Filio & Spiritui fanĉto, erat in principio & nunc, & femper & in fecula feculorum.* Amen.
So we left off.

Trebonæ.

Actionis Tertiæ altera pars.

Preces ad Deum Omnipotentem, pro fua veritate nobis impartienda, ad nominis fuo laudem, honorem & gloriam.

Δ. Note *Arthur* was fet to the ftone, but nothing appeared ; E. K. had brought the powder with him as he was bidden to do. Then I defired him to apply himfelf to fee as he was wont. And fo he did.

E. K. Here appear all in the ftone that appeared yefterday unto me in the air in that moft diforderly and filthy manner. They are in the like apparel as yefterday.

Δ. O God confirm us in thy truth for thine own honour and glory, and fuffer us not to be overcome with any temptation, but deliver us from all evil now and ever.

E. K. There appeared Madimi, II. and the reft : And fo they are here; but now all the reft are gone, and onely Madimi remaineth.

Madimi openeth all her apparel, and her felf all naked; and fheweth her fhame alfo.

E. K. Fie on thee, Devil avoid hence with this filthinefs, &c.

Mad. *In the Name of God, why finde you fault with mee?*

Δ. Becaufe your yefterdayes doings, and words are provocations to fin, and unmeet for any godly creature to ufe.

Mad. *What is fin?*

Δ. To break the Commandement of God.

Mad. *Set that down, fo.*

Mad. *If the felf-fame God give you a new Commandement taking away the former form of fin which he limited by the Law; What remaineth then?*

Δ. If by the felf-fame God that gave the Law to *Mofes*, and gave his New Covenant by Chrift, who fealed it by his blood; and had his witneffes very many, and his Apoftles inftructed by his holy Spirit, who admonifhed us of all cleannefs in words and works, yea and in thoughts, if by the fame God, hofe former Laws and Doctrines be abrogated, and that

* B b b   fufficient

Sufficient proof and testimony to be had herein.

sufficient *proof and testimony* may be had that *it is the same God* : Then must the same God be obeyed : For only God is the Lord of Lords, King of Kings, and Governour of all things.

E K She kneeleth , and holdeth up her hands.

Mad. The Laws of God, and of his Son Christ, stablished by the testimony of his Disciples and Congregation , and by the force and power of his holy Spirit , are not in any particular vocation abrogated, but rather confirmed.

Δ. A priviledge granted doth not abrogate a Law, but doth notifie the force of the law in it self otherwise.

For oftentimes it falleth out , that God being offended at the wickedness of any man, or of some man private, sendeth down his Spirit of Death, infecting and tempting another mans minde ; so that he becometh void of Reason, and riseth up against him, whom God is offended with, and striketh him, so that he dyeth. This, before man, is accounted sin, before God it shall be imputed unto him for righteousness. Even so whatsoever the Spirit of God teacheth us from him , though it appear sin before man, is righteousness before him.

* Arthur was smitten in a swound and E.K. saw one in a long white garment make as though he would smite him. He was very sick for the time. Justice. S. Paul lecherous. Good Angels. The wisdom of God, of us ncomprehensible.

Therefore assure your selves , that whatsoever is seen and heard amongst you, is from above, and is a sign and testimony even this day before you; for I that touched thy Son, * might also have taken away his breath.

But O, you are of little understanding : But behold I teach you.

That unto those that are accounted righteous (through the good will of God) sin is justly punished, but not as unto the wicked. For whatsoever you have done unto other men, even the self-same shall light upon you , but happy is he that receiveth not justice through the terror of malediction, but through the grace and mercy of God.

The Apostle Paul abounded in carnal lust : he was also offensive unto his brethren so that he despaired, and was ready to have left his vocation, untill the Lord did say unto him , My mercy and grace sufficeth thee.

Beleeve me, that we are from above.

Which considered : Consider also , That as you cannot comprehend the heavens, so likewise can you not comprehend the wisdome of God, which saith, I will be merciful unto whom I list, and unto whom I will not, I have none in store : Foolish is he that asketh why ?

And behold I say unto you, Stumble not against God. Who be is that made you? Who is he that hath given you power to look up towards heaven ? You are fools ; and of little understanding : This day saith God unto you,

Behold you are become free : Do that which most pleaseth you : For behold, your own reason riseth up against my wisdome.

Not content you are to be heires, but you would be Lords, yea Gods, yea the Judgers of the heavens : Wherefore do even as you list, but if you forsake the way taught you from above, behold, evil shall enter into your senses, and abomination shal dwel before your eyes, as a recompence, unto such as you have done wrong unto : And your wives and children, shall be carried away before your face.

Δ. The Almighty God of heaven and earth be my comfort , as I desire comfort in his service, and give me wisdome as I desire it for his honour and glory; Amen.

E.K. I see a white pillar, and upon the pillar, I see four heads.

The Chrystaline pillar

Shee tieth the pillar round about with a list.

The four heads are like on two heads, and on two Wolves heads.

Now there cometh a thing like a white Crown of Christal , and standeth upon all our four heads. The heads seem to be inclosed by the necks within the pillar.

Now she taketh the pillar and goeth up with it.

Now she bringeth an half Moon down , and written in it as followeth.

Injustum nihil quod justum est Deo.

Now she goeth round about upon a thing like a Carpet ; she goeth now beyond where is an Orchard; she cutteth branches of two trees, and shee seemeth to insert them, or graff them into another.

Now she goeth into a black place behinde the wood, and bringeth a thing with her in a chain : An ugly thing like a Devil.

Mad. —— Behold, seest thou this : wherewithall thou thoughtest to overthrow, and must infect, thou art utterly overthrown, and shalt never return again.

E.K. Now he leapeth, and the ground openeth, and he sinketh in :
and

and there feemeth a ftink of brimftone to come to my Nofe from the pit.

Now the grafts are all grown in the tree, as if they were all of one tree.

Now fhe cometh out of that orchard. Now fhe goeth round about the orchard, and leaveth a darknefs like a cloud round about the orchard.

Mad. ...... *Vifible to God, but invifible to man.*

E.K. Now fhe cometh again upon her Carpet.

Behold, if you refift not God, but fhut out Satan (through unity amongft you) thus it is faid Unity, *unto you, Affemble your felves together every feventh day, that your eyes may be opened, and* An offer of *that you may underftand by him that fhall teach you*, what the fecrets of the holy books (deli- every 7th vered you) are : That you may become full of underftanding, and in knowledge above day to be common men.

And in your works go forward, and detract no time, that you may alfo have fruit. fecrets of the
Unto *William* I will be merciful for ever, according to my promife. But I will buy ved.
him no Kingdom, after the manner of man, with money. But what I have determined The holy
unto him, fhall happen unto him : And he fhall become mighty in me. books deli-

¶ And this Powder which thou haft brought here, is appointed for a time by God, vered.
and cannot be ufed until then, without offence. Happy is he that heareth my words ·Our works this day : and happy is he that underftandeth them. to go on.

But if you deny the Wifdome of the Higheft, and account us his Meffengers,Crea-⎫ The Lord tures of darknefs. *This day you are made free.* ⎬ *Rofenberg.*

And look that you lay up all things that is fpoken of from above ; and whatfoever hath⎱ The powder *been taught you,(as well the books as inftruments.)* here.

You fhall fhortly have to do again with the cruelty of the Emperour, *and the* accurfed⎰ *Omnia repo-Bifhop.* *nenda.*

Whereunto, if you go forward with God, you fhall be taught to anfwer. If you leave off, Caefar & as foon as you hear of it be going into Germany, *left you perifh before then.* *Papa brevi*

I have no more to fay unto you, but my fwiftnefs is from above. *nos infefta-*

E.K. Now fhe maketh her felf ready, &c. bunt denno.

Mad. ...... *If my friendfhip like you not, I befeech God fend you as good will, as I (in power)* bear towards you.

I have not one word more given me to fpeak.

E.K. Now fhe is gone.

Δ. I was glad that an offer was made of being every feventh day to be taught the fecrets of the books already delivered unto us : Thinking that it was eafie for us to perform that unity which was required to be amongft us four ; underftanding all *after the Chriftian and godly fenfe.* But *E.K.* who had yefterday feen and heard another meaning of this unity required, utterly abhorred to have any dealing with them farther, and did intend to accept at their hands the liberty of leaving off to deal with them any more : which his underftanding,as it was ftrange and unpleafant unto me,fo I earneftly requefted to be refolved therein in manner as followeth.

At the fame time, and in the fame place this enfued.

N O T E.

Δ. Upon Mr. *Kelly* his great doubt bred unto me of *Madimi* her words yefterday, fpoken to him, *that we two had our two wives in fuch fort, as we might ufe them in common*, it was agreed by us, to move the queftion, whether the fenfe were of *Carnal ufe* (contrary to the law of the Commandment) or of Spiritual love , and charitable care and unity of mindes, for advancing the fervice of God.

E.K. Upon a Scroll, like the edge of a Carpet, is written,

De utroq; loquor.

Δ. The one is exprefly againft the Commandement of God : neither can I by any means confent to like of that Doctrine. And for my help in that verity, I do call down the power of Almighty God, the Creator of heaven and earth, and all the good Angels, (his faithful Minifters) to affift me in the defence of my faithful obedience to the law of the Gofpel, and of his Church.

Affift me, O Chrift.   *Affift me, O Jefu.*   *Affift me, O holy Spirit.*

* B b b 2   E.K.

E. K. It appeareth written upon a white Crucifix, as followeth,
Mea gratia, major est mandato. Gratia enim hec mea est, ut hominibus insanis concedera-
tur beatitudo : Et que ita dicta sunt, Vel sint, vel hodie libertas vobis restituitur: Amen
dico vobis, quia si dicerem hominis; Eas, & fatrem Jugula, & non faceret, silim est pec-
cati & mortis. Omnia, enim, possibilia & licita sunt superis. *Neque magis odiosa*
sunt pudenda illis, quam mortalium quorumcumque vultus.
Ita enim fiet, spurius cum fillo (quod magis absurdum est) copulabitur. Et oriens cum occidente,
Meridies quoque cum septentrione coadunabuntur.

E. K. Now it is vanished.

Δ. Hereupon we were in great amazement and grief of minde, that so hard, and (as
it, yet seemed unto me) so unpure a Doctrine, was popounded and enjoyned unto us of
them, whom I alwayes (from the beginning hitherto) did *judge and esteem, undoubtedly, to*
be good Angels : And had unto E K. *offered my soul as a pawn,* to discharge E.K. his credit-
ing of them, as the good and faithful Ministers of Almighty God. But now, my heart
was sore afflicted upon many causes : And E.K. had (as he thought) now, a just and sufficient cause, to forsake dealing with them any more. As his prayer to God of a long
time hath been (as in the former part of this Action may appear.)

After our going out of the Chappel, and at our being at dinner, when we four (whose
heads so were united, in a pillar shewed, as is before set down, I found means to make
some little declaration of our great grief (mine chiefly) now *occasioned,* either to try us,
or really to be executed, in the common and indifferent using of Matrimonial Acts a-
mongst any couple of us four : Which thing was strange to the women : And they hoped
of some more comfortable issue of the cause. And so we left off.

After Dinner, as E. K. was alone, there appeared unto him little creatures of a cubit
high : and they came to the Still where he had the spirit of Wine distilling over out of
a *Retorto :* And one of them (whose name they expressed Ben) said that it was in vain so
to hope for the best spirit of the Wine : And shewed him how to distill it , and separate
it better. And moreover how to get oyl of the spirit of Wine, as it burned in the lamps:
And began to ask E. K. what Country-man he was? And when he had answered an
English-man, he asked then, how he came hither ? he answered by Sea : Then said he,
And who helped you to pass the marvellous great dangers of the Sea. And so took occasion
to speak of the benefits which God had hitherto done for us, very many. And this Ben, said

Ben was the   than among very many other things (as Mr. E.K. told me on Saturday night after Supper
deliverer of   holding on his talk almost till two of the clock after midnight) *That he it was that deliver-*
the powder   *ed him, or gave unto his hands the powder.* And also he said either than or the next day at
to E.K. at   the furthest, that *unleast* he would be conformable to the will of God in this last Action
the digging   declared, *That he would take the vertue and force of the powder from it :* That it should be
in England.   *unprofitable : And that he should become a beggar.*
Note, un-   And of me also he said that I did evil to *require proof,* or testimony now, that this last
least condi-   Doctrine was from God Almighty, and said that I should be led prisoner to *Rome,*&c.
tionally.   He told of England, and said, That about *July* or *November* her Majesty should from
Q. El.   heaven be destroyed ; and that about the same time the King of *Spain* should dye. And
K. Phi.   that this present Pope at his Mass should be deprived of life before two years to an end.
And that another should be Pope, who should be   *Decimus quintus* of his
name; And that he would begin to reform things, but that shortly he should of the Cardinals be stoned to death. And that after that there should be no Pope for some
years.

England.   Of *England* he said, That after the death of our dear Queen, One *of the house* of Austria
made mighty by the King of *Spain his death, should invade and conquer the land,* &c. He said,
One (now abroad) should at *Milford-haven* enter , and by the help of the *Britans subdue*
the said Conqueror : And that *one* Morgan a Britan *should be made King of the* Britans,
and next him, *one Rowland,* &c.

Fr. Garland   He said also, That this *Francis Garland* was an espy upon us from the Lord *Treasurer of*
Edw. Gar-   *England :* And that *Edward Garland* is not his brother : And that so the matter is agreed
land.   between them, &c.

That my Lord *Rosenberg* should be in danger of poysoning for these certain months
to come.

Enochs   That my Tables of *Enoch,* were in some places falsly written.
Tables.   Of Antichrist he spake, and of his appearing.
Antichrist.   Of *Ely* and *Enoch* coming out of Paradise : And of Saint *John Evangelist,* that he dyed
Ely, Enoch.   *not,* but in *Pathmos had his invisible* being : And that he it was, who did give *Julianus*
Johannes   *Apostata* his deaths wound.
Evangelista   He said also that he hath at divers times preached visibly since the time of *his invisible*
state entred.

                                                 He

He confirmed the words of the great Famine and Blood-shed that should come shortly.

He said that on every side of us, people should be slain, but that we should (by the Divine protection) escape. *God our Protector.*

He said that shortly this *Francis Garland* should go into *England :* And that we should be sent for. But that it were best to *refuse their calling us home.* *F. Garland into Engl. Refuse calling home.*

He said that there were four other, who were made also privy of God his mysteries as we were, with whom we should meet at *Rome.* *4 alii participes horum mysteriorum.*

He said that *Mary* and one more in *England,* should see the wonderful days to come. *Madimi* appeared to him there also. *Mary my old Maid.*

The same *Ben* went once away mounting up in a flame of fire : and afterward upon occasion of asking him somewhat, he came down so again. *Ben.*

And of the manner how to draw the oyl of the Spirit of wine being burnt, he brought thither the instruments of two silver dishes, whelmed one upon another with an hole passing through the middle of them both, and with sponge between them : in which the oyl would remain, &c.

After all these, and many other things told me by the same Mr. E. K. we departed each to his bed, where I found my wife awake, attending to hear some new matter of me from Mr. *Kelly* his reports of the apparitions, continued with him above four hours, being else alone, I then told her, and said, *Jane,* I see that there is no other remedy, but as hath been said of our *cross-matching,* so it must needs be done. *About 2 of the clock after midnight. Iane Dee.*

Thereupon she fell a weeping and trembling for a quarter of an hour : And I pacified her as well as I could ; and so, in the fear of God, and in believing of his Admonishment, did perswade her that she shewed her self prettily resolved to be content *for God his sake and his secret Purposes,* to obey the Admonishment.

△ *Note,* Because I have found so much halting and untruth in *E. K.* his reports to me made, of the spiritual Creatures, where I have not been present at an Action : and because his memory may fail him, and because he was subject to ill tempters, I believe so much hereof as shall by better trial be found true, or conformable to truth. *April 20.*

△ *Note* ...... E. K. had this day divers apparitions unto him in his own Chamber, and instructions in divers matters *which be regarded not,* but remained still in his purpose of *utterly discrediting* those Creatures, and not to have any more to do with them. But among divers apparitions he noted this of one that said unto him.

...... *Joyn Enoch his Tables.*
...... *Give every place his running number.*

E. K. What mean you by places ?

...... *The squares. Which done, refer every letter in the Table to his number, and so read what I will, for this is the last time I will admonish you.*

E. K. A man standeth in the Air in a fiery Globe of my heighth, accompanied with some hundred of Puppets : on the one side of him standeth a woman, and about her are four Clouds all white.

The

The man upon a white Triangle ▲ shewed these Numbers with spaces, as you see following.

▲	49	466	495	46	395	152
228	218	597	63	607	254	418
409	410	502	—	228	566	82
	505	550	306	179	423	—
	—	119	473	141	—	320
	603	264	517	141	214	491
	149	312	363	22	261	390
	173	24	247	403	59	414
	197	338	271	370	494	366
174—	175	411	367	97	517	239
	177	—	89	243	116	—
272—	273	603	65	80	103	182
	416	604	—	552	—	460
	—	150	11	—	405	—
225—	226	414	46	295	170	163
	441	395	267	46	—	175
250—	251	467	228	163	25	171
	586	519	331	418	606	73
	83	—	97	311	466	—
131—	132	53	269	—	490	418
251—	253	59	244	222	620	214
	277	68	400	150	—	—
	39	418	23	253	53	4
303—	304	444	75	395	32	98
	401	355	178	538	196	96
	496	497	586	156	224	188
	592	20	545	46	512	331
	90	116	18	55	20	136
	355	287	43	7	338	—
	618	—	—	—	290	335
	20	604	25	123	244	408
	501	610	17	433	72	452
	597	480	—	151	340	424
		182	165	197	195	97
		98	93	—	314	
		401	52	285	495	
			511	335	284	
			175	621		
			170	544		
				352		
				295		

▲. I perceive that commonly one is to be abated of the number.

▲. Note :

Δ. Note ; When E.K. had shewed me this Note, I by and by brought forth my book of *Enoch* his Tables, and found the four letters r T b d to be the four first letters of the four principal squares standing about the black Cross : and that here they were to be placed otherwise than as I had set them. And in the first placing of them together, I remember that I had doubt how to joyn them ; for they were given apart each by themselves.

Secondly, I found out the 4 Characters ; saving they were inverted somewhat, and one of them closed : wherof I found none like, but very near. These Characters were of every square one.

Thirdly, I did take these numbers contained between the lines (some more and some fewer) to be words to be gathered out of the Table of letters : so many words as were distinct companies of numbers ; it is to wit, 41.

Hereupon we began to number the squares wherein the letters stood in *Enochs* Tables as I had them, but we could not exactly finde the words, but somewhat near. Hereupon being tired, and desirous to know the sense of that Cypher, we left off till after supper, and then we assayed again : but we could not bolt it out, though we knew very near what was to be done by the instruction of *a spiritual Voice,* now and then helping us toward the practise.

At length E.K. *was willed to go down* into his Chamber, and I did remain still at our Dineing Table till his return, which was within an hour or somewhat more. And at his return this he brought in writing.

		r			Δ.
r z ı l a f	a y t l p a	t a o a d v	p t d n ı m		24
a r d z a ı	d p a l a m	a a b c o o	r o m e b b		48
c z o n s a	r e y a v b	t o g c o n	x m a l g m		72
t o ı t t z	o p a c o c	n h o d d ı	a l c a o o		96
s ı g a s o	m r b z n b	p a t a x ı	o v s p s n		120
f m o n d a	t d ı a r ı	s a a ı x a	a r v r o ı		144
o r o ı b a	h a o z p ı	m p h a r s	l g a ı o l		168
t n a b r v	ı x g a s d	m a m g l o	ı n l ı r x		192
o ı ı ı t T	p a l o a ı	o l a a d n	g a t a p a		216
a b a m o o	o a c v c a	p a l c o ı	d x p a c n		240
n a o c o t	T n p r n t	n d a z n z	ı v a a s a		264
o c a n m a	g o t r r ı	ı ı d p o n	s d a s p ı		288
s h ı a l r	a p m z o x	x r ı n h t	a r n d ı]		
b o a z a r	o p h a r a	d o n p a t	d a n o a a		336
v ʌ n a x o	p s o n d n	o l o a g e	o o b a v a		360
a ı g r u n	o o m a g g	o p a m n o	v g m d n m		384
o r p m n ı	n g b e a l	a p l s t e	d e c a o p		408
r s o n ı z	ı r l e m v	s c m ı o o	n a m l o x		432
ı z ʌ ı c	z ı a m h l	v a v s g d	l v r ı a p		456
m o r d ı a	l h c t g a	o ı p t e a	a p d o c e		480
o c a n c h	ı a s o m t	x s v a c N	r z ı r z a		504
a r b ı Z m	ı ı l p ı z	s ı o d a o	ı n r z f m		528
o p a n a l	a m s m a p	d a l t t d	n a d ı r e		552
d o l o p ı	n ı a n b a	d ı x o m o	n s ı o s p		576
r x p a o c	ʃ ı z ı x p	o o d x z ı	a p a n l ı		600
a x t ı ʃ v	a s t r ı m	r g o a n n	q a c r a ʃ		624

My applying of Numbers for more easie reckoning.

······ *The black Cross is right, and needeth no mending. But thus much I do, to let thee understand, that thou mayest consider thy self to be a man: And beneath this understanding, unless thou submit all into the hands of God, for his sake; who else leaving you, all naked, provideth in his creatures to his own glory.*

······ *Cara tibi uxor, carior tibi sapientia, charissime tibi ego sum. Electus tremie, & besitando pecca: Noli igitur ad genium, & carmen sapere; sed obtempera mihi: ductor enim tuus sum & autor spiritus omnium. Hec omnia à me sunt, & licita vobis.*

······ *I admonish you as the children of God, to consider your vocation, and the love of God towards you; and not to prefer your reason before the wisdome of the highest, whose mercy is so great towards you,* That you are chosen from the number of men to walk with him, and to understand his mysteries, and with all to execute his justice and praise throughout the Nations and people of the earth. *Consider that if he finde you obstinate, the plagues of baynous sinners, and contemners of the gifts of God shall fall upon you, to your great overthrow: This is the last time of your trial. Therefore shew your selves lovers of him that hath led you, and covered you with a mighty shield: Or shortly look for the reward of such, as have contemned the Wisdome and Majesty of the Highest.*

      I Raphael, *counsel you to make a Covenant with the Highest, and to esteem his wings more then your own lives.*

Δ. When *E.K.* had brought me these things, I greatly rejoyced in spirit, and was utterly resolved to obey this new Doctrine to us, peculiarly, of all people of the world enjoyned. And after some little discourse and conference hereof, we went to bed, this *Aprilis* 20. 20. day of *April*, at night.

Aprilis 21.

Δ. Thus, am I resolved, O Almighty God, as concerning the case, so hard to flesh and blood, to be resolved in, thus: And thus I desire, that we all four, might with one minde and consent, offer and present unto thee, this writing as a Vow, Promise, and Covenant, if it so please thy divine majesty to accept it.

WEE four (whose heads appeared under one Chrystalline Crown, in one pillar united, and inclosed) do most humbly and heartily thank thee; O Almighty God (our Creator, Redeemer and Sanctifier) for all thy mercies and benefits hitherto received, in our persons, and in them that appertain unto us: And at this present, do faithfully and sincerely confess, and acknowledge, that thy profound wisdome *in this most new and strange doctrine* (among Christians) propounded, commended, and enjoyned unto us four only, is above our *humane reason, and Christian profession to like of*: For that in outward shew of words, it seemeth to us expresly to be contrary to the purity and chastity, which of us, and all Christians, thy followers, is exactly required. Notwithstanding, we will, herein, captivate, and tread under-foot all our humane timorous doubting of any inconvenience, which shall, or may fall upon us, or follow us in this world, or in the world to come, in respect or by reason of our imbracing of this Doctrine, listened unto, of us, as delivered from our true and living God, the Creator of heaven and earth; who only hath the true original power and Authority of sins releasing and discharging: And whose pardoning, and not imputing of sin unto us, through our lively faith in the most worthy merit, and precious blood of the Lamb Immaculate, shed for us, is and shall be our justification and salvation. We, therefore (according to blessed *Raphael* his counsel last given) most humbly and sincerely require thy Divine Majesty, to accept this our Covenant with thee (for that, thy merciful promises made unto us, may be to us performed; and thy divine purposes in us and by us, may be furthered, and advanced and fulfilled.) *That*, as we acknowledge thy divine wisdome and grace offered unto us in this thy last mystical Admonishment: And dost most earnestly will us to *accept the same, as lawful and just with thee;* Which Admonishment standeth upon two parts: That is to wit, upon our true Christian charity spiritual between us four, and also upon the Matrimonial licence and liberty, indifferently among us four *to be used*: So we the same foun (which hereunto will subscribe) covenant with thy Divine Majesty, upon the two principal respects before rehearsed, truly and unfainedly to accept and perform henceforward amongst us four, in word, thought and deed, Christian charity, and perfect friendship, and all that belongeth thereto: And as for the Matrimonial-like licence, and liberty, we we accept and allow of it, and promise unto thee (O our God) to fulfill the same, in such fort, as the godly are permitted to fulfill, and have been by divers testimonies commended for, and by Divine doctrine willed to fulfill, in Matrimonial conversation, whensoever thy motions and allurements (Matrimonial-like) shall draw and perswade any couple of us. Beseeching thee, as thou art the onely true Almighty and Everlasting God, Creator of Heaven and Earth, Thou wilt, in thy infinite mercies, not impute it unto us for sin, blindness, rashness, or presumption, being not accepted, done, or performed upon carnal lust, or wanton concupiscence; But by the way of *Abraham*-like *faith and obedience*, unto thee, our God, our Leader, Teacher, Protector and Justifier, now and for ever. And hereunto we call the holy Heavens to be witnesses, for thy honour and glory (O Almighty God) and our discharge, now and for ever. *Amen.*

I Edward Kelly by good and provident (according to the Laws and ordinances of God) determination and consideration in these former Actions, that is to say, appearings, shews made, and voyces uttered, by the within named in this Book, and the rest whatsoever Spirits have from the beginning thereof (which at large by the Records appeareth) not only doubted and disliked their insinuations and doctrine uttered, but also divers and sundry times (as coveting to eschew and avoid the danger and inconvenience that might either by them, their selves, or the drift of their doctrine ensue, or to my indamagement divers wayes, happen) sought to depart from the exercises thereof : and withal boldly (as the servant of the Son of God) inveighed against them : urging them to depart, or render better reason of their unknown and uncredible words and speeches delivered; and withall often and sundry times friendly exhorted the Right Worshipful Master JOHN DEE (the chief follower thereof) as also in the Records appeareth, to regard his souls health, the good proceeding of his wordly credit (which through Europe is great) the better maintenance to come of his wife and children, to beware of them, and withall to give them over : wherein although I friendly and brotherly laboured; my labour seemed to be lost and counsel of him despised, and withall was urged with replies to the contrary by him made, and promises, in that case, of the loss of his souls health, if they were not of God : Whereunto upon as it were some farther taste of them, or opinion grounded upon the frailty of zeal, he ceased not also to pawn unto me his soul, &c. which his perswasions were the chief and onely cause of my this so long proceeding with them : And now also at this instant, and before a few dayes having manifest occasion to think they were the servants of Sathan, and the children of darkness; because they manifestly urged and commanded in the name of God a Doctrine Damnable, and contrary to the Laws of God, his Commandements, and Gospel by our Saviour Christ as a Touchstone to us left and delivered, did openly unto them dislike their proceeding, and brotherly admonished the said Worshipful, and my good friend Mr. JOHN DEE to beware of them : And now having just occasion to determine what they were, to consider all

C c c

these

these things before mentioned by me, and wisely to leave them; and the rather because of themselves, they (as that by their own words appeareth) upon our not following that Doctrine delivered, gave unto us a *Quietus est*, or pasport of freedome : But the Books being brought forth *, after some discourse therein, after a day or two had, and their words perused spoken heretofore, did as it were (because of the possible verity thereof, *Deo enim omnia sunt possibilia*) gave us cause of further deliberation : so that thereby, I did partly of my self, and partly by the true meaning of the said Mr. DEE in the receiving of them, as from God ; and after a sort by the zeal I saw him bear unto the true worship and glory of God to be (as that was by them, promised) by us promoted, descend from my self, and condescend unto his opinion and determination, giving over all reason, or whatsoever for the love of God : But the women disliked utterly this last Doctrine, and consulting amongst themselves gave us this answer, the former actions did nothing offend them but much comforted them : and therefore this last, not agreeing with the rest (which they think to be according to the good will and wholesome Law of God) maketh them to fear, because it expresly is contrary to the Commandement of God : And thereupon desiring God not to be offended with their ignorance, required another action for better information herein; in the mean, vowing, fasting, and praying, Mrs. DEE hath covenanted with God to abstain from the eating of fish and flesh untill his Divine Majesty satisfie their mindes according to his Laws established, and throughout all Christendome received. To this their request of having an action, I absolutely answer, that my simplicity before the Highest is such as I trust will excuse me : And because the summe of this Doctrine, given in his name, doth require obedience which I have (as is before written) offered, I think my self discharged : And therefore have no farther cause to hazzard my self any more in any action. Wherefore I answer that if it be lawful for them to call this Doctrine in question, it is more lawful for me to doubt of greater perril ; considering that to come where we are absolutely answered were folly, and might redound unto my great inconvenience. Therefore beseeching God to have mercy upon me, and to satisfie their Petitions, doubts and vows, I finally answer, that I will from this day forward meddle no more herein. 22. of April, 1587.

Marginal notes:
* April 22. at night.

The women.

An action required by the women.

By me

EDWARD KELLY.

Aprilis

Aprilis 24.   *Trebonæ.*

Δ. PRayers to God made in respect of this strange and new doctrine, requiring his Divine Majesty to be merciful unto us, and to give us wisdom and faith that we may herein please him ; and that we cannot finde how we may do the thing required, *being contrary* to the Laws of *Moses,* Christ, his Church, and of all Nations. Therefore seeing God is *not contrary* to himself, we desired that we might not be contrary to him or his Laws, *&c.*

Δ. Not long, lo, there appeared a great flame of fire in the principal Stone, (both standing on the Table before *E.K.*) which thing though he told me, I made no end of my Prayer to God. And behold, suddenly one seemed to come in at the south window of the Chappel, right against *E.K.* (But before that, the stone was heaved up an handful high, and set down again well, which thing *E.K.* thought did signifie some strange matter toward.) Then after, the man that came in at the window seemed to have his nether parts in a cloud, and with spred-abroad arms to come toward *E.K.* At which sight he shrinked back somewhat, and then that Creature took up between both his hands *the stone and frame of gold,* and mounted up away as he came. *E.K.* catched at it, but he could not touch it. At which thing being so taken away, and at the sight thereof *E.K.* was in a great fear and trembling, and had *tremorem cordis* for a while. But I was very glad and well pleased.

¶ Here appeareth a fire in this other stone also, and a man in the fire, with flaxen hair hanging down upon him, and is naked unto his Paps ; and seemeth to have spots of blood upon him. He spake, and said as followeth.

If I had intended to have overthrown you, or brought you to confusion, or suffered you to be Christus. *led into temptation beyond your strength and power, then had the Seas long ago swallowed you. Yea, there had not a soul lived amongst you.*

But the law and tidings (to mankinde) of gladness, are both grounded in me, I am the Be- The Law & *ginning and the Ending : And behold, happy is he that delighteth in me, for in me is truth and* the Gospel. *understanding. Whatsoever you have received, you have received of me ; and without me you have received nothing. Behold, I my self was even the figure of misery and death for your sins. Why (therefore) disdain you to be figured after me ? I will gather the four quarters of the earth together, and they shall become one.*

And as I have made you the figure of two people to come, and amongst them, the Δ. and *E.K.* *executors of my Justice : So likewise have I sanctified you in an holy Ordinance, giving you* a figure of *the first fruits of the time to come. Happy is he that is a Serpent in the wilderness hanged* two people *up upon the Cross, being the will and figure of my determination, and Kingdom to come : I am* to come. *even in the doors ; and I will overthrow all flesh. I will no more delight in the sons of men.*

* Contrary to my self, I teach you nothing.

For this Doctrine is not to be published to mortal men : but is given unto you, to Δ. * He ans- *manifest your faith, and to make you worthy in the sight of the heavens, for believing in* wereth to a me of your vocation to come.   phrase of my
                                                                                                        prayer or
Therefore I say unto you, Rejoyce, and be not careful for to morrow : for I, even I, have discourse. *provided for you : Sin no more.*   This doctrin

Behold ! None of the Orders, either of Heaven or Earth, are armed to open their mouthes in is not to be *my Name, teaching or opening this Doctrine, unless it were of me, for I am the First and the* published to *Last. And I will be Shepherd over all, that the Kingdom of my Father may come, and that my* any man. *Spirit may be upon all flesh, where there shall be no law, nor need of light : I my self am their* Note. *lanthorn for ever.*   *Unus pastor
                                                                                                        & unum o-*
And behold, I will be as a Rock between you and the teeth of Leviathan, which seek- vile. *eth to set you asunder, and to bring you to confusion.*   *Conatus Di-*

And I am, and am holy, and holiness is self : Out of me cometh no unclean thing.   *aboli.*

For even as the time of Moses *was wonderful to all the Gentiles, even so shall those days* Moses. *to come be unto the Nations and Kings of the earth. I am a law for ever. And behold, power is given unto me from above : And I have visited the earth, and have thrown my curse* Sterilitas *upon her : And lo, she shall become barren.*   Terra.

He that fasteth and prayeth doth but that which is commanded : He that also fulfilleth my will, is justified before me : for who is he that raiseth up, or who is he that casteth down ? Yea, even I it is that have taken you four Trees out of the forrest of the world, and have covered The shew of *you hitherto with my wings. And behold, this that is taken away shall be restored again to you* 4 trees, what *with more power. And Might shall be in it, and a brestplate unto you, of Judgement and* it meaneth. *Knowledge.*   Pectorale

And if there be any of you that seeketh a Miracle at my hands, and believeth in my words, cum Urim & *let him or her present themselves here the next Monday, with the rest, and he shall perceive that* Thummim. *I was the Judge of* Abiram, *and the God of* Abraham : Walk before me as the sons of my Num.

* Ccc 2   Father,

Father, in all righteoufnefs. *And follow you that which you call unrighteoufnefs even with gladnefs : for I can make you whiter then fnow.*

Our unity of what importance it is : eft finis exordii meffis futuræ. Your unity and knitting together is the end and confummation of the beginning of my harveft. *I will not daily with you, but I will be mighty in deed amongft you. And lo, I will fhortly open your eyes, and you fhall fee: And I will fay,* ARISE, *and you fhall go out. What I am, I am.*

E.K. The flame and all is difappeared.

The ancient token and watchword forefhewed us : *Arife, come and fee my judgements.* Δ. *Gloria Patri, & Filio, & Spiritui Sancto, ficut erat in principio,& nunc, & in fempiterna feculorum facula.* Amen.

E.K.

...... faid after, that his body had in it like a fiery heat, even from his breft down unto all his parts, his privities and thighs.

Deo Omnipotenti, Mifericordi & Regi feculorum fit omnis laus, honor & gloria nunc & femper. Amen.

J.D. E.K. J.D. J.K.

Aprilis 18. ann. 1587. WEE four (whofe heads appeared under one Chryftalline Crown, and in one pillar united and enclofed) do moft humbly and heartily thank thee (O Almighty God, our Creator, Redeemer and Sanctifier) for all thy mercies and benefits hitherto received in our own perfons, and in them that appertain unto us : And at this prefent do faithfully and fincerely confefs and acknowledge, that thy profound wifdom in this moft new and ftrange Doctrine (among Chriftians) propounded, commended and enjoyned unto us four onely, is above our humane Reafon, and our Catholick Chriftian Profeffion to like of : for that, in outward fhew of words, it feemeth to us exprefly to be contrary to the purity and chaftity which of us and all Chriftians (thy followers) is exactly required. Notwithftanding, we will for thy fake herein captivate and tread under foot all our humane timerous doubting of any inconvenience which fhall or may fall upon us, or follow us (in this world, or in the world to come) in refpect, or by reafon of our embracing of this Doctrine, liftned unto of us, as delivered from thee, our true and living God, the Creator of heaven and earth, who onely haft the true original power and authority of fins releafing and difcharging ; and whofe pardoning, or not imputing of fin unto us, through our lively faith in the moft worthy Merit and precious Blood of thy Lamb immaculate, fhed for us; is and fhall be our Juftification and Salvation. We therefore, **Aprilis 20. molte profunda.** (according to bleffed Raphael his counfel lately given) moft humbly and fincerely require thy divine Majefty to accept this our Covenant with thee (to the intent that all thy merciful and gracious promifes made unto us four, and any of us, may be to us performed : and alfo that thy divine purpofes in us, and by us, may be furthered, advanced and fulfilled) That as we acknowledge thy divine wifdom and grace opened unto us in this thy laft myftical Admonifhment of univerfal unity to be between us : And doft moft inftantly and earneftly will us to accept and ufe the fame, as both myftically moft needful, and alfo lawful and juft with thee : (which Admonifhment ftandeth upon two parts ; that is to wit, upon true and confummate Chriftian Charity between us four unviolably to be kept. And alfo upon the New Matrimonial-like licence and liberty indifferently amongft us four to be ufed :) So we the fame four above-named (which hereunto will alfo fubfcribe our Names) do this day Covenant with thy Divine Majefty (befides all other refpects, chiefly upon the two principal intents and refpects * before here reherfed) truly *** Before at this mark:** and unfeignedly to accept and perform henceforward amongft us four (in word, thought and deed, to the uttermoft and beft of our power) a perfect unity, and with incomparable true love and good Chriftian Charity, friendfhip, imparting and communicating each unto other, all and whatfoever we have or fhall have hereafter during our lives. And as for the Matrimonial-like licence, we accept and allow of it : And promife unto, thee (O our God, the Almighty, Creator of heaven and earth) to fulfil the fame in fuch fort as the godly are permitted to fulfil, and have been (by divers teftimonies) commended for, and by divine Doctrine willed to fulfil in Matrimonial-like converfation, whenfoever thy motions and allurements Matrimonial-like fhall draw and perfwade any couple of us thereunto : Befeeching thee, as thou art the onely, true Almighty and everlafting God, Creator of heaven and earth, Thou wilt in thy infinite mercies not impute it unto us for fin, blindnefs, rafhnefs or prefumption ; being not accepted, done or performed of us upon carnal luft, or wanton concupifcence, but by the way of Abraham-like faith and obedience unto thee our God, our Leader, Teacher, Protector and Juftifier, now and for ever. And hereunto we moft humbly and faithfully require thy Divine Majefty to be our witnefs : And moreover we call thy holy Angels, and to bear record for thy honour and

and glory, and for our difcharge, now and for ever. And for a further confummation of this New Covenant on our behalf, (by thy will and permiffion) made with thee (the God of heaven and earth) we the fame four firſt notified, and particularly and vulgarly named *John Dee, Edward Kelley, Jane Dee,* and *Jone Kelley,* have faithfully, obediently, willingly and wittingly fubfcribed our Names with our own hands 　　 day of *May,* *Anno* 1587. In *Trebon* Caſtle.

And finally, as thou haſt warned us (O God) that this doctrine and doings fhould unto no mortal man elfe be difclofed, but among us onely the above-named four to be, kept moſt fecret : and haſt faid, that whofoever of us fhould by any means difclofe the fame, and he alfo or fhe to whom the fame fhould be difclofed, fhould prefently and immediately be ſtrucken dead by thy Divine power : So we all and every of us four do requeſt thee moſt earneſtly, and Covenant with thee as our God, that fo all this doctrine and doing may be kept moſt hid and fecret ; and alfo that the fudden and immediate bodily death may light and fall on the difclofer, and on him or her to whom the fame doctrine or doing any manner of way fhall be difclofed or known. *Amen, Amen, Amen.*

　　　　JOHN DEE.

Note and remember, That on Sunday the third of *May, Ann.*1587. (by the new account) I *John Dee, Edward Kelley,*and our two wives,covenanted with God,and fubfcribed the fame, for indiffoluble and inviolable unities, charity and friendfhip keeping between us four, and all things between us to be common, as God by fundry means willed us to do. *Ad Dei honorem, laudem & gloriam in fide & obedientia Factum eſto. Amen.*

---

1 5 8 7.　　　 *Trebonæ,* in the fine Chappel.

A. **T**He forefaid Covenant being framed by me *John Dee,* as near as I could according to the intent and faith of us required, to be notified and declared by the works of unity both fpiritual and corporal. *Now it was by the women as by our felves thought neceſſary to underſtand the will of God and his good pleafure, Whether this Covenant and form of words performed,* is and will be acceptable, and according to the well liking of his Divine Majeſty : *And that hereupon,* the act of corporal knowledge being performed on both our parts, It will pleafe his Divine Majeſty to feal and warrant *unto us moſt certainly and ſpeedily all his Divine, Merciful and bountiful Promifes and Bleſſings* ; and alfo promifes us wifdome, knowledge, ability and power to execute his juſtice, and declare and demonſtrate his infallible verity amongſt men, to his honour and glory.

Hereupon E.*K.* and I went to the Chappel to the South Table. **A.** To this intent I prayed to the Almighty God, Creator of heaven and earth, fatherly, favourably and mercifully to regard the finglenefs and ſtraits of my heart, defiring him to encreafe the faith, and to open the eyes of my heart, that I may fee *Opera digitorum & mirabilia ejus, nobis ſicuti neceſſaria,* for his fervice and glory, and for the confufion and overthrow of his enemies. *Amen.*

I read over the Covenant (*verbatim*) before the Divine Majeſty, and his holy Angels.

　　　　Pauſa ¼ horæ.

E. K. Here appeareth Madimi.

As a thing like a head with three eyes cometh upon her head, and one of the eyes feem to come one into another.

Mad. ...... *Pepigiſti.*
A. *Pepigimus.*
　　Ratum eſt : perimpite ſunt vobis omnia communia.
　　Dei, non hominis eſtote : Promiſſa quæ ſunt, poſſidete : Vobis deſtinata, vera ſunt :
　　Æternus ſum.

E. K. She is gone.

E.K. My thought an infinite number of fpiritual Creatures ſtood afar off behinde her like as in an half Moon.

　　A. *Illi qui Æternus eſt Omnipotens, Sapiens, Bonus, Verus, Mifericors, & rerum omnium Creator, Redemptor noſter & Illuminator omnium (lumine vero Colluſtratorum) Sit omnis gratiarum actio, laus, benedictio, honor & gloria : Nunc & in fempiterna faculorum facula.* Amen.

　　　　　　　　　　　　　　　　Trebonæ.

1587.   *Trebonæ.*

Wednesday
morning
Maii 2c.

PReces *ad Dominum Creatorem Cæli & terra, &c.* Then as concerning the Covenant which was made subscribed and delivered in, but the next day required again of Mr. E.K. and in his wifes name to put out his name, &c. But when he had it, he cut it into equal parts; keeping that half wherein his subscription and his wifes were, and delivered unto me, the other half but after a few dayes desired to have the fight and reading of both together; and then he kept the other part from me also: But afterward *Madimi* did with her *finger draw on the two papers make them whole again, &c. and then she gave the print of my Characters, and said a red Circle should* alwayes appear in the Stone to all mens fight, *&c.*

Quasi Chri-
stus.

E. K. There is here a great Globe of fire hanging in the top of the Stone; and in the Globe a man standing with a purple Robe like Christ, I cannot well perceive his face.

...... *Who sitteth upon the Cherubins, and is carried abroad with their wings : Who is he that is lifted up in thunders, and in the voyce of many waters exalted and magnified through the power of a Seraphin (which is the power of him that made him?) Who is he that stretcheth out his arms and imbraceth all things ? Who is he that is not, and is ? Who is he that numbreth the Stars as the letters of a Volumne ? or entreth down into the waves ? In the multitude of his wonders who is he that harboureth his Whelps there, where the Sea glideth, and keepeth them in Chains, till the day of his stretch-forth power come ? Who is he that maketh his habitation in the Sun, or filleth the Moon with a perpetual River ? Who is he that hath made Winter and Summer, times and seasons ? Who is he that is the Lord of all beasts and fowls ? Who is he that hath made you of nothing ? even he it is that hath led you out, even he it is that hath carried you to the Seas even he it is, that hath kept you sleeping, and preserved you waking : Even he it is that hath tyed his thunders underneath your   and hath harnished your*

With the Whirlewind of vengeance against the people of Ethan, yea even be it is (I say) that is, and liveth for ever   and hath provided you as the chiefest reapers; yea and over-seers of his harvest, which hath made you a promise : That the Kings of the earth shall be inriched by you, and hath made you free from all men, against the day when you shall see me. But O you of little faith and understanding, O, I say, you of little faith and understanding, how long will you be your own masters, may your own servants, how long do you contemn, the profound and unspeakable floods of my wisdome, and fore-knowledge in you.

How long (I say) will you run after your own imaginations and contemn the present counsels which I give you, binding the power that is ready to fall upon you, O you of little faith and understanding.

Behold I have prepared a banket for you, and have brought you even unto the doors; but because you smell not the feast you disdain to enter, happy is be that entreth in through me : For I am the very gate to all felicity and joy, and without me is nothing : Are you more disereet then I am wife ? or more honest than I am holy ? Righteousnesse, and righteousnesse is that, which is rewarded with honour.

Joshua

Behold I made all things, Is it not contrary to Nature, that the lights of heaven should stand : Why therefore at the prayer of the Carpter call you upon the Son in my name, Calling (I say) upon my name did the Sun stand still. Rebuke him therefore if he hath done amisse; or teach him, why he so abused Nature, O you wretches, I say unto you, you are the last of

Figuration

the beginning of the times to come, so figured by my determination and eternal purpose : And behold the Son and Moon shall stand still, even at your voyces, and the Mountains shall bring themselves together before the face of man, at your commandement, that the people and Kings of the earth may say, Lo this is the finger of him that hath created all things.

Be therefore obedient and full of faith.

All things
one.

And see that all things be one amongst you, and cleave not asunder, lest I take vengeance upon you, for behold Sathan hath power to cast you asunder, but a little together but be should be faithful therefore, and provident, be watchful, and take heed for you have made a Covenant; and behold it is written before my face in heaven, even as whatsoever I have spoken unto you,

ACovenant

is laid up in my treasures. Take heed that you run neither to the right hand, neither to the left; but that you cast away your selves for me : At I humbled my self to death, wherein the unity between my Congregation and me, was before my Father perpetually sealed, whereby I am alwayes present with such as put their trust in me. Even so as the East and the West, the North, and the

Potentia
magna ex
deo futura.

South, Esau and Jacob, shall be gathered together through the power I will give you, and united for ever in the Kingdome of my Father which is to come, in one holy and eternal fellowship, so be you contented also to be the figures of the things that are to come by you, that it may be a perpetual testimony before the heavens, and before men, of your perfect and sound faith:

Figures.

And thou, even thou that hast tore in peeces even this morning again this Covenant which thou hast

haſt made with me, Behold the time ſhall come that thou ſhalt be torn in peeces thy ſelf, and I will turn even my face away from thee for a time : And even as thou baſt obſtinately and ignorantly, blaſphemed the company of my holy meſſagers, *even ſo ſhall the people of the earth obſtinately and ignorantly throw thee out from Town to Town : And even as thou haſt done unto me, even ſo ſhall men do unto thee.* But becauſe thy minde was inwardly *never to forſake me, even ſo ſhalt thou never be forſaken of me, but I will return again unto thee.* And now behold, thou haſt made a bargain, and behold thou thinkeſt to take thee up a new dwelling place, and thou ſhalt not do ſo : But who ſo receiveth thee *into his houſe ſhall as* truly as I am, both he and his family ſink down into the very lake of hell. But before thou enter in, I will by dreams and viſions *warn him; therefore run not abroad :* Take heed of the Tempter, *Thou made a Covenant with me, which thou canſt not in* breaking *of the papers put out ; for my regiſter is eternal : And thoſe that bear witneſs before me are the* compaſs *of my wings.*

And lo behold Carpio *hath for his former intent of ſeparating you, cut off the day of his* Father, *and is become fatherleſs: Behold even ſhortly* ſhall his mother periſh alſo.

And, if hereafter, he attempt any farther, I will throw the vengeance *of Juſtice upon him,* that he ſhall be a laughing ſtock to the people amongſt which he was born: Wo be unto them that riſeth up againſt me.

‥‥‥ *After a while I come again.*

E. K.　I thought we ſhould have nothing elſe, but

△. I read this over to E. K.

E. K.　He is here again.

He that pawneth * *his ſoul for me, loſeth it not, and he that dyeth for me, dieth to eternal life. Behold you ſhall both as Lambs be brought forth before men in your latter dayes, and ſhall be overthrown and ſlain, and your bodies toſſed to and fro : But I will revive you again, and will be full of power : And you ſhall be comforted with the joyes of your brethren, for I have many that ſecretly ſerve me, and when you have ſhewed your obedience, the ſecond day after, come here again before me ; for I will lead you into the way of Knowledge and Underſtanding : And Judgement and Wiſdome ſhall be upon you, and ſhall be reſtored unto you : And you ſhall grow every day, wiſe and mighty in men.*

This was ſaid becauſe I had pawned my ſoul, upon my avouching the ſpiritual creatures which have dealt with us, to be of God and good: which my bargain E. K. had by word & writing, diſdainfully charged, and of late threatned me withall.

E. K.　He is gone ; and in going he made a Croſs (toward us) of bleſſing.

The ſecret ſervants for God. Sapientia & potentia in Deo.

Rerum omni Creatori, Omnipotenti, Miſericordi & Juſto, Domino noſtro & Deo noſtro, ſit omnis laus, honor, gloria, gratiarum actio & Jubilatio : Nunc & in ſempiternus ſæculorum ſæcula. Amen.

I can, and by our two Conſents, and at the requeſt of *Jane* △ ‥‥ *unto the women.* And Mr. E. K. hereupon ſaid to his wife, *That his boots were now put off, and changed his purpoſe of going away with Carpio now.* God confirm his minde in all good purpoſes according to the well-pleaſing of the Higheſt. Amen.

Carpio.

‥‥‥ △ ‥‥‥ As I, and E. K. walked out at the new ſtairs, into the new Orchardward along the little River to view the ſmall fiſh, and returning to the fore ſtairs again, E. K. ſaw twain as high as my ſon *Arthur* fighting by the River ſide with ſwords; and the one third to the other, thou haſt beguiled me : Then I at length, ſaid unto them, Can I take up the matter between you? one ſaid yea that you can : in what is it quoth I ? Then ſaid he, I ſent a thing to thy wife by my men, and this fellow hath taken it from him. They fought ſore, and at length, he that had it was wounded in the thigh, and it ſeemed to bleed. Afterward he that was wounded, did bring a yellow ſquare thing out of his boſome; then I gueſſed it to be my Stone that was taken away. *The other ſaid unto him, let it be carried,* ſuddenly he ſeemed to have been out of ſight, and to be come again; he threatned the other that had wounded him, and ſaid he would be even with him. The other ſaid, *Haſt thou laid it under the right pillow of the bed where his wife lay yeſternight.*

Friday afternoon about four of the clock.

Lapidis ſancti reſtitutio.

At length they both went (one after another) into a little Willow tree body on the right hand near the new ſtairs into the garden ; the tree ſeemed to cleave, or open, and they to go in.

Hereupon we went away: And I coming to my Chamber, found my wife lying upon her bed (where I lay yeſternight) and there I lifted up the right pillow, upon which ſhe lay reſting herſelf (being not well at eaſe) And in manner under her ſhoulders there I found my precious Stone, that was taken away by *Madimi :* Whereat E. K. greatly wondred, doubting the verity of the ſhew. But I and my wife rejoyced, thanking God.

Saturday

Saturday May 23. *Mane circa* 9. ⁒

PReces ad Deum fundebantur,&c. And then we requested that the act of obedience performed (according to our faith conceived of our vocation, from the Almighty and Eternal God of heaven and earth) might be accepted: And that henceforward we might be instructed in the understanding and practice of wisdome, both such as already we have received some introductions Mystical, and also of all other what the Almighty God shall deem meet for us to know, and execute for his honour and glory, &c.

Δ E. K. *Took Pen and Inks, and wrote the request here adjoyned; and he read it to me,* and he requested me to read it to the *Divine Majesty ;* and so *I did ,* and hereupon *we waited both to the first* my prayer and *to this Petition, the Divine answer.*

Δ. *Omnipotens sempiterne, vere & vive Deus mittas lucem tuam & veritatem tuam ut ipsa nos ducant & perducant admontem, sanctum Syon, ex hac valle miseria & ad Coelestem tuam Jerusalem.* Amen.

E. K. From the beginning of this our coming, there appeared a purple Circle as big as a star in the Circumference of the holy Stone, which yesterday was brought again: And that it should so be, Madimi had forewarned E. K. when she shewed it unto him, when also she gave the prints of the letters of the backside of the bottome of the gold frame of it.

Equus albus ...... E. K. There appeareth here a great man all in bright harness sitting upon a white horse : he hath a spear all fiery in his left hand, he now putteth into his right hand : he hath a long sword by his side : he hath also a target hanging on his back, it seemeth to be of steel: It hangeth from his neck by a blue lace;it cometh up behind him as high as the top of his head. The horse is milk white, all studded with white : a very comely horse it is. The man is in compleat harness,the top of his helmet hath a sharp form.

Sun. Upon his Target, are many Cherubins, as it were painted in Circles : there is one in the middle : About it as a Circle with six in it, and then a Circle with eight, and then a great Circle with ten in it, and in the greatest are twenty ; and about the Circle of twenty are seven parts : at each of which points is a Cherubin ; Their faces be like burning gold, their wings be more brighter and as it were   their wings coming over their heads do *Cherubin.* not touch together. His horse is also harnished before and behind. The horse legs behind are harnished as with boots marveilously contrived,for defence as it were of his hinde legs.

E. K. He is ridden away, he seemeth to ride through a great field.

E. K. Here is now come Madimi.

E. K. She is gone into the field, that way which he rode.

E. K. Here is another, like a woman all in green.

E. K. Here cometh another woman : All her attire is like beaten gold; she hath on her forehead a Cross chrystal, her neck and breast are bare unto under her dugs : She hath a girdle of beaten gold slackly buckled unto her with a pendant of gold down to the ground.

I am

I am the Daughter of Fortitude, and ravished every hour from my youth. For behold, I am Understanding, and Science dwelleth in me; and the heavens oppress me, they covet and desire me with infinite appetite: few or none that are earthly have imbraced me, for I am shadowed with the Circle of the Stone, and covered with the morning Clouds. My feet are swifter than the winds, and my hands are sweeter then the morning dew. My garments are from the beginning, and my dwelling place is in my self. The Lion knoweth not where I walk, neither do the beasts of the field understand me. I am defloured, and yet a virgin: I sanctifie, and am not sanctified. Happy is he that imbraceth me: for in the night season I am sweet, and in the day full of pleasure. My company is a harmony of many Cymbals, and my lips sweeter than health it self. I am a harlot for such as ravish me, and a virgin with such as know me not: For lo, I am loved of many, and I am a lover to many; and as many as come unto me as they should do, have entertainment. Purge your streets, O ye sons of men, and wash your houses clean; make your selves holy, and put on righteousness. Cast out your old strumpets, and burn their clothes; abstain from the company of other women that are defiled, that are sluttish, and not so handsome and beautiful as I, and then will I come and dwell amongst you: and behold, I will bring forth children unto you, and they shall be the Sons of Comfort. I will open my garments, and stand naked before you, that your love may be more enflamed toward me.

As yet, I walk in the Clouds; as yet, I am carried with the Winds, and cannot descend unto you for the multitude of your abominations, and the filthy loathsomness of your dwelling places. Behold these four, who is he that shall say, They have sinned? or unto whom shall they make account? Not unto you, O you sons of men, nor unto your children: for unto the Lord belongeth the judgement of his servants. The four, Δ. E.K. I.K. & I.Δ.

Now therefore, let the earth give forth her fruit unto you, and let the Mountains forsake their barrenness where your footsteps shall remain. Happy is he that saluteth you, and cursed is he that boldeth up his hands against you. And power shall be given unto you from henceforth to resist your enemies: and the Lord shall alwayes hear you in the time of your troubles. A blessing for obedience according to faith. *And I am sent unto you to play the harlot with you, and am to enrich you with the spoils of other men. Prepare for me, for I come shortly. Provide your Chambers for me, that they may be sweet and cleanly; for I will make a dwelling-place amongst you: and I will be common with the father and the son, yea and with all them that truly favoureth you: for my youth is in her flowers, and my strength is not to be extinguished with man. Strong am I above and below, therefore provide for me: for behold, I now salute you, and let peace be amongst you; for I am the Daughter of Comfort. Disclose not my secrets unto women, neither let them understand how sweet I am, for all things belongeth not to every one. I come unto you again.* Preparare nos met debemus. Salutatio prima. Secrecy from women.

E. K. She is gone along that green field also.

Δ: I read it over to our great comfort.

Δ. We most humbly and heartily thank thee, O God Almighty, the onely fountain of Wisdome, Power, and all goodness: Help us now and ever to be faithful and fruitful servants to thee, for thy honour and glory. *Amen.*

E.K. The field appeareth a very level ground, covered with pretty grass even to the brinks of the...... It is bright if the Sun light, but I see not the Sun, but the clear sky over it.

Δ. *Pausa semihora unius.*

E.K. Now cometh the horseman, and rideth by into the field, and so doth Madimi. Now cometh the third, and so goeth away into the field.

Now cometh she that was left here: she standeth still: she hath a book in her hand covered (as it were) with Mofs three inches at the head, and four inches long, and a finger thick: it hath no Clasps; it is plain. A book 3 inches.

Pausa.

The fourth hour after dinner, repair hither again: And whatsoever you shall reade out of this book, receive it kneeling upon your knees; and fee that you suffer no Creature female to enter within this place: Neither shall the things that be opened unto you, be revealed unto your wives, or unto any Creature as yet: for I will lye with you a while, and you shall perceive that I am sweet and full of comfort, and that the Lord is at hand, and that he will shortly visit the earth, and all his whole Provinces. Secrecy required.

D d d   E.K.

Dominus
propz:est.

E. K. She turneth her self into a thousand shapes of all Creatures :
and now she is come to her own form again.

She hangeth the Book in the air.

Give God thanks, and so depart.

Δ. All laud, thanks, honour and glory be to our God, our King and Saviour, now
and ever. *Amen.*

1587.   *Saturday* the same day.

AFter Dinner, about four hours, or somewhat less we resorted to the place.
A voyce to E.K. Kneel toward the East ; so he kneeled at the table of Covenant,
with his face toward the East, and I at my table opposite to him.

Δ...... In the Name of God the Father, God the Son, and God the Holy Ghost.
Amen.

*Recte sapere & intellegere docato nos (O Dominu) nam sapientia tua,totum est quod quærimus
Da verbum tuum in ore nostro & sapientum tuam in cordibus nostris sige.*

E. K. The Book remaineth hanging in the ayre.

A voice ...... *Kelly,* I know it is troublesome for thee to kneel : Sit.   *Pausa magna.*
Δ .... So E.K. rose from kneeling, and did sit.

...... E. K. Now she is here, that last advertised us.

She taketh the book and divideth it into two parts : and it seemeth to be two books : the half cover adjoyning to one, and the
other half cover belonging to the other, the sides with the covers are
towards me.

The book
div.ded.

...... *Wisdome is a piercing beam, which is the center of the spiritual being of the holy*
Spirit , touching from all parts from whence the Divinity sendeth it out : and is proper to
the soul, or unto substances , that have beginning, but no ending , so that, whatsoever shall have
end, can never attain unto that which is called Wisdome : Neither can things that are subject to
the second death, receive any such influence , because they are already noted , and marked with
the seat of destruction. Happy is he whom God hath made a vessel of salvation ; for unto him be-
longeth joy, and a crown of reward : Adam (your forefather and first parent) *in respect of his*
creation, that is to say, in respect of his imaginative composition received no strength, but by the
Holy Ghost; for the soul of man is free from all passions and affections, until it enter into the body,
unto the which it is limited : so that, being neither good nor bad (but apt unto both) he is left,
by Divine providence and permission joyned together to the end of the one, or the other : But
wheresoever wisdome dwelleth, it dwelleth not with the soul , as any property thereof, but according
to the good will of God, whose mercy concurreth on every side into him , and taketh up a mansion
therein; to utter out, and manifest his great goodness : And even as the heavens are glorified con-
tinually with the Spirit of God : So is the soul of man glorified , that receiveth sanctification
thereby, for no man is illuminated, that is not sanctified : neither is there any man perfectly san-
ctified, that is not   *illuminated. I speak this (my brethren) for that you shall un-*
derstand, That no man did, or can ever attain to wisdom (that perfect wisdome which I speak
of) without he become a Center in his soul unto the mercies, and good will of God comprehend-
ing him , and dwelling in him , therefore lift up your eyes and see, Call your wits together , and
mark my words, To teach you, or expound unto you the mysteries of the Books that you have al-
ready received , is not in my power , but in the good will of God, after whose Image I am :
Which good will of God, is the descending of his holy Spirit abundantly upon you,
and into you, opening all your senses, and making you perfect men : for Adam *understood by*
that grace, and his eyes were opened so that he saw and knew all things that were
to his understanding : So have all those more and less, that have been counted wise, received the
gifts of the Holy Ghost , which setteth the soul on man so on fire that he pierceth into all
things, and judgeth mightily. The Apostles which knew even the thoughts of men,
understood all things , because the holy Spirit made a dwelling place in them : even so
shall it happen unto you : For you are the chosen of this last dayes, and such as shall be
full of the blessings of God, and his Spirit shall rest with you abundantly. Mark therefore what
I have to say unto you.

Ad imagi-
nem Dei
factus erat.

The con-
ceiving the
exposition
of our for-
mer books,
The good
will of God.
Adam his
knowledge.

The Apo-
stles.
Wu.

4

A hundred dayes are limited unto you during the which time, you shall every seventh, present your selves in this place, and you shall laud and praise God. *And behold I will be present among you.*

And before these dayes pass, when power is given me so to do, I will enter out of this Stone unto you. *and you shall eat up these two books, both the one and the other : and wisdome shall be divided between you, sufficient to each man.*

Then shall your eyes be opened to see. and understand all such things as have been written unto you, and taught you from above. But *beware ye take heed, that you dwell within your selves,* and keep the secrets of God, untill the time come that you shall be bid SPEAK; *For then shall the Spirit of God be mighty upon you ; so that it shall be said of you,* LO *were not these,* the Sorcerers, *and such as were accounted Vagabonds : Other some shall say,* Behold let us take heed, *and let us humble our selves before them : For the Lord of* Hoasts *is with them.*

And you shall have power in the Heavens, and in the lower bodies : *And it shall be taught you at all times inwardly, even what belongeth to the hearts of men :* Then shalt thou E. K. *have a new coat put on thee, and it shall be all of one colour.* Then shalt thou Δ. also have power to open. that book, which God hath committed unto thee ; *but use your selves as men, yea even then remember such as may receive the mercies and grace of God :* And let all peace and unity be amongst you· *For even as the Sun looketh into all things from above, so shall you into all the creatures that live upon the earth ; yea the one of you shall have his lifted, and shall enter into the fourth or fifth heaven, for unto him that is worldly knowledge be given ;* and unto him that hath been patient, shall greater things descend. Notwithstanding both sufficiently satisfied: In the mean season, The seventh day hence, shal thou bring in such things, as the Lord hath given thee : And in this place they shall be disposed according to the knowledge that is given me : *And herein thou best pleased the Lord ;* For that thou hast dealt streight, and according to brotherly meaning.

Δ. Now cometh the time that the Whore shall be called before the Highest, and the tenth Month hence, shall the Turk and the Moscovite make a perpetual league together, and in the thirteenth month, shall Poland be assaulted, with the Tartarians, and shall be spoyled : yea even unto the very ribs, so that in the sixteenth month they shall fall all together from Christ : And the hand of God shall run in vengeance, vengeance, even through this Kingdome, and through Germany, and into Italy ; and in the 23. Month Rome shall be destroyed, so that one stone shall not be left standing upon another, and vengeance shall be on all the earth, and fear upon all people, for the Lord is gone out against them : They eat and drink, and say, Let us be merry : Wo be unto them, for the know not the time of their visitation. For lo Justice shall visit them and tread them under foot : And ✦✦✦ this Kingdome shall dure for a while ; that is to say, This wicked triumph. And behold in the North shall rise that Monster, and shall pass forth with many Miracles, but you seeing all these things shall be at quietness untill such times as it shall be said unto them, Revenge. Happy is he that is not partaker of the love of such as shall be vexed these latter dayes.

E. K. She is gone.

Δ. I read these over to E. K. To his great comfort.

...... Make an end, I have no more to say

Δ. Deo nostro Omnipotenti, Patri, Filio, & Spiritui sancto sit omnis laus gratiarum actio, honor gloria & Imperium nunc & in sempiterna saeculorum secula. Amen.

Marginal notes:
An hundred daies limited every 7th day.
Personal apparition.
The understanding of such things as have been delivered us mystically.
Silence untill.
Power to be given us.
Vide actiones nem an.1583 men fis die, of his divers spotted coat. Note and remember. Entrance in the 4th. and 5th. heaven.
Δ O Lord I thank thee that thou hast accepted my patience.
Maii 30.
The books of Dunstan and the powder.
Mense 10. forte mense pro ann.eris.
A Prophesie
Mense 13. Poland.
Mense 16. Bohemia. Germania. Italia.
An.1589. Bohemia. Antichristus
Untill. Revenge.

Magnifici viri fratres & amici Chariss. *Hodie hora* 9.. *ante meridiem istæ mihi allatæ sunt literæ a Domino* Schombergio, *quæ datæ sunt* 5 Marcii, & debebat jam deveniße in manus meas antea. *Ex quibus intelligo ipsum cum Domino* Holek *expectare reſponſum* Munſterbergii. *Quandoquidem Omnipotens ille omnium rerum moderator, & rector vos delegaverit ad hoc ministerium & opus perficiendum. Ego nihil ſcio quid agendum, nec ullum meum Conſilium eo accedere poteſt, ut diſponere aliquid poſſim, ſciam aut velim; niſi quod ſapientiſſimo illi moderatori viſum fuerit. Proinde omnia vobis tranſmitto, Orate ſedulo, & quod placuerit Altiſſimo & Potentiſſimo Domino hoc fiat, & me etiam in omnibus informate & in tantis libenter obedire cupio & volo : Et ita nolim neq; diem iſtam prætermittere quin ſtatim rurſus ad vos tranſmittam. Interim vos & meipſum Dei omnipotentis bonitati immenſæque miſericordiæ commendans.* Dat. Cromoviæ, 16 Marcii, *Anno* 1587.

Veſter amicus & frater,

Guilielmus   manu propria.

Magnificis viris Domino *Joanni* Dee & Domino *Edvardo Kelleo* & ad manus proprias.

1587. *Recepimus tandem* Trebonæ *Aprilis* 2. *Nos enim a* Reichſtenio *abiveramus & rediveramus antequam ad* Reichſtenium *nuncius venit.*

Magnifici Domini Chariſſimi amici & fratres, ad literas veſtras nihil reſpondere potui, quandoquidem per ſuas mihi literas D. *Schomberg.* de ſuo & ſocii ipſius a . . . . tu ſignificaveras, volui primum quæ mihi . . . . necentur audire. Et ſi aliqua nova eſſent vel non audita, dominationem veſtram magnificam denuo certiorem reddere. Hæri noctu ſolus ad me venit D. a *Schomberg.* relicto ſocio in monaſterio meo. Coronienſi dimidium ab hinc milliare, & de negotiis mihi multa expoſuit, de quibus uti intellexi, ex ipſo & Rom. veſtris Mag. ſignificaverit, Uti potui intelligere, ſatis circumſpecte & provide negotia ſunt tractata uſq; huc, & ſpero etiam fideliter : Ad omnia iſta reſpondi, prout ſepiſſime a me intellexiſtis, & nuper etiam literis quæ illi dicenda putabam Dom. veſtræ ſcripſi. Tota res videtur conſiſtere in adjuvandis aliquibus perſonis pecuniarum aliquo auxilio, & prout & ſcriptum ſive . . . . memoriale mihi tradidit, quod tranſmitto Dom. veſtris perlegendum & conſiderandum, & poſt, mihi remittatur oro. Chariſſimi Domini ſcitis quæ ſit voluntas Domini, *proxima actio & aliæ,* (mihi videtur) annuunt ipſos adjutandos, fiat ſecundum ipſius cujus omnia ſunt voluntate & miſericordiſſima diſpoſitione & expediantur eo celerius, prout cum Domino *Edvardo* locuti ſumus. Ipſi reſpondeant Domino altiſſimo & potentiſſimo de fide quam ipſi præſtabunt, ſin vero aliter viſum fuerit Omnipotenti Domino fiat ita. Rogo Dom. veſtras Magn. quam amantiſſime piis ſuis ad Deum orationibus & mediis a Domino vobis traditis & conceſſis promovete, & adjuvetis Domini Dei noſtri opus & voluntatem exequi.

Socius remanſit in monaſterio, ut ſupra dictum, & concluſi cum Domino *Schombergio,* ut neq; videam neq; tractem cum illo, certis de cauſſis, quas vobis ſignificabit, & a me etiam intelligetis ; tamen ut eo ſit melius contentus de *duobus vel tribus millibus* tallerorum ipſi procurabitur ad quædam ſibi neceſſaria comparanda in lucio ſperat ipſum bene fore contentum pro tempore modo cætera quæ majora ſunt propter reliqua ut ſupra ſcripſi procurentur.

Ego

Ego non fum ab Imperatore vocatus, fed meam de aliquibus expetivit fua Majeftas fententiam de quibus refcripfi ut decuit. De actione intellexi Dom. veftras paratas ad præfcriptum diem effe velle, bene eft. Semper nos paratos effe decet & convenit ; Ipfe benigniffime quæ in nobis defunt, fua mifericordia & clementia inenarrabili perficiat : Placet mihi fententia Dom. veftrarum & quæ initio & in prœmio actionis proponere velletis, de quo me informabitis, ad hoc me componam & expectabo humiliter refponfum.

Quæ proponenda putabam nulla funt alia nifi illa.

1. Si Imperator de rebus *Polonicis* a me quicquid fcifcitari vellet, aut fufpicione aliqua de me concepta aut fingendo fibi aliquid *quomodo me gerere debeam.*

2. Si Imperator de fucceffione Regni hujus pro fratre aliquid tractare vellet quomodo me gerere debeam.

3. Si electio *Polonica* fucceffura fit, quid de bonis meis paternis difponat Dominus, & mihi quid faciendum.

4. Debeo-ne de negotio *Polonico* aliqua cum Electore *Brandenburgico* aut aliquo Principe Imperii confidenter conferre, vel non. Cum quibus, quando & qua ratione.

5. Si miles aliquis conducendus & quando.

6. Si Pontifex aut Imperator de perfonis Dom. veftrarum vellet aliquid attentare, vel *eas iterum relegare,*vel quovis modo perturbare, quid agendum & ipfis refpondendum.

7. Si de Thefauro *nobis concredito* aliquid Cæfari fit communicandum, quando, quantum, & quomodo.

8. Si Imperator mea opera uti vellet pro agendis Comitiis in *Moravia* & *Silefia,* fi hoc fufcipere munus debeam.

De cæteri humiliter fupplicent ut me ita difponere dignetur altiffimus ut fibi foli placeam & ferviam fideliter & conftanter ad fui nominis æternam gloriam & Reipublicæ Chriftianæ falutem.

Si Dom. veftræ putant aliqua omittenda, aut quæ offendere poffent per amorem Dei oro, bene confidèrent : omittant aut emendant pro fua pietate & prudentia.

Unum eft quod omifi de propofitionibus ; Quod conftitueram in animo de *Thefauro Domini mihi benigne* conceffo aliquas fundationes, hic in patria ifta conftituere. Deus fcit mentem meam quem nihil latet. Si placet hoc meum mifericordiffimo Domino propofitum vel non.

Et præfertim fi mihi alio (divina ita difponente gratia) fit commigrandum, vellem patria mea cognofcat, & tota pofteritas quod amaverim illam, & optime de falute ipforum & pofteritatis fenferim.

Dat. *Cromoviæ* færia 5. poft Pafcha, *Anno* 1587.

Vefter ex animo, & frater & amicus
fincerus

Guilielmus   manu propria.

In

In nomine Patris, & Filii, & Spiritus Sancti.   Amen.

Gloria Patri, & Filii, & Spiritui Sancto : ſicut erat in principio &
nunc & ſemper & in ſecula ſeculo rum.   Amen.

In Actione Tertia, proponenda.

1. *D*Eo Omnipotenti, *Patri, Filio & Spiritui Sancto, offerimus nos humili-*
mè, paratos ad Divina Oracula, monita, inſtructiones, informationes,
& alia quæcunq; in hac generali Actione, ſuſcipienda, intelligenda, & exe-
quenda, quæ ſua Divina Majeſtas, pro ſua gloria & noſtra conſolatione
maxima fore, præviderit & decreverit.

2. *Humiliter requirimus, an hic plenaria hæc tranſigetur Actio : vel an no-*
bis ad Cromoviam, *cum neceſſariis noſtris rebus, (& quibus illis quidem) pro-*
perandum fuerit.

3. *Hæ noſtri Domini* Roſenbergii *Quæſtiones* 12 *generales, & alia quæ-*
cunq; in eiſdem particulariter continentur, humiliter offerimus, tam ejus quam
noſtro nomine, illa & talia expectantes reſponſa quæ & qualia a ſede Maje-
ſtatis Divinæ, in ſuorum ſervorum conſultationibus procedere, & olim &
ſemper ſolent.

4. *Et quia in eiſdem Quæſtionibus, nulla facta eſt mentio de uſu pulveris*
quem ſibi divinitus conceſſum habet, & aliquoties prius dictum fuerit, quod in
hac Actione, informaretur de illius pulveris uſu, nos, jam humiliter illam de-
ſideramus informationem.

5. *Et quia extraordinarius iſte vehemens favor Moſchovitici Principis erga*
me incognitum jam eſt mihi & multis aliis conteſtatus, & manifeſtus, (ago
Deo Optimo Maximo gratias quantas poſſum maximas) & quia incertus ſum
ad quem finem Deus illum ejus favorem erga me, dirigere velit : humiliter peto
& mihi a te (Omnipotens Deus) informatio aetur de iſto fine, & voluntate
tua in hac parte, & quo modo ejuſdem Nunciis reſpondere debeam, ſi qui jam
venerint de cætero.

6. *An non debeamus nos met aſſponere, (ut alias, aliquoties præmonitum eſt)*
ut hic, lapidem Philoſophorum ex methodo Dunſtani *conficiamus : quæ me-*
thodus, quia mihi non conſtat, ſæpe me hactenus fecit videri quaſi in hoc labore
tardum, otioſum, vel ignavum. Vbi, contra, quam eſt paratus animus meus
& manus & pedes & omnes vires tam animi quam corporis mei, Tu noſti, Tuq;
(O Deus) teſtis eſto meus.

7. *Illa Praxis, cum poculo ferreo, canali vitrea, calce &c. nondum nobis*
ſuccedit ; idcirco, ad illius quoq; Concluſionis veritatem practicam obtinen-
dam, libenter ſciremus, quid eſt quod nos hactenus impedivit, vel quid nobis
deeſt, ad veram intelligendam, & perficiendam praxim illam.

8. Thomæ Kellei *decumbentis valetudinem & ſanitatem, tibi (O Deus)*
commendamus, & ſupplicamus, ut illi, nobiſque propitius eſſe velis : il-
lumq; ſanum & ſalvum nobis reddere & confirmare digneris ad nominis tui
laudem, honorem & gloriam, ex fideli ejuſdem poſthac ſervitio, & officio :
erga divinam tuam Majeſtatem. Amen.

9. Joanna, *uxor* Ed: Kellei *noſtri, Omnipotenti Divinæ Majeſtati tuæ*
ſupplicat per me, & ego humilimè (ejuſdem Joannæ *nomine) tibi (O Deus)*
ſupplico, ut illi velis eſſe miſericors, clemens & benignus ; & ut ejus multi-
plices ad te preces pro fæcunditate cum hoc ejus marito obtinenda, paterna re-
ſpicias charitate : & ut illi hoc contribuere velis gaudium, & quaſi ſui fide-
lis ſervitii (erga hunc ſuum maritum) præmium, ut prole per eundem &
cum eodem gaudere poſſit beata : reſpice quæſumus hanc noſtram petitionem,
ut a multis olim piis fæminis & viris eandem accepiſti, & etiam conceſ-
ſiſti

sisti petitionem Misericordissime Pater, per Filium tuum, Dominum nostrum Jesum Christum. Amen.

10. *Pro mea* Jana (O *Deus*) *humilimè gratias ago, quod hactenus tam clementer & pie illam liberaveris a suæ radicalis infirmitatis contagione: contra quam & medicinam facere, me docuisti: & me ut facerem adjuvisti, factæque eam virtutem concessisti, ut illa remedii optati nobis præberet signa, qualia nostra imperitia magis sperat esse bona & certa, quam recta ratione dijudicare potest, hoc igitur symptona egestionis sanguinolentæ quid sit nescimus, an morbi alterius indicium, an dictæ Medicinæ adhuc in sua virtute & efficacia procedentis, operatio. Tuum* (O *Deus*) *ne dedigneris impartire mihi consilium: & de fluxu illo frequenti, ex ejusdem* Janæ *auribus, libenter audire vellemus remedium aliquod.*

De Angliæ *&* Reginæ *ejusdem statu, si aliquid scire nobis expedit, libenter audiemus.*

✦✦
✦✦

London,   At Mrs. *Goodman* her houſe.

Martii 20 *à meride hora* 4 ¼

J E S U S

Omnipotens ſempiterne & une Deus.

M*Itta lucem tuam & veritatem tuam, ut ipſa me ducat & perducat ad montem ſanctum tuum & Tabernacula.* Amen.

. . . . . . *I am bleſſed* Raphael, *a bleſſed meſſenger of the Almighty, I am ſent of God, who is bleſſed for evermore.* Amen.

John Dee, *I am ſent of God for thy comfort firſt to certifie thee thou ſhalt overcome this thy infirmity, and when thou art ſtrong in body, as God in his goodneſs will make thee,* THEN thou ſhalt have all made known unto thee of ſuch things being not come to paſs as have been before ſpoken of, *becauſe that thou ſhouldeſt take comfort in God, that thou art not left from the comfort of Gods bleſſed creatures. Now God hath ſent me at this time whereby thou ſhalt be ſatiſfied,* THAT *when* thy body is able to abide the time of my ſervice from God to be delivered unto thee by me *Raphael :* Thy friend John Pontoys *yet liveth, but his time is likely to be ſhort.*

          Ask at your will.

Δ . . . . . . O God, I am beaten into a great attempt, to make the counſel privy, of my beggery, and to offer the Earle of *Salisbury,* ſuch my duties as I may perfect to his content. How ſtandeth this with your good liking?

          Δ. Spiritual.

Thou ſhalt have friends, in thy ſuit, and thou ſhalt have foes, but through Gods mercies, thy friends, ſhall overcome thy foes and thou ſhalt ſee how that God in his goodneſs will work mightily in his power for thee.

Proceed in thy ſuit ſo ſhortly as thou canſt finde thy health in body able : And for thy health uſe thy own skill, that God hath, and ſhall guide thee withall to thy good and perfect receiving of thy perfect health.

Δ . . . . Of the blood, not coming out of my Fundament, but at a little, as it were a pin hole of the skin.

Raph. *That the which thou hadſt no knowledge to help thy weakneſs, God in his mercies did ſend thee therein preſent help, the which but only for that iſſue thou couldeſt not have lived. And for the cure and thy help, the ſame God will work with thee in thy heart and minde ſo, that it ſhall be known unto no man, but by Gods merciful goodneſs delivered unto thee, ſuch wayes and means as ſhall be thy help, and reſtore thee to health again. This God of his mercy hath ſent me to deliver this ſhort meſſage, becauſe of thy weakneſs, Thou art not ſtrong to indure them, therefore ſuch is Gods goodneſs to let you to underſtand that after the tenth day of* April, *I will then appear again, and thou ſhalt underſtand much more what Gods will and his pleaſure is to be done in Gods ſervices, and for your good, and ſo for this little ſhort meſſage, I have declared unto you the will of* Jeſus Chriſt *: And ſo for this time,* In the Name of the moſt higheſt Creator and maker of Heaven and Earth, *I do now return at his will and commandement, and I am ready at all times when he ſhall command me to appear to thy comfort. His Name be praiſed evermore.* Amen, Amen.

          Δ. Amen.

Friday

Friday 24 *Martii hora* .9 $\frac{1}{2}$

DEus *in adjutorium nostrum intendas* **D. D. R. R.** .... *Zebaith* .... *The Omnipotent God be praised for evermore, his holy Name be glorified.* Now John Dee, I Raphael *am now come at Gods pleasure, and at his commandement to speak with thee, and make known unto thee as far forth as in my power lieth to speak God hath sent me to declare unto thee: the cause of thy desire now at this time,* John Dee, *as thou art an earthly man, if thou dost desire to have help from God of such things as earthly men cannot be without while they have time here in this mortal life, thou desirest to have knowledge as concerning things hid, the which I* Raphael *have no delight, neither pleasure in speaking of any such earthly matter, or earthly cases. But my delight is in the Almighty, and in his wisdome. But notwithstanding at this request, and thy inward desire in God to be certified of this treasure, the which these two men whom thou knowest do speak of, they ever had a time appointed of God for it, and it was not used accordingly as they should have done. Now this second time, because you have a desire to have help and knowledge at the hands of the Almighty, I* Raphael *do command thee and those men whom thou knowest, that they shall not intermeddle, or to take it in hand before the tenth day of* January *be past, for if they do, they shall not prevail, for that is a time that God hath best appointed for the said purpose, and for the quiet enjoying of it; so when that day is past, then let them in the name of God enter into that work. And if they will be such men as they ought for to be, and as Gods will is that they should be, to deal faithfully and truly one with the other in deed and in word, God will then bless their good purpose, and bring it to their head when they shall take in hand to open the earth, God will presently at that instant then suffer their good purpose to take effect, and the matter to be effected and had, so that they shall not be put off, if they shall beare or see any thing that they shall dislike, but safely to stand in the hope, and craving at Gods hand to have that good help to be a warrant between them, and all hurt and danger whatsoever may behappen, and so overcome. I say, If they will faithfully pray unto God with their whole trust in God, God will bless their good success, if they be otherwise, then as good never stir, and their good success will be against them. So I* Raphael *have made known unto thee Gods purpose in this thy request.*

     For this I have said.

     John Dee, I Raphael, *did make known unto this desire of that secret, and that great gift that gave unto thee in such order and manner as thou knowest where thou hadst it, and that never as yet hadst the knowledge*   *and the wisdome that God will give thee as concerning that, and many mo such*   *unto thee : So this rare gift being taken away from thee by them thou knowest, by taking thy key, and so taking of it from thy keeping, it was the will and purpose of God, that I* Raphael *should give such ... that thou shouldest have knowledge ... of the same. Thou shalt take such course .... thou mayest obtain it again, and when thou hast it, thou shalt put it into the same chest again, and commit it into the custody and keeping of thy very friend* John Pontoys, *and he shall, and will deal faithfully and friendly with thee in keeping the same until such time as by that ... the which thou knowest is promised unto thee, that thou shalt receive the perfect understanding of the hid knowledge and secrecie of God that is not as yet made known unto thee, and .... as hath been said, so shalt thou have such wisdome delivered unto thee by me* Raphael *that shall come in such ... and order as hath been late made known unto thee for thy good in such short and speedy time to be performed, and so thus much I have made known unto thee, as God hath in store for thee to be performed. Thus much I have now said, and given thee cunning to keep it in such maner as I have spoken, or else thou wilt be disappointed of that, and ... it will bide such purpose as God will have come to pass, so in his mighty power command me to come. I have for this matter finished; If thou have any thing speedily, ask in ... for I am to depart.*

     John Dee, If *thou wilt have all thy cause then .... as thou must shew unto thy liking and bers what thou hast drawn, and crave for good assistance it ... of ... desiring his help, and ... unto her the disease. ...to go to such men that should give thee further instruction thy best as I have said to shew unto her that thou hast done .... and he will .... in thy case unto ...... and* Canterbury, *and so the faith shall triumph in short time, and if this be ....*

               Julii 9: *hora* 4. *a meridie.*

   Δ. After my Prayers for a quarter of an hour, a Voice said,   *Westminster*
      I am Raphael *whose voice thou dost hear : To morrow morning at nine of the clock God*   *Three Kings*
      will send me to thy sight.   *in Kings-*
   Δ. So with thanks to God I ended.   *street.*

Δ. *Mittas lucem tuam & veritatem tuam, quæ nos ducant & perducant ad montem sanctum tuum & cælestia tua tabernacula.* Amen.

Barth. As for you, the Creator of God doth appear.

Δ. *Benedictus qui venit in nomine Domini Halleluia.*

...... *Blessed be God the Father, and God the Son, and God the holy Ghost. All honour and power be ascribed unto the living God for evermore. Amen.* Δ. *Amen.*

John Dee, *I am* Raphael, *one of the blessed and elect Angels of the Almighty; and at his will and his good pleasure, he hath commanded me to appear here at this time, to set forth the will and pleasure of the Almighty God.*

John Dee, *my message that I have at this time to deliver unto thee, is of great force, in that God would have thee to do. And whereas it was said at my last appearing at this beholder, that I would appear again, and now it hath pleased God to send me to perform and make known according to that which was then said,* that all things before promised should be made plainly known what Gods will is to be done in all that hath been before said.

Now I do make known unto you the plain meaning and understanding thereof.

First thou hast been promised the secret knowledge and understanding of the Philosophers Stone, *of the Book of St. Dunstans, to have the knowledge of them.*

It is since a long time, as thou knowest to mans reason, and to the minde of man, a few years is with men thought to be big; and now God hath been thy keeper; and most chiefly created thee, and hath suffered thee to have time to live unto this age: and furthermore, thou dost like unto thy Nativity, and considering thy great age that the course *of Nature for age, is likely; by thy reason, to take place.* BUT *John Dee, thou dost well remember unto whom, in the holy Scriptures, that God in his mercies did adde and put to fifteen years longer than the time was set him:* So *think not but God in his mercies will be as great unto thee. And now to come to the matter whereby to let thee to understand why thou hadst not thus these rare gifts and promises performed unto thee, it was the will of God to keep them away, and to suffer the heart of thy supreme head and governour, under God, to be hardned against thee, that thou art no better account made of unto him, but to be such an one that doth deal with Devil and by Sorcery, as you commonly term them Witchcraft: and who doth, and who hath informed him, to be thus evil and hardly informed against thee, but only the Devil, and by the hatred of thy secret enemy whom thou knowest* (Salisbury I mean) *and all malice and enemies that he can by his Devils,* Maserien, Hermeloe, *the four wicked ones, the which are accounted the four Rulers of the Air, whose names be* Ories, Egym, Paynim, *and* Mayrary: *They be the Devils that he doth deal withall, that be through their enticing and his, be thinketh to be pleasant and good wisdom that he receiveth at their hands;* That he and his Devils do seek thy overthrow in all good things, and doth and shall, *so far forth as God will suffer them, seek all the malice and hindrance in all good causes* to be done to thy good. *Therefore now* John Dee I am *to let thee to understand plainly what Gods will and his great purpose is to have thee to do, although it may seem hard to thy good liking, considering as thou dost think, the weaknesse of thy body, and course of age: yet notwithstanding, that same God that hath been thy protector and keeper until this present time of years, that same merciful God shall keep thee, and make thee able to perform things that shall be made known unto thee; for God will not bestow such rare gifts as I have before said, amongst those which be unworthy of such great blessings from the Almighty. For God will not bestow* Pearls *amongst those that will not believe nor understand that God hath any such blessings to bestow upon men: for I say unto thee,* John Dee, *that if God should or would bestow those blessings upon thee, even at this present, or at any time to be shortly performed and delivered unto thee: Then, except that thou shouldst make all things plainly known of Gods secrets delivered unto thee, unto thy supreme head under God here upon earth, and likewise thy enemy to be partaker in these secrets and great gifts of God, if thou wouldst not perform as much unto them, as God should give wisdom unto thee, therein, thy life would and should, by the envy and malice of those wicked ones, and by thy great enemy thou shouldst speedily be cut off from this life, but God will not have it so. So if thou wilt do as God shall command thee by this message,* thou shalt have all these *messages, promises and wisdom, both for the* Philosophers Stone, *the book of* S. Dunstans, *the secret wisdom of that* Jewel *that was delivered, as thou knowest, in what manner it is plainly known unto thee.*

So now it is the will of God to suffer thy supreme Head *his heart to be hardned against thee; and likewise for thy great enemy for his wicked instructions against thee, God doth suffer it so to be, even as* Pharaoh *his heart was hardned against the children of God, so standeth the matter against thee with them. It is the will of God so to suffer it to their great account that they shall have to make, when it shall please the Almighty that that time shall be, that they must render unto God their accounts. Now* John Dee *it is the will of the* Almighty *to send me* Raphael *to deliver unto thee this* Message, *the which will seem unto thee to be very hard: yet as thou art the servant of God, and one whom God doth favour and love (although the world by wicked enemies doth hate thee) willingly and obediently follow that course the which God in his mercies at this time shall make known unto thee.*

Thou

Thou fhalt (if thou wilt obey the commandment of God, by me made known unto thee) take a long journey in hand, and go where thou fhalt have all thefe great mercies of God performed unto thee, *and God will fhew thee as great favour in the fight of God, as ever he did fhew unto* Jofeph, *who was fold into bondage, as thou knoweft, and in all his imprifonment and troubles God was with him, and delivered him : So, if thou wilt follow this commandment from God delivered unto thee by me* Raphael, *that thou fhalt not doubt, nor waver in thy mind, but God will be merciful unto thee, both in this life and in the life to come : and think God will not command thee to take fuch a journy in hand, but that he doth know that is beft for thee,* and he will preferve thee, and keep thee in thy journy. *And thou fhalt find in thy journy, that God fhall and will deal mercifully with thee in finding eafe of the infirmity of the ftone, that the Angels of God fhall direct thee in thy heart and mind, how thou fhalt ufe thy body, to the* health and comfort of thy ftrength. *And when thou art at thy journies end amongft fuch friends beyond the feas as thou knoweft, God fhall and will raife thee as faithful friends (as now I have faid before) as* Jofeph *had, fo fhalt thou be favoured with God and man ; for it is the will and purpofe of God to have thee to be obedient unto this the which I do make known unto thee, becaufe thou fhouldft not remain here, to be beholding unto thofe that are thy mortal enemies, and had rather to bear of thy end, than otherwife to hear of thy well-doing, or any good to be done unto thee by any man ; it is a grief and a fpight in head and mind unto them, that thou fhouldft come to any help,* or things neceffary for mans ufe *here upon earth, the which man cannot be without. And* John Dee, *I am to command thee, that fo fhortly as thou canft by all means poffible,* fet thy things in order, for thy Wardenfhip, *and in all other caufes of worldly affairs. And for maintenance to further thy journy, God will moft gracioufly raife thee up fome good friends to be helping unto thee, that thou maift have maintenance in thy journy. And thy very friend* John Pontoys *fhall by Gods favour* John Pontoys. come home, *and he fhall and will be a great aid unto thee, to perform this courfe the which God by me hath commanded thee to undertake : That where thou doft live now in want, and to be beholding unto thofe, who do not love thee, neither in heart do wifh thee well ; fo God would have thee to be where thou fhalt do him fervice, and God will give thee long days in fo doing, and fulfiling this his* Long life. *commandment and will by me* Raphael, *the which meffage I am at Gods will and his pleafure plainly to make known unto thee, that it is his will to have thee to follow this courfe, in which God will have thee to enter into, Not fearing nor miftrufting the weaknefs of thy body, but that God will preferve thee for that time, as fhall be his good will and pleafure, that thou fhalt have life here in this world, to be as merciful a God to deliver thee from all hurts and dangers, and from all infirmities, even with as much health as thou haft had in this time as thou haft lived thus many years ; fo God will have thee to follow his will in this direction, and then thou fhalt have all things aforefaid performed unto thee, and thou fhalt then have fuch favour, that thou fhalt behold his bleffed Creatures with thefe thy mortal eyes : and if thou wilt perform to the uttermoft of thy power this meffage from God by me delivered ; Then God will in his mercies perform all that is promifed unto thee. And except thou wilt be willing and dutiful, fo much as in thee lieth to make good this,* the which I have through Gods means declared *what courfe thou muft take ; and if thou doft it not, then God will not no more fend unto thee, to the beholding of any mans earthly eyes, any of his bleffed Creatures. Therefore I command thee from God, as I am his faithful Minifter and bleffed Angel of God, that thou fhouldft not doubt to take this journy in hand, for God will be with thee and for thee, and his* △ Si Deus bleffed Angels *fhall be thy comfort, even as the Angel of God was the comfort unto young* Tobias *in* nob fcum his journey, *fo God will deal with thee in thine. And fo I have delivered unto thee what God will* quis contra have thee to do. nos.

It *is the will and favour of God to give the as much underftanding of Gods mercies towards thee yet for to come, as ever mortal man had delivered unto him by any fpiritual Creature from God. So now I have fully ended my meffage. Therefore, fee that thou* John Dee *be as ready to perform it to the greateft of thy power, as lovingly in giving God thanks for this meffage delivered, becaufe I would have thee to be fuch an one as fhall not end his dayes in reproach, and rejoycing of thy enemies, but thou fhalt have time and days to live, that when thou dieft, and fhalt depart this world, thou fhalt die with fame and memory to the end, that fuch an one was upon the earth,* Miracula: *that God by him had wrought great and wonderful Miracles in his fervice. And thus to Gods honour and his glory, I have ended my meffage, yielding unto God all honour, and praife, and thanks for all his bleffings, and his great benefits beftowed upon his Creatures, both now and for evermore.* Amen. *Bleffed be God in all his gifts, and holy in all his works. Praifed be God.* Amen, Amen.

△. Amen.

△. Now, O God, as I have willingly yielded unto thy will and commandment of undertaking a Journey : fo I befeech thee that it may ftand with thy good pleafure to notifie unto me the Country, Region or City unto which thou wouldft have me direct my courfe from hence-forward.

△. Nothing appeared.

A Voice . . . . . . A Voice . . . . . . *In the Name of God, to morrow at ten of the clock.*

△. So be it.

△. All thanks, praife and glory be to God the Father, God the Son, and God the holy Ghoft, now and for ever. *Amen.*

A Note to be confidered.

Mr. *Eccleſtone*.

In the houſe at the breaking up of the place were theſe : *James Bolton,   Lettice Goſtwich* a Maiden, Cook and Dairy-maid.

TO know the houſe and place therein where it is, or if it be in many places divided, which they are.
Or if any other be privy of it, who may give any evidence.

And whatſoever may make this a perfect work, to Mr. *Eccleſtones* reaſonable contentment, moſt humbly and heartily I beſeech God to make known now unto us, and ſo the praiſe and thanks due to God for his mercies, to the beſt of our power to be yielded unto him.

Saturday, *Julii* 11. *hora* 10. *ante meridiem.*

Note, In the Original two Schedules are pinned acroſs this page.

The firſt Schedule.   To enquire,

1. *THe Name of the place whether I am to direct my total Journey.*
     2. *Whom ſhall I have in my company beſides* John Pontoys.
3. *What of* Patrick Sanders.
4. *What of my daughter* Katherine.
5. *What of my ſtanding Books and other appurtenances.*
   What of Mr. Bardolf *to go with me?*   Or,
   Of Mr. Dortnall *his Companion?*
6. *What ſhall my Son* Arthur *do, to his help and comfort in his intended travel?*
7. *Shall not I at any time return hither into* England *again?*
   Shall I make account to keep ſome title of enjoying my houſe at my return?

Mr. Eccleſtone *his Caſe.*

Junii 27.   1607.   The ſecond Schedule.

THe Name of my Houſe is Eccleſton of Eccleſton, *the mans Name whom I ſuſpect is* Thomas Webſter *Carpenter, of the age under fourty, not more, within the County of* Lancaſter.
   The place was in a falſe Roof adjoyning to a Chimney called New Chamber *Chimney.*

                                 Edward Eccleſtone.

Thomas Webſter the Thief.

Note :

Note : There being a Figure in a fingle leaf of paper, and the fame having no direction where it fhould be placed, I thought beft to place it here, the page immediately aforegoing making mention of one *Webfter* a Thief ; and here being words which (if I miftake not) relate to fuch a bufinefs, *an unquam recuperabitur,* whether that was ftoln fhall ever be recovered ; and, *In quo loco jam eft,* In what place *Webfter* the Thief is at prefent.

1. *Significat Domina Afcendentis & octavæ, recuperari poffe.*
2. *Applicans per fed cum receptione, recuperari poffe fignificat, perari poffe fignificat, fed cum difficultate aliqua.*
4. *Nota locum, & fignum eft : & Ancilla vel fœmina aliqua confideranda eft.*
4. *Luminaria fefe mutuo refpicientia, non pofterdum fore denotat* 5. *& maxime cum Dominus medii cæli carpere* 7. *fexali radio refpiciat fed interim* 7'. *domum comburat.*

J E S U S

A Domino factum eft iftud & eft mirabile in oculis noftris. Ex ftercore erigit pauperem ut collocet eum cum principibus populi fui. *Amen.*

Mittas (O Deus) lucem tuam & veritatem tuam, ut ipfa nos ducant, mirabilem in me fac mifericordiam tuam, & fapientiam tuam in corde meo figas.

A Voice. I *Am* Raphael *that fpeak, if you will have me to appear, proceed in hafte, for God hath appointed me great fervice to do.*

Δ. In the Name of Jefus, we defire your anfwers and inftructions to thefe Articles here flightly noted.

1. Raph. *In the Name of Jefu Chrift, I Raphael am now fent unto you to deliver unto you your queftion fo far forth as God his will and pleafure is to command me, and I muft make a fhort continuance with you, for I have fervice of God commanded me in hafte to be done, in his bleffed Name I am come to fulfil his will in your defires, and therefore in his Name go on.*

1. Δ. The name of the place.

Raph. John Dee, *thou haft been a Traveller, and God hath ever yet at any time provided for thee in all thy Journeys, fo much Gods favour and his mercies is fuch toward thee, that this thy requeft and defire to be known,* What Country is beft *for thy good :* God hath referred it to thy own will to make choife, *in what Country or City thou haft thy beft minde unto ;* and *when thou haft made thy choife, if it be Gods liking, and to thy good, it* fhall *be directed unto thee ; otherwife, if it fhall be made known that fome other place fhall be better for thee : Therefore take thy own choife and liking.*

Δ.
Raph. John Dee, *be that hath commanded thee to take this Journey in hand, he will provide for thee in* Germany, *or any other Country wherefoever thou goeft. Therefore let thy good will and liking be in placing thy felf, if thou wilt be near unto* England *or far off.*

Δ. Whether is beft, I know not.

Raph. *I have faid, that wherefoever thou wilt, God doth prize thy willing defire, to fulfil that God doth command : think, but thou fatisfie and reft in taking thy own choife, God will provide for thee, whither and to what City thou haft a minde or will to enter into, and always* Gods good Angel fhall hold thee, *and ever give thee to underftand,* what and where fhall be ever beft for thy good liking, *when thou art there. Therefore take no care, be, that Almighty will provide for thee, that thou fhalt be fo governed with his goodnefs, that all fhall ftand well with thee.*

2. Δ. Whom fhall I have in my company befide *John Pontoys ?*

3, 4. Raph. John Dee, *thou of thy felf doft beft know that* without thy daughter ; thou

canft

canst not be without her : and likewise God hath sent thee a very honest and well-disposed young man to go with thee in thy Journey. And for *John Pontoys,* he shall be one, as thy greatest comfort and special ayd, next unto the Almighty. *And for any other else, it is at thy own good will and well-liking whom thou wilt chuse to make fit thy purpose for necessary uses, for helps about thee,* Servants I mean.

5. Δ. What of my standing books, and other appurtenances?

Raph. John Dee, *thou hast spoken already of a very good course to send them away,* not all at once, *but some at one time, and some at another, and God shall and will give thee good*

John Pon-
toys.

success therein: and let thy friend John Pontoys, *let him provide for all such purposes, and so shalt thou do well.*

Δ. As I have been heretofore hindred of many of good purposes fulfilling, so perchance the King will not be willing now to grant me licence to pass over sea.

Raph. *He shall and will grant thee licence.*

6. Δ. For my Son *Arthur,* do to his help and comfort in his intended travel.

Raph. *If thy Son do like his course to travel, he shall in the mean while do well, for thy sake, being a father unto him, God will favour him. And when thou art in place where God hath commanded thee to go,in short time after thy being there,thou shalt be able to do him good,in helping him for such things as he now wanteth, and then thou shalt take him near unto thee, so that he may have a comfort of thy fatherly help, and thou to have comfort of his well-doing : and so for this I have certified thee.*

7. Δ. Shall not I at any time return hither into *England* again?

Raph. *Thou shalt be better able in health and strength of thy body to come into England again, if thou wilt : but thou shalt see and perceive thy self so mercifully provided for, that thou wilt have but little minde or willingness to come into England again, such shall Gods great mercies be towards thee.*

Δ. Then I perceive that I shall not make any great account of keeping my house at *Mortlake* for any my return hither.

Mr. Eccleston his Case of his money taken away by one Thomas Webster, &c.

Raph. *Thou dost take an hard matter in hand. This man* Thomas Webster *had it,* and hath it in his keeping as yet, *but he will not yield that he hath it. And for* Eccleston *to deal by extremities with him, he shall prevail little, he shall not thereby obtain his purpose. But by friendly dealing with the party, and in proffering him to be a partaker with him, he may yield unto* Eccleston. *But otherwise, the matter will grow hard. I would from God advise thee,* John Dee, *to enter or few of those matters as may be, for this will not be compassed, except that he shall proceed into the mans house according unto Law ; and then he shall entangle himself into trouble, and for the thing never the better : but, as I have said, by friendly dealing be may yield, and so far forth as it shall please God,* I will work by Gods favour to make him yield. *And thus much I have said, and let it suffice.*

It doth remain as yet in a Coffer that is somewhat of a white colour; but he will, if he be stirred,he will then remove it, and hide it in the ground in a little Parlour that he hath. And so I have spoken and answered thee at this time, as concerning

Δ. Money I had sent me from the Emperour by *Hans Bik:* I marvel that it is not yet come hither.

Raph. *For that,* John Pontoys *will make known unto thee, all to thy good. And in whose Name,and in his whose Power I came, so now again I return to that place,to the which in his mercies bring all his blessed Creatures, yielding all honour and praise unto his holy Name, I end. Amen, Amen.*

Δ. Amen.

<hr>

<h1>14 day of July, hora 11½.</h1>

Δ. AS I sate at Dinner with *Bartholomew Hickman,* my Daughter, *Patrick,* and *Thomas Turner,* about the end of the Dinner *Bartholomew* heard a Voice, saying, To morrow half an hour after 9 of the clock, give your attendance to know the Lords pleasure.

Δ. As near as I remember, so he said, or to that effect.

1607.

1607　　　*Julii* 15. *hor.* 9 ¹₂. *ante meridiem.*

J E S U S

In nomine Dei Patris, & Filii & Spiritus Sancti.　Amen.

Mittas lucem tuam & veritatem tuam, sapientiam & omnimodum auxi-
lium tuum, Domine Deus, ut tibi serviamus sancte, fideliter & con-
stanter omnibus diebus vitæ nostræ.　Amen.

Barth. . . . . . The Creature.

I*N the Name of him that created me* Raphael, *and all the blessed Creatures, and likewise in* **Jesus Christ**
his power made all the world, and all things therein contained : Jesus Christ *of his great good-*
nes hath sent me now at his will, and so I am bound at his will to return, when his pleasure is. All
honour be given to him being God Almighty for evermore.　Amen.

　John Dee, *I am* Raphael *that last appeared unto you, and I through Gods good pleasure*
did set down and made known unto thee, what pretended course God would have thee to enter into,
and his will is such, that so far forth, and so speedily as thou canst, to proceed in it, because that
God hath great service for thee to do, when thou shalt be there placed.
　And now I do let thee understand, that as concerning Eccleston *his suit and matter that I did* Mr. Eccle-
at my last being here speak of, so far forth as it pleased God to give me his free will : and now ston.
God hath sent me for favour that God doth bear unto thee, and not for no cause else, I Raphael
do now tell thee, that this matter, and all such like unto it, are not for me to enter into, neither
for any such as be of that high Society and Calling as I am of. Yet notwithstanding, I am
ready by Gods merciful goodness to command those whom God hath and doth appoint to Raphael his
serve under me : *and such his blessed Creatures being those that do stand in his presence, I* Ra- inferiours.
phael *will at Gods pleasure* command those that shall deal in *Ecclestons* suit, *in* constraining
by such Creatures as I have made known unto you, that they shall force and constrain these
parties, as he which he had in hand ; he is one, James Bolton *is another, and the Treasure was* car- The Trea-
ried to the Carpenter his brothers house ; *and there, as I did shew unto thee,* a Coffer of sure.
white colour. *Those parties are so troubled in minde, that they cannot be quiet, how or where*
to place the Treasure, *because they* would keep it close. *But let this suffice and satisfie for*
the whole answer in this his suit : I Raphael *through Gods power will* command such Creatures Raphael his
that shall constrain those parties to *bring the matter to* true light, and confess the said command-
Treasure ; *and he,* the party the owner to have his money *again, in so short time as may be* ment.
pleasing and acceptable unto the Almighty. God will have the whole matter made known *in*
this order, without any further trouble unto the parties : but it is his will that he shall examine them in friendly manner, *if they will not yield,* then by the force of a Justice in exa- How they
mination ; *but* they will not yield till such time as I by these Creatures *shall make them to* will & shall
yield, through Gods help, to their *sorrow ; and so the party the owner shall so* come by his goods yield.
again. *And now I have answered you in as ample manner as God will have me ; for as I have*
said,) such matters are not for me, but that course that I have now declared, by Gods help shall
be performed. And so in the Name of the Highest for this I do now end, giving praise to the
Almighty. And furthermore, John Dee, *in few words, for thy sake,* If this Window by his Δ. By this
Creatures, *should have medled in the cause,* they *should have had a great labour. But not-* Win-
withstanding, that which I have spoken of, is sufficient, praised be the Name of God : and so dow to be
I end.　　brought in,
　Δ. If it should not offend, then I would gladly know the sum of the Treasure.　　　&c.
　Raph. *Two thousand and a half, and odde money.*
　Δ. How, in gold and silver ?
　Raph. *More then three parts thereof in gold.*
　Δ. Most humbly and heartily I thank the Almighty for . . . . . .
　Raph. John Dee, *if thou dost doubt of any thing as concerning the entring into the course*
of thy Journey ; and likewise, if thou dost doubt of any thing that shall be against thy good success
when thou art there, Now speak, and I shall through Gods mercies make thee answer, as it may
and shall please God to the good direction of any thing that thou shalt doubt of, for God will not
command thee to enter into that Journey, but that he will most mercifully and graciously be thy
keeper, and deliver thee from the hands of thy enemies in thy Journey. And for the good health
of thy body, God will so carry thee in good health, that thou shalt set forth such service when
thou art there placed, what shall be thy great comfort unto Gods honour, in making of his marvellous works *to be known. And thus much for thy comfort through Gods merciful goodness I*
have made known unto thee : *and so I end.*

Δ . . . .

Δ. . . . . .
John Dee, *God doth know all this that thou dost speak of. In few words, to end many words, he will so direct thy wayes in ending such troubles, as shall be to thy good and speedy finishing.*

Δ. . . . .
John Pontoys, *before such time as thou shalt have any great cause to use his aid, and furthermore, God will so work for thee in the heart of his Master (whom he is Factor for)* Stapers *I mean, that* Stapers *shall with all the aid and help that he can to further thy good proceeding. And so God in all cases will thus graciously deal with thee. And now is my full time to depart in Gods peace, and to serve him from whom I came, his mighty Name.*

Δ. I fearing his sudden departure, did earnestly urge at his hands, to know the truth of *Tobias* his history : and so half unmannerly did interrupt his speech with my question.

John Dee, *I am* Raphael *that is appointed of God to be thy Guide in this thy Journey ; and I am that same* Raphael *that was the Guide unto young* Tobias *in his long Journey, and delivered him from the power of the wicked Spirit* Asmodeus, *who had, as thou knowest, how many he had destroyed : and I brought him through Gods power home again, and delivered him in health unto his own parents. And thus much I have made thee plainly to understand without any doubting to the contrary. And so now once again I do depart. All honour and glory to the everlasting God, both now and for evermore. Amen, Amen.*

Δ. Amen.

---

17 *July*.

AFter dinner (*horam circiter* 4 ½.) as *Bartholomew* and I talked of divers of my doings with Mr. *Kelley*, a Voice produced this to *Bartholomews* hearing,

A Voice. . . . . . *I,* John Dee, *I have heard you all this while.*
Thou shalt be able to do, and to see, and to understand more than all this as thou hast spoken of, according as God hath promised thee.

Δ. Blessed be his holy Name, and his mercies be magnified on me, to the honour of his holy Name. *Amen.*

Δ. *Note* . . . . . Upon occasion of further talk and *speech of my Jewel* that was brought, I asked *Bartholomew* if ever he had seen it since it was set in gold ; and he thought that he had not seen it : Whereupon I went speedily to my Chest, unlocked it, and took it out, and undid the Case, and set the Stone in his due manner.

And by and by did *Raphael* appear in the Stone, and in voice said thus, as followeth :

Raph. *In the Name of* Jesus Christ, *I am* Raphael *whose voice thou didst hear right now. And now, in Gods holy Name, for thy good, and for thy comfort, I have, now, here, in this Pearl entred Possession, in token hereafter to be that blessed Creature, to be obedient unto Gods Commandment, to serve thee at all times, when thou art placed in thy Journey, which God hath commanded thee. And likewise thou shalt have the book from whence this came. And that Dust which thou hast in keeping, (the which thou dost make account of no better but dust) Then it shall be turned to the right use, from whence it was : and to that good purpose, that God hath ordained for to do. And now it was the will of God, that I should speak unto thee a few words of this good comfort to be performed. Praise God, honour his holy Name, for his great blessings now and for ever ; That it did please the Almighty to send me to your presence, in token of his love, for his great mercy. And so now, in his Name I go again into the presence of the Almighty, whose Name be ever praised, with all his elect Angels, and all the blessed Creatures of God, and all the blessed Creatures upon earth, praise his Name for evermore. Amen, Amen.*

Δ. Amen.

Dei do-
mum
Vid. Ar-
batel.

1
2
3

Δ. O Lord God, most humbly, heartily and sincerely I honour thee, praise thee, and extoll thy mercies, and most loving kindness, for these, and all other thy graces and blessings on me. Accept, O God, my hearty thanks, and enable me so to thank thee, as may be a most acceptable sacrifice unto thy Divine Majesty. *Amen, Amen, Amen.*

1607. Sept. 5. *hora* 9 ½. *Mortlak.*

יהוה

Mitte lucem tuam & veritatem tuam Domine, quæ nos ducant & per-
ducant ad montem sanctum tuum & ad cælestia tua tabernacula.
Amen.

Barth. He is in the Stone now.
Benedictus qui venit in nomine Domini.

O Most *merciful Lord and Saviour Christ Jesu, who is and was the Creator and Redeemer*
of Mankinde, and of all his blessed Creatures. In his power I Raphael am now come at
his will and commandment, and so likewise at his good pleasure I must then return at such time
as he hath commanded me.

John Dee, *in the Name of the Most Highest, I am come to deliver unto thee this my*
Message, the which God in his goodness hath commanded me.

First, I Raphael am sent of God at this time most chiefly to put thee in that good remem-
brance of my last appearing to your presence, to let thee to understand, that look what course
God in his mercies did set then down, what way thou shouldst take to enter into this Journey,
the which God in his goodness is most willing that thou shouldst enter into. For, John Dee,
God hath declared, and made manifestly known unto thee at my last appearing, what service
God would use thee unto, and all such purposes that were the last time spoken of, shall be by Gods
favour and his merciful good gift performed unto thee : and fear thou not, but God will
safely help and preserve thy body in thy Journey, to that end, that thou shouldest be
in that place wherein thou mightest have time to enter into all such service as Go·l hath
by me made known unto thee. *For,* John Dee, *such hath Gods mercies been in suffer-*
ing wicked men to prevail against thee, and do make a scorn of thee here
in this thy Native Countrey : *So it is with thee as it was with Christ and his Apostles, being*
most cruelly used in their own Native Countreys ; so John Dee, *God hath suffered those wic-*
ked men to pluck thee down in worldly affairs, the which should be maintenance for thee and
for thine, and without such maintenance man cannot be without, while he is here in this vale of
Misery. Such wicked men have most cruelly used thee, even as Job *by Gods sufferance, who*
suffered the Devil to prevail against him : yet Gods mercies be so great unto thee, that although
they (most wickedly) have robbed thee of thy possession, yet God would not suffer those wicked
ones by any of their malicious practices to prevail in any wise to hurt thy body, as Jobs *was :*
For if they (through their wicked purposes) could have wrought such cruelty against thee, thou
hadst not been a man living here upon earth until this time. So John Dee, *thou dost know who*
is thy mortal enemy, who, rules next unto your earthly King.

Δ.

Why thou maist well know, for I have made it known before time unto thee, that he is not thy
friend, though thou hast not offended him in any wise. Therefore, because that this thy Na-
tive Countrey is not a place fit for Gods purposes in his wisdome to be bestowed upon thee
here. Therefore at my last Message, God did send me to make known unto thee, whether he
would have thee to go ; that there thou mightst be a man, that man, whom God hath
appointed to make his Wisdome known : *for thou art that man whom God hath chosen, that*
(accordingly as it was said yesterday) that no mortal man in flesh, but onely *Enoch,* had
or shall have the. like wisdome made known, plainly to be understood by any man, or
thou thy self shalt understand and receive at the hands of the Almighty. Therefore it is his
will and purpose of God, that he would have thee in that Countrey, for this thy Native Countrey is not worthy of gifts that thou shalt receive at the hands of God, to come, and
to be made known unto those which be not worthy of such great gifts of Gods wisdome, to come amongst those that be unworthy.

Therefore, John Dee, *in all these matters the which in favour at this time made known*
unto thee, the chief and greatest cause of this my coming unto thee, is to make the matter
plainly known, that God in his mercies would have thee with all diligence that thou canst possibly,
to haste thee to that Countrey where God doth command thee, and at my last being here thou

knowest

knowest what was my Message, therefore do thy diligence to fulfil it as thou canst, and God will put his great helps unto thee, in strengthning of thy body, and otherwise, which shall be to thy good. And thou being once in that place where God would have thee to be, thou shouldst well perceive and plainly understand, that God will most mercifully work with thee for thy good in performing all such promises, the which hath been both at the last time and at this time made known unto thee.

John Dee, I do put thee in remembrance, that whereas thou didst say, that thou hadst a portion of money sent thee from the Emperour unto thee; I tell thee, that the Devil in working in the heart of one of thy enemies (Cook I mean) did seek some wayes by his false important ill speeches, in most false manner, unto one that did in somewhat let the Emperour to understand, what he had most falsely, to thy discredit (as he thought) to hinder thee, that thou shouldst not come to any help or credit at the Emperours hand. But John Dee, be of good comfort, The Emperour of all Emperours will be thy comfort, and aid thee, and evermore put down thy enemies ; that the Emperour (that thou shouldst have received that portion of) it shall be so with thee, that he shall have more need of thee, in such wisdome as God shall deliver unto thee; for thou shalt have no need of him, but onely to keep good will and friendship betwixt him and thee, in shewing thy self friendly unto him, as God shall hereafter give thee plainly to understand.

Now, John Dee, I have made known unto thee what Gods will is in this my message. This is the greatest and the most principal cause, why God hath sent me unto thee at this present time. And now I have through Gods mercies delivered this his Commandment unto thee ; and for this I have now said and finished.

Δ. Blessed be the Almighty God, now and for ever.

Gladly I would have understood how much the portion was which the Emperour would have sent me.

John Dee, let it go, and speak no farther of it ; for thou maist be joyful, whereas it is said unto thee, that he should have need of thee, and not thou of him. Therefore reason no more in that matter.

Δ. As concerning Mr. Eccleston.

John Dee, in few words I answer thee, He hath dealt with the parties in those affairs, but the chief party will not, as yet, yield any thing to be made known, but doth stubbornly and stoutly stand in his own defence : And Gods Creatures have wrought with him, and nothing he will (as yet) yield unto, except that those Creatures should deal so cruelly with him, as it were to pull him apieces : this is his wicked stubbornness. But God will bring the matter to light ; but Eccleston hath not dealt so in the matter as he might have done, he is too too slack in his own cause. Therefore if the fault be in him, then do not blame the Creatures of God. For God could (as you very well do know it) command that said Treasure to be brought : but he will not have it so to be, because it shall come by other means among men : So God hath a great care and purpose to do all for your good, to keep matters out of blame and slander of the world, as it might come to passe, if it should come by any other wayes, but by this plot which is laid down to decline. And when it is the will of God that it shall be delivered, God will so perform it, if man will do as he should do, in all reverend manner towards God-ward. And so now I let you to perceive, and to know, that it is not as yet obtained.

Δ. Whether hath the other party confessed any thing ?

Raph. He hath not as yet yielded openly : but he hath in secret manner perswaded his fellow, that the matter might be made known unto Eccleston, in confessing of all the whole matter, but the other will not yet yield : but it were better for him to yield at the first, then to tarry any longer, the lesse would be his punishment from God therein. And so I let you to understand, that you shall give God his time to work in that matter at his pleasure, and then shall it be so the good of the owner, and of you likewise. And now I have said.

Δ. As concerning the bereaving me of my own goods, I would gladly understand who hath my silver double gilt bell-Salt, and other things here of late conveyed from mee.

Raph. John Dee, This is the will and purpose of God to command thee, although thou dost suffer wrong because thy goods be so taken away from thee, yet Gods will is such, that he will have thee to be a peace-maker in this cause : for it is past help to have it again : But as thou art a mortal father, so use that matter as a father, for thy son had it, although he would not, neither will confess it. And likewise for such things of late missing about this house, thou shalt hereafter as plainly know who had them, and how they were gone, as thou dost plainly understand for thy Salt, but thou shalt stay and proceed no further, till such time as I Raphael shall speak further of it ; for God will have all things to be done well, and to his best liking, So for that I have now said.

Δ.

Δ.
John Dee, *it is in the hands of God and his power to send thee such helps as thou dost seek of the* Treasure *to be brought unto thee, but God will not have it so to be,* the while thou art in this place (England *I mean*) *for God will not have thee to come into any disdain, or slander might take some advantage against them, but be content with that little that can be made of thy right in the* Colledge *matters. And furthermore, thou shalt see that God will send thee soon some ●such small helps by man, that thou shalt have some feeling of help, to help thee whither thou shouldst go ; and therefore I* Raphael *have now said.*

Δ .... John Pontoys.
John Dee, *be not too much inquisitive, but what shall be best to your liking in any good cause whatsoever you or be shall think good to be done for your good, God will put his assistance and help that you shall perceive Gods favour therein. And thus much I have said : at Gods commandment I came, and so on his mercifull goodnesse, and his power, I must presently depart.*

Δ ... Bartholomews *request of* George Sherman *his earnest oft and dreaming of Treasure to be under the foundation of the* wall called *De la pry* wall, a Nunry in times past within in half a mile of *Northampton,* Sir *William* Tate *his house is within that wall in three parts.*

That man may lawfully have it, if he take heed in the breaking of the   the three places, for it is for the greatest part under the bottom of the wall, and many roots of thorns and trees that will let and hinder the working for it, if be do not work much as slope as you can, to go under the roots, the which he may well and lawfully do. So doing, be may well obtain his purpose ; and now you have plainly understood the truth.   500.

300.

The one part of that Treasure *was laid by an old Nun, that was of that house, at that time, and one   that was her brother, and the other was laid even at the same time, that the same travel the which you took, the last day saving one, to know of that battel, it was bid at the same time by one of the Lords that was there killed, and so it hath remained ever since, the one place more easier to come at then the other, but with the favour of God, and in his mercy, that good fortune to be desired at parties hand, it may be had and compassed by the said party. And so now I have made the matter known unto you. And now in the name of the Almighty, and mercifull God, at whose will and pleasure I came, so now I depart in Gods peace. The mercies of God be upon you, both for this life, and for that which is to come, his name be glorifyed for evermore.* Amen, Amen.

Δ. Amen.

1607.   *Munday* 7. *Sept. hora* 7.

Δ. *His* morning as Bartholomew had intended to be going homeward in the morning, and I not intending to move an action now, but committed all to God, Bartholomew was spoken unto by Raphael.

..... *Command* John Dee *to come up into this place.*   A voice to Bartholomew.

Δ .... In the name of Jesus, and to the honour and glory of the most blessed Trinity. *Amen.*

Mittas O omnipotens sempiterne & une Deus lucem tuam & veritatem tuam, que nos ducant & perducant ad montem sanctum tuum & cælestia tua tabernacula. Amen.

Barth. ..... He is here.

Δ .... *Benedictus est, qui venit in nomine Domini.* Amen.
The Almighty God be blessed and praised of all good creatures, give praise unto his holy name, for evermore. *Amen.*
John Dee, *I am the same blessed creature* Raphael, *that did appear the last day but one in this place, I am at the commandment of the most highest to come unto your presence at this time, because thou shouldest very well know that I* Raphael *am very ready at all times, to come, when God shall command me ; but* John Dee, *I have no long message, at this time, for thou hast Gods full purpose and his will, in what he would have thee to enter into, and because that thou shalt well know that even now at your departing, the one from the other, it hath pleased God to send me to let thee to understand that for this time no more matters (as concerning what thou art taught) shall not (at this time) no more be spoken of, untill such time as God shall appoint, at your next meeting and coming together, that then, if there be any thing, that is not done of you, so far forth as it is in your power to fulfill it, if any such default in you be, I will then put you in remembrance of it, and help you in any thing which you shall doubt of : and if you have any question or demand to ask of me, even now, I am very ready in few words to answer you, and then in his*
F f 2   *name.*

name, who hath sent me (that is the Almighty) I must return therefore, if you have to ask do it.

Δ .... As concerning Mr. John   of the Isle of Man, his pitiful case hath moved my compassion.

Raph. .... John Dee, assure thy self, that as thou dost most heartily, with a good faith in God, that thou mightest be that man wherein God will most mercifully help his distressed case, therefore I answer thee, that God hath, and he will bear thee, to thy comfort therein, and to the great comfort of the man whom that cause doth belong unto. God will mercifully help the cause so shortly, as his will and pleasure is to be done in it. So much I have said for this.

Δ .... I thank God most heartily for his so great mercies.

Δ .... John Pontoys, my great friend, earnestly desireth to know his good Angel.

Raph. .... John Dee, for thy sake he shall know his good. Angel, but let it not be with him hereafter to have a pride in mind, that God hath made known unto him his good angel, for no man upon the face of the earth can have a better then he hath, for Uriel is his appointed Angel from his birth to this day, and so shall continue with him to the appointed time, that God will take his life away in separating his soul from his body, for Uriel hath been under God his deliverer forth of many dangers, and so he shall be his defence under God to his lifes end. And for this, I have made the matter plainly known unto you. Procede.

Δ .... Secondly, John Pontoys is desirous to know the end of the Polish troubles.

Raph. .... John Dee, in few words, for that matter, I answer thee. Those troubles will somewhat end to his losse; but it shall be no great matter, so that God will work the case that it shall end to his liking. And thus much for this I have said.

Δ .... As concerning the man and the Treasure, I am desirous to know whether he will be content to assign his title to Bartholomew, upon some portion thereof delivered unto him; and what other he hath made acquainted with the matter; and whether it may not by Gods good liking be set up without digging.

Raph. .... John Dee, in all this I hear thee, and I know thine intent herein. That man may be reasonably ruled, but yet he will not put over his title therein; but he hath 4. that beknowing how the matter doth stand with him, and so much as he doth know, he hath made them to know as much as himself: Therefore assure thy self that he shall be ruled, and that it shall not be as he will. If he will not be ordered in such sort and good councel as I Raphael shall give unto this Bartholomew at that time, that then he shall have no part of it, but I certifie you that he will be ruled; but onely the others, which I have made known unto you, they will not come to so good course in the matter as he will. Therefore let it rest, I will direct Bartholomew in the matter which shall be to his good, or else it shall not come to his hand, the which you have to know of. And for this, now I have said.

John Dee, it is the will and purpose of God, that it shall come by breaking of the ground, because that God will have all things done well, that no discord may break out betwixt the parties hereafter. And so now in Gods name I have said.

Δ .... Most humbly I thank and praise Almighty God for his infinite mercies and favour, beseeching him to assist me evermore. Amen.

Δ .... John Pontoys would shortly fall to work somewhat, to win some help for mony by distillations and Alchymicall conclusions, till we were otherwise holpen, and we are utterly unable to provide things necessary for lack of sufficient provision of money.

Raph. .... Trouble not thy self (as yet) with these causes.

Δ .... If Captain Langham will lend me an hundred pounds or more, as he promised me, for which my servant Patrick expecteth his performance at this hour.

Raph. .... Not (in such time) TO DO YOU GOOD.

Note. John Dee, that is the plain meaning, wherein it is said, not to do thee good, because it will be something too long (for thou art ready for it, if it were now, therefore with all haste, so much as is in Gods will to be done in it, it shall be hastened forward to do thee good.

And now I have plainly spoken unto thee in this case, my time appointed of God is at hand.

John Pontoys note. John Dee, thou hast fulfilled two questions, as concerning John Pontoys, look in thy Note.

John Pont. Oh that I might be fit to serve you in Bartholomews absence.

Raph. .... John Dee, In the name of the most highest I answer thee, to this his desire wherein he doth crave at the hands of God, for to obtain the sight of his blessed creatures; but hereafter it shall be made known unto thee, what God will do for him in that his desire. And now, all power and glory be given to the Almighty who hath made heaven and earth, his name be magnified, and praised everlastingly. Amen, Amen.

Δ .... Amen.

Δ .... All praise, all thanks, all honour and glory be yielded unto God of all his creatures, now and for evermore. Amen.

Δ. John

CPSIA information can be obtained
at www.ICGtesting.com
Printed in the USA
BVHW01s1954090218
507501BV00003B/52/P